ONTARIO SERIES
VI

MUSKOKA AND HALIBURTON
1615-1875

MUSKOKA
AND
HALIBURTON
1615-1875

A Collection of Documents

Edited with an introduction by

Florence B. Murray

THE CHAMPLAIN SOCIETY
FOR THE GOVERNMENT OF ONTARIO
UNIVERSITY OF TORONTO PRESS
1963

FOREWORD

THE PRESENT VOLUME is the sixth in the Ontario Series since *The Valley of the Trent* first appeared in 1957 and it follows on others dealing with the Kingston, Windsor, and Toronto districts. With *Muskoka and Haliburton* the Ontario Series returns to the same general locality as the first work—the vast country of forests, lakes, and rolling, rocky hills stretching off to the north, away from the shores of the St. Lawrence Waterway. During the 1820's and '30's when the Trent sector was being occupied, Muskoka and Haliburton were just then receiving their first concerted explorations. It was another generation before the tide of advancing settlement first began to penetrate the country treated in these pages.

Here we can trace the progress of Muskoka and Haliburton since the far-off days, 350 years ago, when the Jesuit Fathers began their ministry to the nomadic Indians of that region. Gradually the country was explored and surveyed, treaties were made with the Indian inhabitants, lumbermen began to thin the dense forests, and colonization roads were built to encourage settlement. Agricultural progress was disappointingly slow; but thanks to improved communications as well as the natural scenic beauty Muskoka began to blossom forth as the popular vacation land with which we are familiar.

Miss Florence B. Murray, an Associate Professor at the Library School, University of Toronto, has long been interested in the history of Muskoka and Haliburton. Born and raised in the District of Muskoka, Miss Murray has kept up her connection with the country through frequent visits and has come to know the region and its past as few other persons have done. This volume demonstrates the wide range of her interests and the painstaking care with which she has collected, arranged, and studied the documents relating to her subject.

In her researches Miss Murray, like many another, was assisted by the then Prime Minister of Ontario, Hon. Leslie M. Frost, to whose concern for preserving the history of this province this series owes its inception as a joint endeavour of the Champlain Society and the Government of Ontario. A resident of Lindsay in Victoria County, Mr. Frost has always had a particular interest in that sector of the province. He has derived much pleasure retracing the routes and uncovering the campsites of the pioneer explorers and surveyors of the rugged, beautiful country between the Ottawa and Georgian Bay. Mr. Frost has helped scholars with documents and maps, has put them on the track of important records, and given them invaluable advice based upon his intimate knowledge of the country and its people. In a sense this volume, in the progress of which he has taken much interest, is a tribute to Mr. Frost's many great services to the cause of historical study in Ontario.

The previous volumes of the Ontario Series are proving their worth by stimulating inquiry into Ontario's past and are helping awaken in the public a desire to pay homage to worthy forbears and to take pride in being citizens of a storied province and nation. I wish to thank Miss Murray for her spendid achievement in placing the history of the District of Muskoka and the County of Haliburton, a previously neglected section, within the context of the development of this province as a whole. By so doing she has significantly widened our historical horizons.

JOHN P. ROBARTS
Prime Minister of Ontario

PREFACE

THE REGION now known as Muskoka and Haliburton occupies a strategic position on the land barrier that separates the Ottawa River from Georgian Bay and displays the rugged terrain characteristic of the southern part of the Laurentian Shield. These physical factors largely determined its history, from the first exploration of the navigable rivers to the great days of the lumber camp and the sawmill, and the beginnings of the tourist trade.

In the first section of this volume, which treats a period for which the present-day boundaries are meaningless, documents frequently include material relating to adjacent districts. Indians whose hunting grounds lay inland from Georgian Bay, around the Muskoka Lakes, or along the Gull River have a place in the history of the area, although their nominal homes may have been further south. Reports by the Royal Engineers concerning attempts to trace a practical water route from Lake Simcoe to the Ottawa River include country well to the east of Haliburton, but are printed in full in order to give a complete account of the expeditions. The selection of documents in the latter part of the volume, which deals with settlement and the organization of community life, is limited more strictly to the present District of Muskoka and County of Haliburton.

Muskoka and Haliburton are treated as a unit in this work whenever possible. They have in common the rocks and hills, the countless lakes and rivers which have made them well-known holiday resorts. They share the cold winters and deep snows, the profusion of spring flowers, and the unforgettable colours of autumn. But they are separated by a height of land which divides the waters flowing west into Georgian Bay from those flowing south by the Trent system, and since they were explored and settled in a period when transportation depended on the waterways, their historical development followed different paths. From the days of the early explorers who went by the Toronto Portage, Lake Simcoe, and the Severn River to Georgian Bay, Muskoka has had a close relationship with Toronto. The first settlers looked to Orillia and indirectly to Toronto as their trading centre. Haliburton was linked through the Kawartha Lakes with the towns on Lake Ontario east of Toronto, and its market centres were Lindsay and Peterborough. Because of this historical division, in some sections of the volume the two districts are treated separately.

The purpose of the Ontario Series is to portray the development of a region through a selection of documents as nearly as possible contemporary with the events. This has meant the exclusion from this volume of certain topics such as the history of the Indians before the coming of the white men, for which there is only archaeological evidence, or the wanderings of the Indian tribes after the destruction of the Hurons, known mainly through oral traditions. In somewhat the same way it has been necessary to exclude the many interesting accounts of pioneer days which have appeared in recent years in such papers as the Bracebridge *Herald-Gazette*, the Huntsville *Forester*, and the *Haliburton County Echo*.

Names of persons and places have presented the problems commonly found in works dealing with periods of exploration and early settlement. Indian names, such as Musquakie and Aisance, were handed down from generation to generation and often used without forenames, so that it is difficult to distinguish one individual from another. Place names are also subject to duplication. At least six rivers in the Muskoka system were referred to as the Muskoka, and the names Kushog and Kashagawigamog were both used at the same time for each of two long winding rivers in Haliburton. Until recent years there has been little consistency even in official sources in the spelling of such names as Magnetawan. In the Documents, of course, the place names appear as in the originals, but in the Introduction, footnotes, and Index the decisions of the Canadian Board on Geographical Names have been followed.

Irregularities of spelling, capitalization, and punctuation, common in a collection of documents of this nature, have been reproduced without the addition of the word "*sic*" except where necessary to avoid misunderstanding. Similarly, since so many of the documents fall into the period of the Province of Canada, 1841 to 1867, the phrase "Province of" is omitted in the Introduction and footnotes if the date makes the reference clear.

The material in this volume has been collected over such a long period and with the help of so many people that it is impossible to name more than a few. Dr. W. Kaye Lamb, President of the Champlain Society, Dominion Archivist and National Librarian, merits special gratitude. By his expert counsel he has done much to bring the work to completion. The staff of the Public Archives of Canada also have given unfailing assistance.

Since the latter part of the volume relates mainly to topics that fall under the control of the provincial government, the Ontario Department of Public Records and Archives has been the source for a large number of documents. Dr. George W. Spragge and his staff have made available manuscripts, books, pictures, and maps and have offered many valuable suggestions. Special thanks are due to Mr. A. W. Murdoch who prepared the map on Colonization Roads. The Ontario Department of Lands and Forests provided much of the material relating to surveys and roads. Gracious permission was given by the Surveyor General of the Lands and Surveys Branch for the use of a portion of the map of Southern Ontario as an end paper. Mr. W. Eric Carroll, Chief Clerk of the Surveys Section of the same branch, was an unfailing source of information on problems relating to maps and surveys.

The University of Toronto Library and the Toronto Public Library were the major sources for printed materials. Thanks are expressed to librarians of the University of Toronto, especially those of the Department of Rare Books under Miss Marion E. Brown, and to the staff of the Reference Department of the Toronto Public Library, and Miss Edith G. Firth of the Baldwin Room. The Ontario Legislative Library, the Archives of the United Church of Canada, and several other institutions in and around Toronto provided information on special topics. Collections examined further afield included the Library of Congress, the New York Public Library, the Burton Historical Collection at the Detroit Public Library, the British Museum, the Royal Commonwealth Society, and the Public Record Office in London. Unpublished Crown-copyright material in the Public Record Office has been reproduced by permission of the Controller of Her Majesty's Stationery Office.

The Honourable Mr. Leslie Frost, the former Prime Minister of Ontario, to whom the series owes its inception, generously made available his own maps and documents relating to the history of an area in which he has long had a special interest.

Thanks are due to the Champlain Society, to Dr. Patrick C. T. White, former editor of the Ontario Series, and to Dr. Morris Zaslow of the Department of History of the University of Toronto, editor of the Champlain Society Publications. Dr. Zaslow gave unstintingly of his time, offered valuable suggestions for the inclusion and organization of material, read manuscript and proofs, and arranged the details of publication. His contribution to the work cannot be overemphasized. Appreciation is expressed to Dr. W. S. Wallace, Librarian Emeritus of the University of Toronto, to Dr. James

Watson Bain, for permission to use his father's papers, to Mr. W. R. Wadsworth, Q.C., for permission to print his father's reminiscences, to Mr. Claude Snider of Gravenhurst for the opportunity of examining his collection of photographs, and to Mr. Harley Cummings of Ottawa for information concerning the settlement of Haliburton and for permission to use documents in his possession.

It is a pleasure to acknowledge the assistance given by my mother over many years in collecting and copying the documents, and in the tedious, final preparation of the work for publication. Thanks are due also to the staff of the Library School of the University of Toronto for encouragement and suggestions, and especially to Miss Margaret Cockshutt for help in compiling the index.

Finally thanks are extended to Major C. C. J. Bond for his excellent cartographical work in adapting a number of maps for reproduction, and to the University of Toronto Press, and especially to Mrs. Marion Magee, for editorial supervision.

FLORENCE B. MURRAY

CONTENTS

Major Roads of Muskoka and Haliburton

THE MUSKOKA ROAD

THE PARRY SOUND ROAD

ILLUSTRATIONS

LINE DRAWINGS

PLATES

(between pp. lxxx and lxxxi)

MUSKOKA AND HALIBURTON, 1615–1875

INTRODUCTION

A. TRAVELLERS AND MISSIONARIES ON GEORGIAN BAY AND THE SEVERN RIVER, 1615–1823

THE FIRST EUROPEAN KNOWN to have caught even a glimpse of Muskoka or Haliburton was a French youth, usually identified as Etienne Brulé, and the year was 1610 or 1611. In 1610 the chiefs Ochateguin, a Huron, and Iroquet, an Algonkin, who had been at a trading fair on the St. Lawrence, at Champlain's insistence took home with them a French lad, and Champlain in turn took a young Huron whom he called Savignon, to Paris. No definite statement is available to show whether the French lad wintered with the Algonkins or with the Hurons, but he came back with the Hurons the following June. Champlain told of returning Savignon to the Indians and added, "I also saw my French boy who came dressed like an Indian. He was well pleased with the treatment received from the Indians, according to the customs of their country, and explained to me all that he had seen during the winter, and what he had learned from the Indians."[1]

In 1611 a young Frenchman, again unidentified, but probably Etienne Brulé, went home with the Charioquois or Huron Indians, and Savignon's brother, Tregouaroti, promised to show him as much as he could. The Hurons' usual route home from Quebec was by the Ottawa River, Lake Nipissing, and the French River, then south past the multitude of rock islands along the Muskoka shore to Matchedash Bay, and so to Huronia. A simpler route would have been by Lake Ontario and the Trent system or the Toronto Portage to Lake Simcoe, and overland to Huronia, but that presumably was barred by the Iroquois domination of Lake Ontario.

The next Europeans to see the shore of Muskoka of whom there is record were the Recollet, Father Joseph Le Caron, and twelve Frenchmen, who, accompanied by some Hurons, set out for Huronia by the Lake Nipissing route in the summer of 1615. The good Father, clothed in his long robe, his bare feet in sandals, guarding the vessels for the mass, probably had little interest in the islands of Georgian Bay. Samuel de Champlain who followed Father Le Caron a week later passed by canoe along the same shore in the last days of July, 1615. From his pen came the first description of any part of Muskoka or Haliburton (A 1).

[1]Champlain, *Works*, ed. Biggar, v. 2, p. 188.

A few years later Gabriel Sagard, called Théodat, a Recollet, spent a few months in Huronia, 1623–4, and then returned to France where he wrote an account of his journey. Of the route along the Georgian Bay shore, on his way to the Huron country, Sagard said only, "Two days before our arrival among the Hurons we came upon the Freshwater sea,[2] over which we passed from island to island, and landed in the country so greatly longed for on Sunday, the festival of St. Bernard, about midday, with the sun beating down perpendicularly upon us."[3] On the return journey, Sagard and his company spent a day in an Algonkin village, thought to have been on Beausoleil Island which lies in the entrance to Matchedash Bay and is geographically part of Muskoka (A 2).

Although the Recollets were the first missionaries in Huronia they were not strong enough to undertake alone the task of Christianizing so numerous a people. In 1625 the Jesuit Fathers also began work among the Hurons and in time opened missions for the Algonkins on Georgian Bay, Lake Huron, and Lake Nipissing.

The Muskoka and Haliburton area, with its chains of lakes and rivers, its fur-bearing animals, its fish, wild fruit, and maple sap, would have supported a large Indian population, but written evidence suggests that until very recent years it has harboured only nomadic groups. In historic times it has been a hunting ground for three Indian peoples in turn, the Algonkin, the Iroquois, and the Ojibwa. The disposition of tribes at the beginning of the seventeenth century is comparatively well known through the writings of the Jesuit Fathers and the early French explorers. There were two main linguistic groups in the Great Lakes region, those speaking the Algonkian tongue and those speaking the Iroquoian. The lands of the Algonkian peoples stretched from the Maritime Provinces to Lake Winnipeg and included the Laurentian Shield. The Iroquoian people were mainly south of Lake Ontario and the St. Lawrence, but included the Hurons, one of the most important Indian peoples in the history of the Canadian fur trade.

In the time of Champlain the Hurons, twenty to thirty thousand in number, lived to the south of Muskoka, between Lake Simcoe and Georgian Bay. Although they were an Iroquoian-speaking people they were bitter enemies of the Five Nations to the south of Lake Ontario, and on friendly terms with the Algonkins to the north. They lived a comparatively settled life, cultivated the soil and raised corn, beans, and squash. They knew the waterways and

[2]Lake Huron.
[3]Sagard, *The Long Journey to the Country of the Hurons*, ed. Wrong, p. 69.

travelled far in their canoes for trade or war. As early as 1609 they were carrying furs to the French on the St. Lawrence and by the following year had gained a position of dominance in the fur trade. They gathered their furs, mainly by barter, from an area including and stretching far beyond Muskoka and Haliburton to the east, west, and north. During the first part of the seventeenth century a comparatively stable economy evolved around them as middle men.

The Algonkian peoples were to the north of the Hurons. When the French first went up the Ottawa River through Lake Nipissing to Georgian Bay they passed the lands of several Algonkian groups. On the shores of Lake Nipissing were the Sorcerers, or Nipissings, who obtained furs by trade from far to the north and west and traded them again with the Hurons. They often wintered near the Hurons, just to the south of Muskoka, in the neighbourhood of Lake Couchiching. The Algonkian peoples though divided into several groups had many things in common: they were nomadic, migrating from one place to another in their birch bark canoes; they lived in wigwams, and subsisted by hunting, fishing, and trading (A 7). Though agriculture was known to them it was of slight importance in their economy. Du Creux said of them, "They wandered from place to place and lived only for the day, with no fixed abode and no garner or store; they lived by hunting and fishing and sowed no crops."[4]

To what extent the people of Algonkian stock hunted the beaver, bear, and fox, or fished in the lakes and rivers of Muskoka and Haliburton can never be known. They came in small groups or families, camped a brief time and were gone. Summers' growth and winters' storms have long since obliterated almost all traces of the fleeting camps. There is no definite evidence to show that either the Hurons or the Algonkins knew the water routes which led from Georgian Bay across the Muskoka and Haliburton area to the Ottawa. Certainly the Hurons were accustomed to take the longer route by way of the French River and Lake Nipissing on their trading expeditions to Quebec.

The wealth of material which has come down to us in the *Jesuit Relations* concerning life in Huronia merely emphasizes the poverty of early material on the district to the north and east in which Muskoka and Haliburton lie. The Jesuit Fathers found that, difficult as it was to Christianize the Hurons, it was as nothing compared with the hardships involved in following the wandering

[4]Du Creux, *The History of Canada, or New France,* ed. Robinson and Conacher, v. 1, p. 46.

Algonkins from camp to camp (A 6). The *Jesuit Relations* show no missions which can definitely be located in Muskoka or Haliburton but include two to the Algonkins, the mission of Ste. Elizabeth and the mission of the Holy Ghost, which no doubt served some of the Indians who hunted in the area. The mission of Ste. Elizabeth was started between 1640 and 1644 for Algonkins who had been driven from the St. Lawrence Valley by the Iroquois and had sought refuge among the Hurons, and for other Algonkins who went south to winter near the Hurons (A 3). This mission has been located by Du Creux[5] and by Father A. E. Jones[6] as being at the north end of Lake Couchiching, two or three miles south of the present territorial limits of the Muskoka District. The Church of the Holy Ghost, or St. Esprit, was established for the Algonkins of Lake Nipissing and other bands who wintered in that area, and was as nomadic as some of the Indians whom it served. Father Claude Pijart began the mission on May 8, 1641, and spent several laborious years, assisted at times by Father Leonard Garreau (A 4, A 5, A 7).

The economic system which revolved about the Hurons might have lasted many years had trouble not come from the outside. For the Iroquois who lived south of the Great Lakes and traded with the Dutch and English, the impact of European civilization brought almost insoluble problems. They became dependent for their very way of life upon European tools and firearms, but lacked the beaver skins with which to buy them. Beaver, which had never been plentiful south of Lake Ontario, became more and more scarce as the seventeenth century advanced. Inevitably the Iroquois looked to the rich fur lands to the north, and to the profits which were falling into Algonkin and Huron hands. At first they attempted to gain a share by treaty but when that failed they resorted to war. A thousand Iroquois spent the winter of 1648–9 north of Lake Ontario, some of them probably in the Haliburton area, and in the spring destroyed the Huron nation and massacred many Nipissings and others of the Algonkian tongue. After the dispersal of the Hurons in 1649, the Jesuit Fathers followed their remaining flocks and ministered to them on the islands of Georgian Bay and in the forests to which they had fled. Soon, however, the land was abandoned to the Iroquois as far north as Lake Nipissing.

After 1666 small bands of Iroquois settled along the shore of Lake Ontario where the waterways and trails led to the north, but

[5]*Ibid.*, v. 2, map.
[6]Jones, "*8endake Ehen*," or *Old Huronia*, pp. 70–3.

as far as is known they used Muskoka and Haliburton only as a hunting ground. No records have been found of white men in or near the area for many years after the destruction of the Hurons, though the English and Dutch traders who came up the Mohawk River to Lake Ontario may well have followed the Indians north into the fur grounds.

Although the Iroquois held the land north to Lake Nipissing they could not gain absolute control of the fur empire they had hoped to snatch from the Hurons, and gradually the Ottawa, an Algonkian people, slipped into the trade that the Hurons had vacated. The power of the Iroquois declined until, in the final third of the seventeenth century, Europeans at last were able to enter Lake Ontario and use the trails and waterways across the peninsula of southern Ontario. In 1669 Jean Peré[7] apparently left Lake Ontario by the eastern branch of the Toronto Carrying Place, and crossed by Lake Simcoe and the Severn River to Georgian Bay. No record of his trip has been found but his route is indicated roughly on the Galinée[8] map of 1670.

A few years later, René Robert Cavelier, sieur de La Salle, navigated the Severn River at least three times and possibly four. In 1680 he went from Fort Frontenac, now Kingston, to the Iroquois village of Teiaiagon, in the present Toronto area, north by the Toronto Carrying Place to Lake Simcoe (which he called Lake Toronto) and then by the Severn River to Georgian Bay (A 8).

In the days when water transportation took first place, the Severn River as the outlet of navigation across the peninsula of southern Ontario had obvious strategic importance. One of the first to recognize this was the Baron de Lahontan. He argued that if France's Indian allies were to attack the Iroquois in their own country they must have forts. Accordingly he suggested that three "forts supposés" or "little castles" be built, one at the mouth of Lake Huron, one at the mouth of Lake Erie, and one near the mouth of the Severn (A 9). By the time that Lahontan published his work the power of the Iroquois was already broken and the forts were

[7]Jean Peré came to Quebec in 1660 and became a fur trader. In 1669 he was sent with Jolliet to explore for the copper mine on Lake Superior, and in 1684 travelled as far as Hudson Bay. He had returned to France by 1690.

[8]Robinson, *Toronto during the French Régime*, pp. 18–20. The several variant copies of the Galinée map are discussed by James H. Coyne in "Exploration of the Great Lakes, 1669–70, by Dollier de Casson and De Bréhant de Galinée," Ontario Historical Society, *Papers and Records*, v. 4, 1903, pp. 78–89; also by Robinson in "Galinée's Map of the Great Lakes Region in 1670," *Canadian Historical Review*, v. 20, Sept., 1939, p. 293; and in the Percy Robinson Papers, III A, no. 18.

unnecessary, but the Toronto Portage with the Severn River continued to hold a strategic place.

The extent to which the lakes and rivers of Muskoka and Haliburton were known in the French period is shown not only by the writings of explorers and missionaries, but also to some degree by the contemporary maps, although it is unlikely that the maps indicate with any accuracy the full extent to which the Indians and *coureurs de bois* knew and travelled the waterways. Many of the fur traders were illiterate and, in addition, many were unwilling to risk official disapproval for engaging in the trade or to reveal to rivals the sources from which they obtained their furs. In spite of this the maps gradually showed a more accurate coastline and gave some indication of the existence of chains of lakes and rivers in the Muskoka area.

One of the first of interest is the well-known Champlain map of 1632.[9] South of Lake Nipissing between Georgian Bay and the Ottawa River are the words "Chasse descaribous" and in the Muskoka and Haliburton area and toward the Ottawa there are signs for Indian wigwams. The 1656 Sanson map[10] shows lakes in the Muskoka region and names of Indian bands between Georgian Bay and the Ottawa.

The map "Novae Franciae Accurata Delineatio 1657" (Plate I) again shows chains of lakes in Muskoka, one of which has some resemblance to the Muskoka Lakes. North of this, near Georgian Bay, is the word "vlamitans" or "clamitans," the meaning of which has not been ascertained. An inset[11] published with this map which shows a different and more accurate coastline marks Lake Couchiching, "Contarea lacus," and an island, which is almost certainly Beausoleil, "Kiondechiara." This name, spelled "Khionchiara," had been used previously for the Severn River on a map "Description dv pais des Hvrons"[12] which was probably of the year 1651. The name was repeated by Du Creux[13] as "Chionkiara" for the Severn River and as "Schiondekiaria" for Beausoleil Island. Father Jones[14] believed that these similar names used for the Severn and Beausoleil Island referred to the rock formation found at both places.

---

[9]Copy in Public Archives of Canada (P.A.C.). Reproduced in Champlain, *Works*, ed. Biggar, portfolio.

[10]Copy at P.A.C.

[11]Copy at P.A.C.

[12]Copy at P.A.C. Reproduced in Du Creux, *The History of Canada, or New France*, v. 2.

[13]*Ibid.*

[14]Jones, *"8endake Ehen," or Old Huronia*, pp. 205–13.

A map dated about 1679 in Pinart's collection[15] shows "Mis-sisagé" in the Lake Muskoka area and marks the centre of the Huron-Ottawa tract as the place from which the Wolves and Iroquois drew the greatest part of the beaver which they carried to the English and Dutch. Lake Simcoe is shown as "Lac de Taronto," and the portage to Lake Ontario at the Rouge River is clearly marked, as well as Toronto—"Teyoyagon."

On the so-called Belmont map[16] of 1680, Lake Simcoe is again "Lac de Tarenteau," and the Severn River, "R de Tarenteau," flows into a wide bay filled with islands, marked "Ga8endogué." Coronelli's map[17] of 1688 shows "Les Missisaghe" between Lake Nipissing and "Lac Taronto," "Algonquins Peup:" to the east of these, nearer the Ottawa River, and "Baye Sakinam" north of the Severn River.

In London in 1755, Dr. John Mitchell, a botanist who had lived in Virginia, published "A map of the British and French Dominions in North America"[18] which summed up the knowledge of the continent to the end of the French period. It shows a number of lakes and rivers in the Muskoka and Haliburton area and indicates the limits of the Iroquois territory (Plate II).

At the beginning of the British period in 1760, Major Robert Rogers[19] heard of the Severn route from the Indians living near the site of old Fort Toronto, when he was on his way to take possession of the former French forts for the British, and in 1764 Alexander Henry,[20] travelling with some Indians from the upper lakes to Fort Niagara, apparently went by way of the Severn, though his description of the river is characteristically inexact. Around the year 1785 the Chevalier de Rocheblave, who had served as an officer in America with the French, Spanish, and English successively before coming to Canada, petitioned insistently for compensation for losses in the war. With considerable astuteness he asked for land on the portage from Toronto to Lake Simcoe and the Severn River. In a long memorandum headed "Observations générales que propose philipe de rocheblave sur les deux provinces du bas Canada"[21] Rocheblave commented on the central position of

[15]Pinart, *Recueil de cartes, plans et vues*, no. 15.
[16]Copy at P.A.C.
[17]"Partie occidentale du Canada ou de la Nouvelle France." Copy at P.A.C.
[18]Copies at P.A.C. and many large libraries.
[19]Robert Rogers, *Journals* (London, 1765), p. 206.
[20]Alexander Henry, *Travels and Adventures in Canada and the Indian Territories* (New York, 1809), pp. 178–9.
[21]Ontario, Department of Public Records and Archives (P.A.O.), Simcoe Papers.

Toronto, and on the "petite rivière" which led to Lake Huron. If he had received the compensation which he requested it might well have included the first land grant in Muskoka, but changes of administration frustrated Rocheblave's plan.

The Peace of Paris, 1763, which transferred Canada from French to British control had little immediate effect on areas so far removed from Quebec as Muskoka and Haliburton, but the American Revolution brought more results. An inrush of United Empire Loyalists and an uncertain boundary line, legacies of the Revolution, forced the British government to begin the survey of territories in Upper Canada, and to examine the water routes. The ever-present danger of war with the United States and the importance of the fur trade with the northwest alike demanded better lines of communication between the St. Lawrence and Lake Huron. A route was required which was shorter and less hazardous than that by the Ottawa and Lake Nipissing, removed from the American frontier, and unobstructed by Niagara Falls. Inevitably Lake Simcoe and the Severn River which were connected with Toronto by the Carrying Place, and with the Bay of Quinte by the Trent system, aroused the interest of military officers and traders.

In May, 1780, General Haldimand issued orders for a party of white men and Indians to survey the Toronto route (A 10). Probably as a result of these instructions a party went up the Toronto Portage, by Lake Simcoe and the Severn, turned north through Baxter Lake and came to Georgian Bay at Honey Harbour. They then turned south down the Bay to the Severn River, followed their course back through Lake Simcoe, and proceeded to Niagara (A 11). Only an incomplete, unsigned copy of the diary kept on this expedition has been found. It is inaccurate in its distances and difficult to follow for directions, but nevertheless of considerable interest as the first detailed description of the Severn River.

In 1788, with the thought of defence uppermost in his mind, Lord Dorchester determined on a survey of the fortifications and harbours of the Great Lakes. On May 29 he instructed Gother Mann, Commanding Royal Engineer, to undertake such a survey and to examine "the mouth of the French river, and that of the River Matchadosh upon Lake Huron" (A 13). On December 6, Mann made his report covering the islands of Georgian Bay, Matchedash Bay, and the Severn River. His report on the Severn was not favourable. Not only did he doubt that a settlement at the mouth of the river would ever become "a place of much importance," he also thought that the rapids on the river and the length of the portage from Toronto were "very strong obstacles to any business being carried on this way upon the great scale of Trade" (A 14).

John Graves Simcoe, first Lieutenant Governor of Upper Canada and a former captain of the King's forces in the American Revolution, never lost sight of the importance of military preparedness for his young colony. Water communications between the upper and lower lakes occupied his mind continually and at least by the spring of 1793 he had determined to cross from Toronto to Lake Huron (A 15). On September 25 he and his party set out along the shore of Lake Ontario and up the Humber and Holland River trail to Lake Simcoe, Lake Couchiching, and the Severn River, which they reached on October the first. The journey down the Severn and later to Beausoleil Island, which they called "Isle de Traverse," is of interest for the history of Muskoka (A 16). While at Matchedash the party visited Cowan, a fur trader who had been settled there for fifteen years, and who, as Simcoe later said, practically governed the Indians with whom he resided.

Simcoe was always certain that some route must be opened from Lake Ontario to Georgian Bay by way of Lake Simcoe, and he made provision for the purchase of the right of way from the Indians (C 2). The only portion of the route open to question in his mind was the Severn River, which not only added unnecessary miles but also was encumbered with falls and rapids. Simcoe's insistence on a road to the upper lakes far removed from the American border was justified by the War of 1812, when desperate efforts were made to open a line of communication from Lake Simcoe to Georgian Bay. The route chosen however was south of the Severn, by Kempenfelt Bay, the Nine Mile Portage to Willow Creek, and down the Nottawasaga River, or by a winter road to Penetanguishene.

In 1815, immediately following the conclusion of the war, and while the importance of the control of the lakes was still strong in all minds, another survey of the Great Lakes was carried out. Sir E.W.C.R. Owen had been appointed Commodore and Commander in Chief of the British naval forces on the lakes, and his younger brother, Captain William Fitzwilliam Owen, was appointed to survey part of the lake frontier. Captain Owen was instructed by Commodore Owen to examine, among other things, "The Range of Manitoulin Islands and the navigation north and east of them to the Bay of Matchidash"[22] which should have included the Muskoka

[22]P.A.C., C 500, pp. 64–70.

shore. Unfortunately illness and other difficulties prevented the survey from proceeding as rapidly as had been expected and Muskoka, except for the Severn River, received no attention. Captain Owen left a map of the Severn, and in 1822 a memorandum, based on the map, was compiled which gave distances between the falls and the lengths of portages (A 17). Although Captain Owen did not have time to carry out an accurate survey of the islands of Georgian Bay, he chose as an assistant in 1815 Henry Wolsey Bayfield who accomplished the task in 1820 (A 18).

About 1819 the British government had turned its attention to the search for a direct water route between the Ottawa River and Georgian Bay south of Lake Nipissing and French River, and as part of the search sent Lieutenant Joseph E. Portlock to examine the Severn once more. Portlock made a lengthy report on his exploration with recommendations for dams and canals to avoid the falls (A 19), a report which is of special interest because of later changes on the Severn necessitated by power developments and the construction of the Trent canal system.

B. EXPLORATION OF THE WATERWAYS
OF THE INTERIOR, 1819–1837

AFTER THE WAR OF 1812 when the British government began a deliberate search for a water route which would connect Georgian Bay and the Ottawa, officers of the Royal Engineers crossed and recrossed Muskoka and Haliburton following the chains of lakes and rivers, using Lake Simcoe as a pivot. In 1819, the year that Portlock examined the route from Lake Simcoe to Georgian Bay (A 19), Lieutenant Catty crossed from Lake Simcoe and the Talbot River to the Ottawa by way of the Madawaska (B 1). His is the earliest account of a journey across this part of the Laurentian Shield and gives Catty a claim to be the first recorded white man to have set foot in Haliburton. It is a brief report on a journey past rapids and falls, through lakes and rivers then unnamed and now almost impossible to identify. Catty's own map has not been found but his route is shown on several maps, nearly contemporary, those by Lieutenant Marlow (Fig. 3), by Lieutenant Briscoe (Fig. 4), by Lieutenant Walpole,[1] and by J. G. Chewett (Fig. 5), and also on a map used by Robert Gourlay in his *Statistical Account of Upper Canada*, 1822. Unfortunately these maps do not determine Catty's route with any exactitude nor even make it clear whether he followed the Madawaska River or the York River to its junction with the Madawaska. Walpole who was assigned the task of verifying Catty's route in 1827 went by way of Lakes Kashagawigamog, Drag, and Kennibik to the York River, and left two maps (one detailed, one a sketch) as well as his report in which he assumed that he was following Catty (B 17), but J. G. Chewett who accompanied Walpole submitted a map on which Catty's line is shown well to the north. No explanation has been found for this curious discrepancy in the maps made by two men on the same survey.

An unpublished work by Dr. James Watson Bain[2] supports the view that Catty followed the York River and lists the lakes as Balsam, Mud, Moore, Gull, Kashagawigamog, Grass, Head, Drag, and Kennibik. If the northern route by the Madawaska River proper were used Catty would have continued further north on the Gull River chain then crossed by Kennisis, Madawaska, and Bark

[1]Public Record Office (P.R.O.), W.O. 55/864.
[2]Bain, "Early Explorations in the Muskoka and Haliburton Districts" (typescript).

lakes. If he used the intermediate route shown on Chewett's map he might have gone from Drag Lake north to Haliburton Lake, and to the York River in Bruton Township. Catty's general conclusions as to the possibility of establishing a water communication from Lake Simcoe to the Ottawa were discouraging but did not prevent British government officers from sending out other exploratory surveys. One point in Catty's report which they found of special interest was the mention of a lake from which there flowed "a river which runs in the direction of and discharges itself near Kingston." Obviously such a river would afford a water communication from Kingston to both Lake Simcoe and the Ottawa.

In 1825 a commission of which Sir James Carmichael Smyth was president made a report to the Duke of Wellington on fortifications, communications, and troops in Canada (B 3). Smyth who was especially concerned with water communications accepted the Severn River as a possible connection between Lake Simcoe and Georgian Bay, but remarked that it would require £30,024 to make it navigable. For the waterways from Lake Simcoe to the Ottawa which were unknown except for Catty's report, he planned a series of exploratory surveys in 1826, starting with the Black and Talbot rivers.

From early days the Black River, which empties into the Severn River below the first fall north of Lake Couchiching, had been of interest. The Pilkington map of 1793 bears the note "The source of this River is reported to be near the head of the Rideau. Canoes go up it a great distance" (Fig. 2). The Duke of Wellington had mentioned the Black River in his Instructions to the Commission under Carmichael Smyth, and Smyth in his Memorandum to Colonel Durnford wrote that "Some intelligent Canadian Boatmen reported to us that the Black River falls into those Lakes forming the communication between Lake Simcoe and the Ottawa, as explored by Lieut. Catty, and which from the Lay of the Country we are disposed to think is probably the case" (B 2). Consequently, Lieutenant W. B. Marlow of the Royal Engineers and Lieutenant Smith of the Royal Artillery received instructions to leave Kingston on the twenty-third of August, 1826, in order to explore the Black River and "ascertain its head & carefully examine the country between its Source & the Talbot" (B 6).

At the conclusion of the survey Marlow and Smith submitted a report (B 7) and a map (Fig. 3) of the route they travelled, but as is the case with many expeditions through unnamed lakes and rivers, it is difficult to trace their course with any certainty. Although Marlow and Smith assumed that they followed the Black River to its source, their report and sketch map suggest that they traced the Black River only to its junction with Anson Creek and then followed the latter east through Longford Township. That the name Black River was given to more than one stream is shown by Lieutenant Baddeley's reference in 1835 to the "easternmost" and "westernmost" branches. Incidentally, his report causes some confusion by attributing this exploratory survey to Walpole, not Marlow (B 27).

After reaching the head of the river Marlow continued east probably through Hindon Township to the Gull River system. Lieutenant Walpole's large map of 1827 bears a note beside Gull Lake that "Lt Marlow entered this Lake after reaching the source of the Black River, in 1826" and markings on the map suggest that he came in at the west side of the lake. Marlow's own map indicates that he reached a lake further north, perhaps Twelve Mile Lake, and then turned south to Gull Lake. Whatever may have been the exact route that Marlow followed, his exploration put an end to the long-held belief that the Black River might be an important link in water communication. Smyth summarized the result in his statement, "although it does not appear that any use can be hereafter made of the Black River, it was absolutely necessary that it should be explored" (B 10).

In February 1826, Lieutenant Henry Briscoe of the Royal Engineers had also received instructions to survey the Talbot and Black rivers. In April he proceeded to Holland Landing but found neither the canoes nor Indian guides ready. In May he went a second time to the Landing but again failed to obtain guides and returned to York (B 5). At the end of August he set out the third time and finding no satisfactory guide for the Talbot, accepted one for a more northerly route which led by the Muskoka and Madawaska systems to the Ottawa (B 8). By this decision he became the first white man known to have crossed the heart of Muskoka.

Briscoe and his party descended the Severn River to within half a mile of the third fall where they turned up Morrison Creek to Morrison Lake and Muldrew Lake (formerly Leg Lake), and then portaged to Muskoka Bay at the southern end of Lake Muskoka. On leaving this lake they went up the South Branch of the Muskoka River to the Lake of Bays (which Briscoe called Lake Baptiste on his map), then by the Oxtongue River and a series of lakes, rivers, and portages to Madawaska waters, Lake Opeongo, and the Petawawa River to the Ottawa (B 9).

Although Briscoe had not been able to carry out his instructions, Smyth considered the deviation from orders an advantage and concluded that "Lieut: Briscoes journey shews what vast facilities for internal navigation & communication the Country between the Ottawa and Lake Simcoe will afford to future settlers" (B 10). The Duke of Wellington took a less kindly view of the surveys of 1826. In a memorandum he complained that the officers "go wandering over the Country they don't know where, and report upon any thing excepting what they were sent to examine and report upon." His conclusion was "Let these Surveys be made again next season" (B 11).

Smyth proposed that two parties be sent out in 1827, one under Lieutenant Briscoe, accompanied by Lieutenant Greenwood of the Royal Artillery, to repeat the first part of Briscoe's route of the previous year, then endeavour to find the river mentioned by Catty as branching off toward Kingston, and finally to continue by the Madawaska to the Ottawa; the other under Lieutenant Walpole, accompanied by J. G. Chewett of the Surveyor General's office, to verify Catty's route and to meet Briscoe where the river branched off toward Kingston (B 12). Briscoe and Greenwood, who found no sign of the river alluded to by Catty, submitted a sketch map of their route (Fig. 4) and a report condemning the Madawaska as impracticable for navigation (B 15).

Meanwhile Walpole and Chewett proceeded up the Talbot River, through Balsam, Gull, Kashagawigamog, Head, Drag (which Walpole called Porcupine), Miskwabi (which he called Owl), Grace, Farquhar, Elephant, and Baptiste lakes, and down the York River to the Madawaska. Walpole found no lake "having a River flowing from it, and discharging itself near Kingston." He did however see a small river that emptied into the waters of the Trent near Balsam Lake (which may have been a branch of the Irondale River flowing out of Grace Lake). Walpole submitted a report (B 17) and at least two maps of the route.[3]

The next recorded exploration of the Ottawa-Georgian Bay tract had a somewhat different motive and started from the reverse direction, the Ottawa. By the 1820's settlement had straggled north to the present site of Arnprior, lumbermen had pushed still further, and there was much interest in the possibility of opening the lands of the upper Ottawa. It was also the great era of canal building. The Erie was opened in 1825, and the Oswego feeder in 1828, linking Lakes Erie and Ontario with the Atlantic by a southern route. Cana-

[3]See *supra*, p. xlv.

dians watched with dismay the trade of the rapidly expanding western states by-pass the St. Lawrence. Only a water communication from Georgian Bay to the Ottawa, which would provide the shortest route to the sea from the upper lakes, seemed likely to regain the western trade for the St. Lawrence River.

Charles Shirreff of Fitzroy Harbour on the Ottawa actively promoted such a development. One of his sons, Alexander, acted as an assistant overseer of works on the Rideau Canal for Colonel By, who was himself interested in finding better communications from the Ottawa to Lake Huron (B 23). Another son, Robert, was interested in the establishment of a land company to develop the Ottawa-Huron tract and build a canal. In January, 1829, Charles Shirreff wrote an eloquent report in which he proposed a route from the Ottawa to Georgian Bay by Lake La Vieille, through a chain of lakes which appears to be the Muskoka, and by the Moon River which he called the Moose (B 22).

An opportunity of checking the proposed route came in the autumn of the same year, 1829. Shirreff's son, Alexander, explored from the Ottawa River to Penetanguishene and back to the Ottawa with the twofold purpose of examining the waterways and of learning for himself the fitness of the land for settlement. From his observations of the character of the rivers and the levels he became convinced of the superiority of the existing Lake Nipissing route over any that might be developed by the Muskoka chain. His judgment of the quality of the land, however, was far less reliable. He firmly believed that if land grew hardwood trees it was suitable for agriculture, ignoring the fact that often, even in the best areas which he examined, only a thin layer of vegetable mould covered the Precambrian rocks.

Shirreff left the Ottawa at Deux Rivières on the 30th of August, 1829, with a crew of five. By portages, lakes, and rivers, they crossed to the Petawawa system, then to Trout (now Radiant) Lake, upstream to Cedar Lake, and down a chain of lakes and rivers to the South Branch of the Muskoka River, the Lake of Bays, Lake Muskoka, and out to Georgian Bay and Penetanguishene. Their return was by the Severn River, through Morrison and Muldrew lakes to Lake Muskoka, and then again by the South Branch of the Muskoka River and the Madawaska and Petawawa rivers to the Ottawa (B 24).

Four years later the House of Assembly set in motion the first large-scale exploratory survey of the interior of the Muskoka and Parry Sound district. Following an address of the House on January

3, 1834 (B 25), Lieutenant Governor Colborne issued instructions for an exploring party to examine the country north from the Township of Mara to Lake Nipissing, or, in other words, to continue the division line between the Home and Newcastle districts and to make lateral excursions from the line. The officers were to examine the capacity of the country to support settlers, the courses of the rivers, the dimensions of lakes, and the geological and mineralogical structure of the terrain. The party was led by Lieutenant John Carthew, Royal Navy, with Lieutenant F. H. Baddeley, Royal Engineer, as geologist, Samuel Richardson and William Hawkins as surveyors, Mr. Beman in charge of provisions, as well as the usual canoe men, axemen, and chain bearers (B 26). Between July and November, 1835, they ran a line about 77 miles in length, north between the modern townships of Morrison and Ryde, Muskoka and Draper, Monck and Macaulay, Watt and Stephenson, across Skeleton Lake, between Cardwell and Stisted, and on into the Parry Sound district where it was discontinued in Chapman or Lount (B 27).

The most interesting part of the report[4] covers the work of Carthew, Baddeley, and Hawkins, who in lateral surveys explored most of the large rivers, such as the Black, Severn, Muskoka, and Magnetawan. The first mention of many a lake and river, later well known to settlers and tourists, is found in these reports, lakes then unnamed and the shores still unsurveyed. The account by Lieutenant Baddeley, who was not only a geologist, but also a naturalist with a keen eye for the plant and animal life about him, is more readable than the one by Lieutenant Carthew. References creep into Baddeley's report, often under scientific names, to be sure, to many a tree and flower: sarsaparilla, iris, cardinal flowers, ferns, cherry trees laden with fruit, juniper berries, and blueberries. He mentions the whippoorwills and the bears, and comments on the habits of hornets. It is difficult to see how he could have spent September and October in the Muskoka area without being moved by the blaze of colour and the calls of the wild fowl gathering for their long flight south, but he made no mention of these things. He did however observe the first fall of snow and noted that "by settling on the bushes and trees it has changed their sombre green into a brilliant and feathery white, at once novel and attractive."[5]

As late as 1837 the possibility of establishing a practical water communication between Lake Huron and the Ottawa was still in question. Consequently, on March 4, 1837, the Legislature passed

[4]Upper Canada, House of Assembly, *Journal*, 1836–7, app. 37.
[5]*Ibid.*, p. 29.

"An Act to provide for a Survey of the Ottawa River, and the Country bordering on it, together with the Country and Waters lying between that River and Lake Huron" (B 28). A three-man commission was appointed which included the Honourable John Macaulay, John S. Cartwright, and Francis H. Baddeley (then a captain). The same year three exploring parties were sent out: one under Lieutenant David Taylor[6] by the French River, Lake Nipissing, and the Turtle Lakes to the Ottawa; a second under William Hawkins[7] from the Shawenaga (now the Magnetawan) eastward to Allumette Island and return by Lake Nipissing and the French River; and the third through the Muskoka and Madawaska route under David Thompson, the famed explorer of the Columbia River.

In 1837 David Thompson was a man of 67. His exploits in the northwest were far in the past, and the fame which now enshrines his name still in the future. The best contemporary description of him is a favourable one by Dr. J. J. Bigsby in *The Shoe and Canoe*. Captain Baddeley spoke more doubtfully and mentioned "there are rumours abroad that Mr. T. is not trustworthy as to reporting of facts" and that "there is something in his conversation which I do not like and which makes me suspect his candour" (B 30). In spite of these doubts, Thompson was appointed to make the Lake Huron to Ottawa survey, and from him came the first accurate, systematic notes and maps of the Muskoka River waterway.

Detailed records of Thompson's route have been preserved. The most valuable, perhaps, are the four finely-drawn maps of his course, which are on file at the Ontario Department of Lands and Forests. He also left numerous written records including "Journal of Occurrences from Lake Huron to the Ottawa River" which gives the most complete account of the trip. Details of soil and rocks, mileages, observations for latitude and longitude, written in Thompson's fine hand, often in faded ink, make a document intelligible only to a specialist. But here and there glimpses of the human side of the journey are revealed, from which selections appear in this volume (B 32).

In July of 1837 at Holland Landing Thompson supervised the making of cedar canoes for the expedition, against the advice of Captain Baddeley who preferred that tin canoes be used (B 31). At the end of the month the exploring parties set off from Pene-

[6]David Taylor, "Report of the Route between Lake Huron and the Ottawa River via Lake Nipissingue, Turtle Lake and Matawa River" (P.A.O., Macaulay Papers).
[7]F. H. Baddeley to J. Macaulay, Oct. 2, 1837 (P.A.O., Macaulay Papers).

tanguishene and on August 6 Thompson succeeded in finding the mouth of the Muskoka River. From there his route may be traced as follows: up the Muskoka River, past the junction of the Gibson River, through Go Home Lake, past the junction of the Moon River with the Muskoka, and into Lake Muskoka. The party remained in that district from August 14 to 26, and surveyed the three lakes, Muskoka, Rosseau, and Joseph. Dotted lines on Thompson's map indicate the great extent of the work accomplished (Fig. 6). On August 26 Thompson continued up the South Branch of the Muskoka River to Lake of Bays, which he called Forked Lake. He left the Lake of Bays by the Oxtongue or Muskoka River, came to Oxtongue Lake, which he called Cross Lake, and then to South Tea Lake which he called Canoe Lake. There the party stayed for two weeks, built two lighter canoes necessary for crossing the height of land, and surveyed as far as the north end of the present Canoe Lake. Finally, near the end of September they left by the southeastern route through Smoke, Ragged, Big Porcupine, Bonnechere, Harness, and Head lakes, and the Madawaska River route to the Ottawa.

Although Thompson left voluminous material on this expedition there is little in the nature of a summary. He praised a few districts, such as Lake Muskoka and Lake of Bays; he had only harsh words for others, and complained continually about the poverty of wild life. But of all the early explorers he is one of the very few who commented on the matchless autumn colouring of the Huron-Ottawa region: "The woods in all their Foliage have suddenly changed & assumed all the vivid tints of October, and begin to fall freely, one cannot help a sigh at such a quick change" (B 32, September 24).

The reports and maps that Thompson submitted to the government do not appear to have been known to later surveyors. Alexander Murray in 1854 said that he was unacquainted with any accurate survey of the interior which he was about to visit (D 10), and V. B. Wadsworth said that J. S. Dennis had to make a canoe traverse of the lakes connected with the Muskoka River as there was no surveyed record (D 16). T. M. Robinson in 1862 wrote to James Bain concerning the recent discovery of Lake Joseph "not before known to white men" (J 2). No explanation has been found for this total disregard of the first detailed survey of the lakes and rivers of the Muskoka chain done by David Thompson.

C. THE INDIAN IN THE MUSKOKA AND HALIBURTON REGION

As the power of the Iroquois declined in the second half of the seventeenth century, the way was open for other Indians such as the Ojibwa from the north and west to move into southern Ontario. The Ojibwa, "people whose moccasins have puckered seams," were of Algonkian stock and were often known as Chippewas. There are no records to show definitely which bands came first, or to indicate their relationship with the Algonkins who had been there in the days of the Hurons. They were divided into two closely related groups, one known as Mississaugas or Mississagues, and the other known simply as Chippewas or Ojibwas. There was no clear-cut division between the lands claimed by the two groups, but in general the Mississaugas spread from Georgian Bay along the Trent waterway, then eastward toward the Ottawa, or south toward Lake Ontario, while the Chippewas remained in the vicinity of Georgian Bay. Some Mississaugas, however, lived at Matchedash Bay and became known as the Matchedash Indians. These, no doubt, were the Indians Alexander Henry found on the Severn River in 1764, and John Graves Simcoe met at the mouth of the Severn in 1793.

Although in later years it was customary to differentiate between Mississaugas and Chippewas, in the French period and at the beginning of the British period, this was not done. John Collins recorded an agreement with the "principal Chiefs of the Missisaga Nation" (C 1) and J. B. Rousseau, probably referring to the same agreement, spoke of the "Chippaway Indians" (C 3). A letter from Peter Russell used the name "Chippewas" but the enclosure used "Mississagas" to denote the Indians of whom Yellowhead was chief (C 5).

There is no written evidence to show at what date Ojibwas were first in or near Muskoka. Maps in Pinart's collection,[1] which have been dated about 1679, show the "Missisagé" or "Missisaghé" in the Muskoka area. "Les Missisaghe" are shown again in the same region on Coronelli's map[2] of 1688 with "Algonquins Peup:" toward the Ottawa River. In 1718 it was stated, "On the opposite or North shore of Lake Huron you have Matechitache; some Missis-

---

[1]Pinart, *Recueil de cartes, plans et vues*, no. 15–16.
[2]"Partie occidentale du Canada ou de la Nouvelle France."

sagués are there, whose manners are the same as those of the Outaouaes."[3] An "Enumeration of the Indian Tribes" of 1736 showed Mississaugas at a number of places in southern Ontario including Matchedash, and stated, "The principal tribe is that of the Crane. Warriors 150."[4]

In the first half of the eighteenth century the Iroquois, although much diminished in power, still remained in southern Ontario, as indicated by the Mitchell map of 1755 (Plate II). Mississauga traditions[5] tell of a great battle between the Mississaugas and the Mohawks on the Island of Skulls at the lower end of Georgian Bay, of the advance of the Mississaugas by way of the Severn River and Lakes Couchiching and Simcoe, and of further fighting in Haliburton and the country to the south. There is some archaeological evidence that such battles took place, but written records suggest that for many years both the Mississaugas and the Iroquois occupied lands in southern Ontario. By the end of the French period, however, the Ojibwa nation claimed much of the province, including Muskoka and Haliburton.

The band under Yellowhead, later known as the Chippewas of Lakes Simcoe and Huron, were the Indians most closely connected with the Muskoka district, and from their chief, Yellowhead— Mesqua Ukie or Mesquakie—Muskoka probably derived its name. When they first appeared in the records they were living in the unsettled lands in the rear of the Home District, that is in the Lake Simcoe area, and from an early period they were officially recognized by the British government and received annual presents. In 1797, disturbed because the government had neglected them for a few years, a party of 140 under Yellowhead visited the posts at York and Niagara to voice their complaints (C 5). They received an attentive hearing, since the unsettled relations with the United States following the American Revolution made even the Indians remote from Lake Ontario an important factor in plans for the defence of the border. Added to this, settlement was rapidly expanding northward, and the families in the vanguard were at the mercy of their Indian neighbours. The government found it necessary to maintain good relations with the Indians in order to obtain sur-

[3]"Memoir on the Indians of Canada as far as the River Mississipi, with remarks on their Manners and Trade, 1718," in *Documents Relative to the Colonial History of the State of New-York*, ed. O'Callaghan, v. 9, p. 889.

[4]"Enumeration of the Indian tribes connected with the Government of Canada; the Warriors and Armorial bearings of each Nation, 1736," *ibid.*, v. 9, p. 1056.

[5]Paudash, "The Coming of the Mississagas," Ontario Historical Society, *Papers and Records*, v. 6, 1905, pp. 7–11.

renders of the tracts of land required for the ever-increasing white population. Although the Ojibwas had moved into southern Ontario only toward the end of the seventeenth and early eighteenth century and had used much of the land only as hunting grounds, the government recognized their right of ownership, and from time to time negotiated for the purchase of certain parcels of land.

Yellowhead's band claimed the lands about Lake Simcoe and the Severn River, and so controlled the northern end of the communication from Toronto to Georgian Bay. As early as 1780 Governor Haldimand ordered the route to be examined (A 10). On May 22, 1785, Henry Hamilton instructed John Collins to survey "the Communication between the Bay of Quinté, and Lake Huron by Lake La Clie,"[6] and to note "What tract of land it might be necessary to purchase, and at what rate."[7] On August 9 of the same year, at "Lake le Clie," John Collins and William R. Crawford, with Jean Baptiste Rousseau as interpreter, made an agreement with the Mississaugas which gave the King the right to make roads and carry on trade through their country (C 1). No details were given, but ten years later Rousseau certified that the purchase included "one mile on each Side of the River which empties out of Lake Simcoe into Matchidash Bay" (C 3). If Rousseau's memory was correct, this agreement which included both sides of the Severn was the first known surrender of any land in Muskoka or Haliburton.

Rousseau's statement in 1795 was probably necessitated by the carelessness with which some of the first Indian surrenders had been recorded. In 1793 and 1794, Governor Simcoe, disturbed by the absence of formal documents at York, had a search made for them in Quebec without success.[8] On September 12, 1794, D. W. Smith, the Surveyor General, instructed Alexander Aitkin to proceed to Matchedash Bay and make arrangements for a new agreement (C 2). The Severn River was not specifically mentioned and even at that date seems to have been superseded by the overland route to Penetanguishene.

Although the next three cessions by Yellowhead's band were for territory to the south and west of Muskoka they are of interest as

[6]Several spellings occur, such as Le Cli, La Clie, and Les Claies. It was renamed Lake Simcoe by Governor Simcoe in honour of his father.
[7]Hamilton to Collins, May 22, 1785 (Ontario, Department of Lands and Forests, Instructions to Land Surveyors, Book 1, pp. 13–15; also printed in P.A.O., *Report*, 1905, pp. 371–2).
[8]Joseph Chew to E. B. Littlehales, Nov. 14, 1794, and Dorchester to Simcoe, Jan. 27, 1794 (P.A.O., Simcoe Papers).

showing the way in which these Indians sold their land piece by piece until little remained to them. On May 19, 1795, they surrendered the Penetanguishene area in what was apparently a preliminary agreement which was followed by a formal treaty on May 22, 1798.⁹ On November 17 and 18, 1815, they surrendered parts of Simcoe County¹⁰ and on October 17, 1818, about 1,592,000 acres south and west of Lake Simcoe.¹¹

The Indians most closely associated with Haliburton were Mississaugas, described by the government as "The Chippewa Nation of Indians inhabiting the back parts of the New Castle District." They were divided into bands, including the Eagle, Reindeer, Crane, Pike, Snake, and White Oak. The Crane tribe, which had been mentioned as early as 1736, was led by Pahtosh or Paudash, a name later given to Paudash Lake in Cardiff Township, Haliburton. On November 5, 1818, by Treaty number 20, these Indians surrendered a great tract of land, 1,951,000 acres in extent, which included parts of Muskoka and Haliburton south of the forty-fifth parallel (C 6). In the agreement the description of the boundary line was so confused that "the line forty-five" was said to strike a bay at the northern entrance of Lake Simcoe, instead of Lake Muskoka.

H. C. Darling, reporting to Lord Dalhousie in 1828, stated that the Mississaugas of Rice Lake had expressed a desire to be collected into a village and have lands allotted to them for cultivation (C 7), and soon after this date they were settled on reserves. The problems which faced these and other Indians with the growth of the white population are indicated by a petition to Colborne in 1829: hunting grounds converted into settlements, encroachment by other hunters on the land which still remained to them, unjust seizure of their furs by white men, and attacks upon their women (C 8). In 1837 T. G. Anderson reported that there were about 500 Indians of the Chippewa nation in the Newcastle District, living on three reserves known as Alnwick, Rice Lake, and Mud Lake (C 13). Certain changes in the location of the reserves occurred in later years, but all remained far to the south of Haliburton.

The Chippewas of Lakes Simcoe and Huron all recognized Yellowhead as their head chief but were divided into three bands under Chiefs Yellowhead, Aisance, and Snake. Before 1830 they had

⁹Treaty number 5, Canada, Department of Indian Affairs, *Indian Treaties and Surrenders*, v. 1, pp. 15–17.
¹⁰Treaty number 16, *ibid.*, pp. 42–5.
¹¹Treaty number 18, *ibid.*, p. 47.

wandered at will in the Lake Simcoe district, but about that date Sir John Colborne,[12] disturbed by their nomadic habits, set aside land for them between the Narrows at Orillia and Coldwater on Matchedash Bay, and made provision for houses and farms and for religious instruction. The Chippewas accepted Colborne's plan and in September, 1830, the chiefs and headmen of Yellowhead's band wrote that they were about to settle at the village that was being built for them (C 9). The band under Yellowhead was established at the Narrows, the band under Aisance at the Coldwater end of the reserve, and the one under Snake on Snake Island in Lake Simcoe.

Sir Francis Bond Head was as much concerned about the Indians as Colborne had been, but believed that their problems were caused by contact with European civilization and that the only hope lay in removing the Indians far from white settlements. To effect this he assembled them at conferences held at the Narrows and Coldwater and suggested that they sell their lands and move farther from the white population (C 14). After some consideration the chiefs met in Toronto in 1836 and signed an agreement for the sale of their lands in return for the interest on one-third of the proceeds. Later, in 1842, they complained that they had not received any money and were not satisfied with the terms of sale (C 18). They were not the only critics of Head's policy. The news of his action brought an immediate outcry in Britain from missionary organizations, the Aborigines' Protection Society, and other well-wishers, and resulted in a series of investigations into the management of Indian relations which culminated in the appointment of a commission of inquiry[13] in 1842.

Before Yellowhead and his tribe moved from the Narrows, rebellion broke out in Upper Canada and Head returned to England. During the border crisis of 1838, Head's successor, Sir George Arthur, called upon the Indians of Lakes Simcoe and Huron to serve their Queen and country. A camp was set up for them at Holland Landing in November, 1838, but was disbanded in January of 1839. The Indians who had been deprived of the opportunity of hunting in the north at the winter season, naturally demanded rations for their families as well as pay for themselves, and bickering over the settlement continued for some time (C 15, C 16).

[12]Colborne to Sir George Murray, Oct. 14, 1830 (Great Britain, Colonial Office, *Aboriginal Tribes of North America*, pp. 128–9).
[13]Canada, Commission Appointed to Inquire into the Affairs of the Indians in Canada, *Report* (Legislative Assembly, *Journals*, 1844–5, app. EEE).

When Sir Francis Bond Head persuaded the Chippewas to sell their land in 1836, Yellowhead and his band bought 1,600 acres which had been abandoned by white farmers at Rama on Lake Couchiching. In 1839 they prepared for the move (C 17) and settled on land which they have held to the present day. Aisance and his band moved to Beausoleil and the Christian Islands, and Snake remained for a time at Snake Island.

The Rama band, although probably the best known, was never very numerous. It numbered 184 in 1842, and 201 in 1857. In 1858 the Special Commission Appointed to Investigate Indian Affairs reported, "This Band are much given to hunting and basket making, consequently avoid tilling the soil, and are dragging through a life disgraceful to humanity" (C 20). Muskoka was their favourite hunting ground, and there the families had their traditional trapping limits, Yellowhead in the district between Lake Muskoka and Lake of Bays, and the Bigwin family around Lake of Bays where the name is perpetuated in Bigwin Island. Although the Rama Indians usually hunted in Muskoka they also went to the Gull River waters in Haliburton, where V. B. Wadsworth met Rama women in 1860 (D 16).

The Chippewas under Chief John Aisance who moved to Beausoleil Island in 1842 numbered 232 persons in 1842 and still only 233 in 1857 (C 20). They were predominantly Roman Catholic in contrast with the Rama Indians who were Protestant. By 1858 they had cleared 300 of the island's 4,000 acres, though they did not cultivate the whole amount in any one year. Often they were obliged to make their gardens on surrounding islands because Beausoleil did not lend itself to gardening, and Indian methods of agriculture quickly exhausted the soil. About 1856 they moved to the Christian Islands.

The Sandy Island Indians were sometimes referred to as Ojibwas to distinguish them from the Chippewas of Lakes Simcoe and Huron, but the distinction had little meaning since they too acknowledged Yellowhead as their head chief. They were divided into two bands, one the Sandy Island or Shawanaga Indians with Solomon James as chief, and the other the Muskoka or Miskoka Indians, for many years led by Chief Mekis or Megis and after his death about 1858 by Begahmegahbow (C 22). In 1857 the Sandy Island Indians numbered 145, and by 1867 had increased to 174. The Special Commission of 1858 described them in rather unflattering terms (C 20).

For many years the Muskoka Indians occupied a tract of land between Lakes Muskoka and Rosseau where Port Carling now stands; the village was called Obajewanung, occasionally Baisong Rapids, and later, Indian Gardens or Indian Village. They and the band under Chief Solomon James both claimed Parry Island as a reserve and carried on long, involved discussions with the government as to the lands to be occupied by these two related groups (C 24, C 25). Some of the Muskoka Indians under Chief Begahmegahbow were still living at the Indian Village when the first steamboat, the *Wenonah,* made its maiden voyage in 1866, but soon after they moved to Parry Island.

Although the government was concerned for the religious and temporal welfare of the Indians it was equally or more concerned with obtaining the surrender of Indian lands on favourable terms. In 1850 William B. Robinson arranged a treaty for a large, ill-defined area which stretched from Penetanguishene to Batchawana Bay on Lake Superior, together with the islands off the shores, and inland to the height of land which separated the territory of the Hudson's Bay Company from Canada (C 19). This surrender was interpreted to include lands hitherto unceded in Muskoka and Haliburton. The agreement was made by the principal men of the Ojibwa Indians inhabiting and claiming the above lands, but Yellowhead and his band, although they held hunting grounds in Muskoka, had no part in the treaty. Following this, in 1856, by Treaty number 76,[14] the Chippewas of Lakes Couchiching, Simcoe, and Huron surrendered certain islands in Lakes Simcoe and Couchiching and all the islands in Georgian Bay to which they claimed ownership, except the Christian Islands. This treaty covered a comparatively small acreage, but it included Beausoleil Island.

The Huron-Ottawa territory was divided into townships; roads were built and settlements made, but the Chippewas and Mississaugas still pressed claims for compensation for certain lands which they considered had not been rightfully surrendered (C 26). In 1923, after an official inquiry, the governments of the Dominion of Canada and the Province of Ontario acknowledged the justice of these claims, drew up the Williams Treaty,[15] which included parts of both Muskoka and Haliburton, and paid compensation to the Chippewas and Mississaugas.

[14]*Indian Treaties and Surrenders,* v. 1, pp. 203–5.
[15]Canada, Department of Indian Affairs, *Indian Treaties* (processed copy); also Morris, *Indians of Ontario,* p. 61 and map.

To what extent the Indians in the nineteenth century knew the waterways of Muskoka and Haliburton, trapped and fished in the area, or cultivated a few acres of its soil is difficult to estimate. The best evidence comes from the brief, scattered references in the writings of explorers, surveyors, and early settlers. Thus in 1819 Lieutenant Portlock commented that a certain river, apparently the Kahshe, "is stated by the Indians to be a considerable stream" (A 19). Lieutenant Catty in 1819 and the Royal Engineers who surveyed the water routes in 1826 and 1827 made almost no references to Indians except as guides (B 1, B 8, B 9). Alexander Shirreff met few Indians on his exploratory journey in 1829 and his guide was an Indian canoe man who knew nothing of the route. Concerning the Muskoka River, Shirreff said, "This river, by the traders, is called the Muskoka, after the Mississagua chief, who hunts in some part of its neighbourhood" (B 24).

Carthew and Baddeley encountered more Indians in their survey of 1835. In his report Carthew mentioned a number of Indians including a band under Pamosagay who had cleared forty acres of land and were growing corn and potatoes on an island in Lake Rosseau (C 11). David Thompson in 1837 reported Indian lodges on an island in Lake Muskoka, and an "Islet where Indians have formerly been" in Lake Joseph. On Lake Muskoka he met two Indians and a sick boy on their way to Lake Rosseau (B 32), and at Canoe Lake he saw an old camp, apparently Iroquois. Alexander Murray reported that on the survey of the Muskoka and York rivers in 1853 he was informed by the Indians of Lake Rosseau that numbers of their tribe resorted during the hunting season to the area north of Fairy and Peninsula lakes to trap beaver (D 10).

J. S. Dennis gave no account of the Indians he met in his surveys of 1860 and 1861 (D 15) but in a letter of February 21, 1862, he reported on his efforts to settle the Muskoka Indians' request for land between Lakes Rosseau and Muskoka (C 24). Vernon B. Wadsworth, who was a student of Dennis's at the time of the surveys, later told about the Indians he had met, in one of the few descriptive accounts which are available (C 23).

The surveyors laying out the townships of the Muskoka district frequently saw signs of Indian occupation. In the Lake of Bays area, for example, George Rykert in his survey of Ridout Township in 1862 noted that it was the favourite hunting ground of the Lake Simcoe Indians who also made large quantities of sugar, and Robert T. Burns in his report on McLean Township said, "A few acres have been cleared by the Indians on which I noticed corn and potatoes growing."[16] J. P. Vansittart reported of Brunel Township, "it is highly valued by the Indians as a hunting ground, two or three families of whom camp here every fall and winter."[17]

Reminiscences of early settlers frequently mentioned the Indians. Alfred Kay of Port Sydney wrote, "Each fall would see the Indians with their families from the Rama reserve canoeing past our place on the river making their way to their hunting and trapping grounds far up in the North. In the spring they came back laden with furs and pelts. Chief Bigwin and Menominee were among the tribes and I knew the latter quite well. He was a fine old man."[18]

[16]Kirkwood and Murphy, *The Undeveloped Lands in Northern & Western Ontario*, p. 93.
[17]*Ibid.*, p. 96.
[18]Reminiscences of Alfred Kay as told to Mildred I. Hoth (*Pioneer Days in Muskoka*, p. 15).

D. SURVEYS FOR SETTLEMENT

DURING THE YEARS in which exploring expeditions were searching for water communications between Lake Huron and the Ottawa River, land surveyors were gradually working north toward the southern boundaries of Muskoka and Haliburton. By 1826 at least one surveyor, John Huston, was examining the land north of the Kawartha Lakes and probably in the southern part of Haliburton. In November of that year he had received instructions to ascertain whether a range of townships fit for settlement could be found north of Verulam, Harvey, Burleigh, and Methuen (D 1). According to the reports which he submitted in 1827 he examined the land north of Harvey for a depth of more than one range of townships, which would have taken him into the southern part of Snowdon or Glamorgan, and for the depth of nearly two townships north of Burleigh, which would have taken him through Monmouth, but he found little land fit for settlement (D 2, D 3).

In 1830 Charles Rankin surveyed in the Newcastle District,[1] starting from the Talbot River and proceeding north and east. He found much poor land and concluded, "what we saw agreeing with report of traders & they also having stated to us that the same description continued Eastwardly to water emptying into Balsam Lake & northwardly to Gull Lake we thought it advisable to abandon the survey as useless." In 1834–5 John Smith, Junior, explored land to the rear of Fenelon, in Somerville Township, and also between Balsam Lake and Thorah Township.[2]

Although Carthew and Baddeley were instructed in 1835 to direct their attention to "the courses of rivers, and dimensions of lakes and creeks," they were to report as well on "the capacity of the country required to be explored, as regards the interests of settlers" (B 26). David Thompson also observed the quality of the land along the route of his exploratory survey in 1837 and later wrote to the Provincial Secretary: "Although the examination of the Muskako River for a canal was a failure, yet it brought us acquainted with a valuable tract of Country for settlement." He estimated that there were 1,024,000 acres of land along the Mus-

---

[1]Ontario, Department of Lands and Forests, Surveyors Letters, Book 8, no. 32.
[2]John Smith, Junior, "Survey of tract of land in rear of Fenelon, East of Balsam Lake &c." (P.A.O.)

koka fit for cultivation which would give 200 acres to each of 5120 families (D 4).

An Order in Council in 1847 directed the Commissioner of Crown Lands to open the waste lands in the rear of the Midland, Victoria, and Colborne districts. Two surveying parties were to start from the Madawaska River at Bark Lake, one under John Haslett to work east to the Bathurst District, the other under Robert Bell to work west to the place where the boundary line of the Home District crossed the Muskoka River, not far from the site of the town of Bracebridge. Bell's instructions[3] required that he engage assistants who, when the line passed through land unsuited for roads or settlements, would explore to the right and the left.

The survey party left the Madawaska River on August 26, 1847, and reached the Home District boundary the middle of February. On his survey from Bark Lake to the Muskoka, Bell ran a direct line and on the return eastward explored a road line which inevitably deviated somewhat from the original line (D 5, D 6). The length of the exploring line—over eighty miles—greatly increased the difficulties of obtaining men and supplies. More than once Bell had to send back to the Ottawa for additional workers "willing to engage in a service that was universally dreaded." Supplies had to be carried from Bark Lake; cattle were driven to the camp and butchered as needed to avoid carrying the quantities of pork otherwise necessary.

Bell's Line ran between the present townships of Bangor and Jones, Wicklow and Lyell, McClure and Sabine, Bruton and Clyde, Harburn and Eyre, Guilford and Havelock, Stanhope and Sherborne, Hindon and Ridout, Oakley and McLean, Draper and Macaulay, and Bell himself made careful observations of the country through which the survey passed. At one point in Harburn Township he walked about fifteen miles to the south of the line where he climbed a rocky pinnacle to view the land, and on Christmas Day he explored several miles southward in Stanhope Township. He summarized his impressions in his report: "With respect to the features & character of the Country I would beg to state that from the Madawaska River [to] the Muskako River the country is uneven and hilly throughout, but in my opinion the chief part of it is quite fit for settlement." Later in his report he admitted "The greatest objection that at all exists in respect to the whole territory is the great abundance of Rocks" (D 6).

[3]Instructions to Land Surveyors, Book 5, pp. 93–6.

After the Robinson Treaty of 1850 (C 19) brought a large but ill-defined area, newly acquired from the Indians, under the control of the government, the Territorial Divisions Act (I 1) was passed which added this land to the older settled counties. In May, 1852, Simcoe County petitioned to have the tract which had been annexed to it surveyed for settlement (D 7), and in November of the same year an Address was presented by the Legislative Assembly to the Governor General praying for a survey of the country bounded by the French River, Lake Nipissing, the Ottawa River, Lakes Huron and Simcoe, and the settled parts of Upper Canada (D 8).

Even before the petition was presented, J. W. Bridgland had been instructed to survey the township of Carden and a road line from the Eldon Portage to the Muskoka River. When the Township of Carden proved unfit for settlement he was instructed to continue his line by the south bank of the river to Georgian Bay. Bridgland's report was probably the most critical to come from the pen of any surveyor in the Muskoka district: "The general quality of the land," he wrote, "is extremely rocky, and broken, so much so indeed, that, in a district explored of abt. five hundred square miles, not a portion, sufficient for a small township, could be obtained in any one locality, of a generally cultivatable nature." He warned the government against "incurring future expenses in the subdivision of a country into Townships, and farm lots, which is entirely un-fitted, as a whole, for agricultural purposes " (D 9). Unfortunately, with the Legislative Assembly urging the opening of the Ottawa-Huron tract for settlement, little heed was paid to his warning.

The next important exploration of the Muskoka and Haliburton country was carried out by Alexander Murray in 1853 for the Geological Survey of Canada as part of a geological and topo-graphical survey of the territory lying between Lake Huron and the Ottawa River (D 10). As stated previously Murray does not seem to have been acquainted with David Thompson's work for he commented that little or nothing was known to him of the country through which he would have to pass, and "Not being acquainted with any accurate surveys of the portion of the interior I was about to visit, the main water courses naturally afforded the greatest facilities for my work." The survey conducted by Murray might be considered the completion of an era of exploration of the water routes of the Huron-Ottawa country which began with Catty in 1819, and lasted a third of a century, but its real importance lies in the analysis of the rocks and soil.

Murray's route began, as did Thompson's, with the southern

branch of the Muskoka River, often known as the Muskosh. Murray did not survey Lake Muskoka in detail, nor did he go up the Indian River to Lake Rosseau although he mentioned the latter by the name of Rousseau. At the forks of the Muskoka River above Lake Muskoka he chose the North Branch (whereas Thompson took the South) and so went by Lakes Mary, Fairy, Peninsula, and across the portage to the Lake of Bays. These names he gave to the lakes and they have persisted to the present day. From the Lake of Bays he followed the Oxtongue or Muskoka River to the lake which he named Oxtongue because of its shape, and then to Canoe Lake where he built a canoe, a very few miles from where David Thompson had built his canoes in 1837. Both Thompson and Murray gave the name Canoe Lake to the lake on which they found cedar for the building of their canoes but Murray's name has been retained for the northern one and Thompson's lake, immediately to the south, has been renamed South Tea Lake. Here once more the two routes separated. Murray continued through Jo Lake, Burnt Island, Otter Slide, White Trout, and the Petawawa River to the Ottawa, and returned by the York River route: Mud, Golden, and Round lakes, the Little Madawaska, Barry's Bay, Lake Kamaniskeg, York River, Baptiste and Benoir lakes, southwest through Harcourt Township by the lakes and rivers of the height of land to Farquhar and Grace lakes, then to Drag and Kashagawigamog lakes, the Gull River, and so to Balsam Lake.

In 1856 and 1857 Michael Deane ran exploration lines connecting the northeast corner of Somerville with the Gull River and with Bell's Line (D 11, D 12). He found some land "well adapted for agricultural purposes" but other parts "rough rocky and unproductive." He recommended a road from Fenelon Falls to Bell's Line but did not consider a road from Gull River to Bell's Line at the Muskoka River advisable, because he thought the route to the lands in the valleys of the Muskoka and Black rivers should be by way of Beaverton.

In the same year, 1857, instructions were issued for the survey of the boundary lines between several of the townships in the Haliburton area "with the view of opening up for settlement this section of the Ottawa and Huron Territory." John Lindsay[4] was to survey the boundaries between Minden and Snowdon, Dysart and Glamorgan, Dudley and Monmouth, and Harcourt and Cardiff, and James W. Fitzgerald those between Minden and Stanhope, Dysart and Guilford, Dudley and Harburn, and Harcourt and Bruton (D 13).

[4]*Ibid.*, pp. 331–5.

Fitzgerald's survey followed the line which a year or two later was adopted as the Peterson Road in preference to the line about one township further north which had been surveyed as a road by Robert Bell. His estimate of the proportion of good and bad land and the quality of the timber was summed up in the words: "it is my opinion that at least 40 p cent of the whole is well adapted for immediate cultivation besides a large proportion would in the course of time be rendered available" (D 14). This estimate is especially interesting because six of the eight townships, Dysart, Guilford, Dudley, Harburn, Harcourt, and Bruton were among the nine townships in Haliburton later selected by the Canadian Land and Emigration Company, and on which B. W. Gossage and Edward Miles gave very conflicting estimates of the number of acres of land fit for settlement (F 43).

In 1860–1 John Stoughton Dennis carried on, or directed, a number of surveys in the Muskoka district which are of special interest because they occurred just at the time the country was opened for settlement. Fortunately, in addition to Dennis's factual report (D 15), there are available the more colourful reminiscences of his assistant, Vernon B. Wadsworth (D 16). Dennis took his party up the Muskoka Road, and by Lake Muskoka and the North Branch of the Muskoka River to High Falls where he established a store camp and decided on a crossing. He connected this point with the bridge newly erected over the South Branch and then proceeded north to Mary, Fairy, and Peninsula lakes. According to Vernon B. Wadsworth, Dennis discovered Vernon Lake and gave it, as well as the river which flows from Vernon to Fairy Lake, the name of his young pupil. He determined the place for a crossing of the Vernon River, and there a few years later the town of Huntsville developed. From the crossing of the river Dennis ran a line northeast to the thirty-fifth mile north of High Falls and out to the Bobcaygeon Road, but owing to the rough country between the head waters of the Muskoka and the Magnetawan could not get a line fit for a road beyond the thirty-fifth mile. Following this, Dennis surveyed westerly from the Muskoka Road, passing between Lakes Muskoka and Rosseau at Indian Village, then south-west to the mouth of the Muskosh River, where he examined the harbour.

At a period when transportation by water was more practical than by land it was of vital importance to find an outlet on Georgian Bay for the townships to be opened by the Muskoka and Bobcaygeon roads. In 1852 J. W. Bridgland had made a cursory examination of the harbour at the mouth of the Muskosh and given a favourable report on it (D 9), but Dennis considered it "anything but a good one" and abandoned the idea of using it as a shipping port for the new district (D 15). As an alternative he examined Parry Sound harbour which he found "commodious and safe." A party of surveyors under Dennis's direction then ran a line from Parry Sound to the Bobcaygeon Road as far north as the present Scotia Junction, but again found the land unsuited for road or settlement. Accordingly Dennis suggested that a road be opened from Parry Sound to the Muskoka Road near Lake Vernon and from there to the Bobcaygeon Road. Had this been done it would have given the northern part of Muskoka and Haliburton direct access to a good harbour on Georgian Bay. Instead, however, a survey was begun for a road line from Parry Sound through Indian Gardens to the Muskoka Road just north of Bracebridge (E 19). Dennis's surveys were among the last of the large-scale exploratory investigations which laid the groundwork for the location of the colonization roads in Muskoka.

E. THE COLONIZATION ROADS

THE ROAD WAS THE KEY to settlement on the Laurentian Shield. In the southern part of the province good farming land lay along the Great Lakes and on the banks of navigable rivers; but the Georgian Bay shore was rocky and forbidding, and good land was to be found only in the interior, difficult if not impossible of access by water alone, and as a result "insurmountable to individual enterprise."

During the 1850's and 1860's ambitious plans for colonization roads were announced by the government. Some of the roads, based on systematic exploration, were carried to completion, some never went beyond the planning stage, others were abandoned when they reached country too rough for roads or settlement. Those roads that did develop were the ones which led directly to good agricultural land. Grandiose schemes to provide transportation between distant points were doomed from the beginning. The day of long distance hauling by land had not yet arrived; neither the vehicles nor the road builders were ready.

Since the government intended to open the tract from the Ottawa River to Georgian Bay more or less as a unit, the old dream of a route connecting the two waters found expression in the road plans of the early 1850's. The key road was to be the Ottawa-Opeongo, a great curving line to run from the Ottawa River in the Township of Horton, Renfrew County, northwesterly to Opeongo Lake and later to be extended to Georgian Bay at the mouth of the Magnetawan River. South of this, branching off the Opeongo Road in Brudenel Township, Bell's Line (some maps called it the Muskoka Road) was to run due west to the Muskoka River (E 1). Intersecting one or both of these there was to be a series of roads parallel to one another and running in a south to north direction. Commencing with the easternmost the most important of those actually constructed were the Frontenac, Addington, Hastings, Burleigh, Bobcaygeon, Victoria, and Muskoka (E 2). The Opeongo which had been planned as an overland route from the Ottawa River to Georgian Bay did not even reach Lake Opeongo.

The problems which beset the government in building roads in the Ottawa-Huron tract were much greater than those in the less rugged country to the south. Straight lines were impossible; lakes, rivers, rocks, and hills caused wide deviations. Numerous rivers and creeks required bridges, swamps required causeways, and parts of the country were so rough that no practical road line could be obtained. Work on the Muskoka and Haliburton roads was carried on at first mainly by contract, later under direct control of the government. When it was done by contract, the contractor sometimes bid so low that either he failed to complete the work or he built an inferior road which in turn often was not properly inspected.

The labour supply and the wages varied with the financial condition of the day. At times overseers found it almost impossible to get workers because of the competition of other occupations that were offering better terms (E 49). Many of the new settlers, anxious to clear their land, only agreed to work on the roads when they were in dire need of money for seed grain or food for their families. Wages were low even by the standards of the period. In 1866 they advanced from 90c to $1 per day for labourers and from $1.25 to $1.50 for foremen[1] while board and lodging cost at least $3 per week (E 49). Workers were seldom permitted to live at home (E 5) and the food in the boarding houses was poor. If the men dared to talk of a strike they were threatened with instant dismissal (E 3).

When the roads were completed the government's problems were by no means at an end. Newly made roads were "ploughed into the deepest ruts and mudholes by the heavy provision loads of lumbermen" (E 6) and bridges and causeways were burned through the carelessness of settlers in clearing the land, or by fires in the debris left on the ground by the lumbermen (E 32, E 40). The government paid the cost of surveying and building a colonization road, then required the settlers along the road to keep it in repair. When the road ran through a settled area, the men, busy clearing their farms, were not likely to do more repair work than they were forced to do, while on such roads as the Peterson and the Monck there were long stretches with no settlers who could be held responsible for maintenance. Year after year the government was forced either to allow the roads to deteriorate, or to provide more money for improvements and repairs.

The Muskoka Road

The Muskoka, perhaps more than any other colonization road, in time fulfilled the dream of those who planned it. The route chosen for it determined the location of villages and the flow of

[1]Andrew Russell, Circular to Crown Land Agents, May 19, 1866 (P.A.O., Colonization Roads Papers, Letter Book 2, p. 205).

men and supplies for generations to come. When the government decided to open Muskoka for settlement it issued instructions on October 11, 1856, and April 17, 1857, to Charles Unwin to survey trial lines to the Great Falls on the Muskoka River, one from Atherley on the east side and the other from Orillia on the west side of Lake Couchiching (E 8, E 9). Both proved to be too costly and David Gibson surveyed a third line, from the end of navigation at Washago to a junction with Unwin's easterly line some nine miles distant (E 10). The first grant for the Muskoka Road was made in 1857, and the Minister of Agriculture, in his annual report for that year, announced plans for a road "to run from the head of navigation of Lake Couchiching at a point called Washago Mills to the grand falls at Muskoka, where it will intersect the line known as Bell's line, along which it is proposed to construct a main or base line road eastward from Lake Muskoka until it meets the Ottawa and Opeongo Road."

David Gibson gave out contracts for a bridge over the Severn River and for the first part of the road (E 10). The work began at Washago in 1858 with St. George and O'Brien the contractors, and Charles Rankin, surveyor, responsible for laying off farm lots along the road. Rankin received his instructions in November, 1858 (E 11) but asked permission for his partner Mr. Spry to do the actual work (E 12). The survey was carried out in March, 1859, and in October the first location tickets were issued for lands adjoining the road. The Report of the Board of Agriculture and Statistics for 1859 stated: "From the termination of the navigation on Lake Couchiching where a wharf has been erected, to the Great Falls of Muskoka—a distance of about 21 miles—all streams have been substantially bridged and the road has been levelled and cross-wayed. A very good road between these points has been opened, and the country along it is being rapidly settled." The announcement, however, may have been a little premature. Vernon Wadsworth stated that in 1860 the road was located to the falls on the South Branch of the Muskoka River but was only open to the present site of Gravenhurst, and that the travelled section of the road was so rough that a team could haul but eight hundred pounds of provisions (D 16).

In 1861 the bridge over the North Branch of the Muskoka River at Bracebridge was partly constructed, and by the end of 1863 the road was 24 miles beyond the falls, in the vicinity of Vernon and Fairy lakes where Huntsville now stands (E 15), but the bridge over the Vernon, or Muskoka River was not completed until 1870.

Meanwhile repairs were continually required, and in 1870 the government planked eight of the eleven miles between Washago and Gravenhurst. Even with this improvement the road remained steep, narrow, incredibly rough and dusty. Mrs. King travelled over it by stage coach in 1871 and left a graphic description of her experiences (E 18).

After the Free Grants and Homestead Act of 1868 (F 15) was passed, lots in the northern part of Muskoka were rapidly located. Settlers in Macaulay, Stephenson, and Brunel petitioned for the extension of the road, and settlers in Chaffey Township, to the north and west of Huntsville, petitioned for a bridge across the East River which flows through that township to Vernon Lake (E 16). By 1872 the road was north to the unsubdivided Township of Perry in Parry Sound District. Long before the road had reached the northern limits of Muskoka, settlers were demanding secondary roads to serve localities to the east and west. Some of the roads opened at early dates were: the Muskoka Branch or Alport Road, from the Muskoka Road to the Alport settlement near Lake Muskoka at the mouth of the Muskoka River; the McLean Road east through McLean Township; and the Brunel Road east through Stephenson, Brunel, and Franklin townships.

The Parry Sound Road

In 1861 the government apparently accepted J. S. Dennis's recommendation that Parry Sound be chosen as the outlet on Georgian Bay for Muskoka and Haliburton (D 15), and instructed Dennis to survey a line from the Muskoka Road to Parry Sound and to examine the capability of the country as a field for settlement. A survey party, organized in July of that year, set up a store camp at the head of Lake Rosseau (where the village of Rosseau now stands) and surveyed westward to Parry Sound and eastward to a junction with the Muskoka Road a few miles north of Bracebridge. The line recommended by Dennis was regarded merely as a preliminary one and in December of 1862 James A. Gibson, the well-known surveyor from Willowdale, was instructed to locate the final road line (E 19). The route he selected started a little further north on the Muskoka Road and differed considerably from Dennis's. Tenders for the road were called on November 6, 1862 by David Gibson, Superintendent of Colonization Roads (Plate XII). James Cooper began work on the first six miles in 1863–4 but failed in his contract, and the section was completed by R. J. Oliver in

1865 (E 20). The remainder of the road was constructed by William Beatty of Thorold who found it impractical in places to follow the surveyed line and made still further deviations (E 21).

The final route was described by the Crown Lands Department as follows: "The road commences at a point on the Muskoka road, near to the 9th mile-post north of the Falls of Muskoka, and follows the west boundary line of Stephenson to a point near to the south end of the 6th concession, where it proceeds in a north-westerly direction to Parry Sound." Bridgland announced that the road had been completed in 1867, that it was "a very fair line of road," about 45 miles in length, and had cost $28,154.59, including a bridge which cost $1,800.[2] The Parry Sound Road gave access to two other roads already under construction, the Rosseau and Nipissing Road and the Northern Road which ran from Parry Sound north and eastward.

The Bobcaygeon Road

The Bobcaygeon Road was projected to run north from Bobcaygeon along the easterly boundary of Verulam, Somerville, Lutterworth, Anson, Hindon, Ridout, and Franklin townships, and from there an extension was surveyed to Lake Nipissing "that deviated but slightly from a straight line." In 1856 a grant was made by the government for the new road. W. S. Conger, member of the legislature for Peterborough, was anxious that the road should start at Bobcaygeon, run north between Verulam and Harvey, then bear northeasterly, and that it should be called the Bobcaygeon Road (E 22, E 23). The government accepted the name but not the route.

Construction began on October 16, 1856, and by the end of 1857 the Bureau of Agriculture and Statistics reported that the road was "nearly completed to the rear of Galway and Somerville, within a hundred yards of the Burnt River."[3] There it crossed into Haliburton. On September 7, 1858, Michael Deane noted that it was open for wheeled traffic about one mile north of the Burnt River (E 24). By the end of 1859 thirty-six miles had been completed and as well a winter road had been made three miles further to the north concession of Minden.[4] To prepare for the settlers who

[2]J. W. Bridgland, "Brief History of Colonization Roads Ontario" (P.A.O., Colonization Roads Papers, Reports, 1862–8, p. 376).
[3]Canada, Bureau of Agriculture and Statistics, *Report*, 1857.
[4]*Ibid.*, 1859, pp. 18–19.

were waiting for locations along the road, Michael Deane laid out a tier of lots on both sides of the road from Somerville to Bell's Line during the months from April to July, 1858 (E 24), and J. S. Dennis later laid out the lots along the road north of Bell's Line (E 28).

Meanwhile the government had not abandoned its plan to extend the Bobcaygeon Road north to meet the projected Ottawa and Opeongo Road at Lake Nipissing. On May 19, 1859, the surveyor, J. K. Roche, was instructed to explore for a road from Bell's Line to Lake Nipissing.[5] He commenced the work, but, on September 13, was drowned while crossing Balsam Lake by canoe during a storm. Crosbie Brady continued the survey during the winter of 1859–60, and in spite of unfavourable weather, reached Lake Nipissing at the end of March, and completed the work on June 23 (E 26). The tragedy at the beginning of the survey was followed by a second during the winter in the death of David, another member of the Roche family, and the illness of two other men in the party from scurvy. It was a needless loss of life for the northern part of the road was never built.

In the summer of 1861, James W. Bridgland reported that the road was under construction at the junction of the Peterson line (E 27), and by 1863 it had reached the Oxtongue River in the Township of Franklin (E 29). It progressed little further and the northernmost miles were apparently soon abandoned. Instead, at the demand of the settlers in the 1870's, a spur of the Muskoka Road built eastward from a point just north of Huntsville wound its way along Fairy, Peninsula, and the Lake of Bays to meet the Bobcaygeon Road not far from Dorset.

The southern part of the Bobcaygeon Road has continued in use and has been incorporated into the present system of highways. The northern part, from Minden to Dorset, was altered considerably in the 1930's and now passes to the east, instead of the west of Boshkung Lake.

The Burleigh Road

The Burleigh Road, like the Bobcaygeon, ran north into unsettled lands on the Laurentian Shield. According to the original plan it was to extend from Burleigh Rapids through the townships of Burleigh, Anstruther, Chandos, Cardiff, Monmouth, and Dudley to an intersection with the Peterson Road. Instructions were issued

[5]Instructions to Land Surveyors, Book 5, pp. 400–2.

to James W. Fitzgerald on August 9, 1860, to explore from Burleigh Rapids to the rear of the Township of Burleigh, and supplemented on December 24 with instructions to continue to the Peterson line.[6] Fitzgerald's report on the survey was unusually confident, and concluded: "I have no hesitation in saying that it is capable of becoming in the course of a few years one of the most prosperous of any of the new Colonization Roads being now opened up for settlement in Canada" (E 30).

By the end of 1862 the road extended twenty-three miles north of Burleigh Bridge, but complaints were already being made concerning its condition. J. W. Bridgland, in his report for 1863, recommended the continuation of the road to a junction with the Peterson, but later he added a memorandum that the formation of the Monck Road would render this unnecessary (E 31). In 1866 he noted that expensive yearly improvements were required owing to "irregular, tortuous and injudicious location" and charged that "There appears to have been no clearly conceived purpose, as to where its general direction should lie or tend" (E 33). The townships through which the Burleigh Road ran were settled slowly, if at all, and in consequence it never developed the importance of some of the other colonization roads.

The Peterson Road

As early as 1847 the government was interested in the possibility of opening a road to connect the Ottawa River with the Muskoka River and so with Georgian Bay. In that year instructions were given to Robert Bell to lay out not only an exploring line from the Madawaska to the boundary of the Home District at the Muskoka River, but also as he returned eastward to the Madawaska "to project the best site for the road line."[7] Ten years later, when preparations had been made to build that road, and the contracts had been let, it was realized that for at least part of the way a better route than Bell's Line might be found a few miles to the south. Bell himself agreed that the land to the south of his route was of much better quality than the country he had examined (E 34), and J. S. Peterson, a surveyor, also recommended a more southerly line (E 35). At first it was assumed that the road would follow this southern route only part of the way and then veer northwest to Bell's Line for the remaining portion. However, the entire route

[6]Ibid., pp. 477 and 485.
[7]Ibid., pp. 93–6.

was built about one township south of Bell's original line except for a few miles at the western end where it deviated sharply to the north. In the report of the Minister of Agriculture for 1857 the road was called "Bell's Line" (E 37) but in 1858[8] the name "Peterson" appeared and Peterson Road it remained.

Work on the road commenced at both the eastern and western ends. Twenty-one miles from the eastern end westerly to the Hastings Road had been completed by 1858. In the next year, ten more miles were opened (E 38) and the following year ten more, which brought the road to the northwest of Harcourt Township. By the end of 1861 it had reached the northwest angle of the Township of Dysart and was under contract to the Bobcaygeon Road.[9] Meanwhile the Muskoka section was surveyed in 1859 (E 38) and by 1860 seven and a half miles were opened south and eastward from a point on the Muskoka Road near the Great (Muskoka) Falls, through the township of Draper. The settlers going to, or coming from, the Muskoka Road found this indirect line, southeast through Draper, inconvenient, and as a result in 1866 instructions were given to R. J. Oliver to open a branch from the angle on the Peterson Road directly westward to the Muskoka Road (E 41).

Although the Crown Lands report for 1863 referred to the road as being completed from the Muskoka Road to the junction with the Ottawa-Opeongo and capable of admitting an ordinary wagon with fifteen hundredweight (E 39), the road was never satisfactory. Vernon B. Wadsworth went on foot over the western end of it as far as Guilford Township in 1862 and said, "The Peterson Road for most of the distance was cut out but not travelled by teams excepting by timber teams in the winter and there were not more than a dozen settlers on our whole route of travel" (D 16). As some parts were being cleared in 1863 the underbrush was springing up in others, especially on sections passing through the townships owned by the Canadian Land and Emigration Company (E 39). These the government refused to clear and repair, insisting that the Company keep the road in order as part of the purchase agreement.

J. W. Bridgland recognized that the road was a failure and wrote in February, 1865, "I doubt whether the road has really ever been travelled by waggons throughout its whole length at all, and hence as a grand communication between the Ottawa and Lake Huron

[8]Canada, Bureau of Agriculture and Statistics, *Report*, 1858 (Legislative Council, *Journals*, 1859, app. 3).
[9]Canada, Department of Agriculture, *Report*, 1861.

has never been a realization." He laid the blame on insufficient expenditure, only $338 per mile, and poor supervision, and he called for some action for its improvement (E 40). However, from year to year only a few hundred dollars were spent on repairs; the wilderness won the struggle and parts of the road were overgrown and closed to traffic as early as the 1870's.

The Monck Road

The watchful and at times suspicious attitude of Upper Canada toward the United States after the War of 1812 made it inevitable that the government would give special consideration to all possible lines of communication between the Ottawa River and Lake Huron remote from the frontier. Though the emphasis was on water communication, as early as 1822 it was suggested that a road be built in the rear of the settled townships.[10] In 1823 the Surveyor General, Thomas Ridout, reported that a line of road "through the most Northern line of Townships" was impractical, but suggested one from Lake Simcoe through Georgina, Brock, Mariposa, Ops, Emily, Smith, Douro, Dummer, Belmont, Marmora, Madoc, Elzevir, Kaladar, Kennebec, Olden, and Oso, "connecting with the Military road by the way of Perth and Richmond to the Ottawa."[11] Had this road developed it would have run about three townships to the south of the route selected for the Monck Road forty years later.

The Monck Road was built with a twofold purpose—to provide a military route at a time when relations with the United States again were tense, and to open up new territory for settlement. At first it was regarded as an extension westward of the Mississippi Road, but about the end of 1863 it was given the name Monck (E 42) in honour of the Governor General. Bridgland referred indirectly to its military purpose in 1864 (E 43) and in 1866 he said, "The great advantage of a thorough internal communication road from the navigable waters of Lake Huron to those of the Ottawa by which Military stores & troops may be transported and deposited can hardly be overestimated, indeed it seems to have become in the present threatening emergency an indispensible necessity." He went so far as to suggest blockhouses and arsenal depots at thirty- or forty-mile intervals (E 48). The road was started by J. A. Snow "upon a broader, and more substantial basis, than the

[10]Lord Bathurst to Sir P. Maitland, Dec. 7, 1822 (P.A.C., Q 60, p. 95).

[11]Thomas Ridout to George Hillier, May 30, 1823 (Ontario, Department of Lands and Forests, Surveyor General's Office, Letters Written, v. 26, pp. 36–7).

ordinary Colonization Roads, that in case of necessity, it might be useful for military purposes" (E 49). However, the plan of building a wider roadway and more substantial bridges was followed but a short time, and through most of its length the road was little better than parts of the Peterson.

The Monck Road as finally built was described by the Crown Lands Department as "leading from the upper end of Couchiching Lake in the Township of Mara in an Easterly direction, to unite with the Mississippi at its intersection with the Hastings Road."[12] Using present-day names the route might be described as passing through North Mara, Rathburn, Sebright, Dartmoor, Uphill, Head Lake, Norland, Kinmount, Furnace Falls, Irondale, Gooderham, Monck Road, and Bancroft.

The survey of the road began in 1864. Peter Gibson surveyed the western part and Thomas Weatherald surveyed ten and a quarter miles eastward from the Bobcaygeon Road (E 45) before withdrawing owing to the death of his brother. His work was continued by Robert Gilmour who surveyed from Snowdon Township to the Hastings Road (E 46). In 1866 John A. Snow re-examined the westerly part which had been surveyed by Gibson in order to locate a more favourable line, and in the spring of 1866 superintended the beginnings of construction at the western terminus in Mara (E 49). The road was not completed until 1873 and never was satisfactory. The government expected the settlers along the road to keep it in repair, but they were too scattered and too few in number, and by 1875 the Monck Road was reported to be in a "deplorable state" (E 50).

[12]J. W. Bridgland, "Report of Colonization Roads operations during 1866" (P.A.O., Colonization Roads Papers, Reports, 1862–8, p. 296).

F. THE BEGINNINGS OF AGRICULTURAL SETTLEMENT

DURING THE EARLY 1830's it seemed possible that the Ottawa-Huron tract would fall into the hands of a land company and be settled from the Ottawa River. The project of opening a regular line of communication between Montreal and Lake Huron by way of the Ottawa and settling the neighbouring country was said by Robert Shirreff to have been first suggested by his brother, Alexander Shirreff, in a pamphlet published in 1824 (F 1), but such a possibility must have been evident since the days when Champlain and the Jesuit Fathers first toiled over the long portages.

Charles Shirreff and his sons Robert and Alexander all were strong advocates of the opening of the tract for settlement. Alexander made the exploratory trip in 1829, already described (B 24), and when Robert went to London about 1832 he acted as an agent to stir up interest in the formation of a land company. For some men the opening of the tract for settlement was a mission in life, for others, especially land company officers, it was probably nothing more than a specious argument for obtaining large grants of free or cheap land upon which to build their fortunes.

On September 29, 1832, Robert Shirreff wrote to Viscount Howick, Undersecretary of State for War and the Colonies, outlining the advantages of connecting the Ottawa with Lake Huron and suggesting that grants of land be given to a company willing to undertake the task (F 1). For the next few years projected or actual companies, with variant names but often the same officers, badgered the British government for grants of land and privileges.[1] A proposed Ottawa Land Company paralleled, or was identical with, the North American Colonial Association, which in turn was closely related to the North American Colonial Association of Ireland, or the Irish North American Colonial Association, or the General Colonial Association of Ireland.

Compelling arguments based alike on conditions in the old and in the new world were marshalled by the projected companies to justify demands for large grants of land: the poverty and lack of

[1]Lengthy correspondence may be found in P.A.C., Q 219, pts. 1–2, and Q 224, pts. 2–3.

employment in Ireland and other parts of the British Isles; conditions on the sailing ships used by the poorer classes of emigrants; and the wretchedness and despair experienced by persons arriving in a strange land with none to help (F 6). To strengthen these arguments the land companies pointed out that regular communication between the Ottawa River and Lake Huron would bring the commerce of prosperous American communities of the west to Montreal and Quebec; that by such a route the distance to Montreal from the point where Lakes Huron, Michigan, and Superior meet would be 500 miles, while from that point to New York by the Erie Canal was 1,100 or 1,200 miles;[2] that in time of war a route far from the frontier would offer safety for military and commercial shipping, and a well-disposed group of immigrants settled along the way would afford further protection.

In spite of much talk there was considerable uncertainty, or deliberate indefiniteness concerning the actual route, the kind of communication to be built, and the speed with which it would be made ready. Before Alexander Shirreff explored from the Ottawa River to Lake Huron, the Shirreff family had been in favour of a Muskoka River route, but later apparently they and others took the Lake Nipissing and French River route for granted. Some writers assumed an all-water route. Robert Shirreff referred to "canals or railroads" (F 1), and still others regarded an improved water communication as a natural outcome of settlement (F 2). The tract of land requested for colonization was stated by Lord Fitzwilliam in a letter to T. Spring-Rice as "that which lies between the River Ottawa and Lake Huron, to the South of Lake Nipissing, and in the rear of the present Settlements in the Newcastle and Midland districts, but separated from them by an extensive and barren space" (F 4). A map by Maria Knowles, enclosed with the letter, indicated the area more exactly (Plate III).

At times it looked as though the requested land grant was about to be made, but changes in the British government and the cross currents of political life intervened. The final blow came in April, 1835, in a message from Lord Aberdeen to J. G. Ravenshaw which conveyed "the conviction to which his Lordship had been led by a consideration of the documents connected with the Subject, that it is not expedient to establish any new Land Company whatever in Canada" (F 7).

[2]"Comparative Remarks on Two Projected Communications with Lake Huron" (P.A.C., Q 224, pt. 3, pp. 708–20).

The Opening of Muskoka and Haliburton

Almost a quarter of a century elapsed after the futile attempts of the land companies to obtain the Ottawa-Huron tract before the government opened it for settlement. The decision to turn the heavily forested land of the Canadian Shield to agricultural use has been a target for criticism during the last one hundred years, and can be understood only in the light of conditions at the time in the British Isles and in the settled parts of the province. Many public-spirited men, moved by the poverty which still existed in England and even more in Ireland, believed that homes should be found for the needy immigrants on the unsettled lands in Canada. Others, influenced by economic arguments, hoped that an increase in population and in the area under cultivation would bring financial prosperity. They were seriously disturbed to see emigrants from Great Britain going to the United States where wages were higher and land could be had on easier terms than in Canada. Only in the north—for the prairies were still locked in the grip of the Hudson's Bay Company—was there to be found free or cheap land. Upon this tract many Canadians fixed their hopes of free land for themselves, their sons, and their friends.

When Muskoka and Haliburton were opened, the conditions on which land was available for purchase or as a free grant were determined by "An Act to Amend the Law for the Sale and the Settlement of the Public Lands," 1853 (F 8). This provided for the sale of land at a price fixed from time to time, and for free grants to actual settlers in the vicinity of a public road in any new settlement, under regulations to be made by the Governor in Council. The free grants on the public roads were expected to provide a body of settlers who would keep the colonization roads in repair and so relieve the government of that expense. Late in the summer of 1858 two Crown Land Agents were appointed (F 9), and in the following July a number of townships were opened for sale (F 10, F 11, F 12). Several problems developed almost at once: some townships settled quickly, but in others few locations took place; settlers who purchased lands on instalments found they had no way of earning money for the payments; speculators bought the land, stripped it of its pine and abandoned it, or left it uncleared and so a handicap to other settlers on the road.

Since a number of the Muskoka townships had been added to Simcoe County, the Simcoe County Council was in a position to observe the weaknesses of the system. In 1865 it presented a memorial to

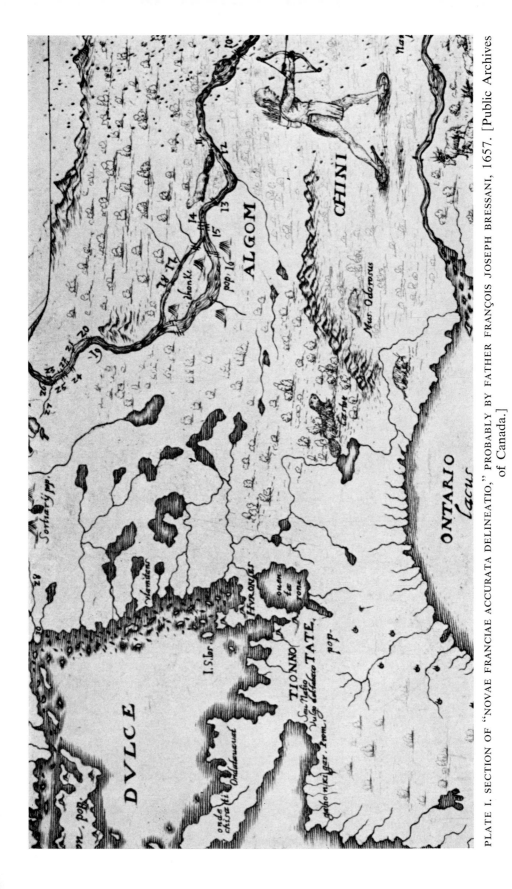

PLATE I. SECTION OF "NOVAE FRANCIAE ACCURATA DELINEATIO," PROBABLY BY FATHER FRANÇOIS JOSEPH BRESSANI, 1657. [Public Archives of Canada.]

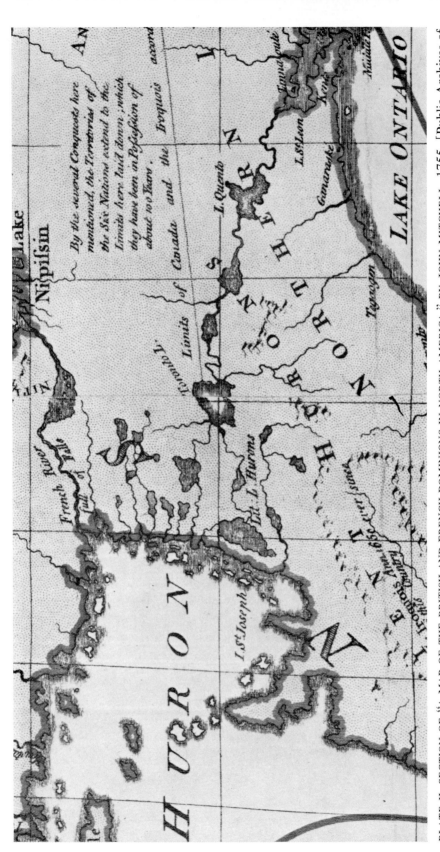

PLATE II. SECTION OF "A MAP OF THE BRITISH AND FRENCH DOMINIONS IN NORTH AMERICA," BY JOHN MITCHELL, 1755. [Public Archives of Canada.]

PLATE III. MAP BY MARIA KNOWLES SHOWING THE "TRACT OF LAND PROPOSED TO BE COLONIZED" BY THE LAND COMPANIES, 1834. [Public Archives of Canada.]

PLATE IV. INDIAN VILLAGE AT RAMA, A WATERCOLOUR BY TITUS HIBBERT WARE, SEPTEMBER, 1844. [Ware's Diary, Toronto Public Library.]

PLATE V. THE SEVERN RIVER, BY MRS. JOHN GRAVES SIMCOE, BASED ON A SKETCH BY LT. ROBERT PILKINGTON, 1793. [Department of Public Records and Archives, Ontario.]

PLATE VI. VERNON LAKE, PENCIL SKETCH BY GEORGE HARLOW WHITE, 1875. [John Ross Robertson Collection, Toronto Public Library.]

PLATE VII. LAKE MUSKOKA, 1883, BY EDWARD ROPER. [Roper's *Muskoka, the Picturesque Playground of Canada.*]

PLATE VIII. CLERGY HOUSE, MINDEN, PROBABLY BUILT ABOUT 1870 AS A DEPOT FOR A LUMBER COMPANY AND LATER ACQUIRED BY THE ANGLICAN DIOCESE OF TORONTO. [Department of Public Records and Archives, Ontario.]

PLATE IX. MADILL CHURCH, STEPHENSON TOWNSHIP, BUILT BY THE WESLEYAN METHODISTS, 1872–3. [Ontario Department of Travel and Publicity.]

PLATE X. PORT CARLING, SKETCH BY S. PENSON, 1879. [From W. E. Hamilton's *Guide Book & Atlas of Muskoka & Parry Sound Districts.*]

PLATE XI. EARLY LOCOMOTIVE AT HALIBURTON. [Department of Public Records and Archives, Ontario.]

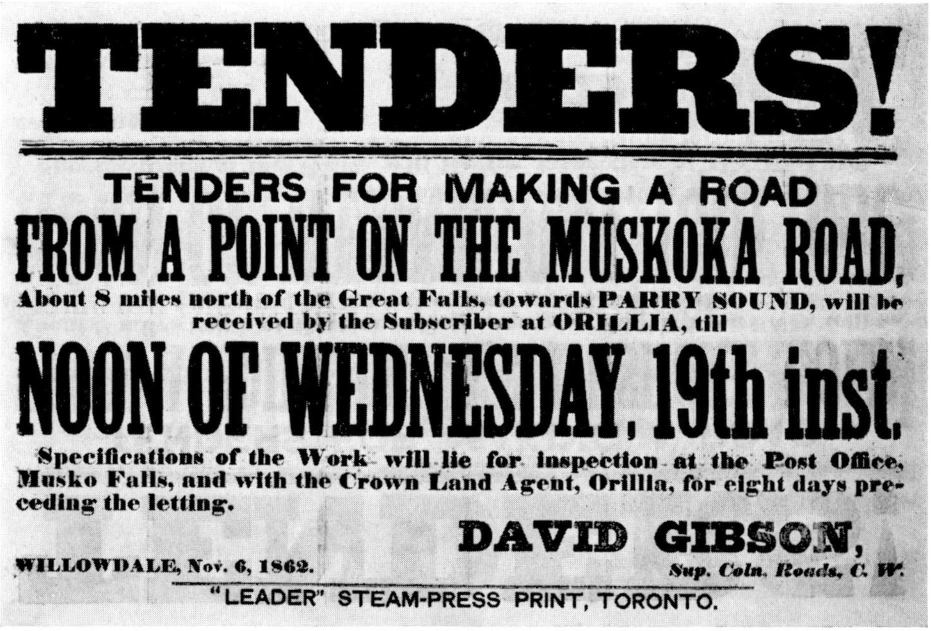

TENDERS!

TENDERS FOR MAKING A ROAD
FROM A POINT ON THE MUSKOKA ROAD,

About 8 miles north of the Great Falls, towards PARRY SOUND, will be received by the Subscriber at ORILLIA, till

NOON OF WEDNESDAY, 19th inst.

Specifications of the Work will lie for inspection at the Post Office, Musko Falls, and with the Crown Land Agent, Orillia, for eight days preceding the letting.

DAVID GIBSON,

WILLOWDALE, Nov. 6, 1862.   Sup. Coln. Roads, C. W.

"LEADER" STEAM-PRESS PRINT, TORONTO.

PLATE XII. ADVERTISEMENT FOR TENDERS FOR PARRY SOUND ROAD, NOVEMBER 6, 1862.

THE RESIDENCE OF   "THE GROVE,"   THOS. MCMURRAY. ESQ.
BRACEBRIDGE.

PLATE XIII. LETTERHEAD OF THOMAS MCMURRAY, 1874. [Immigration Papers, Department of Public Records and Archives, Ontario.]

Pratts Hotel   *Rosseau*

PLATE XIV. ROSSEAU HOUSE, COMMONLY KNOWN AS PRATT'S HOTEL, WATERCOLOUR BY ARTHUR ELLIS, AUGUST 15, 1881, FOR PUBLICATION IN THE *Canadian Illustrated News.*

the Governor General stating that the manner in which the lands were being disposed of was "injurious to the best interests, and materially retards the progress and settlement of the country" (F 14). The Council advocated free grants of land with stringent conditions of settlement and forfeiture of lands held by speculators if purchase money was in arrears.

In 1868 the Province of Ontario passed the "Free Grants and Homestead Act" making it lawful for the Lieutenant Governor in Council to "appropriate any Public Lands considered suitable for settlement and cultivation, and not being Mineral Lands or Pine Timber Lands, as Free Grants to actual Settlers" (F 15). Muskoka and Haliburton were included in the area in which such grants could be made. Strict settlement duties were set forth: to clear and have under cultivation at least fifteen acres, two acres of which were to be cleared and cultivated annually during the five years following the date of location; to build a house at least sixteen by twenty feet; and to have actually and continually resided upon the land for five years after date of location. A clause, providing that one hundred acres of land was to be given to each settler over the age of eighteen years, was amended the following session to two hundred acres,[3] and later provision was made for an extra allowance of land, on request, to compensate for rocky portions.

Following the passing of the Act, the Department of Crown Lands gave notice that the townships of Humphry, Cardwell, Watt, Stephenson, Brunel, Macaulay, McLean, Muskoka, Draper, McDougall, and Foley were open for free grants, and that part of the lands in Cardiff, Chandos, Monmouth, and Anstruther was also open (F 16). Unfortunately the "Free Grants and Homestead Act" made no provision for relief for the settlers who had purchased lands in some of these townships and who still owed payments on them. Petitions were presented, among them one from Monck Township (F 17), pointing out the injustice of making the early settler who had contended with the greatest hardships pay arrears on his land while new settlers obtained free grants.

The Settlement of Muskoka

In 1859 R. J. Oliver was appointed "Agent for the settlement of the Severn and Muskoka Road" (F 13) and in October he met the waiting applicants and issued the first location tickets. By the end

[3]"An Act to Amend 'The Free Grants and Homestead Act of 1868,' " (Ontario, *Statutes*, 1868–9, 32 Vic., c. 20).

of the year he reported 54 locations and stated that some settlers were planning to buy Crown land in the rear of their free grants, that already they were asking for postal service and preparing for a schoolhouse and a place of worship (F 18). The number of persons on the free grants had risen to 190 in January, 1861 (F 19) and to 287 by the end of 1862 with a further 743 on the Crown lands (F 20). The government of Ontario advertised the free grant lands in the late 1860's by pamphlets and posters distributed in Canada, Great Britain, and a number of European countries, and sent an Emigration Commissioner to Great Britain. Partly as a result of this, the census showed a steady rise in the population of Muskoka: 5,360 in 1871; 12,973 in 1881; 15,666 in 1891; 20,971 in 1901; then little increase or even a decrease in the ensuing decades.[4]

Although the total population of Muskoka was rising until the turn of the century, the rural townships had begun to decline much earlier. Discontent with the quality of the soil was evident from an early date. In 1867 A. P. Cockburn, member of the provincial legislature, addressed a meeting on the advantages of forming a Settlers Association, at which he admitted "that very often people had come in here with exaggerated ideas of the country and had left in consequence of the disappointments they had met with" (F 22). In 1870 the Alport farm, probably the best in Muskoka, was offered for sale. The list of stock and equipment (F 23) and the description of the farm (F 24) show what could be done with Muskoka land, but the fact that Mr. Alport had decided to sell his property and leave Muskoka hinted that all was not well.

With the opening of the Muskoka townships the controversy concerning the quality of land on the Laurentian Shield became a practical question affecting the welfare if not the very life of the settlers. As with most controversies, bitter and exaggerated statements were made on both sides. A. P. Cockburn, R. J. Oliver, and Thomas McMurray were among the most vocal supporters of Muskoka. According to McMurray, by 1871 R. J. Oliver had written "not less than 83 Editorials and Letters in defence of the country."[5] McMurray admitted that there were some cases of poverty "but such is the exception not the rule." He summed up his position in the words "if the right class will only come, they will do well" (F 26).

Joseph Dale was probably the most violent critic. In his pamphlet, *Canadian Land Grants in 1874*, he criticized every feature of

[4]Canada, Dominion Bureau of Statistics, *Seventh Census of Canada*, 1931, v. 1, p. 349.
[5]McMurray, *The Free Grant Lands of Canada*, p. 14.

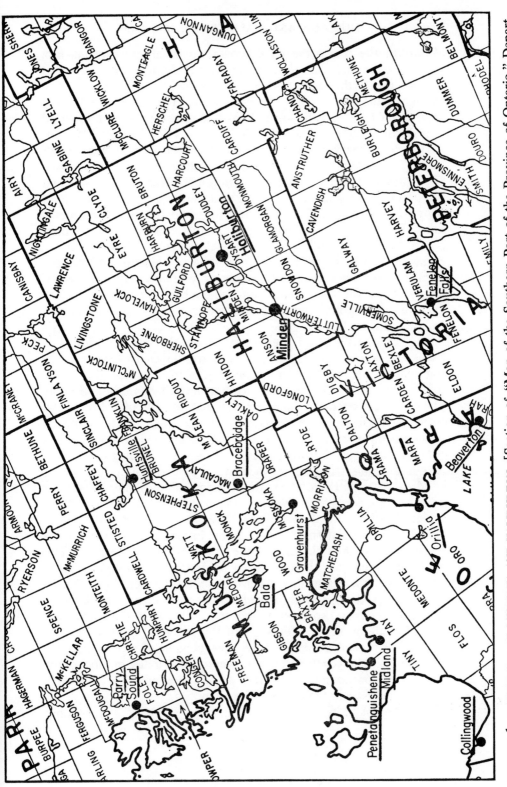

FIGURE 1. TOWNSHIPS OF MUSKOKA AND HALIBURTON. [Section of "Map of the Southern Part of the Province of Ontario," Department of Lands and Forests, 1961.]

Muskoka: the rocks, the dark brown water, absentee ownership, the roads, the difficulty of obtaining deer and other game, expenses of settlement, the poverty-stricken shanties, and above all, the quality of the land. "I have known instances where so great is the quantity of rock that the ground has had to be made; and a mound of earth has been sought for, and looked upon as a treasure" (F 29).

Between the two extremes were writers such as Mrs. King, author of *Letters from Muskoka*, who settled near Utterson. Mrs. King gave a very harsh picture of life on the free grant lands from the point of view of "poor ladies and gentlemen" who, she said, "form the worst, or at least the most unsuccessful, class for emigration." For "the lower Classes" she thought that Muskoka offered a hard life but some chance of eventual success (F 28). It is interesting to note that the Reverend A. Styleman Herring of London, England, who knew at first hand not only the poverty from which some of the settlers had come, but also the hardships which awaited them on a Muskoka farm, was one of the most active promoters of emigration.

"Rock" was the word used most frequently by the critics. The defenders pointed out that extra land was given to the settler to compensate for the rock, to which the critics replied that loose stones were found everywhere and that the soil was thin and poor. The defenders cited statistics to prove that, in spite of the rock, the crops in Muskoka were equal to those of some of the southern counties, and pointed to the mammoth turnip which weighed 32½ pounds, the largest known to have been grown in Canada (F 19).

It is hard to credit some of the statements concerning early crops in Muskoka and Haliburton, when today, along many roads, the fields, once cleared, are given over to weeds and rock. Part of the explanation was stated as early as 1872 by a member of the Canadian Press Association: "In too many instances the settlers have made the mistake of clearing off the timber from the rocks. . . . The result has been that the soil being no longer held by the fibrous roots of the trees, is readily washed away by the rains" (F 27). In many places the soil was indeed thin, a few inches on the Precambrian rock, and so an easy prey to erosion when the lands were cleared of the protecting forests. But it was fertile, built of the leaf mould and vegetable matter of the ages, capable of growing magnificent crops. The vegetables and flowers grown today on pockets of deeper soil or on newly cleared ground are proof of the early settlers' claims as to the fertility of the land.

All the abandoned farms were not the result of soil erosion.

Some were caused by a changing economy: specialized farming
that developed with the opening of the west, and cheap, rapid
transportation that came with the building of the railways. It was
no longer important that Muskoka could grow a few thousand
bushels of wheat when the prairies produced more than the Dominion could consume. It was uneconomical to grow apples in a
climate noted for its hard winters and late spring frosts, when the
Niagara Peninsula grew enough fruit for the province.

Many settlers who became discouraged with the woods and rocks
of Muskoka and Haliburton "went West" to start new farms on
homesteads free both of tree and rock. The greatest exodus took
place after the period covered by this volume, but was so serious,
even as early as 1879, that one writer referred to it as the "Manitoba fever."[6]

The Settlement of Haliburton

Settlement in Haliburton was divided between that on the Crown
lands and that on the lands of the Canadian Land and Emigration
Company. In the summer of 1858, Richard Hughes, agent for the
Bobcaygeon Road, was appointed agent for the sale and settlement
of Crown lands in the townships of Somerville and Galway, and
for six townships now in the County of Haliburton—Snowdon,
Lutterworth, Minden, Anson, Stanhope, and Hindon (F 9). Some
settlers, however, had not waited for the lands to be declared officially open. J. W. Fitzgerald, proceeding on a survey in October,
1857, saw squatters along Gull River and Moore Lake, also on
Gull Lake and five miles still further up the Gull River. He found
one man who had been settled in the Township of Stanhope between Big and Little Boshkung Lakes for six years, and who had
cleared about ten acres of land (F 30).

Richard Hughes in his 1859 report on free grants on the Bobcaygeon Road showed 168 settlers, 776 acres cleared and 126 houses
built, with a total population of 697 (F 32). Twenty-five families
had settled on the boundary line between Stanhope and Minden
and a post office had been opened at Gull River in Minden Township. By the end of 1862 a thousand lots had been sold, containing
over 90,000 acres, and a number of sawmills and grist mills had
been built (F 34).

In December, 1861, George G. Boswell was appointed agent for

[6]W. E. Hamilton, Dec. 26, 1879 (P.A.O., Immigration Papers, Correspondence,
1879, no. 8732).

the northerly part of the Bobcaygeon Road. In January, 1863, he reported that a settlement had been formed at the Narrows at the Lake of Bays, and that there was a settler at the point where the road crossed the Muskoka River, about seventy miles north of Bobcaygeon.[7] The following year he had to admit that there had been little improvement, partly owing to the state of the road north of Bell's Line (F 35).

Canadian Land and Emigration Company

Although the proposed settlement of the Ottawa-Huron tract by a land company did not develop in the 1830's, a more restricted area, consisting of ten townships was sold to an English company in the 1860's. Nine of the townships were in Haliburton—Dysart, Dudley, Harcourt, Guilford, Harburn, Bruton, Havelock, Eyre, and Clyde—and the tenth was Longford in Victoria County (F 38). In 1859, after regulations had been issued which permitted the sale of land *en bloc* (F 36) the Canada Agency Association, acting through John Beverley Robinson of Toronto, made tentative inquiries concerning Crown lands available for purchase (F 37). An English company which purchased land through this agency was incorporated under the name Canadian Land and Emigration Company, Limited (F 40), but was occasionally called the Canada Land and Emigration Company. The Honourable Mr. Justice Haliburton, better known as Thomas Chandler Haliburton, author of *Sam Slick*, was the first chairman.

Lengthy negotiations were carried on between the Company and the Department of Crown Lands concerning the selection of townships and the terms of sale.[8] The Department agreed to pay for the survey of the outlines of the townships but the Company had to pay for the survey of land within the townships and the subdivision into lots (F 39). B. W. Gossage with other surveyors under his direction began work in the townships of Longford and Dysart. As many as sixty or seventy men were employed on the project at one time, and large sums of money were required for wages and provisions (F 42).

According to the terms of sale an allowance was to be made for

[7]Guillet, *The Valley of the Trent*, pp. 82–3.

[8]The establishment of the Canadian Land and Emigration Company is traced in a series of documents printed in Ontario, Provincial Secretary, *Return to an Address of the Legislative Assembly . . . for Copies of the Agreements between "The Canada Land and Emigration Company" and the Government (Sessional Papers*, 1868–9, no. 34).

swamps. When the survey was completed it showed 403,125 acres in the ten townships of which 41,000 were deducted as swamp, leaving 362,125 acres to be paid for at 50c per acre (F 44). B. W. Gossage submitted a report in which he divided the land into five grades according to its fitness for settlement. Edward Miles also examined the land and gave a very different and more critical report (F 43). Unfortunately the latter's estimate of the number of acres suitable for agriculture proved to be the true one in the experience of the settlers.

Although the Company had to pay for all land except swamp, the final terms demanded that settlement duties be performed only on land considered fit for settlement, which was set at 261,544 acres. The Company had to settle one-ninth of this acreage in three years, four-ninths in the next ten years, and another four-ninths in the next fifteen years (F 44). Settlement duties required that there be one *bona fide* settler for every two hundred acres of land, that ten acres for every hundred acres be cleared and under crop, and that a house be built for every two hundred acres. The date from which the time for the fulfilment of settlement duties should reckon was originally January 1, 1865, but when the Company encountered difficulties beyond its own control the government extended the date to January 1, 1868 (F 46). Ten per cent of the purchase money was also allowed to the Company by the government for the building of roads.

From the outset the Company had difficulty in selling the lands. The distance of the townships from the settled parts of the province, the absence of good roads, the rough nature of the country, the Civil War in the United States, the Fenian raids on the border, and the rival attractions of Western Canada, all combined to discourage sales (F 46). When free grants were offered in Muskoka and in other parts of Haliburton, the Company found settlers were even more reluctant to purchase Company lands (F 47, F 49). The number of acres sold to the end of 1864 was 3,798 including 12 town lots in Haliburton (F 45) and by 1870, 16,560 acres had been sold or leased, of which 2,226 were cleared (F 50).

From 1862 to 1866 Charles R. Stewart was resident agent. He was then replaced by Alexander Niven, P.L.S., as resident agent and Charles J. Blomfield as manager. In 1883 J. M. Irwin, a lumberman, and W. H. Lockhart Gordon, a Toronto lawyer, became commissioners and in 1889 the Company's holdings were transferred to the Canadian Land and Immigration Company of Haliburton. At times it appeared that the Company's operations could be made profitable, but financial difficulties persisted even throughout the days of the lumber boom and became acute in the depression of the 1930's. During the Second World War the Company finally surrendered its charter.

The settler's life differed but little whether he occupied a free grant or a Canadian Land and Emigration Company's lot. A graphic description of one settler's first years in Haliburton was given by A. Parsonage in a letter to his son Charles: poverty to the verge of starvation, and incessant hard toil, but with this the bounty of the crops, a healthy climate, and hope for the future. In spite of all its drawbacks, Parsonage found Canada "a large and beautiful country" (F 52). C. L. MacDermott, a young Englishman who went to Haliburton in 1868, gave a more factual account: prices, wages, the nature of the soil, the cost of clearing the land (F 53). In spite of some favourable comments, settlement in Haliburton progressed more slowly than in Muskoka, and in the latter part of the century the lure of the Canadian west left a trail of deserted Haliburton farms.

G. LUMBER, FUR, AND GOLD

Lumbering

MUSKOKA AND HALIBURTON were fortunate in having a wealth of timber available for export in a period when wood was all important.[1] When cutting first began on the Laurentian Shield the demand on the British market was for "square timber," pine trees squared ready for use as ship masts or as rafters to support the heavy English roofs. Square timber had to be made from the tallest, soundest trees, trees that were straight and free from black knots, and had an average diameter of at least twenty-one inches. Great waste resulted from the discarding of logs which did not meet these requirements, and from the squaring of the trees.

The square timber trade always had an element of speculation, being dependent on the demands of the British market, and the lapse of time between the cutting of the timber and delivery in Great Britain allowed unusual fluctuations in price. The trade was strong in the period when cutting first began in Muskoka and Haliburton, reached its peak about 1865, then declined and had almost disappeared by the heyday of Muskoka and Haliburton lumbering, which came around the end of the century. Meanwhile the British market had begun to purchase "deals," or planks, three or four inches thick; and by the end of the 1860's the export of these exceeded that of square timber.

The American market for Canadian lumber developed later than the British since there was no shortage of lumber in the United States as long as settlement was confined to the eastern region of the continent. But the population in the east was increasing rapidly and at the same time settlement was pushing west to the treeless prairies. As a result great quantities of timber were needed for building purposes both on the New York and Chicago markets. During the 1860's even the Michigan forests were being depleted and American lumbermen were importing logs from the Canadian shores of Lake Huron or operating camps themselves in Canada. The American market was much less demanding than the British as to quality, and so offered more advantageous cutting. The timber exported to the United States was partly in the form of saw-logs,

[1]A number of the documents referred to in this section are summarized or reprinted in "A History of Crown Timber Regulations" (Ontario, Bureau of Forestry, *Annual Report*, 1899, p. 29–139).

many of which were taken across Lake Huron from the Muskoka district, and partly in the form of planks and boards.

The most valuable tree on the Laurentian Shield was the pine, red and white, which grew from Georgian Bay to the Ottawa River. The red pine was more plentiful in the western part and usually grew on higher land. When the market for other woods developed toward the end of the century, Muskoka and Haliburton offered a great variety: cedar, spruce, tamarack, balsam, black ash, yellow birch, maple, beech, basswood, and oak. Hemlock was of little importance for lumber before the 1880's but was valued for its bark which was used in tanning.

Problems inherent in the timber trade—the conflicting interests of the settlers and lumbermen, destruction of the forests through fire, losses during financial depressions, the difficulties the government met in collecting timber dues—all were familiar long before the forests of Muskoka and Haliburton were brought into the market, but some of them were aggravated by the land policies in these districts. The sales or free grants of land by the government to the settlers and the licences for timber berths to the lumbermen within the same area, inevitably gave rise to conflicts between the three parties, government, settlers, and lumbermen.

Settlers and lumbermen had widely divergent interests, but were also mutually dependent on each other. To the settler, even one who understood clearly the regulations concerning occupancy, the sight of a lumberman with a licence to cut pine on his farm, without compensation, must have brought bitter resentment. On the other hand in some parts of Muskoka and Haliburton, so dependent was the settler on the lumberman both for employment and markets, that when the lumberman had stripped the pine from the area and moved on, the settler had to abandon his clearing and follow (G 21). From the lumberman's point of view the settler was a mixed blessing. Although the farm produce was desirable for the camps, the settler was gradually cutting and burning the forest on which the timber trade depended. Over the years there were continual complaints that lands which grew magnificent forests were being turned into worthless farms. In 1863 a Committee of the Legislative Assembly admitted that "It appears from the evidence that settlement has been unreasonably pushed in some locations quite unfit to become the permanent residence of an agricultural population."[2]

[2]Canada, Legislative Assembly, Select Committee Appointed to Enquire into and Report on the State of the Lumber Trade of Canada, *Report*, May 12, 1863 (Legislative Assembly, *Journals*, 1863, app. 8).

There were two major points of conflict: the right of the settler to sell the timber on his land, and the right of the lumberman to cut timber on land for which he had obtained a licence, but on which a settler had located. The "Act to Amend the Law for the Sale and the Settlement of the Public Lands," 1853,[3] was in force when settlement began in Muskoka and Haliburton. This act placed no restriction on the settler's right to his pine, and as a result so-called settlers purchased land for the sake of the timber and stripped it, even though the land so purchased might be in a timber limit already under licence. In 1860 "An Act Respecting the Sale and Management of Public Lands"[4] provided that the settler's right of occupation "shall have no force against a License to cut timber existing at the time of the granting thereof." More stringent regulations issued the same year permitted the settler to cut and sell his timber only if the value was applied to the purchase money due to the Crown, and the conditions of settlement had been fulfilled.

In spite of laws and regulations the abuses continued and were cited by the Crown Timber Agent, J. F. Way, in 1867 (G 21). Settler and lumbermen alike connived at violations of the laws when their interests were at stake. Squatters sold timber on land to which they had no possible claim. Settlers sold timber in defiance of the act or in ignorance of it, but many of them were so poor that even Mr. Way, asked for leniency (G 18). Disputes arose between the men belonging to rival companies concerning timber bought from settlers and Way remarked "as is usually the case the men disputed about timber which neither had a right to cut" (G 17).

The settler's right to cut pine was stated more definitely in the Free Grants and Homestead Act of 1868 (F 15). This reserved to the Crown all pine trees except timber necessary for building and fencing or that which had to be cut in actually clearing the land, until the issue of the final patent. All pine trees disposed of with the above exceptions were to be subject to the same dues as were payable at the time by holders of licences to cut timber or saw-logs. New Crown timber regulations[5] followed in 1869 which made it illegal for a settler to sell his pine until he had completed all the conditions of location, unless under settlers' licence. A further Order in Council, issued May 27, 1869,[6] provided that all pine trees on land located or sold under the Free Grants and Homestead Act

[3]Canada, *Statutes*, 1852–3, 16 Vic., c. 159.
[4]*Ibid.*, 1860, 23 Vic., c. 2.
[5]"A History of Crown Timber Regulations" (Ontario, Bureau of Forestry, *Annual Report*, 1899, p. 106–9).
[6]*Ibid.*, pp. 115–16.

should be subject to any timber licence in force not only at the time of location or sale, but also granted within five years subsequently, and might at any time before the issue of the patent be cut and removed. Under these regulations a law-abiding settler had little hope of reaping much profit from his pine.

Although the major cause of disagreement between settler and lumberman was the ownership of the pine, other factors led to friction. Disastrous fires destroyed both the settlers' homes and the timber on which the livelihood of the lumbermen depended, and each blamed the other, with justification. Settlers also charged that the lumbermen's heavy loads destroyed the colonization roads (E 6) to which the lumbermen replied that they built other roads and improved the waterways which gave the settlers access to market for their timber and farm produce.

Muskoka and Haliburton are fortunate in having networks of waterways, but most of the streams are obstructed by rapids and falls which made timber driving difficult. The government did not build slides and dams in this area to the extent which it did in the Ottawa Valley and lumbermen often had to make their own improvements (G 13, G 20). Owing to this, cutting developed more slowly than would otherwise have been the case, and much timber was lost or damaged on the way to market.

Partly as a result of these natural obstructions on the waterways, the history of the lumber trade on the Shield is closely connected with the building of the railways. In the 1850's the Cobourg to Peterborough and Port Hope to Lindsay lines were opened.[7] The former, between 1854 and the year 1860 (when it was abandoned), carried great quantities of timber from the Kawartha Lakes district to Lake Ontario. Areas to the north of the Kawarthas were also cut, and no doubt some logs came from the Haliburton region. In 1853 the Northern Railway reached Allandale and, in 1855, Collingwood. This opened up the pine lands of Simcoe County, and included some along the Black River in Muskoka. As the Northern Railway pushed on to Orillia in 1871, Washago in 1872, and Gravenhurst in 1875, a great development took place in the lumber trade. By the 1880's Gravenhurst had fourteen mills and was a centre for the sawmilling industry.

At the time when Muskoka and Haliburton timber was first marketed the lumberman paid for the privilege of cutting in three ways: by a charge for the licence, by ground rent, and by timber

[7]Stevens, *Canadian National Railways. 1. Sixty Years of Trial and Error*, pp. 428–36.

dues. Under the Regulations of 1851[8] there was provision for the licences to be sold by auction in certain circumstances with an upset price to be set by the Commissioner. This practice became quite general under the Regulations of 1866,[9] and the sum obtained beyond the upset price was known as a bonus. When the market was strong, valuable timber limits brought considerable sums (G 10, G 11).

Lumbering operations extended to the Laurentian Shield in three lines of attack, by the rivers falling into the Ottawa, by those falling into Georgian Bay, and by the Trent system. By the middle of the 1850's lumbermen were cutting pine on the fringe of Muskoka and Haliburton. In May, 1854, Joseph Fraser Way was appointed Crown Timber Agent for a large area which included Haliburton (G 15) and in June, 1855, Alexander William Powell was appointed to the same position for the Huron and Superior Territory which included Muskoka (G 2). In 1856 licences were granted for cutting on the Severn, Muskoka, Seguin, Moon, and Black rivers (G 3), and by 1861 lumbering operations had moved further into the interior. In that year licences were granted for Muskoka, Morrison, Ryde, Draper, and Macaulay townships, and in 1866 for Oakley and Monck (G 6). Among the early lumbermen and companies in this district were Quetton St. George, Andrew Heron, George Caswell, Joseph Smith, and Peter Christie (G 3, G 6). By 1871 a number of large companies were cutting including: Dodge and Company; Clarke, White and Company; Hotchkiss, Hughson and Company; Cook Brothers; Bell Ewart Company; and Silliman and Beecher of Albany. The largest companies such as Dodge employed as many as eight hundred or a thousand men (G 8, G 9).

After the opening of several of the townships of the Muskoka district for free grants, a public auction was held of the timber berths in the unlocated sections of the townships, November 23, 1871 (G 10). Unusually high prices were bid because the market was strong at the time (G 14). Unfortunately for the lumber companies a severe depression occurred in the autumn of 1872 and the panic on the New York market occasioned a slump in the lumber industry which caused the failure of a number of companies. As a result in 1876 the licence holders successfully petitioned the Ontario government for a reduction in the rate of dues charged in Muskoka and Parry Sound (G 14).

Timber licences in the Haliburton area probably date from 1860.

[8]Montreal, *Canada Gazette*, Aug. 16, 1851, pp. 11216–18.
[9]Ottawa, *Canada Gazette*, June 23, 1866, pp. 2150–2.

In that year licences were issued for limits in Lutterworth and Anson, in 1861 for Minden, Stanhope, and Snowdon, and in 1863 for Monmouth, Glamorgan, and Cardiff (G 16, G 19). Among the best known companies lumbering in that area were Harris and Bronson, later Bronson and Weston of Ottawa, Gillies & McLaren, William McDougall & Company, Mossom Boyd, and Boyd and Cumming (G 16). Mossom Boyd of Bobcaygeon, "Lumber King of the Trent River," held extensive timber berths both on Crown lands and in the townships belonging to the Canadian Land and Emigration Company (G 23, G 24, G 25, G 26) and established depot farms to raise supplies for his camps. In 1871 C. R. Stewart reported that on Boyd's farm in Havelock Township nearly seventy acres were under cultivation (F 50).

The early sawmills were built mainly to meet the needs of local communities and were placed at accessible points where water power and timber were available. The first of which a record has been found, in or near Muskoka, was at the mouth of the Severn River. In 1830 a mill was built at the first fall up the river from Georgian Bay; it was later surrendered to Aisance and his band (G 1). Lieutenant Baddeley commented in 1835 that "At the mouth of the river are saw mills built by government but now going to decay it is said that the pine which was brought down the river for the supply of the mills was for the most part bad" (B 27). Much later, in 1852, sawmills were built for Quetton St. George and Company on the Severn River at its outlet from Lake Couchiching at the place later known as Washago. These mills were mentioned by David Gibson in 1858 (E 10) and by Vernon B. Wadsworth in 1860 (D 16). A mill was also built at an early date at the first fall on the Muskoka or Muskosh River. Alexander Murray reported that between the date of his visit to the river in 1853 and the writing of his report in February, 1854, "Mr. W. B. Hamilton, of Penetanguishene, has erected a saw-mill on or near the first falls, about two miles from the mouth of the river, where he is said to have an almost inexhaustible supply of pine within easy distance" (D 10). The lumber was shipped mainly to Chicago, but some also went to Owen Sound and Collingwood. In later years very extensive mills and docks were built at the mouth of the Muskosh and known as Muskoka Mills.

In 1852 a sawmill was built on the "lower rapids of the Gull River" (D 10), which would be a little south of Haliburton, and in 1858 J. W. Fitzgerald reported a sawmill on the Gull River between Mud Turtle (now Shadow) Lake and Moore Lake (F 30). Richard

Hughes wrote in 1859 that "A saw-mill has been erected at Kin-mount during the last six months, and is found of great benefit to the settlers, as it saves 18 miles of carriage for lumber." He added that parties were prepared to build mills on the Gull River as soon as the privileges were ready for sale (F 32). In 1861 he reported that three sawmills had been completed on the Bobcaygeon Road one of which was as far north as Minden (F 33).

Fur Trapping and Trading

The oldest industry in Muskoka and Haliburton was not lumber-ing but trapping. Unfortunately no journals kept by trappers or fur traders in this district have been found, and as a result it is usually impossible to tell who first traded on a given lake or river, or who built the make-shift trading posts. In the days of the Hurons, furs from the Muskoka and Haliburton region went by the great Huron trading fleets to Quebec; in the time of Iroquois domination they went by the Toronto Portage or the Trent system to Lake Ontario and south to Albany and New York. At the beginning of the Eng-lish period the Indians carried their furs from the Muskoka and Parry Sound area to traders on Georgian Bay, or to Lake Simcoe and the Holland River, or exchanged them with traders who had set up temporary trading posts in the hunting grounds.

The fur traders were almost all French or English. The trappers at first were usually Indian, but according to George S. Thompson, by the 1870's "Most of the trappers in the Haliburton district were white men, though quite a number were Indians" (G 31). Early settlers, or sons of settlers, often supplemented their income from the farm with money obtained for furs (G 32). Beaver was the most sought after skin in the early days, but in Haliburton in the 1870's otter, bear, wolf, marten, mink, muskrat, and fox were also being trapped (G 31). Certain sections of the country were especially rich in fur and these were often claimed by Indian chiefs or princi-pal men as the traditional family hunting grounds, even after the land had been surrendered to the government.

At the end of the eighteenth century the trader who probably obtained the majority of the furs from Muskoka was George Cowan, also known as Jean Baptiste Constant or Constance, who had a trading post at the southeast of Matchedash Bay, described in McDonell's journal of Governor Simcoe's trip in 1793 (A 16). An equally colourful figure in the early trade was Quetton St. George, a French Royalist who came to Canada in 1798, opened several stores in the southern part of the country, and began trading with the Indians to the north. One of his posts is said to have been at the Narrows between Lakes Simcoe and Couchiching, and this, no doubt, attracted some of the trappers from the Muskoka district. Although many of his papers have been preserved, the story of his trading expeditions to the Indians is based mainly on tradition.[10]

The Holland River which flows into the southern end of Lake Simcoe was an early centre for the fur trade from the north. At Newmarket, Borland and Roe carried on an extensive business. Jean Baptiste Sylvestre, born 1813, while still a young lad worked for Mr. Roe and many years later gave a brief account of one of his fur trading adventures with his father, also called Jean Baptiste Sylvestre, who traded "among the Muskoka lakes and at Sylvestre's Lake in Parry Sound" (G 28). William Benjamin Robinson,[11] born in 1797, brother of Chief Justice John Beverley Robinson, was another fur trader from Newmarket. He succeeded to the business of his step-father, Elisha Beman, and carried on trade with the Indians in Newmarket and in Muskoka. He and his partner set up two trading posts, one at the mouth of the Muskoka River and one on the island in Lake Muskoka now called Yoho.

All through the first half of the nineteenth century Penetanguishene was also a centre for the trade. George Gordon[12] went from Drummond Island to the Penetanguishene district about 1825, built a trading post, and soon became a prominent merchant. Indians came to him to exchange their furs for flour, pork, and clothing, and he in turn sent traders to the Indian hunting grounds. His half-brother, Jean Baptiste Rousseau, who travelled far and wide collecting furs is probably the man for whom Lake Rosseau is named. Another trader from Penetanguishene who may have been in the Muskoka region at an early date was Andrew Mitchell. In 1835 Lieutenant Carthew met six Indian families on Lake Rosseau and remarked in his journal "They trade with Penetanguishene through one of Mr. Mitchell's traders" (C 11).

A little north of Muskoka in the present district of Parry Sound, there was a trading post at Shawanaga, "old" in the 1830's, at which

[10]The Toronto Public Library has in its possession a Mississauga-French dictionary applying to the region between York and Lake Simcoe, probably compiled by St. George, which includes notes on quantities and prices of furs. It was printed in part in A. F. Chamberlain's *The Language of the Mississaga Indians of Skŭgog* (Philadelphia, 1892), pp. 74-9, and also described in J. C. Pilling's *Bibliography of the Algonquian Languages* (Washington, 1891), p. 361.

[11]Jarvis, *Three Centuries of Robinsons*, pp. 144-7.

[12]Wallace, "The Early History of Muskoka," *Queen's Quarterly*, v. 49, autumn, 1942, pp. 247-50.

Mr. Morrison was the trader. Carthew[13] and Baddeley[14] both referred to it. Another post, Bourassa, just south of the Seguin River,
near the present site of Parry Sound, was mentioned by John Bigsby
in 1823 (A 20). At a much later date, about 1862 to 1879, the
Hudson's Bay Company had an agent, Thomas Goffatt, at Orillia,
and no doubt many of the furs collected by the Rama Indians in
the Muskoka district were carried to Goffatt's store (G 30).

There were no large fur-trading posts actually in Muskoka or
Haliburton. Instead there were fur traders' cabins, with perhaps a
log hut for stores, temporary in character, occupied only at some
seasons of the year and abandoned when the need had gone. References to such buildings appear in the journals of the early explorers.
Alexander Shirreff said in 1829 that Trading Lake (now Lake of
Bays) "appears to have been long a principal station of the traders.
There are here vestiges of two old establishments, besides a commodious house in good repair, but deserted when we passed." He
also spoke of a lake about two days' journey up the North Branch
of the Muskoka River (possibly Doe Lake) which had a trading
station to which the common route was by the Neyetewa or Magnetawan River (B 24).

The Muskoka River, between Lake Muskoka and the junction of
the North and South Branches, was a strategic point at which to
intercept the Indians coming down from the more northern parts.
Lieutenant Carthew mentioned that in 1835, one mile up the river
from the lake, there was "an old trading post and clearing of small
extent on the south bank of the River,"[15] and Baddeley referred to
the same building (B 27). Years later, Vernon B. Wadsworth,
describing the surveys of 1860, said, "We reached the mouth of the
Muskoka River after a paddle across the Lake of some ten miles,
and passed up the River to the first falls, where Bracebridge now
stands. Near the mouth of the River we saw a log house with a
small potato garden around it, and found that it was the trading
post of Alexander Bailey who was then at his permanent home in
Penetanguishene" (D 16). Apparently there were similar traders'
cabins in Haliburton at an early date. Lieutenant Walpole noted
"Traders Houses" at the northern end of Gull Lake, on the map[16]
of his exploratory survey in 1827.

There is a persistent tradition that the Hudson's Bay Company

---

[13]Upper Canada, House of Assembly, *Journal*, 1836–7, app. 37, p. 6.
[14]*Ibid.*, p. 26.
[15]*Ibid.*, p. 3.
[16]P.R.O., W.O. 55/864.

had a post on Bigwin Island in the Lake of Bays in the 1860's. No contemporary evidence has been found, but it is possible that Thomas Goffatt, the Hudson's Bay Company agent at Orillia, had an outpost on that island. Goffatt made trips to the north to collect furs and on one at least went as far as Lake Nipissing.[17]

Regular fur sales for the trappers of the district have been held for many years. In 1865 Mr. Thompson's sale at Penetanguishene amounted to $14,959 (G 29). Two sales were held each year at Haliburton, and, according to George S. Thompson, buyers came from "New York, Boston, Toronto, Quebec, Peterborough, and other cities and towns" (G 31).

Rumours of Gold and other Minerals

From early days the rock formations of Muskoka and Haliburton have encouraged dreams of gold, silver, copper, lead, iron, and other minerals. Traditions of Indian mines persisted (G 33), and settlers had specimens of rock tested, sometimes with encouraging results (G 34). Men searched for gold in Muskoka, and a few claimed to find it (G 35, G 36). In Gravenhurst in 1877 a flurry of excitement occurred when gold was "discovered" but hopes died almost as rapidly as they had arisen.[18] In Haliburton deposits of iron were discovered as early as 1870, and a number of men invested heavily without any satisfactory return. The Snowdon Iron Mine Company was formed and a spur of the Victoria Railway was built to the mine, but no large-scale developments followed.[19] The radioactive minerals, for which Haliburton is now well known, became of importance only in the twentieth century.

[17]Orillia, *Times*, Dec. 17, 1874.
[18]Hamilton, *Guide Book & Atlas of Muskoka and Parry Sound Districts*, pp. 5–6.
[19]*History of the County of Peterborough*, pp. 475–8.

H. TRANSPORTATION

WHEN THE COLONIZATION ROADS were opened into Muskoka and Haliburton, farmers along the fringe of settlement found it profitable to supply teams and wagons to haul the settlers' belongings to the newly acquired lots. As time went on, regular stage coach services developed (H 1, H 2, H 3, H 4, H 5), operating at fixed charges for passengers and freight. Since the roads were unbelievably rough and dusty, many people preferred to use the steamboats on the lakes and rivers in summer when such were available, and the stage coach routes were adjusted to meet the seasonal demands. Thompson's stage,[1] for example, ran from Haliburton to Minden in winter, but in summer a boat carried passengers and freight to the foot of Lake Kashagawigamog and a stage covered only the few remaining miles.

The stage coach industry was at its height in Muskoka in the period shortly before the railway reached Bracebridge in 1885, when settlers by the hundreds were entering the free grant lands and industries were springing up in the villages. The most important company was that of John Harvie who was said in some years to have employed from seventy to one hundred teams. The noise and congestion caused by the heavily loaded wagons or sleighs on the narrow roads disappeared almost overnight with the arrival of the railway. Only a few smaller companies remained, such as Caverley's which ran from Bracebridge to Huntsville, and they too disappeared one by one as better methods of transportation became available.

Boats, Canals, and Locks

The first boat on the Muskoka Lakes larger than a canoe was for the use of the surveyors under the direction of J. S. Dennis in 1861 (H 6). A large row-boat followed in 1862, a sail-boat in 1863, and another sail-boat in 1864. These were used for both freight and passengers. William Holditch built a horse-boat, a large flat boat propelled by paddle wheels worked by horses, but it proved unsatisfactory and made only one trip from Bracebridge to Muskoka Bay (H 10).

In 1866, A. P. Cockburn placed the first steamer on the Muskoka

[1]Thompson, *Up to Date, or the Life of a Lumberman*, pp. 11–18.

Lakes, the celebrated *Wenonah* or "first born daughter,"[2] which was the admiration of all visitors and brought immediate practical benefits to the settlers. Regular service was made available for the transportation of passengers, livestock, and farm produce (H 8) and freight rates dropped to one-half (H 10). The *Wenonah* was followed by the *Waubamik,* and in 1871 by the *Nipissing.* Cockburn's enterprise developed into the Muskoka Lakes Navigation Company which was famous for many years for its "Hundred Mile Cruise."

A steamer, the *Northern,* eighty feet in length, was launched at Port Sydney on June 18, 1877. It ran from Port Sydney on Mary Lake, by way of Huntsville to the head of Lake Vernon and returned to Huntsville and Fairy Lake, a trip of fifty-six miles (H 10). These were the beginnings of steamship services on the major navigable waterways of Muskoka. With the coming of the automobile and the paved highways, the need for the boats disappeared and it is difficult now to realize the part they played in opening the area for settlement.

Haliburton, although well-endowed with lakes and rivers, lacks the long navigable waterways found in Muskoka, and moreover did not attract the same number of settlers and tourists in the nineteenth century. As a result there were fewer boats on its lakes at an early period. The first steam-boat on Lake Kashagawigamog, nicknamed the "Royal Mail Steamship 'Bull of the Woods,' " is humorously described in George S. Thompson's *Up to Date, or the Life of a Lumberman.*

Some engineering works were required to connect the major waterways in Muskoka, but none of an extensive character. Lakes Rosseau and Muskoka, connected by the Indian River, differed in level only a few feet, though the shallowness of the river in places increased the difficulty of navigation. In February, 1865, J. W. Bridgland asked permission of the Commissioner of Crown Lands to examine the river (H 11), and in June, 1867, he made a detailed report in which he suggested a tram road across the narrow strip of land instead of a canal and lock (H 12). But the settlers in the area were of another mind (H 13) and their member in the legislature was A. P. Cockburn, who was a strong believer in the future of Muskoka and had himself placed the first steamer on Lake Muskoka. The lock and canal were begun in July, 1870 (H 14) and completed the following year. At the same time, to avoid the

[2]Thomas, "The Beginning of Navigation and the Tourist Industry in Muskoka," *Ontario History,* v. 42, April, 1950, pp. 101–5.

obstructions in the Joseph River, a cut was made from Lake Joseph
to Lake Rosseau at the point now known as Port Sandfield (H 14,
H 15).

Navigation on the northern chain of lakes—Vernon, Fairy, Peninsula, and Mary—required a lock between Fairy and Mary, and a
canal between Fairy and Peninsula which were connected only by a
marshy creek. In 1873 work was begun on the lock between Mary
and Fairy (H 16) and was completed in 1877, but the canal between Peninsula and Fairy lakes was not opened until 1888. The
Lake of Bays, though only a mile from Peninsula Lake, is over a
hundred feet above it; consequently no attempt has been made to
connect the two by water. Instead a railway was built between them
about 1906—one of the shortest railways in the world—and the
miniature train, which hauled incredible quantities of lumber and
supplies, was the delight of tourists for several decades.

Railways

Muskoka and Haliburton were settled in an age of railway building,[3] when plans for new lines sprang up wherever commerce
beckoned. The dream of direct communication between Lake
Huron and the Ottawa River was revived, with the railway, rather
than the waterway or road, serving as the hoped-for connecting
link. T. C. Keefer pointed out in 1864 that a railway across this
part of Canada would provide the shortest route between east and
west for the carriage of lumber, and supplies for the lumber trade,
as well as fish and grain (H 17). However, in spite of such arguments, the south-to-north lines were built before the east-to-west.

When the first settlers entered Muskoka the Northern Railway
was already in operation from Toronto through Allandale to Collingwood on Georgian Bay, and in 1867 a spur was laid to Barrie.
Several groups were interested in extending the line north into the
interior. Businessmen who had caught the "railway fever" were
always ready for one more venture, and a line which would carry
to market the pine of the northern part of Simcoe County seemed
to them a profitable investment. The settled areas around Lake
Ontario, especially Toronto, were interested in any railway which
would guarantee "cordwood, or any wood for fuel" at a low rate
(H 18). Lumbermen were anxious for a railway through Muskoka
and Haliburton because falls and rapids on the major rivers ham-

[3]The history of the railways of Muskoka and Haliburton is included in Stevens,
Canadian National Railways, v. 1, chaps. 12–13.

pered the log drives and prevented the sawmill industry developing on the Shield.

To the settlers in Muskoka and Haliburton a railway meant reduced freight rates, increased sums for the pine trees, and, above all, access to the cities and towns at the "Front" where a market could be found for their produce. A. P. Cockburn told the settlers that "it was not possible for them to become a very prosperous people without a railway" (H 19).

During 1869 a group of prominent businessmen planned an extension from the Northern Railway at Barrie to Orillia, with the authority to build to Lake Muskoka, and in December of that year they obtained incorporation under the name of Toronto, Simcoe and Muskoka Junction Railway Company (H 21). The Northern Railway, under the management of Frederic Cumberland, pursued an attitude of caution to the proposed line and left the communities that desired the railway to initiate action and raise funds. But it was obvious that the Northern Railway, which had derived much of its revenue from hauling the pine of Simcoe County, sooner or later would have to follow the lumberman onto the Canadian Shield. Meanwhile, ratepayers in Gravenhurst and Bracebridge lost no opportunity of urging the advantages of continuing the line northward and in August, 1869, invited the officials of the Northern to visit the district (H 19).

The Toronto, Simcoe and Muskoka Junction Railway was slow in building, but it reached Orillia on April 1, 1872, Washago on August 8, 1873, and the southern boundary line of Muskoka, the Severn River, in September, 1874. It was at Gravenhurst in August, 1875, and at Muskoka Wharf, Gravenhurst's port on Lake Muskoka, in November. The citizens of Gravenhurst and officials of the Northern Railway Company celebrated the arrival of the railway on November 13, "the locomotives and steamers whistling without cessation for about five minutes, the brass band on the Nipissing playing an appropriate air" (H 25). The length of time which had elapsed between the incorporation of the company and the opening of the line to Gravenhurst was explained partly by the roughness of the country through which the track had to be laid, and partly by the hesitation of the company in building through such a sparsely settled district. In view of these difficulties the company asked special subsidies from the government (H 23) as well as from the communities. The line continued very slowly northward and reached Bracebridge in 1885 and Huntsville in 1886. Here, as in all districts, the railway by its choice of route brought prosperity to some settlements and destroyed others. Huntsville in time became a thriving town while its rival Hoodstown,[4] left without a railway, disappeared.

Some confusion in the names applied to this company results from a series of amalgamations.[5] On December 27, 1871, the Toronto, Simcoe and Muskoka Junction Railway united with the North Grey Railway to form the Northern Extension Railways Company, and on June 3, 1875, the Northern Extension Railways Company was absorbed by the Northern Railway Company, which became part, at a later date, of the Grand Trunk Railway, and still later of the Canadian National Railways.

Although the Northern Railway was the one finally extended through Muskoka it was not the only line which considered building into the north. Another well-organized railway, the Port Hope, Lindsay and Beaverton Railway Company, which changed its name on December 24, 1869, to the Midland Railway of Canada, was casting glances toward Georgian Bay in the late 1860's. It ran from Port Hope to Lindsay, with a branch to Peterborough and Lakefield, and in 1870–1 extended its main line to Beaverton with authority to continue to Lake Huron. Although some settlers expected this line to reach Muskoka (H 20), the extension to Lake Huron did not develop.

Settlers in both Muskoka and Haliburton looked hopefully to the Toronto and Nipissing Railway Company which had been incorporated by William Gooderham, March 4, 1868, with the stated purpose of proceeding to the north. Construction began in 1870 on a line which was to run from Scarborough through Uxbridge and Cannington to Coboconk. The Canadian Land and Emigration Company, which was seriously handicapped by the lack of a railway, supported the incorporation of this railway with a petition (H 26) and, in the spring of 1870, C. J. Blomfield was considering means of obtaining a further extension to Haliburton village (H 29). His plans were doomed to failure; the railway reached Coboconk near the mouth of the Gull River in November, 1872, but progressed no further.

Another company planning a railway to Haliburton, also supported by Blomfield, was incorporated in 1869 under the name Peterborough and Haliburton Railway Company (H 27). A petition for aid was addressed to the Lieutenant Governor by the in-

[4]Hoodstown, originally called Port Vernon, is described by F. M. De la Fosse in *English Bloods*, pp. 88–9.
[5]Stevens, *Canadian National Railways*, v. 1, p. 411.

habitants of the Town and County of Peterborough (H 28). In September, 1870, at a meeting of the provisional directors in Mr. Blomfield's office, proposals were outlined for building a railway with iron rails if necessary, from Peterborough to Chemong and wooden rails from Chemong to Haliburton (H 30). This company, like many others, proceeded little beyond the paper stage.

The railway which was to reach Haliburton in 1878 began as a combined settlement and railway scheme in the mind of George Laidlaw. The settlement aspect of his plans did not develop far, but the railway was incorporated on March 22, 1872, as the Lindsay, Fenelon Falls and Ottawa River Valley Railway, with the object of reaching the iron ore in Haliburton, as well as the pine forests of Haliburton and Lake Opeongo. In March, 1873, the name was changed to the Victoria Railway Company. So anxious were the townships of Haliburton, then a part of Peterborough County, to obtain an extension of the railway into their territory that they were willing to support it with a substantial bonus. When Peterborough was reluctant to permit them to tax themselves for this purpose, they agitated for separation and obtained an act establishing the Provisional County of Haliburton, 1874 (I 10). The new county at once promised $55,000 to the railway and on November 23, 1878, welcomed its arrival at Haliburton. Although the railway was a boon to the settlers, the financial problems which resulted from the bonus were to plague the county for years to come.

I. COMMUNITIES AND INSTITUTIONS

THE TERRITORIAL DIVISIONS ACT, passed in 1851, added the territories recently acquired from the Indians to the older settled counties. By this act the land west of the line between the former Home and Newcastle districts, from the Severn River and Rama on the south to French River on the north became part of Simcoe County (I 1). In 1858, however, four townships now in Muskoka—Ryde, Draper, Macaulay, and Oakley—were added to Victoria County. Although this disposition of the four townships looked reasonable on a map it was a hardship to the incoming settlers, since access to all four was from the Muskoka Road and their trading centre was Orillia, not Lindsay. Three Haliburton townships—Lutterworth, Anson, and Hindon—were attached to Victoria, and twelve to Peterborough—Snowdon, Minden, Stanhope, Guilford, Dysart, Glamorgan, Monmouth, Dudley, Harburn, Bruton, Harcourt, and Cardiff (I 2). At the time this act was passed, Victoria and Peterborough were united, and when they separated in 1863 the Haliburton townships continued with their respective counties.

The settlers soon found that some municipal organization was needed to regulate local affairs, especially assessments, taxes, schools, and roads. The inhabitants of Morrison and Muskoka petitioned the Simcoe County Council that they be united and organized into a municipality. The petition was considered by a committee in June, 1864, reported upon favourably,[1] and the necessary by-law was passed (I 3). In 1867, Draper, Macaulay, Stephenson, and Ryde were also organized into one municipality by the County of Victoria and the next year Oakley was added. The settlers, however, found that area too large, and as the population increased, petitioned the Legislature in November, 1869, that separate municipalities be formed.[2] This was a pattern followed by other townships in Muskoka and Haliburton. By 1867 four of the Haliburton townships had separate municipal organizations—Snowdon, Stanhope, Minden, and Dysart (14).

Settlers in the Muskoka townships found the obligation of going to Orillia or Lindsay to settle even minor court actions intolerable. In January, 1868, Morrison, Muskoka, Monck, Watt, Humphry,

[1]Simcoe County, Municipal Council, *Minutes*, June, 1864, app. p. 37.
[2]P.A.O., Ontario Sessional Papers, Petitions, 1869–70, no. 128.

Stephenson, Brunel, Macaulay, and Draper petitioned the government for a Division Court and Registry Office to be set up at Bracebridge (I 5). In March the necessary act[3] was passed, in April notices were published for Division Courts to be held at Bracebridge during the year (I 6), and by June preparations were under way for two buildings to house the Registry Office, Court Room, and Lock-up.[4]

Although the act provided for a Division Court and Registry Office, the administration of justice in general remained with the counties of Simcoe and Victoria. In 1869 this division in administration proved so inconvenient that under the leadership of A. P. Cockburn, the member for the North Riding of Victoria, meetings were held and a petition circulated asking that the townships be united into a junior county temporarily annexed to Simcoe (I 7). This move, however, brought objections from some of the settlers, and although a bill was introduced into the legislature it was not passed. A protest meeting was held at Bracebridge to express regret and indignation (I 8) and the Lindsay *Expositor* openly attacked William Lount for the failure of the bill.[5]

The administration of justice at a point distant from the townships was a hardship equally for the settlers in the townships and for the county which had to bear the costs of administration. During the latter half of the 1870's Simcoe County sent memorials to the Ontario government protesting the expense of administering justice in an unorganized district from which it derived no income (I 9), but not until 1888 was Muskoka separated from Simcoe.[6] Meanwhile the townships that had been attached to Peterborough County had also become restive and agitated for a separate county. In 1874 "An Act to Incorporate the Municipality of Haliburton, and to Provide for its Becoming a Provisional County" was passed (I 10), and on June 18 of that year the first municipal council of Haliburton met at the town hall in Minden (I 11).

Politics and Elections

When the Muskoka district was added to Simcoe County in 1851, its representative in the legislature was nominally the member for that county, the Honourable W. B. Robinson. After the

[3]Ontario, *Statutes*, 1867–8, 31 Vic., c. 35.
[4]P.A.O., Colonization Roads Papers, Copy Book 1865–8, p. 713.
[5]Lindsay *Expositor*, March 24, 1870.
[6]"An Act Respecting Muskoka and Parry Sound" (Ontario, *Statutes*, 1888, 51 Vic., c. 13.

Parliamentary Representation Act of 1853[7] divided Simcoe into two ridings, the North Riding, which included Muskoka, elected Angus Morrison in 1854, 1857, and 1861. Confederation[8] brought a new distribution of the townships by which Macaulay, Draper, Morrison, Muskoka, Monck, and Watt were included in the North Riding of Victoria. In 1867, A. P. Cockburn, "scarcely 30 years of age" and a "staunch reformer" (I 12), won the seat. After a successful experience in the provincial legislature he turned to the Dominion Parliament in 1872 and contested a new riding, which included Muskoka and Parry Sound, against D'Arcy Boulton of Toronto. (I 14, I 15, I 16). In spite of the fact that Boulton had the support of his leader, Sir John A. Macdonald, Cockburn was elected, and in 1874 was successful again over another candidate, John Teviotdale of Bracebridge.

The Haliburton townships added to Victoria and Peterborough in 1858 were nominally represented by the members for those constituencies. In the redistribution at Confederation, Anson, Hindon, and Lutterworth were included in the North Riding of Victoria, and Snowdon, Minden, Stanhope, and Dysart were included in the East Riding of Peterborough.

Principal Early Villages

The sites for future towns were often selected by the surveyors. Robert Bell, for example, said in his report on the survey of 1847, "I chose a site for a town at the Great Falls on the Muskako River" (D 6). A town site was later laid out there, now known as Muskoka Falls, but when steamer service developed on Lake Muskoka, Bell's site was eclipsed by Bracebridge, more favourably situated at the head of navigation on the North Branch.

In general, a town grew up where a major road crossed a navigable river, such as at Severn Bridge, Bracebridge, and Huntsville, or at a natural terminus of navigation such as Gravenhurst near the southern end of Lake Muskoka, Bracebridge at the first falls on the river, Port Carling on the Indian River between Lakes Muskoka and Rosseau, and the village of Rosseau at the northwestern end of that lake. Kinmount developed where the Bobcaygeon road crossed the Burnt River, Minden where it crossed the Gull River, and Dorset where the road touched the Lake of Bays. The presence of a falls which provided water power for a grist mill or sawmill was

[7]Canada, *Statutes*, 1852–3, 16 Vic., c. 152.
[8]"British North America Act, 1867," Schedule 1, pt. B.

an added factor in the formation of a settlement. When the railways came, the lines of transportation changed, and villages dependent for their prosperity on water routes, if ignored by the railway, usually declined and even disappeared.

Severn Bridge, the first community in Muskoka, was begun about 1858 (I 17). Vernon B. Wadsworth said that in 1860 "At this crossing of the Severn River there were two or three houses, and a store kept by one Jackson" (D 16). Although good water-power was available, the population grew slowly, and was soon exceeded by that of Gravenhurst and Bracebridge.

Gravenhurst was entirely uninhabited when Wadsworth reached there in July, 1860. The Muskoka Road was under construction, but not even a path led to Muskoka Bay, about one mile distant on Lake Muskoka. Among the first settlers were James McCabe and his wife who opened a tavern before the summer of 1861 (J 1). When A. P. Cockburn placed the *Wenonah* on Lake Muskoka in 1866, Gravenhurst became the southern terminal of navigation. In summer, passengers and freight alike came by stage from Washago and transferred to the steamer for Bracebridge or one of the other ports of call (I 19). The coming of the railway in 1875 confirmed Gravenhurst's position as the distribution centre for Muskoka, and, even more, made it the "Sawmill City." When the extension of the railway to Bracebridge in 1885, and the gradual decline of the lumber industry at the beginning of the century, closed the mills one by one, other industries such as the tourist trade developed.

Bracebridge in 1861, according to W. E. Hamilton, "consisted of the log huts and potato patches of Messrs. John Beal and David Leith, James Cooper's log house, and a small brick tavern and store, built on the south side of the river (there being no bridge save a large pine tree, which spanned the Falls) by Hiram Macdonald."[9] But with its strategic position on the Muskoka Road, and River, with an abundance of water power, and above all with a number of active, determined promoters, Bracebridge grew rapidly in population and in importance. It served as a natural meeting place for farmers from Monck, Macaulay, Muskoka, and Draper townships. On July 1, 1867, the settlers in the neighbourhood gathered with the inhabitants of Bracebridge to celebrate "The natal day of our new Dominion . . . with becoming loyalty and eclat" (I 20). By 1870 Bracebridge had free schools, several

[9]Hamilton, *Guide Book & Atlas of Muskoka and Parry Sound Districts*, p. 22. This may be compared with a description of Bracebridge in 1871 in McMurray, *The Free Grant Lands of Canada*, p. 27.

churches, at least three hotels, stores, sawmills, a newspaper, and a developing tourist trade. That year Charles Marshall found "the little town" romantic and picturesque, but also bustling and prosperous (I 23).

Huntsville,[10] on the Muskoka Road about twenty-five miles north of Bracebridge, at the crossing of the Muskoka or Vernon River, was not settled until the late 1860's, although it had trappers' cabins at an early period. The first trapper on record in that area was William Cann of Orillia who had a shanty on the west side of the river, probably from the late 'fifties, which he visited each year, and later shared with a Mr. Hildritch. In 1861 James Hanes and his family settled at Utterson, about ten miles south of the present site of Huntsville, but built a fishing shanty at Hunter's Bay, at the east end of Lake Vernon, which they occupied as a permanent home from about 1863. Travellers in 1865 found about a dozen shanties, most of them with an acre or two of cleared land, belonging to trappers along the southern and eastern shores of Lake Vernon (J 5). In 1869 Captain George Hunt settled with his family on land later included in the original town site of Huntsville, and he is regarded as the founder of that town. Other settlers followed into the same area, although the Muskoka Road was still not completed for the last three miles. Captain Hunt superintended the work required to open the road, assisted by another settler, Nathan Norton, who cut the timber for the roadway. The next year, in January, 1870, a post office was established (I 24), named Huntsville in honour of Captain Hunt.

Many smaller centres developed in Muskoka, such as Bala, Beaumaris, Baysville, Port Carling, Port Sydney, Utterson, Dwight, and Ilfracombe, each one differing in character from the others, and to the present day carrying the stamp of the first settlers who chose the locality and established community life.

Minden, on the border between Minden and Anson townships, where the Bobcaygeon Road crosses the Gull River, is the oldest community in Haliburton. It already had a number of settlers before it was surveyed as a town plot. Among the first was Daniel Buck who opened a tavern principally for the men working on the road which reached the Gull River in 1859. By 1860 there were a number of buildings including two small stores (I 28), and Mr. Buck was already building a larger hotel (I 27). At first the name of the settlement was Gull River but apparently this was changed

[10]The facts concerning Huntsville mainly are from *Huntsville's Old Home Week*.

to Minden with the establishment of the post office (I 26). Schools and places for worship were set up almost at once, and the community rapidly became a market centre for a large part of Haliburton. With the establishment of the County of Haliburton in 1874 it was made the county town and a newspaper appeared soon after (I 30).

The village of Haliburton, on Head Lake, is in Dysart, one of the townships bought by the Canadian Land and Emigration Company, and its early development was dependent on that company. Dysart was surveyed in 1861-2 but no settlement was made until 1864, although a few trappers were in the neighbourhood. The surveyor, B. W. Gossage, reported three squatters on Lake Kashagawigamog in 1861, two of whom had taken in their families (F 41), and Wadsworth in 1864 met a trapper, Dave Sawyer, from Drag Lake (I 31). In 1864 C. R. Stewart, manager of the Canadian Land and Emigration Company, became the first settler. The report of the Company given at the annual meeting in March 1865 showed twelve lots in the town plot of Haliburton already sold (F 45).

The Churches

The first settlers, as soon as the immediate need for shelter and food had been satisfied, gave thought to a church and a school. Many of them had been accustomed to attend religious services regularly, and, using the materials at hand, they tried to establish in the wilderness a replica of what they had known at home. Sometimes all that could be accomplished was a gathering at one of the log cabins. Mrs. King, writing to her son said, "We greatly felt, after we came into the Bush, the want of all religious ordinances; but we soon arranged a general meeting of all the members of the family on a Sunday at your sister's, when your brother-in-law read the Church of England service, and all joined in singing the chants and hymns."[11] As soon as possible, settlers erected special buildings for worship. Mrs. King mentioned one which was in her neighbourhood but too far away to attend, "Here Church of England, Presbyterian, and Wesleyan ministers preached in turn." One of the first buildings erected at Haliburton by C. R. Stewart was for church services. In the centres of settlement these rough shanties were replaced by regular churches at an early date.

The clergymen who followed their members into "the bush" faced serious hardship. Many of them had to travel by horseback,

[11]King, *Letters from Muskoka by an Emigrant Lady*, pp. 48–9.

by canoe, or on foot in all weathers to widely scattered meeting places or settlers' homes. The Reverend George Henry Kenney ministered to nine townships in the neighbourhood of the Gull and Burnt rivers, and Lakes Kashagawigamog, Boshkung, and Maple (I 34). When clergymen were not available "local preachers" held services, and colporteurs distributed tracts and preached. George Buskin, one such "Gospel Worker" in the Ryerson Settlement and Doe Lake district just to the north of Muskoka, left an account of his experiences in his autobiography *More than Forty Years in Gospel Harness*. Clergymen of various denominations visited the lumber camps and usually met with an attentive hearing from men of all creeds. The Roman Catholic clergymen made a special effort to reach the camps in which French Canadians were working, but Protestant and Roman Catholic clergy alike visited the other camps.

From the days of the first tourists down to the present time campers and cottagers on some of the lakes and rivers have met together for Christian worship on Sunday morning. James Bain and his young companions held such a service, led by John Campbell, at their camp on Lake Rosseau (J 4). The Muskoka Club, which grew out of their early camping trips, continued the tradition of outdoor services for many years at Yoho,[12] in Lake Joseph, with the same John Campbell, then Dr. John Campbell, of the Presbyterian Church, in charge.

The Schools

Schools and churches are closely associated in pioneer settlements. In Muskoka and Haliburton a schoolhouse was often used for religious services, and a clergyman, probably the best educated person in the community, frequently served as the local superintendent of schools or even taught the children of nearby settlers. In 1865 A. Parsonage wrote "we have a resident Clergyman living on the next lot to ours Little Fred and Marian go there to School almost every day" (F 52).

At the time Muskoka and Haliburton were opened for settlement, common schools were established under legislation of 1850 and 1853 which provided for support by voluntary subscriptions, rate bills paid by the parents, or assessment on property. Inspection was by local superintendents, such as the Reverend Walter Wright

[12]A photograph of a service at Yoho about 1895 is given in Mason, *Muskoka; The First Islanders*, p. 20.

and the Reverend Frederick Burt (I 38, I 39). By the School Improvement Act of 1871[13] the common schools became free public schools, and full-time inspectors, who were qualified teachers, were appointed. As in any pioneer district, the schools of Muskoka and Haliburton for many years were inadequately supported (I 41); access to them was difficult owing to the distance between farms and the lack of roads (I 40); attendance was irregular, and teachers but poorly trained. However, provincial grants, the continuous pressure of the inspectors, and the work of some of the more progressive trustees gradually raised the standards.

[13]"An Act to Improve the Common and Grammar Schools of the Province of Ontario" (Ontario, *Statutes*, 1870–1, 34 Vic., c. 33).

J. THE FIRST TOURISTS

THE ROCKS AND HILLS of the Laurentian Shield, which spelled ruin
for many a settler, attracted the city-dweller intent on hunting and
fishing, and so laid the foundation for a tourist trade which compensated the inhabitants of Muskoka and Haliburton to some
degree for the agricultural deficiencies of their land. There are a
number of factors essential to the growth of a successful tourist
business: the proximity of a large urban population from which to
draw visitors; transportation services and hotels pleasing not only
to the men but to their wives and families; active businessmen willing to put time and money into making the region known; and
above all, beauty of lakes and rivers, fishing and hunting, and a
climate known for its health-giving qualities. All these Muskoka
had by the middle of the 1860's. Haliburton, though equally
endowed by nature, did not possess some of the other requirements
until a later period.

Holiday-seekers from Toronto and the thickly settled peninsula
of western Ontario rode in comfort on the Northern Railway from
Toronto to Lake Simcoe and then continued by boat and stage.
Adventurous Americans, attracted by descriptions of the northern
lakes and accounts of the profusion of game and fish, came to
Toronto, often by way of Niagara Falls, and then followed the
same route north. In later years when the railway was opened to
Gravenhurst and Bracebridge, businessmen from Pennsylvania,
Ohio, and other parts of the United States, as well as from Ontario,
built luxurious summer homes on the Muskoka Lakes which
rivalled those on the St. Lawrence.

The first tourists, visitors with no other motive than to see the
country and enjoy a holiday, found their way to Muskoka about
the beginning of the 1860's. James Bain and John Campbell, aged
eighteen and twenty, went as far as Lake Muskoka in July, 1860,
and returned year after year on camping expeditions (J 4), until in
1872 they bought islands and built their cottages on Lake Joseph.
Two other young men, H. P. Dwight and Mr. Townsend, made
annual fishing trips to the Muskoka River from about 1863 (J 9)
and years later were members of the Dwight-Wiman Club noted
for its hunting expeditions. There were no doubt other tourists in
those early years, but most of them have left no record. One of the
most ambitious trips to Muskoka and Haliburton was that of a
group of men from Oshawa who, in 1865, went by way of the

Severn River, Lake Muskoka, and the North Branch of the Muskoka River to Mary, Fairy, and Vernon lakes, then to Peninsula Lake, over the portage to the Lake of Bays, and south by the Gull River route (J 5).

The citizens of Muskoka, led by their very active member of the legislature, A. P. Cockburn, lost no opportunity of displaying the beauty of the country to such influential guests as the Ontario government (J 7), the Canadian Press Association (J 10), and the officials of the Northern Railway (H 19). Thomas McMurray and other writers continually advertised the scenery, the fishing, and the hunting, while the railways produced guide books to lure travellers to both Muskoka and Parry Sound.

Thomas M. Robinson, who helped James Bain and his friends plan some of their trips and accompanied them as leader, may be considered the first, or at least one of the first, hosts for the tourist trade. Mr. Robinson later advertised his home on Muskoka Bay: "Quiet Private Board in retired locality. Terms: $1.00 per day, with the use of boats."[1] For some years the only taverns and hotels were those intended for settlers and businessmen, but gradually tourist resorts were opened which offered good fishing, attractive surroundings, and suitable accommodation for family parties. The best known of the early hotels was built in 1873–4 by an American, W. H. Pratt, on Lake Rosseau just outside the limits of the present Muskoka District. It was named Rosseau House, but was usually called Pratt's, and was considered the best hotel in the north (J 6 and Plate XIV). Unfortunately it burned on October 6, 1883, and was not rebuilt.

To the citizens of Muskoka their most important guests in the early period were Lord and Lady Dufferin in 1874 (J 11). Lady Dufferin described the trip from Gravenhurst to Bracebridge, "When we left our carriages we got on to a steamer covered with flags, and steamed along a lovely place, called Muskoka Bay, into Muskoka Lake, and then through a most curious, narrow river, in which we twisted and turned round islands, and had only just room to move; sometimes we appeared to be going straight ashore, and then turned suddenly to one side and were saved. This river brought us to Bracebridge. . . . A band and a crowd met us on the wharf, and we drove through the town, the band preceding us, the Governor-General's carriage in front, and mine behind."[2]

[1]*Guide to Muskoka Lakes, Upper Maganetawan & Inside Channel of the Georgian Bay*, p. 106.

[2]Hariot Georgina, Marchioness of Dufferin and Ava, *My Canadian Journal, 1872–8*, p. 161.

MUSKOKA AND HALIBURTON

DOCUMENTS

A. TRAVELLERS AND MISSIONARIES ON GEORGIAN BAY AND THE SEVERN RIVER, 1615–1823

A 1 SAMUEL DE CHAMPLAIN[1] ON GEORGIAN BAY, 1615
[*Champlain*, Works, *ed. Biggar, v. 3, pp. 45–7*]

... The next day we parted, and continued our journey along the shore of this Lake of the Attigouautans,[2] in which there are a great number of islands; and we made about forty-five leagues, keeping along the shore of this lake. It is very large, being nearly four hundred leagues in length,[3] from east to west, and fifty leagues wide, and in view of its great size I named it the Freshwater Sea. It abounds in many kinds of excellent fish, both those we have and those we have not, and principally in trout, which are of enormous size; I have seen some that were as much as four and a half feet long, and the smallest one sees are two and a half feet in length. Also pike of like size, and a certain kind of sturgeon, a very large fish, and marvellously good to eat. The country bordering upon this lake along the north shore is partly rugged and partly flat, uninhabited by savages, and slightly covered with trees including oaks. Then afterwards we crossed a bay[4] which forms one of the extremities of the lake, and made some seven leagues until we reached the country of the Attigouautan, and came on the first of August to a village called Otoüacha.[5] Here we found a great change in the country, this part being very fine, mostly cleared, with many hills and several streams, which make it an agreeable district. I went to look at their Indian corn which at that time was far advanced for the season.

This district seems to me very pleasant in contrast to such a bad country as that through which we had just come. ...

A 2 GABRIEL SAGARD[6] AT AN ALGONKIN FEAST IN 1624
[*Sagard*, The Long Journey to the Country of the Hurons, *ed. Wrong, p. 247*]

... We left that spot[7] when the canoe that had been brought us was ready, and we made such speed that about noon we came upon Etienne

[1]Samuel de Champlain (1567?–1635), the founder of Quebec, went to the Huron country by the Ottawa River and Lake Nipissing in 1615. His description of Georgian Bay, Muskoka's western boundary, is the first recorded comment on the area.
[2]Lake Huron. The Attigouautans were Huron Indians.
[3]"This is almost three times the length Champlain himself gives it in his map of 1632. The real distance from the end of Matchedash Bay to St. Joseph Island is about 175 geographical miles." (Champlain, *Works*, v. 3, p. 45).
[4]The bay in the southeastern part of Georgian Bay, into which the Severn flows.
[5]Otoüacha was probably near Thunder Bay in Tiny Township.
[6]Gabriel Sagard, called Théodat (d. 1650), was a lay brother of the Recollet Order. He came to Canada in 1623, spent several months in the Huron mission,

Brulé[8] with five or six canoes from the village of Toenchain,[9] and all together we went to take up our quarters in an Algonquin village.[10] According to my custom I went about, visiting the lodges in the place, and I was invited to a feast of a large sturgeon which was boiling in a great cauldron over the fire. The master of the feast, who invited me, was alone, sitting beside the cauldron and singing continually for the success and glory of his feast. I promised to be there at the appointed hour, and returned thence to our own lodge, where I had scarcely arrived when the man appeared who was charged with the summons to the feast. To everyone whom he invited he gave a small piece of stick as long and as thick as one's little finger, as a token and sign that one was among those invited, and not those others who could not produce the same. There were nearly fifty men at this feast, and they were all more than sufficiently satiated with the great fish, of which everybody had a good piece, and with the meal that was stirred into the broth. The Algonquins, one after another while the pot was being emptied, showed our Hurons that they could sing and fence as well as our men, and that if they had enemies they had also enough courage and might to overcome them all. At the close I talked to them a little about their salvation, and then we withdrew. . . .

A 3   FATHER JÉRÔME LALEMANT'S[11] REPORT ON THE MISSION OF SAINTE ELIZABETH,[12] 1643-4
[Jesuit Relations, ed. Thwaites, v. 27, p. 37]

The Iroquois, who make themselves dreaded in the great river St. Lawrence and who every winter for some years past have been hunting men in these vast forests, have compelled the Algonquins who dwelt

and returned to France in 1624. He was especially interested in the customs and language of the Indians and in the plant and animal life of the country. In 1632 he published his *Grand Voyage du pays des Hurons*.

[7]After leaving Huronia, Sagard and the Indians had to land at a cove and wait for another canoe to be brought.

[8]Etienne Brulé (1591?-1633) came to Quebec with Champlain in 1608. He spent the winters of 1610-11 and 1611-12 with the Algonkin and Huron Indians and was probably the first white man to see Georgian Bay. He lived for many years with the Hurons, travelled widely with them, and at the time of this quotation was on his way back to Quebec. In 1633 he was murdered in Huronia.

[9]Toenchain, a village not far from modern Penetanguishene.

[10]This Algonkin village was probably on Beausoleil Island which is now a national park but is geographically part of the Muskoka district. "That the feast described by Sagard took place on Beausoleil island is supported by a variety of circumstances. It was a village of the Missisaugas at a later date" (Sagard, *The Long Journey*, note on map at end of volume).

[11]Father Jérôme (Hierosme) Lalemant (1593-1673) ministered to the Hurons from 1638 to 1645. He was Superior of the missions in New France from 1645 to 1650 and again after 1659. He wrote the *Relations* of the Huron missions, 1639 to 1643, and those for New France from 1646 to 1648 and 1660 to 1664.

[12]The mission of Sainte Elizabeth was probably near the north end of Lake

on the banks of the river to abandon not only their hunting grounds, but also their country, and have reduced them this winter to come here near our Hurons, in order to live more in safety,— so much so, that a whole village of these poor wandering and fugitive Tribes came near the village of saint Jean Baptiste.[13] We were obliged to give them some assistance, and for that purpose to associate with Father Antoine Daniel[14]— who had charge of the Huron Mission of which I had spoken in the preceding chapter— Father René Menard,[15] who, having a sufficient knowledge of both languages, had, at the same time, charge of this Algonquin Mission, to which we have given the name of sainte Elizabeth. . . .

A 4   LALEMANT'S REPORT ON THE MISSION OF THE HOLY GHOST, MAY 15, 1645
[Jesuit Relations, *ed. Thwaites, v. 28, p. 97*]

. . . The seventh[16] Church, called that "of the holy Ghost," consists of Algonquins, several Tribes of whom wintered together this year on the great Lake of our Hurons, about twenty-five leagues[17] from us. This compelled Father Claude Pijart[18] and Father Leonard Gareau[19] who were appointed for their instruction, to pass the Winter[20] with them,— with inconceivable trouble and labors, but not without consolation, when they see that they prepare Spouses for Jesus Christ within these woods, and amid these lakes and rivers. . . .

Couchiching, two or three miles south of the district line of Muskoka. Thwaites points out that the mission, like the Indians for whom it was intended, was nomadic.

[13]The village of Saint Jean Baptiste is thought to have been near Bass Lake in the northeastern part of Oro Township.

[14]Father Antoine Daniel (1601–1648) came to Canada in 1632 and went to the Huron mission a year or two later. He remained there, except for the years from 1636 to 1638, until his death in the Iroquois attack on St. Joseph, July, 1648.

[15]Father René Menard (1605–1661) was sent to Canada in 1640. He worked at Huronia, first with the mission of the Holy Ghost, later with that of Sainte Elizabeth. After the destruction of Huronia in 1649 he ministered to the Iroquois and to the tribes on Lake Superior.

[16]The other six churches were for the Hurons and were more or less stationary.

[17]Twenty-five leagues from Huronia would be a little north of the Muskoka district.

[18]Father Claude Pijart (1600–1683) was sent to Huronia in 1640 to open a mission for the Nipissings. He worked with them and other Algonkins until the Huron mission was destroyed by the Iroquois.

[19]Father Leonard Garreau (1609?–1656) came to Canada in 1643 and went to the Huron mission the following year. For almost two years he worked with the mission of the Holy Ghost and later with the Huron churches. For a time after the destruction of Huronia he was one of the priests in charge of the Hurons on the Island of Orleans.

[20]The winter of 1644–5.

A 5   FATHER PAUL RAGUENEAU'S[21] REPORT ON
ALGONKIN MISSIONS, 1645
[Jesuit Relations, *ed. Thwaites, v. 30, pp. 109, 87, 89*]

... Father Claude Pijart and Father Leonard Gareau, who had wintered with the Algonquins on the shores of our great lake, and in the midst of the snows, which cover these countries more than four or five months, followed those same tribes throughout the Summer, upon the bare rocks which they inhabit, exposed to the heat of the Sun; and thus spent with them almost all the past year. ...

... They had left us at the end of the month of November; after four or five days' journey,— in which they had to combat the winds, the snows, and the ice which was beginning to form in every direction,— they saw themselves constrained to leave their canoe, still distant more than three leagues from the place where they were aiming to land. ...

Father Jean de Brebeuf[22] went, toward the end of Autumn,[23] to a place named Tangouaen,[24] where dwell some Algonquins, and where some cabins of Hurons have taken refuge, in order to live there more sheltered from incursions by the Iroquois; for it is a retired country, and surrounded on all sides by lakes, ponds, and rivers, which make this place inaccessible to the enemy. It was a journey extremely difficult for the Father, and for a young Frenchman who accompanied him thither: but their consolation much surpassed their hardships, when they found in the midst of those profound forests and those vast solitudes a little Church which they had gone to visit. By this, I mean a whole family of Christians, who find God in those woods ...

The Father, having spent some days in that solitude, was in haste to accelerate his return, fearing to be surprised by the ice and the winter which was beginning, and which in fact stopped him on the way, and placed him in danger of dying from both hunger and cold, and of perishing in the lakes and rivers which they had to cross. ...

[21]Father Paul Ragueneau (1608–1680) came to Canada in 1636 and served in Huronia from 1636 until its destruction, except for the years 1640 and 1641. From 1645 to 1649 he was Superior in Huronia and from 1650 to 1653 Superior of all Canadian missions. As such he wrote the *Relations* of the Huron missions for 1645 to 1649 and edited the general *Relations* from 1649 to 1653.

[22]Father Jean de Brébeuf (1593–1649) first came to Canada in 1625, and worked among the Montagnais, Hurons, and Neutrals. He was head of the Huron mission from 1634 to 1638. Along with Father Gabriel Lalemant he was put to death by torture by the Iroquois in March, 1649.

[23]The autumn of 1645.

[24]There is no direct evidence to show where the Algonkins were living at this time. The *Jesuit Relations* (ed. Thwaites, v. 36, p. 247) suggests that Tangouaen was on the north side of the Severn River, in Baxter or Wood Township. However, Father A. E. Jones, from a study of the time required to go there from Huronia, places it north of Lake Nipissing (Jones, *"8endake Ehen,"* or *Old Huronia*, pp. 165–6).

A 6   RAGUENEAU'S REPORT ON ALGONKIN MISSIONS, 1648
[Jesuit Relations, ed. Thwaites, v. 33, pp. 151, 153, 155]

. . . On the South shore of this fresh-water sea, or Lake of the Hurons, dwell the following Algonquin tribes: Ouachaskesouek, Nigouaouichirinik, Outaouasinagouek, Kichkagoneiak, and Ontaanak,[25] who are allies of our Hurons. With these we have considerable intercourse . . .

Had we but enough people and enough means, we would find more employment in converting those peoples than would suffice for our lifetime. But, as there is a dearth of laborers, we have been able to undertake only a portion of the task,— that is to say, four or five Nations on this Lake, in each of whom there are already some Christians who, with God's aid, will be the seed of a still greater conversion. But it is impossible to conceive the fatigues or the difficulty of preserving the little fruit that can be gathered there; because we are often six, seven, or eight months, and sometimes a whole year, without being able to meet these truly scattered flocks. For all these Tribes are nomads, and have no fixed residence, except at certain seasons of the year, when fish are plentiful, and this compels them to remain on the spot.

Therefore, they have no other Church than the woods and forests; no other Altar than the rocks on which break the waves of this Lake. . . .

. . . Last Winter, many of those Algonquin Tribes came to winter here among the Hurons. Two of our Fathers,[26] who have charge of the Missions in the Algonquin language, continued their instruction until Spring, when they dispersed. At the same time, our Fathers set out to follow them, carrying on two different Missions,— one for the Algonquin Tribes dwelling on the Eastern shore of our freshwater sea, and for the Nipissiriniens; the other for the Tribes of the Algonquin language who dwell along the Northern shore of the same Lake. The former of these Missions is that which we call "the Mission of the Holy Ghost;" . . .

A 7   RAGUENEAU'S ACCOUNT OF THE MISSION OF
THE HOLY GHOST, 1649–50
[Jesuit Relations, ed. Thwaites, v. 35, pp. 179, 181]

This Mission was established for the Nations speaking the Algonquin tongue, who have— as little as the fish, by taking which they subsist— no certain abode along the coasts of the Great Lake, where they dwell sometimes in one place, sometimes in another, conformable to the different seasons of the year; or according as fears of the Iroquois compel

[25]According to Thwaites (Jesuit Relations, v. 73, p. 202) this is a misprint for Outaouak.
[26]Jones gives Fathers Claude Pijart and Joseph A. Poncet de la Rivière as the missionaries to the Algonkins in 1647–8 ("ꞗendake Ehen," or Old Huronia, p. 404).

them to move farther away from the peril which every day threatens them. This means that our Fathers who have had the care of that mission have led a wandering life among this wandering people, and have lived almost always on the water, or on desolate rocks beaten by the waves and storms. . . .

It was time that God should give to them[27] the spirit of faith; for, when Springtime came, bands of Iroquois, coming from a distance of two hundred leagues, surprised a party of these good Neophytes in a place where they deemed their lives perfectly secure; dragged them into Captivity, men, women and children,— not sparing even the young, but committing them to the flames with a cruelty beyond conception. . . .

A 8   LA SALLE[28] ON THE SEVERN RIVER AND GEORGIAN BAY, 1680
[*Margry, Découvertes, v. 1, pp. 500–1, as translated in Robinson,*
Toronto during the French Régime, *pp. 36–7*]

. . . He arrived on the fifteenth [of August, 1680] at Teiaiagon,[29] a village of the Iroquois situated sixty leagues from the fort, towards the extremity of the north side of Lake Frontenac.[30] He remained there till the twenty-second, because of the necessity of transporting all his baggage overland to Lake Toronto,[31] which discharges itself into Lake Huron by a river[32] which is navigable only by canoes and runs from east to west. . . . On the twenty-third, the Sieur de La Salle arrived at Lake Toronto, on which he embarked with all his people and descended the river which comes out into a bay full of islands. Thence he turned north to follow the north shore of Lake Huron because there are more harbours and places in which to shelter than on the south side, and because there is protection there from the great winds afforded by three long islands which are six or seven leagues from the shore. . . .

A 9   BARON DE LAHONTAN'S[33] PROPOSED FORT ON THE SEVERN ROUTE, 1703
[*Lahontan,* New Voyages to North-America, *reprinted from the English edition, 1703, v. 1, pp. 317–8*]

. . . To the North-West[34] of this River,[35] there lies the Bay of *Toranto*,[36] which is twenty, or five and twenty Leagues long, and fifteen

[27]The Algonkins.

[28]René Robert Cavelier, sieur de la Salle (1643–1687) came to Canada in 1667. He carried on a series of ambitious fur-trading and exploring expeditions in which he made extensive use of the route by the Toronto Carrying Place, Lake Simcoe, and the Severn River. According to Dr. Percy J. Robinson he crossed the Carrying Place on three and possibly four occasions, once in 1680, twice in 1681, and possibly once in 1683 (Robinson, *Toronto during the French Régime,* p. 36).

[29]Teiaiagon was in the present Toronto area, probably at the mouth of the Humber River.   [30]Lake Ontario.   [31]Lake Simcoe.   [32]Severn River.

[33]Louis Armand de Lom d'Arce, baron de Lahontan (1666–1715?), came to

broad at its Mouth. This Bay receives a River[37] that springs from a little Lake of the same name, and forms several Cataracts that are equally impracticable both upon the ascent and descent. Upon the side of this River you'll see a Man's Head mark'd in my Map, which signifies a large Village of the Hurons, that was destroy'd by the *Iroquese*. You may go from the source of this River to the Lake *Frontenac*, by making a Land-carriage to the River of *Tanaouate*,[38] that falls into that Lake. Upon the South side of the Bay of *Toronto*, you see the Fort call'd Fort Supposé, which I mentioned in my 23d Letter, and about thirty Leagues to the Southward of that, you find the Country of *Theonontate* which being formerly inhabited by the *Hurons*, was entirely depopulated by the *Iroquese*. . . .

A 10   ROBERT MATHEWS[39] TO LIEUTENANT COLONEL
MASON BOLTON[40]
[*Public Archives of Canada (P.A.C.), Haldimand Papers,
B 104, p. 125*]

Quebec
19th. May 1780

I am commanded by his Excellency General Haldimand[41] to acquaint you that being desirous to open a Communication with Michilimakinac from Niagara by way of Toronto, He desires you will, without loss of time, Dispatch an Intelligent officer either of the Garrison or Lieut. Col. Butler's Rangers[42] with a necessary party of White Men and Indians to explore that useful route making observations upon the Navigation of the Rivers or Lakes, and the length and nature of the ground and woods by which they are intercepted — a report[43] of which you will please to transmit for his Excellency's Information.—

Canada on military duty in November, 1683. He served against the Iroquois and carried on extensive explorations. After his return to Europe he published his memoirs in both French and English. He proposed that the French build and maintain three forts against the Iroquois, including the one here described.

[34]An error for southeast.

[35]French River.   [36]Matchedash Bay.   [37]Severn River.

[38]Probably the Trent system, though the reference to land carriage suggests the Toronto Carrying Place.

[39]Robert Mathews, Major of the 53rd Foot, military secretary to Governor Haldimand from 1778 to 1786.

[40]Lieutenant Colonel Mason Bolton, Commandant at Niagara, drowned in November, 1780, in the sinking of the *Ontario*.

[41]Sir Frederick Haldimand (1718–1791), Governor in Chief of Quebec from 1778 to 1786.

[42]A loyalist corps organized by Colonel John Butler in 1776, and commanded by Captain Walter Butler in the attack on Cherry Valley in 1778.

[43]No report has been found, but the following memorandum (A 11) probably concerns this expedition.

A 11   "FROM A MEMORANDUM BOOK BORROWED OF M. HARE"[44]
[*Ontario, Department of Lands and Forests, Field Notes,*
v. 1, pp. 181–6]

"And swampy where we crossed the Creek before mentioned, seems now
to run N. E. We encamped about 12 Miles, the Indians being tired and
bad travelling, prevented us to go further, although we might have gone
[blank] further, the Sun being about 2 Hours high.

Sunday 25th. June 1780—.
    Set off and went 8 miles, came to a pond,[45] here we rested, went on
about 2 miles further, where we came to a thick Cedar Swamp— from
here our Course was N. N. W— went that Course about 5 miles &
came to the end of the carrying place to a Creek[46] 8 yards wide, which
came from W. N. W. here we stopped about an Hour, the Creek runs
E. N. E. set off hence 2 miles, then we entered a large meadow, where
the creek runs through — went about 2 miles and came to a Creek 10
yards wide, which emptied in this — came from S. S. W—upon our
right hand as we went down the Creek three miles further came to
another Creek, about 9 yards wide on our left hand, comes from N.W.—
    Mountains of [*sic*] each side of the Creek we now go, at the Creek
above mentioned we slept.

Monday — 26th —
    Set off in the Morning, & from here the Creek is about 50 yards wide
and runs very crooked. went down about 23 miles, then we entered a
small Lake[47] in breadth about 6 Miles, the Creek runs East: where the
Creek enters, the Meadows are 4 Miles in breadth —
    This Lake runs from appearance from the Mouth of the Creek N by
W. — On the East Side of this Lake are a great many Indians, We go
down the West Side — Went about 12 miles and encamped, the Shore
rocky & thick bush, and opposite is an Island[48] about 2 miles long.

[44]An incomplete copy of a journal of an exploratory trip by way of the
Toronto portage, Lake Simcoe, and the Severn River to Honey Harbour on
Georgian Bay and return to Niagara. It was tentatively attributed by Dr. Percy
J. Robinson to William Hare, an Indian trader. However the extant copy gives
no author, and states merely that the journal was "borrowed of M. Hare." If the
author was someone of the name of Hare it would seem more likely that he was
a member of the United Empire Loyalist family of that name at Niagara. Peter
Hare (1748–1834), a captain in Butler's Rangers, would fulfil Haldimand's specifications (A 10).
    A copy of the journal apparently was sent to Haldimand and is referred to in
a letter from Major Bolton to Haldimand, Niagara, September 14, 1780, "You
have, Sir, a journal of the party I sent to Lake Huron by way of Toronto." However the journal has not been located in the Haldimand Papers. This journal is
discussed by Dr. Percy J. Robinson in "The Toronto Carrying Place" (*Ontario
History*, v. 39, no. 1, March, 1947, p. 42) and further material appears in the
Percy J. Robinson Papers at the Ontario Archives. Some of the following footnotes are based on Dr. Robinson's research.
    [45]Hackett Lake.
    [46]Holland River.   [47]Cook Bay, Lake Simcoe.   [48]Snake Island.

Tuesday — 27th:

We leave this in the Morning, go about one mile, where are two more Islands, here the Lake widens greatly, can't perceive what breadth believe it to be about 10 miles; went about 15 miles further and came to a Bay[49] runs West that is about 8 miles deep & ½ mile broad; At the end[50] of this Bay Indians used to go across to Matchetash in two days, but the way being bad and no Canoes at the other side they go round: Here the Lake appears to be 20 miles broad: Here we stayed about 3 Hours the wind being too high to cross the Bay, in the Evening crossed & went about 4 miles where we encamped; Still a rocky Shore & very low thick woods; opposite where we slept is another Island[51] about 8 miles from the North Shore about 2½ miles long.—

Wednesday 28th —

Set off in the morning crossed several Bays & passed two Islands about 8 miles from the N. shore & 10 miles distant from one another — went about 10 miles and came to the mouth of the River, where went past several Islands where Indians had corn-fields on. Our course from here is North the River[52] here is about 1¼ mile wide several Islands in it: One small Island in the middle of the River, where about 10 Hutts of Indians, who saluted us as we came nigh the Shore, & we returned them the Compliment — remained there about an Hour, the Chief wanted us to remain there as it was likely for Rain, but excused ourselves and went on about two miles, and began to blow very hard, was obliged to encamp on a large Island[53] about two o'Clock, remained there all night —

Thursday 29th —

The Wind still blowing very fresh, & rain was obliged to remain here all night —

Friday 30th:

Set off about 7 o'Clock went about 5 miles, our course then N. E. went about 3 miles further, came to a very broad Island, went down the West side about 1½ miles, where the Water runs rapid, and at each end of the Island there is a small Fall[54]—here we carried over our Canoes & Baggage the Carrying place is about 50 yards broad: Here the River is about fifty yards broad —Here the River is about fifty yards wide [sic]—Rocks on each side; about ½ a mile from the carrying place, runs in a Creek[55] comes seemingly from S. E. is about 20 yards wide.— We now go N. N. W— went about 3 miles came to another Carrying place[56]

---

[49]Kempenfelt Bay.

[50]The portage from Kempenfelt Bay, later known as the Willow Portage, ran to Nottawasaga Bay, not to Matchedash.

[51]Thorah Island.   [52]Lake Couchiching.   [53]Chiefs Island.

[54]The first fall on the Severn River. Writers are divided in the numbering of the seven falls; some start at the source, some at the mouth of the river. The numbering supplied in these notes agrees with that used in the journal of Governor Simcoe's trip (A 16) and Captain Owen's table of distances (A 17).

[55]Black River.   [56]The second fall.

about 30 yards wide where we carried our Baggage & Canoes over; from this our Course is West — Several small Islands — went about ten miles & came to a small Lake[57] about one mile wide and 3 long, Here we encamped; very low Land until we came to this Lake —

Saturday 31st —

Set off about 7 o'Clock, went a mile N. E. then turned North— went about 3 miles, where the River is 100 yards wide & several rocky Islands; three miles further came to a Fall[58] about 20 yards wide, here we carried our Canoes across over a rocky [blank] about ¼ mile long. Went about One mile further where came to another Fall[59] of Water, descends very rapid — here we carried our Canoes across, is about ¾ of a mile long & very rocky — went about 12 miles where we came to another carrying place[60] — The Fall is about 15 yards wide and 50 yards descending. About ½ mile further came to another carrying place[61] — The River runs about ¾ of a mile N.N.W. and then turns round to S.S.E. we cross the carrying place S.S.W. it is about 150 yards across, where come again into the River — Here we encamped —

Sunday — 1st: July —

Set off in the Morning, went round to W. by N. about ½ a mile then turned S.W. and came to a large opening[62] about 2 miles long and 3 broad, and a great number of rock Islands — Went two miles that Course & then N. west — Here we left the River which runs W. S. W. and enters in a Bay of L. U.— went into a Bay[63] were we carried our Canoes over into a Pond — Still our Course N.W — this Pond resembles a River — it is about 100 yards wide, and in some places more or less — went about four miles, when we carried our Canoes over into another Pond — went about a mile and then came into a large opening[64] which is very full of Islands and Bays & difficult to find the way through them, we were several times obliged to turn back and go another way. We went about six miles through those Islands, & then went West by South about 2 miles, then came into a deep Bay[65] of Lake Uron — several Indians planting Corn; It is low land — Here we arrived about 2 o'Clock —

NB. In this Bay is where the Indians go the nigh cut[66] to where we saw them on the Island —

Monday 2nd July 1780 —

Left this about eight o'Clock in the morning, went towards the Head of the Bay— Our Course E.S.E. about 5 miles where we come to the

[57]Sparrow Lake.   [58]The third fall.   [59]The fourth fall.
[60]The fifth fall.   [61]The sixth fall.   [62]Gloucester Pool.
[63]The party turned north through Baxter Lake and South Bay to Honey Harbour, thus avoiding the last fall on the Severn.
[64]Honey Harbour.
[65]Probably Matchedash Bay, but directions and distances are not clear.
[66]The Indian path from Lake Couchiching to Matchedash Bay is shown in Figure 2.

River, it empties into this bay W. S. W — ¼ mile up the River we came to a Fall[67] where carried out Canoes over, the carrying place but about 20 yards — from here went [blank] two Falls & slept— Here

Tuesday — 3rd —
From there went to the small Lake;[68] here we encamped —

Wednesday — 4th —
Set off from here went about four miles — very low and swamp Bush at the West side is a fine large Bay; went about 3 miles further, came to a carrying place which crossed over the two first we went over going down, it is about a mile long, and goes South, we came into the River about 3 miles above the Falls & struck across about 5 miles below them — and is about 3 miles from the opening of the River — as you go down to this short Cut the course is N.N.E — went as far as Miskoteyank[69] & encamped here —

Thursday — 5th —
Set off from here and encamped about Eight miles from the Mouth of the Creek[70] —

Friday — 6th; July —
Went this Day as far as where we encamped by a Creek where we forgot a pipe Tomahawk —

Saturday — 7th —
Went about 20 Miles from the Landing

Sunday — 8th —
Went to the Lake[71] —

Monday — 9th —
Went as far as Messinegan River — about 12 o'Clock encamped— The Wind blowing hard ahead, and Rain —

Tuesday 10th: July 1780 —
Went as far as 40 Mile Pond —

Wednesday —
Went as far as Niagara —
NB.—Forgot to mention, that where the Indians lay, opposite in a Bay on the N. shore, was a Road,[72] strikes to the Lake, can go to in ¾ of a Day —

[67]The seventh fall on the Severn.   [68]Sparrow Lake.
[69]Dr. Robinson assumed that this was the island on which the Indians were living near the entrance to Lake Couchiching.
[70]Holland River.   [71]Lake Ontario.
[72]It is not clear whether this refers to the same path as that in footnote 66 or not.

Low Land and thick Bush from the small Lake to where the Indians
Plantations are —

A 12   BENJAMIN FROBISHER[73] TO HENRY HAMILTON[74]
[*Public Record Office (P.R.O.), C.O. 42, v. 47, p. 661; also printed in
Guillet*, The Valley of the Trent, *p. 134*]

Montreal 2nd. May. 1785.

. . . I am told Lake La Clie will admit of the Navigation of small
Vessels, and there is no want of Water in the river[75] already mentioned,
that runs from it, into Lake Huron, but it seems there are in it several
Falls of Water, which with other obstructions occasions Six or Seven
Carrying places, all of them short ones— large Canoes have gone up and
down it at different times, but I am told it is not practicable for Boats
untill some of the Carrying places are levelled so as to get them over
upon rollers— To avoid this river there is no other way of getting to
Lake Huron from Lake La Clie, but by a road overland as before described of about 18 miles some parts of which are low Marshy Ground
of a considerable extent so that embrasing every object for the purpose
of Establishing a sure and short Communication between the two Lakes,
I am of opinion from the present knowledge we have of the Country, it
can only be accomplished by the Carrying place of Torronto to Lake
La Clie, and thence down the river to Lake Huron . . .

A 13   LORD DORCHESTER'S[76] "INSTRUCTIONS TO CAPTN. [GOTHER]
MANN[77] COMMANDING ENGINEER"
[*P.R.O., C.O. 42, v. 20*]

Head Quarters Quebec 29th. May 1788

Whereas it is expedient for the King's Service, that the fortifications
at Ontario, Niagara, Erie, Detroit, and Michilimakinac, be kept in a
proper state of defence, you are hereby ordered & directed to proceed
without loss of time to these several Posts, thoroughly to survey and
report their condition . . .

[73]Benjamin Frobisher (1742?–1787) emigrated to Canada and became a fur
trader at least as early as 1765. In later years he was in partnership with his
brothers and supervised the Montreal aspect of the business.
[74]Henry Hamilton (d. 1796) was Lieutenant Governor of Quebec from 1782 to
1785 and, after Haldimand's departure for England in 1784, became Administrator of the government.
[75]Severn River.
[76]Sir Guy Carleton, first Baron Dorchester (1724–1808), Governor in Chief
of British North America.
[77]Gother Mann (1747–1830) was Commanding Royal Engineer in Canada
from 1785 to 1791 and again from 1794 to 1804. As such he made an extensive
examination of the fortifications and surveyed the navigable water routes. After his
return to England he became a general, July 19, 1821, and served as Inspector
General of Fortifications from 1811 until his death. From 1825 to 1828 he was
again concerned with Canadian water routes (B 4, B 10, etc.).

You will examine the mouth of the French river, and that of the River Matchadosh upon Lake Huron likewise Torrento upon Lake Ontario, and give every information how far they will answer for shipping and of what size, whether the Country adjacent is propitious for settlements, and if these by the nature of the ground can at a small Expence be defended. . . .

A 14   GOTHER MANN'S REPORT TO DORCHESTER
[P.R.O., C.O. 42, v. 20]

Quebec, 6th. Decr. 1788.

. . . From French River to Matchadosh Bay is about 44 or 45 leagues, and the description I have already given of the North Coast of the Lake will also nearly answer for this District, as it appears equally barren and rocky. There is a Cluster of Islands which line almost the whole extent of it, in some places not spreading more than half a League from the Main Shore, and in others three Leagues, but no where more: there are however other Islands detached and scattered about in this part of the Lake at various distances.

Matchadosh Bay lyes to the Eastward and Southward of French River, it is of considerable extent being of about 12 Miles deep and of an irregular breadth, from five to seven Miles: at the entrance from the Lake, there are several Islands, the best Channel through them for a Vessel is next to the West Main Shore. Throughout the greatest part of the Bay, there is depth for Vessels of any Draft of Water, but towards the bottom of the Bay it is Shoal, having only 6 feet Water within about a Mile and a half from the Shore. There are several small Rivers or Creeks which fall into the bottom of this Bay, but not any one in particular which bears the name of Matchadosh, adverting however to that[78] which leads to Lake La Clie and by which there is a Communication (sometimes used) to Toronto on Lake Ontario; I therefore examined the entrance of this river particularly, and found that there was a Bar with only Six feet Water, within that there was two Fathom, and at a quarter of a Mile up a Rapid.

The Banks of the River are Rock, and continue so as I am informed the greater part of it's course: it therefore does not seem a proper situation for a Settlement: but if it should ever be thought an object of consequence, in the view of a Communication to Lake Ontario: Storehouses may be built at the entrance & protected on the South Shore. But it is, I apprehend, to be doubted, whether it can ever become a place of much importance even in this respect, if, as I am informed, it is impracticable to pass with large Canoes, on account of the Rapids and difficult carrying Places, and if to this is added the great length of Portage from Toronto to Lake La Clie, and the being obliged to keep Canoes upon that Lake, these seem altogether at the first view, to be very strong

[78]Severn River.

obstacles to any business being carried on this way upon the great scale of Trade . . .

A 15   JOHN GRAVES SIMCOE[79] TO ALURED CLARKE[80]
[*Ontario, Department of Public Records and Archives (P.A.O.), Simcoe Papers, Letter Book 4, p. 58; also printed in* Simcoe Correspondence, *ed. Cruikshank, v. 1, p. 340*]

Navy Hall Niagara
May 31st. 1793.

. . . I have not as yet been able to cross from Toronto to Lake Huron. — This I propose to do in the Autumn. But I have good information that a road is very easy to be made to communicate with those waters which fall into Lake Huron.— The distance by Land is only 24 miles the River which flows into Lake Huron is interrupted by very few portages, which may be surmounted without much expence, or difficulty, the advantages that may in future be derived from this communication are of a most extensive nature, and in the present situation of affairs may possibly become of military importance. . . .

A 16   ALEXANDER MCDONELL'S[81] JOURNAL[82] OF SIMCOE'S
TRIP TO GEORGIAN BAY, 1793
[*P.A.O., Simcoe Papers, v. 35*]

Journal from York on Lake Ontario, to Matchetache Bay on Lake Huron, & from thence back to York, 1793.

Sept. 24th. Left York on Tuesday evening in company with Lieut.

[79]John Graves Simcoe (1752–1806) was appointed Lieutenant Governor of Upper Canada in 1791. In 1796 he was appointed Governor of San Domingo but did not formally resign his command in Canada until 1798. Simcoe was deeply concerned with the defence of Upper Canada in case of war with the United States, and was especially interested in discovering a route to the upper lakes removed from the American frontier.

[80]Major General Alured Clarke (1745?–1832) was Lieutenant Governor of Quebec from 1790 to 1791 and of Lower Canada from 1791 to 1796. In the absence of Lord Dorchester he acted as Administrator from 1791 to 1793, and in 1797 was created a Knight Bachelor.

[81]Alexander McDonell (1762–1842) was born in Scotland, served with Butler's Rangers in the American Revolution, and settled in Canada in 1784. He was Sheriff of the Home District, 1792–1805, and for several years represented Glengarry in the House of Assembly.

[82]This copy of McDonell's journal in the Simcoe Papers varies slightly from the one at the Toronto Public Library which was printed with a few changes in *Transactions of the Canadian Institute,* 1889–90, and in Simcoe's *Correspondence.* The copy from the Simcoe Papers, given here, is on paper watermarked 1809, and is followed by tables, signed by McDonell, comparing shipping costs for freight from Lachine to Michilimackinac by way of Lake Simcoe and by way of the Ottawa River.

Pilkington[83] of the Royal Engineers, Lieut. Darling[84] of the 5th. Regt., Lieut. Givens[85] of the Queens Rangers, Mr. Aitken,[86] Deputy Provincial Surveyor, two Lake la Claie, & two Matchetache Indians, went in a Batteaux to St. John's[87] on the River Humber, & slept there that night—

. . .

Oct. 1st. . . . got to the head of the Lake,[88] entered the River Matchetache[89] & encamped—

2d. Proceeded down the River, & in the course of two hours had to carry our Canoes &c. over two portages— A little below the first carrying place the Black River falls into the Matchetache, & changes the color of that River to a dusky brown from which it does not vary, until it enters the Bay of the same name upon Lake Huron— Below the second Portage the River widens; six or seven miles further on we crossed a small Lake[90] about six miles in circumference, put on shore & dined upon a point where we found various kinds of berries— Mr. Pilkington's Canoe, & mine leaky, were hauled up and gummed here— After dinner got on board, & pushed off, at sun set came to a third carrying place, where after bringing our Canoes &c. on shore we encamped— This place is said to be much infested, during the summer, with Rattle Snakes; it certainly has the appearance of it, being almost a solid rock, with a few scrubby pines & Oak growing on it— John Vinsall[91] a Swede one of the

[83]Robert Pilkington (1765–1834), Lieutenant of the Royal Engineers, came to Canada in 1790. He served on Simcoe's staff from 1793 to 1796, accompanied him on some of his journeys, and made maps and sketches (see Fig. 2 and Plate V). He returned to England in 1803.

[84]Henry Darling (d. 1835) became Lieutenant in the 5th Regiment in 1783, Captain in the 68th Regiment in 1795, and Major General in the Quartermaster General's Department in 1821.

[85]James Givins or Givens (1759?–1846) came to Canada as a young man and was employed for a time in the fur trade. He became a lieutenant in the Queen's Rangers and accompanied Simcoe on some of his journeys. About 1797 he was appointed Agent at York for Indian Affairs. From 1816 to 1830 he was Superintendent, and from 1830 to 1837 Chief Superintendent, of Indian Affairs for Upper Canada.

[86]Alexander Aitkin (d. 1799) was Deputy Surveyor for Mecklenburg and the Midland District of Upper Canada. He was employed on a number of surveys including York harbour, Penetanguishene harbour, and Lake Simcoe. The name is spelled in several ways: Aitkin, Aitken, Aickin, etc.

[87]Jean Baptiste Rousseau (1758–1812) often signed his name Rousseaux, and was frequently referred to as Mr. St. John. He was a fur trader long established at the mouth of the Humber River near York, and frequently acted as Indian interpreter. In 1795 he moved to Ancaster where he built a grist mill and became an officer of the militia.

[88]Lake Simcoe.

[89]Severn River.

[90]Sparrow Lake.

[91]John Vinsall's name was also spelled Vincall and Vencal. Mrs. Simcoe mentioned him in her *Diary*: "Vencal the Swede rowed the Boat very intelligent man born at Unterburgh in Sweden."

Rangers cut one of his toes almost off here— Near this portage is a fine fall, & below that an impetuous rapid[92]—

3d. Had the Canoes &c carried across early in the morning, after breakfast proceeded down the River, went thro' several rapids, & crossed two more carrying places; at 2 o'clock arrived at & had every thing carried over a fifth— The scene at this place is pleasing & romantick— the Portage is a rock, in most places covered with moss & Acorns, & a few small pines & oak growing out of the fissures, the falls such as may easily conceived to be, from an immense body of water, having a great descent & being condensed between two rocks, at not more than 15 feet asunder— After dinner continued our journey, crossed a sixth portage, & shortly after re-embarking it began to rain, & we encamped upon a small Island about two miles below the last mentioned carrying place—

4th. Loaded our Canoes early in the morning, & embarked, the wind being fair hoisted sail & in about 2 or three hours arrived at a seventh & the last portage; having crossed our Canoe &c & again got on board, at 11 o'clock we entered Matchetache Bay— The Indians having been informed (by an express over land from the village on Lake Simcoe) of the Governor's being near at hand, were assembled upon a point a short distance from the last Portage; upon seeing them we steered towards the point, when we got within a few yards of the shore, they complimented His Excellency with a feu de joie which we answered with three cheers, & immediately landed; after the ceremony of shaking hands was over, the Chief presented two dozen of Ducks to the Governor, His Excellency thanked him & told him that he should be happy to see him & his Band in the evening at Mr. Cowan's[93] on the opposite side of the Bay— We then parted & re-imbarking sailed across in little more than an hour; it blew so fresh before we arrived that we were forced to lower our sails— Upon landing, unloaded, & hauled up our Canoes, encamped in the woods a small distance from the Lake, & about half a mile from Mr. Cowan's house, or rather Fort, for it is a regular square enclosed with good pickets; his house is in one, his store opposite to it in another, an out-house for Corn, Potatoes &c in a third, & the gate in the fourth; he does not allow the Indians to get drunk within this Garrison— Soon after encamping the Indians arrived, & his Excellency filled their pipes by ordering each of them some tobacco— At 8 o'clock Mr. Cowan who had been out hunting during the day, being returned, came to pay his respects to the Governor— Mr Cowan is a decent, respectable looking man & much liked by the Indians; he was taken prisoner when a boy by the French at Fort Pitt, during the war, in the year 1759; he has

[92]Ragged Rapids.
[93]George Cowan (d. 1804) was also known as Jean Baptiste Constant or Constance. In 1796 he was appointed official interpreter for the Mississaugas, and in 1804 was drowned on the loss of the government schooner *Speedy*.

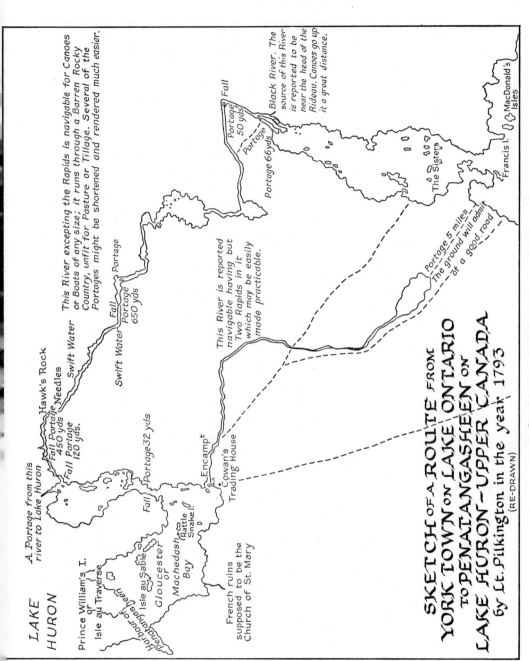

LAKE HURON

A Portage from this river to Lake Huron

This River excepting the Rapids is navigable for Canoes or Boats of any size; it runs through a Barren Rocky Country, unfit for Pasture or Tillage. Several of the Portages might be shortened and rendered much easier.

Hawk's Rock

Swift Water

Needles

Fall Portage 450 yds

Fall Portage 120 yds.

Fall

Portage

Swift Water

Portage 650 yds

Fall

Swift Water

Portage 32 yds

Prince William's I. or Isle au Traverse

Gloucester or Isle au Sable

Harbour of Refuge

Fall

Machedash or Rattle Snake I. Bay

Encamp.t

Cowan's Trading House

This River is reported navigable having but Two Rapids in it which may be easily made practicable.

French ruins supposed to be the Church of St. Mary

Portage

Portage 50 yds

Fall

Portage 66 yds

Black River. The source of this River is reported to be near the head of the Rideau. Canoes go up it a great distance.

The Sisters

Portage 5 miles. The ground will admit of a good road

Francis I.

MacDonald's Isles

SKETCH OF A ROUTE FROM YORK TOWN ON LAKE ONTARIO TO PENATANGASHEEN ON LAKE HURON~UPPER CANADA by Lt. Pilkington in the year 1793

(RE-DRAWN)

FIGURE 2. [Original in Public Archives of Canada.]

adopted all the customs & manners of the Canadians, & speaks French much better than he does English; he has been settled at Matchetache upwards of 15 years, without once going to Lower Canada; he makes an annual trip to Michillimackinac, to meet his supplies, & forward his furs from thence to Montreal; he has in general six Canadian Engagés with him, & is well known to that class of people by the name of Constant—

5th. Mr Cowan having been desired by the Governor to attend this morning to interpret arrived after breakfast & the Indians being met, addressed His Excellency with "they were happy to see their Father in good health, & they were much obliged to him for taking the trouble of visiting his children in their own Country"— The Governor replied that he should always be happy to see them & hear of their prosperity; begged they would attend to their hunts during the winter, & assured them that he wished for nothing more than seeing them & his children the whites live in harmony & friendship together; he promised them a kegg of rum, which should be delivered the day of his departure from the the [*sic*] Bay, & told the Chief that he would send to him from York, a Silver medal & a Flag, the usual badges of distinction, which this Chief had not as yet received; they then shook hands & went off well satisfied—

I must here observe that the Lake Simcoe Indians, were much mortified at the Governor's not taking the Beaver blanket, when offered to him, this they communicated to the Matchetache Indians, by the express which went overland, to which they simply replied, that their Father did right not to take it then, that they should have made his bed, upon his arrival at York, (as they did) & not wait till he came to their village— The Matchetache Indians, had made a bed for their Father at York, by presenting him in a similar manner with a beaver blanket—

Soon after the departure of the Indians, His Excellency, the Gentlemen of his party & Mr. Cowan, embarked in one of that gentlemans large Canoes (worked by five Canadians) intending to visit Pinatanguashine, a place supposed to be a good harbour for vessels; the wind blew so fresh, that we could not effect our purpose, especially as we had a wide traverse to make, we landed upon an Island[94] opposite to it, & from its appearance, & the account Mr. Cowan gave of the depth of water, I believe His Excellency was satisfied with its sufficiency in every point of view, for the reception of Vessels of 80 or 90 Tons— judging from the wood, the land about it seems good— Pinatanguashine lays six miles within Matchetache Bay, & nine miles from Mr. Cowan's — we walked about a mile & a half farther, & had a fine view of Lake Huron, then returned to the canoe & dined, after which we re-embarked, hoisted sail, & arrived at our encampment a little after sun-set—

[94]Beausoleil Island.

6th. Between 9 and 10 o'clock, the Tent being struck, & every thing in readiness, launched our Canoes, & set off on our return home; put in at the point where we had met the Indians on the morning of the 4th. Inst— His Excellency gave them the Kegg of Rum agreeably to his promise— After some little ceremony on their part in returning thanks, & wishing their Father fair weather & a clear sky, we pushed off from shore, upon which they saluted as they did the day we arrived in the Bay, we gave them three cheers, paddled on, & soon arrived at the Portage, carried Canoes &c. across & without stopping pursued our journey; went 5 or 6 miles further on, & landed on an Island— The Indian in the Governors canoe getting sick, Mr. Givens with a white man, & the other two Indians, returned to the point to bring home the sick man, & get another in his place; but before they got down, the Indians on the point had got so drunk that they could not go, even if any of them was willing, Mr. Givens therefore put the sick man on shore, pushed off, & joined us in the evening, & finding it too late to proceed after his return we encamped—

7th. Got every thing on board before sun-rise; in consequence of our losing an Indian the preceeding day, the one that was in my Canoe, was removed to the Governor's, & a Ranger sent into mine in lieu— Paddled up the River, crossed two carrying places, upon the second of which we breakfasted (the same on which we dined on the 3d.) after which His Excellency, & the gentlemen of the party, crossed to the opposite side of the River, to view a fall, which could not be seen from that which we were upon; having satisfied our curiosity, we re-crossed, embarked into our different Canoes, & pushed off, carried over two more portages, upon the second of which we encamped about sun set—

8th. Some of the Canoes being leaky were gummed here, after which we got on board, paddled pretty hard, crossed the two remaining carrying places, & before sun-set got to the head of Lake Simcoe, & encamped on the spot we occupied the night of the 1st Inst— . . .

A 17   CAPTAIN WILLIAM OWEN'S[95] EXPLORATION OF THE
SEVERN IN (1815?)
[Ontario, Department of Lands and Forests, Surveyors' Letters,
Book 18, no. 131]

Report on the communication explored by Captain Owen of the Royal Navy; from Penetengushene in the Home District, to the mouth of the River Trent in the Bay of Quinty, being about 227 miles, following the course of the waters—

[95]Captain William Fitzwilliam Owen (1774–1857) was appointed to survey the Great Lakes in March, 1815, and returned to England in May, 1816.

Captain Owen states by his Sketch[96] the distance from Penetengu-
shene, across Matchadash Bay, to Tent Island to be
about   miles 11
Thence Northerly up the River Severn, to the lower or 7th. Fall
— Portage 30 yards   1¾
Thence to Gloucester Pool   3¼
Thence along the East shore of Gloucester Pool to the 6th fall,
of 6 feet,— Portage 120 yards   4½
Thence to the 5th. fall, of 55 feet, Portage 460 yards   1
Thence to the 4th. fall of 18, or 20 feet, Portage 780 yards   11
Thence to the 3rd fall of 12 or 14 feet, Portage of 400 yards   1½
Thence to Welsh Pool   5
Thence crossing Welsh Pool[97]   4½
Thence to the 2nd. fall of 10 feet— Portage 60 yards   7½
Thence to the 1st, or upper fall of 9 feet. Portage 60 yards   4
Thence to the Narrows on Lake Simcoe   10¾
                                                                        ———
                                                                 Miles 65¾

. . .

9th July, 1822

A 18   Henry Bayfield[98] to Commissioner Robert Barrie[99]
          [*P.R.O., Admiralty 1, v. 3444*]

                                              Naval Establishment
                                              Penetengushene
                                              20th. Octr. 1820.

I have the honor to inform you that I ceased working on the North
coast of Lake Huron on the 10th. of this month, in order to return to
this place according to your directions, but having very bad weather, I
was prevented from obtaining some observations and did not arrive here
till the 15th. in the afternoon.

[96]This map is at P.A.C., 410—Trent—1818.
[97]Welsh Pool is an early name for Sparrow Lake.
[98]Henry Wolsey Bayfield (1795–1885) entered the Royal Navy as a child and
served in Canada in the latter part of the War of 1812. In 1815 he was selected
by Captain Owen as an assistant for the surveys of the Great Lakes. In 1817 he
was appointed Admiralty Surveyor in British North America, and in 1867 became
an admiral. He spent most of his life in a long series of naval surveys in Canada.
[99]Robert Barrie (1774?–1841) was appointed Resident Commissioner on the
Great Lakes in 1819, and served as Commodore from 1827 to 1834. In 1815 he
was made a Companion of the Bath, in 1840 a Knight Commander; on June 10,
1837, he became a rear admiral.

During the 10 Weeks, that I have been absent from Penetengushene I have surveyed 45 Miles to the North Westd (in direct distance) along the North shore of the Lake, excepting Gloster and Machidask Bays with their Islands, which, as being close to this place I have purposely left till the last.

I have no doubt Sir, but that you will think 45 Miles of coast in 10 weeks, very slow progress, but I trust you will think otherwise, when I inform you, that, in that distance we have ascertained the shape, size & situation of upwards of 6,000 Islands, Flats and Rocks: the main Shore too is broken into deep Bays and Coves and together with the Islands is composed of barren Granite Rock.

From the immense number of the Rocks and Reefs, this part of the coast is almost unnavigable for Vessels of any size, but is very favorable to Boat Navigation: large Boats might row for many miles in the Channels within the Islands in any wind or in any weather.

I met with no Streams which would admit a Boat far up them; the few which were large enough for that purpose, were obstructed by rapids or falls.

I was informed by the Indian traders, that these rivulets run out of small Lakes not far inland, where the Indians hunt for Beavers &c: I also learnt that the barren rocky country ceases at about 8 or 9 Miles back, within which they said there was good soil and timber.—

As the Islands become much less numerous and the coast less broken, as we proceed up the Lake, I am in hopes we shall be able to complete its Survey next Summer and the better to enable me to accomplish that much desired object, I intend to take out the Boats for a fortnight in the Indian Summer, to work in the vicinity of Machidash, if Captn. Roberts has no objection and which I hope you will approve of.—

The Survey of this coast and its numerous Islands, has been a work of great difficulty and labour and has put both our perseverance and patience to the test: from Mr. P.E. Collins, Mid I have received the most zealous assistance and my men have behaved in the most exemplary manner: amongst Islands so numerous, where we had to run lines in many different directions, in a day or even in an hour, we could make no use of our Sails and I could seldom or ever spare them the Sunday: their work therefore in this part of the Season has been far more severe than that of any other year, in consequence of which I am induced to submit them to your consideration for allowance of Fatigue Pay[100] for the last 10 weeks of the Season.

On my arrival here I was honored by the receipt of your letter acknowledging receipt of the quarterly abstract of Provisions up to 30th. June last & accompanying this is the abstract up to the 30th. September inclusive.

I delivered Mr. Collins the letter enclosed in mine relating to his time.

[100]Fatigue pay was not allowed (P.R.O., Admiralty 1, v. 3444).

A 19   LIEUTENANT PORTLOCK'S[101] "REMARKS[102] ON THE RIVER SEVERN," 1819

[P.A.C., R.G. 11, Report on Water Communication, pp. 37–43]

A   It is unnecessary to Speak of this point[103] it having been personally observed by His Excellency.[104] The Strait is shallow (In many Places only 7½ feet in depth) and much contracted by rushes— As the Lake again expands the land appears to be good on both shores, that on the west, rising considerably towards the interior—

B   Yellow head's Island,[105] small rather low and nearly cleared, the Indians partially cultivate it and obtain Indian Corn, Pumpkins &c.

C   At this point there are some fine Strata of Stone admirably adapted for Building—

D   A small rocky Island on which are two Childrens graves. The land to the west does not appear so high, but is still good— The E. Shore is low and covered with Cedars and young Poplars.

E   The River[106] here commences and is about 40 yards wide. The Banks are generally Rocks low and partially covered

F   with young timber— An Island divides the River into two streams which are precipitated down their respective Falls[107] — The Northern is contracted to about 30 feet and rushes with great force through this narrow Channel, having a descent in 100 feet of six. A Canal, the necessary remedy for this obstacle, would be attended with great expense: it might indeed be short not exceeding 50 yards, but the Rock a low, hard, mass of Granite must tend to render labour highly difficult. In Preference I should recommend damming up the Northern Channel and after the removal of Loose Stones turning it into a Canal which indeed nature has almost formed it. The small width of the Channel would greatly aid this Plan and render it much less expensive than any other. From the Bay to the west two other Channels proceed as marked

[101]Joseph Ellison Portlock (1794–1864), geologist and naturalist, was the son of the explorer, Captain Nathaniel Portlock. At the time of this expedition down the Severn he was a first lieutenant of the Royal Engineers. Later he was employed for several years on the ordnance survey of Ireland and in 1849 was appointed Commander of the Royal Engineers, Cork District.

[102]The map to accompany this report has not been located, but most of the places can be identified from the description.

[103]The Narrows between Lakes Simcoe and Couchiching.

[104]Sir Peregrine Maitland (1777–1854), Lieutenant Governor of Upper Canada, 1818–28.

[105]Now Chiefs Island.

[106]Severn River.

[107]The first fall on the Severn.

on the sketch (the dotted lines signifying that they were not personally observed) They are equally obstructed by Falls. On my return I carried my canoe etc over an Indian Path thereby avoiding two Falls and meeting the Western Channel This Walk gave me an opportunity of observing the Soil, which on the northern half is exceedingly rich and abounds with fine Timber, but on approaching the River the Masses of granite again expose their barren surface, pointing out that the foundation is of that nature and merely covered in Particular and low spots with alluvial deposits.

G   The Black River enters here; it is about 40 yards wide and appears a fine stream— The water being exceedingly dark renders its name highly appropriate—

H   In several Places the River is exceedingly deep and here I found the depth more than Six Fathoms— A huge Mass of rock forms at this Spot the E. Bank, the left (an Island) is low—

I   A small island divides the River and Occasions two Falls[108] — The descent is seven feet nearly perpendicular, and much obstructed by broken Rocks— The Portage (50 yards in length) is covered with Soil and bordered by fine Timber, but the summits of several Masses of Granite projecting from the ground, point out again the difficulty of Cutting a Canal and induce me to recommend the same method here as at at [sic] the last fall, viz turning one of the Falls into a Canal—

J   Road to the western Channel already commented on— The Banks have hitherto been low with occasional projections of Rocky [sic] and chiefly covered with Pines —

Between
J and K   The Banks are low and bear strong marks of Periodical Inundation— The Soil is rich and covered with Oak, Elm, and Maple— The Small Creeks marked on the sketch are scarcely deserving of notice and indeed are frequently imperceptible—

K   At this spot the Scenery totally changes as the River expands into a beautiful Lake.[109] The Banks acquire a grander Character— Masses of Rock covered with pines now bound the scene and rocky Island [sic] burst from the tranquil bosom of the Lake— On the Right the thick growth of Timber warrants a favourable opinion of the soil— A River[110] enters this Lake, it is stated by the Indians to be a considerable stream I think from its situation it may prove a Channel of Communication with Lake Nipissang—

[108]The second fall.
[109]Sparrow Lake.
[110]The Kahshe River flows from Kahshe Lake and forms no connection with Lake Nipissing.

L   A strong rapid. The water is shallow and rolls over a Mass of Rocks having at the Summit a chûte of ft1/6. A towing Path might be found on the south Bank— On the north the Eddy aids greatly the ascent and it would be easy to cut through the rocks— On the south a canal might be formed with fallen stones or on either Bank— Machinery might be erected for putting up Boats— I descended this rapid in the canoe and ascended by putting [sic] after landing the greater

M   part of my baggage— A Fall[111] in two seperate discents of about 12 feet— The Upper one is in the form of a Semicircle and boils up in the centre over a Rock to the height of the fall— The Granite Banks 30 feet high, defy improvement— A Portage (in consequence of uneven Surface) 450 yards long joins two small Bays— near it is a ravine marked on the Sketch) which on examination I found much choaked with masses of broken Rock and now overgrown with young trees— From the appearance of this River I doubt not that the River formerly passed through it and now recommended it as the proper situation either for a Canal or Portage— which might be here easily formed—

N   In the distance of 500 yards there is a discent of 30 feet nearly— This fall[112] is divided into several Chûtes, connected by rapids, the channel is narrow, from 60 to 90 feet, and the immense Banks of granite preclude the formation of a canal except at an enormous expense. There is a method of forming a Canal immediately over the stream and this would be facilitated by the small width of the stream but being novel, I should to reflect [sic] before giving a decided opinion as to its practicability. The Portage is 1000 yards over Rocks and excessively steep at the extremities— The difficulty of giving temporary vent to the Water prevent [sic] the adoption of the Plan before recommended for the other falls—

O   A strong rapid —The eastern Channel is the deepest, and as only a small Portion is bad it might be remedied by a towing Path—

P   Two strong rapids close to each other— only the summits are difficult of ascent— Towing Paths might be constructed or the upper Rapid which is the worst might be avoided by making a Canal to the north of the little Island, following the Plan before recommended—

Q   At this Point the Bank is an immense perpendicular Rock at the foot of which is a depth of 46 feet of water—

R   One of the most picturesque spots[113] in nature. The river

111The third fall.
112The fourth fall.
113The fifth fall.

descends in 220 yards nearly 50 feet. At the summit the channel is contracted to 12 feet and the Water falls 9 feet a rapid succeeds and two inferior chûtes of each 4½ feet— The Water forming from the former falls then gushes through a narrow pass 40 feet in width broken by rock and declivities until at the end of 35 feet, it falls nearly 10 feet. To the north of the Island forming one boundary of this grand chûte is a perpendicular Fall of 18 feet. The river endeavouring to burst from restraint covered with foam and hurled with violence from one rock to another and the Pines throwing an air of Solemnity over the whole, form a scene too beautiful for description—

A Canal at this place would be attended with the usual difficulties, I fear here insurmountable— The Portage is 490 yards in length over Rocks fifty feet high, and excessively steep at both Ends—

S   A branch[114] of the River tending to Penetanguishine but possessing equal obstacles with the main branch.

T   A fall[115] of 7 feet in 60 yards. I think either a canal might be cut through the Rocks here low, or from a large mass dividing the fall the Principle of Damming made use of as before recommended—

U   Branch[116] of the River having two Falls near Lake Huron. The Lake[117] now passed is beautiful in point of Scenery but the Banks (as they have been generally) are either covered with stunted Pines and dwarf Oaks or exhibit a naked surface of stone—

W   The last fall[118] in the River— The Descent is about 4½ feet and by following the Plan so often recommended the north Fall which rushes through an opening of not ten feet might with ease rendered [sic] the Scite of a canal

After leaving this Fall the Banks lose The grand character they have hitherto had, and become low and covered with hard Wood—

X   At this Island I terminated my progress into the Lake— Penetanguishine bears nearly West, the land from the River Wye, gradually veering to the North—

The Northern Channel between X and the main Land being much confined I sounded across to the entrance of a deep Bay and found sufficient water as expressed in the sketch. The mouth of the River is shallow having not more than 8 feet of water—

[114]Probably the route through Sixmile Lake.
[115]The sixth fall.
[116]The route through Baxter Lake and South Bay to Honey Harbour.
[117]Gloucester Pool.   [118]The seventh fall.

Y   This Bay is deep but shallow— The Land to the South gradually rises and appears good— A Road[119] to Lake Simcoe runs from the bottom of the Bay and must be very short, respecting the River Wye I could gain no other information than before received tending to destroy all hopes of its utility. There is another River near it stated by the Indians as a large Stream, this is to be seen on the maps—

I have now concluded my remarks on a river which displays Scenery of the most picturesque description and is indeed a noble stream, yet offers the greatest obstacles to improvement— Most of these are surmountable as I have pointed out and when they are overcome I do not consider the remainder as beyond the reach of science.

The depth of water is generally sufficient for every purpose and sometimes exceedingly great— The usual breadth from 80 to 100 yards— The barren Rocks of a great part of the River render the formation of settlements impossible and the other part tho' rich bears such marks of inundation as render it equally unfit— Wherever a Ravine occurs the soil is admirable but this is a rare occurrence in the rocky part of the River.

In point of expense, I think £20.000 would remove all but the two great Falls and that this sum might be reduced one fifth by adopting the Plan I have recommended—

I regret that want of Provisions and the intractable indolence of the Indians deprived me of the Power of visiting the other Branches of this noble River I hope however to have some future opportunity of so doing—

A 20   DR. J. J. BIGSBY'S[120] DESCRIPTION OF GEORGIAN BAY, 1823
[*Bigsby*, The Shoe and Canoe, *v. 2, pp. 90–2, 94–5*]

. . . We now crossed to a naked islet on the direct way to the North Main, holding Gloucester Bay on the east.

Gloucester Bay is large, and very irregular in its outline. Its lower end takes the name of Matchedash, and receives the river Severn of Lake Simcoe.

From this point (the barren gneis islet), a sudden change of scenery took place. The deep water, regular outlines, and fertility of the main (based on limestone before) ceased. The intricate region of islets, of reefs, and marshes, began.

[119]The Indian road shown in Fig. 2.
[120]John Jeremiah Bigsby (1792–1881), medical doctor and geologist, came to Canada in 1818. In 1822 he became British secretary and medical officer of the Canadian Boundary Commission and in 1823 accompanied a surveying party of that commission from Kingston to Lake of the Woods.

The view from hence, our dining place (where my compass would not traverse) is very fine. The capacious mouth of Gloucester Bay, partly barred by islands, is on the east, bounded by high woods and headlands. Looking south, past the lofty Giant's Tomb, partly hiding the Christian Isles, we see the successive capes we had just skirted. Northerly, we beheld the thousand rocks of the north shore, backed by ranges of pine forests.

We now made directly north, and encamped for the night on the slippery top of a mound of granite, twenty feet high, some little distance from Rennie's[121] Bay (so named by Captain Bayfield).

Whether we were really on the main or not, I cannot tell. We were among a labyrinth of dough-shaped mounds, rushy marshes, and thin groves of stunted cedar, birch, alder, and red oak. We could not see 500 yards into the interior.

Our tent was only secured by laying poles loaded with stones along the bottom of the canvas.

The evening had been lowering, but afterwards became partially clear and starry. I left the tent at about eleven o'clock, and was much struck by the picture before and around me.

Our men were asleep at the fire— all, save the cook on duty, who was feeding it with wood, and stirring the soup. The cool wind was shaking the birch trees, and the waves were whispering and rippling among the reefs below. Looking towards the head of Gloucester Bay I saw several solitary red lights wandering over the surface of the lake, which lay here and there in shadow. These were the canoe-torches of Indians spearing the fish attracted by the flame. When they chanced to draw near, the flare of the light, and the frequent streams of cinders dropping into the water red-hot, were reflected beautifully on the dark men and their craft. . . .

The next morning early we started for the old trading post of Bourassa. The whole intervening north shore, thirty miles long, is as much cut up, and as full of fiords and inlets, as the coast of Norway. These are sometimes several miles deep, and receive rivers, such as the Muskoka, Moon, and Seguine. It is faced, too, with a multitudinous belt several miles broad, of rocky or tolerably-wooded islands, invested by marshes, rushy basins, and lagoons, so numerous and intricate as to baffle the most experienced guide. Captain Bayfield counted in this part of the lake 7000 islets and islands within forty-five square miles. It was small blame to us, therefore, that we were lost in the deep bay, which is honoured by the name of Franklin, east of Parry's Sound, choked with reedy islets and half-drowned cranberry grounds.

. . .

[121]Lieutenant Rennie was one of Bayfield's assistants on the survey of the lakes.

B. EXPLORATION OF THE WATERWAYS
OF THE INTERIOR, 1819–37

B 1 LIEUTENANT J. P. CATTY'S[1] REPORT TO HIS EXCELLENCY
SIR PEREGRINE MAITLAND ON A WATER ROUTE BETWEEN
LAKE SIMCOE AND THE OTTAWA

[P.A.C., R.G. 5, A 1, v. 45; another copy in R.G. 11, A 1, v. 9, pp. 25–30; also printed in Guillet, The Valley of the Trent, *pp. 142–5]*

Montreal, 1st October 1819

I have the honor to report to your Excellency that in pursuance of your instructions I proceeded to examine the course of the waters laying between Lake Simcoe and the Otawa.

I left the Lake by a river which I have every reason to suppose the Talbot river, but which I cannot determine without seeing Captain Owen's Survey of it. We had not ascended it more than two miles before we found our course impeded by the stream being completely choaked by trees fallen across it. We here commenced the first carrying place of about twelve miles through a flat country very finely timbered and the land to all appearance of the first quality   We now and then came upon the river and found the channel narrower & shallow, not more than two feet water in deepest parts. The river however rises two feet at least, in the spring which would make this part navigable for Batteaux were it cleared of the timber. At the end of this Portage the River widens into a fine deep stream with about twelve feet water on an average which continues for about five miles when the river again becomes shallow and unavigable even for canoes wherever there is deep water it so narrow that there appears scarce room for a batteau to pass— The bed of the river about ten miles miles [*sic*] higher up is entirely dry and the Water passes under ground for about half a mile, and there seems but little appearance of any channel for boats, even when the water is highest— From this place to the first carrying place to the Lakes the river is navigable though very much choaked by fallen trees. The Land on each side is low but of good quality— The course of the river about S S W. the carrying place to the first lake is about four miles in length over very fine Land but hilly— This neck or ridge of land appears to form the division between the head of the waters which fall into Lake Simcoe and those which take their course toward Lake Ontario in the direction of Kingston. The first lake[2] is about seven or eight miles in length, the banks rocky and producing little else but

[1]James Patrick Catty became First Lieutenant in the Royal Engineers, July 21, 1813, and came to Canada in 1814. He served in Lower Canada until 1818, and at York from 1818 to 1820. He was promoted to Second Captain on January 15, 1826, but does not appear in the army lists after 1834.   [2]Balsam Lake.

Pine timber. On the Eastern side it discharges itself by a small river into another Lake[3] which I understand communicates with some river falling into Lake Ontario near the Bay of Quinte. We left it by the North East end and ascended a fine broad and deep stream[4] for about seven miles into a chain of small narrow lakes which communicate with each other by separate streams—

From the second to the third Lake the Navigation is interrupted by four separate falls of about twelve feet each, and after passing the third Lake, we were generally obliged to carry from one to the other as the streams which joined them were so filled with trees as to prevent our taking up the canoes— The Lakes[5] are ten in number the two last very shallow and the land in the neighbourhood of the last connecting stream nearly all low land & swamp. The whole distance from the first to the last lake is about ninety miles. The Land has uniformly the same appearance on the banks of these lakes viz—high rocky and barren but I observed whenever we left the immediate vicinity of the Lake and advanced into the interior the land appeared to improve— At the South East end of the last Lake is a river[6] which runs in the direction of and discharges itself near Kingston. We here commenced a portage of about four miles over very high but fine land. This ridge divides the waters falling into Lake Ontario from those falling into the Otawa. Our course had hitherto been from N.N.E. to N.E. The Lake to which we carried the canoes is about five miles in length and in appearance shallower than any of the others— We left it by a fine broad and deep stream running in an Easterly direction through a flat and low country rather marshy. We went down the river about sixteen miles without interruption to a large swampy lake very shallow which is the commencement of a chain of Lakes about ten miles in length the remainder are however deep and have much the same appearance as those already passed. At the East end of the Lakes, is a fall of about thirty feet with rapids for about half a mile below. These lead to a fine river with low sandy banks and on an average about six feet water. The stream is here and there blocked up by trees but we proceeded about thirty three miles with little interruption, we here came to some strong rapids about half a mile in length, which were succeeded by about eight miles of smooth water— The river here makes a circuit of seven or eight miles and becomes very rapid with three separate falls. The carrying place across is not more than one mile and over very fine land. We then proceeded about forty miles with little interruption down to the river's junction with the Madawasca which takes place in a large plain bounded on every side by high land—

[3]Cameron Lake. Catty refers here to the Trent waterway system.

[4]Gull River.

[5]The ten unnamed lakes are impossible to identify with certainty. For a discussion of possible routes see *supra*, pp. xlv–xlvi.

[6]This river, which would have formed an important link in the water communications of Upper Canada, was a main object of inquiry in the explorations carried on by the Royal Engineers in 1826 and 1827.

The Madawasca comes into this plain from the South. About six miles below the rapids commence which occasioned us to make small carrying places for about one mile when the river is again navigable for six or seven miles We then arrived at a succession of rapids for about sixty miles over ledges of rock—The river here enters a very fine Lake[7] with high banks and finely timbered with beech, elm, and maple—The Lake itself is about seven or eight miles in extent. Immediately upon leaving the Lake the river assumes its former appearance and becomes a continued strong rapid with falls of four or five feet here and there, for about forty five miles when it falls into the Otawa about eight miles above the rapids and falls of the Chat.—

From this sketch of our cursory passage through the country Your Excellency will perceive that the only part which offers any encouragement to the hope of establishing a batteau communication is the first chain of Lakes and the river which falls into the Madawasca, and even this presents many obstacles, as the communications from Lake to Lake are generally very bad and would require great labour to render them passable for light boats. Should these difficulties be overcome, some other communication than by the Madawasca must be found as its whole course is almost an uninterrupted rapid, when the water is low, scarce affording enough to float canoes in safety over the Rocks, when high, rising to such a degree and flowing with such rapidity as to preclude the possibility of taking up batteaux and much more of bringing them down.

The Talbot river may be navigable in the spring, when the waters are high but is so shallow in the fall as scarcely to afford water enough for a canal. The Land I have reason to believe is good in every part except in the immediate Vicinity of the Lakes and rivers— These Sir are the Principal observations I have been able to make during my Journey through the country which has been much more tedious and less satisfactory than might have been expected from the first accounts I received

B 2   "COPY OF MEMORANDUM ADDRESSED BY THE COMMISSION OF WHICH MAJOR-GENERAL SIR JAMES SMYTH[8] IS PRESIDENT, TO COLONEL [ELIAS] DURNFORD,[9] COMMANDING ROYAL ENGINEER IN THE CANADAS"
[Smyth, Copy of a Report to His Grace the Duke of Wellington, app. C, pp. 6–7]

Quebec, July 27th. 1825

. . . His Grace the Master General[10] attaching much value to the practicability of a communication between the Ottawa and Lake Simcoe,

[7]Calabogie Lake.
[8]Sir James Carmichael Smyth, Baronet (1779–1838), military engineer, was promoted Major General in 1825. He worked closely with the Duke of Wellington and in 1825 was sent to inspect fortifications in Canada. His report in 1826

it will be necessary that the journey performed by Lieut. Catty in 1819.—should again be undertaken, and the Officer employed upon it instructed not to hurry himself but to give himself sufficient time to make every observation which may hereafter be of use to the service.— It will be also necessary to ascertain the rise and source of the Black River, which has its Mouth in the narrows of the Lake Simcoe.—

If you could employ two officers on this duty the Service would be better done, as they could penetrate up each River, the Talbot and the Black River simultaneously— Some intelligent Canadian Boatmen reported to us that the Black River falls into those Lakes forming the communication between Lake Simcoe and the Ottawa, as explored by Lieut. Catty, and which from the Lay of the Country we are disposed to think is probably the case. It will be necessary, however, that the Course of this River, as already explained, should be verified and reported upon.

B 3   EXTRACTS FROM SMYTH'S REPORT ON WATER COMMUNICATION
[*Smyth,* Copy of a Report to His Grace the Duke of Wellington, *pp. 2, 77–8, 80, 82–3*]

Halifax 9th September 1825.

. . . The Coasts of Lake Huron (with the exception of some Country about Penetangushene Harbour) . . . being as far as the British are concerned, as yet, in a state of Nature and covered with impenetrable Forests: . . .

Two modes of communicating from Penetangushene to Lake Simcoe have been suggested. The first by cutting a canal from the head of Kemperfeldt Bay into the Nottaswaga Creek. . . .

The other mode that offers itself is by the Severn or Matchadash river.

Upon the same data as those we had the honor to submit to your Grace as the foundation of our Estimate for the water communication between the Bay of Quinte and Lake Simcoe, it would require £30,024 to make the Severn, or Matchadash, Navigable. Altho' the River flows only a distance of about 60 miles, yet it falls 120 feet.

The difference of level is divided into seven different falls, one of which is 55 feet, and another of 20 feet. . . .

That part of the Coast of Lake Huron which belongs to His Majesty, from Penetangushene to the falls of St. Mary communicating with Lake Superior, is a bleak, barren, and inhospitable coast, entirely uninhabited. . . .

In our Instructions your Grace alluded to a Water communication

was but one of his many military writings. He was Governor and Commander in Chief of the Bahamas, 1829–1833 and Governor of British Guiana from 1833 until his death.

[9]Elias Walker Durnford became Lieutenant Colonel of the Royal Engineers, July 21, 1813, and Colonel on March 23, 1825.

[10]The Duke of Wellington, Master General of His Majesty's Ordnance.

between Lake Simcoe and the Ottawa. In 1819, an officer of Engineers, Lieut. Catty, explored this route. From his Report, which we have read, the distance appears to be about 400 miles, 150 only of which can be accounted navigable. The Black River, which is also mentioned by Your Grace, flows into the narrows above Lake Simcoe. It is understood to issue from one of the Lakes upon the communication before mentioned. We have, however, requested Col. Durnford to cause this matter to be verified, as also to have the route, which was merely penetrated by Lieut. Catty to ascertain its practicability, examined with more attention. . . .

B 4   SMYTH TO GENERAL GOTHER MANN
[*P.R.O., W.O. 55/862*]

Nutwood. Ryegate. 16th. November 1825.

In the memorandum I left with Colonel Durnford, a copy of which is attached to the Report, you would perceive that in furtherance of the views of His Grace the Master General & in compliance with my Instructions I requested of that officer to take the necessary steps to have the Talbot & the Black Rivers surveyed; as also to have the practicability of communicating from Lake Simcoe to Lake Huron by the South River ascertained; which River terminates in Gloster Bay & is supposed to have its source in a mud Lake or Swamp not far from Lake Simcoe—

I have now the honor to lay before you the enclosed copy of a letter from Capt. Melhuish[11] to Colonel Durnford forwarded to me by the latter; by which you will perceive that after proper & due enquiry it has been determined to give up the attempt to explore the course of the Talbot & the Black Rivers until next May, for the reasons therein assigned and which I take the liberty to add appear satisfactory— The Survey of the South River was however immediately to be commenced upon by Lieut. Walpole[12]—

Colonel Durnford is anxious that I should lay before you the circumstances of the very heavy extra expences which must necessarily be incurred by the officers while employed in these remote situations in procuring provisions for themselves & their Servants; as well as the other various contingent charges to which they must be liable— He has suggested that a Guinea per day should be allowed to each of them whilst

[11]Samuel Camplin Melhuish became Second Captain in the Royal Engineers, September 28, 1824, and First Captain on February 24, 1829. The letter referred to is found in P.R.O., W.O. 55/862.

[12]John Walpole (1798?–1864) had a long career in the Royal Engineers. His promotions were: Second Lieutenant 1816, First Lieutenant 1825, Second Captain 1839, Captain 1846, Major 1848, Lieutenant Colonel 1854, Colonel 1854, Major General 1863. In June, 1848, he was made Major of Brigade of the Royal Sappers and Miners. He was the son of the Honorable Robert Walpole who was nephew of Robert Walpole, the Prime Minister. His obituary appeared in the *Gentleman's Magazine*, February, 1864, p. 267.

employed upon these surveys to cover their extra expences— Before I took the liberty of addressing you upon the subject I thought it my duty to look at His Majestys Warrant relative to the extra Pay & allowances for the Corps of Engineers in order that I might not lay before you inadvertently what might subsequently appear to be an improper application. Upon referring to the warrant I observe it is directed that upon Surveys where the duties are extremely laborious & the unavoidable expences very great, that in all such cases an allowance of Extra Pay & travelling charges shall be proportionate to such Expences— under these circumstances the officers appear to be justly entitled to a fair remuneration; & I humbly conceive the allowance of a Guinea per diem will not more than cover their unavoidable expences—

There will be of course further expence in the hire of canoes, Indians & Canadian guides. These charges will in the first instance be defrayed by the Commissariat out of the extra-ordinaries of the Army upon the authority of the Commander of the Forces— It will be no great sum, but probably the ordnance will be called upon to repay it.

B 5   LIEUTENANT HENRY BRISCOE[13] TO COLONEL ELIAS DURNFORD
[*P.A.C., C 426, pp. 140–2*]

York U.C. 14th. May 1826

With reference to the General Orders of the 18th. & 20th. February last, I have the honor to report to you, that I left Kingston on the 21st. ultimo to commence the Survey of the Talbot & Black Rivers assisted by the officers detailed in the General Orders.

On my arrival at this place I was informed by the Commissary (Mr. Billings[14]) that by proceeding to New Market & Holland Landing I should be furnished with every assistance & information by a resident of the former place:— I was there informed to my great disappointment that the canoes were not ready, neither had the Indian guides arrived— I was however informed that every thing would be prepared on the 2d. May— I therefore returned to York & having procured the necessary provisions &c. I proceeded to the landing (accompanied by the party). I then found that three of the voyageurs had been sent to Penetanguishine for two canoes & were not returned. I was advised to proceed to the head of Lake Simcoe, in expectation of meeting the three voyageurs with the canoes & with the assurance of finding the Guides. I accordingly went thither & remained at the mouth of the Matchedash several days during which time the canoes were brought in, but not

[13]Henry Briscoe (d. 1838) was commissioned Second Lieutenant of the Royal Engineers, July 21, 1813, First Lieutenant on December 15, 1813, Second Captain on June 24, 1831. He served in Canada in the War of 1812, and later was in charge of a section of the Rideau Canal. He returned to England in 1832, served in Ireland for a time, and died in Demerara in 1838. He married while in Canada and had three sons and four daughters.

[14]Francis Thomas Billings, Deputy Assistant Commissary General at Quebec and then at York.

being able to procure the Guides I determined to return to the Landing, leaving two trusty Canadians at the Narrows with orders to remain there 4 days in expectation of the Indians coming in from the hunting grounds. At the expiration of the time allowed the Canadians returned without success, & finding that no further hopes could be entertained of procuring guides, I thought it most adviseable to bring back the party to this place to return to their posts.

During the time we were detained at the head of the Lake, I took the opportunity of examining the mouth of the Black River which empties itself into the Matchedash about a mile & half from its mouth between the 1st. & 2d. fall. I found it a very rapid stream, I was informed by a very intelligent Indian trader that he had the greatest difficulty in ascending 30 miles up the river in a light canoe with an Indian, which occupied two days being obliged to make eight portages & that he returned with ease in half a day.

Before I conclude I must beg leave in justice to my own arrangements to state, that upon the promulgation of the General Orders of 18th. & 20th. Feb. I wrote to the Commissary at this post informing him that I should positively arrive here on the opening of the navigation & requesting him to have every thing provided by that time, & was assured by him in reply, that there would be no difficulty in procuring adequate means.

In conclusion I beg further to offer my opinion derived from the best information, I have been enabled to obtain, that the fall of the year would be the most proper season for these surveys.

1st. Because in consequence of the waters at that time being low a more accurate estimate could be formed of the expense of rendering any communication navigable, than in the spring.

2d. The passage of canoes would then be much safer than at present when the rivers are full, & consequently extremely rapid, & numerous snags & fallen trees concealed below the surface of the water, which could only be avoided in the fall of the year when they are perceptible.

3d To avoid the musquitoes, which are so insufferable that the Indians leave the woods & establish them selves on islands in Lake Simcoe during the Summer season, & it is doubted whether they could be induced to act as guides at this time.

B 6   CAPTAIN SAMUEL ROMILLY[15] "TO THE OFFICERS APPOINTED
FOR PARTICULAR SURVEYS"
[P.R.O., W.O. 55/863]

Royal Engineer Office
Kingston 10th. Aug. 1826

The officers appointed for particular Surveys by the General Orders of the 18th. & 20 Feby. & 8th. August 1826, will hold themselves in

[15]Samuel Romilly was promoted Captain in the Royal Engineers July 21, 1813. In 1826 he was Commanding Royal Engineer in Upper Canada.

readiness to leave Kingston on the 23d proximo. Whilst acting together the Senior Officer Lieut. Briscoe will assume the command and direction of the whole party.

Lieut. Marlow[16] with Lieut. Smith[17] Rl. Ay. will follow the course of the Black river which has its mouth in the Narrows of Lake Simcoe, ascertain its head & carefully examine the country between its Source & the Talbot, as there is every reason to believe it heads very near that River or the Rice Lakes from which it flows, the length of the portages & the most feasible methods of opening a communication with the Talbot to be minutely stated. This party will then return by the earliest route to Kingston.

B 7   LIEUTENANTS W. B. MARLOW AND WILLIAM SMITH TO COLONEL J. R. WRIGHT,[18] COMMANDING ROYAL ENGINEER IN UPPER CANADA, ON SURVEY OF BLACK RIVER
[P.A.C., C 428, pp. 64–76; another copy in P.R.O., W.O. 55/863]

Kingston September 22d 1826

Agreeably to the General Orders of the 18th. and 20th. February and 8th. August 1826, as also the Orders we received from Captain Romilly, Commanding Royal Engineer in Upper Canada (an extract of which we herewith enclose) we proceeded to the mouth of the Black River,[19] which we found did not empty itself into the Narrows of Lake Simcoe as was supposed, but into the Matchadash or Severn River about a mile and a half from its head on the right bank.

The Severn River discharges the Waters of Lake Simcoe and the Black River into Lake Huron.

The right Bank of the Black River is rocky and between forty and fifty feet in height chiefly covered with Pine Timber; The left swampy, the Trees Elm and Ash. The breadth of the River is Sixty Yards, & the depth of Water nine feet with a current running at the rate of one mile per hour— Proceeding a mile up the River we came to a small rapid extending in length one hundred Yards; here the breadth was contracted to thirty feet; half a mile from this both Banks became rocky and from forty to fifty feet high.

At four miles and a half from the Mouth of the River is a fall of three feet, to avoid which we made a Portage of three hundred Yards over level ground, and came again to the River, the banks of which were fourteen feet in height, steep and rocky; having passed up a small shoot

[16]William Biddlecomb Marlow (1795?–1864) was made First Lieutenant in the Royal Engineers, March 23, 1825, Captain in 1837, Major in 1846, Colonel in 1854, and Major General in 1862. After leaving Canada he served as a Commanding Royal Engineer in New Zealand in 1845 and 1846.

[17]William Mein Smith became Second Lieutenant in the Royal Artillery in 1822, First Lieutenant on November 6, 1827, Captain in 1839, and went on half pay in 1842.

[18]John Ross Wright became Lieutenant Colonel of the Royal Engineers, March 23, 1825.   [19]The route taken in this survey is discussed in *supra*, xlvi–xlvii.

of Water and proceeded a mile further, we came to a Rapid, 200 yards in length; after which the River resumes its former depth, vizt from 13 to 14 feet having rocks and Islets interspersed in various directions—

At seven miles and a half from the mouth of the River we found our progress obstructed for 200 yards by fallen Timber to avoid which we made a Portage, and proceeding 2 miles we passed our Canoe up a small shoot of Water where the River was contracted to fifteen feet in breadth; after which it expanded to 60 feet, continuing for the space of 5 miles with a good deep channel— At fourteen miles from the mouth of the River it is 18 feet broad and four deep— Proceeding a quarter of a mile, we made a Portage to avoid a shallow Rapid of 250 Yards; 2 miles and ¼ from this we made another Portage of 200 Yards, the River falling over large Rocks of Granite for a distance of 300 Yards, the difference of level from the Head to the foot of the fall, being 90[20] feet—

Nineteen miles from the mouth of the River we came to another fall of 20 feet in height and made a Portage—

Twenty-two miles from the mouth of the River the depth of the water decreases to 2 feet and continues at this depth for 50 feet farther, it then resumes its usual character vizt from 12 to 14 feet in depth, the speed of the Current being one mile per hour. Five miles beyond this, the depth of the water is 4 feet, the Bed of the River being filled up with rotten Vegetation and sand, this continues for 50 feet when it again becomes 12 feet in depth

At 29 miles and a half from the mouth, of [sic] the River dashes thro' a narrow Channel, extending in length about 200 Yards, between two precipices of granite rock about 120 feet in height, the difference of level from the Head to the foot of the Fall is about 30 feet— At about one mile from this we came to a fall 30 feet in extent, the difference of level from the foot to the Head of which is 8 feet; in the channel of the Fall the Rocky Banks of the River are contracted to 8 feet in breadth; three quarters of a mile farther there is another fall and rapid the Channel of the River being very much contracted and full of Rocks, and in one place entirely lost under a huge mass of granite, the whole extent of the Rapid and fall being 200 Yards and the difference of level from the head to the foot of the Fall at least 40 feet—

After making this Portage which was on the left Bank we again came to smooth Water, the breadth of the River increasing to 50 feet, and 13 feet in depth; immediately below the Fall we observed the highest Water Mark to be 20 feet above the present level—

At 300 yards from last fall we came to a Rapid and made a Portage of 50 yards in length on the left Bank of the River, the difference of level from the head to the foot of the Rapid is 8 feet.

At 32 miles and ¼ from the mouth of the River we passed up a Rapid extending for 50 yards (difference of level 3 feet) the River is here shallow and interspersed with Rocks for the space of a mile when

[20]P.R.O. copy reads "20 feet" which agrees with Marlow's map (Fig. 3).

it becomes choked up with fallen Timber, making a Portage to avoid this of 100 yards, the depth of the River we found to be 15 feet and 60 feet wide—

At 37¾ miles from the mouth of the River there is a Rapid of 150 yards in length over loose Rocks falling from a height of 12 feet (We here made a Portage) after passing this Rapid the river resumed its usual depth and appearance.

Two miles farther on we were again interrupted in our progress by fallen Timber and made a Portage over a bed of Stones extending for 300 yards through which part of the River flowed. We now came to a small Lake about 400 Yards in length and the same in breadth; Crossing the Lake we came to a fall of Water over Rocks of Granite full 50 feet in height, the length of the Fall is 200 Yards; We made a Portage on the left bank. 700 Yards from this we passed a small Rapid, the difference of level from the head to the foot of which, was 4 feet and made a Portage on the right Bank. Forty one miles from the Mouth of the River the breadth increases to 100 yards and the depth is 15 feet with rocky banks, it continues in this manner for nearly 2 miles when it contracts to 20 yards in breadth and filters through a bed of loose Rocks for the space of 20 Yards; making a Portage over the Rocks we came into a Lake a mile in length and 1200 in breadth, with 3 small Islands in the centre   our course through this Lake lay E By N average depth 29 feet, the banks being high and rocky composed of granite, in floods the water rises three feet—On arriving on the opposite side of the Lake we again came to the River the average breadth of which is 60 feet—

At 43 miles and ¾ from the mouth of the River we arrived at a small Rapid the River running over loose rocks, this being too shallow for the Canoes to pass we made a Portage of 100 yards to avoid it, the difference of level being about 3 feet—Proceeding 700 Yards we came to another Rapid similar to the last (difference of level 4 feet) from this we passed into a Lake of three quarters of a mile in length and the same in breadth; Crossing this in a Northerly direction we came to another Lake of half a mile in length and a quarter in breadth having a large Island in it, from this into another small Lake at the N.E. extremity of which we came to the River, flowing through a bed of Rocks, and made a Portage of a quarter of a mile on the left bank. Proceeding 200 yards we came to a Lake 400 yards wide and the same nearly in breadth—During our course through these Lakes we observed several Rivulets flowing into them from the surrounding country, which in many places was low and swampy.

At 46 miles from the mouth of the River we came to a fall of 8 feet in height, after which the River resumed its former appearance for the space of 2 miles and a half when it filters thro' a swamp. Having made a Portage to regain the River of ⅞ a mile, we embarked and proceeded 600 yards farther but finding the River a complete morass impassable for a Canoe even when unloaded, we made a Portage Easterly over

rocky and uneven ground interspersed with swamps Tracing the River in this manner for 2 miles, we arrived at its Source a small streamlet, of 2 feet in breadth, flowing out of one of the surrounding Morasses.

The general course of the Black River is E.N.E. but winding very much. The land throughout is bad, but improves as you proceed into the interior. The Timber on each bank is principally Pine.

Leaving the source of the black River we proceeded in an Easterly direction 3 miles and a half, through a Morass and arrived at a Lake 150 Yards in breadth and three quarters of a mile long, on the banks of this Lake are many Swamps from one of which at the S.E. end flows a small Rivulet which winding thro' a ravine joins into another Lake about 100 yards in length, and 100 broad: to this Lake we made a Portage of 3 miles over very uneven ground occasionally interspersed with granite rocks. Crossing the Lake in a direction S. by E. we passed thro' a small channel into another Lake of a mile in length, and a quarter of a mile in breadth, the Banks low and marshy— crossing this Lake in a direction S.S.E. we made a Portage Southerly of one mile, over a ridge having on each side (but particularly on the East) low and deep ravines, and arrived at one of the Rice Lakes—

Proceeding in a Southerly direction through this Lake, we came to a Rapid 50 yards in length, the difference of level from the head to the foot of the fall being 6 feet; having a Portage on the right bank, we descended the River for 5 miles, when we came to a Fall and Rapid 15 feet in height; 200 Yards from this we made another Portage of 200 Yards to avoid fallen Timber that obstructed the navigation.

Proceeding onwards in a South direction for 2 mile we came to another Fall, 10 feet in height, and made a Portage on the left bank, a quarter of a mile farther we arrived at another fall and Rapid, in length 200 feet, the height of the Fall is ten feet, making the Portage on the left Bank and proceeding 4 miles and a half we entered into a Lake of six miles (called in Captain Catty's Survey Kinaskinguash[21]) Crossing the Lake we proceeded in a South direction down a shallow River having a Rocky uneven bottom with a Rapid at the Head the current of the River running 3 miles per hour and the depth being in some parts 8 feet and in others scarcely 2— Two miles onwards we passed down a very shallow rapid, a mile in length running over a rugged bed of Rocks, after which the River deepens and becomes wider— Five miles from this we entered the Balsam Lake crossing which in a S.S.W. direction we made a Portage of 4 miles to the head of the Talbot River over hilly ground— Proceeding for 100 yards on the Talbot River we made a Portage of half a mile to avoid some fallen Timber, and again Embarking we descended the River for 4 miles when it lost itself under a bed of Rocks flowing under ground for a mile and a half and appearing again in a very shallow Stream— Proceeding 4 miles farther (during

21Gull Lake. The name Kinaskinguash does not occur in Catty's report (B 1). It is used on Marlow's map for the first lake northeast of Balsam Lake. On Shirreff's map it is spelled Kanashingiquash.

which we were obliged to walk a great part of the way in the water, it being too shallow to permit our canoes passing and the Land being swampy on either side) We found the River completely blocked up with fallen Timber, we here made a Portage of 12 miles, and again embarked on the River, which descending 4 miles without any obstructions we arrived at Lake Simcoe.

Relative to the probability of making a communication to the Ottawa by means of the Black River, (which is extremely winding throughout) we do not think it can be so easily accomplished as by means of the Talbot— In the Black River there are numerous falls some of which are of great height and the Bed of the River is composed throughout of red granite, a stone very difficult to work— The Talbot which runs in a much straighter direction, has but few falls, and none of any great height— The Bed of the River is also composed of a soft lime stone—

Should it however be thought adviseable to endeavour to make the Black River navigable to its Source (which from our observations we are led to suppose would be attended with very great difficulty) a Communication between its source and the Talbot by way of the Rice Lakes, could be easily effected by a Canal through the Morass of 3½ miles in extent into the first Lake we arrived at after leaving the head of the Black River— crossing this Lake the Communication might be continued by deepening the rivulet (which is 3 miles in length) into the Second and Third Lake.—From this third Lake a Canal communication might be made of a mile in length through the deep ravine on the east side which would bring the communication to the Rice Lakes.

We trust the accompanying Plan will serve to explain what we have here observed—

These Sir, were the principal observations we were able to make during our progress through the Country, which has been attended with much more difficulty this year than it otherwise would owing to the very low state of the Water, The Indian Guide (the same that formerly accompanied Captain Caddy [sic] on his Route and probably one of the most intelligent Indians we could have met with) assuring us that he had never known the Black River so shallow as it is this year, that during the Spring it is upwards of 15 feet higher, than at present, which was evidently the case from the Water marks on the Rocks and the dead Weeds &c left on the branches of the trees— At that season of the Year the River is extremely rapid.

B 8   BRISCOE TO WRIGHT

[P.R.O., W.O. 55/863; also printed in Bain, "Surveys of a Water Route"; another copy in P.A.C., C 428, pp. 78–80]

Kingston U. C.
16th. Oct. 1826

With reference to my letter to you dated from the West Shore of Lake Simcoe of the 29th. August reporting the necessity of my returning to Holland Landing to procure fresh provisions & to one dated from the Landing of the 31st. August last, stating that a guide had been procured for the Talbot route; I have now the honor to report, that the Indian alluded to was found on examination to be very imperfectly acquainted with the Country through which he had undertaken to guide us & the morning after his arrival deserted; most unfortunately the Indian who accompanied Lieut. Catty in the year 1819 was engaged for Lt. Marlow to explore the Black River & no other Indian could be procured who knew the Talbot route, as will be perceived by the annexed copy of a letter from Mr. Givens of the Indian Dept.

In this predicament I happened to hear of a half Indian an Iroquois from the Lake of the two Mountains who had frequently passed between the Sault du Chat & Lake Simcoe. On interrogating him he was ignorant of the Talbot River but described his route as commencing from the Severn beyond the Black river & spoke in very high terms of a very large Lake[22] & fine river connected by minor Lakes & rivers with the Madawasca; he appeared remarkably intelligent & bore an excellent character with every one who knew him; under these circumstances I thought it most advisable to proceed immediately in exploring his route as no chance remained of procuring a guide for the Talbot & I beg leave to inclose herewith a report of the expedition which I regret to say was most unsatisfactory.

When we had been out about 20 days & were descending a branch of the Madawasca we met an Indian who had been a month coming from the Chat; he informed us that it would take us three weeks to arrive there by the Madawasca, in consequence of the extreme lowness of the water & as we had then but ten days provision left, owing to the great delay & difficulties we had experienced from the cause stated viz: from the lowness of the water, high water mark averaging from 5 to 6 feet, I determined to pursue the most expeditious route to the Ottawa's taking advantage of a Chain of Lakes connected with a large but very rapid river which brought us out upon the Ottawas, about 9 leagues above a trading post of the Hudsons Bay Company called Ft. Cologne.[23]

B 9   BRISCOE'S REPORT OF A SURVEY FROM LAKE SIMCOE
TO THE OTTAWA
[*P.A.C., C 428, pp. 81–5; another copy in P.R.O., W.O. 55/863;
also printed in Bain, "Surveys of a Water Route"*]

Report of a Survey undertaken in pursuance of the General Orders of the 18th and 20th February and 1 July 1826 to examine the Water Communication between Lake Simcoe and the River Ottawa.

[22]Apparently Lake Muskoka.
[23]Fort Coulonge, frequently spelled Cologne or Coulonge, at the junction of the Ottawa and Coulonge rivers. A fur-trading post, established there by Louis d'Aillebboust, sieur de Coulonge, Governor of New France, 1648–51, was later operated by the North West and Hudson's Bay companies. Settlement of the area dates from 1843.

The party left Holland Landing on the 4 Septr. and proceeding to the Narrows of Lake Simcoe, descended the Severn until within half a mile of the third Fall. Here we left the Severn on the 7 Septr. by a small winding Creek[24] running in about a S.W. direction— its breadth varies between 5 & 20 yards— in the course of ½ a mile it is obstructed by two small Falls 3 or 4 feet high; the Creek then widens into a Lake[25] about 2½ miles in length and 200 yards wide— We then proceeded up the Creek[26] for nearly a mile, in the course of which there are 4 Falls; one 15 feet high, the others 4 or 5— The Bed of the Creek is composed of red Granite. The Banks generally low; the greatest rise of Water about 5 feet; the soil of an indifferent quality— The Creek takes its rise from a Lake[27] which we crossed 5 miles in a N:W direction and 3 S:E bounded by high rocky banks— From this Lake we made a Portage of 2½ miles into a Large Lake[28] which we crossed N N W 2 miles, & N & by E 7 miles. We left it by a large River[29] running W S W 50 yards wide at the mouth and 10½ feet deep. We ascended about 11 miles where it is obstructed by a Rapid and Shoals and ¼ mile further by two contiguous Falls,[30] the lower one 80 feet and the upper one 30 feet high— In the course of the next 12 miles it is impeded by three falls: the first 30 feet, the second 15 feet and the third 5 feet and by upwards of a Dozen rapids. In the next 9 miles there are 5 Falls of 4 or 6 feet, and as many rapids—

The River here widens into a fine Lake[31] containing numerous Islands. We crossed it in a N.N.E direction 9 miles and left it by a continuation[32] of the River we had been ascending; which was 20 yards wide at the entrance, and about 12 feet deep: the current sluggish— In the course of 8 miles it is obstructed by one fall[33] of 20 ft and 5 Rapids and then exceedingly interrupted by Rapids and Shoals for 4 miles, when it becomes a Lake[34] one mile in length— Two miles beyond this Lake there is a fall of 70 ft and half a mile higher up another Fall of 60 ft— Above this fall the River is a continued Rapid for ½ mile— The Succeeding 6 miles are without any obstruction except a few fallen trees— The breadth of the River here is 12 or 15 yards and is then a succession of Rapids & Shoals for 1½ miles: after which we crossed a shallow Lake[35] 2 miles in length— From this Lake we crossed 3 more[36]

[24]Morrison Creek.

[25]Morrison Lake.   [26]Muldrew Creek.

[27]Muldrew Lake, formerly Leg Lake.

[28]Lake Muskoka. Apparently this route from the Severn River to Lake Muskoka was well known to the Indians.

[29]Muskoka River. At the forks they turned into the South Branch.

[30]Known as South or Muskoka Falls.

[31]Lake of Bays.

[32]Usually called Oxtongue River, but regarded by the early explorers as a continuation of the Muskoka.

[33]Marsh Falls.   [34]Oxtongue Lake.   [35]South Tea Lake.

[36]Dr. J. W. Bain gives the lakes as Smoke and probably Ragged and Big Porcupine ("Surveys of a Water Route," p. 21). Miss Saunders gives Smoke and Hilliard (*Algonquin Story*, p. 14).

by Portages into Each: the first 3½ miles, and the other two a mile or 1½ miles long—

These Lakes are connected with each other by small Streams not navigable—

The difference of level between these Lakes is very considerable. Here we made a Portage of 9 miles; in the course of which we observed several small Lakes and some little streams running in a direction contrary to those we had been ascending— From the end of the Portage we crossed two Lakes ½ mile each across by a Portage of ¼ mile between them—

From the last Lake,[37] the Madawasca or rather I should think a branch of that River takes its rise— We now began to descend the Waters— Immediately on entering the River there is a considerable fall. It is about 7 yards wide and not deep enough to float a laden Canoe— It runs 2 miles N E. through a Marsh—In the next 9 miles there is one fall of 15 feet, and three of between 4 and 5 feet—

The banks are generally very low, but the River enlarges, and the banks are higher in the last 3 or 4 miles, which are much obstructed by fallen Trees—

It was here we met the Indian from whose information I determined to proceed by the route[38] of Fort Coulogne— This was on the 23 Sept.— The River now enters a Lake[39] which we crossed Easterly 2 miles, and then re-entered the River, the next 2 miles of which are interrupted by a Rapid, several Shoals and fallen Trees— We now left the Madawasca and crossed a chain of Lakes,[40] 9 in number, making Portages from one to the other, for a distance of about 21 miles—

The 6th is a very large Lake said to extend to within a short distance of the Ottawas— We left the 9th Lake by a shallow muddy River with low banks 4 miles long, and then crossed two more Lakes, the first, half, the second one mile in length, connected by a River 60 yards across, and ¼ mile long—

We then descended a small and very shallow River 16 or 17 miles obstructed by 4 or 5 Rapids ½ a mile in length— We afterwards crossed a Lake in a N E direction 8 miles which we left by a River 12 or 15 yards wide obstructed by 5 Falls and Rapids in the course of 2½ miles— We then made a Portage of 1½ mile and descended 4 or 5 miles impeded by a Fall of 20 feet and several Rapids— This River enters a larger one the course of which is generally E for about 45 miles, averaging 50 yards wide—

[37]Head Lake; or Source Lake if he followed the Hilliard Lake route.

[38]The route by the Petawawa River which flows into the Ottawa above Fort Coulonge.

[39]Lake of Two Rivers.

[40]Dr. Bain suggests that the nine lakes were Kearney, Pond, Little Rock, Sunday, Sproule, Opeongo, Wright, Bonfield, and La Vieille, and that Briscoe then continued by the Crow River to the Petawawa ("Surveys of a Water Route," p. 21). Miss Saunders shows the last three lakes as Proulx, Hogan, and Radiant (*Algonquin Story*, p. 14, and map).

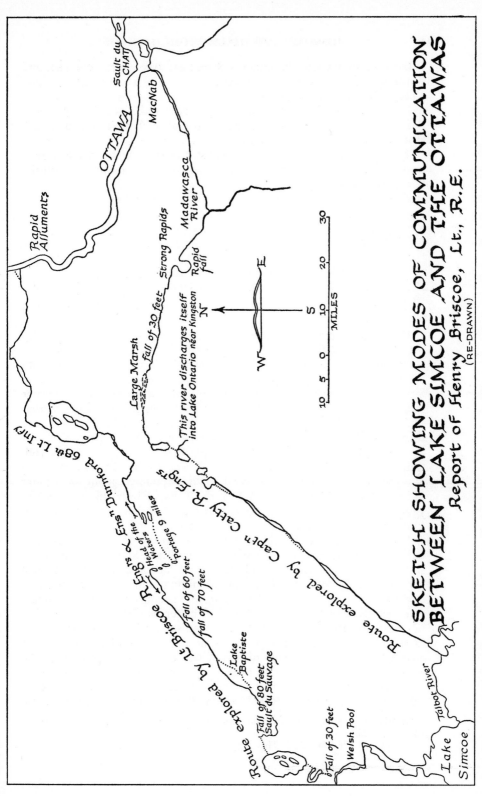

FIGURE 4. ORIGINAL SKETCH DATED "COMMANDING ROYAL ENGINEERS OFFICE, QUEBEC 28TH. OCTR. 1826." [Public Archives of Canada.]

It then empties into the Ottawas 8 leagues above Fort Coulogne, and is nearly one entire Rapid— Its banks are very high and rocky; in many places 60 & 100 feet perpendicular—

In the last 20 miles, it forms several small Lakes— We left it by a Portage of 1 mile to avoid the Rapids and Falls with which it is impeded, at its junction with the Ottawas—

The average greatest rise of Water throughout the route was 5 feet— The land we passed over, was generally bad, particularly on the borders of the Lakes and Rivers.

The Party arrived at Fort Coulogne on the 2d October.

Kingston U C
16 October 1826

B 10   SMYTH TO GENERAL GOTHER MANN
[*P.R.O., W.O. 55/863*]

Nutwood. Ryegate. December 28th. 1826

I have the honor to acknowledge the receipt of your orders of yesterday as conveyed to me by Colonel Mann[41] in his letter of that date. I have read with every attention Lt: Walpole's report[42] of the 26th September relative to the proposed water communication between Lake Simcoe and Penetangasheene; and have also referred to his former statement of the 14th November of last year, together with my observations (as contained in the letter of the 19th January of the present year which I had the honor to address to you) upon the same subject— I have perused with much interest Lieut. Briscoe's report of the 16th October of his expedition from Lake Simcoe to the Ottawa; and have also read Lieut. Marlow's letter of the 22d: September giving an account of his examination of the Black & of the Talbot Rivers. In obedience to your command I respectfully submit such observations as have occurred to me upon the perusal of these several papers—

However desirable the object, it does not appear that a continuous or uninterrupted water communication between Lake Simcoe & Penetangasheene can be effected but with very great labour and at considerable expence. . . . I take the liberty of submitting, with every respect, that any attempt to connect Lake Simcoe with Penetangasheene by the waters of either the North or South River had better be abandoned— Neither of these undertakings could be accomplished without a very heavy expenditure. It therefore appears to me that it would be much more adviseable (whenever a sum of money can be allotted to connect Lake Simcoe with Lake Huron) to avail ourselves of the Severn or Matchedash River, the natural outlet of the former, and by means of locks & canals to turn the Severn Rapids which at present impede its navigation.

[41]Probably Cornelius Mann who was made Colonel in the Royal Engineers, July 29, 1825.
[42]P.A.C., C 428, pp. 52–62. This copy is dated September 25.

This is an operation which we are certain can be done; and we are as sure Lake Simcoe will afford an inexhaustible supply of water— The small streams, as the country is cleared, lose a great proportion of their waters—as, whether we make use of the South, the North, or the Severn Rivers a considerable sum must be expended, I respectfully submit that we had better undertake that operation which we know we can effect. . . .

Lieut. Briscoe who was employed to explore the water communication between Lake Simcoe and the Ottawa did not, I observe in his Report, ascend the Talbot River & pursue the route formerly accomplished by Captain Catty, according to the memorandums I left with Colonel Durnford; but, owing to accidental circumstances & a mistake about a Guide, penetrated the country by advancing up a creek from the Severn; and, with his canoe, reached the Ottawa in 34 days— I conceive this deviation to be advantageous to the Service, & more useful than if Lieut. Briscoe had followed Captain Catty's footsteps. Our knowledge of the country is in consequence more extended; &, I take the liberty of adding, the accomplishment of Lieut: Briscoes journey shews what vast facilities for internal navigation & communication the Country between the Ottawa and Lake Simcoe will afford to future settlers—When a dense population comes to be established between the Ottawa and the St. Lawrence; & between the Ottawa & the Lakes which supply the St. Lawrence, the military features of Canada will assume a very different appearance.

Lieut. Marlow's report respecting the Black and the Talbot Rivers is very satisfactory; in so much as although it does not appear that any use can be hereafter made of the Black River, it was absolutely necessary that it should be explored; & the possibility of being able to penetrate by it to the chain of Lakes, by which Captain Catty reached the Ottawa, ascertained— Lieut: Marlow's remarks upon the Talbot River appear very correct and judicious— As the Province of Upper Canada advances in population and means I have little doubt but that this River will be made useful in contributing towards a water communication from Lake Simcoe to the Bay of Quinté near Kingston— There does not appear a great deal to be done to obtain, even now, a water conveyance from Lake Simcoe by the Talbot & the Balsam Lake to the Upper Rice Lake— I have very little doubt but that on the completion of the Rideau Canal the Provincial Legislature will attempt that important communication.

I have returned the Papers & the Sketches which accompanied them;

B 11   W (Duke of Wellington), Minute on Reports of Surveys
          [*P.R.O., W.O. 55/864*]

10th January 1827.

I have perused these Papers. It is in my opinion a point of the greatest importance to open a communication by Water between Kingston or the

Bay of Quinté, preferably the former, and Lake Simcoe; and the latter
& Gloucester Bay in Lake Huron.

No point ought to be spared in ascertaining the preferable line for this
Communication. Until this shall be effected, we shall have completed
only half our business.—

The information contained in these Papers is interesting and shews
what we shall be able to do by and bye by means of the Ottawa.

But I confess that I have read them with pain. They afford a fresh
proof of the inaccuracy with which all the Military Business of this
Country is done. The reason is because nobody does his own.

Here are certain Officers in time of Peace ordered to make specific
Reconnoissances. They do not so arrange matters as to procure to a
certainty the Provisions necessary to enable them to perform their duty;
nor do they, where guides are requisite, take measures for providing
such guides as are capable of conducting each Officer on the road he is
to go.

The consequence is that they go wandering over the Country they
don't know where, and report upon any thing excepting what they were
sent to examine and report upon.

Let these Surveys be made again next Season.

Let any Officer who reads these Papers reflect upon what would be
the consequence of the immediate operations of an Army depending
upon such performance of this important Duty!

With such assistance what Officer at the Head of an Army would
venture to form a Plan; or to order its execution with vigour.

B 12   SMYTH TO GENERAL GOTHER MANN
[P.R.O., W.O. 55/864]

Nutwood. Reigate. 2d: February 1827.

I have read with every respect and attention His Grace The Master
Generals minute of the 10th: ultimo on the subject of the late Surveys
of the Water communications, therein alluded to, in Upper Canada; and
in obedience to your orders, as conveyed to me by Colonel Mann in his
letter of the 29th of the same month, directing me to submit such observations as might occur to me after the perusal of His Grace's minute;
I take the liberty of pointing out that as His Grace has ordered that the
Officers should be again employed during the approaching Season upon
their duties, I am of opinion that it would be advantageous to the Service
if a little alteration should be made in the routes to be explored this
year from those which were ordered to be surveyed last autumn— In
the sketch which accompanies Lt Briscoe's report I observe that at
about 80 miles from Lake Simcoe & the same distance from that part of
the Ottawa called Lake du Chat (a very few miles only above the mouth
of the Rideau) a River is marked, said to communicate with Kingston
on Lake Ontario— As this is a point of such very great importance to
ascertain I am confident His Grace the Master General will approve of

the best exertions and talents of the Officers being directed to this subject— I feel therefore disposed respectfully to recommend that in consequence of this report of a River running from the situation I have described to Kingston, the Engineer Officers to be employed in survey- ing, during the ensuing Summer, should be divided into two Parties only, instead of into three as last season— That one Party should survey the course formerly explored by Lieut. Catty from Lake Simcoe to the Ottawa, detaching an Officer with such assistance as he may require to follow the course of the River branching off from this communication, at about 80 miles from Lake Simcoe, to Kingston— The other Party to go over again Lieut: Briscoe's late route from the Severn to the Ottawa only continuing their course by the Madawaska to the head of the Lake du Chat on the Ottawa, instead of making for that River higher up either at Fort Cologne or any other point. Accurate Reports of these different water communications, particularly of that leading to Kingston, are, I take the liberty of observing, of the utmost consequence— Lt. Marlow's report of the Talbot River (running into Lake Simcoe) is very satisfactory; and added to the knowledge we already were in pos- session of relative to the Trent and the Rice Lakes gives every reason to hope that whenever a sufficient sum of money can be allotted to the purpose there will be no difficulty in establishing a water communica- tion from the Bay of Quinté to Lake Simcoe— We also know that by the Severn we can reach Gloster Bay in Lake Huron at the expence of the Locks and short canals required to ascend & descend the Rapids, the necessary water for which would be supplied by the inexhaustible reservoir of Lake Simcoe itself, situated fortunately on the highest level— I was in hopes that by means of the South River this object might have been to have been [sic] accomplished at a cheaper rate and which line of communication if feasible would have been moreover more desireable from the Mouth of the South River being so much nearer Penetangasheene than that of the Severn— Lt. Walpole's report however of the height of the intervening ground (which I could not judge of at the moment from the whole country being covered with wood) does not hold out much encouragement to this plan. We are however certain of being able to accomplish the object of getting into Lake Huron from Lake Simcoe by the Severn, whenever the establish- ment of a communication from Kingston or the Bay of Quinté into the latter, shall have rendered it necessary.

B 13   Fitzroy Somerset[43] to General Gother Mann
[P.R.O., W.O. 55/864]

Office of Ordnance
10th. February 1827

Having brought under The Master General's consideration your letter of the 7th. Instant communicating the further suggestions of Colonel

[43]Lord Fitzroy James Henry Somerset (later Baron Raglan) (1788–1855) was

Sir James Smyth for the more effectual fulfilment of His Grace's orders and intentions respecting a Water communication between Lake Simcoe and Penetangasheene and Lake Simcoe with the Ottawa, I am directed to express the Duke's concurrence with the suggestions of Sir James Smyth, and His desire that Orders may be issued accordingly for the Surveys next Season.

B 14   WRIGHT'S INSTRUCTIONS TO OFFICERS FOR FURTHER SURVEYS
        [*P.R.O., W.O. 55/864; also printed in Bain,* "Surveys of a
        Water Route"]

Royal Engineers Office
Kingston, 24th. August 1827.

Lieut's Briscoe & Walpole will hold themselves in readiness to proceed on the 27 Instant on the particular Surveys ordered by the Master General of the Ordnance.

Lieut. Briscoe, accompanied by Lieut. Greenwood[44] of the Royal Artillery as authorized by the General Order No. 3 of the 26th Ulto. will go over again the Route he went last year except that he will proceed to the Ottawa by the Madawasca instead of the Route by Fort Cologne.

Upon reaching that part of the River that runs into the Madawasca where Captain Catty fell in with it on his route from the Talbot, he will retrace a small portion of Capt. Catty's Route until he reaches the Lake at the N.E. Point of which a River is marked on his sketch as branching off and discharging itself into Lake Ontario near Kingston and endeavour to find it out.

Lieut. Walpole accompanied by Mr. Chewit[45] of the Surveyor General's Department, should His Excellency's permission be obtained, will proceed from Lake Simcoe by the Talbot along the Route explored by Capt. Catty until he arrives at the Point of the Lake where the River is marked as branching off towards Kingston and his attention along the whole of this Route will be particularly directed to ascertain whether any River branches off towards Lake Ontario that affords a probable expectation of a Water communication with that Lake.

Lieut's Briscoe & Walpole will endeavour if practicable so to time their movements as to arrive at the Point above mentioned nearly at the same time and meet each other. Should they not immediately discover the said

---

made Military Secretary at the Horse Guards in 1827 and worked closely with the Duke of Wellington.

[44]William Greenwood (d. 1861?) became First Lieutenant of the Royal Artillery in May, 1815, Captain in 1834, Major in 1842, and Lieutenant Colonel in 1854. He was made a Companion of the Order of the Bath.

[45]James Grant Chewett (1793–1862), son of William Chewett who was Surveyor General of Upper Canada, became a surveyor on March 6, 1819. About 1824 he received an appointment in the Surveyor General's office and later was given the office of Deputy Surveyor General which he held until 1841.

River they will trace in opposite directions to endeavour to find it out, returning in three or four days to the place of their mutual departure.

Lieut. Briscoe will then continue his route to the Ottawa by the Madawasca and Lieut. Walpole should the River be discovered will proceed to trace its course and ascertain the facilities it affords for a Water communication between Lake Simcoe and Lake Ontario for which purpose he will minutely report upon the several Rapids and Falls, the Portages, Depth of Water, nature of its Banks, and every particular necessary to form a correct opinion of its practicability.

Should Lieut. Walpole arrive at the place appointed and discover the River previous to meeting with Lieut. Briscoe he will proceed on the survey of it, leaving some token or memorandum, of his having done so, for the information of that Officer.

Should the River not be discovered Lieut. Walpole will retrace his Route to Kingston by the most expeditious way his guide recommends.

B 15   BRISCOE TO WRIGHT
[P.R.O., W.O. 55/864; also printed in Bain, "Surveys of a Water Route"]

Royal Engineer Office
Kingston Upper Canada
13th October 1827

Agreeably to Genl. Orders No 3 of the 26th of July, and in obedience to your order of the 24th Aug., I left this place, accompanied by Lt. Greenwood R.A. to retrace a part of my former route, & proceed to the Ottawa by the River Madawasca, instead of the route by Fort Cologne, and we beg leave to refer you to my former Report upon that part of our route which lies between the third fall on the Severn and the head of the Waters (having nothing additional to communicate upon that part of the journey). On arriving at this point, we entered a small Lake[46] from whence the Madawasca takes its source; we proceeded about two miles, when we were obliged to make a portage of a few hundred yards, the river being choked with fallen trees and obstructed by a fall of 6 or 7 feet; reentering the river, we advanced 6 or 7 miles, when we met with a succession of 6 small Lakes, but were invariably obliged to make portages from one to the other, the connecting streams being obstructed by rapids & falls. From the 6th lake[47] to the 7th, a distance of about 20 or 25 miles, the navigation of the River is impeded by a succession of strong Rapids & Falls. The last mentioned Lake is 6 miles long which we crossed in a S.E. direction; pursuing the course of the river about 5 miles (the character of which is the same as already described) we

[46]Probably Head Lake. Briscoe's map (P.R.O., W.O. 55/864) suggests that he and Lieutenant Greenwood followed the same route as in 1826 to a point a little east of Lake of Two Rivers.
[47]Galeairy Lake.

arrived at two lakes, one about 4 miles,[48] and the other ½ amile[49] [*sic*] long: after quitting the Lakes, we had to encounter the usual difficulties in the River, making constant portages, the rapids being of a dangerous character; proceeding about 2 or 3 miles, we arrived at a large Marsh about 4 miles long, answering to that described by Capt. Catty Rl. Engr. in his report: on leaving the Marsh we made a portage, there being a fall of 7 feet in the river; from this point to the Sturgeon Lake[50] (a distance of about 25 miles) we found the River in most cases, a succession of Rapids with numerous falls, which compelled us to make as frequent portages.— We crossed the above mentioned Lake by a N.E. course 4 miles— From this Lake to the Ottawa the river is altogether obstructed by dangerous rapids, rendered still more difficult by the unusual lowness of the water, varying between 3 & 4 feet below high water marks; the average breadth of the River from Sturgeon Lake to the Ottawa is about 40 yards. With respect to establishing a water communication on the line of the Madawasca, we perfectly agree with Captain Catty in the impracticability thereof and beg leave to add, from our own knowledge of that part of the River unexplored by Captain Catty, that the upper waters present difficulties of a still more decided character.

The Country through which we passed was uniformly, with a very few exceptions, of a sterile nature, the bed of the river, and the banks thereof, which were generally steep, being one continued line of Granite, to within a few miles of the Ottawa.

B 16   LIEUTENANT JOHN WALPOLE TO WRIGHT
[*P.R.O., W.O. 55/864; also printed in Bain,* "Surveys of a Water Route"]

Royal Engineer Office
York U C 12th. Novr. 1827.

I herewith have the honor to transmit you a report and Sketches of the route— I was directed by you to proceed upon in August last—

I have already informed you I discovered no River that flowed in the *direction of Kingston*; and that prior to my leaving Lake Simcoe I learnt from the Indian who went with Capt. Catty (but from illness was unable to go with me) that he knew of none, that had its rise in any of the Lakes I was to pass through—

I was fortunate in procuring the Guide—Lt. Marlow[51] had last year, of whom that officer spoke so highly—

I also found him extremely intelligent, and perfectly conversant with the waters he guided me through—

[48]Bark Lake.
[49]Kamaniskeg Lake.
[50]Calabogie Lake.
[51]Apparently an error for Briscoe. In 1826 Marlow used the guide who had accompanied Catty (B 8).

B 17   Walpole's Report of Survey from Talbot River to the
Madawaska, November, 1827
[*P.R.O., W.O. 55/864; also printed in Bain,* "Surveys of a
Water Route"]

A report of the route (as far as the Madawaska river) explored by
Captn. Catty in 1819 and Lt. Walpole in 1827—

Soon after entering the Talbot River, in consequence of the very great
quantity of drift-wood that impedes its navigation, a Portage of 7¼ Miles
is made over very flat and low Lands. The River then becomes navigable
for four or five miles, when a small Rapid obliged us to make a Short
Portage— with the exception of two Shallows, and where the River
loses itself under a bed of Lime Stone, we were enabled to proceed without interruption 'till we left the River to pass over to Balsam Lake— It
will be seen by the Sketch, in this Portage two Elbows of the River are
crossed— The Land between Balsam Lake and the River Talbot forms
itself into a ridge, and is rather high— It was by no means apparent to
us, that the level of Balsam Lake is above that of the River, unless it be
so, some difficulty will be encountered in getting a water communication
through that part of the Country, for it would be injudicious to direct
the water of the River Talbot, as it is near the Source, but a small Stream
— After leaving Balsam Lake we ascended a fine stream; a short distance up, there are four Rapids, easy of ascent— above the Rapids the
River expands into a Lake, called the Lac des Isles,[52] the Lake is
bounded by Rocks of a very hard description— It may here be observed
that after passing the Rapids below the Lac des Isles, we remarked no
more Lime Stone through the Route until we arrived at the Mouth of
the Madawaska.

From the Lake we again entered the River and soon arrived at the
foot of a small Rapid, above which there are two others at short distances from each other—

They are severally 12, 8 & 16 feet high, but with facility might be
rendered passable for Batteaux. From there the River continues broad
and navigable for a few Miles, when a Portage of 75 yards is made to
avoid a small fall, called Moore's fall, here the operation of damming up
one of the Channels of the Fall might be easily performed— Having
passed these Falls, we entered upon a fine Lake six Miles long, called
Gull Lake, but with extremely Sterile and barren Shores.

This Lake is left by a sinuous but navigable Stream, flowing through
a flat Country— after ascending it for about 6 Miles, we arrived at the
foot of a strong rapid— There a portage is made over some very broken
and high Land— It will seem this Portage no longer follows the course
of the River we ascended, but brought us to the side of a small Creek—
The Creek & the small Lake from which it flows, cannot be less than

[52]Shadow Lake.

200 feet above the level of the River, at where, we commenced the Portage— The Creek takes a circuitous Route and falls into the River below the Portage. Though practicable, to form a communication be- tween the small Lake and the River the great difference of level would render it a work of great labour and expence—

From the small Lake there is a Portage of a Quarter of a mile to another Lake— the two Lakes are totally unconnected, & the latter is about 20 feet below the small one— The Land between them is not very favorable for making a communication, and it may be a question, whether by doing so, it would be considered advisable to open another outlet to the small Lake—

The next Lake[53] is nearly twelve Miles long, its shores are much in- dented, varying from 1000 yards in breadth to small Straits from 30 to 50 feet wide— This Lake gives rise to a River called Burnt River, which discharges itself near Balsam Lake—

Leaving the long lake, we passed up a narrow and sluggish Stream at the extremity of which there is a small lake; from the lake we again got into a small Stream; the navigation soon became intercepted, by drift wood and shoal water, but a portage of ⅝ Mile brought us to where the Stream is again navigable.—

At the distance of about a Mile there are some strong rapids and falls, of 50 feet descent.— A portage of 684 yards avoids them:— it was observed the banks of the river here are very unfavorable for making a Cut, being high and rocky.—

We now passed without interruption to the lake, called Porcupine Lake,[54] extending several miles to the North, We passed near the South- ern extremity of it, and made a portage of one mile to a small one— These two lakes are on the same level, and the ground is favorable for connecting them. From the small Lake there is a portage of ½ Mile to Owl Lake[55]— Though the portage is made over high ground, it appeared to the southward, there would be no difficulty in making a communica- tion between the Lakes— from the small Lake and Owl there are small Streams flowing in the direction of the waters below Balsam Lake—

At the extremity of Owl Lake there is a small Stream rising in a boggy and marshy Lake, from which we passed over a portage[56] of ¾ mile to another of similar description: in the Spring, the guide informed us, the two are connected by the low & swampy land— there would therefore be no difficulty in securing a communication at all times, were a cut deep enough from one to the other to be made;— for it will have been observed that the waters from thence [corrected in pencil to read: these] two Lakes flow in opposite directions. A portage of 220 yards and an- other of 968 yards were made to arrive at the Lake marked (a):—

[53]Kashagawigamog Lake.
[54]Drag Lake.
[55]Miskwabi Lake.
[56]In margin: "vid. sketch."

Communications might be easily made were [*sic*] the Portages are, for there are but small differences of Level between the Lakes and the small Connecting Streams would require little else than damming up.

From the Lake[57] marked (a) it is necessary to make two very small portages with a pond intervening to get upon the uppermost Lake[58] (b) which is described in Capt. Cattys Sketch as having a River flowing from it, and discharging itself near Kingston. Nothing but a very Little shallow stream runs from it; which was ascertained to make a winding course for about 1 mile & a half and fall into the Lake (a).

From the Lower Lake there is however a small river[59] that empties itself into the waters of the Trent near Balsam Lake, as I was assured by the Guide. This river is I have every reason to suppose the same as that alluded to in Capt. Catty's Sketch, although inaccurately described as having its source in the uppermost Lake— It was never meant to be inferred (so it is conceived and the observation is made with due deference) that this River discharged itself near Kingston without first forming a junction with the waters of the Trent, which certainly may be said to discharge itself near Kingston for, by referring to the Sketch B drawn to a smaller scale it will be seen that the courses of the several rivers that flow into the Trent between its source and Kingston forbid the inference.

The Trent having been frequently explored and perfectly well known I did not think it my duty to pass over to it, I therefore proceeded on Captain Catty's route.

To pass the high Lands dividing the waters that fall into Lake Ontario from those falling into the Ottawa a portage of little more than 2¼ miles was made.

At the extremity of the portage there is a small Lake. From the lands being very high & extremely broken it is difficult to pronounce which of the Lakes, is situated on the higher Level.— The land appeared to be generally of so unfavorable a nature, that the operation of forming a Canal between them would be one of extreme Labour.

From the small Lake a portage of 1¹/₁₀ mile was made to another; the one described in Captain Catty's report as being extremely shallow— The shallow Lake[60] is certainly not less than 200 feet below the small one— the stream from the latter has at first a very precipitous fall. Here the work of making Locks &ca. from the great difference of Level would also be Laborious and expensive.

We left the shallow Lake of the Shanwashkong river, meaning marshy; this we descended without interruption for manny [*sic*] miles— we passed the Lake noticed by Capt. Catty as being shallow as well as those that are deeper & bounded by rocky shores— After passing the Lakes we came to a falls of about 35 feet and then two rapids at short distances of 25 and 7 feet fall— for several Miles rapids do not occur and the

[57]Grace Lake.   [58]Farquhar Lake.
[59]A branch of the Irondale River flowing out of Grace Lake.
[60]Elephant Lake.

navigation is only interrupted by drift wood— The next rapid we arrived at had about 40 feet fall and at the interval of a few miles at another about 12 feet— The banks of the river at all these rapids vizt. those that were passed after the fall of 35 feet, are not very high, averaging about 10 feet high, therefore the operation of forming cuts &c. by the sides of the rapids would not exceed the ordinary Labour and expence in works of the Kind. Soon after we came to the bend in the River, where there are several falls & rapids, the portage is a mile, & the circuit that the river takes is considerably greater, the difference of Levels at the extremities of the portage cannot be less than 200 feet, the ground here is unusually high compared with what we had seen it at the banks of this river, the river is navigable from these rapids & falls with the exception of two small rapids till it meets the Madawaska river flowing for the distance of two or three miles through a large marshy Lake (Shanwashkong Lake) bounded by high & sterile Lands as mentioned by Captain Catty.

It was at the junction of Shanwashkong River with the Madawaska that Lieut. Briscoe & his party came upon the route, that Officer having received Orders to report upon this part of it— I descended the River and in obedience to Orders proceeded to Kingston without loss of time.

As far as my observations went I found the River as Capt. Catty has described, an almost uninterrupted succession of rapids.

There can be but one opinion respecting the very great difficulty there would be in overcoming the obstacles that at present oppose the navigation of it:— the great height to which the waters of this River rise in the Spring,— observable by the timber that has floated and been deposited on its banks, and the extraordinary rapidity with which it descends into the Ottawa are circumstances which would render the operation, if not infeasible, certainly enormously expensive and laborious.

In the former part of my report I have endeavoured to shew what difficulties separately exist to forming a water communication wherever it is at present intercepted, thereby enabling an opinion to be formed of this route from Lake Simcoe to the Ottawa, that though it comprises a large quantity of navigable water, possesses some obstacles that could only be overcome by more than an ordinary degree of labour and expence.

It may be added that the Country through which We passed unusually bore a most barren and cheerless aspect.

B 18   WRIGHT TO COLONEL ELIAS DURNFORD
[*P.R.O., W.O. 55/864*]

Royal Engineers Office
Kingston 17th. Novr. 1827.

Herewith I have the honor to transmit Lt. Walpole's Report & Sketches of the Route he was directed to explore conformably with your

Orders of the 24th. May. A copy of the Instructions issued to him & Lt. Briscoe dated the 24th. August was transmitted to you with Lt Briscoe's Report on the 14th. Instant.

The Sketches accompanying Lieut. Walpole's Report consist of one on a large scale marked A,[61] on which his route appears to be shewn with great correctness, the other marked B, is a general Sketch of his Route upon a small Scale.

Captain Catty's Report has been verified by these Surveys with the exception of the River marked on his Sketch as proceeding from a small Lake & discharging itself into Lake Ontario near Kingston.

From the Lake so marked on Capt. Catty's Sketch, only a very small Shallow Stream appears to run from it, connecting it with another lower Lake, from which there is a small River that the Guides assured Lt. Walpole emptied itself into the Trent near Balsam Lake; & which he concludes with great apparent probability must be the River alluded to by Capt. Catty.

Lt. Walpole states that he did not think it necessary to trace the course of the River leading only to the Trent, which has been frequently explored & is well known, but continued to pursue the remainder of Capt. Catty's Route to the Madawasca & from thence to the Ottawa as being the most convenient route by which he could return to Kingston

B 19   COLONEL ELIAS DURNFORD TO COLONEL MANN
[*P.R.O., W.O. 55/864*]

Rl Engineers Office
Quebec 27th. Novr. 1827.

I have the honor to forward, for Genl. Mann's information, copies of Letters from Lt. Colonel Wright, dated 14th. & 17th. Inst., transmitting the Reports of Lieut Briscoe R.E. with Lt. Greenwood Rl. Arty., and of Lt. Walpole R.E. who was accompanied by Mr. Chewit of the Surveyor Generals Department who has been much accustomed to traverse the woods, and volunteered his Services, for which I hope He, as well as Lt. Greenwood will be compensated, the Report of the former being dated 13th Octr. and of the latter the 12th Novr. 1827.

It appears that Lt. Briscoe did not perceive any sign of the River alluded to on the Sketch made by Captain Catty, nor does he appear to have made any discovery, from which any favorable conclusions, respecting the principal object of his excursion, can be drawn.

Lt. Walpole has entered into very minute detail from various matters that appeared important to him, and particularly as he fell upon a small River marked (a), and which he concludes, with great probability, must have been the one alluded to by Capt. Catty, but rather incorrectly marked on his Sketch.—

[61]Both maps, A and B, are found in P.R.O., W.O. 55/864.

It is much to be regretted that he did not explore its' course, rather than have proceeded to the Ottawa, although I think it was natural for him to rely upon the information of his Guide.

B 20   SMYTH TO GENERAL MANN
[P.R.O., W.O. 55/864]

Nutwood. Reigate. 24th April 1828

In obedience to your desire as communicated to me by Lieut:Colonel Ellicombe[62] on the 18th instant I have read with attention Lieutenants Briscoe's & Walpole's reports of the 13th October & of the 12th November last upon the water communication between the Ottawa and Lake Simcoe; & I have examined the four[63] several sketches transmitted by these Officers— I take the liberty of submitting with every respect, the following observations—

2. From the concurring testimony of Captn. Catty, of Lieut: Briscoe & of Lt. Walpole who have each, at different periods, explored the country between Lake Simcoe and the Ottawa there can be very little doubt but that a water communication can never be established by the Madawasca— The Madawasca which is about 130 miles in length seems to offer a series of rapids and waterfalls; & the River itself to be of too impetuous a character to make it an eligible navigation— as far as we yet know of this unfrequented track of Country it would appear that the shortest and most eligible line of communication will be found to be that taken by Lieut: Briscoe, in consequence of the advice of his Guide, in 1826 which brought him upon the Ottawa above an old Station belonging formerly to the North West Company called Fort Cologne & about 80 miles higher up the Ottawa than the mouth of the Madawaska—

3. From Lieut: Marlow's report of the Talbot River (in 1826) and which is now fully confirmed by that of Lieut. Walpole in his report of the 12th November of last year, The Talbot River is that which promises to be of the greatest consequence to this part of Canada as holding out a prospect of being able to effect, by its means, a communication from Lake Simcoe to the Balsam Lake.— From the Balsam Lake, as the Country becomes more settled & improves in its resources, we know a water communication can be made by the Rice Lake & the River Trent to the Bay of Quinté.— Thus the Talbot may at some future period be the means of establishing the connection between Lake Ontario & Lake Simcoe— It would moreover appear from Lieut: Walpoles sketch & report that it is by the Talbot & the Balsam Lake that the communication with the Ottawa from Lake Simcoe is to be effected— From Lieut.

[62]Charles Grene Ellicombe became Lieutenant Colonel in the Royal Engineers, March 23, 1825.

[63]In margin: "Say 3 sketches — the sketch A was in two pieces but it is now joined together."

Briscoes report the Severn is not (decidedly) the line by which we are to get to the Ottawa, although that by the Severn we will have to communicate with Penetangasheene & Lake Huron I think (after the report upon the South River of 1826) does not admit of a doubt—

4. I think that it is to be lamented that Lieut: Walpole did not verify the course of the River issuing from the Lower Lake marked A on his sketch (about half way between Lake Simcoe & the Ottawa) and which he was told by his Guide fell into the waters of the Trent near the Balsam Lake— From what he states I think it is very probable that the River is not of that consequence nor likely to afford that assistance which it had been conjectured it might have yielded in establishing a communication with Lake Ontario— As however it was reported to flow into the Trent & the Trent runs into Lake Ontario it will certainly upon some future occasion be adviseable that it should be explored. I also recommend that when an Officer can be allotted for this duty the nature of the Burnt River should be ascertained— I observe in Lieut: Walpoles large sketch the Burnt River[64] is dotted in as being supposed to connect Balsam Lake with these waters originally explored by Captain Catty at about 30 miles from that Lake— The Burnt River may afford a better line than the Gull Lake & the Lake des Isles— At any rate it will be desirable to ascertain this point at a convenient future opportunity.

5. The foregoing observations contain every thing which has occurred to me upon the subject after having read the reports; which are herewith returned.

B 21   LIEUTENANT COLONEL JOHN BY[65] TO COLONEL
ELIAS DURNFORD
[P.A.C., C 48, p. 1]

Royal Engineers office
Rideau Canal 16th. March 1829

I have the honor of transmitting for the information of His excellency Sir James Kempt[66] a report from Mr. Shirreff[67] on the advantages that

[64]On Walpole's sketch the Burnt River flows from the southeast section of Lake Kashagawigamog, which probably is meant to indicate the Drag River, a branch of the Burnt River, which comes from Lake Canning. This comment by Smyth supports the view that Catty went by the York River route.

[65]John By (1781–1836), military engineer, was in Canada from 1802 to 1811. In 1826 he returned as Lieutenant Colonel of the Royal Engineers to design and construct the Rideau Canal. He went back to England in 1832.

[66]Sir James Kempt (1764–1854), Administrator of the Government of Canada from 1828 to 1830.

[67]Charles Shirreff, a merchant from Leith, settled at Fitzroy Harbour on the Ottawa River in 1818. He had four sons and a daughter. The family became prominent in the development of the area and owned extensive property and mills. Charles Shirreff and his sons were active in promoting the idea of a canal from the Ottawa River to Georgian Bay, and the settlement of the Ottawa-Huron tract. The name was spelled in several ways: Shirreff, Shirrif, Sherriff, Sheriff, etc.

must accrue to the country by forming a water communication from the Ottawa to Lake Huron; and as I believe a Canal would be executed of sufficient size to pass steam boats for the sum of £800-000 I have enclosed a sketch[68] showing the route of the proposed Canal and request you will also have the kindness to lay it before His Excellency.

B 22   CHARLES SHIRREFF'S "OBSERVATIONS ON THE ADVANTAGES OF A CANAL FROM THE OTTAWA TO LAKE HURON WITH INFORMATION COLLECTED RESPECTING ITS PRACTICABILITY"
[*P.A.C., C 48, pp. 2–14*]

The improvement of the great water communications, which nature has formed on the Continent of America, will long be a prominent and important object, and the Public Works, now in progress with this view in Canada, must accelerate the growth of the Colony in a degree hitherto unknown. One important undertaking however, is still wanting to complete a plan of inland navigation not to be equalled in the world.

Government have already made some attempts to discover a line of water communication between the Ottawa and Lake Huron. But the reports on that part of the country which has been explored for this purpose have not been favorable. The route of the Hudson Bay Company by Lake Nipissing besides being circuitous is impeded by numerous falls and rapids particularly in the upper part of the Ottawa. A strong impression of the advantages of a direct Eastern outlet from Lake Huron led the writer to make particular enquiry respecting the space of land, which lays between the routes already explored, and that by Lake Nipissing, and from the information he has obtained, chiefly from the Indian traders who are accustomed to traverse that part of the country in all directions, he is now enabled to state, with a great degree of confidence, that by ascending the Ottawa about one hundred miles above Bytown, at the entrance of the Rideau Canal, a point will be reached, from whence a waterway to Lake Huron might be formed with great facility. The distance of Lake Huron from the Ottawa, at this point, does not appear to exceed 120 or 130 miles. In favorable weather it is an Indian journey of only three days, a communication therefore in this direction, would bring to our very door the immense waters of the Huron, the Michigan and even of Lake Superior; all of which have hitherto lain hid in the forest, and almost inaccessible.

From the Lake des Allumettes, where the Canal would leave the Ottawa, the line passes through several lakes, and over some carrying places, the last of which, at the height of land, is one mile and a half long. The distance here from the Ottawa is 40 miles. Beyond the portage is situated a lake called by the Indian traders La Vieille, said to be 60

[68]P.A.C., map 400, 1829.

miles in circumference, from which a river, widening in several places into small lakes, runs in a westerly direction to a lake[69] of considerable size being the third on a river called Moose,[70] and 45 miles distant from Lake Huron. Bateaux with goods for the Indian trade are brought up the river, which is said to be as large as the Rideau, and to have a good harbour at its mouth 70 miles from French River.

This part of the country is described as an extensive tract of good land, as lower and more level than the lands adjacent either to the South or North. The declivity from Lake La Vieille (situated on the highest ground in the route) to Lake Huron is said to be very small.

The rapid increase of inhabitants in the direction of the Ottawa, the improvement of its navigation, and the settlements which are taking place in the Western Territory of the United States combine to bring this object into present view, which, till lately seemed reserved for the consideration of a future age. But still, it may not have been closely contemplated that the time is now come when it might be accomplished with every prospect of immediate advantage.

. . .

The unbounded liberality with which England is improving and fortifying the Canadas would make a further call on the public purse appear unseasonable, nor would it be necessary for the present work which possesses such great inducements for the investment of Private Capital. The Canal would commence under circumstances peculiar to itself. It would be formed through a country not yet appropriated, so that not only would the expense of purchasing individual property be saved, but it would be in the power of Government to secure a Company against even the possibility of loss, by putting into their hands a quantity of land along the Banks of the Canal, which would soon become valuable, while at the same line [sic] this would not be a great sacrifice on the part of the Government, as these lands must if not thus opened out, remain for many years waste and uncultivated. Looking, however to the extensive commerce, which must soon be concentrated on the Canal, a grant of land might not be considered necessary to ensure its success.

. . .

If then this measure were carried into effect, which, it is presumed might be done safely and easily with British capital, we might venture to look into futurity and without the imputation of chimera or enthusiasm view this wonderful collection of inland waters, which are navig-

[69]The distance given from Lake Huron suggests that this refers to the Lake of Bays.
[70]Muskoka River.

able for the largest vessels and surrounded by coasts extending some thousands of miles, brought forward as a new and vast field for enterprise affording an additional opening for the commerce of Great Britain protected from all foreign intrusion by carriers composed of her own colonies. We might see the busy intercourse which is now established between Quebec and Montreal, extended up the Ottawa and along the Huron Canal to a city starting into existence and importance as our medium of communication with this new Mediterranean, and we might see the prosperity of Canada increasing rapidly with the settlements and improvement of the western regions, having its foundation and security in the very form which the Creator has given to continent of North America.

Fitzroy Harbour
January 1829.

B 23   By to Sir James Kempt
[P.A.C., C 48, pp. 226–7]

Royl. Engrs. Office.
Rideau Canal. 9th. May 1829.

I have the honor to state for the information of your Excellency, that the bearer of this, Mr. Sherrif, knows of a person who is willing to act as Guide through the Line of the proposed Canal from the Ottawa to Lake Huron, reported on by Mr. Sherrif, a Copy of which report I had the honor of transmitting to your Excellency through Colonel Durnford; and as a Son[71] of Mr. Sherrif has been employed by me for some months as an Assistant Overseer of Works on the Rideau Service, and has proved himself very useful in taking Levels &c &c. I am induced to take the liberty of suggesting that much useful information might be derived by sending Mr. Sherrif Junior, & the Guide through the proposed line of Canal, the expense of which I suppose would not exceed £150.

I trust your Excellency will excuse the liberty I take in again mentioning the subject of this Canal; but as there is generally great difficulty in procuring Guides for such a Service, & one being at present in the vicinity of By-Town I have thought it my duty to report the circumstance, in case your Excellency should wish to have Mr. Sherrif's report verified.

[Endorsed] It is desirable that the Country should be explored and the water communication traced & ascertained but it is a service for wh. I have no funds at my disposal, and should be undertaken by Upper Canada. J.K.

---

[71]Alexander, son of Charles Shirreff.

B 24   ALEXANDER SHIRREFF'S EXPLORATION FROM THE
OTTAWA RIVER TO GEORGIAN BAY, 1829
[*Sherriff* [*Shirreff*], "Topographical Notices of a Country Lying Between
the Mouth of the Rideau and Penetanguishine on Lake Huron," *Literary
and Historical Society of Quebec,* Transactions, *ser. 1, v.2, 1831, pp.
243–309*]

The extent of country along the Ottawa River, above its present
settlements, and stretching from thence to Lake Huron, forms perhaps
the most important portion of Upper Canada, yet to be explored with a
view to settlement. . . .

As to the main body of the country between Lake Huron and the
Ottawa, its southern extremity from the Simcoe waters to the last surveys on the Ottawa, has been traversed by two exploring parties,[72] and
in this direction a barren rocky range of high lands is described to
extend nearly across the whole. Respecting the lands north of this, it has
hitherto been very difficult to obtain any distinct intelligence, as they
have been frequented only by a few illiterate servants of the traders.
But it appearing almost certain, from various corroborating reports,
that immediately to the north of these explored tracts, the country
became less elevated and more fertile, the journey, of which the following observations are the result, was undertaken in order to examine into
these important circumstances.

The nature of the country as far as a journey of this kind could
ascertain it, though differing materially from what report had described,
has far exceeded my most sanguine expectations.

. . . It is a common opinion that land without a growth of hard-wood
is unworthy of occupation; but this idea, though it may generally hold
good farther south, should be entirely lost sight of in exploring these
northern parts of Canada.— The white pine frequently forms the main
growth on excellent clay soils, with but a small mixture of hardwood,
and sometimes none whatever. The red pine, also well known to be so
abundant on the Ottawa, is by no means so infallible a sign of inferior
soil as is generally asserted. It certainly grows to a considerable size on
almost bare rocks, and on arid sands, it is seen in places the sole tree
for miles. But it is on strong clays that the red pine is found in the
greatest perfection, and here it is usually accompanied with white pine
or other firs, and frequently a mixture of hard-wood. . . .

. . . In no view are the advantages of a navigation between Lake
Huron and the Ottawa more evident than with regard to the lumber
trade. By such a communication the winter supplies of the timber cutters
would be obtained from the fertile countries south and west of that great
lake, at one-third the cost now incurred in procuring them from Mont-

[72]Probably refers to Catty (B 1) and Walpole (B 17).

real, and the certain result would be an ample and steady supply of timber below the lowest of the present varying prices. If, therefore, there was no other object in view, but that of insuring a regular supply of necessaries, at the cheapest rate, for working the great red pine fields of the Ottawa, it is highly interesting to ascertain what natural facilities may exist, for a communication between Lake Huron and the upper waters of that river. . . .

. . . On the upper des Allumettes are two trading houses, one belonging to the Company,[73] called Fort William, and the other to some private traders. At these stations we had made little doubt of obtaining some distinct accounts of the country towards the Hurons [corrected to read: Huron], and also of procuring a guide acquainted with it, in our intended direction, at least until fairly past the division of the waters; but in both these particulars I was disappointed. The lands of the Algonquin Indians frequenting the Ottawa, do not extend quite to the height of land, at least on the Nesswabic;[74] and the traders on the Grand river,[75] have no communication with the Mississaguas, who hunt beyond the Algonquins. All the information obtained, therefore, amounted to this, that along the upper waters of the Nesswabic was a great extent of fertile level country, and that by following up the most westerly branch of this river, canoes could pass to the streams running in an opposite course. We had previously received information of a considerable river rising in that direction, and flowing south-westerly to lake Huron; but whether it was this or some other that might be reached by the above route, I could not ascertain.

As to a guide, after some fruitless enquiry, I was obliged to be satisfied with an Indian canoe-man, in the employ of the traders. He had travelled no part of our intended route, but was an expert tracer of hunting tracks and portages, and could act as interpreter, in obtaining information from the Indians we might fall in with. . . .

. . . To the south of lake Nipissing is a great level tract, abounding in a rich heavy soil, and extending, with little rise, many miles southward. These lands are traversed by two considerable streams, the largest, called the South river, entering lake Nipissing, not far from the outlet. As far as I could hear, this river has a course, of eighty or one hundred miles, nearly north. The source[76] is near that of a northern branch of the Muskoka, and by this route canoes sometimes cross the country towards Penetanguishine: about four days are required to reach the source of the South river. The first fifteen or twenty miles is described to be without rapids; and through very fine lands, which, indeed, continue more than

[73]Hudson's Bay Company.
[74]Now the Petawawa River.
[75]An old name for the Ottawa River.
[76]A connection could be made from the South River to the Muskoka River through Doe, Buck, Fox, Vernon, and Mary lakes, and the North Branch of the Muskoka River, but it would require much portaging.

halfway up its course, and on the upper parts of the river, the lands, though inferior, are said to be still perfectly habitable. . . .

. . . The lake[77] which we had now reached, is within the Mississagua hunting bounds, and along the south shore, I was directed to look for the portages leading to the Huron waters. From the Cedar lake, thus far, it had proved a three days' journey, travelling leisurely, though, by the help of Constant's chart, without much delay in tracing out the route. After a little searching we found a portage-path which led to a small lake, and from thence ascending a brook still belonging to the eastern waters, we soon arrived at another carrying place, which, from its westerly direction, and being distinctly tracked and marked, I did not doubt to be the proper route. Having proceeded along it nearly a mile, we were met by an Indian, only the second we had seen since leaving the Ottawa. It could not have occurred in better time, for I now found that we had missed the main route, and begun to follow an interior hunting track.

After retracing our way for a little, the Indian conducted us to an extensive piece of water, which he called Otter lake.[78] Its waters run into the Nesswabic by the most southerly of the two branches, meeting at the swamp before spoken of, and which is only five or six miles distant from Otter lake. Of course this southerly branch should have been our route; but I had no reason to regret our wandering, as it was the means of throwing us in the way of this Indian, without whose information we must have incurred much more serious delay.

He was one of the Iroquois tribe, who reside with the Algonquins, at the Lake of the Two Mountains. They are generally robust enterprising fellows; and, having no hunting territory of their own, frequently ascend the Ottawa, and passing over the grounds of their Algonquin friends, make free with the beavers and otters, on those of the Mississaguas. These Iroquois, from their roving habits, are the best guides through this part of the country. The hunter we had fallen in with, and his father, had been rambling round this neighborhood for a twelve month, and described it as *bonne terre partout partout,* and every where abounding with small lakes. A few hours journey northward from the lake, on the northern branch of the Nesswabic, (and the shores of which are above described as peculiarly fertile) he says the streams run off in a northwesterly direction, and no doubt it must be to the south river, so that it seems almost certain that there is no material alteration in the nature of the country, before reaching the waters running into lake Nipissing. Indeed, from every thing that came under my observation, there appears to be no distinct continuation of heights dividing these level tracts, either towards the north or the west.

A few weeks previous to our meeting with the Iroquois, he had made an excursion to Penetanguishine, and I now learned that a few miles more would bring us to the head of a considerable river, running in that

[77]Probably White Lake.
[78]Probably McIntosh Lake.

direction. With the lowest part of this river, however, he was not acquainted, having left it some distance above the mouth, by a route[79]
crossing to the Severn. I procured from him a chart of his whole journey,
as near as he could recollect it, and also a sketch of the various streams
of waters forming the heads of the rivers, running both ways from this
vicinity.

Round Otter lake the lands have very little rise and are timbered with
hard-wood and a considerable mixture of white pine. Where we chanced
to encamp, the soil was very good and free from stones. From this lake
their is no further ascent on the waters, in the direction we now proceeded. A still channel, in places scarcely twice the breadth of the canoe,
winds for a mile or two through a tamarac swamp, and ends in a basin
of a remarkably circular shape, near a quarter of a mile in diameter. I
think it probable that, at some points, this swamp continues un-inter-
rupted to the first western stream, not a mile distant; but, on the route,
the marsh is crossed by a sandy bank, twenty to thirty feet high, and
about fifty paces over, and close to the round pond, from which is a
miserable sinking portage, of half a mile to the first Huron water, a deep
pool two or three acres in extent. The surface of this was raised to its
utmost brim, by a beaver dam near the outlet, which accounted for the
wet and yielding nature of the portage. The beavers have, in fact, nearly
effected the junction of the Huron and Ottawa waters.

After crossing this pond, there is a further portage of about three
quarters of a mile, over an uneven rocky tract, to a lake[80] appearing to
be of considerable extent to the right of our rout, and from which flows
the river which was to bear us to lake Huron. It is here a fine clear
stream, with a gravelly channel, twenty or thirty feet wide, and already
with sufficient water, even in the dry season in which I passed, for the
easy navigation of a three-fathomed canoe, excepting at a few rippling
shoals. This river, by the traders, is called the Muskoka, after the Mississagua chief, who hunts in some part of its neighborhood. The Indians
have some other name for it, which I could not learn. . . .

. . . About the first lake on the Muskoka, the shores are rocky and
fir-timbered, and they continue so for a mile or two farther down the
stream. In half a mile it touches upon another piece of water,[81] extending to the left, and a mile further, after passing a fall two or three feet
high, is a very picturesque lake,[82] extending also to the left, apparently
several miles. Here the country resumes its fertile appearance, and
retains it, with some inconsiderable exceptions, to the mouth of the river.
Immediately beyond this lake, is a short rapid and portage, a little below
which, the river is joined by a considerable stream[83] from the north, and

[79]The route by Muldrew and Morrison lakes.
[80]This may be Blackbear Lake.
[81]Littledoe Lake.
[82]Joe Lake.
[83]Potter Creek.

soon after enters a fine open piece of water,[84] about two miles in extent. Within three miles below this, are two more small lakes,[85] and from this point, which is about twelve miles from the first basin, the water ceases to widen out in this way, now forming a regular river channel, in which are only three more lakes on the whole course.

A little above the lowest of these basins, the Madawaska route, by which we recrossed the country, strikes off from the channel of the Muskoka . . .

. . . I now return to the Muskoka:— As already noticed, this river ceases to widen out into lakes, about twelve miles from the first one on the route, and from this point it continues to flow in a regular channel for about twenty miles. On the first seven or eight miles of this space, there are several small rapids, and for the ensuing ten or twelve, is a smooth stream, winding in a most extraordinary manner, through a level sandy valley, timbered chiefly with balsam, tamarac, and poplar, beyond which, however, the hard-wood rising grounds are seen, seldom a mile distant on either side. The river here is of a very uniform breadth, from sixty to eighty feet; the depth is six feet and upwards quite across the channel, and the current about one mile per hour.

This winding channel is terminated by a great and sudden descent in the river. First is a little rapid water, and then succeeds a fall, nearly perpendicular, of about thirty feet. Below this are some rapids, for half a mile, which suddenly and [corrected to read: ends] in a great slanting fall, descending perhaps fifty feet. Neither of the portages at these falls exceed a furlong in length. On the lower one is a curious variety of the rock. When broken, it is of a light carmine colour, and resembling free-stone in the grain. Not much of it is seen above ground, but it appears to be in regular beds, three or four feet thick, and though rather hard near the surface, it would probably be found, on more thorough examination, a fit and beautiful material for building.

These falls may be considered as the western verge of the interior table lands. In a direct line this point is probably about twenty miles from the division of the waters. The route of the Muskoka, thus far, continues nearly in the same direction as that on the upper parts of the Nesswabic, and the whole direct breadth of the level country on this route appears to be about fifty miles. The perpendicular rise within this space, from either side to the height of land, I should not suppose to exceed seventy feet.

The streams running in every direction from these uplands, have a much more steady supply of water, and are far purer than the lower tributaries of the Ottawa. The channels are generally very moderate in breadth, appearing to be little troubled with floods, which, from the marks along the shores, seldom seem to rise above two feet (perpendicularly) in the streams, and fifteen or eighteen inches in the lakes.

[84]Canoe Lake.
[85]South Tea Lake.

These favorable distinctions are readily accounted for in the form and nature of this interior country, consisting of a vast level, generally with a light free soil devoid of marsh, and interspersed with hundreds of small deep reservoirs, retaining and refining the water again and again, before it passes to the main rivers.

The singular facilities which this plain country possesses for water communication, within itself, must be evident. Were there any possibility of leading a population into it, the channels and basins of still water, intersecting it in every direction, might quickly be completed into a ramification of water ways, which for general utility, and natural beauty could scarcely find a parallel. Sufficiently deep and expansive for the largest steam-boat, and yet too small, or too well sheltered by the bold shores, to be dangerous for the smallest skiff. But without some main line of navigation from the inhabited parts of Canada, this pleasant and commodious region must, for obvious reasons, remain a desert.

In less than half a mile below the great fall, a narrow lake[86] is entered, which appears to extend a number of miles north and south, along the base of the ridge, but we saw neither extremity, merely passing with the flow of the water about a mile across the middle of the lake. From hence the river continues a rapid descent for about eight miles, through fine hard-wood forests to the next lake. In this space the fall, which must be considerable, is principally in rapids, it being the only part of the river where there is any considerable descent of this kind.

The piece of water[87] to which this leads, with its surrounding shores, is the finest in appearance which we met with. It extends about ten miles nearly south, and towards the lower part is a wide inlet to the east, much farther than I could distinguish. Several islands of various sizes, rise boldly from the water, and in the entrance of the great eastern bay, just mentioned, there is one[88] appearing to contain three or four hundred acres of good land. On the west, the shores rise quickly to a considerable height, timbered with hard-wood and white pine. On the east, they form a long gradual slope of the richest appearance, and without a fir for miles.

A large southern branch of these waters flows into the eastern arm of this lake.[89] Its course is through several considerable lakes, and by it canoes may pass to the Trent or lake Simcoe. I did not see this branch, but was informed of it by a trader well acquainted with this vicinity. He further asserted that saltpetre is found on a certain part of the stream, not far from its mouth. The fine central basin which receives these rivers

[86]Oxtongue Lake.
[87]Lake of Bays.
[88]Bigwin Island.
[89]The reference is not clear. Shirreff may be confused by the Black River which rises not far south of the Lake of Bays and flows into the Severn River. The only major river flowing into the eastern arm of the Lake of Bays is Hollow River. This supposed southern branch is shown on Shirreff's map, and in more detail on that by Maria Knowles (Plate III) where it is marked South Branch.

appears to have been long a principal station of the traders. There are here vestiges of two old establishments, besides a commodious house in good repair, but deserted when we passed.

The Muskoka flows from the southern extremity of the lake, apparently doubled in size. It is now from one to two hundred feet wide, containing about as much water as the Rideau, and continually interrupted by small falls, with here and there a short rapid, among which obstructions there is seldom four miles of still water together. The channel between the falls is alternately composed of sand and a firm compact gravel. The portages, which are now well tracked, are generally over even ground, the shores of the river being seldom rough or precipitous, even near the falls and rapids. Considering the great descent of the country, the canoe route is as good as could be looked for, consisting, with little exception, of smooth runs and short portages, and this continues to be its character to the end. In returning we made our way up the river about as expeditiously as we had descended.

This succession of small falls continues for about twenty miles from the Trading lake, when the river again makes a great and sudden descent.[90] There are first two falls, from fifteen to twenty feet in height, and then a sloping fall of of [sic] sixty or seventy, all within a quarter of a mile, and in a straight range down the ridge, forming together a wild interesting scene. A little below this, the river is joined by a large branch from the north, and it now winds gently with a broad deep and still channel to its last and largest lake,[91] about six miles distant from the great fall.

There are altogether fourteen portages on this river, and the difference in level of the two lakes, is, I think, about two hundred and fifty feet. The channel here is not remarkably winding except at two points, for a few miles. The course continues much the same as on the upper parts of the river, averaging about S.S.W. until half way between the lakes, when it makes a decided turn nearly westward for the remaining part of the route. The lands retain their promising appearance along this part of the river, being almost every where covered with timber of nearly the same description as that in the centre of the country. In returning I examined the vicinity of most of the portages, and almost invariably found a light soil of fair quality, though frequently uneven and strong [corrected to read: stony], as might be expected near the falls.

The large stream which flows in from the north at the lower part of this run, is the same by which, and the south river, (as before hinted) there is a canoe route to lake Nipissing. On a lake[92] about two days

[90]South or Muskoka Falls.
[91]Lake Muskoka.
[92]Possibly Doe Lake, which connects with the Magnetawan and could be reached by portages from the North Branch of the Muskoka River by way of Fox and Buck Lakes; but more than "2 days travel" would be required. C. F. Miles, in his survey of McMurrich Township in 1870 mentioned a route through Doe Lake often used by the Parry Sound Indians.

journey up this branch, is a trading station to which the common route is, not by the Muskoka, but along a considerable river flowing out of, or through a large lake not far to the westward of the station, and entering lake Huron, (as I am told,) about thirty miles from the French river. It is called the Neyetewa, and the country along its upper parts, and on the northern branch of the Muskoka, is said to be much of the same nature as that which we passed through.

The last Muskoka lake is a great body of water extending chiefly north-westerly, and containing hundreds of islands, some of them very large, but appearing mostly barren. From the entrance of the river, the route runs westerly through the islands, about ten miles to the outlet of the lake, which we found without much delay, having fortunately met with an Indian, (only the third we had seen,) the night before, who directed us how to steer, and but for this, we should, in all probability, have spent days in searching for it. It was impossible to form any idea of the extent of this piece of water to the northward, on account of the multitude of islands. To the south west, it extends about ten miles from the outlet. In this direction it is less crowded with islands, and has a fine appearance. Where the main shores could be distinguished, they generally seemed to be of a habitable nature, continuing round the water in an even moderate elevation, with, however, a greater proportion of white pine than I had before usually observed. At the lower end of the lake, the appearance is not favorable, the growth, as far as seen, being of the fir kind.

From the southern extremity of the lake to the Severn river, the distance is only eight or nine miles, and over this space is the common route by which the fur traders reach the waters of the Muskoka. From the lake is a portage of about three miles, leading to a rivulet which passes through two small lakes, and enters the Severn, half a mile above the fifth portage from Penetanguishine bay. On my return I ascended the Severn and regained the Muskoka by this route. The long portage, close to the large lake, is mostly over a good, though uneven soil, but from that to the Severn, the country gradually assumes a barren aspect. Along this river from the fifth portage to its mouth, a distance of fifteen or sixteen miles, the shores are uniformly barren, consisting, in fact, generally of solid rock, even on the smooth water. The limestone of Penetanguishine bay does not extend up the Severn, the stone of this river appearing exactly of the same nature as along the Muskoka. Both streams evidently flow from the same ridge of country, though the sources of the Severn, are without doubt in a much lower part of it. The elevation, however, of lake Simcoe above the Huron, must be considerable, there being seven portages altogether to this lake, and five of these which I passed, certainly form an ascent not far from one hundred and twenty or thirty feet.

At the outlet of the large Muskoka lake, is a fine fall[93] sixteen or tweenty [sic] feet high, with a heavy body of water. The river now

[93]Bala Falls.

appears to contain considerably more water than the Severn, and probably three times as much as the Rideau. A mile or two below this fall, the channel is divided. The principal branch[94] runs north-westerly, and enters the Huron at Moose point, said to be about thirty mils [sic] from Penetanguishine. The lower branch appearing to lead off about one third of the water, continues in a westerly course thirteen or fourteen miles to a small sequestered bay on the lake, about ten miles north of the same place.

We followed the lower stream. There are on it ten short portages chiefly passing moderate falls, which, with some rapid water, form a descent from the Muskoka lake, of probably about one hundred and fifty feet. The breadth of this channel is very irregular, particularly towards its outlet, where it spreads out into ponds full of rocky islands. The lands along it continue good, and even appear to increase in fertility as we approach the lake. The soil at the portages is richer than I had generally observed close to the river, and often free from stones to the brink of the falls and rapids. Within three or four miles of lake Huron, a sudden change takes place, and nothing is now seen but low, solid, and frequently bare masses of rock. We reached the [corrected to read: this] immense expanse of water the seventeenth of September, the eighteenth day from the Ottawa, and a long swell from the boundless north-west drove our now little canoe speedily into the bay of Penetanguishine. . . .

. . . With regard to the nature of the whole body of the country, extending from the sources of the Madawaska to lake Nipissing, and from lake Huron to the Ottawa, I cannot, from merely passing through it in one or two lines, pretend to speak with certainty. The central part, however, of this wide region is, without doubt, generally good, there being, as already stated, every reason to suppose that the soil increases in fertility as we descend from the elevated tracts on the head waters of the Nesswabic and Muskoka, towards lake Nipissing. As to that part nearer lake Huron, and south of the French river, I have obtained but little distinct account, which is favorable, however, as far as it goes. On the whole, every thing I have seen or heard, enables me at least to state that in this, hitherto, unnoticed part of Canada, a fine habitable country will be found, to the extent of millions of acres; and I have now only to express my hope, that it will, ere long, be rendered accessible to population.

B 25   HOUSE OF ASSEMBLY ADDRESS REQUESTING EXPLORATION
OF LANDS NORTH OF LAKE HURON
[*Upper Canada, House of Assembly,* Journal, *1833–4, pp. 59–60, 63*]

To His Excellency Sir John Colborne,[95] Knight, Commander of the most Honorable Military Order of the Bath, Lieutenant Governor of

[94]Now known as the Moon River.
[95]Sir John Colborne, later first Baron Seaton (1778–1863), was Lieutenant Governor of Upper Canada from 1828 to 1836.

the Province of Upper Canada, Major General Commanding His Majesty's Forces therein, &c., &c., &c.

May it please your Excellency:

We, His Majesty's most dutiful and loyal Subjects, the Commons House of Assembly of the Province of Upper Canada, in Provincial Parliament assembled, respectfully beg leave, to request that Your Excellency will be pleased, during the ensuing season, to send out an exploring party to penetrate from different given points on the north shore of Lake Huron,[96] in continuous right lines, some fifty or sixty miles into the heart of the country. We beg permission to suggest, that if a practical Surveyor were sent out to produce the lines, and take field notes of the soil, timber, water, &c., and a gentleman of science were to accompany him, and report upon the geology and mineralogy of the interior, as well as on the borders of the Lake, the results could not fail to be highly beneficial to the interests of this Province, as well as those of the Empire at large, and that the expenses which might be incurred thereby be paid out of the Territorial Revenue.

Commons House of Assembly   Archibald McLean
4th January, 1834   Speaker

B 26   COLONEL WILLIAM ROWAN[97] TO LIEUTENANT JOHN CARTHEW[98]
       [*P.A.O., Crown Lands Papers, shelf 72, box 5*]

Govt House
14 July 1835

With reference to the accompanying copy of a communication to the Surveyor General respecting the information required to be obtained of the country, to the Northward of the shore of Lake Huron; I am directed to acquaint you that the Lieut Governor requests you will proceed to Penetanguishine immediately and lose no time in proceeding with the party placed under your charge, to explore the lands traced in the Diagram forwarded to the Surveyor General for your use. The chief objects to which your attention will be directed are the following   1st to report on the capacity of the country required to be explored, as regards the interests of settlers.   2dly Its Topographical outline as regards the courses of rivers, and dimensions of lakes and creeks, the bearings and relative altitude of the ranges of mountains and hills.   3dly To determine the latitude and longitude of as many points as may insure geographical accuracy in exploring the country.   4th To report on the geological and

---

[96]The phrase "north shore of Lake Huron" was frequently used to include the east shore of Georgian Bay, as shown in the instructions to Carthew (B 26).

[97]William Rowan (1789–1879) was civil and military secretary to Sir John Colborne. He was knighted in 1856.

[98]John Carthew was commissioned Lieutenant in the Royal Navy, November 24, 1815.

mineralogical structure of the country. Lieut Baddely[99] of the Rl Engineers will be responsible for the geological survey and general report of the country. The two Depy Surveyors Mr. Hawkins[100] and Mr. Richardson[101] will with your assistance run a line, NW in prolongation of the western boundary of "Rama" till it strikes the French River. It is supposed that this line will be generally about thirty miles from Lake Huron.

Great accuracy will be required in running this line, as it will remain as the base line of all future observations and operations. Lieut. Baddely will probably extend his observations as far as he may find it convenient to the North-east of this line towards Lake Nipissing. You will give such attention in examining the country to the South-west in the direction of Lake Huron, as will convey correct information of the general character of the lands between the base line and Lake Huron as far as French River.

The two Depy Surveyors will be employed in running the line, while you and Lieut. Baddely are making your observations on the country on each side of it; and will be required to make field notes as they proceed, and one of them may occasionally diverge for the purpose of examining the country to the Lake Huron side of the line, and of reporting on the quality of the soil.

Mr Beaman,[102] who will have charge of the conveyance of the provisions, will proceed to the points, which you may on consultation with him fix with the provisions and take care that you are constantly supplied; he probably will meet you on Moon River, or any River to which it may be more convenient to convey the supplies.

By leaving provisions at the entrance of the River, on the left bank and then proceeding up the River, to the points near which he may suppose the base line may run, there can scarcely any delay take place in your receiving supplies.

The number of men to be employed in carrying provisions, and as axe-men and boat men will not exceed fifteen. When you arrive on

[99]Frederick Henry Baddeley (d. 1880?) became Lieutenant in the Royal Engineers in 1814, Captain in 1835, Major in 1846, Colonel in 1854, Major General in 1856. In 1828 he was on an exploring expedition in the Saguenay country; in 1835 he was sent to Toronto to take part in the exploration with Carthew; and in 1837 was Commanding Royal Engineer in Upper Canada.

[100]William Hawkins (1807–1868) came to Canada from Ireland in 1832. He qualified as a Deputy Provincial Surveyor on October 31, 1832, and for the rest of his life was active in government surveys and private practice. Hawkins' report of the survey of 1835 is printed with those of Carthew and Baddeley (Upper Canada, House of Assembly, *Journal*, 1836–7, app. 37).

[101]Samuel Richardson (1796?–1843), land surveyor, came to Canada from Wales and lived for several years at Penetanguishene and later at Kempenfelt Bay. He carried on a number of surveys in the Lake Simcoe and Penetanguishene area. He was the treasurer of Simcoe County at the time of his death.

[102]Eli Beman (1799?–1869), son of Elisha Beman of Newmarket. He had a schooner on Lake Simcoe before the introduction of steamers, and in 1831 was government contractor for building Indian houses along the Coldwater Road.

French River, if you can examine the country, from Lake Nipissing to "La Cloche", and that on the shore of Lake Nipissing the value of your report will be much increased.

You will endeavour to complete this survey without the least delay. The following are the rates at which the party are to be paid.

	£	s
Lieut Carthew		
Lieut Baddely	1—	5—each—per diem
Two Depy surveyors—	1—	each
Mr. Beaman————————————		15——
Two chain-bearers		
at the usual rate		
Axemen and voyageurs at————		3–9————

B 27   SELECTIONS FROM F. H. BADDELEY'S EXPLORING REPORT
[*P.A.O., F. H. Baddeley, Exploring Report; also printed with slight changes in Upper Canada, House of Assembly,* Journal, *1836–7, app. 37*]

[July 16, 1835] I left the Capital of Upper Canada, in company with the other gentlemen of the party, for Lake Simcoe, in the neighbourhood of whose waters, it was proposed that our labours should commence. Our party from hence consisted of Lieutenant Carthew R.N. (in charge of the whole) myself as geologist, and Messrs. Richardson and Hawkins surveyors.

. . .

August 6th. Upon departing from our encampment this morning, we soon after (one quarter of a mile) came upon the left bank of a River, whose course is westward, width about one hundred feet— depth considerable— (upwards of ten feet) current slow and water blackish; from the latter appearance it has obtained the name of the Black River, and it is, I believe the one which Lieutenant Walpole Royal Engineers ascended in his way to the Ottawa about nine years ago.[103] We followed the course of this river downwards, for about two miles of very broken rocky country covered with soft timber, and a sandy soil, and then reached a fall across which Mr. Richardson was attempting to throw a tree in order to pass his party; . . .

. . .

[103]It seems unlikely that Lieutenant Walpole was on the Black River at that time. In 1826 he was examining the rivers to the east of Lake Simcoe (P.A.C., C 428, pp. 52-62) and in 1827 he went up the Talbot River, not the Black River (B 17). Carthew may be confusing Walpole with Lieutenants Marlow and Smith who went up the Black River in the summer of 1826 (B 7).

August 20th. . . . I learn from Croteau[104] that about eight years ago he crossed from the Boncher river on Lake Chat, to Lake Simcoe. He started the 15th. August from the head of the Chat rapid, met Lieut. Walpole[105] R.E. on the 12th Septr. on height of land or the dividing ridge, between the Ottawa and Lake Huron, reached Lake Simcoe, by passing down the Talbot river, on the 27th September. He described the land through which he passed as in general very good, but the best he noticed was on the Madawaska river (Large Prairie) he noticed very little rock the heights or dividing ridge, consists of land covered with a fine growth of maple. The longest portage met with was nine miles on the Talbot river, through excellent land. He adds that in the Spring of the year you may pass in canoe from Lake Simcoe to By Town in eight or nine days. . . .

August 21st. . . . At some falls, about six miles above our last Encampment, meridional observations for latitude were taken; about one mile and a half above these falls a fork in the river[106] was reached, having been informed that the eastern-most branch[107] had been ascended by Lieut Walpole on his way to the Ottawa, we chose the westernmost, which conducted us by a very winding and tortuous course through some of the best alluvial lands we had seen from the beginning judging from level timber and the absence of rock: the soil however wherever pierced and wherever seen on the banks was found to be sandy.

. . .

August 25th . . . We reached another fork[108] in the afternoon and observed that immediately after taking its western branch, that the river had lost much of its breadth and depth. Since navigating above the first fork we met with few appearances which would lead us to suppose that the river is much frequented even by Indians; but on a portage round a fall we reached to-day we were somewhat surprised to meet with the work of white men: we observed several large trees had been cut down, a labour which indians never undertake, contenting themselves for firing with the smaller ones, for cutting which their tommy axes are better adapted; the form of the camp, also, hard by, was another sign that the white man had been here— These were the only signs of his presence we saw on the river. . . .

[104]Croteau served as canoe man, explorer, and guide.
[105]Miss Saunders (*Algonquin Story*, p. 15) assumes that Croteau accompanied Walpole, which does not agree with Baddeley's comment.
[106]Black River.
[107]If Baddeley is referring to Lieutenants Marlow and Smith (see footnote 103) this supports the view that they turned up Anson Creek at its junction with the Black River.
[108]A fork in the Black River.

August 30th. . . . Upon leaving this lake[109] we took a western course for about one mile of land partly rocky and partly good, when we reached another lake, which we crossed and came to an indian portage on the western side where we encamped

Upon reaching this spot Croteau recognized it as one he had visited about four years ago with his young wife, and the recollection evidently gave him pleasure he was then on his way from Lake Simcoe to Lake Nagatoagomon;[110] he considers the distance from hence to Lake Simcoe (Lake Coochaching) to be about thirty miles on a Southern course— Lake Nagatoagomon is he says about twenty miles to the north east of us— In starting from Lake Coochaching the first fifteen miles are almost all rock, thence to Lake Nagatoagoman, maple is greatly the prevailing timber. In the whole interval between the two lakes, he traversed twenty one lakes the largest of which was seven mile long and is ten miles on this side Coochaching; he has been often on this lake we are upon in his way to the upper lake, to which it is the usual indian track. A river[111] runs out of Nagatoagoman into the Severn, which we shall (according to Croteau) probably fall in with on our way to the line.

August 31st. Coursed the Lake this morning, while so employed we observed a doe drinking on its borders, we stealthily gained the shore and Croteau with indian caution stole upon the poor animal and shot her a useless sacrifice of life as we had as much provisions as we could carry, and after partaking of one mess of venison we were obliged to abandon the rest. The lake we are upon is of a rounded form and about three miles in circumference; its shores are partly rocky and partly swampy and we observed no good land close upon them. . . .

This river Nagatoagoman[112] we are now in is the same as that described by Alexr Sherriff, Esqr. in his Topographical notices, inserted in the 2nd Volume of the Transactions of the literary and Historical Society of Quebec and commencing at page 243; he there calls it the Muskoka river but hints, that among the indians, it has another name. It flows from a large lake of the same name and is where we struck it from one hundred and fifty to five hundred feet wide and differs from the one we have just left being larger, much less winding and in having several rapids and falls; the shores are also are [sic] often steep and rocky on this river neither of which characters belong to the other In the intervals between the falls and rapids the waters are sluggish and deep. The timber on the shores as noticed to day, was of a mixed description both hard and soft, but the elevated portions seem in general clothed for the most part with maple— soil as usual, almost always sandy.

In descending we saw Mr Richardson's name, with the date (24th

[109]One of the small lakes in the northern part of Oakley Township.
[110]Lake of Bays.
[111]There is no river which runs from the Lake of Bays to the Severn.
[112]Muskoka River. They were on the South Branch.

[corrected to read 23d] August) blazed on a tree and afterwards Mr Carthew's (20th August) patches of alluvial land one or two acres in depth were frequently seen at the salient and re-entering angles of the river but this feature is common enough to many rivers; we stopt to encamp at a granitic point on the right bank of the river.

Note. In passing we beg to call the readers attention to Mr. Sherriff's communication as one well deserving of his perusal we think however generally that he has drawn too favourable an inference from level and quality of timber neglecting the more important consideration of soil which almost every where throughout the country appears to be excessively light and sandy and often very shallow.

September 2nd. Upon sending out the men to notice the land they brought back the intelligence that to south westward a fine timbered slightly hilly rockless land was met with for the distance travelled (one third of a mile) the soil of which was a deep clayey loam of a yellowish colour a specimen of which was brought back. Croteau who went S.E. about half a mile, found good timber, but very rocky land.

Soon after leaving our Encampment we reached a large fall,[113] over granite the whole descent of water here could not be less than fifty feet near the foot of these we again saw Mr R's initials and date (24th. August) a little below this we stopped to read the following notice "Exploring party propose passing the river one quarter of a mile below this at the falls— 20th. August." Accordingly we soon reached these falls,[114] which consist of three distinct descents of water in all I conclude amounting to one hundred and fifty feet; they are by far the largest we have seen and rush through rocky scarps of gneiss and mica slate, or hornblende schist. At the head of the middle fall the line passes and here, across a gut about ten feet wide, we found a couple of spars over which the line party had passed At the base of the last fall, the most considerable of the three, we discontinued taking courses in consequence of supposing Mr. Carthew had rendered that labour unnecessary. Upon resuming our voyage, in the interval of an hour, we cut the line again twice, which shows that the river must here trend northward as well as westward. About one eighth of a mile above the last intersection we observed a river[115] coming in on the right bank apparently from the northwestward and thinking to strike the line again by this route we ascended it about one mile and a half, as far as some falls[116] (fifty feet descent) but finding it took us too much to the eastward, we returned to the main river and proceeded down it about eight miles to a large Lake ("Muskoka" according to Mr Sherriffs "Chimie" as we were informed) on an Island near the eastern side of which we encamped. We are now on our way to Penetanguishene for provisions not having a sufficient

[113]Trethewey Falls.
[114]South or Muskoka Falls.
[115]Muskoka River, North Branch.   [116]Bracebridge Falls.

quantity left to undertake any fresh excursion and hoping to meet Mr Carthew on the way (who we have ascertained from a note we found fastened to a pole is expected with a fresh supply for the line) which meeting would prevent any loss of time on our part. The river we were desirous of ascending[117] is evidently the one Mr Sherriff speaks of at page 304 as leading to the south river which flows into Lake Nipising. In our descent to the lake the land on both sides of the river was observed to be very level, low and usually well timbered and we noticed clay as forming much of its soil one of great rarity in the country we have hitherto traversed; rock also was not seen another favourable sign: towards the mouth of the river we passed one or two old trading posts now deserted and covered with brush wood

The Lake we are upon is evidently a very large one and is full of rocky islands; the rock upon which we are encamped is composed of granite and gneiss, the former traversing, the latter, in veins usually composed of large crystals of red felspar and white quartz.

September 3rd. As the lake we have to traverse is liable, like most large lakes, to be rendered impassable for canoes by comparatively light breezes, we rose very early with the intention of availing ourselves of the calm which usually prevails at this time of the year before the Sun rises, so early indeed as to catch a fine large pickerel napping in a hole in the rock within reach of the paddle with which he was despatched; from the appearance of this fish in such a place and from the quantity of fish bones noticed on the rocks, we are disposed to think that the lake must be very fishy. Upon embarking we steered through a great number of islands towards the northwestern end of the lake for about six miles but failing to discover the portage we were in search of, and seeing nothing of Mr. Carthew, I thought it better to return to the Line and take my chance of getting a supply of provisions there, and in case of not succeeding to return to the lake and make a second effort to find the portage. Accordingly we reached the last intersection of the Line and river in time to allow of a noon day's observation for latitude after which Croteau was dispatched forward along the line with a letter and we encamped on the shore to await his return. In my letter an application was made for provisions to enable me to ascend the river to eastward of us or the one which Mr Sherriff was informed led towards Lake Nipising.

September 4th. We have much hardwood at our encampment the soil is a reddish or yellowish sandy loam— Walked about one mile along the line and saw a tree marked 26 miles from N E corner of Mara, August 2nd, from which I infer that the party is some distance forward— Met with the same description of land as at our encampment. Upon calculating my observations for latitude taken here and at the Black river I find the results agree nearly with the measured distance

117Muskoka River, North Branch.

September 5th. Impatiently expecting Croteau's return I walked forward again on the line to meet him; he overtook me on my way back and was accompanied by Baker and an other man of the name of Lamorie, an old employé of Capt. Bayfield's, when that officer was engaged surveying Lake Huron. Croteau brought letters from Messrs. Richardson and Hawkins, by which I learn that they are encamped on a lake[118] about forty two miles from the starting point and consequently seventeen miles from our encampment that they have barely enough provisions for themselves. In consequence I am obliged to return to Penetanguishene and as Croteau and Paressinue will not engage to return I must take the other two men with me, there being dearth of hands at the settlement, all being engaged in the fisheries. The weather being rainey we remained encamped the rest of the day.

September 6th. A rainey night is succeeded by a rainey morning, tired of our encampment, however, we desire to proceed having no courses to take. Shortly after noon we reached Lake Chomie, or Muskoken, or Kitshisagin[119] for it has all these names, the latter implying "big mouth of the river". . . .

September 7th. We started again this morning in search of the portage leading to some small lakes, and ultimately to the Severn, but our guide, Croteau (usually a sure one) carried us a second time too much to the northward in which direction we passed Island after Island; these islands which have the same bearing longitudinally as the lake, northward and southward are as before said rocky. . . . Losing all hope of finding the portage by following our guide I assumed the direction myself and turning back proceeded towards the southwest angle of the lake instead of the northwest. Fearing however to overlook the portage, which we were informed was at the bottom of a small bay, we steered into every inlet large or small we met with, which gave us an opportunity of observing the remarkably indented nature of the western shore of this lake and of forming some opinion of its extent. Should the eastern shore be incisive, like the western which I believe it is not the lake following all its bendings must be one hundred miles in circumference; it is I should think at least twenty five miles long by eight or ten wide and is very little smaller than Lake Simcoe, from which it is seperated to the northward by an interval of about twenty miles; this interval should be explored as well as the eastern shore of the lake in which direction as far as could be noticed from the lake, favourable appearances were seen, not so however to westward, where all is rock and evergreen. After a hard days paddling we at last reached the portage, and puting on shore we crossed it, a distance of about two and a half miles The first portion was through hardwood land which soon becomes swampy and ultimately rocky The

[118]Probably Skeleton Lake.
[119]Printed copy reads "Kelshesagin."

portage terminates at the south eastern extremity of a rather long but narrow lake[120] which we crossed in a few minutes and landing again on the opposite side encamped for the night.

September 8th. Crossing the portage, about half a mile of swampy land, we came upon another small lake which also crossing to its outlet, a small river, we descended it to a small fall, where we stopt to breakfast. The country we are in is most barren, consisting of little besides rocks. To reach the Severn we made four more portages none of them long and always on the continuation of the river on which one or two more lakes occur, the last extending to the Severn the distance between which and the Muskoka lake by this route may be about nine miles I was much disappointed in the size of the Severn, for excepting in the places where it expands into lake like extensions of water, which are somewhat of frequent occurrence, it is not much wider than the Black river, one of its tributaries whereas from having heard so much of it, I had supposed it to be a large river. We are informed that a remarkable difference is perceived in the colour and transparency of the two streams where they first attempt to mingle their waters, which is done slowly and reluctantly, both preserving for some distance below their confluence, their distinguishing characteristics; blueness and clearness on the part of the Severn, and darkness and opaqueness on that of the Black river. Nothing can exceed the sterile aspect of the northern shore of the Severn from the point we struck it to almost its mouth in the Matchadash, a distance of about twenty miles, except it be the southern, the former is clothed with some degree of vegetation but the latter, its aspect of native sterility apparently assisted by the operation of recent fire, presents one almost *vegetationless* scene from one extremity to the other. . . .

At the mouth of the river are saw mills[121] built by government, but now going to decay it is said that the pine which was brought down the river for the supply of the mills, was for the most part bad, we can easily give credit to this report, for during our journey we have seen very little good for anything; that we met with was usually crooked and full of gum knots. . . .

September 13th. Early this morning I baptized the quarry with rum to prevent the recurrence of intoxication which I had observed in one of the men the preceding evening, and having entered into the journal a memorandum never to take any more on similar excursions, we embarked . . .

September 14th. This morning I proceeded with the indian to the mouth of the river, leaving Mr Beaman to follow; we reached the indian wigwams after about one hour and a half hard paddling. The object of my visit was to procure if possible a good canoe man and guide, and

120Muldrew Lake.
121Built about 1830 (G 1).

attempts had been already made to hire our indian visiter, which were now renewed, but womans influence, strong even here, prevailed and we were disappointed.

I did not hear the name of this river,[122] the indians of whom we made many enquiries, either would not or could not understand us. Upon the arrival of Mr Beaman, I decided to ascend it with the hope of meeting Mr Carthew on his return from the Line, and with the intention of reaching Lake Huron by another river which descends from a lake we shall pass through, according to the information we have received, but as the early part of our rout has been coursed by Mr Carthew, in his ascent to the line, it is, as before, unnecessary to repeat the task

About three quarters of a mile from our starting point, which may be half a mile above the actual mouth of the river in the lake, we met with rapids, with a portage on the right bank, over bare granite; one mile above these rapids, falls occur, where the land is very rocky on both sides; the portage here is short but steep, and a mass of granite divides the falls into two parts; proceeding we soon after saw a river[123] from northward foaming in at right angles to our course and where there is a portage, but observing the waters we are in to flow uninterruptedly from the Eastward we pursued them through a somewhat contracted channel at first, between rocks, but which brought us into a lake like expansion, which we pursued for two or three miles, when finding no outlet at its upper end and that it became shallow and full of rushes we returned again to our Encampment.

September 15th. A white frost on our blankets this morning, and a thick vapour rising from the river— Thermometer at 6 AM 30 in air 55 in the river. Seeing nothing of Mr Carthew, I thought it advisable to recommend Mr Beaman to forward a portion of the provisions intended for the line, up the river with the hope of falling in with him, and I decided to accompany the same; ascending therefore as far as the portage we saw yesterday, we crossed it and found it very short. On re-embarking, our course upwards was found to lay between N.70 E.and S.70 E. and soon after we reached rapids and falls where there is another portage (short) on the right bank as before, but rough steep and rocky; about another mile further other falls or bad rapids occur; here the river turns to the right and enters a succession of Lakes in one of the largest[124] of these, while exploring for an outlet, we met Mr Carthew on his return from the line, who requested me to go back with him to the mouth of the river. The aspect of the country we have passed through to-day, as seen from these waters is rocky & infertile. We reached our encampment a little after dusk

[122]Muskoka River.

[123]Muskoka River. The Muskoka, coming in from the north, and the Gibson River from the east meet at this point. Baddeley proceeded east by the Gibson River a short distance, then returned to the junction and turned north.

[124]Probably Go Home Lake.

September 16th. The bare rock we are encamped upon, and which as before said is about half a mile up the river, is a gneiss veined by granite. The men were very successful in catching black bass at the foot of the first falls above, an occupation which contrary winds forced upon them. Mr Carthew and I were engaged tracing off two or three copies of an indian plan of the country, furnished by Payette, a half breed of considerable intelligence, who with some difficulty, and not without increase of wages, was inclined to remain with us; his presence, however, was essential as we had no indian guide capable of taking his place, and when appealed to by Mr Carthew as to the expediency of retaining him, I readily advised it, and should if his retaining fee had been higher, as the safety of the party on the line depends upon having him; an error was committed when hiring the men, in not having bound them by a written agreement for a specified time, the consequence of which was that as the fishing season approached many were desirous of leaving us and some did so; we were also too late in our selection as most of the best men were engaged. . . .

Quebec 8th March 1836

B 28 "AN ACT TO PROVIDE FOR A SURVEY OF THE OTTAWA RIVER, AND THE COUNTRY BORDERING ON IT, TOGETHER WITH THE COUNTRY AND WATERS LYING BETWEEN THAT RIVER AND LAKE HURON" [*Upper Canada,* Statutes, *1836–7, 7 Will. IV, c. 57*]

(Passed 4th March, 1837.)

WHEREAS it is highly important to the Commercial interests of this Province, that the River Ottawa, and its tributary Streams, and the Country lying between the River Ottawa and Lake Huron, be Surveyed, and efficient measures taken to ascertain the practicability of making a Navigable Communication between the two Waters: *And Whereas,* it is necessary to provide for the expense of such Survey: *Be it therefore enacted* . . . That it shall and may be lawful for the Governor, Lieutenant Governor, or Person Administering the Government of this Province, to pay a sum not exceeding Three Thousand Pounds Currency, out of such monies as are in his hands, and unappropriated, to be applied in the employing of a Surveyor and Engineer, to ascertain the nature of the country lying between the River Ottawa and Lake Huron, and to report the practicability of establishing a communication by Water between the same.

II. *And be it further enacted by the authority aforesaid,* That it shall and may be lawful for the Governor, Lieutenant Governor, or Person Administering the Government of this Province for the time being, to nominate and appoint, under His Hand and Seal, such person or persons as he shall think fit to be Commissioners,[125] and in case any vacancy or

[125]The Commissioners appointed were John Macaulay, John S. Cartwright, and F. H. Baddeley.

vacancies should happen in the said Board of Commissioners, by death, resignation or removal from Office, it shall and may be lawful for the Governor, Lieutenant Governor, or Person Administering the Government, to fill such vacancy or vacancies.

III. *And be it further enacted by the authority aforesaid,* That the said Commissioners shall be, and they are hereby authorised, to engage an Engineer and Surveyor, and pay them such salaries as they may deem just and reasonable, to carry into effect the Provisions of this Act.

IV. *And be it further enacted by the authority aforesaid,* That so soon as the said Survey shall have been completed, the Commissioners shall, without delay, transmit a report of all proceedings had under the provisions of this Act, together with a detailed statement of the expenses attending the same, to the Governor, Lieutenant Governor, or Person Administering the Government, to be laid before the Legislature, at its next Session. . . .

B 29   DAVID THOMPSON[126] TO JOHN MACAULAY[127]
[*P.A.O., Macaulay Papers*]

Kingston May 30. 1837.

On Sunday morning I arrived here, and put up at Mr. Donalds and yesterday at 9 Am I walked over the Bridge to see Captain Badely, and after much conversation on the business in which he detailed all he had done &c he remarked, that he could not go on the Survey &c himself, as the business of the Engineers Department devolved on him, that I might depend on his vote, and that having your vote also, I might consider myself as being the Engineer and Surveyor, but that no plan of operations could be finally settled until the return of Mr. Cartwright;[128] he fully agreed with me that it was not necessary for a Commissioner to go until a Route had been examined from Lake Huron to the Ottawa River, when a Commissioner could inspect that Route, or any other part of the country.

He invited me to dine with him and at 5 Pm I was with Capt Badely; when he told me that not being at liberty to take an active part in

[126]David Thompson (1770–1857), the well-known explorer and geographer, was born in England, and while still a boy was apprenticed to the Hudson's Bay Company in 1784. In 1797 he joined the North West Company and later became a partner. From 1807 to 1811 he traced the Columbia River from its source to its mouth. Thompson's map-making laid the basis for the future maps of western Canada, but unfortunately his work received little attention during his lifetime, and he died in poverty.

[127]John Macaulay (1792–1857) was appointed a member of the Legislative Council of Upper Canada in 1836 and continued as a member for the Province of Canada in 1841. He was appointed Surveyor General in 1836.

[128]John Solomon Cartwright (1804–1845), businessman and banker, was elected for Lennox and Addington to the House of Assembly of Upper Canada in 1836, and to the Legislative Assembly of the Province of Canada in 1841.

the Survey, and the business of his Department requiring much of his attention, he had written to the Governor resigning his situation of Commissioner. Thus all is uncertainty and delay. Mr. Cartwright is expected here the morrow when I shall wait on him. I cannot close this letter without expressing my deep sense of your great kindness and attention to me.

B 30   BADDELEY TO MACAULAY
[P.A.O., Macaulay Papers]

Kingston May 31st 1837

. . . Mr. Thomson dined with me yesterday and I shall introduce him to Mr. Cartwright when that gentleman returns to Kingston; he is highly qualified for the duty in point of scientific and professional acquirements, and with a young man like Mr. Hawkins, who from personal knowledge I can strongly recommend, much may be done. I think it is necessary, however, from the confidence which has been placed in me, and my desire to see the service properly conducted to acquaint you that there are rumours abroad that Mr. T is not trustworthy as to reporting of facts, This I mention without knowing what degree of credit to attach, although I must confess that there is something in his conversation which I do not like and which makes me suspect his candour. I am told Mr. McClean, the Speaker to the House of Assembly, can give you accurate information on the subject, which it behoves you to procure on all accounts. Before I heard these rumours I had pledged my vote on the strength of your opinion as well as my own and Sir Francis's but of course my resignation cancels it. I need not remind you that I write confidentially. . . .

B 31   BADDELEY TO MACAULAY
[P.A.O., Macaulay Papers]

Kingston July 19th 1837—

Yours of the 17th inst is now to be answered having written yesterday in reply to previous favors I find I was under a mistake respecting Mr Taylors[129] departure he goes off this morning and will deliver this It would have been better in all respects if tin canoes had been employed We were nearly purchasing one in 1835 and then heard them much recommended it was against my opinion that Cedar canoes were built, but Mr Thomson seemed so pressing on this point that it [was] conceded to him—

[129]David Taylor was instructed to explore a route further north than Thompson's route. His "Report of the Route between Lake Huron and the Ottawa River via Lake Nipissingue, Turtle Lake and Matawa River" is found in the Macaulay Papers.

With respect to the Sextant I can have no objection that Mr. T should have his own if it should arrive in time in which case you perhaps will have the goodness to get from him and return to me the one he has of mine . . .

Place Mr. Taylor on the same independent terms as Mr. Hawkins is with regard to Mr T The latter I perceive writes about being employed 3 or 4 months after his return in making out his reports &c &c. This seems to me to be a *feeler* In my opinion he is bound to furnish report calculations and both free of expense and it would be better to tell him so at once. He seems throughout to be trying to make the best bargain for himself. We shall require a compiler of the reports and I think Mr Taylor would answer that purpose best, for such a service he of course should be paid but not for his report &c &c. You are at liberty to tell the gentlemen my sentiments on this subject which I trust are in unison with your own and Mr. Cartwright's and if so it would be well that they should know them explicitly before their departure

B 32   EXCERPTS FROM DAVID THOMPSON'S "JOURNAL OF OCCURRENCES FROM LAKE HURON TO THE OTTAWA RIVER" [*P.A.O., David Thompson Papers, v. 28, no. 66*]

1837 August 1st. Tuesday. New moon at 7 AM A cloudy windy morning SSWd[130] at 7 AM began to moderate, the waves lowered & at 9 AM left our campment on the sandy Point of the south Christian Island. The Wind at times freshened & we had a tumbling Sea partly from the west & from the south until we doubled the Point opposite the Giants Tomb— then light waves aft. The Christian Isles appear to be 7 in number. the 3d very large say 3 Miles by ½ M. at 2½[131] PM came to the Sand Bank, or Knowl about 5 Miles from Penetanguishene here we put ashore, dined a few minutes and at 3¼ PM Messrs. Macaulay, Taylor & Hawkins in 2 Canoes went to Penetanguishene, and I remained. Wrote to my wife— to Mr Macaulay on my Theodolite-Sextant, my £30 indian payments. Accounts inclosed to him &c &c.

. . .

August 5th Saturday . . . On crossing to the great Isld. at the north end of which we are led to believe we should find the Southern Branch of the Muskako River[132] I soon found from the appearances of all about us that we had to find the Main land, as all before us were rocky, granite

[130]South southwestward.

[131]Thompson's abbreviations for time, and for distance, vary greatly. Time is here expressed as a fraction, in other places with one or two dots separating the hour and minutes, with or without special signs over the figures.

[132]Thompson regularly uses the spelling "Muskako." In his "Report on the Exploratory Survey" (Macaulay Papers) he calls the Muskoka River the "Muska ko skow see pie, or Swamp Ground River."

Islands, in order to be sure to find the River we were in search of. We had much difficulty in getting to the main Land, & in following it. In hopes of finding Rivers we were led into Channels & Bays like Rivers from which we had to return. We followed the main Land in all its windings to 4..40 PM when seeing a good place for observation for Latde & Longde we put ashore . . . A very fair day. Shortly after I set off this morning Messrs Taylor & Hawkins set off each with 3 men & each having the Cedar & a small Canoe. Mr Hawkins a tin canoe of 14 ft & 40 In[133] on the Mid Bar & Mr Taylor a similar Canoe of Birch Rind.

Augst. 6. Sunday . . . altho Sunday I was anxious to find the River we are in search of, and we examined closely all the Shores, & went into several Bays &c from which we had to return, at length we perceived driftwood on the Shores, which gave us hopes that a River was near us and at 2¾ PM may be said to have entered it. . . .

Augst 7th Monday . . . it was now 6¼ PM & we camped worried with Musketoes & Sand Flies with a few Midges. . . .
The whole of the Country we have come over these 3 days from the time we came to the main Shore is a very rude Country of Quartz and sienite granite with small scanty Wood, mostly Fir, Cand[134] Pines, some Red Oak & Aspins in low sheltered Spots, no Birds or any thing, all is desolation, and very little frequented by the Indians.

. . .

Augst 13 Sunday. . . . Rain in Showers again came on— but our Things were tolerably dry & we exd. the Provisions & put all in the best order we could. The Tent is all mildewed getting full of small holes & will soon be useless. We camped for the Night. Showers of Rain & Calm — but, thank God not many flies to what we have had. . . .

Augst 14 Monday . . . came to Swamp Ground Lake[135] . . . crossed to N. 40 E. to an Islet 500 yds & camped where Indians have been. . . .

August 15 Tuesday. Wind Southerly, cloudy. breakfasted & at 7.30 AM set off— sketched the Lake about us, many Islands . . . saw an indian Lodge,[136] & in hopes of getting information went to it, about 1½

[133]Abbreviation for inches.
[134]Abbreviation for Canadian. Probably a reference to the red pine.
[135]Lake Muskoka. In his "Report on the Survey of the Rivers, Lakes, &c" p. 97 (Thompson Papers) he gives the name "Mus ka ko skow, oo, Lak a hagan or Swamp Ground its Lake" and says: "From the fine surrounding Country I was induced to survey the Shores of this large lake."
[136]This Indian lodge may have been on Eilean Gowan Island. On August 16, Thompson camped at the lodge and said it was on a large island about three-quarters of a mile from the river which they had to go up (Muskoka River). His map shows a faint dotted line connecting the mouth of the river and the south tip of an island in the vicinity of Eilean Gowan.

M off, but no Person, suppose they have gone to Lake Huron for presents & they have left a Cat & many of their utensils &c with many Rolls
of very good Birch Rind for Canoes. I asked my Men if they would have
a Birch Rind Canoe made. They said not, as it would not stand the
required rough usage which our business must have. We returned, to
where we came from, & contd the Survey of the Lake. At the indian
Lodge fine ground & hard wood, a small patch of Potatoes look well but
the Potatoes are yet very small. . . .

August 16 Wednesday . . . At a Narrows which leads to the Matchedash River[137] by a C P[138] &c &c found a piece of Birch Rind, with
several names of 1831 but could not make them out, further in this
Narrows abt 300 yd small Horns of Deer on the ⊂ [left][139] then exd. the
Bay & found the C P leading to the Matchedash River of about 1000 yd.
in length, a small Brook crosses the path, twice or thrice, & enters a
small Lake[140] at end of the C P. The Brook is from this Lake. . . . returned . . . camped at the indian Lodge— bad campment at 6.10 PM—
the Cat but no Person. Many Flies— Thank God, we have had a very
fine day, & employed it well. The Country appears as barren of Berries
as of everything else. Agriculture may do well here, but nothing else
will— The Whole of the Large Isle on which we camp is mostly good
Land. The River we have to go up is abt ¾ M from us. . . .

August 17th Thursday All night SE Wind & cloudy. Musketoes bad.
At 5.35 set off At 7.25 put ashore to Breakfast. Wind NE & cool cloudy,
but fine— soon changed to SE 1 to ½ threatening Rain— At 2'0 PM put
ashore to dine— we have caught 3 fine Bass. . . . Killed a small Collar
Snake,[141] bluish color, with a Ring of yellowish Red about its neck,
close to the head it was about 1 foot in length & girth in proportion. . . .

Augt 18 Friday— Cleared in the Night— Wind North and cool—
64° took up the Net, not a single Fish. These Lakes do not seem to
have much Fish —all we can get is a chance Bass with the Hook. Breakfasted. Woods within mostly hard Maple & some fine Bass wood. At 6.46
AM set off to a River[142] . . . Came to a strong Rapid abt. 2 ft descent
and about 260 yd above it a strong shoal Rapid of large Stones of abt
2 ft descent— in all say 5 ft descent. . . . The C Pl is on the ⊂ N 60 E 50
yd very good to a Bay of still water— easy to make a Lock. Soil shallow
upon grey Sienite, as usual. Woods of Hemlock- Cedar- Maple, Red
Oak &c— We now left the Cargo, & only taking what we thought necessary for a few days, took the Light Canoe over the Rapids, & set off at

---

[137]The well-known route from Lake Muskoka to the Severn River.

[138]Thompson usually used "C.P.," an abbreviation for carrying place, to indicate a portage.

[139]Contrary to modern usage, Thompson seems to use the sign ⊂ for left, and
⊃ for right. It is possible that his sign, which varies somewhat in form, was originally an arrowhead.

[140]Pine Lake.

[141]Probably a ring-necked snake.   [142]Indian River.

10.38 AM & surveyed a fine Lake[143] bordered to the Water frequently, with fine hard woods & the same brown subsoil . . . At 3.40 PM at a small Fall of the same River, descent abt 18 In— abt 50 ft wide with from 4 to 8 In water over a smooth Rock of grey Sienite. handed the Canoe up it, the C.P. is on the ⊂ of a few Feet— say 4 or 5 yds into still water, and to a lake,[144] which we surveyed on the ⊂ & the Bays seemed to bring us almost back to the 1st Fall.[145] at 6 PM we camped on an Islet of small yellow Fir clean and tall, as most of the Firs are but only 4 to 10 In dia. A W N W wind has blown fresh since noon, clear and cool. So far the whole of this Lake appears surrounded by good Land, and fine hard woods, often down to the water Edge, especially all the Bays. The Points as usual have a border of Rock and woods of yellow Fir, with some Birch, Red Oak &c &c. but this border is not wide 50 to 100 yd or so— a few Musketoes.

August 19 Saturday. . . . At 7¼ AM put ashore to breakfast & examine the Land, as usual a border of Rock & yellow Fir & then Birch . . then Maple &c &c veget Mould & a warm sandy brown Clay or light brown, some places appear a brown yellow but all support a fine healthy vegetation. . . . At 1.#.7′ PM put ashore & dined— speared 5 Bass, saw many today but they will not take bait such as we have— a bit of salt Pork. At 6 PM put up on an Islet where Indians have formerly been. A very fine day, thank God & as usual well employed.— The men foolishly took only 2 days provision of Pork.[146] 68°[147]

. . .

August 21st Monday . . . continued the Survey . . . at 1..3 PM at the 2nd Fall. handed down the Canoe &c and the Men's provisions being out set off for the 1st C P where we left the Cargo— on the way detained abt ½ h with Rain & the Men dined on Soup & Biscuit— at 3½ PM arrived at the 1st C P. for the last ½ hour, a heavy Storm of Wind & Rain, we got all wet, when we arrived at the C P it was some time before we could camp for the violence of the weather. . . .

. . .

[143]Lake Rosseau. In this report Thompson refers to Lakes Rosseau and Joseph as 2nd and 3rd lakes respectively. But in his "Courses, Distances, &c" he uses the heading Trade Lake for both. The name Trade or Trading Lake was more frequently applied by travellers to the Lake of Bays.
[144]Lake Joseph.
[145]The southern end of Lake Joseph is only a short distance from the falls on the Indian River.
[146]Most of the provisions had been left at the carrying place between Lakes Muskoka and Rosseau. After returning for more provisions Thompson continued with the survey of Lake Rosseau.
[147]The sign used by Thompson for degrees of heat varies and is often indecipherable. In printing these extracts it has been standardized to the usual form.

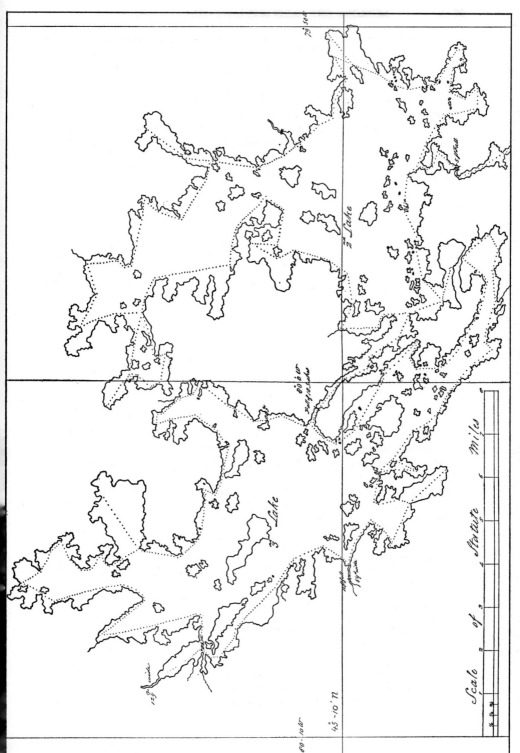

FIGURE 6. LAKES JOSEPH AND ROSSEAU BY DAVID THOMPSON, 1837. [Re-drawn from original map at Department of Lands and Forests, Ontario.]

Augt 23rd Wednesday . . . set off and went to the place of the Deer Horns[148] and surveyed the ⊃ side of the Lake. . . . we camped upon a Pt of Rocks bad but no better in view. We have come about 2 Miles along a Bank of Rocks[149] which to [*sic*] rise about 180 ft in height above the Level of the Lake, where highest, and come to the Lake in rude Slopes— cold chilly day, suffered from it. Killed 2 young stock Ducks.[150] All the M Land, & some of the Islands, good hard Woods & good Land, but almost every where the Lake &c is bordered by rude Rocks & Firs, with a few Red Oak & Aspins & the past 2 M have been burnt some years ago, & have young woods of Firs & Aspins &c. . . .

. . .

August 25 Friday . . . at 5.#.41′ AM set off Co[151] S 38 E. to a Pl we came to on the 1st Survey of this Lake, & we now follow on to the place of obsn & put ashore for Fog, we could not see. breakfasted. At 7½ AM cleared & went off and surveyed to the Pl of Deers Horns, and proceeded to the C.P. The weather fine, but light thin clouds, did not allow me to observe for longde. At 9 A.M. arrived at the C.P. and found all well. took the canoe down the Rapids,[152] loaded with everything & at 9.32 set off. met 2 Indians, very old Men & a sick Boy. They are on their way to the 2nd Lake.[153] held on the Survey to the Islet[154] on which we camped the first day from the 12th Fall, dined and set off for the upper River[155] at 1½ PM. At about ½ M from the mouth of the Upper River camped at 5..6 PM as there is no camping for some distance up the River. . . .

Augt 26 Saturday . . . Early a few showers. At 8..6 AM ventured to set off to the River. At 8.23 AM entered the River. abt 50 yd & appears very fine, deep Alluvial Soil, with fine hard woods very fine for Meadows . . . Exd a marked Line which crossed the River. The Line runs N 10 W to S 10 E blazed Trees on both sides led to a Branch . . . the ⊃ Fork[156] having the great body of water, and by a strong rush of Current cut across the ⊂ Fork[157] . . . all along steady Cur at 1 to 1½ M per Hour . . . heard a Fall. Land rising on both sides with Firs &c . . .

[148]Thompson notes deer horns in more than one place in his "Courses, Distances, &c." Apparently the place referred to here was on Lake Rosseau near the Indian River.
[149]Probably the rocky cliffs on the northeast side of Lake Rosseau between Rosseau Falls and the head of the lake.
[150]Mallard ducks.
[151]An abbreviation for "course" which Thompson uses frequently.
[152]On the Indian River between Lakes Rosseau and Muskoka.
[153]Lake Rosseau.
[154]Mentioned under August 14.
[155]The Muskoka River above Lake Muskoka.
[156]Probably the South Branch of the Muskoka River.
[157]Probably the North Branch of the Muskoka River.

This brought us in view of a high Fall[158]. . . Paul La Ronde[159] now finds that it was the Branch of this River that we left to-day up which he once passed a few years ago in the winter. carried all over by 3½ PM we had to clear the Path for the Canoe. The Path is over very uneven stony & rocky ground Roots of Trees & wet places from small Springs— and high at times on Shed of the path, which leads as near the Falls as possible— This Fall rushes down a very great height thro' a rift or ravine in the Rocks, in places very narrow. . . The Fall descends abt. 122 ft. . . . About the middle of this C.P. near the edge of the Fall is a Hemlock Tree marked on 4 Sides.[160] one blank   2nd William Hawkins L.S. 3d 20th August 1835 God Save the King— and a Line, not readable. The 4th side 23 Miles N.E. corner of Mara. This line comes from S 10 E to N 10 W. . . .

. . .

August 31st Thursday. . . . Saw a Deer descend the River as we were setting off, came near us Paul fired at & severely wounded it, crossed & followed but did not come up with it. The Land within good hard wood & Soil. . . . No rock appears along the River since this morng except at the Falls & Rapids, & all has a mild appearance, fit for cultivation. . . [Came] to the Lake of the 2 Bays[161] [inserted above: Forked] . . . The name of the Lake Nun ge low a ne goo mark Lak a hagan. . . There are interruptions of grassy swampy Pine Inlets along the River, but not on the Lake, where the fine hardwoods always show a prominent bold aspect and in the Bays to the water edge— The Land crowned with these fair woods rises every where boldly from 50 to 180 ft above the Lake. . .

September 1st Friday. . . The trees are large & fine of Maple, Bass & Iron Wood blk Birch some Elm & Ash very few Beech to be seen. The Land every where rises from 50 to 180 ft above the water in bold slopes, & in places much precipitous Rock along Shore, Sienite & Quartz—

[158]South, later Muskoka Falls.

[159]In his "Accounts" Thompson lists "Paul la Ronde Canoe man engaged June 15th at £3 per month for the first month and £3 15 per month for the rest of his Time."

[160]Marks of the Carthew and Baddeley survey (B 27).

[161]Lake of Bays. In "Report of the Survey of Rivers, Lakes, &c" Thompson says: "This Lake is called by the Natives Nun ge low e nee goo mark Lak a hagan or the Lake of Forks from the many deep Bays and Points of Land. The fineness of the Country induced me to explore all the Coasts of this Lake, and it was also necessary to do so, to learn what water may be depended on from it, in dry Seasons." In "Report on the Exploratory Survey" Thompson says: "Nun ge low e nee goo mark so Lak a hagan or the Lake of the Forks from its many deep Bays and Points of Land . . . The Forked Lake may be called, for this part of the Country, a large Lake. The surrounding lands are fine, and I surveyed its Shores, but the direct distance across this Lake may be 10 miles."

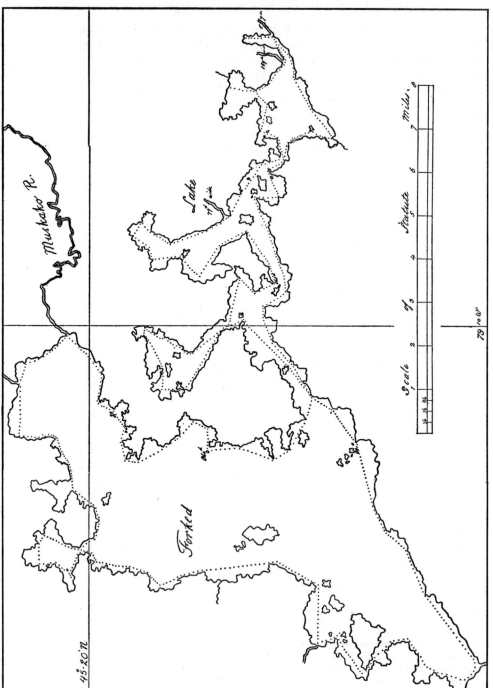

Muskoka R.

Lake

Forked

45°20′N

Scale of Statute Miles

79°10′W

FIGURE 7. LAKE OF BAYS BY DAVID THOMPSON, 1837. [Re-drawn from original map at Department of Lands and Forests, Ontario.]

some of the Isld have some good Wood, but are generally bad. Rock with yellow Firs. So far this Lake appears very fit for agriculture & capable of maintaining many Inhabitants, fit for wheat or any other northern grain. . . .

. . .

Septr 5 Tuesday . . . remarked a large dry Log, cut at both ends with a large Axe— Perhaps some White Hunter[162] . . . many Loons, killed one last evening— Saw 2 Otters & many Tracks of them along this Lake. All the Fish we have seen is the coarse speckled Salmon Trout, caught only 3 of them— small 1–2 lbs. but not a Squirrel, Hare or Mouse to be seen or heard— small Birds very scarce as well as all others except Loons. . . .

Septr 6th Wednesday 58° a very fine morning, lightly cloudy. breakfasted & set off at 6.50 AM surveyed & finished this Lake at 2½ PM when we came to the entrance of the upper River[163]— went on to the Embarras[164] . . . then . . . to the foot of the Fall[165]— 27th C P. and bad unloading. an Islet at foot of Fall— a steep bank to carry up. Rain— 3.40 PM— got all over by 4¾ PM & camped. The rain contd steady with many Flies. very Troublesome. 2 PM 77° — 4 PM 69°— 9 PM 64°.

Septr 7th Thursday. . . . The descent of the Fall about 30 ft. by examining the quantity of water passing down this Fall it appears that about 3/5 of the water of the lower River is lost, & that only 2/5 now remains. . . .

. . .

Septr 9 Saturday . . . At 2½ PM finished the Survey of Cross[166] Lake, and entered the River . . . to the 32nd Fall & C P on the ⊃ at 3¼ PM— this is by far the worst C P we have had: it is a kind of Ravine between 2 banks of Rocks— encumbered with wood & very steep to near the head of the Falls. by 4¾ P.M. carried all over & set to work to clear a way to get the Canoe over this C.P. which we effected by 5 of us dragging & pushing the Canoe up on its bottom & myself with a double line round a Tree holding what we gained, & carried the Canoe the latter part, as we could not camp on this rude place, we loaded by 6..10 PM

[162]Baddeley also noted that the large trees were never cut down by Indians (B 27).

[163]Muskoka or Oxtongue River.

[164]The word "embarras" was used frequently by Thompson for a mass of fallen trees and other material obstructing a river.

[165]Marsh Falls.

[166]Oxtongue Lake.

and went to the foot of the next Rapid N 25 E 150 yds & at 6..20 PM camped. good. it was dark before we got all in order. . . .

. . .

Septr 13 Wednesday . . . The fog so dense we are obliged to put ashore until it passes as we are now close to a Lake[167]— which I surveyed in the two upper Bays.— each has a River of about the same water— but which we are to take we know not. Mr. Sheriffs map[168] my only Guide shows only one River; both of them very shoal— also on the south side of the Lake a Brook with marked Trees & Willows broken, as if a C P to another Lake. . . . As we are now at the 1st Lake of the height of Land[169] I resolved to do what I have long seen necessary from the shoal waters, Rapids &c. The necessity of exploring the Country to know what it is according to my Instructions &c and our large Canoes being too heavy for shoal Water, and also that with one Canoe we cannot separate ourselves to examine two Rivers at the same time &c I determined to make two small Canoes which should be able to take all our Provisions, Baggage &c— for this purpose we crossed to the north side where we had seen Cedar Trees, & exd. the Ground, and in deep sandy Bay, thank God, we found on a bank of abt 25 ft high sufficient good Cedar for our purpose.— We then brought up all the things necessary to close to the cedar grove, and camped— made Floats for the Net, and set it— got the Axes in order. & with the crooked Knives &c &c with 2 men I split out 33 Timbers for the Canoes. 2 PM 60° 4 PM 59° 9 PM 51° Clear & fine.

Septr 14 Thursday 45° cold clear Morng. dense Fog— visited the net, nothing in it— All hands at work. 3 men knifing Timber. 2 men with myself split out the Gunwales for the Canoes to be 19 ft in length. brought them to the Camp. Split out 40 more Timbers— Set the net in another place . . . My Mercury getting rather short of the quantity required for an Obsn. exd. my Mercury in stock, found the Bottle broke, but the Leather tied round it had kept it in. The Bottle too thin by far for such a purpose. Lost an Hour with one Man in getting it collected and cleaned, lost about ½ lb of it, and what my Bottle for Obsn. could not contain, put in a Flagon for Liquor, as I have no other means . . .

Septr 15th Friday 40° a mild night, cool clear morng. Calm at 9 AM Westerly Wind . . . Visited the net, nothing, let it stand. all hands at work, by noon with 2 Men split out 33 Boards for the Canoes . . . For

[167]South Tea Lake. Thompson refers to it as Canoe Lake, and says: "This Lake I count the first Lake of the Height of Land." He spent about two weeks there building two canoes, surveying the district, and searching for the water route.

[168]A map was included in Shirreff's *Topographical Notices*, published in 1831.

[169]Height of land dividing the waters which drain into the Georgian Bay from those which drain into the Ottawa.

want of something fresh find myself weak, took Chocolate for Dinner with Crackers and much better, in the afternoon with 2 Men split out 53 Boards for the Canoe, in all 88 Boards, tho' some not good, which I think will be enough. Split out the Bars &c so that we have mostly completed splitting out all that is required for 2 Canoes of 19 ft length on the Gunwales— or abt 18 ft length direct. very fine day. Wind westerly & clear 2 PM 64° 9 PM 54° much better.

Septr 16. Saturday. 52° A fine clear morng. Visited the Net nothing in it, so that we find there are only a few small Fish in all these Lakes that we have passed. The whole Country seems nearly destitute of living Animals, & Birds, as well as Fish, not a single squirrel, mouse, or any thing of the kind has been seen or heard since we set off. Partridges very scarce— we have only killed abt 4— Ducks the same— in short there is a desolation or destitution of animal life of all Kinds. Knifing Boards &c all the Timbers for the Canoes are turned & drying &c— Sent Baptiste[170] to look for 4 young Trees with curved Roots for Stems which he brought . . .

Septr 17 Sunday . . . Each of the Men, except Antoine[171] making himself a Shirt of the Cotton I brought, put much of my field drawings in Ink warm close day— At 9 PM Rain came & contd all night. at times heavy showers & squalls of wind

Septr 18 Monday 56° S E Gale with steady Rain, working hard to get all ready to begin a Canoe, when the weather permits, as we have no shelter from the Rain & every thing is wet. Knifing Boards for the Bottom, Sides &c &c cleaned a place for the building of the Canoes. I put the Bars in the Gunwales, got the stems partly ready, &c &c heavy showers at times, in the evening heavy Rain which contd at intervals most of the night. 2 PM 55° 9 PM 50°

Septr 19. Tuesday. 50° Wind S Wly. promising better weather but heavy Showers came on & contd to the afternoon— put the Bottom & Stem on the Canoe Bed & by 1 PM got in the necessary Timber, put one round of Boards along the Gunwales, cut Logs for the Canoe to rest on, & put one round on each side of the bottom. to 6 PM clear fine night. 49° flyg Clouds. 40° cold clear night.

Septr 20th Wednesday 32° Ice abt ⅒ of an Inch thick in a Kettle abt 4 yd from the Fire— dense Fog to 8 AM then clear fine weather. Early all at work. Two men collecting Gum for the Canoes. put all the Boards abt the Canoe & took it off the Bed— & gave it to Baptiste to

---

[170]In his "Accounts" Thompson listed "Jean Baptiste Taron gee kee ra ree" as a canoe man.

[171]"Antoine Sae te ron quis" was also listed as a canoe man in Thompson's "Accounts."

finish. Cut down Two Cedars & split out 14 Boards. we have employed more time for want of nails. The Canoe is 19 ft on the Gunwales by 42 In[172] width & 20 In depth. 2 PM 56° 9 PM 36° very fair day, but cold evening—

Septr 21 Thursday . . . put the 2nd Canoe on the bed . . .

. . .

Septr 23 Saturday . . . Early got the Canoe finally boarded in, & set to work on getting the rest of the Timbers in, &c &c. which occupied all day with the 2 Canoes. pegs instead of nails, we have not one third enough of nails. picked an old piece of Line into Oakum to help the stopping the Seams of the Canoes . . .

Septr 24th Sunday . . . Men employed on the Canoes running gum into the seams, caulking slightly &c &c. We had 300 lb of Biscuit, & we have expended at the rate of abt ⅛ lb[173] per man per day, or less. The allowance is ½ lb per day. abt ½ Bag of Flour is also expended. but we have 3 Boxes of Pork abt 220 lb & abt 60 lbs of Beef remaining— Since Wednesday morning the 20th Inst. Ther 32° and water frozen to Ice— The woods in all their Foliage have suddenly changed & assumed all the vivid tints of October, and begin to fall freely, one cannot help a sigh at such a quick change. . . .

[172]Abbreviation for "2 inches."
[173]This figure is not clear in the manuscript.

C. THE INDIAN IN THE MUSKOKA AND HALIBURTON REGION

C 1 JOHN COLLINS'[1] MEMORANDUM[2] ON INDIAN PURCHASE
[P.A.O., Simcoe Papers]

At a conference held by John Collins and William R Crawford[3] Esqr. with the principal Chiefs of the Missisaga Nation Mr. John Russeau Interpreter— it was unanimously agreed,[4] that the King shall have a right to make roads through the Missisaga Country, That the Navigation of the Rivers and Lakes, shall be open and free for his Vessels and those of his Subjects, that the Kings Subjects shall carry on a free trade unmolested, in and through the Country, That the King shall erect Forts, Ridouts, Batteries, and Storehouses &ca. in all such places as shall be judged proper for that purpose— respecting Payment for the above right, the Chiefs observed they were poor and Naked, they wanted Cloathing and left it to their good Father to be a judge of the quantity

Lake le Clie 9th. Augt. 1785—
John Collins, D S G.

C 2 D. W. SMITH[5] TO ALEXANDER AITKIN
[Ontario, Department of Lands and Forests, Instructions to Land Surveyors, Book 2, pp. 482–5]

Sur. Genl. Office, Upper Canada
12. September 1794—

You will pass over Lake Simcoe to Matchedosh Bay—
You will send to Mr. Cowan or Constant, and endeavor to get him to meet you—

[1]John Collins (d. 1795) came to Canada in 1759 and was appointed Deputy Surveyor General in 1764. On May 22, 1785, he was instructed by Henry Hamilton "to take a survey of the Communication between the Bay of Quinté, and Lake Huron by Lake La Clie" and to note "The Indian Tribes, on the Communication, their numbers disposition, &ca. What tract of Land it may be necessary to purchase, and at what rate." (Ontario, Department of Lands and Forests, Instructions to Land Surveyors, Book 1, pp. 13-15.)

[2]Another copy of this memorandum, also in the Simcoe Papers, has "(Signed) J. B. Rousseaux enterprer" as well as John Collins' name.

[3]Captain William Redford Crawford was born in America about 1743, came to Canada and settled at Fredericksburg, and was a magistrate and sheriff of the Mecklenburg District. According to R. A. Preston (Kingston before the War of 1812, p. 33) "It was he who persuaded the Mississaugas to sell the title to their land in 1783."

[4]This agreement is probably the one referred to by J. B. Rousseau, May 21, 1795 (C 3). If so, it included one mile on each side of the Severn River.

[5]David William Smith, or Smyth (1764–1837), came to Canada about 1790. In 1792 he became Acting Surveyor General of Upper Canada and in 1800 Surveyor

You are herewith furnished with a map, which may elucidate our Purchase of the Indian Lands—

You will talk with Mr. St. John[6] (on the subject) who was present at the Treaty—

You are to do away if possible, all Jealousy & discontent (should any exist) among the Indians, relative to these purchases.

If upon Enquiry and the accumulation of incidents, you may think it prudent, that further presents be made to satisfy the Indians, should they appear Jealous or discontented, you will report to me, in circumstantial Detail, and if it shall be thought proper that a fixed time should be settled at York,– you will estimate the particulars, of what they may expect; as a most complete ratification of the Cessions of the Indians must be then obtained—

You are principally to survey the communication pointed out by Mr. Cowan as more easy of access than the old Route. This Tract, if found expedient, must be exchanged in Lieu of that which has formerly been supposed to have been purchased; The object is to establish at the End of Lake Simcoe a Settlement, and another at Matchedosh Bay, with intervening Lands, sufficient for the purpose of Portage, and Farm Lands, to facilitate on the Plan of Yonge Street, one Lot therefore on each side of the Road might be sufficient—

In case it be necessary to meet the Indian Chiefs this Autumn, you will be pleased to give me the most early and necessary information, perhaps however it may be held the ensuing Spring, with greater Effect — Mr. Cowans possessions, and as much Lands, as he shall require, not inconsistent with public purposes, and the power of Government to grant, will be secured to him— The Provisions he furnished the Party who accompanied his Excellency the Lieut. Governor, to Lake Huron, may be replaced in Flour—

In answer to the Memorandum which you left at this office, I am authorised to inform you by His Excelly. the Lieut: Governor, that the Kings Horses at York, will be ordered to your assistance; for which purpose you will call on Major of Brigade Littlehales,[7] to receive the order— If necessary you may give a little Rum, & a few trifling things to the principal Men among the Indians, but this, had better be managed by Cowan or Constant, as well as the fixing of any time for their meeting at York— The Quantity of Land wanted for the use of Government, is pointed out in the foregoing Parts of these Instructions, that is to say, "For a Settlement at the End of Lake Simcoe, and for another at Matchedosh Bay, with intervening Lands for the purpose of Portage and Farm Lands, to facilitate on the Plan of Yonge Street; One Lot therefore on each side of the Road might be sufficient,"— Should you

---

General. He returned to England, and retired from the office of Surveyor General in 1804. He was created a baronet in 1821.

[6]Jean Baptiste Rousseau.

[7]Edward Baker Littlehales, later Sir Edward Baker, Bart. (d. 1825), Simcoe's military secretary.

find the communication pointed out by Mr. Cowan, to be more easy of access, than the old Road, you will lay it off into Farm Lots after the same manner that you have already commenced the Yonge Street, between York and Lake Simcoe, provided the Indians make no objection to this subdivision, and making due allowance for the settlement at the End of Lake Simcoe, as well as that at Matchedosh Bay—

I am further authorised to inform you, you may tell Mr. Cowan, that he is to be paid, well, for his trouble; the Rate pr Day, must be arranged between ye, it being certain, however, (to use His Excellency's Expressions) He must have, *almost* what he demands[8]—

As you have attended His Excellency on this Rout,[9] and are personally acquainted with his Views relative to this Communication, it is needless for me to swell these Instructions with further detail; I make no doubt, but you will execute this Business, with fidelity and dispatch—

C 3   SEVERN RIVER PURCHASE CERTIFIED BY J. B. ROUSSEAU
[P.A.O., Simcoe Papers]

I certify that the purchase[10] made from the Chippaway Indians between Lake La Clie, now Lake Simcoe & Matchidash Bay, as nearly as I can recollect, was as follows—vizt—One mile on each side of the foot path from the Narrows at Lake Simcoe to Matchidash Bay, with three Miles and a half Square, at each end of said Road or foot path, for the building of Stores or any other public purpose, also one mile on each Side of the River[11] which empties out of Lake Simcoe into Matchidash Bay for the purpose of carrying on the Transport—

York 21st. May 1795

C 4   PETER RUSSELL[12] TO SIMCOE
[Russell, Correspondence, ed. Cruikshank, v. 1, p. 117]

Niagara, 31st December, 1796

. . . I beg leave to trouble your Excellency with the enclosed speech to Major Smith[13] from some Upper Lake Indians who lately visited the Post at York by which it appears that something should be soon done to conciliate the affections of the tribes in the rear of York, who, for want

[8]In margin "Confidential to Mr Aitken."
[9]Simcoe's trip to Georgian Bay by the Severn River (A 16).
[10]Probably the agreement of August 9, 1785 (C 1).
[11]Severn River.
[12]Peter Russell (1733–1808) was Administrator of Upper Canada from 1796 to 1799.
[13]Samuel Smith (1756–1826) was born in New York State and served with the Queen's Rangers in the Revolution. He came to Canada and in 1791 was commissioned in the Queen's Rangers which had been re-organized by Simcoe. In 1798 he became Lieutenant Colonel, and was Administrator of Upper Canada in 1817 and again in 1820.

of some such attention, may become unfriendly to the British name and harass the back settlements by their depredations, I communicated their speech to Captain Claus[14] who succeeds Colonel Butler[15] in the Indian Agency at this place but his instructions bind him up so close that he cannot deviate from the line chalked out for him, and I find by them that, should I obtain the supply by my personal requisition, the value thereof would be charged against myself unless the service for which it was asked might meet with the Commander in Chief's approbation. Not having presumed to trouble the Duke of Portland[16] upon the subject, I leave it to your Excellency to mention it to His Grace or not as you may judge proper. . . .

C 5   PETER RUSSELL TO ROBERT PRESCOTT[17]
[*Russell*, Correspondence, *ed. Cruikshank, v. 1, p. 287*]

Upper Canada, 25th Sept. 1797.

I take this opportunity of transmitting to your Excellency a few Copies of the Acts passed in the last Session of the Provincial Parliament of this Province.

I beg leave to transmit at the same time the Copies of Speeches made by Yellow Head[18] (who with a Party of about 140 Chippewas lately visited the Posts of York and Niagara) to Major Shank[19] and myself with our answers.

INCLOSURE

Speech of Yellow Head, a Chief of the Mississagas, accompanied by several other Chiefs, and about one hundred and forty Indians from

[14]William Claus (1763–1826), an officer in the Indian Department, was appointed Deputy Superintendent of Indian Affairs in 1799.

[15]Colonel John Butler (d. 1796) came to Canada after the American Revolution and acted as Superintendent of Indian Affairs until his death.

[16]William Henry Cavendish Bentinck, third Duke of Portland (1738–1809), was Home Secretary from 1794 to 1801.

[17]Robert Prescott (1725–1816) was appointed Governor in Chief of Canada in 1797.

[18]This was probably "The Yellowhead," father of William Yellowhead or Musquakie. He and his son served in the War of 1812 and took an active part in the defence of York in April, 1813. After the war he was succeeded by his son as Principal Chief of the Chippewas of Lakes Simcoe and Huron.
William Yellowhead (d. 1864) also known as Musquakie, with many variant spellings, was born about 1765. His face was scarred from a wound received in the War of 1812. He lived with his band at the Narrows from about 1830 to 1839, and while there the government built him a house, which later became the parsonage for St. James' Church. About 1839 he moved with his band to Rama. His hunting grounds were in Muskoka, especially in the Lake of Bays area, and from him Muskoka probably takes its name. There is a tablet to his memory in St. James' Church, Orillia.

[19]David Shank (d. 1831) was the senior officer of the Queen's Rangers next to Simcoe and was commanding at the post of York.

Lake Simcoe, to Major Shank com'ding His Majy's Post at York, 4th Sept. 1797—

Present Majors Smith, Shaw, Lieut. Givens, Ensn. McGreer, Surgeons Gamble and Fleming, &c., &c.

We are exceedingly poor, have come a long way to see our Father, and hope that now we are here he will prove charitable to us, we are much grieved to see ourselves so long neglected by our Father, and desire to know at once if we have offended him, or if he wishes us to come no more to see him, if so we will go and come no more to trouble him.

Sir William Johnson[20] and Colonel Butler used formerly to give us like other Indians attached to the British Government annual Presents; And altho' we have complained repeatedly, we have received very little for several years past.— We are poor and cannot purchase Guns &c., of our Traders; but if you cannot now supply our wants, we wish you to allow Mr. Givens to accompany us to Niagara to see our other Father,[21] that we may make known our grievances to him, and that you will give us little of what you have in Store for our Women and Children to return home with, and some of your Milk and Provisions for us to proceed to Niagara—

MAJOR SHANK'S ANSWER

Brothers,

You have no ways offended your Great Father the King.— His Majesty has the same confidence in your Loyalty and Attachment he ever had; and you cannot say but that the King's Officers have been on all occasions charitable and kind to you at this Post; with regard to your annual Presents I hope more attention will be paid hereafter; the reason I cannot answer you fully and with more certainty on this head is that we have no person of the Indian Dept. at this Post; but this matter shall be fully represented to His Honor the President, and to Capt. Claus, Superintendent of Indian Affairs at Niagara.

C 6 INDIAN SURRENDER OF PARTS OF HALIBURTON AND MUSKOKA
    [*P.A.C., Indian Treaties and Surrenders, R.G. 10, ser. 4, v. 2,
    Treaty no. 20; also printed in* Indian Treaties and Surrenders,
    v. 1, pp. 48–9]

ARTICLES OF PROVISIONAL AGREEMENT entered into on Thursday, the Fifth day of November, 1818 Between the Honorable William Claus, Deputy Superintendent General of Indian Affairs, in behalf

[20]This is probably an error for Sir John Johnson (1742–1830) who was appointed Superintendent of Indian affairs in British North America in 1783.

[21]Peter Russell, Administrator of the Government. The Indians proceeded to Niagara where they repeated their statements and were assured by Russsell that another "Council fire" was to be lighted at York to which they could go for their presents (Russell, *Correspondence*, v. 1, p. 289).

of His Majesty, of the one part, and Buckquaquet, Chief of the Eagle Tribe; Pishikinse, Chief of the Rein Deer Tribe; Pahtosh,[22] Chief of the Crane Tribe; Cahgahkishinse, Chief of the Pike Tribe; Cahgagewin, of the Snake Tribe; and Pininse, of the White Oak Tribe, Principal Men of the Chippewa Nation of Indians inhabiting the back parts of the New Castle District, of the other part, Witnesseth: that for and in consideration of the yearly sum of Seven Hundred and forty pounds Province Currency in Goods at the Montreal price to be well and truly paid yearly, and every year by his said Majesty to the said Chippawa Nation inhabiting and claiming the said Tract which may be otherwise known as follows, A tract of Land situate between the Western Boundary Line of the Home District and extending Northerly to a Bay at the Northern Entrance of Lake Simcoe, in the Home District, Commencing on the Western Division Line of the Midland District at the North West Angle of the Township of Rawdon— then North sixteen degrees west thirty three miles, or until it strikes the line forty-five; then along said line to a Bay at the northern entrance of Lake Simcoe;[23] then southerly along the Waters edge to the entrance of Talbot River; then up Talbot River to the Eastern Boundary Line of the Home District— then along said Boundary Line south sixteen degrees east to the North West angle of the township of Darlington, then along the Northern Boundary Line of the Townships of Darlington Clarke Hope & Hamilton to the Rice Lake, then along the southern shore of said Lake and of the River Trent, to the Western Division Line of the Midland District then north sixteen degrees west, to the place of Beginning, containing about one million, nine hundred and fifty one thousand Acres. And the said Buckquaquet, Pishikinse, Pahtosh, Cahgahkishinse, Cahgagewin and Pininse, as well for themselves as for the Chippewa Nation inhabiting and claiming the said Tract of Land as above described, Do freely, fully, and Voluntarily surrender and convey the same to His Majesty without Reservation or limitation in Perpetuity. And the said William Claus, in behalf of His Majesty, does hereby promise and agree to pay to the said Nation of Indians inhabiting as above mentioned yearly and every year forever the said sum of Seven Hundred and forty Pounds Currency in goods at the Montreal price, which sum the said Chiefs and Principal People parties hereunto acknowledge as a full consideration for the Lands hereby sold and conveyed to His Majesty.

In witness whereof the parties have hereunto set their Hands & seals on the day first above mentioned in the Township of Hope, Smith's Creek.

[22]This name was also spelled Paudash, Paudaush, Pautash, Potash, etc. It belonged to a well-known line of Mississauga Indian chiefs and is perpetuated in Paudash Lake, Cardiff Township, Haliburton. George Paudash, head chief, lived in the settlement at Rice Lake for many years, and was succeeded by his son M. G. Paudash in 1863.

[23]The line forty-five strikes Lake Muskoka, not Lake Simcoe. The error is repeated as late as 1863, by W. R. Bartlett (C 26).

Signed, Sealed and Delivered in the
  presence of
"The word forty having first been
  written over the figures 45"

J. Givins, S.I.A.
Wm. Hands, Sen., Clerk Ind. Dept.
Wm. Gruet, Interpreter, I. Dept.

W. Claus, Dy Supt
  Genl. I.A. on behalf
  of the Crown.
Buckquaquet, [totem]
Pishikinse, [totem]
Pahtosh, [totem]
Cahgahkishinse, [totem]
Cahgagewin, [totem]
Pininse, [totem]

The manner in which the yearly payment was to have been made to you, for the lands which you had ceded to the Crown on the fifth day of November 1818 not having been sufficiently explicit and defined in the Provisional Agreement. In order to obviate any difficulty or misconstruction which might hereafter arise I have called you together for the purpose of explaining to you the manner in which it is intended that the payment shall be made and in order that you may subscribe your names on the back of the Provisional Agreement as acquiescing and approving of the same as follows viz Every Man, Woman and Child to receive to the amount of ten dollars in goods at the Montreal prices, so long as such Man, Woman or Child shall live, but such annuity to cease and be discontinued to be paid in right of any Individual who may have died between the respective periods of payment, and the several individuals then living, only, shall be considered as entitled to receive the yearly payment of ten dollars in goods as above stated.

[Endorsed] No 20. Provisional Agreement with the Rice Lake Chippewas for the surrender of 1951000 Acres signed 5th. November 1818

C 7   H. C. DARLING'S[24] REPORT TO LORD DALHOUSIE,[25] 1828
[*Great Britain, Colonial Office, Aboriginal Tribes of North America,*
p. 27]

Quebec, 24 July 1828

. . . MISSISSAQUAS of Rice Lake, consisting of 317 souls, and Mohawks of Bay of Quinti, not exceeding 319 souls.— Of these, the Mississaquas of Bay of Quinti and the Rice Lake have recently been converted to Christianity by the Methodist Society, who have introduced missionaries among the Indians here and in every part of Upper Canada where they have been able to obtain a footing. These missionaries come

[24]Henry Charles Darling (d. 1845) entered the army in 1794 and became a major general in 1825. In 1820 he was appointed military secretary to Lord Dalhousie. About 1827 he became Deputy Superintendent General of the Indian Department of Lower Canada, and later Superintendent General. In 1833 he was appointed Lieutenant Governor of Tobago.
[25]George Ramsay, ninth Earl of Dalhousie (1770–1838), Governor in Chief of Canada, 1819–28.

chiefly from the United States, and belong to the "Canada Conference Missionary Society, auxiliary to the Missionary Society of the Methodist Episcopal Church of the State of New York," from which they receive a small salary, seldom exceeding 40 £ a year.**** It is undoubted that they have done some good, by influencing the Indians to embrace Christianity, and have inculcated the first principles of civilization, which shows itself in the desire which they have recently expressed to be collected in a village, and have lands allotted them for cultivation.

. . .

CHIPPAWAS under Chief Yellow Head.— These Indians amount upon an average to 550 souls; they occupy the lands about Lake Simcoe, Holland River, and the unsettled country in the rear of York. They have expressed a strong desire to be admitted to Christianity, and to adopt the habits of civilized life; in these respects they may be classed with the Mississaquas of the Bay of Quinti and Rice Lake, but are at present in a more savage state. . . .

C 8   PETITION OF THE MISSISSAUGAS
[*P.A.C., Indian Affairs, R.G. 10, v. 5, pp. 3–6*]

To His Excellency Sir John Colborne K. C. B. Lieutenant Governor of the Province of Upper Canada &c. &c. &c.
    The Petition[26] of the Messissaga Indians of the Rice Lake in the New Castle District.
                    Humbly sheweth,
    That we and our Fathers having been in a long sleep have lately been roused up by the word of the Great Spirit, our eyes are now open and we see that there is light and truth by Jesus Christ for Indians as well as for our white Brothers.
    That our hearts are grieved for the abuses which are done us by some white men. Our hearts are true and we will speak plainly, white men seize on our furs, and take them from us by force, they abuse our women and violently beat our people.
    That your Red Children look for protection, We pray that late abuses, which we have suffered may be inquired into. Some white men tell us that we have no right to complain of Roberies on our hunters, and violence on our women, we believe you know, and if white men do not understand that Red men are to be protected, you will please to say, to what priviledges in law the Indians are entitled to.
    That we are poor in lands and have few places for hunting, much of our hunting grounds are covered by white Settlement, and the small

[26]A further petition, August 11, 1830, with 37 Indian names, protested against certain individuals who "have made it a practice to come annually into our country & have carried off from our neighbouring forests Fur to the amount of several hundreds of dollars p ann." (P.A.C., R.G. 10, v. 5).

remainder left to us are invaded by the hunters from Lower Canada, they come upon our hunting grounds, and wantonly kill and destroy all the animals old and young, that come in their way. We have told them of their injustice and urged them to depart; but our words are feeble and they will not listen. None but our Great Father can make them hear, when he speaks they must obey.

And your Petitioners further pray, that in case the existing Laws do not afford to the Indians a mutual and just protection, that Your Excellency may be pleased to recommend a Legislative Enactment whereby Offenders may be brought to Justice, in a Sumary manner.

York Jany. 27th. 1829—   Signed   their marks
                                 George Pautash

                                 John Cow[27]

                                 John Crow

                                 Peter Nogin[28]

                                 Peter Wauson

C 9   INDIAN CHIEFS TO SIR JOHN COLBORNE
[*P.A.C., Indian Affairs, R.G. 10, v. 5, pp. 577–80*]

Yellowhead's Island[29] Sept 15th. 1830

Father, Seven young men belonging to this tribe & perhaps some of the Snake tribe, will settle on the portage road from this to Majedush

[27]This is probably "Handsome Jack" Cow who appears in the literature of the early settlers, and for whom Jack Lake in Methuen Township is named. Handsome Jack claimed as his hunting grounds Methuen and Chandos townships (*History of the County of Peterborough*, pp. 218-20).

[28]The name is also spelled Nogie, Nogy, Noogie, Nogee, etc. Nogies Creek, Harvey Township perpetuates the name (See Guillet, *The Valley of the Trent*, p. xxix).   [29]Chiefs Island, Lake Couchiching.

next spring. As for us old men, we intend to settle at the village[30] you are building for us, & end our days there, & our children will be kept at school.

Father, We are always greatful to receive your instructions, & ready to obey them, but it is getting so late in the season, we shall not be able to clear much this fall, but early next spring we will commence as you desired us.

Father, We are poor yet & have no mochasins; we wish to hunt this fall, & get some meet & deerskins against the cold winter.

Father, We are glad of the money you sent us for our work this season, & we wish to know when you can pay us the remainder. We shall be going to our huntings in about two weeks, & should be glad of the money before we go, & if you can accomodate us we should be glad of some in small change such as three, two & one dollar bills with some 2/6 pieces.

We are your children.

Chiefs & head men	his William X Yellowhead mark his Bigwin[31] X mark his Waumbone X Youngs[32] mark his Isaac X Johns mark his Big X Shilling[33] mark

[30]At the Narrows between Lakes Simcoe and Couchiching.

[31]Probably Chief James Bigwin. The name is also spelled Big Wind, Bigwind, Big Wing, etc. The Bigwin family traded with other Indians for furs at Bigwin Island, Lake of Bays, and the name is perpetuated in that of the island. The earliest examples of the name Bigwin have surname only, but from the 1830's to the 1850's the name of James Bigwin appears on a number of land surrenders. John Bigwin who died in 1940, supposed to be over 100 years old, was well known to the early settlers in Muskoka.

[32]In the Treaty of November 26, 1836, the name appears as Wahbone Young.

[33]Chief Big Shilling's name was given as Nebe-non-a-quet in a list of Indian forces at Holland Landing, December 22, 1838 (P.A.C., R.G. 10, v. 124).

C 10   COLBORNE TO R. W. HAY[34]
[*Great Britain, Colonial Office,* Aboriginal Tribes of North America,
pp. 136–7]

Upper Canada, York, 15 December 1831.

With reference to your Despatch of the 4th August, transmitting the copy of a statement from Mr. Peter Jones, a missionary of the Methodist Episcopal Church, I beg leave to observe, that most of the Indian tribes residing in Upper Canada have large tracts of land reserved for them by recorded agreement, and they are all confident that their lands will never be taken from them. The Rice Lake Indians, about 80 families, have a right to occupy the islands on the Rice Lakes; but the agents of the New England Company[35] having built a village for them, and having offered to support a school, they petitioned that about 1,200 acres of the waste lands of the Crown might be granted to the company for the use of these Indians. This measure was recommended to be complied with by the Secretary of State. . . . The Indians on Lake Simcoe have three islands set apart for them on that lake; I have, however, considered it more for their benefit to collect them on the northwest shore of the lake, and to form two establishments for them on a road which they have cleared between Lake Simcoe and Lake Huron, and to locate them on the lands of the Crown. All these Indians receive an annuity from His Majesty's Government. The Indians from Drummond's Island are located on the same tract.

The Indians will never find any difficulty in obtaining as much land as they can be induced to cultivate. Many of the tribes indeed are in possession of tracts of land too extensive for their present numbers. As certain families become civilized, and are able to manage their own property, lots might be secured to them by deeds; but I strongly recommend that in their present state His Majesty's Government should continue to act as their guardian, and not suffer their lands to be removed from under a control which it is necessary to retain for the benefit of the Indians and their posterity.

With respect to Asance's[36] tribe, and their application for money, it

[34]Robert William Hay was appointed Permanent Undersecretary for War and the Colonies in 1825.

[35]The New England Company, the oldest English Protestant missionary society, was founded in 1649 by the Long Parliament with the name "Society for Propagation of the Gospel in New-England." It worked among the Indians of New England, and after the American Revolution, in Canada. The founding and early history is covered by William Kellaway's *The New England Company, 1649-1776* (London, 1961).

[36]The name is spelled in many ways: Aisance, Asance, Aisence, Ascanse, Aissans, Aasance, etc. It appears at least as early as 1798. On June 8, 1811, at a conference which led to the surrender of land at Penetanguishene, "Young Aisainse" referred to his "Garden Ground" at Penetanguishene Bay (P.A.C.,

should be stated that they have mentioned their desire to have part of their annual payments in money instead of goods. We have already expended more than 3,000 £ for the tribes at the Matchadash and Lake Simcoe, in building houses and clearing land for them, and in purchasing cattle.

The preachers of the Episcopal Methodist church have received in every instance protection and encouragement from the superintendents of the Indian department.

C 11   JOHN CARTHEW'S MEETING WITH INDIANS ON LAKE ROSSEAU, SEPTEMBER, 1835
[*Upper Canada, House of Assembly, Journal, 1836–7, app. 37*]

. . . we entered a large Lake studded with beautiful islands, but the haze and rain prevented my observing its extent— The voyageurs said it extends to the NW 20 or 30 miles, and they name it Rousseau's Lake.[37] 4h 48m N by W, 4h 51m ENE, 4h 55m N, 5h fell in with 6 families of Indians— received information from them that one of our party and two men had been on the shore of this Lake, and that they had met the main party on the 2nd of September, but they gave me little or no information as to what Lake or what portage the main line might cross. These Indians were very civil, and after making some enquiries as to their mode of life, they took me to their village. I was surprised to find about 40 acres of good clearing, planted with corn and potatoes. I learned from them that they had made this in 4 years. The plantation is on an island in the Lake, but only a small part of the island is good land — The chief's name is Pamosagay. I made the Indians a few presents of tobacco and provisions, as they promised us any assistance we might require. They appear to reside here all the year round, taking plenty of white fish and trout. They trade with Penetanguishene through one of Mr. Mitchell's[38] traders— These Indians were very cleanly, with good wigwams and new canoes. . . .

Indian Treaties and Surrenders, R.G. 10, ser. 4, v. 2). Early occurrences of the name give surname only, but in the 1830's the name John Aisance, chief, appears. About 1830 Aisance and his band were settled at Coldwater by Colborne, but later moved to Beausoleil Island, and about 1856 to the Christian Islands.

[37]This is the earliest use of the name Rousseau's Lake which has been found. Vernon B. Wadsworth attributed the origin of the name to Jean Baptiste Rousseau, the trader at the Humber River. However, it seems more likely that the lake was named for the Jean Baptiste Rousseau who was a trader from Penetanguishene, and half-brother and clerk to George Gordon. Rousseau is said to have travelled extensively through the wilderness collecting furs from the Indians. The change in spelling from Rousseau to Rosseau was gradual, both forms occurring at least until the 1870's.

[38]Andrew Mitchell, a fur trader at Penetanguishene, came with his father and brother from Drummond Island. Andrew Mitchell kept the first, and for many years the only, store at Penetanguishene.

C 12   T. G. ANDERSON[39] TO COLBORNE

[*Great Britain, Colonial Office,* Return to an Address of the Honourable
the House of Commons, dated 11th June 1839, for Copies or Extracts
of Correspondence. . . . Respecting the Indians, *pp. 118–20*]

Coldwater, 24th September 1835.

May it please your Excellency,

In support of my recent Applications to your Excellency for further
Assistance to the Indians, and particularly the Heathen Indians assemb-
ling on the North Shores of Lake Huron, I have the Honour to submit
the following Observations on the Indian Establishments under my
Care.

It is now Five Years since, by the Direction of your Excellency, I
undertook the Settlement and Civilization of Three Tribes of Indians at
Coldwater and the Narrows of Lake Simcoe, numbering about 500
Souls. The Tribe under the Chief John Aisance, and that of the Pota-
ganasus under Chief Ashawgashel, were fixed at Coldwater, whilst the
Tribe under Chief Yellowhead were settled at the Narrows.

It will be necessary to look at the past Condition of these people and
compare it with the present. Many anxious Friends of the Indians occasionally express Disappointment that greater Progress has not been
made; and to every one it must be Matter of Regret, that Instances
occur of individual Misconduct, which create Doubts as to the Propriety
of interfering to amend their Condition.

It is only therefore by keeping in view their actual State before
Measures were taken to assist their Civilization, that any fair Estimate
can be formed of the Advantages or Disadvantages of those Measures.
I have also to urge that it may be borne in Mind that much Opposition
has continually arisen from the Necessity of mixing different religious
Persuasions.

Prior to the Year 1830 these Tribes had become much demoralized
from their long Residence near White Settlements.

They were in the constant habit of drinking spirituous Liquors to
excess; not one of them could read or write; and they scarcely knew any
thing of Religion.

Their Hunting Grounds were exhausted, their Government Presents
were exchanged for Whiskey, they were in Debt to all the Traders, and
unable to obtain more Credit, and thus were constantly in a State bordering on Starvation.

Their Suffering and Misery were strongly marked in their personal
Appearance and the Condition of their Wigwams; the latter, imperfectly

[39]Thomas Gummersall Anderson (1779–1875) had a long career in Indian
affairs, stretching from 1815 to 1858. He was Superintendent at Coldwater from
1829 to 1837, and Chief Superintendent of Indian Affairs for Canada West from
1845 to 1858.

made, and very insufficiently supplied with Fuel, could scarcely be said
to afford Shelter to the ragged and emaciated Frames of the elder
Indians, whilst the wretchedly diseased Appearance of the Children
spoke still more forcibly of the Intoxication and Want of Food of the
Parents.

Miserable as was their State, it will hardly be credited that their
Minds were so debased, their Listlessness and Lethargy so great, that
it required considerable Persuasion to prevail on them to accept the
Bounty of Government.

By studious Attention to their Habits and Prejudices, they were at
length gradually brought to assist, and the general Result has been that
each Indian with a Family has now a little Farm under Cultivation, in
which he raises not only Potatoes and Indian Corn, but also Wheat,
Oats, Pease, &c.; his Wigwam is exchanged for the Log House; hunting
has in many Cases been altogether abandoned, and in none appears, as
formerly, to be resorted to as the only Means of Subsistence.

Habitual Intoxication is unknown, the Sabbath is carefully observed,
their Religious Duties carefully attended to, and Reading and Writing,
with a moderate Knowledge of Arithmetic, is almost universal among
the young People.

I attach great Importance to their Habits of Drunkenness being overcome. At the first it was necessary to prohibit the bringing of Spirits
within the Bounds of the Settlement; the near Approach of the White
Settlers has rendered this Restriction no longer possible, and yet Instances of Intoxication are very seldom met with, whilst numerous
Examples may be brought forward of total Abstinence from ardent
Spirits.

The Log Dwelling Houses for the Indians were erected by Government. Frame Houses for the Superintendent and the Two Chiefs, Aisance
and Yellowhead, with Schoolhouses at Coldwater and the Narrows, were
also built at the Commencement of the Establishment. Since that Time
a Saw Mill and a Grist Mill have been added at Coldwater, and a Saw
Mill is in Progress at the Narrows. About 500 Acres in the whole have
been cleared and are under Cultivation, and it is very gratifying to
observe this Year that many of the Indians are, of their own Accord,
and unassisted, erecting Log Barns and Stables.

Another strong Mark of Amendment is in the Article of Dress. All
the Indians here, compared with Indians in a wild State, are well
clothed, and have in most Instances abandoned the Indian Dress for
that of their White Neighbours. They have also become anxious to
possess Furniture, and some have exercised their Ingenuity in the Manufacture of Articles of Household Furniture, for themselves. All have
advanced to a Knowledge of the Difference between Barter and Cash
Transactions, the main Source of Imposition by the Trader; and they
are alive to the Advantages of pursuing their Fishing in the Fall as a
Source of Profit, and not merely for their own Food. To enable them

to do this more extensively they have built for themselves Two Batteaux, each capable of holding Forty or Fifty Barrels of Fish.

I must not omit what I consider highly in their Praise, that, although obliged frequently to submit to irritating and extremely unjust Treatment on the Part of the neighbouring White Settlers, no Indian has, during the whole Period of my Superintendence, been complained of for any Breach of the Laws, with one solitary Exception, for the Removal of Part of a Fence, and that done in Ignorance.

Every Indian throughout the Settlement is possessed of the Means, with moderate Industry, of providing himself with an ample Supply of Food and Clothing, and he has acquired sufficient Knowledge of the Arts of civilized Life to avail himself of these Advantages; the Minds of the younger Branches are opened by Education, and Religion has fixed itself upon the Attention of all.

Can it then be said, because a few Individuals still pursue their Winter's Hunt, because others are idle, and have done little towards extending the Clearings on their Farms, or because some still give way to the Temptations of the Whiskey Bottle, that nothing has been done? Far from it; the Prospect is a very cheering one, and if the innumerable Obstacles thrown in the way of this Settlement be taken into account, this Experiment will appear incontestably to prove, that the Indian, under proper Treatment, is capable of being weaned from his savage Life, and of being made, under the Blessing of the Almighty, a good Member of the Church of Christ, and a dutiful and loyal Subject.

C 13   REPLIES BY ANDERSON TO QUESTIONS ON THE INDIANS
OF THE NEWCASTLE[40] DISTRICT, 1837[41]
[*Great Britain, Colonial Office*, Return to an Address of the Honourable the House of Commons, dated 11th June 1839, for Copies or Extracts of Correspondence . . . Respecting the Indians, *pp. 146–7*]

INFORMATION CALLED FOR.
From Captain Anderson, Rice Lake.

Query 1st.— The Number of Tribes and of Indians resident within this Province?
Answer.— There are Three Tribes of Indians of the Chippewa Nation in the Newcastle District; their Numbers about 500.

Query 2d.— The Pursuits of each Tribe, with the Number of fixed Locations occupied by the Indians?
Answer.— The Pursuits of the Indians in the Newcastle District since

[40]These are the "Chippewa Nation of Indians inhabiting the back part of the NewCastle District" who surrendered a large area in Haliburton and Muskoka in 1818. Since the reserves on which they settled were well to the south of Haliburton, no further extracts concerning their life on the reserves will be included.
[41]Covering letter by Anderson dated Coldwater, May 15, 1837.

they embraced Christianity are principally agricultural. There are Three fixed Locations; viz. Alnwick, Rice Lake, and Mud Lake Indian Settlements.

Query 3d.— The Situation of the Locations of the settled Parties or of Hunting Grounds occupied by the other Indians?
Answer.— The Alnwick Indian Settlement is situate on the South Side of the Rice Lake, about One and a Half Mile back from the Lake. The Rice Lake Indian Settlement is on the North Side of the Lake. The Mud Lake Indian Settlement is situated on a Point of Land on that Lake.
The Hunting Grounds is the Tract of Country through to the Ottawa River.

Query 4th.— The extent of the Lands set apart at the different Locations for the Use of the Indians, or of the Hunting Ranges?
Answer.— The Extent of the Alnwick Indian Settlement is about 3,000 Acres, that of the Rice Lake about 1,200 Acres, and that of the Mud Lake about 1,600 Acres; the Hunting Ranges consist principally of Deer, with which the Country abounds.

Query 5th.— The Number and Description of the Clergy or Teachers attached to each Tribe or Party?
Answer.— There is a Missionary and Schoolmaster of the Wesleyan Methodist Persuasion at the Alnwick and at the Rice Lake Settlements. That at Mud Lake having been principally under the Management of the late Mr. Scott, Agent for the New England Company, the Methodists have never supplied that Settlement with a resident Missionary or Schoolmaster.

C 14   SIR FRANCIS BOND HEAD[42] TO LORD GLENELG[43]
[*Great Britain, Colonial Office,* Return to an Address of the Honourable the House of Commons, dated 11th June 1839, for Copies or Extracts of Correspondence . . . Respecting the Indians, *pp. 150–1*]

Upper Canada, Toronto, 15th August 1837.

. . . In the course of the inspectional Tour which I last Year made of the Province, I assembled, in the Months of August and September the Indians at each of these Places,[44] and after explaining to them how much better, in my Opinion, it would be for them to receive Money for their Hunting Ground than to continue on it, surrounded as it was by the White Population, and consequently deprived as it was of its Game, I

[42]Sir Francis Bond Head, Baronet (1793–1875), Lieutenant Governor of Upper Canada, 1836 to 1838.
[43]Charles Grant, Baron Glenelg (1778–1866), was Colonial Secretary from April, 1835, to February, 1839.
[44]At the Narrows, at Coldwater, and with the Moravian Indians on the Thames.

left them to reflect by themselves on what I had stated. At the Expiration of several Weeks I ordered the Superintendents to bring the Matter again before the Consideration of the Indians, who at their Councils gravely discussed the Subject.

The Chiefs of the Narrows and of Coldwater, after a long Debate, became unanimously of Opinion, that the Offer I had made to their Tribes was advantageous. They accordingly, on the 26th of November, came down in a Body to Toronto to beg me to carry it into effect. An Agreement[45] was accordingly made out and signed by the Chiefs in Presence of the County Members of the Provincial Parliament, and when the Transaction was thus formally closed, the Head Chief, Yellowhead, stepping forward, said to me, "*Father*, our Children, and our Children's Children, will pray to the Great Spirit to bless your Name for what you have this Day done for us!" . . .

C 15   GERALD ALLEY[46] TO S. P. JARVIS,[47] TORONTO
[*P.A.C., Indian Affairs, R.G. 10, v. 124, no. 135*]

Indian Camp Holland Landing
December 30. 1838

I have the honor to enclose you the accompanying recapitulation of the ration returns, for the embodied Indian Warriors[48] of Lakes Huron & Simcoe, encamped at this place, and commencing Novr. 16th. and ending Dec. 31.

To guard against confusion in the provision accounts, I have furnished Mr. Henderson with the ration return for the period between the 16th. and 23d. Novr. and requested him to hand over the amount to Messrs. Dallas and Roe of Orillia, from whom the provisions were obtained.

The balance of those gentlemen's accounts for provisions furnished by them, to some of the Indian families at Orillia, I propose to liquidate with the pay of those warriors, whose families have been supported & to this arrangement those warriors have assented.

[45]Treaty number 48, November 26, 1836, for surrender of lands on the Coldwater Road. It is of special interest for the totems which include that of Bigwing (Bigwin).

[46]Gerald Alley, one of the first white settlers in Orillia, was employed by the government in 1833 to instruct the Indians in farming. In 1835 he was made postmaster at Orillia.

[47]Samuel Peters Jarvis (1792–1857) was Chief Superintendent of Indian Affairs from 1837 to 1845. He organized the Queen's Rangers in the Rebellion of 1837.

[48]The Indians were called to arms by Sir George Arthur to strengthen the forces against the American border raids which followed the Rebellion of 1837. Although the Indians were detained in camp but a short time, it was at the winter season when they would have been in their hunting grounds to the north, and considerable hardship resulted. The names of Yellowhead, Bigwin, and other Indians with hunting grounds in Muskoka were included in the list of chiefs and warriors at the Holland Landing camp (P.A.C., R.G. 10, v. 124).

As the number of families that have been rationed does not amount to 1/3 of the Warriors encamped, the remaining portion expect their pay from the commencement of their services, and in preferring to supply their own families have contracted debts on that account.

I have drawn my returns to the 31st. inclusive that there may be no broken days in the present year—

C 16   ANDREW BORLAND[49] TO ALLEY, TORONTO
[*P.A.C., Indian Affairs, R.G. 10, v. 124, no. 172*]

Holland Landing Jany 30th 1839

Since your absence the Indians have been Complaining most bitterly that they should be called out for so short a time Comming many of them a long distance to serve their Queen & Country & their pay to be stoped at so early period it is going to leave them destitute of means to return to their places from whence they started, they say if their great Mother sends them off in this way, their familys must starve, before they can reach their Hunting grounds, & not only that, but calling them out at that Season of the year, has destroy the means of their making a living for the remaining part of the Winter, notwithstanding those difacultys they are always ready to serve their great Mother when calld upon, but at the same time their great Mother will not forget the wants of her Children, they hope their father at Toronto will make some further provision for them, pay is stoped Rations also stoped, they intend going to Toronto to call on the Governor or their father, if there is nothing more done for them they cannot think of starving on their return home in the middle of a hard Winter.

[Endorsed:] The Lt Gov approves of the Holland Landing Indians receiving Rations up to 28th February. 1839. By command F Halkett[50] A M S.

C 17   CHIEFS OF THE NARROWS INDIANS TO JARVIS
[*P.A.C., Indian Affairs, R.G. 10, v. 128*]

We the undersigned Chiefs of the Narrows Indians who are about to remove to Rama[51] herein enclose a list of the names of our tribe who wish to go to work at once in that township, to clear up some new land for a crop of wheat for the ensuing year, as this work must be done at once, and as we intend as soon as it is completed to go and hunt in order to pay our debts to those we have been so long owing, we have with the consent of our tribe to request that you will be pleased to

[49]Andrew Borland, of Borland and Roe, fur traders and merchants at Newmarket. Borland was in command of a company of two hundred Indians.

[50]Frederic Halkett (d. 1840), Captain of the Coldstream Guards and assistant military secretary.

[51]This move to Rama was necessitated by the sale of their lands in Treaty number 48.

order twenty five pounds worth of flour and twenty five pounds worth of
pork to be furnished for this purpose out of our land payments or any
other monies that may be due unto us. We are induced to go thus to
work, because all other Indians are doing so and we have to hope that
a similar aid will be afforded us, so to do, as was given to John
Sunday, and whereby alone we can enjoy the benefits you have intended
in our new village
Narrows July 1 1839

their

Chief	Yellowhead
Chief	Naingiskkung[52]
Chief	Big Shilling

marks

P.S. That there may be no delay in enabling us thus to go to work we
send a young man down to Toronto to whom you will please to pay
fifteen dollars as we have agreed with him.

C 18   RAMA, SNAKE ISLAND, AND COLDWATER INDIANS
TO SIR CHARLES BAGOT[53]
[*P.A.C., Indian Affairs, R.G. 10, v. 128, no. 545*]

To His Excellency the Right Honourable Sir Charles Bagot Knight
Grand Cross of the Bath Governor General of British North America
&c &c &c
  May it please Your Excellency,— We the Indians residing at Rama,
Snake Island, and Coldwater having met in Council to take into consideration an agreement[54] of a sale of Land we made with Sir F Bond
Head, very humbly desire to approach Your Excellency to obtain an
equitable settlement of the same. The Land in question is situate between
Coldwater, and the Narrows of Lake Simcoe, and according to the
agreement above referred to, we were to receive one third of the interest
arrising from the principal of the money from the said Tract of Land,
annually; another third to be applied to the use of the Indians throughout the Province; and the remaining third "to be applied to any purposes (but not for the benefit of the said Indians) as the Lieutenant
Governor may think proper to direct." We wish to state to Your Excellency that when Sir F Bond Head insisted on our selling this Land and
the bargain he had previously drawn out for us to sign, we were not
made sensible of the full purport, so that we knew not the nature of the
bargain. It may be proper for us to state to Your Excellency that the

[52]The name of Chief Thomas Naingishkung (also spelled Nenageshkung, Nan-
ingishkung, etc.) appears on many Indian documents from the 1830's to the
1860's. In August, 1858, his authority was transferred to his son Joseph Benson
Naingishkung, often known as Joseph Benson.
[53]Sir Charles Bagot, Baronet (1781–1843), was Governor General of British
North America from 1841 to 1843.
[54]Treaty number 48. The clause concerning the distribution of money, which
the Indians are protesting here, was apparently not carried out.

said article of agreement bears date "Toronto 26th. Nov 1836," and up to the present period we have not received any money from the sale of the said Land. May it please Your Excellency— We are not fully satisfied that other people should participate in the money arrising from this sale— We conceive it to be our right to reap the benefit and not others. Also the article of agreement is not satisfactory as it does not specify what the principal of the money comes to. We should like to know, how much per acre is given? and how much the whole comes to? the same as when we sold our Land to our Great Father at other times. In writing to Your Excellency we wish to state particularly that the Grist Mill at Coldwater, and the Saw Mill near the Coldwater road are not included in the agreement and hence we shall continue to consider them as Indian property. If Your Excellency should deem it necessary that we, the heads of our people, should meet at Kingston in order to a final adjustment of the said Land we are ready to repair thither at any time, only we would add, it is the opinion and wish of our people that a moiety of the money be paid down, the other to be deposited in the Bank of Upper Canada that we may draw the Intrest annually.

We beg to renew our expressions of attachment to our Great Mother the Queen and our grateful feelings for the care our Great Mother is ever taking of us. Also in Your Excellency we repose the fullest confidence, and we pray the Good Spirit to make Your Excellency more and more happy and Your Excellencys children throughout British America more peaceful and more contented.

Rama Lake Simcoe
May 26th 1842
                    Signed
          Head Chief Wm. Yellowhead's

          Chief Joseph's[55]

          Chief John Ascanse's

          Chief Thos. Nangashking's

          Chief Big Shilling's

          Chief Peter Katahkgwn's[56]

          John Snake[57] Interpreter

[55]Probably Chief Joseph Snake of Snake Island. He died in 1861 and was succeeded by Simpson Bigsail.

[56]This name has variant spellings: Ketawkegkwn, Gade-que-gunn, Gadahgegwin, etc.

[57]John Snake of Snake Island was interpreter and chief's orator.

C 19   The "Robinson" Treaty

[P.A.C., Indian Treaties and Surrenders, R.G. 10, ser. 4, v. 4, Treaty no. 61; also printed in Indian Treaties and Surrenders, *v. 1, pp. 149–52]*

THIS AGREEMENT made and entered into this ninth day of September, in the year of our Lord one thousand Eight hundred and fifty at Sault Ste: Marie, in the Province of Canada, BETWEEN the Honorable William Benjamin Robinson[58] of the one part, on behalf of Her Majesty the Queen, and Shinguacouse, Nebenaigoching, Keokouse, Mishequonga, Tagawinini, Shabokeshick, Dokis,[59] Ponekeosh, Windawtegowinini, Shawenakeshick, Namassin, Naoquagabo, Wabakekek, Kitchipossegun by Papasainse, Wagemake, Pamequonaishung, Chiefs, and John Bell, Paqwutchinini, Mashekyash, Idowekesis, Waquacomiek, Ocheek, Metigomin, Watachewana, Minwawapenasse, Shenaoquom, Ouingegun, Panaissy, Papasainse, Ashewasega, Kageshewawetung, Shawonebin, and also Chief Maisquaso (also Chiefs Muckata, Mishoquet and Mekis[60]), and Mishoquetto, and Asa Waswanay and Pawiss, Principal Men of the Ojibway Indians inhabiting and claiming the eastern and northern shores of Lake Huron from Penetanguishene to Sault Ste. Marie, and thence to Batchewanaung Bay on the northern shore of Lake Superior, together with the Islands in the said Lakes opposite to the shores thereof, and in land, to the height of Land which separates the territory covered by the Charter of the Honorable Hudson Bay Company from Canada, as well as all unconceded Lands within the limits of Canada West to which they have any just claim of the other part, Witnesseth, that for and in consideration of the sum of Two thousand Pounds of good and lawful money of Upper Canada to them in hand paid, and for the further perpetual annuity of six hundred Pounds of like money; the same to be paid and delivered to the said Chiefs and their Tribes at a convenient season of each year, of which due notice will be given, at such places as may be appointed for that purpose; they the said Chiefs and principal Men, on behalf of their respective tribes or bands, do hereby fully, freely and voluntarily surrender, cede, grant, and convey unto Her Majesty, Her Heirs and Successors for ever, all their right, title and interest to and in the whole of the territory above described, save and except the reser-

[58]William Benjamin Robinson (1797–1873) was a brother of Chief Justice John Beverley Robinson. After the death of his father in 1798, his mother married Elisha Beman, and W. B. Robinson lived in his step-father's home at Newmarket. As a young man he traded in furs with the Indians in the Muskoka district and is said to have had trading posts on Yoho Island and at the mouth of the Muskoka River. He represented Simcoe County in the House of Assembly from 1830 to 1841, and in the Legislative Assembly of the Province of Canada from 1844 to 1857. He served as Inspector General from 1844 to 1845, and as Chief Commissioner of Public Works from 1846 to 1847. In 1850 he negotiated the so-called Robinson Treaty.

[59]Chief Dokis or Dukis was the leader of a band on Lake Nipissing.

[60]Mekis or Megis was the chief of the Muskoka Band at Sandy Island. He died about 1858, and was succeeded by James Begahmegahbow (C 22).

vations set forth in the schedule hereunto annexed— which reservations shall be held and occupied by the said Chiefs and their Tribes in common for their own use and benefit— and should the said Chiefs and their respective Tribes at any time desire to dispose of any part of such reservations, or of any Mineral or other valuable productions thereon, the same will be sold or leased at their request by the Superintendent General of Indian Affairs for the time being, or other Officer having authority so to do, for their sole benefit, and to the best advantage. And the said William Benjamin Robinson of the first part on behalf of Her Majesty and the Government of this Province hereby promises and agrees to make or cause to be made the payments as before mentioned, and further to allow the said Chiefs and their Tribes the full and free privilege to hunt over the territory now ceded by them; and to fish in the Waters thereof, as they have heretofore been in the habit of doing, saving and excepting such portions of the said territory as may from time to time be sold or leased to individuals or Companies of individuals and occupied by them with the consent of the Provincial Government. The parties of the second part further promise and agree that they will not sell, lease or otherwise dispose of any portion of their reservations without the consent of the Superintendent General of Indian Affairs or other officer of like authority being first had and obtained; nor will they at any time hinder or prevent persons from exploring or searching for Minerals or other valuable productions in any part of the territory hereby ceded to Her Majesty as before mentioned. The parties of the second part also agree that in case the Government of this Province should before the date of this agreement have sold, or bargained to sell, any mining locations or other property on the portions of the territory hereby reserved for their use, then and in that case such sale or promise of sale shall be perfected by the Government, if the parties claiming it shall have fulfilled all the conditions upon which such locations were made, and the amount accruing therefrom shall be paid to the Tribe to whom the reservation belongs. The said William Benjamin Robinson, on behalf of Her Majesty, who desires to deal liberally and justly with all her subjects, further promises and agrees that should the territory hereby ceded by the parties of the second part at any future period produce such an amount as will enable the Government of this Province without incurring loss to increase the annuity hereby secured to them, then and in that case, the same shall be augmented from time to time, provided that the amount paid to each individual shall not exceed the sum of one Pound Provincial Currency in any one year, or such further sum as Her Majesty may be graciously pleased to order; and provided further that the number of Indians entitled to the benefit of this treaty shall amount to two thirds of their present number, which is fourteen hundred and twenty two to entitle them to claim the full benefit thereof, and should they not at any future period amount to two thirds of Fourteen hundred and twenty two, then the said annuity shall be diminished in proportion to their actual numbers.

The said William Benjamin Robinson, of the first part further agrees on the part of Her Majesty and the Government of this Province that in consequence of the Indians inhabiting French River and Lake Nipissing having become parties to this treaty the further sum of one hundred and sixty pounds Provincial Currency shall be paid in addition to the two thousand pounds above mentioned. . . .

C 20   THE CHIPPEWAS IN 1858
[Canada, Special Commission . . . to Investigate Indian Affairs in Canada, Report, 1858, pp. 80–5, 286]

THE CHIPPEWAS OF LAKES HURON AND SIMCOE.

This Tribe having originally migrated from Lake Superior, occupied as their hunting ground, the vast tract stretching from Collin's Inlet on the north-eastern shore of the Georgian Bay to the northern limits of the land claimed by the Mississaguas.

Of this they have surrendered at different times nearly the whole; having ceded in 1795[61] 28,000 acres for a payment of £100, in 1815[62] a further tract of 250,000 acres for £4,000. These were absolute sales, and the Indians now derive nothing from these surrenders.

They subsequently in 1818[63] gave up to the Crown 1,542,000 acres for a perpetual annuity of £1,200. In 1836,[64] they surrendered the tract of 9,800 acres on the Portage road from Simcoe to Coldwater, on which they were located by Sir John Colborne six years previously. This land was to be sold, and under the terms of the Treaty, the proceeds were to be applied for the benefit of Indians generally. This however has not been carried out, and the Lake Huron and Simcoe bands enjoy the whole benefit of the surrender.

This is in conformity with the usual terms of land surrendered, and as they have received the money for so many years, it would be unwise to disturb the present arrangement.

Their present reserves consist only of 1,600 acres purchased out of their own funds at Rama on the east side of Lake Couchiching, some Islands in that Lake and Lake Simcoe, and the Christian Islands in the Georgian Bay.

The Tribe has split into three Bands, called respectively from the locations of the Villages, The Rama, Snake Island, and Beausoleil Bands. They have lately surrendered the Island occupied by the last named Band, who intend to remove to the Christian Islands.

As the three divisions have nothing in common but their annuities, the present condition of each will be best seen by considering them separately.

[61]Treaty number 5 for Penetanguishene area (*Indian Treaties and Surrenders*, v. 1, pp. 15–17).
[62]Treaty number 16 for Oro, Medonte, Tiny, and Tay (*ibid.*, pp. 43–5).
[63]Treaty number 18 for the Collingwood area (*ibid.*, p. 47).
[64]Treaty number 48 (*ibid.*, p. 117).

The revenue of the whole Tribe is at present $5,658 composed as follows:

Annuity for land ceded in 1818, $4,800.

Proceeds of land sale in the tract surrendered in 1835, $858.

They may expect an increase in their income, when the lands given up, but not yet sold, are brought into the market.

CHIPPEWAS OF RAMA

This Band was located on its present Reserve in 1838. It affords one of the most striking and lamentable instances of the deterioration which has taken place in the condition of the Indians by reductions in the number of officers appointed to superintend and direct them in the road to civilization. . . .

Their present settlement contains 1,600 acres of land purchased by themselves out of their annuity at a cost of $3,200. Five years after they established themselves there they had cleared 300 acres of land, had built 20 houses, and raised four barns, while they were able to dispose of their surplus agricultural produce to the surrounding settlers.

Their condition in 1857 is described as follows:

"This Band have belonging to the community only one yoke of oxen, though farming implements, oxen, cows, horses and seed grain have been repeatedly supplied, yet, like most of the other Tribes, they have not benefitted by the advantage. A frame church is under construction, they have also a log school-house. The Rev. Peter Jacobs is missionary and school-master, but the Indians inform me, school is not taught more than half the time. The log houses built for them about 13 or 14 years ago, being badly constructed, are all going to decay. Two frame barns which were built at the same time and at great expense are stripped of the weather boards by the Indians themselves, and the frames falling in ruins. This Band are much given to hunting and basket making, consequently avoid tilling the soil, and are dragging through a life disgraceful to humanity."

The Band appears to be on the increase, the census in 1857 shewing a total of 201; in 1842 their numbers were returned as 184. The live stock belonging to individuals is stated to be 5 horses, 3 oxen, 10 cows, 4 pigs and 8 head of live stock. They own 32 houses and 2 barns. Their farming implements consist of 4 ploughs and 3 harrows, and in 1856 they raised only

Indian Corn	77	Bushels
Pease	9	"
Potatoes	940	"
Hay	11	Tons.

Their revenue at present is derived from their share of the annuity receivable by the Chippewas of Lakes Huron and Simcoe, amounting to $1547 33 besides $346 88, the interest of the sales of the Coldwater tract, in all $1894 21. They however, in conjunction with the other

Bands comprised under this denomination, will participate in the proceeds of their lands surrendered for sale and not yet brought into the market.

BEAUSOLEIL BAND

This band were settled by Sir John Colborne in 1830, at Coldwater, Medonté Township, whence they removed in 1842 to Beausoleil Island in Metchadash Bay.

The account given of them by their Superintendent is very satisfactory as regards their moral character and industry. In spite of the disadvantages of their location, they seem to have made considerable progress since the date of the Commissioners' Report in 1844–5. They had then 14 houses and a barn, and had 100 acres under cultivation.

The returns of this year shew an increase of 6 in the number of houses, besides a school house. They keep a considerable quantity of stock, and estimate their crop of Indian corn to have yielded 1200 bushels. They also raised 1000 bushels of Patatoes [sic]. In addition they made about 5000 pounds of sugar and cured 150 barrels of fish caught at the fisheries near the Island which abound in bass and pike.

The Island contains nearly 4000 acres, of which some 300 have been cleared by the Indians. We do not suppose however that all of this was under crop in any one year, as the rude culture adopted by the Indians speedily exhausts the soil. We learn therefore that after a single crop, the clear sharp sand appears in the top, obliging them to seek fresh land, or commence new clearings.

The village is gradually falling into decay, and the Band having surrendered this Island contemplate removing to the Christian Islands which they have reserved for their permanent occupation, and which are estimated to contain 10,000 acres.

They appear to have remained quite stationary in numbers since 1842. They were then reckoned at 232, and the Census of the present year shews their actual strength to be 233.

Their School-master is absent, and the Superintendent reports that "The Band in General Council have resolved that for the present, they will not pay any salaries to Chiefs or others except the Doctor, as it is so much money taken from the funds of the Band, without any corresponding benefit."

The majority of this Band are Roman Catholics.

There are already residing on the Christian Islands a few Pottawatamies and Ottawas, in all 94.

The former, who came from Lake Michigan, remain heathens though every effort has been made to christianise them.

They have no money payments; but the Beausoleil Indians have offered to receive them into their Band and share the annuity with them if they will abandon their heathenish customs and embrace christianity. Like all the unconverted Tribes they are much addicted to intemperate habits.

The Ottawa, in number 45, who are principally Roman Catholics, migrated here in 1854. Having heard that their payments from the United States Government were about to cease, and that the Indians in that part of the Country were to be sent to the west of the Mississippi, they preferred living under the English flag, and the Chippewas of Beausoleil are willing to adopt them as they have no funds of their own. They are described as better Farmers, and more sober in their habits than the Pottawatamies, but no details have been received as to their settlement or the produce raised by them.

The Revenue of the Beausoleil Band is $2,124 44 made up of $1,735 46 alloted to them from their Annuity, and $388 98 interest derived from the funded proceeds of lands sold for their benefit.

SNAKE ISLAND BAND.

The Snake Island Indians derive their name from their location in Lake Simcoe. They only occupy Snake and Machego Islands, but other very valuable Islands are still unsurrendered. They are principally Methodists, but have no resident preacher. The Rev. Peter Jacobs, from Rama, visits them occasionally. Their school is kept by Mr. Law, who sometimes counts 40 children under his tuition. The attendance is, however, very variable, there being frequently but 8 or 10 pupils present, at other times none.

The following statistical Returns shew the band to be generally in a tolerable condition as regards their advance towards civilization; much, however, remains to be done, and we believe that the principle of concentration might be successfully applied in this instance. Were the Islands in Lake Simcoe ceded, steps might with advantage be taken for uniting the Snake Island and Rama Bands, and placing them under a more constant supervision.

The Snake Island Band partakes of the habits of their brethren at Rama. They spend the principal part of their time in fishing and hunting. This disposition is favoured by their location on the Islands in Lake Simcoe, and their buildings on them are fast falling into decay. They have there 20 dwelling-houses and a log barn; besides a frame school house, occasionally used as a church, and 2 frame barns, which are described as literally falling to pieces. The frame buildings are public property. They hold in common 3 yoke of oxen, one plough, a harrow, and 2 carts, while individuals possess 8 horses, 8 head of horned cattle, and 5 pigs. The returns give also 2 ploughs, one harrow and 3 sleighs, as private property.

From 39 acres actually in cultivation, they raised this year:

Fall Wheat	70	Bushels
Spring do.	50	”
Indian Corn	77	”
Oats	60	”
Potatoes	780	”

They also saved 13½ tons of hay. The land cleared by them extends over 95 acres. The greatest quantity cultivated by one Indian is 8 acres, on which were grown 80 of the 120 bushels of wheat above mentioned.

Their revenue is as follows:

Annuity $1036 54/100
Land Fund 232 37/100

[SANDY ISLAND INDIANS]

The Sandy Island Indians are Heathen, and live alternately on the borders of Lake Huron, about 50 miles north-west of Penetanguishine, and in the interior north of that place; they cultivate very small patches of Corn and Potatoes, not as a dependence for food during the Winter but rather as a bon-bouche in the Autumn.

The only farming implements they possess are a few axes and iron hoes, and in absence of the latter, crooked sticks are used as a substitute. When they go to the interior in the Autumn to hunt Beaver and other animals for their skins, they generally carry a supply of dried fish in case of a failure in their trapping.

When they return to the Lake in the Winter, they resort to the precarious mode of procuring food by cutting holes in the Ice and watching for and spearing such fish as may be attracted by a decoy or are casually passing by, in this way they some days kill as many as 100, but at other times they lay on the ice for many days together, and perhaps do not see one, in the meantime hare and partridge snares are depended upon for subsistence.

They have hitherto resisted all the attempts made to civilize them, and cling with uncountable tenacity to the foolish superstitions imbibed from their fathers.

C 21   W. R. BARTLETT[65] TO CHIEF YELLOWHEAD FOR THE
MISKOKO[66] INDIANS
[P.A.C., Indian Affairs, R.G. 10, v. 544]

Indian Office
Toronto August 4, 1859

Your letter of the 12 Inst [sic] applying on behalf of the Miskoko Indians for the grant of a parcel of land North of Miskoko Lake, has been received by the Superintendent General of Indian Affairs, who has instructed me to tell you in reply that he has no power to make Reserves on land which has been already surrendered.

I cannot understand what is meant by the allusion to a promise made by the Government concerning their payments. I cannot ascertain that

[65]W. R. Bartlett was Indian Superintendent at Toronto, 1858 to 1873.

[66]The Miskoko or Muskoka Indians belonged to the Sandy Island band. At this time they were living between Lakes Muskoka and Rosseau. (C 24 and C 25).

any promises have been made to the Miskoko Indians for the payment of money. I would like to know more clearly what payments you refer to.

The Indians however may rest assured that if a promise has been made to them by the Government, it will be performed in good faith.

C 22   BARTLETT TO JAMES BEGAHMIGABOW, ACTING CHIEF OF MUSKOKA, CARE OF WILLIAM SIMPSON, PENETANGUISHENE
[P.A.C., Indian Affairs, R.G. 10, v. 545]

Indian Office
Toronto October 10. 1860

With reference to the document handed me last spring at Penetanguishene signed by Chief William Yellowhead of Rama in which it is stated that you are the present chief of Muskoko I have the honor to inform you that your appointmt. has met with the approval of the Superintendent General of Indian Affairs, and I am to instruct you to continue to act as chief during the minority of the late Chief Megis's eldest son who when he is old enough to perform the duties of that office, will fill the place of his late father.

In conveying to you the Superintendent Generals decision I would beg leave to add that, as it is desirable that every Indian chief should be able to read and write, young Megis will be expected to avail himself of every means that may be afforded him to acquire the elementary parts of a common English education in order that he may qualify himself in some measure for the office he is to fill. He should be also made aware that the Department will not appoint any Indian of intemperate and dishonest habits to the office of Chief.

C 23   VERNON B. WADSWORTH'S[67] REMINISCENCES OF INDIANS IN MUSKOKA AND HALIBURTON, 1860–4
[V. B. Wadsworth, Incidents of the Survey, pp. 1–3, 13–14, 6–7; original in possession of W. R. Wadsworth, Q.C., Toronto]

I met the Indian Medicine Man of the Ojibway Tribe, named Musquedo, at Obogawanung Village, now Port Carling. He was then eighty years of age but strong and vigorous. He had a flag pole in front of his hut with an emblem on top to denote his vocation. He invited me to a White Dog Feast and other pagan ceremonies when Mr. Hart and I were camped at the end of the Indian River on Lake Muskoka. He had

[67]Vernon Bayley Wadsworth (1843?–1940) was articled to John Stoughton Dennis in 1860 and immediately set out on surveys in the Muskoka, Parry Sound, and Nipissing districts. He qualified as a land surveyor May, 1864, and was in partnership for a time with B. W. Gossage and later with Charles Unwin. The firm of Wadsworth and Unwin was active for several years in government, railway, and other surveys. In 1876 Wadsworth became inspector for the London and Canadian Loan and Agency Company and later its general manager. His reminiscences were written in 1926.

a large silver medal conferred upon him for bravery at the battle of Queenston Heights in 1812, in which he participated on the British side with other Indians of the Georgian Bay district. His son, William King, was elected Chief of the band and I stayed one night with King and his sister in their hut en route to join our survey party at Portage Bay, Lake Rosseau.

I feel sure that Muskoka Lake was named after old Musquedo, although other residents of that section say that it was named after an Indian from Lake Simcoe.

Lake Rosseau,[68] in my opinion, was named after an Indian interpreter named Rosseau who was employed by Governor Simcoe in his treaties and interviews with Indian tribes on Lake Ontario and with the Indians of Georgian Bay and Lake Simcoe districts. Rosseau's home was at the mouth of the Humber River on Lake Ontario, near Toronto, and on the Indian portage leading from Humber Bay to Lake Simcoe.

William King, the son of Musquedo and Indian Chief of the Port Carling band, was always dressed in black broadcloth clothes when at Penetanguishene or other outside village centres and also wore a high black hat.

. . .

I met another Indian and his wife and family, named Abram Asey. He was encamped on the Rosseau Village Bay in a wigwam near the present Rosseau steamboat wharf . . . His birch bark wigwam was warm and comfortable and the floor covered with beaver and other valuable furs, and I envied him for possessing such a comfortable lodging as this winter camp. Asey's permanent home was on Beausoleil Island in the Georgian Bay.

When our survey party was at the Bridge site on the Muskoka River (now Bracebridge) the only settler there, named Cooper,[69] entertained our survey party men and staff and had a dance at his log house. Cooper was unmarried and was a fiddler, so he cleaned out the one room of his house to permit of a dance and Asey, the Indian, was one of the party and was requested to give an exhibition of an Indian war dance. To this he agreed and, as he was concluding it, he gave a loud war-whoop, pulled out his scalping knife and quick as lightning seized me by the waist and threw me to the floor on my back, and with knee on my breast and his knife brandished, pretended to cut my throat, much to the amusement of the assembled party all but myself. Asey let me get up with no bodily hurt, but I felt much humiliated and naturally so, being only a boy of sixteen years of age.

The Indian Village of Obogawanung, now Port Carling, consisted of some 20 log huts, beautifully situated on the Indian River and Silver

[68]See footnote 37 to C 11.

[69]This was probably Joseph Cooper (1837?–1933), son of James Cooper, an early settler in Bracebridge. Joseph Cooper owned a sawmill and a grocery and provision business which carried supplies for the lumber camps. He also built houses and timber slides, and for some time was a member of the village council.

Lake with a good deal of cleared land about it used as garden plots, and the Indians grew potatoes, Indian corn, and other vegetable products. They had no domestic animals but dogs and no boats but numerous birch bark canoes.

The fall on the River there, being the outlet of Lake Rosseau, was about eight feet, and fish and game were very plentiful. When Mr. Hart and I were encamped there, Musquedo brought us potatoes and corn and we gave him pork and tobacco in return.

. . .

When the survey party camped at the Portage near the present village of Windermere leading from Portage Bay, Lake Rosseau, to Three Mile Lake, one evening after our dinner when the men were singing their French songs, our dogs commenced to growl and their hair bristled up and we all said there were wolves or bears near. Presently, however, the dogs gave tongue and we heard a rustling of snowshoes on the portage path and instead of animals a small Indian boy appeared in the fire-light. Our men could speak Indian and questioned him as to where he came from and at such a late hour in the woods and in the depth of winter. He stated that he had been visiting Henomenee[70] and family at Mary's Lake and was going to his home at Obogawanung (Port Carling). He had travelled all alone about twenty miles to our camp through the wild woods and then would cross Lake Rosseau to his home. The boy had a fine little Indian pup, carrying it in his bosom—a present from his Mary Lake friends. We soon gave him food and tea and he spent the night at our camp and then started for home the next morning, well fed and in good spirits.

In visiting that Indian Village of Obogawanung, I was informed that many of the Indian men had two wives, which was the custom of those pagan Indians, but not of those Indians professing Christianity. The men who were employed in our surveying operations were great axe-men, packmen and canoe-men and prided themselves on their walking powers. I have known them to walk or run between daylight and dark on their journeys on the ice of Georgian Bay, sixty to eighty miles, and then dance all night, and if occasion required they could do without food for long periods and travel with heavy loads.

. . .

When in the Township of Guilford, I met some Indians from Rama on Lake Couchiching. They were trapping and hunting there and I purchased a dog from them named Wawaskosh (or "Deer", in their Ojibway language). . . .

While in the Township of Guilford I had the ill luck to cut my arm

[70]The name was spelled Menominee by Wadsworth in his "History of Exploratory Surveys" (D 16). Menominee apparently belonged to the Rama Reserve and hunted in the Mary Lake and Lake of Bays region. He was well known to the early settlers there, and his name was given to one of the post offices.

with an axe and I had to keep my arm in a sling. The pork diet did not help to heal the wound and I feared proud flesh was appearing. However, one day two of those Rama Indian women visited our camp to get a good meal and gossip. While there one woman saw my arm in a sling and asked to see the wound and after seeing it she went off into the woods and soon returned munching bark or something like it and presently, after fully masticating the material, she placed the stuff in poultice form on my wound and it proved most efficacious and soon healed the wound. Those Indians, two families, the Yorks and Antoines, still reside in Rama Indian Village . . .

In the Township of Harcourt I stayed with an Indian named Barnard. He came from the Lake of Two Mountains in Quebec. His wife was educated by the nuns in the convent there. There was great fishing near their house on the Madawaska River— grey trout of large size and speckled trout. There were great numbers of deer in that district also. It was interesting to note that on a portage between two lakes, one running into Gull River of Trent River waters and the other into the Madawaska waters and only about 600 feet in length, in the Trent waters there were no speckled trout and they abound in the Madawaska waters such a short distance away. I cannot give the reason for this. I and my men spent a night there with that Indian and enjoyed his hospitality. They belonged to the Huron Tribe of Indians from the reserves in Quebec Province who came up the Ottawa River, and the tributary Madawaska River, to this point.

C 24   COLONEL J. S. DENNIS[71] TO P. M. VANKOUGHNET[72]
[*P.A.C., Indian Affairs, R.G. 10, v. 283*]

Toronto, 21st. Feb 1862.

I consider it my duty to report to you that while on the Surveys back of Lake Muskoka, last month, on the request of the Indians residing at that place I attended a council of the Band, convened for the purpose of adopting an address to His Excellency asking to allow them to exchange the land reserved to them on Lake Huron by the treaty of 1849[73] for a tract where they reside.

[71]Colonel John Stoughton Dennis (1820–1885), son of Joseph Dennis of "Buttonwood," near Weston, was commissioned a surveyor in 1842. He carried on extensive surveys and trained many well-known surveyors. In 1869 he was sent by the Canadian government to set up a system of surveys in Manitoba, a system which was partly responsible for the Red River insurrection. From 1871 to 1885 he served as Surveyor General of Canada.

[72]Philip Michael Matthew Scott Vankoughnet (1823?–1869) was Minister of Agriculture from 1856 to 1858 and Commissioner of Crown Lands from 1858 to 1862.

[73]A reservation attached to the Robinson Treaty in 1850 provided "For Chief Mekis and his Band, residing at Wasaquising (Sandy Island), a tract of land at a place on the main shore opposite the island, being the place now occupied by them for residence and cultivation, four miles square."

By that treaty "Megis" and Band (the Muskoka Band) became entitled to a tract on the main land north of Parry Island— 16 square miles.

When Mr. Keating[74] and myself were sent subsequently to set apart the tract in common with the other Reserves on that Lake— these Indians met us and had a Council at which they desired us to attend the object of which was to ask that Parry Island might be substituted for the tract on the main shore—

After some consideration Mr Keating and myself took upon ourselves to consent to the proposition and since that the Island has constituted their reserve, the majority of the Band however who always remained at Muskoka[75] (the name "Muskoka" being derived from Musk-ko-do —one of the principal men of the community) became less inclined each succeeding year to leave the locality where they had lived for so many years and go out to settle on Parry Island, and some two years back they besought me to bring the matter of the present proposed exchange under the consideration of the government for them— No convenient opportunity however occurred till the other day when the council resulted in a formal proposition to surrender Parry Island and to receive in lieu a tract where they now reside.

Their communication to His Excellency will doubtless be placed in your hands and I would beg to observe that if my opinion as a party conversant with the matter from the beginning and also as knowing the land at both places— were asked— I should say I know of no reason why their request should not be granted — on the contrary I think an exchange might be made which would be mutually advantageous.

I would suggest in case that proposition should be entertained that it should be part of the instructions, to whoever might be sent to effect the exchange with the Band— that the Government reserve the right if at any future time thought desirable to construct a Road through their Reserve at Muskoka and Bridge over the strait between Lakes Rosseau and Muskoka.

C 25   BARTLETT TO WILLIAM SPRAGGE,[76] DEPUTY SUPERINTENDENT
OF INDIAN AFFAIRS, QUEBEC
[P.A.C., Indian Affairs, R.G. 10, v. 546]

Indian Office
Toronto July 11. 1862

Referring to my former letters respecting the Muskoka Indians' claim to Parry Island, I have the honor to state that a few days ago, I met at

[74]John William Keating, surveyor of Rama and other Indian lands. For a time he was Assistant Indian Superintendent at Walpole Island and at Sarnia.
[75]The area between Lakes Rosseau and Muskoka.
[76]William Prosperous Spragge (1808–1874) entered the Surveyor General's Office in 1829 and later became the chief clerk for Canada West. On March 17,

the Christian Island, Solomon James the Principal chief of the Shawanaga or Sandy Island band of Indians, who, at a council held there,
made to me a statement in regard to the position of the Muskoka Indians, and their asserted right to surrender Parry Island.

Chief James assured me, and I have no reason to suspect his statement, that the chief Bagemagabow (successor to Megis) and his band—
and himself (the successor of Muh.Kah.da.mi.zhu quod) & his band,
comprise the Shawanaga or Sandy Island Tribe of Indians— That when
the three Reserves were set apart for them under the Robinson Treaty,
these bands agreed in a Council that their Reserves should be held in
common, and they settled it amongst themselves, that they would all
remove from their reserves on which they resided, and go to Parry
Island, as the land was better than that on the main land.

He assured me that Bagemagahbow was a party to this agreement,
and on referring, on my return from the Island to the Papers in this
office, I find that chiefs name to the Petition addressed to the Hon Mr.
VanKoughnet on the 21st Jany last, transmitted by me to Mr. Walcot
on the 29 March 1862.

Chief James states that, notwithstanding Bagemagahbow now wishes
to set up an exclusive claim to Parry Island and wants to surrender the
same for land at Muskoka, a large majority of the Sandy Island Indians,
comprising these two bands before mentioned, are against its surrender,
and he requested me to say that on behalf of that majority he protests
against the Proceedings of the Muskoka Indians.

These statements of James lead me to believe that the Reserves of
these Bands are held in a similar way to those of the Rice & Mud Lakes,
& the Chippewas of Lake Huron & Simcoe, that is, each band is equally
interested in all their reserves.

This being the case it would not be right to grant the Prayer of the
Muskoka Indians, without further inquiry into the matter.

C 26   BARTLETT TO INDIAN CHIEFS AND WARRIORS OF RAMA
AND SNAKE ISLAND
[*P.A.C., Indian Affairs. R.G. 10, v. 547*]

Indian Office
Toronto Jany 22. 1863.

Having submitted your Petition to His Excellency the Governor General through the Supt Genl of Indian Affairs, in which you put forth a
claim to a large tract of land extending from the River Talbot to the
height of land which divides the waters of Lake Huron from those which
fall into the Ottawa, embracing Lake Muskoka, and other places, I am
instructed to explain to you that the agreement[77] made on the 5th Nov-

---

1862, he was made Deputy Superintendent for Indian Affairs and continued in this
office after Confederation.   [77]Treaty number 20 (C 6).

ember 1818 between the Honbl Col Claus Dep supt Genl of Indian Affairs & Buckquaquet, Peshekins, Potash and others executed at Smiths Creek, has been examined, and from this document it appears that the Indians conveyed to the Crown for the yearly consideration of £740. the tract extending on the South from the Southern Shores of the Rice Lake, River Trent &c to the line 45 on the North and extending from a point about 33 miles in a course N 16° West from the N W angle of the township of Rawdon and from thence along the said line 45 to a Bay at the Northern entrance of Lake Simcoe— This Bay or inlet is of course Lake Couchiching where it flows into the Severn.[78]

The Robinson Treaty signed 9th Sept 1850 embraces all the land on the east coast of Lake Huron Northward and Westward to the Sault Ste Marie coming down Southwest at Penetanguishine to the vicinity of the Severn. It leaves nothing unceded. Such being the case it is not to be supposed that the Government would be prepared to listen to the claim of the Rama Indians, unless it can be shewn that the Treaties alluded to were made with Indians who did not possess the right which they exercised

C 27   DEATH OF YELLOWHEAD REPORTED TO BARTLETT
[*P.A.C., Indian Affairs, R.G. 10, v. 277, B 566*]

Rama, Indian Village,
Feby 1st. 1864.

We have to Report to you the death of our Head Chief— William Yellowhead. He returned from his hunting just after Christmas in his usual health, but was taken ill on Friday the 8th Jany, and on Monday[79] 12th Jany. he died about 9, A.M. having been ill a little over three days. A Medical Gentleman was called in on Sunday, but the disease could not then be checked.

His age was supposed to be upwards of 100 years.

Thos. X Nanageshkung
George X Young
Joseph B Nanegeshkung

C 28   BARTLETT TO JAMES DALLAS,[80] ORILLIA
[*P.A.C., Indian Affairs, R.G. 10, v. 547*]

Ind Office Toronto Feb 11. 1864

I have recd your letter of the 15th ulto enclosing the will of the late Chief Wm Yellowhead.

[78]See footnote 23 to C 6.
[79]Friday was January 8, 1864, and Monday was January 11 not 12.
[80]James Dallas (d. 1872) came to Orillia from Edinburgh in 1835. He was active in municipal life, and in 1843 was appointed a magistrate.

Indians in the eye of the law are looked upon and treated as Minors—consequently wills made by them have not been considered as of any legal value— They may be useful however in shewing the remaining chiefs & Indians of the Band, how the deceased chief wished his effects to be disposed of— Indians you are aware cannot dispose of land—

Since the decease of my Indian assistant Mr Francis Assickinack,[81] I have been quite alone in my office, with such a pressure of work in arrear that I have been unable to reply to your letter before

I herein return the will

C 29   COPY OF YELLOWHEAD'S WILL
[P.A.O., Miscellaneous Mss]

I William Yellowhead, of the Township of Rama in the County of Ontario, Head Chief of the Chippewa tribe of Indians and being of sound and disposing mind and memory do make and publish this my last will and testament hereby revoking all former wills by me at any time heretofore made.

First— I give and devise to my wife Elizabeth Yellowhead all my household goods and furniture.

Second— I give and devise to my nephew Isaac Yellowhead,[82] his heirs executors administrators and assigns all my right title and interest in and unto the following lands— viz— lots number seven and eight situated in the township of Rama containing by admeasurement two hundred acres and may be better known as the land upon which I now reside also that lot of land owned by me on the Black river also my hunting ground situated on Trading Lake and extending from said lake to Trout Lake and better known as the hunting ground belonging to the Chief of the Yellowhead family.

Third— I also appoint and declare my nephew Isaac Yellowhead my sole heir and successor to the Chiefship of the Chippewa tribe and direct that he be installed Head Chief of the Chippewa tribe by my people and the Government of Canada after my death.

Fourth— I also direct that my nephew Isaac Yellowhead is to take care of and provide for my wife Elizabeth Yellowhead and my daughter Jane Yellowhead so long as they remain single and unmarried.

In witness whereof I the said William Yellowhead have hereunto set my hand and seal the 20th. day of September in the year of our Lord 1861—

Signed sealed and published and declared by the said testator William Yellowhead as and for his last will and testament in the presence of us

[81]Francis Assikinack (1824?–1863), an Indian, had been sent to Upper Canada College by S. P. Jarvis, and was later employed as clerk and interpreter in the Indian Department.

[82]Yellowhead was succeeded as head chief, not by Isaac Yellowhead but by Joseph Benson Naingishkung.

who at his request and in his presence and in the presence of each other
have subscribed our names as witnesses thereto.

   Edward Gaudor— of the Township of Rama in the County of Ontario
      Yeoman and
William Gaudor of the same place.

his

William   Yellowhead

mark

C 30   JAMES W. BRIDGLAND[83] TO COMMISSIONER OF CROWN LANDS, ALEXANDER CAMPBELL[84]
[P.A.O., Colonization Roads Papers, Reports 1862–8, p. 260]

Department of Crown Lands
Quebec 7th. August, 1865

   . . . I visited also in the vicinity of Rosseau Lake, the Indian settlement. This settlement is formed by a few families of Pagan Indians, who
hitherto have refused social intercourse with Christian indians, and object
to Missionary visitations. They have under imperfect cultivation, some
30 or 40 acres of land, planted this season with corn, potatoes, pumpkins, and beans. They have log houses, and as many dogs as Human
inhabitants.

   The land occupied is of a sandy quality, and cleared and cultivated
in the most slovenly and wretched manner. Not only do dead standing
trees deform the ground, but fallen ones obstruct and cover much of the
same, and from year to year, the limited crop is planted by this careless
people, with hoes, among all this debris, when a few days expenditure of
industrious, and well applied labour, would clear away the obstructing
rubbish and add 100 % to the crops raised. . . .

[83]James William Bridgland (1817–1880) qualified as a land surveyor and car-
ried on many surveys including that of the Muskoka River in 1852 (D 9). On
January 22, 1856, he became Superintendent of Colonization Roads and after
Confederation continued in the same office for the Province of Ontario.

[84]Alexander Campbell (1822–1892) was a partner and friend of Sir John A.
Macdonald. He held several public offices in the Province of Canada and later in
the Dominion. He was Commissioner of Crown Lands from 1864 to 1867. In
1879 he was given a K.C.M.G., and in 1887 appointed Lieutenant Governor of
Ontario.

D. SURVEYS FOR SETTLEMENT

D 1   THOMAS RIDOUT[1] TO JOHN HUSTON[2]
[*Ontario, Department of Lands and Forests, Instructions to Land Surveyors, Book 4, pp. 165–6*]

Surveyor General's Office
York 2nd. Novemr. 1826

Having received the Commands of His Excellency the Lieutenant Governor to take the necessary measures to ascertain whether a Range of Townships of Land fit for settlement can be found in rear of those of Verulam Harvey Burleigh & Methuen or how near to the same between the line of the waters surveyed by Lieut Catty Royal Engineer and the Eastern Boundary of the Newcastle District I am to request that you will with as little delay as possible enter upon and perform the said service. Enclosed is a plan shewing the relative situation of the Townships and the line of waters above mentioned. The Honble. Peter Robinson[3] whom you will see will explain to you more fully the object of the survey . . .

D 2   HUSTON TO RIDOUT
[*Ontario, Department of Lands and Forests, Surveyors Letters, Book 26, no. 163*]

Cavan 10th
Jany. 1827

I beg lave most respectfully to inform you that your orders and Instructions of the 2nd. and 14th. of November 1826, have been duly recd. by me from the Hands of the Honble. Peter Robinson and agreeable to your commands I proceeded with as little delay as posseable to examine and explore the unsurveyed lands in rear of the Newcastle District— Commenced my journey on the 3rd. Ult. and by the severity of the weather on the 27th. of said Decemb was compelled to desist, during which time the Woods was verry unfavourable by reason of the Marshes,

[1]Thomas Ridout (1754–1829) was born in England, came to Canada after the American Revolution, and obtained employment in the Surveyor General's office. He served as Joint Acting Surveyor General from 1799 to 1810, and as Surveyor General from 1810 until his death.

[2]John Huston qualified as a surveyor on October 28, 1820. He lived in Cavan and carried on government surveys of townships and town plots, including the town plot of Lindsay.

[3]Peter Robinson (1785–1838) was elected to the Legislative Assembly of Upper Canada in 1817, and in 1824–5 was instrumental in forming a settlement of Irish immigrants in the vicinity of Peterborough. On July 19, 1827, he was appointed Surveyor General of Woods and Forests and Commissioner of Crown Lands.

Swamps, and Streams, not being frozen to bear one fourth a mans weight which greatly impeded our progress— formality prevents me of sending you a coppy of the field notes of the part explored until finished that they may be dilivered in due form. However this much I will say as far as I have explored the prospects are not flattering which I am sorry to relate— From a hill on the South side of the River[4] marked on Lieut. Catty's rout the land appeared good north of sd. river a part of which will be in the North of the first range of Townships north of Verulam, and of the West half of Harvey—

I would have written before only I expected favourable weather that I could have finished without troubling you with a letter— from the present depth of the snow it would be verry tedious and would encrease the expence to undertake to finish it now. However I stand ready to go on and do my duty Immediately if required—

D 3   HUSTON TO RIDOUT
*[Ontario, Department of Lands and Forests, Surveyors Letters,
Book 26, no. 164]*

York 8th
June 1827

I beg lave most respectfully to inform you of the cause of me not exploring further towards the Westward - Eastward, and Northward as pr your Order bearing date at York the 2nd November 1826

The Honble. Peter Robinson in explaining to me the object of the Survey gave gave [*sic*] me to understand when I found good land sufficient for one Township to Desist and report. And also estimated the time with the opinion of John Smith Jr.[5] Esqr. that I might explore the land ordered by you (say 40 days) excepting the land north of the Township of Methewen, from Mr Smiths account of that portion of country to the Honble. Peter Robinson he Mr. Robinson directed me not to Explore North of said Methewen, I Explored sufficient to the West and North of Verulam to know the land is not fit for settlement, in rear thereof— between the line of waters Surv by Lieut. Catty. Royal Engineer, and the Northern Boundary of said Verulam. I also explored sufficient to the North and East of Burleigh to Know the land is not fit for settlement, nearly the Depth of Two Townships in rear of said Burleigh.

In rear and North of Harvey I explored North more than land sufficient for one range of Townships,[6] and finding the land in General bad,

[4]Apparently the Gull River, though it is difficult to see how the land north of the Gull River would be in the first range of townships north of Verulam and Harvey.

[5]John Smith, Jr., qualified as a surveyor on April 5, 1825. He helped locate the Peter Robinson settlers in the Peterborough area, and also surveyed the country between Lake Simcoe and Balsam Lake.

[6]This would have taken him into the southern part of Snowdon or Glamorgan.

and I having exceeded the time mentioned by Mr. Smith to the Honble. P. Robinson, I considered myself out of the line of my duty to proceed further & encrease expences, without reporting thereon and await your further Orders.

D 4   DAVID THOMPSON TO J. M. HIGGINSON, PROVINCIAL SECRETARY
[*P.A.C., David Thompson Letters, M.G. 19, A 8, 3, Letter 28*]

Montreal, April 17. 1840

I shall be much obliged to you to do me the favor of laying the following before His Excellency the Governor General.

On the east side of Lake Huron, near it's south end, there is a very interesting and extensive tract of country almost unknown, yet deserving attention from the goodness of the Land, it's fine Forests, and great water powers for every purpose useful to the future inhabitants.

The last year of Lord Seaton's administration of Upper Canada the Legislature voted the sum[7] of £3000 Cy for exploring and surveying a line of country from the east side of Lake Huron to the Ottawa River for a Ship Canal of seven feet of water on the sill of the Locks. He was succeeded by Sir Francis B. Head (1837) who appointed me to explore eastward of Lake Huron to the Ottawa River for the above purpose. Captain Baddeley R E drew up my instructions, which directed me to follow up the Muskako River to its scource in the dividing ridge of Hills between Lake Huron and the Ottawa River; and from this elevation descend by some Stream to the Ottawa River

In vain I represented to him a Canal for Ships could never be found in such a direction; his answer was, that all he wanted to know was the elevation of the dividing ridge and the next year he would go himself. With much difficulty I effected a passage by the Muskako River and Lakes to the height of the ridge of Hills; and by Lakes, and the Madawaska River decended to the Ottawa River. By estimation the scource of the Muskako River is 1209 feet above Lake Huron; and the scource of the Madawaska River about 1400 feet above it's sortie into the Ottawa River. Although the examination of the Muskako River for a Canal was a failure; yet it brought us acquainted with a valuable tract of Country for settlement. The Muskako to the height of land, has 73½ miles of river and 36½ miles of small Lakes of fine clear water. In the 73½ miles of river there are 33 Falls for Mills. In all 110 miles; from this deduct 30 miles for the sinuousities of the River and Lands that may not be good; this leaves 80 miles in depth of good Land from Lake Huron. Allowing only 10 miles in depth on each side of these 80 miles of River and Lakes this gives 1600 square miles of Land covered with Forests of a very fine growth of Maple, Ash, Elm, Bass, Beach and a few Oaks, which always indicate a rich soil. The sides of the Rivers and Lakes have a border of

[7]See B 28.

stately Firs, from 50 to 100 yards in depth, behind which all is hard wood as above. I had an augeer to bore the ground, and always found among the hard woods from 6 to 12 inches of vegetable mould beneath which is a dark yellow soil of good quality. 1600 square miles contain 1.024.000 square acres, and exclusive of the mill sites, at five shillings per acre is worth £256.000 Cy Allowing 200 acres to each family, a settlement is given to 5120 families.

What extent of good lands lie on the east side of Lake Huron to as far north as the French River, is unknown, probably not less than three millions of acres.

The reason why this extensive tract of country is unknown is the whole of this Coast of the Lake is covered by innumerable Isles and Islets (45.000) so that the main shore is never approached but by a few Indians

Should the above meet His Excellency's attention and be thought a fit country for Immigrants, the survey necessary to have this fine country settled, is first a survey of the east Coast from a few miles south of the Muskako River, northward to the French River (about 80 miles) to examine all the Streams that flow into the Lake in this distance, and note the apparent quantity of good Land on each Stream: This survey will require a whole season of open weather; The Map and Report to be done in the winter: from these a tolerably correct idea may be formed of the quantity of land fit for cultivation, and its place. The second year surveys of Townships into Lots of Land for settlers may be made, ready for occupation. The third year sales of Land may take place and Settlements formed as the Governor General may see fit.

One great advantage of this tract of Country is the whole is at the sole disposal of the Crown without any claim whatever on these Lands.

D 5   EXCERPTS FROM ROBERT BELL'S[8] DIARY OF A SURVEY,
MADAWASKA RIVER TO THE HOME DISTRICT
[Ontario, Department of Lands and Forests, Field Notes, no. 1895]

August 5th 1847. Preparing to proceed on the survey. Hired some of the men & bought the provisions.

. . .

[Aug.] 26. Sent the canoes down to the Head of Long Rapids for provisions with 4 men in each. Finding that this was about the required latitude, I started the expling [exploring] line,[9] at this point being on the

[8]Robert Bell (1823–1873) qualified as a land surveyor June 16, 1843. He made a number of important government surveys and was active in the development of the city of Ottawa in which he made his home.

[9]Bell started his survey from a point on the Madawaska River near Bark Lake, surveyed the line to the boundary of the Home District where it crossed the Muskoka River, and on the way back laid out a road line. His route is shown on

North side of the River— Course astronomically N 70½° E & S 70½ W got a meridian altitude of the sun at noon. Then produced the line to the River edge, & got all across to the South side, & parted company with Mr. Haslett.[10]

. . .

[Oct.] 21. Ran to 35½ miles.[11] Wet heavy evening— Wind South Westerly

22. Very stormy. The rain & snow fell so heavy, that little or nothing was got done— South Wind

23. Moved forward the camp to 35½ miles & then continued the line to 35 m. 70 chs. Being anxious to find out the distance from the line at this point, to York River I set out at noon to day to explore Southward,[12] & if within reach to find it, leaving Mr. Burritt to carry on the line. I travelled all the afternoon & passed the night on the shore of a large lake some 7 or 8 miles, from the line—

24th Oct 1847. Sunday. Set out this morning as early as I could see, & steering S by E travelled on at a brisk pace untill near 12 o clock. The country was hilly & uneven, but the soil & timber were of the finest quality. At some places great masses of rock occured, rising abruptly from a smooth regular surface, the rock being really piled up into heaps & forming considerable hills— I saw no limestone, the only kind of rock is a sort of coarse grey granite. The streams at some places, pass over beds of boulders of from 1 to 3 feet diameter. They are nearly round, and appear as if they had been at some time under the action of fire— Some of these boulders are open & porous like the cinders that are sometimes seen in burnt limestone, & contain embedded in them, large pieces of a very hard substance, like melted glass— From the point where I turned back a pretty clear view of the country for some three or four miles round was obtained by climbing to the top of a steep rocky pinnacle that stood on a beautiful hardwood ridge. The appearance of the country on all sides was beautiful. At this place I was not less than 13 or perhaps 15 miles from the line & for that distance & as far as I could see beyond it, I never saw a finer quality of timber or apparently

---

his map "Plan of the Survey of the Westerly Part of an Exploring Line extending from the Bathurst to the Home District, with the Survey of the Road and Township Divisions, executed in Connection therewith" (Ontario, Department of Lands and Forests).

[10]John James Haslett (1811–1878) was born in Ireland and qualified there as a land surveyor. About 1842 he came to Canada and obtained his licence. He carried on many surveys especially in Peterborough and Hastings counties and the surrounding areas.

[11]This point is on the line between Harburn and Eyre townships.

[12]Through Harburn Township.

better soil— As I was now convinced that the York River would be of
no service to me in getting supplies by it, I therefore went no further,
but steered for the camp with all possible speed & got there about an
hour after dark. It was my opinion that the water of the lakes I had
traced for several miles emptied westward. On my arrival at the camp
I found the men there from the canoes & one of the Indians, who knew
the country, & holds the upper hunting ground on York River told me
that the water passing from these lakes emptied westward by the Black
River,[13] & that the Head of the York River was far to the South East.
During the afternoon, had heavy rain & all night—

25th. Being very unwell & as some of the canoe men had got badly
hurt by falls coming out with their loads, & but a small supply therefore
reached the camp, I sent the men down to Bark Lake to bring up some.
Examined the place for the road site from 30 miles out to 33 miles.

26 October 1847. Still unwell. Barely able to move about. Continued
the explorations for the road site. As the country here is very rough, I
examined carefully on both sides, in order to get the best place that it
afforded. Boisterous & snowy, cold. N.West.

27. Felt some better to-day. Made an excursion Northwards, & found
the country much inferior to that lying Southward. It is mostly covered
with a thick growth of green timber, with considerable W Pine of a poor
quality, & the surface generally rough & rocky. Clear night   Took some
observations

28. Made an excursion North Westward & found the country much
the same as that I passed through yesterday Clear & cold got some
observations

29. So unwell I did not go out, got some observations—

30. Fair untill afternoon. Three of the axe men got back with their
loads. The others had to be sent to Bytown, disabled— Ran 20 chs
afternoon.

31st. Sunday —Wind west mild

1st. November, 1847. Wet morning. P M cloudy & sultry. Continued
the line to 36 miles & 30 chs. The going of the worst sort. Uneven surface & thick green timber. The rest of the men able for service, besides
these others [?] had to be employed in the canoes. As mentioned, three
were with me on the line. In the meantime I had sent James Bell down
the River to hire more men & make sure of getting up as much as possible of the supplies before the navigation closed—

[13]If Bell refers to the Black River which flows into the Severn, this must be an
error. The waters flowing west from the section which Bell was then exploring
would go by the Burnt River or the Gull River routes.

2. Carried up the camp, & then continued the line to 36 m 65 chs Dark & sultry. The going of the worst sort.

3. Continued the line to 37 m & 25 c Rained most of the day, going very bad.

4. Stormy. Ran to 37 miles & 50 chs through a thick swampy windfall

5. Continued the line to the River at 37 miles 72c. 15. through going of the worst sort. Then moved up the camp. Boisterous & squally.

6. Had to send the men to Bark Lake for biscuit, leaving only Mr. Burritt & myself at the camp. Chained up the 2 last days work & opened the line to 38 miles & 5 chs— Fair.

7. Sunday. Very cold. Dark & cloudy

8. Rained heavy. Made a short excursion Southward, but the rain fell so heavy, I had to return before going far. The country here is rough to the Northward a very considerable range of hardwood hills are seen extending several miles to the northeast.

9. At work on the line. Cool & cloudy

10. Stormy & boisterous. Wind Northerly. At work on the line

11. Still stormy. Heavy snow having struck on the line

12. This forenoon got the line out to the lake[14] at 38 miles, 68 chs. Then explored a path around the South side of it. Snowy. Wind N west.

13th. Chained up, & laid out the trig points. So wet & snowy got nothing more done only got all ready for moving the camp— The men got back with their loads from Bark Lake—

14. Sunday. Wind N West Cold Snow fell about 4 inches.

15. Moved all forward to the west end of the lake to 40 miles. Stormy & cold. Wind North West.

16. Trying to get the line across the Lake. The air was so thick & hazy & the day so dark, I had great difficulty getting it done— The distance was over a mile. Most of the day wet.

17. Got the trig measure completed & all finished at the lake & ran on to 40 miles & 25 chs. Forenoon clear— Wind west.

18th November 1847. Very stormy. Rain & snow. Worked on the line from 9 A M to 2 P M. & had to quit.

[14]Marsden Lake.

19. Continued to 41¼ miles. Cold

20. Moved up the camp to 41¼ miles & continued the line to 41½ miles

21. Sunday. Seven of the men from the canoes arrived with some pork & flour. The rest had went down the river with one canoe to bring up four barrels of pork that had been brought part of the way by others & left there— Kept 1 axeman to recruit my line party which now amounted to 4 axemen, 1 chainman & one assistant, Mr. Burritt, who was very efficient in any capacity. The others were sent back to Bark Lake forthwith, after taking some dinner, for more provisions, & permanently established on the route as a portage party—

22. Continued the line to 41 m & 75 chs. Heavy rain afternoon—

23. Rained so heavy all day we got very little done on the line—

24. Moved the camp up to 41¾ miles & continued the line to 42 m. 30 chs

25th. Stormy Snow & rain. Worked on the line till noon, & had to quit— Afternoon explored around the lake.

Novr. 26, 1847 Cold & some snow falling. Wind northerly. Continued the line to 43 miles & 15 chs

27. Snowy. Continued the line to 43 miles & 70 chs. J. Bell, D. Mc-Auley & Alexr. Ellis arrived—

28th Sunday— Sent off J. Bell to McNabb to buy oxen & bring them up & sent J. Kaley & Alex Ellis down to Bark Lake to assist in bringing up flour & pork. Wet afternoon

29. Moved the camp forward to the end of the line. Detained a long time getting all across the Lake[15] having to beat a way through sheets of ice nearly a mile. Wind north very cold.

30. Ran the line to 44 miles & 70 c. Very cold. Wind north

December 1st. Very stormy. Snow fell so thick we had to quit work on the line, Then moved forward the camp to 45¼ miles—

2. Out of provisions. Started with all hands down the line & met the portage party at 38½ miles. Took their loads there & returned to the camp Sent off one axeman sick— Owing to the continued wet weather the valleys are so much flooded that the road is almost impassable. The men wading so much in the water can make but very short days

15Little Redstone Lake.

journeys & carry but small loads, & the weather is so cold that they
suffer greatly—

3. Still snowing & every branch loaded with it. Continued the line to
45¾ miles—

4. Cold & boisterous. Ran the line to the large lake[16] at 46 miles &
then made a float for getting all across it. The short piece run to-day
was of the worst sort.

5. Still snowing. Sunday.

6. Moved the camp forward to the outside of the lake, & after much
trouble owing to the snow still falling got the line carried across the lake
in the night by using lights—

7. Continued the line to 47 Miles & 45 chs. Rough bad going Wind
West

8. Some rain. The wet snow falling of [sic] the branches. Wet and
most disagreable   Ran to 48 Miles.

9. Rained heavy. Out of provisions. Started with all hands down the
line for more, every valley flooded & the rain pouring down almost continually, & very cold Staid over night at 35½ miles.

10. Still raining. Met the men at 26 miles & staid there all night.

11th December 1847. Returned with the loads as far as the 35½ mile
camp Sent the portage party down again. Still raining, & very cold.

12. Sunday. Rough & boisterous. Got to the camp late in the evening.

13. Rained heavy till noon. Continued the line to 48 m 30 chs Over
heaps of rocks covered with thick green timber—

14. Continued the line to 49 miles over rocks & green timber. Cloudy
& Wind West

15. Moved from the camp to 49 miles. Took nearly all day the road
was so rough. Then at work on the line. Blowing a hurricane all day

16. Ran to 49 m. 50 chs. Bad going as before, only the timber
heavier—

17. Ran to 50 miles & 20 chs. Very cold

18. Ran to 50 miles & ¾. Still rough.

19. Sunday. Wind north very cold

[16]Kennisis Lake.

20. Ran to 52 miles. Snowy afternoon

21. Snowy day. Moved forward the camp to 52 miles, then ahead on the line. Wind South East.

22. Continued the line to 52 miles and 50 chs. Snow 6 inches deep.

23. Continued the line to 53 miles & 30 chs. Clear & cold Wind West

24. Snowy. Ran to 54 miles.

25. Christmas— Explored the country[17] several miles southward. Clear & cold.

26. Sunday. Very cold. Wind north.

27th December, 1847. Continued the line to 54½ miles, & had the way explored for bring the cattle round by the ice on the lakes from 46 miles to 50 miles. The country along the line is so rough that it is impassable for cattle or almost anything—

28. Moved forward the camp to 54¼ miles. So stormy we could do nothing on the line. J. Bell arrived with 3 oxen. Brought 4 on the line & killed one of them below for the carrying party, which allowed them to carry flour altogether, & so saved the cost of carrying pork—

29. Left Mr. Burritt to carry on the line & set out with the 3 oxen & 4 men, and drove 4 miles ahead on the course of the line, left an ox and two men to butcher it & secure the meat & then return. (3 men had come up with the oxen) & drove on the other two oxen. Went ahead 9 miles with the oxen that day. Wet & rainy.

30. Drove the cattle about 3 miles further, which took the whole forenoon, as the cattle were about fatigued out. Then stopping there we got one dressed that night.

31st December 1847. Still raining. Butchered the other ox & then set to work to make a place to keep it secure.

1848

1. Jany. Rained heavy all day. Got our beef all properly secured after a very hard days work under an incessant torrent or rain   Cold frosty night & no camp.

2. Sunday. Clear & fine— Returned to the camp.

3. Got the line forward to 56 miles & 35 chs. Sent down 2 men to the 41¼ mile depot for flour—

[17]Stanhope Township.

4. Moved forward the camp to 56 m, 35 chs. Then continued the line. Very cold. Wind north.

5. Exceedingly stormy. The snow blew around & fell so thick it was quite impossible to see to carry on the line. Got some beef carried in & explored around the lakes.[18] Clear night

6. Continued the line to 57⅛ miles. Very cold Wind northerly.

7. Ran to 57¾ miles. Cold Wind East.

8. Ran to 58½ Miles do.

9. Sunday. Very cold Wind north.

10. Exceedingly cold. Moved up the camp to 58¾ miles & then continued the line to 58 m. 55 chs. Sent J. Bell down to McNabb for men and supplies, as the complement at work both carrying & at the line were getting reduced by sickness & accidents, & a new supply could not be done without—

11. Continued the line to 59½ miles. Weather moderate. Snow fell about 2 inches to-day. Wind northwest.

12. Sent 2 men down to the depot at 41¼ miles for flour. Snow about 9 inches deep. This day I was so unwell I had to come in to the camp in the afternoon,— Mild Wind westerly. Continued the line to 59 miles & 65 chs

13th— Moderate— Still very unwell & unable to be much out— Ran to 60 miles & 5 chs. Wind west.

14. So unwell I was obliged to stay in the camp. Very wet day. Mr. Burritt & the men continued at the line untill noon & had to quit & come in. Wind South.

15. Still getting worse, unable to get up. Rained heavy all day—got nothing done on the line

16. Sunday. A little better, but still unable to eat or rise.

17. Still down sick— Mr. Burritt had the men at work on the line & ran to 61¾ miles

18th Jany 1848. Being still very sick & quite unable to go out of the camp or do anything, & almost out of provisions, I sent the men all down the line for flour but one who remained with me— The portage party on the lower part of the line owing to the heavy rain, had been quite unable

[18]St. Nora Lake.

to carry up flour enough, & I found it necessary to send the men down one trip to help them.

Until the 22d. I lay sick in the camp— When Mr. Burritt arrived with two men—

23. Sunday. Better to-day. Got some beef brought to the camp. Clear & fine

24. Moved up the camp to 61½ miles. Wind south easterly. Recovering fast. Much better to-day

25. My party being now weakened & not at all fit to get on with the work to advantage & although I had made every effort to get men, could not by any means in my power do so, & finding therefore that to carry the picket line through would be impossible, in order to get the work completed I determined to go on with the compass. The season had now got so far advanced that it was a matter of the utmost importance to proceed with despatch. For if much of the work remained to be done, at 3 months from now it could not be done, as the breaking up of the ice would open the lakes & streams & leave the road for the carrying parties impassable— Besides I saw no reasonable hopes of being able to get men enough to do it—& those now with me were insisting on leaving en masse every day, although most diligent & efficient men, they were all discouraged & unless matters turned more favourable the water in particular, the prospect ahead was most gloomy. I therefore commenced the line with the compass & from 62 miles continued it. Ran to 63 miles & 55 chs. Wind South East cloudy—

26th Jany. 1848. Rained very heavy nearly all day. Explored the little river[19] at 63 miles some three or four miles— got nothing done on the line   Wind South.

27. Light rain. Continued the line to 64 miles and 70 chs Snowed & rained during the night Wind South—

28th January 1848.—Moved forward the camp to 64¾ miles, & got some beef brought to the camp So stormy & the wet snow falling off the branches, we got nothing done on the line.

29. Cloudy. W. Southerly. Continued the line to 66½ miles. Stormy evening

30. Sunday. Rain & snow.

31. Continued the line to 68½ miles. Rough stormy day. Rain & snow Wind southerly.

[19]Black River.

1st. Febry. — Carried up the camp to 68 miles & 10 chs & then continued the line to 69 miles. Very boisterous high wind. Snowy. Wind southwest.

2. Ran to 70¼ miles. Clear day. W. West. Bad tedious going.

3d. Stormy. Sent all hands for beef— Two men arrived from below. Found that a new supply of men were on their way up, & 4 heavy oxen then on the lower end of the line coming on. The breaking up of the lumbering establishment on the Madawaska River had most fortunately thrown so many men out of employment that some had been found willing to engage in a service that was universally dreaded.

4th Feby. Ran to 71¼ miles. Exceedingly tedious, bad going— 3 of the new men arrived. Placed all hands on short allowance of flour, and required them to live almost entirely on beef.

5th. Sent 2 men down the line with orders about the cattle & to assist in driving them up, & also with orders for the regulation of the portage parties below. Moved the camp forward to 70 miles & 53 chs & continued the line to 71½ miles, bad going. Snow about 1 foot deep—

6th Sunday. A M clear. P M cloudy.

7th. Continued the line to the Muskako River, & then made a float & crossed it & got the line ran across the two points to the west side on the main bank.

8. Moved forward the camp to the west side of the Muskako River, & then ran to 73 miles & 70 chs. Got the river examined both above & below the crossing place about 5 miles, & selected the bridge site— Snowy very cold Wind Westerly

9. Continued the line to 75¼ miles. Wind Easterly. Snowy & boisterous.

10. Ran to 76⅝ miles Very cold—

11. Moved up the camp to 76⅝ miles & continued the line to 77¾ miles. Very cold. Wind Northwest.

12th Feby 1848. Continued the line to 79 miles— Two men arrived with an ox at the camp this evening. The other oxen had been killed at convenient places along the line, which saved the carrying of meat & lessened the labour of bringing up the provisions very materially as all hands had to live almost entirely on beef.—

13. Sunday. Very cold got the ox butchered & dressed & all secured

14. Moved forward the camp to 79 miles, & continued the line to 80½ miles. Wind West

15. Continued the line out to the Home District Boundary Went down the River to the Muskako Lake & up the river to the Great Falls.[20] To the lake the country along the river is beautiful Clear & fine. Wind West

16. Explored several miles up the River[21] that empties into the Muskako on the north side about 1¾ miles below the Great Falls. The country on both sides is good, & the river affords water power of the first order— Saw 3 magnificent Falls[22]— Sent three men out to Penetanguishine for some articles we wanted, & to the Post Office— Sent the rest of the men down the line to carry along & distribute the beef & flour at places where we would require it hereafter— Clear & fine. Wind West.

17. Explored up the Muskako & back from the River. The country is mostly pretty fair. The most eligible town site afforded on these rivers is that at the Great Falls. Fair W. West. Got observations—

18. Chained the Boundary line of the Home Dist from the end of the Main to the High Falls, & then explored the road site some two or three miles East ward from the townsite Fair. Got observations

. . .

D 6   BELL TO COMMISSIONER OF CROWN LANDS, J. H. PRICE
[Ontario, Department of Lands and Forests, Field Notes, no. 1895]

Bytown, 6th September, 1848.

Having completed the service required agreably to the instructions of the Honbl. Commissioner of Crown Lands of 9th July 1847 To survey the westerly part of an exploring line extending from the Bathurst to the Home District, I have the honor to submit the following report thereon–

As instructed I proceeded in company with Mr. John J Haslett, who was instructed to survey the Easterly part of the line to a point on the Madawaska River between Kiminiskia & Bark Lakes, in Latitude 45° 22′ 45″ north which was determined by the mean of the meridian altitudes of the sun and several stars and from this point I surveyed a line bearing south seventy & a half degrees west astronomically to the North Easterly Boundary line of the Home District where it crosses the Muskako River, after duly examining that section of the country I

[20]Later known as South Falls and then as Muskoka Falls.
[21]North Branch of the Muskoka River.
[22]High Falls was divided by islands into three separate chutes.

chose a site for a town at the Great Falls[23] on the Muskako River.–
The water power afforded by the Falls is very great, besides the locality
is otherwise suitable. At this point I commenced the line of road which
I surveyed as I returned. On this line at each distance of 101 chains
on the course of the main line, I planted a post of cedar or other
durable wood, & at the township Boundaries planted stone monuments
with broken glass and crockery under them. At the stone monument
planted at the intersection of the road and Township lines a post 6
inches square is also planted, duly inscribed with a marking iron—
None of the posts are smaller then 4 inches square. The townships are
laid out 808 chains in width on the course North 70½ East & the
Township lines drawn back one mile from the Road line on each side
on the courses South 19½ East and North 19½ West— All the courses
here mentioned are the astronomical courses.

With respect to the features & character of the Country I would beg
to state that from the Madawaska River [to] the Muskako River the
country is uneven and hilly throughout, but in my opinion the chief part
of it is quite fit for settlement— In the vicinity of Bark Lake the
Country is extremely rough and rocky. But immediately South of it
towards York River there are several extensive tracts of good land, and
extending Eastward from this section a tract of good land passes out
to the shores of Lake Kiminiskia, after passing three miles beyond Bark
Lake on the line, the country assumes a better appearance & is timbered
with hardwood, W. Pine, spruce and balsam. The hardwood is most
abundant & of a heavy growth— Red pine is hardly seen at all after leaving the neighbourhood of the Madawaska River. The common soil is a
light loam of a good quality— clay is hardly seen, at least near the surface, sand but seldom & no lime stone at all. The surface of the country
presents a series of ridges, lying usually North East and South West, but
sometimes meeting in different directions varying in width from a mile
to a few chains & rising commonly to an elevation of some 80 or
100 feet above the vallies. The Eastern sides of the ridges rise with
a gentle easy slope, are well timbered & commonly good land. The
Western sides are unvariably steep and rocky & at many places present
perpendicular rocky faces. In all cases where a mural face occurs the
line of bearing is North East and South West. The country continues of
this description to about 35 miles from the Madawaska River— Northward of the line it is rather more broken with swamps & rocky hills &
covered more with green timber. Good land occurs in many places but
in isolated prices [sic] & commonly of no great extent Southward the
country is much better, rocky hills & ridges are occasionally met, but
there are large tracts of excellent land. The surface however is decidedly
more uneven & the ridges attain a greater elevation & are more continuous & regular.

[23]South or Muskoka Falls.

From thirty five miles to forty six miles the line passes over a considerable quantity of good land, but the Country is more broken & there is less regularity in its features— From forty six to fifty miles is decidedly the most unfavourable portion of the whole for either road making and agricultural purposes. Good land is seldom seen on this section & then in small quantities. A great part of it is covered with water, Lakes are numerous, & sometimes four or five square miles or even a greater area is covered by one sheet of water. The Lake shores are commonly high and rocky & covered with green timber. The land between these lakes is exceedingly rough and uneven, counting [sic] of parallel ridges of rocks bearing South West and North East, rising to an elevation of some 150 feet to 220 feet and extremely narrow, with perpendicular faces northward. The timber is composed of spruce, W. Pine & hemlock, with some times a little hardwood— I was led to believe from the different appearances observed in my exploration (which extended over several miles on each side the line & some times perhaps near twenty miles) and from the line of its direction that this tract is limited to the immediate vicinity of the head waters of the streams which rise here and flow to either side. Beyond fifty six miles to the Muskako River the Country is less uneven though still rather hilly. There are large tracts of good land along the line & on both sides of it. At several places rocky Hills occur but not to any great extent. The greatest objection that at all exists in respect to the whole territory is the great abundance of Rocks. Along the Muskako River the land is generally good. On the South side from two miles to five miles above the great Falls the timber is chiefly W. Pine, the surface rocky & the soil light and poor, but both above and below this on the same side, & on the other side generally the soil is good & the land well timbered. From the place where the main line crossed the Muskako River at 72½ miles to where it crossed it again near the end, it passes through a good tract of country, & from the point where the main line terminates at the District line down the River to Muskako Lake the land on both sides is good. The Muskako is a very smooth but strong running stream from 200 to 300 feet wide & from 18 to 25 feet deep. Usually where there is a fall the water falls almost perpendicular through a narrow rocky passage & leaves a very short space of broken rough water— The country throughout is extremely well watered, and the Streams are remarkably clear. The rivers afford an almost unlimited amount of available water power. Owing to the various causes above mentioned, getting a suitable site for a road was a difficult matter— The line of road surveyed is very crooked & in some places rough; But of this I am fully satisfied, that the country affords no better site for a road—

I would beg to state further, that on the road line posts were planted at distances of 101 chains on the course of the main line as before stated— but at these places one post only was planted, & no mark made to indicated a road allowance on either side of it. The character of the country is such that if road allowances are laid out, on the straight boundary lines, as is commonly done in the level part of the Province such allowances will seldom be of any use for road purposes— As the country becomes settled road lines will be laid out, where roads can be best made & if the amount of the road allowances be thrown into the lots extra, it will compensate the land owners.

As instructed I have herewith furnished a plan of the survey drawn to the scale of forty chains to an inch, shewing the rivers, Lakes & general features of the country. Also the Field Book containing the astronomical observations both for latitude and bearing & the locality, with the dip and strike of the various fixed rocks & a diary— The specimens of those fixed rocks have been duly forwarded.

I have also furnished an estimate of the probable cost of constructing a road on the line surveyed. The kind of road estimated for is the most economical kind practicable for wheel carriages— Where the surface is smooth dry & hard already it is not intended to have more than ten feet in the centre grubbed, & the timber cut down on each side of the thirty three feet from the centre. But where it is naturaly impassible to make it fit for travelling on at any season. By doing so the whole road can be made passable at the least expence, & unless the bad places be made as good as other parts of the road, the money or labour laid out thereon is in a great degree lost.

For further particulars I would beg to refer you to the Field Notes and Diary.

D 7   SIMCOE COUNTY PETITION FOR SURVEY OF NEWLY ACQUIRED LANDS
[*Simcoe County, Municipal Council, Minutes, May, 1852, p. 32*]

Unto His Excellency the Governor-General in Council assembled.
The Petition of the Warden and Council of the County of Simcoe, humbly sheweth:

That a great and valuable tract of land, lately acquired by treaty with the Indians, annexed to the County of Simcoe, and defined in the Territorial Divisions Act as bounded on the east by the late Home and Newcastle Districts prolonged to French River, on the west by Lake Huron, on the North by French River, and on the south by the River Severn and the Township of Rama:

Your Petitioners believe that this tract of land possesses a vast supply of timber, consisting of oak, pine and other valuable woods. As no part of it has been surveyed they cannot of course offer any opinion as to its fitness for agricultural purposes. It is conveniently situated, being within two days' journey from Toronto, and one from the County town of Simcoe:

May it therefore please your Excellency in Council, to order an immediate survey for settlement of the said extensive and valuable tract of country.

And your petitioners as in duty bound shall ever pray.

D 8   ADDRESS OF LEGISLATIVE ASSEMBLY, PRAYING FOR A SURVEY,
NOVEMBER 8, 1852
[*Canada, Legislative Assembly,* Journals, *1852-3, pp. 432-4*]

On motion of Mr. *Mackenzie*,[24] seconded by Mr. *Hartman*,[25]
Resolved, That an humble Address be presented to His Excellency the
Governor General, praying that he may take into consideration the
propriety of causing an immediate Survey of the uninhabited Tract
of Country bounded by the *French River*, Lake *Nipissing*, the *Ottawa*
River, Lakes *Huron* and *Simcoe*, and the *Georgian Bay*, and by the
settled parts of *Upper Canada*, so far as said Tract is, or may be, ceded
by the Indians; the said Survey to be made by the cardinal points, and
the lands set off into Counties, Townships and Sections,— each Section
to contain one square mile, or 640 acres, and to be subdivided into
four quarter sections of 160 acres each, with a proper allowance for
Roads; the Townships to be square, except where the local position of
the territory surveyed may interfere; each Township where practicable,
to contain 49 sections, nine of which Townships to form a County;
Town Plots, with lots for schools, to be reserved in the several Townships, and a site for a County Town selected in each County; that a
Geological Survey and detailed description of the soil, be carried on
and completed, while the Land Surveyors are establishing the Boundaries of the Sections, Towns, and Counties: and, that to ensure the
more speedy settlement of said uninhabited Tract, to provide homes
for the youth of Canada, encourage immigration, and prevent emigration, every alternate quarter Section of 160 acres be bestowed upon any
actual settler, the head of a family, who, at the time, owns no other land,
—conditioned for a free deed from the Crown to him or her at the end of
five years actual possession and cultivation,—the land thus conveyed
as a free gift, not being liable for any debt that may have been contracted by the settler previous to the issue of the Crown Patent, and
the intermediate lots reserved for actual settlers by purchase only.
   Ordered, That the said Address be presented to His Excellency the
Governor General by such Members of this House as are of the
Honorable the Executive Council of this Province.

D 9   J. W. BRIDGLAND'S "REPORT . . . OF EXPLORING LINES FROM
THE ELDON PORTAGE TO THE MOUTH OF THE RIVER MUSKAKO,"
JANUARY 31, 1853
[*Ontario, Department of Lands and Forests, Field Notes, no. 1897*]

In obedience to your instructions,[26] dated January 2nd. 1852, and
issued to me from your Crown Lands office Quebec, for the subdivision
of the township of Carden into farm lots, and also for the survey of a

[24]William Lyon Mackenzie (1795–1861) represented Haldimand in the Legislature from 1851 to 1858.
[25]Joseph Hartman, member for the North Riding of York.
[26]Instructions to Land Surveyors, Book 6, no. 12.

road line from the Eldon portage road to the Muskako river, I proceeded to the execution thereof upon the 18th. of May 1852, in the
manner, and with the results (so far as the exploration was proceeded
with) which I had the honour to report to you, upon my return in the
following month of June.

You were pleased upon receipt of the report above alluded to, to
change the nature of your instructions, in so much as related to the
survey of the township of Carden, withdrawing your order for the subdivision of the same, and directing me (by your instructions[27] of date
June 21st., to continue the exploration line (already opened some seven
or eight miles) upon the same course untill its intersection with the
Muskako river; exploring to the right and left of the line, as far as
practicable; thence to continue the exploration upon the South bank of
the said river to its influx into the Georgian Bay. Pursuant to this, I left
home again upon 21st. July 1852, proceeding by the same route as at
first, and arrived at Orillia on the following day, leaving the same evening for the field of operations— as per diary.

I took up the line from its terminus upon the 2nd. June 1852, continuing it upon the Astronomical course, North 16° West, to the end
of the 13th. mile, when I changed it one degree further from the
meridian, retaining this direction, and correcting my deviations as
frequently as practicable, by nightly observations of Polaris, untill I
struck the Muskako river, appointed— per instructions— to be the
northern limit of the exploration. The distance on the above line, being,
twenty nine miles and seventy seven chains from the Talbot to the
Muskako. I then run from the twenty seventh mile post, upon a due
West course, Astronomical, untill I struck the great Muskako Lake.
From between the seventh and eighth mile posts, on this line, I turned
South westward, passing around the south east bay of the Lake, and
from thence northwest, and westward, as per plan— and field notes—
in accordance with the general Southern edge of the waters of the rivers,
and the numerous lakes and lake-like expansions upon it, to the terminus of the same, at its mouth, opening into the waters of Lake Huron:
exploring to the right and left (I believe) faithfully; as far as my own
personal labour, and my supervision of that of those beneath my Command, enable me judge, [sic] and I must express my regret and disappointment, in being unable after so much labour and time expended
in the exploration, to report anything concerning the lands examined,
which will prove satisfactory, as to their value, or elligibility.

The general quality of the land — as will be more distinctly seen
by inspecting the map accompanying this report — is extremely rocky,
and broken, so much so indeed, that, in a district explored of abt. five
hundred square miles, not a portion, sufficient for a small township,
could be obtained in any one locality, of a generally cultivatable nature.

The country northward of Black river, may be described as one vast
field of granite rock— distorted— apparently into its present broken

[27]Instructions to Land Surveyors, Book 5, p. 209.

and convolved surface, by the force of aqueous and igneous agency, and presents to the eye the desolate and unfertile picture of a country pitched into hills, mounds and ridges, and scooped into basins, ravines, and rock-girded swamps of all imaginable forms; having at times, this peculiarity— a sudden change from the most barren, and rugged region of rocks, to a vale or belt— two or three chains in width— of the richest soil, and covered with the best timber,—such most generally being the margin of some spring creek, or clear water lake— while the character of the land surrounding the turbid, blackwater streams and lakes, is entirely of an opposite character, being generally of a worse description, even than that more distant from them.

That portion of land to the south of the Muskako, and lying upon the last two or three miles of the exploration line, continued from the Talbot to the first mentioned river (being principally to the east of the line) is most eligible, as to quality of soil, and extent of surface, of any discovered in the exploration.

Westward, from hence to Muskako Lake, and thence southward, and westward, around the Lakes connected with the river, the country is, in general, still more barren, and unpromising; an exception of rare occurence, and of brief continuance, scarcely redeeming the whole from the character of absolute, and universal sterility.— I have alluded in a former Report to a small belt of good land, winding for a distance of some four or five miles in an eccentric direction, near the great Muskako Lake, crossed by the west exploration line, and again met upon the second mile of the southwest line.

After rounding the southern extremity of the great lake, and proceeding westward, the agricultural prospect is still worse; the country being composed allmost wholly, of rocky ridges, and small lakes, and is in general, of a far more swampy character upon the borders of the Lake and river.

From personal observation, and the corroborating reports of traders and hunters, who have traversed the region in all directions, I am fully convinced, that, these unpromising features, continue over all that tract, situated between the Muskako and the Severn rivers.

Here and there, however, around some small lakes, there is found a little bordering of arable land, the beauty and value of which seem enhanced by the barren aspect around it.

The water in the lakes, is generally black-coulored; they are frequently bordered upon one side by marsh, or swamp, and upon the opposite, by banks of precipitous rocks; others again, are entirely surrounded either by swamps, marshes, or steep rocks. Sometimes the water in these lakes is good, and clear; as also in the streams, in which case they are mostly relieved by a margin of fair sloping land covered with hardwood timber; such lakes are fed and purified by some entering, and outflowing stream of spring waters.

Towards the shores of Lake Huron, lakes are of more frequent occurence, the country being dotted with them in every direction, rendering anything like a regular survey of exploration, difficult; while in the spring time, upon the melting of the heavy snows, and the falling of the rains at that season, many of them are united by connecting channels, and low winding flats, in such a manner, as to form almost a general inundation.

As might be expected, in a country comprising such features— and though generally so broken and rugged as to defy cultivation yet possessing no superior elevations— but few streams formed by spring currents are found; being principally, in their larger character, made by the collected drainages of the winter and spring accumulations of snows, and rains, which are sponged up by extensive and allmost numberless, tamarac, and alder swamps, affording a frugal, and deeply dyed supply to the larger streams, during the parching summer months, whilst the smaller and less favoured creeks, are diminished and finally dried up, long ere the fall rains again arouse them into life.

(A consequent feature, therefore, in the streams, is, the smaller— in the mid-summer are usually dry, while the larger have a high water mark some six or seven feet above their lowest ebb.)

The general direction of all the large streams is westward; of tributary creeks, of course at right angles to these, with a westerly tendency. Some indeed, owing to the chaotic character of the country, defy all laws of regularity, and shoot, and wind, in tortuous conformity to every point of the compass.

Falls, and rappids, also, characterize all the rivers met with in this region, from the greatest, to the least, so that in availing oneself of their services as a line of route, the canoes are as often carried, as they carry, making the conveyance of provisions into the interior, laborious allmost beyond description.

The Muskako river, in spring tide, is a powerful stream, having at such time, where its current is about two miles an hour, (its general rate perhaps where there are no perceptible rappids) an average depth of from eight, to fifteen feet, and a width of from two, to three hundred feet. The water is blackish and bitter, abounding in their season, with pickerel, pike, bass, &c. No remarkable superiority, however, characterizes the quality of the soil or the timber upon its immediate banks, on any part traversed by our exploration. The timber on the southern side, consists for the most part, of pine, and hemlock, with a mixture of birch, ash, basswood, and maple. The pine is however inferior, frequently forked, crooked, and punkey, consequently not very valuable for lumber. Notwithstanding these disparagements, taking into consideration the existence (in the vicinity of the terminus of my first exploration line), of the largest tract of arable land I have met with in the survey, and the unquestionable water power easily attainable, I deem this, an elligible locality, for milling, and settlement, if access to it, could be had through any feasible route.

The quality of the timber, in general, is (as a natural consequence of the broken, rocky and sterile nature of the land) of a very inferior description, allthough, in parts, possessing a somewhat level surface, and tolerably free from outlying rocks, it is often surprisingly good, both as regards quality, and size— the soil, being at the same time mere sand, and the continuous rock, lying within six or eight inches of the surface.

The great extent however, of the land explored is timbered with poor stunted wood, the largest trees being white pines, of the gnorliest, and worst description, thinly scattered, with small balsam, spruce, white birch and soft maple, making up between. Thus upon the higher land such produce is found, whilst the swamps, marshes, and swales are filled chiefly with tamarac and alder. Moose-wood, ground-juniper, and ground-hemlock, form the most frequent underwoods.

Proceeding now, upon the southern side of the Muskako river, westward to the Lake of the same name, no general improvement, is observable. To the right, indeed, for about two miles, that section of land, previously noticed as the best seen, stretches out, bounded again at the distance of from two, to three miles, by tamarac and cedar swamps, or the same barren wilderness of rocks before alluded to. In all the distance upon this line, — due west — I did not meet with one spring creek, untill close upon the Lake; our party suffering much at times, from the entire absence of water, of any kind, and at others, from the putrid and sickening quality of that which could be obtained.

But, to recall attention particularly, to the remaining portion of the exploration, would only be to repeat the tedious monotony, of rocky barrens, swamps, marshes, and burnt regions; destitute of good water, good timber, in short of every-thing, necessary to make settlement desirable, or life supportable; regions where even the foraging partridge, and the provident squirrel, seem from their scarcity— scarcely able to exist.

With reference to the geology of the country, your instructions not warranting me in making any particular examinations, and that which was of more importance, and formed the direct substance of those instructions, occupying my time to the fullest extent, I have but little to offer in the shape of information concerning it: besides I am aware that Captain Baddely (I presume, a scientific and practical geologist) has so copiously reported upon these identical regions, as to render it superfluous in me to add any-thing thereto.

Ferruginous sands, and in the neighborhood of large streams and lakes, portions of rock containing some very apparent particles of iron, and pyrites, abound, but I have never seen any specimens of so rich a nature, as to lead me to conceive the vicinity of any great portion of metal.

Local attraction is certainly, in places, very great, but nothing more than may be easily accounted for, from the ordinary existences above alluded to. I do not presume, however, to give it as my decided opinion,

that nothing important of this nature does exist, but only that I saw
nothing in the casual, and superficial examination thus made, to indicate its presence.

After examining all my notes of survey, and making the necessary
comparisons and deductions, I unhesitatingly conclude,— *it is impossible to connect the mouth of the Muskako river, upon the southern
side of the stream and of the lakes, with the point of terminus of Mr.
Bell's road line at the great falls, by a line of road so located, as to
form, throughout any considerable portion of its extent, a good line of
settlement.* If however, Mr. Bell's road line allready laid out, is being,
or is likely to be, settled, there would be no difficulty in connecting the
tract, that I have mentioned as existing at the terminus of my first
exploration line, with it; but if the settlement of that line, is dependant
upon the feasibility, of an egress to Lake Huron, then it is allmost
certain, that, neither the one, nor the other, can be made available, but
through the rendering of the Muskako river navigable.

Having arrived at the mouth of the river, I made a cursory examination of the harbour, which it affords. It may indeed I think be pronounced, a good one, being completely land-locked, having bold shores,
and ample depth of channel. A fleet of ships may ride with perfect
safety in it, while the severest gale rages without.

I beg to refer, here, to the plan of the harbour, accompanying this
report, which delineates the features thereof, and the depth of water —
as far as soundings were made — of the principal channel to the
south west, untill it opens, so much, as to disclose a view of Christian
Island in the distance.

I may add (whatever reliance can be placed upon it) that the Indians, report a considerable section of good land, as existing somewhere
between the Muskako and Lake Nipissing perhaps rather to the east
of the District Line.

I have learned, however, to place but a small value upon the information received from this class of persons; their judgement of the quality
of land, being, in general, exceedingly deficient; their statements as to
the distances to places, and of their localities, being, generally not even
an approximation to correctness; and their far famed property, of acute-
ness in finding out places, being explained, most truthfully, by the fact,
of their ransacking in every tortuous direction, all the area between,
untill they strike at last upon the only thing left, viz. the place looked for.

In conclusion, I beg leave again, to express my regret, as to the
general result of the survey; that after after [sic] the opening out of
about eighty miles of line, and the performance of explorations, in different directions, of more than four hundred miles, so little should have
been discovered, to promise advantage, or to induce settlement; and the
only satisfaction which I can derive from reflecting upon the results of
my labour is, that I have endeavoured to discharge the duty assigned to
me, with faithfulness, and to the extent of my abilities, though at times,

under no ordinary discouragements. The only advantage, perhaps, which your department will realize from it, is, a knowledge of what the country really is, and a consequent safeguard, against incurring future expenses in the subdivision of a country into Townships, and farm lots, which is entirely unfitted, as a whole, for agricultural purposes.

Toronto January 31st. 1853.

D 10   ALEXANDER MURRAY'S[28] "REPORT FOR THE YEAR 1853 . . .
TO WM. E. LOGAN, PROVINCIAL GEOLOGIST"
[*Canada, Geological Survey,* Report of Progress for the Years
1853–54–55–56, *pp. 59–99*]

Montreal, 1st February, 1854.

In the spring of the year 1853, you were pleased to direct me to make an examination of a portion of the unsurveyed region lying between Georgian Bay, in Lake Huron, and the Ottawa River. In this I was engaged the whole summer and autumn following, and I have now the honour of laying before you a Report of the progress then made.

The line of route I had laid down as best calculated to afford general information, promising to be a very long one, and little or nothing being known to me of the character of the country through which I should have to pass, I deemed it prudent to supply myself with a more complete stock of provisions than has usually been required, and to take with me an extra canoe and two additional hands for its navigation, for the first month of our voyage; by the end of that time I was in hopes we should be far enough advanced, and sufficiently lightened, to dismiss the extra canoe, and reach some settled part with the usual complement of four men and two canoes.

Not being acquainted with any accurate survey[29] of the portion of the interior I was about to visit, the main water courses naturally offered the greatest facilities for my work, as it appeared to me that by following some one of the main streams which fall into lake Huron to its source, I might be able to cross the water-shed, and find my way to the Ottawa by one of the rivers falling in the opposite direction. The river selected is a large stream known as the Muskoka; the course of this was followed to its head, beyond which a short portage brought us to the source of the Petewahweh, and by its channel we descended to the Ottawa. Returning we ascended the Bonne-chère River to a sheet of water well known to the Ottawa lumberers as Round Lake, from which we crossed to another

[28]Alexander Murray (1811–1884) was born in Scotland and, after a career in the Royal Navy and some experience in geological work, was appointed assistant to Sir William Logan. In the first half of the 1860's he surveyed largely on the Laurentian Shield and made a special study of the Laurentian series of rocks. He was later Director of the Geological Survey of Newfoundland.

[29]Apparently Murray was not familiar with David Thompson's report and maps. See *supra,* lii.

expansion, likewise well known as Lake Kamaniskiak, on the main branch of the Madawaska. We descended the Madawaska to the York or South-West Branch, known as the Shawashkong or Mishawashkong (the river of marshes); pursuing its upward course to the head, we again crossed the height of land and finally came out on Balsam Lake by the channel of the Gull River. . . .

The Muskoka River falls into Georgian Bay by at least two and probably more outlets; we ascended the most southern of these,[30] commencing where it joins the waters of Lake Huron at the north-east angle of Kennie's[31] Bay, in latitude 44° 57′ N., longitude 79° 53′ W. The ascent of the river from this point takes a general course due north for a distance of from five to six miles, where one of the outlets branches off, and then turning abruptly to the eastward, maintains an easterly direction for about thirteen miles to the exit of Muskoka Lake. This is an extensive sheet of water studded with numerous islands, and bounded by a very irregularly formed coast, which is indented by a succession of parallel bays, with long bold promontaries between. Crossing Muskoka Lake there were, along our line of survey, two general courses, the first a few degrees east of north for about two and a-half miles, the second a few degrees south of east for about eight and three-quarter miles; these reached to the entrance of the main river into the lake. Conforming with the trend of its bays, promontaries, and islands, the length of Muskoka Lake, lying obliquely across the general bearing of the stream, is about N.W. and S.E.; its surface stretches far away to the southward of the latter of the two courses given above, probably from fifteen to twenty miles, but our survey was confined to the northern portion of the lake. Another large sheet of water called Lake Rousseau, lies about four or five miles a little west of north from Muskoka Lake, which[32] receives its water by a stream coming in at the head of the most northerly bay; with the exception of a rapid, falling from eight inches to one foot, which occurs within a short distance of Rousseau Lake, the current on the connecting stream[33] is scarcely perceptible.

Following the main river upwards from Muskoka Lake, in a course north of east, about four miles brings us to a bifurcation shewing two streams of nearly equal size,[34] the one bearing away to the north, the other eastward; it is probable the eastward stream may be considered the main channel, but we ascended by the north one. On a general bearing very nearly due north at a distance of about thirteen miles, we arrived at a series of very picturesque lakes, the lowest of which for distinction I named Mary's Lake. From the foot of this lake, which is about four miles long by an average breadth of from one and a-half to two miles,

[30]The same branch as that ascended by Thompson, through Go Home Lake.
[31]Misprint for "Rennie's."
[32]"Which" refers to Muskoka Lake.
[33]Indian River.
[34]The North and South branches of the Muskoka River.

the course turns to N.N.E., and that bearing being carried on from the head of Mary's Lake for about four miles further, strikes another expansion which I have called Fairy Lake. The main stream[35] comes in at the north-west angle of Fairy Lake, but that we did not follow; we crossed the lake in a direction about N.E. by E. to a small tributary at its eastern end, which we found to fall from a third lake nearly due east, at the distance of a little over one mile. This lake, which lies nearly east and west, is from two to three miles long, and from the peculiarity of its shape was called Peninsula Lake.

Here leaving this branch of the Muskoka, we made a portage of a mile and three-quarters over a height of land, our course being S.E., and reached a long narrow lake stretching away southward for several miles; this we termed the Lake of Bays. The waters of this lake flow into Muskoka Lake, by the channel of the eastern main stream, and as the south-west extremity of the Lake of Bays is not over fifteen miles from the position where the two main branches join, while its level is upwards of a hundred feet above Peninsula Lake, the course of the eastern branch must be extremely rapid, or broken by very heavy falls, the total fall to Muskoka Lake being 323 feet.

Into the Lake of Bays several streams fall, two of which are of considerable size; but the one at the northern end appearing to be the largest, we continued our survey along its course. It falls into a bay at the north-east angle of the lake, in lat. 45° 19′ N., long. 79° 4′ W. nearly; and from this point a bearing of about E.N.E., will in four miles strike the next lake on our course, named from its shape Ox-tongue Lake. The connecting stream[36] between this lake and the Lake of Bays, with many meanders in its course, makes a general curve to the south of the direct bearing that has been given.

Above Ox-tongue Lake the upward course is nearly due north for about two miles, until presenting a succession of heavy falls, where it first turns south of east for about two miles, and afterwards bends to north-east, which course, excluding many minor sinuosities, it maintains for eleven or twelve miles to Canoe Lake,[37] so called from the circumstance of our being detained there for several days to construct a new canoe. Above Canoe Lake our course continued north-eastward through a series of small lakes and ponds, connected by short and narrow streams, generally rapid. The uppermost of the expansions was called Burnt Island Lake, and it is the highest on the Muskoka River. We attempted to follow a small stagnant brook which passes through a marsh at the northern extremity of Burnt Island Lake, but after progressing about two miles, all appearance of running water terminated in a vast

[35]The river flowing from Vernon Lake into Fairy Lake.
[36]Oxtongue River.
[37]Canoe Lake has retained the name given to it by Murray. South Tea Lake, immediately south of Canoe Lake was called Canoe Lake by David Thompson who built two canoes there (B 32).

swamp. From a bay at the north-east end of the lake we then crossed over a height of land, and at the distance of about half-a-mile, in the bearing N.N.E., we came upon a small lake which afterwards proved to be the head waters of the Petewahweh. The place of the portage is in lat. 45° 40′ 30″ N., long. 78° 38′ W. . . .

The country on each side of the Muskoka River, between Lake Huron and Muskoka Lake, is for the most part rugged and barren, bearing chiefly white and red pine, usually of small size. There are intervals, however, of better soil at various distances back from the river, where the pine timber which still prevails is of tolerably stout growth, and may eventually become of commercial importance. Since the time of my visit, Mr. W. B. Hamilton,[38] of Penetanguishene, has erected a saw-mill on or near the first falls, about two miles from the mouth of the river, where he is said to have an almost inexhaustible supply of pine within easy distance. Should this attempt at lumbering prove successful, and the present prices for the manufactured article continue, it is not improbable that establishments may extend still further into the interior before many years, as the river affords every facility for using water power in a great many places.

The portion of the shores of Muskoka Lake which came under my notice, like the banks of the river below, is bold, rocky, and barren, which is also the case with Rousseau Lake, although in the latter some good land occurs in patches, which are partially cultivated by a tribe of Indians who have settled there.

Between Muskoka Lake and the junction of the two main streams above, the river passes through rich alluvial flats producing abundance of good-sized elm, soft maple, ash and other trees, among which there is scattered a considerable quantity of fine white pine. Above the junction for from five to six miles, up to the high falls on the branch which we followed, the forest still indicates tolerably strong land in a stout growth of pine and hemlock, but above that part it becomes less productive, the principal trees being stunted evergreens, mostly balsam-fir, on a light and generally sandy soil.

The coasts of the upper three lakes are occasionally precipitous, and, except in the valleys of little streams, are every where bold and rocky. These precipices, with the hills in the back ground rising three hundred or four hundred feet at a moderate distance, offered very picturesque scenery, which, however, possesses few recommendations for settlement or permanent improvement.

I was informed by the Indians of Rousseau Lake that a very extensive area of country, occupied by vast swamps, or interspersed with innumerable small ponds and lakes, tributary to the north branch, lay directly

[38]William Basil Hamilton (d. 1891) had a general store in Penetanguishene, and was district councillor for Tiny 1846 to 1848 and a justice of the peace. In 1854 he moved to Collingwood and entered the sawmill business. He held various public offices in Collingwood, including that of mayor in 1858.

north from Fairy and Peninsula Lakes, where numbers of the tribe resorted during the hunting season, for the purpose of trapping beavers,
which were represented to be very numerous.

The character of the coast of the Lake of Bays, like that of the chain
of lakes, on the north branch, is rocky, bold, and barren, for the most
part; but the valley of the river above frequently contains wide areas of
alluvial flats, having clay of a drab colour as a subsoil, overlaid by sili-
cious yellow sand. Groves of red pine were observed in many parts, both
on the lakes and on the river, and instances were not altogether wanting
where that timber attained a good sized growth, probably suitable for
squaring into spars. The soil producing red pine, however, is not usually
deemed to be of the best quality. At the height of land between the
Muskoka and Petewahweh, and around the upper lakes, there are great
tracts of marsh and swamp, closely grown over by stunted tamarack and
dwarf spruce, or carpeted by marsh plants. These swamps occupy the
valley between the ranges of hills, which are here widely apart, running
about N.N.E. and S.S.W. On the sides of these hills there are frequently
good hard-wood trees; many of them were white birch, the bark of which
we found of essential service for building our new canoe. . . .

The Shawashkong, as its name implies, flows in many parts through
immense marshes, especially at the lower and towards the upper extremities. . . .

Tracts of good hard-wood land mixed with pine, occur in the valley
of the Sahwashkong [sic], particularly in the flat country around the
Grand Bend and at Kaijick Manitou Lake;[39] but the prevailing forest is
pine throughout the length of the river. Farms have been established at
two places, one at a short distance from the Little Mississipi, by Mr.
Conroy, and another further up and near the Grand Bend, by Mr.
Egan.[40] Lumbering operations have already extended nearly up to Kaijick
Manitou Lake, and I was informed by the Chief of a tribe of Indians I
met there, that preparations were about to be made to bring timber down
from the country above Papineau Lake.[41] The name of Kaijick Manitou
was given the lake in honor of this Chief, who proved of great service to
us by his description of the country we were about to travel through at
the height of land.

Between Kaijick Manitou and Papineau Lakes the river flows slug-
gishly through a vast marsh, making a very serpentine course through
the valley, which is bounded on either side by hills of moderate elevation, frequently clothed with good sized hard-wood trees. Although there
is a perceptible current for the whole distance, the rise in this part is
very small, certainly not amounting to more than six or eight feet. . . .

[39]Baptiste Lake.
[40]These farms may have been depot farms established by the lumbermen. R. &
W. Conroy was a lumber company at Aylmer, Quebec, and John Egan was a
lumberman from the Ottawa Valley.
[41]Lake Benoir, in Harcourt Township.

Above Papineau Lake there are occasional rapids, connecting a chain of lakes at the main source of the river, but the elevation of them was not ascertained; for shortly after leaving Kaijick Manitou Lake, our provisions were exhausted, and we had necessarily to abandon farther measurements, and make the best of our way to the settlements. Fortunately beavers, muskrats, and other game were tolerably abundant, and supplied our necessities until we arrived at Kah-shah-gah-wigamog, where we fell in with a trapper, named Russel, who kindly provided us with venison and bread.

Continuing our journey from Papineau Lake, our course was nearly south-west for about seven miles, within which distance we portaged over to and crossed a succession of small lakes stretching along the water-shed situated between the Ottawa and Lake Ontario. The next course was a little south of west, with a straight distance of about eighteen miles, crossing from one lake to another along the height of land, and at length reaching Kah-shah-gah-wigamog, or Long Lake, the waters of which fall into Cameron's Lake, by the channel of the Burnt River. This lake is narrow, and lying about S.S.W. as a general bearing from its upper end, has a length of a little over thirteen miles. The outlet leaves the lake on its south-east side, not far from the south-western extremity; this we did not follow, but from the south-west end, pursued a course nearly due west for a little over two miles, making in the distance two portages and traversing a small lake, and then striking the Gull River. The course of this stream was followed downwards through Gull Lake and the two Mud-turtle Lakes[42] to Balsam Lake, making a course nearly due south, with a straight distance of about eighteen miles.

The waters of the first part of our course from Papineau Lake probably all belong to the Ottawa side of the ridge, and may fall into the Shawashkong, but all the others evidently go the other way, and most probably are upper waters of the Ottonabee.

The country all along the height of land is more or less broken and hilly, and the sides of the hills are amply covered with hard-wood trees intermingled with pines. The valleys and more level parts, except where swamps or marshes occur, frequently display an excellent soil, yielding a stout growth of maple, elm, birch and beech. There are also good tracts of land around Kah-shah-gah-wigamog and Gull Lake; and I was informed by the trappers I met there, that the country east of the latter lake was well adapted for settlement over a large area. Settlement has already begun on the Gull River, north of Balsam Lake, and will most probably soon extend still farther back. When I visited the same country in 1852, a saw-mill was in progress of construction on the lower rapids of the Gull River, which has since been finished and put in operation; below it there are now several clearings, with houses and barns on them, where all was a wilderness one twelve-month before.

[42]The Lakes between Gull and Balsam are Moore and Shadow.

D 11   MICHAEL DEANE[43] TO JOSEPH CAUCHON,[44] COMMISSIONER OF CROWN LANDS

[Ontario, Department of Lands and Forests, Field Notes, no. 1926]

In compliance with instructions[45] dated the 14th. November 1854, I have surveyed an exploration or guide line from the North East corner of Somerville to Mr. Bell's line, on an astronomical course N. 20° 51′ 40″ W., and explored the country on each side 4 or 5 miles, the Plan and returns thereof are herewith furnished—

The first section, extending from the starting point at the North East corner of Somerville to 6⅛ miles on the main line, the land is of a rough undulating character with occasional valleys and patches of good sandy loam soil, the prevailing timber is hardwood intermixed hemlock and pine.

The next section extending from 6⅛ miles to 12 miles, the land is generally of a good description the soil being composed of a sandy loam, and comparatively free of stone, it is well watered and fit for compact settlement.

The next section extending from the 12th. to the 18th. mile is tolerable land, more stony and undulating than the last section, soil the same as above described, the timber hardwood, mixed with pine and hemlock.

The next section extending from the 18th. mile to Mr. Bell's line, the land on the east side of the line is the same as the last section, but on the west side the land is more hilly stony and hemlocky.

The whole line with some few deviations affords a good direct and practicable site for a road.

The country generally with the exception of the section between the north boundary of Somerville and Gull Lake is adapted for settlement; the whole is well watered being very much intersected by Streams, Rivers and Lakes, those of the latter which are connected by the great chains of water abound with maskinonge, white fish and salmon trout, falls and rapids are very numerous on these waters, affording great facilities for working machinery by water power—

Believing that a colonization road would greatly facilitate and hasten the settlement of this extensive tract, I have on returning home, located a road from Mr. Bell's road to 18½ miles on the main line, where I deemed it advisable to suspend the location of the road, till I have explored the country from Gull Lake to Muskoko River— for in the event of a road being practicable or deemed necessary from the North East

[43]Michael Deane (1819–1897) qualified as a land surveyor on May 26, 1848. He was county surveyor for Victoria County, and also carried out many surveys for the Dominion government in the prairie provinces.

[44]Joseph Edouard Cauchon (1816–1885), a journalist and politician, was Commissioner of Crown Lands from 1855 to 1857. He was interested in the development of the Canadian west, and served as Lieutenant Governor of Manitoba from 1877 to 1882.

[45]Instructions to Land Surveyors, Book 5, p. 238.

corner of Somerville to Muskoko, economy would suggest having one main road to Gull River above the head of Gull Lake, and the two branches from there, one to Mr. Bell's road at the Muskoko River, and the other to Mr. Bell's road at the head of Little Coshogwigmog Lake[46]—

In concluding my report on this line I would earnestly recommend the immediate construction of a road from Fenelon Falls to Mr. Bell's road at the head of Little Coshogwigmog Lake, as I am fully convinced that a road communication into the interior is the only means of settling this extensive tract and developing its resources.

I have also surveyed an exploration line from near the North East corner of Somerville to Gull Lake on an astronomical course N. 65° 51′ 40″ W — 6 miles and 27 chains, and explored the country for the space of four or five miles on each side, in half mile sections.

For the first two miles the country to the north east of the line is very rough and undulating, the naked granite rock appearing at intervals, the soil is sandy, and the timber a mixture of hardwood hemlock and pine in equal proportions, the hardwood consists of maple, beech and birch, and the pine though large is scrubby and of a poor quality, on the south west of the line the land is tolerably good less stony and better pine timber, a large tamarac swamp occurs on this section extending to the north boundary of Somerville, it is too wet to be of any value, on leaving the small Lake at the two mile post a narrow belt of very good land is passed through extending south westerly to lots 7 and 8 in the 14th. Concession of Somerville.

The line then passes through a very rough rocky section, about a mile and a half in breadth timbered with a growth of stunted hemlock spruce and pine, with scarcely any soil, the granite appearing at the surface or merely covered with moss.

The line then intersects a beaver meadow, the land on either side being rough and stony, the timber a mixture of hardwood and hemlock; for the next mile the line passes through a section of country very undulating and stony, the timber is a mixture of hardwood and pine the latter of a good quality— from this point to near the margin of Gull Lake, the land on the line and to the north of it, is rough and stony and intersected with several high ridges; on the south of the line on this section there is a tract of table land of good quality, the soil being loamy and the timber hardwood of a large size, mixed with hemlock and pine— adjoining the lake on the east side of Miner's bay, there is a narrow valley of good land, of a clay soil and hardwood timber—

The route generally from the North East corner of Somerville to Gull Lake is impracticable for a road, owing to its roughness, as well as Gull Lake presenting a permanent obstacle. This locality is very unproductive and holds out but few inducements to the settler, while to the hunter or sportsman its resources are inexhaustible, there being abun-

[46]Probably St. Nora Lake.

dant signs of beaver and otter in the small lakes and creeks, martin and mink are caught in great numbers, and the hardwood ridges abound with deer. . . .

Lindsay 8th Feby. 1856

D 12   DEANE TO CAUCHON
[Ontario, Department of Lands and Forests, Field Notes, no. 1926]

Lindsay 25th. April 1857

I have the Honor to submit the following report upon my explorations in the rear of the County of Victoria, under instructions[47] dated the 16th. May 1856 . . .

Having hired men, and procured supplies, and Camp equipage for the prosecution of my Exploration in the rear of the County of Victoria, I left Lindsay on the 12th. August by steamer Ogemah[48] and arrived at Fenelon Falls on the evening of the same day, and proceeded thence in small Boats to my starting point on Gull River, where I arrived on the 16th., being greatly delayed on my journey by the lowness of the water as well as innumerable portages and wading places.

On Monday the 18th. Inst I commenced the Survey of my exploration line (running a magnetic Course— N. 72°. W. from Gull River, at a point 9 miles and Fifty-four chains on the Main Line which I ran last year from the North East Corner of Sommerville bearing N 20°. 15'. 40″ W. . . .

At Muskako River I terminated my line and formed a junction with Mr. Bridgelands Line,[49] and returned to Gull River, as I considered it unnecessary to continue my line through a section of Country already explored.

On the line I crossed nine Lakes and several Beaver Meadows, owing to which as well as to the general roughness of the route, I decided on not locating a Road on my return, being of opinion that the benefits arising from a Road through that section, would be incommensurate with the cost of construction, as well as being an indirect route to the available lands in the Valleys of the Black and Muskako Rivers, the direct outlet of which in my opinion should be Via Beaverton.

Summing up then, the total of this route, there are 4 miles rough rocky and unproductive, 6 miles tolerable though stoney and somewhat rocky in places, and 12½ miles of a good quality, fit for settlement, and well adapted for agricultural purposes.

The Country generally is well supplied with water the main Chains, viz, Gull River Black River and the Muskako possessing unlimited water power, afford numerous sites for working machinery.

[47]Instructions to Land Surveyors, Book 5, pp. 263-4.

[48]The Ogemah, a caravel, 103 feet in length, is described by H. M. Wallis in "James Wallis, Founder of Fenelon Falls" (Ontario History, v. 53, no. 4, Dec., 1961, p. 266).   [49]See D 9.

The whole route is through the granite region, and from indications in the rocks, I am of opinion that in many places, there is iron ore in abundance.

The lumbering resources are very limited, the pine generally is of an inferior quality, and very little seen, except in the Valley of the Black River, fit for merchantable timber.

I have Sir in this brief report given you such information as I think will enable you to form a general idea of the capabilities and resources of the Country, which you were pleased to appoint me to explore.

D 13 ANDREW RUSSELL'S[50] "INSTRUCTIONS[51] TO PROVL. LAND SURVEYOR JAMES W FITZGERALD[52] TO SURVEY THE BOUNDARY LINES BETWEEN THE TOWNSHIPS OF MINDEN & STANHOPE, DYSART & GUILFORD, DUDLEY & HARBURN, HARCOURT & BRUTON &C, &C"
[*Ontario, Department of Lands and Forests, Instructions to Land Surveyors, Book 5, pp. 336–9*]

Having been directed by an order-in-Council of the 25th Ultimo to survey the outlines of certain townships north of the Counties of Peterborough & Victoria with the view of opening up for settlement this section of the Ottawa & Huron Territory, I have chosen you to perform part of this service; you will in addition to the usual surveying party, engage two assistants, who, with a practical knowledge of the fitness of land for agricultural purposes as well as a knowledge of the various descriptions of Canadian Timber &c, understand the use of the pocket compass & can keep notes, and you will send one of them to explore to the right, and the other to the left of your lines to the distance of from three to five miles in order to ascertain the quality of the land on both sides of your main line. . . .

Sep. 23, 1857

D 14 FITZGERALD'S "SURVEY OF TOWNSHIP BOUNDARIES"
[*Ontario, Department of Lands and Forests, Field Notes, no. 1904*]

St. Mary's June 1st. 1858

In accordance with instructions received from you dated Sept 23rd. 1857 to survey the outlines of certain townships north of the Counties

50Andrew Russell was appointed Assistant Commissioner of Crown Lands on November 22, 1839.

51On August 18, 1857, similar instructions had been issued to John Lindsay "to survey the boundary line between the townships of Minden & Snowdon, Dysart & Glamorgan, Dudley & Monmouth, and Harcourt & Cardiff &c" (Instructions to Land Surveyors, Book 5, pp. 331-5).

52James W. Fitzgerald (1828–1901) was born in Ireland, came to Canada in 1853 and qualified as a land surveyor on July 13, 1857. He surveyed in the northern part of Peterborough and Victoria counties and subdivided Minden Township. He also carried on surveys in western Canada.

of Peterboro and Victoria, I beg to state that I have now completed said survey and shall submit to you the plan, Report, and other documents connected therewith—

. . .

. . . I shall now briefly review the whole including the explorers' daily reports. I will commence with the township of Minden, it contains more good land than any in my survey— The soil is generally a sandy loam, it is advantageously intersected by lakes and rivers the latter affording any amount of water power, the timber is chiefly Beech and Maple, fully 60 p cent of the land in this township is well adapted for cultivation—

Stanhope, the land in this township is more hilly and undulating and the soil is generally lighter, north of a chain of lakes previously referred to flowing into Big Bushkonk are a series of hardwood ridges of moderate height. The soil in the Valleys between them is very rich, but on them is light and stony. The above mentioned water chain flows through several large Cranberry marshes, about 45 p. cent of this township is suitable for farming purposes—

Dysart. This township immediately east of Minden contains several tracts of good land along its westerly and southerly boundary. There is also a good tract of land north of the River flowing out of Drag lake into Kashabagawigamog, the easterly part however is generally rough and hilly, a branch of the Burnt river before alluded to flows through the south part of this township and unites with the principal river flowing out of Kashabagawigamog about 4 miles south of same. The timber is principally hdwood the soil sandy and in several places loamy. This township yields about the same per centage of arable land as the preceeding

Guilford along its westerly boundary partakes of the same undulating character as that adjoining it in Stanhope, towards the north and east however it is very rough and broken with granite ridges in places covered with large stones, the soil along the Valley and on the side of some of the ridges is tolerable, and the timber of the usual kinds of hardwood mixed with Hem. Bal. and Pine. There are a few large lakes in the township in which salmon trout and other kinds of fish is abundant; from 30 to 40 p cent is adapted for agricultural purposes.

Dudley along its western boundary is broken. Drag Lake and its surrounding ridges are in the westerly part of this township, the easterly part is very good land and contains large tracts of excellent land, the soil is sandy loam, the timber chiefly hardwood with a good proportion of Hemlock & Pine— fully 40 p cent of this township is good arable land and well suited for farms

Harburn This township though rough and broken along its westerly boundary gradually becomes more even and uniform towards its easterly extremity, the timber is of a very mixed kind and not very gross The soil resembles that of Dudley and would average nearly the same p centage

Harcourt There are some good tracts of land along the north and west of this township An extensive pine Valley is situate in the easterly part stretching northwards into Bruton. The soil is generally light & sandy but of considerable depth in places. Towards the southerly part of the township the land is broken and the timber also is inferior The York branch of the Madawaska River flows through the N E. corner of this township The p centage of arable land is about 35—

Bruton The westerly part of this township is covered chiefly with hardwood timber, in places it is low and swampy. The easterly part is for the most part covered with white and Norway pine the soil is sand and generally free of rocks and stones from 40 to 45 per cent of this township is capable of being cultivated

Having thus reviewed the eight townships comprising the survey with which I have been favored, stating as near as possible the proportions of good and bad land the description and quality of the timber and soil, it is my opinion that at least 40 p cent of the whole is well adapted for immediate cultivation besides a large proportion would in the course of time be rendered available—

D 15   J. STOUGHTON DENNIS'S "REPORT . . . OF THE SURVEY OF THE MUSKOKA ROAD LINE, NORTH OF GRAND FALLS, PARRY SOUND ROAD LINE, & EXPLORATION TO MOUTH OF MUSKOKA RIVER"
[*Ontario, Department of Lands and Forests, Field Notes, no. 2211*]

Toronto, 19th April 1861

I have the honour to report to you upon the various surveys comprising
1st The Survey of the Muskoka Road line North of the Grand Falls to the Bobcaygeon Road—
2. The Exploration from the District line out to the Mouth of the Muskoka and the character of the Harbour at that point—
3. The advantages possessed by Parry Sound as a Harbour and the result of the Survey and exploration from this point to the Bobcaygeon Road— performed under your instructions[53] dated respectively the 26th June and 6th of August of last year—
1   The Muskoka Road line
The Survey of this line occupied from the 24th of July on which day I left Toronto, till the 26th day of September following—at which time we arrived back at the District line from the Bobcaygeon Road, and commenced the exploration line from thence out to the Muskoka River
I took my party and supplies in by Lake Simcoe to the Severn at the foot of that Lake— thence by the Muskoka Road as constructed up to

[53]Instructions to Land Surveyors, Book 5, pp. 473-4, 477.

the South Easterly Bay of Muskoka Lake and from thence by canoe up to the high Falls on the North Branch of the River at which place I established my store camp— and commenced work—

Upon a "reconnaissance" of the River and country in the vicinity of the North Falls[54] I came to the conclusion that at no point to be found for miles on that Branch did the same facilities exist for crossing the stream as immediately at the Falls— Here the high banks will be very easily surmounted— a shallow Ravine occurring precisely where required on the South side and on the North side the ascent being so gradual as to be admirably adapted for a Road—

The Bridge itself will be very inexpensive— The width of actual waterway is not more than a chain and the facilities afforded by two rocky Islands in mid channel render any long span unnecessary –

I therefore proceeded to connect this site with the Bridge which had been lately erected over the South Branch of the Muskoka at the Grand Falls—

The line was then continued Northerly and Westwardly to the District line the general direction of which was followed up to 6 chs and 13 lks on the 9th mile, and from this point I diverged on the general bearing of N.9° E. Magnetic— varn. 4° 9′ West — to the end of the 18th mile— Here having first examined the Country North of Fairy Lake and determined on the point at which to cross the Muskoka River North of the Lake mentioned— the Course was changed to the general direction of N.40° E. upon which the Survey was continued to within 20 chs of the end of the 34th mile when it was altered to N.71° E. on which direction I ran out to the Bobcaygeon Road— intersecting the same at 9 c 41 lks north of the 23d mile post—

A line for road was located by my Survey up to the end of the 35th mile from whence although no pains were spared in exploring it was found impossible anywhere in the vicinity of the Survey to get a line however crooked upon which a road could be opened at any reasonable expense for construction—

I then proposed to deviate from the line Surveyed say at 33 miles 60 chs and continue North Eastwardly and so get around if possible the rocky and broken country referred to— and with this view deferred any examination of the country in that direction until the survey of the exploration line from Parry Sound, which I expected to pass a few miles north of this, would give me a better knowledge of the features in that direction— proposing, should it prove practicable to get a road on that line, to extend this up North Easterly from the point mentioned and join in with it Westerly of the Bobcaygeon Road—

I may now mention that this was subsequently found to be impracticable— Neither the country on the Parry Sound line or between the two although thoroughly examined was found to be such that a road could

[54]Site of the present town of Bracebridge.

be made anywhere North Easterly— or in that direction out to the Bobcaygeon Road—

It would appear to be part of the height of land between the heads of the Muskoka (North Fork) and the Maganitawan— and which no doubt extends North Easterly to the sources of the Petawawa—this region is so rocky, swampy and mountainous that the construction of a road through it would be immensely expensive and the idea of locating one was therefore abandoned—

Had my stock of provisions permitted while inland after discovering (in Jany. last) that a North Easterly route was impracticable— I should have made a Survey from say the 29th mile on the Muskoka Road line in an Easterly direction out to the Bobcaygeon Road in hopes of finding a more favourable country— This however for the above reason— it was not in my power to effect—

I am inclined to think from general observations that the Muskoka Road may be continued out in that direction— and before closing this report will again refer to the subject proposing a route for examination—

No bridges of consequence will be required on the road as far as located excepting the one across the Muskoka River between Lake Vernon and Fairy Lake at which point also the crossing is under very favourable circumstances

This Bridge however will of necessity be of a more expensive character than the one over the river at the Falls— the stream here being about one hundred feet wide— but I should say from appearances that little danger may be apprehended from Freshets—

The general character of the land over which the line passes up to the 35th mile— particularly that part of it between the Township of Macaulay and Lake Vernon— is undulating country covered with Hardwood — the soil is sandy and gravelly loam with clay developing itself in many places, and presenting altogether very attractive features for settlement. I think it will be found that the land comprised in the outlines shewn on the official maps of the Department as the Townships of Stephenson and Brunel will be for agricultural purposes much above the average quality of that of the Ottawa country generally—

Observations taken from Marys Lake Fairy Lake and Lake Vernon would confirm this opinion—

2. Exploration line from the Old District line out to the mouth of the River Muskoka and the character of the Harbour at that point—

In returning from the Survey North-Easterly to the Bobcaygeon Road of the Muskoka Road line— I took up this Exploration commencing it on the 27th of September and getting out to the mouth of the River on the 30th of Oct. following — With reference to this line I became satisfied in the course of the Survey that in consequence of the nature of the country passed over, the number and extent of Bridges, and the large item in causeways which would be involved, nothing but the circumstance of the mouth of the river being the best Harbour (if not the only one) on that shore would justify its selection for the contemplated leading road out to Lake Huron—

On examining the Harbour upon my arrival out to the Coast— I found it anything but a good one, the Channels being narrow and tortuous— so much so that it is impossible to navigate them with certain winds—

I found that whenever vessels were bound to the Mills[55] on the Muskoka River which Mills supply a certain number of cargoes of Lumber every season, it was always necessary to get a certain Pilot to take them in and out through the Channels leading to and from the Harbour at the mouth of the River— After being loaded they were liable to detention— as with certain winds it was impossible for them to get out—

I obtained the services of this Pilot in the examination of the Harbour at this place, as also of that at Parry Sound, and from the information afforded by him together with my own observation, came to the conclusion that all consideration of this route and Harbour for the contemplated Road would have to be abandoned . . .

Before leaving the question of the Exploration line out to the mouth of the Muskoka Road it is necessary to say something as to the character of the country along it— This may be described generally as follows—

Between the District line and the North fork (known as the Moose River[56]) of the Muskoka the country is pretty much the same— generally Hardwood— though mixed with pine timber in many places— This timber although of small size generally is frequently found of excellent quality— Soil sandy and gravelly loam— affording say ⅓d of the surface fit for settlement— the remainder rocky and swampy—

In some places however— for instance— North Easterly from Lake Muskoka— and again for a few miles West of the outlet of Lake Rosseau— exist considerable portions together of land desirable for settlement.

From the Moose River fork of the Muskoka out to the mouth, the country as may be seen by the Map is very much broken and is so rocky and swampy particularly West of the 23d mile as to afford little or no land fit for farming purposes—

3— Harbour at Parry Sound and Exploration line to Bobcaygeon Road

From my observations at this place together with information derived from the Pilot mentioned, and from Mariners— all being corroborated by the statements of Mr Warren the gentleman in charge of the extensive Mills erected by Mr Gibson, I am led to believe this to be a commodious and safe Harbour—. . .

4. Exploration line to Bobcaygeon Road—

The character of the country along this line is not as favourable as from previous accounts I had been led to expect —The Plan exhibits the features so fully that any particular description is unnecessary—

[55]See G 4.
[56]Now known as the Moon River.

Up to the 34th or 35th mile through which extent a road might be located without difficulty it may be taken to be a fair sample of the average of the Ottawa country generally— that is— that part with which I am acquainted— but from thence out to the Bobcaygeon Road it is impracticable either for the construction of a Road or for settlement— partaking of the same character precisely as observed on the Muskoka Road East of the 35th mile—

The country between this line and that of the Muskoka Road was traversed and explored without finding any better route— Under the circumstances I should recommend that the Road from Parry Sound should run from that point joining with the Muskoka Road just East of Lake Vernon say at the 24th mile on the latter and continue out from thence on the proposed Easterly route as here-in-before indicated, to the Bobcaygeon Road—

I have now respectfully to solicit your attention to a subject the importance of which will no doubt be readily admitted—

It is the necessity which exists for opening up a road upon the North Shore of the Georgian Bay connecting the settlements West of French River with those in the County of Simcoe— being in fact the continuation of the great Northern Road Southeasterly for Postal and general communication particularly during the Winter Season—

The greatest want which will be experienced in the formation of settlements at the few points on that shore favourable for the purpose— will be found to arise out of the difficult and uncertain nature of the communication with the old Townships to the South East.

For some 6 or 7 months of each year this coast is a sealed book excepting by the precarious means afforded by the ice— It is well known that the mails from Penetanguashine to Manitowaming Bruce Mines Sault De Ste Marie even once a post was established have during the Winter season been carried by a Dog Train on the ice— No winter passes without the carrier suffering hardships during these trips, unheard of anywhere excepting in connection with Polar Expeditions— beside the constant risk of the loss of the mails—

Supposing the country inland to be utterly unfitted for settlement— the increasing necessities of a regular winter communication between the points mentioned— looking to the probable formation of large settlements west of the French River, would justify the construction of a road from the South East to join the great Northern supposing the same to be practicable— In this case there can be little doubt but that it is practicable and also that at some points along it more or less land would be developed fit for settlement— As necessary also in other respects to perfect a system of Roads for the Ottawa country with which it would be connected by the Muskoka and Parry Sound lines— I feel that no apology is needed for my referring to it as a subject deserving of immediate consideration.

I think it probable a road might be located upon a line generally parallel with the shores of the Georgian Bay keeping back of the rocky coast line— intersecting the Muskoka Road say at the District line and running up so as to cross the French River at the first convenient point— say at the Recollet Falls—

It might be found upon examination that a road might be made upon a more direct line from Orillia Northerly through Matchedash and West of Lakes Muskoka and Rosseau— This would be much the more direct route and as it might be made to intersect a tract of land of fair quality and of considerable extent observed during the exploration out to the mouth of the Muskoka River lying in a Northerly and Southerly direction West of Lake Rosseau circumstances altogether might justify its examination—

In case it were found impracticable I would try the other upon which although not so direct, I think a road might be located— . . .

D 16   Vernon B. Wadsworth's "Reminiscences of Surveys, 1860–64"

[Wadsworth, History of Exploratory Surveys, pp. 1–13; also printed in Association of Ontario Land Surveyors, Annual Report, 1926, pp. 156–67]

In May 1860 I became an articled pupil of J. S. Dennis of the City of Toronto, being a youth then sixteen years of age, having passed my preliminary examination in the old Parliament Buildings on Front and Wellington Streets, Toronto, in April 1860.

The Government of that day decided to develop for settlement, lumbering, etc., by means of colonization roads throughout the above districts, as at that time the only isolated settlements in those districts being for lumbering purposes, and to a very small extent. In fact the only settlement of those extensive districts comprised a few people at the Severn Bridge about 14 miles north of Orillia, and a small sawmill village at Parry Sound.

The Muskoka Road at that time was extended twelve miles from the crossing of the Severn River to where Gravenhurst is now situated, and at Parry Sound three or four small houses and a small sawmill were located, but no road thereto, nor were there any farms or settlers in that vicinity; nor indeed was there any settlement from the Georgian Bay and the Severn River northward to Lake Nipissing, and northward beyond, excepting the Hudson Bay Company's posts and these were few and far between.

To develop this large forested country the Commissioner of Crown Lands of that time, instructed J. S. Dennis to make exploration surveys throughout the districts, and if the exploration surveys reached a country suitable for farming settlement, then roads were to be opened to be based on those survey lines with outlets on suitable Georgian Bay harbors.

The instructions to J. S. Dennis comprised the location and extension of the Muskoka Road northeastward to the north branch of the Muskoka River with suitable bridge crossing over the Muskoka River, starting from the end of the located road at the Falls on the south branch of the Muskoka River, and thence easterly and northerly north of the Muskoka River to the surveyed line of the Bobcaygeon Road.

On completing this exploration for road survey, an exploration line was to be surveyed westerly through the Indian Gardens, now Port Carling, from a point about five miles north of the crossing of the north branch of the Muskoka River, and to terminate at the mouth of the Muskosh River,[57] the outlet of Lake Muskoka on the Georgian Bay.

Failing to find the country traversed suitable for settlement on this last mentioned line, then the survey party was to proceed to Parry Sound and run an exploration line easterly fifty miles or so to the intersection of the Bobcaygeon Road line, and thereafter to survey a line from a point about five miles or so north of the crossing of the Muskoka River northward to the north end of Lake Rosseau, and westward to Parry Sound, which, if found to be the best navigable harbour for the Georgian Bay trade, was to be adopted as the terminal point for that road, and the lakeport for the district.

Thereafter a line was to be run from the north end of Lake Rosseau to the mouth of the South River, falling into Lake Nipissing. This line was estimated at eighty miles in length and was to be a theodolite line with explorations on each mile extending for a distance of three or four miles east and west of the main survey line, and to locate by diversions the site of the future colonization road where the main line was unsuitable.

These surveying operations were very extensive, and required a more intimate knowledge of the district and the lakes therein than the Government maps of that time disclosed.

Mr. Dennis organized his surveying party about the 1st of July, 1860, hiring the axe-men, cook and packers at Penetanguishene, Indians and Half-breeds— the best of men for such work. The staff associated with J. S. Dennis were John L. Oliver, Milner Hart,[58] student, V. B. Wadsworth, student, and MacDonald to be store camp keeper, and he was succeeded by Mr. Gentle who overlooked and guarded the provisions etc.

The men were to meet us at Orillia supplied with their axes, blankets, clothes and other necessaries.

Mr. Dennis and the staff left Toronto travelling by the old Northern Railway, which then ran to Collingwood, passing through Allandale,

[57]An alternative name for the South Branch of the Muskoka River from Lake Muskoka to the Georgian Bay. It is also spelled Musquash.

[58]Milner Hart (1837–1920) qualified as a land surveyor July 11, 1863. He was surveying in the Red River settlements at the time of the Riel Rebellion and later worked in Manitoba. In 1890 he took a position with the London and Canadian Loan and Agency Company of which his friend Vernon B. Wadsworth was manager.

and with a switch from Lefroy to Belle [*sic*] Ewart on Lake Simcoe where we took passage on the steamer "Morning" in charge of the late Captain May, and proceeded to Orillia, touching at Jackson's Point, Beaverton and Atherley and arrived at Orillia about 2:00 p.m.

There was a great storm on Lake Simcoe that day and it was very rough and very difficult for the steamer to touch at the respective points, and seasickness was common amongst the passengers.

On our arrival at Orillia we took rooms at Stafford's Hotel and our men from Penetanguishene were there awaiting us.

The next morning we hired two or three row boats and started up Lake Couchiching and duly reached the north end, a twelve mile row, to the outlet of the lake, being the Severn River which falls into the Georgian Bay on the north shore opposite Port McNichol. There are three outlets of the Severn River from Lake Couchiching.

We camped near the saw-mill, owned and operated by the late Quetton St. George,[59] and waited there for one Harvey[60] who with his team was to transport our provisions and camp equipment, etc., to Lake Muskoka, distant about twelve miles northward.

The then travelled road, known as the Muskoka Road, terminated there, and the road was so unfinished that a loaded team could only haul about 800 pounds of provisions, etc. and consequently to supply our party, Harvey had to do a lot of teaming to forward our supplies to Lake Muskoka.

We spent the day at St. George's mills amidst the rattlesnakes which at that time abounded there, some exhibited in cages. The next day we walked along the Muskoka Road, crossing the main Severn River and then entered the Laurentian Rocky Country of Muskoka. High rocks barred the way and presented a poor prospect for the settler accustomed to the fertile lands of Southern Ontario.

At this crossing of the Severn River there were two or three houses, and a store kept by one Jackson,[61] and I there met my friend, W. A. Browne,[62] whose father was surveying the Township of Morrison.

From this point northward the road passed through a very rocky,

[59]Henry Quetton de St. George (1820–1896), son of Laurent Quetton de St. George who had been in Canada from 1798 to 1815. Henry Quetton de St. George inherited his father's estates, and came to Canada in 1847. He built the sawmill on the Severn River in 1852.

[60]John Harvie, the stage owner, or one of his brothers. See H 3.

[61]James H. Jackson was one of the first settlers at Severn Bridge, having gone there in 1858. In January, 1861, he became the first postmaster, and from 1870 to 1881 he was representative for Morrison Township on the Simcoe County Council. *The County of Victoria Directory for 1869-70* lists Jackson as "Dealer in Dry Goods, Groceries, hardware, glass, china, earthenware, boots, shoes, &c."

[62]William Albert Browne (1843–1912), who had a long professional life as a surveyor, was the son of John O. Browne (1808–1881). John O. Browne came to Canada in 1847 and qualified as a surveyor on November 18, 1848. This survey of Morrison Township, mentioned by Wadsworth, was Browne's only government work.

sandy country, timbered principally with pine, hemlock, birch, etc. We followed Harvey's team on foot through an unsettled country, and in the afternoon reached the termination of the travelled road (now Gravenhurst). No one was there. Even the men who had been constructing the road had left for their homes at Orillia and other outside points. There was no road-way fit for a team or even a pathway to the south Bay of Lake Muskoka where we intended to camp and obtain canoes for travelling across Lake Muskoka to where our surveys commenced, on the south branch of the Muskoka River. However, our men quickly cut out a roadway to the Bay shore, about a mile distant, and suitable for a wagon to pass over and we camped there.

Harvey, day after day, brought in our required supplies from Orillia, till we were fully supplied for the season's operations. Our food was principally flour, and Chicago mess pork in barrels, and tea, and at first some beans.

Mr. Dennis's desire was now to obtain a birch bark canoe to make a Canoe Traverse of the lakes connected with the Muskoka Rivers, as there was no surveyed record[63] of the lakes and rivers in the district we were to survey. We had no canoes with us, and expected to obtain them from the Indian Village, which was about 25 miles northward of South Bay, Muskoka (now Port Carling). Fortunately our men found an old birch bark canoe concealed by the Indians in one of the Bays, and having duly repaired same and made paddles, Mr. Dennis and two men proceeded to the Indian Village of Obojawanung (now Port Carling) and returned in a couple of days with sufficient canoes to transport the party and supplies across Lake Muskoka to the mouth of the Muskoka River and thence up the river to the first Falls thereon, where Bracebridge is situated today.

The Lake was calm and beautiful, many rocky islands on our course, clothed with pine and hemlock, making altogether a charming prospect. As we passed from South Bay into the main Muskoka Lake at the Narrows, we saw the first encampment of Indians, namely Menominee, his wife and two grown-up daughters. Menominee was clad in Indian style with shirt, breech-cloth, leggings and moccasins, no hat and long black hair reaching to his waist— a wild looking Indian. His permanent camp and home was on Mary's Lake and there is now a post-office named after him near that Lake.

We reached the mouth of the Muskoka River after a paddle across the Lake of some ten miles, and passed up the River to the first falls, where Bracebridge now stands. Near the mouth of the River we saw a log house with a small potato garden around it, and found that it was the trading post of Alexander Bailey[64] who was then at his permanent

[63]Dennis, as well as Alexander Murray, was unfamiliar with David Thompson's survey.

[64]Alexander Bailey of Penetanguishene had a fur-trading house near the mouth of the Muskoka River, and a trading house and store at the North Falls, later

home in Penetanguishene, passing en route the mouth of the south branch of the Muskoka River flowing from Lake of Bays. We soon reached the basin at the foot of the Falls, a beautiful circular basin of several acres in extent and the Fall itself is upwards of fifty feet in height— an impressive sight. Mr. Dennis arranged for a permanent store camp at the foot of the Falls on the south side of the basin and at the base of a high perpendicular rocky hill there situate, with Mac-Donald as storekeeper.

There were no white settlers in all the route we had travelled excepting at the Severn Bridge. It was a virgin wilderness. The rivers and lakes teemed with fish, bass, salmon trout, speckled trout, pickerel, etc., and the woods with red deer, partridge and many beaver and other fur animals. Moose were not seen there in those days. They were confined to the Ottawa River region.

Mr. Dennis with three men and a birch bark canoe now commenced his Canoe Traverse of the lakes and rivers in that district, and passing up the Muskoka River he reached Mary's Lake, Fairy Lake and Peninsula Lake and discovered Vernon Lake and Vernon River (named after the writer).[65] He did not go to the Lake of Bays, or Trading Lake as the Indians called it from the fact that an Indian, one Bigwin from Snake Island in Lake Simcoe, traded somewhat with those Indians in that Lake.

On returning to our base store camp at the Falls, Mr. Dennis then made a Canoe Traverse of the shores of the connecting lakes, Muskoka, Rosseau and Joseph,[66] which latter lake he discovered and named after his father at that time residing at Buttonwood near Weston. He also traversed the Muskosh River from its outlet in Lake Muskoka to the Georgian Bay where a sawmill was there in operation. Having thus obtained the location of the lakes and rivers in the district to which our surveys were confined, and with Bayfield's Chart of the Georgian Bay Coast, we were fully equipped for the surveying operations required.

We now proceeded southward about four miles to the falls about one hundred feet high on the south branch of the Muskoka River where the existing Muskoka Road terminated, and after selecting the bridge site crossing on the north branch of the Muskoka River, where Bracebridge is now situated, we there found the Muskoka Road cut out to this south falls and the necessary timbers collected to construct the bridge, but otherwise not a sign of civilization.

These falls were very beautiful, the river passing through a rocky gorge

Bracebridge. In 1863 he bought land from James Cooper on the north side of the river, above and below the falls, and built a sawmill in 1864, and also a grist mill. For some time he acted as postmaster. His son, Captain George Bailey, served for sixty-one years as captain and commodore for the Muskoka Lakes Navigation Company.

[65]Usually known as the East or Big East River.

[66]Lake Joseph had been mapped by David Thompson in 1837 but not named.

with high precipitous banks— a wild and beautiful scene clothed with pine and evergreens.

Our surveying operations now commenced and we located by compass lines the road line between the two falls on the north and south branches of the Muskoka River and thence ran northerly for several miles along the old District Line, the west boundary of the then surveyed Township of Macaulay, to Falkenberg Village of this day, and thence north-easterly, locating the road en route and keeping north of the Muskoka River until we reached Vernon River, the outlet of Vernon Lake, where the Town of Huntsville is now situated, and thence proceeded eastward north of Fairy and Peninsula Lakes until we reached the surveyed line of the Bobcaygeon Road. The country passed through was well timbered with pine, hemlock and hard-woods with not much rocky land and well suited for settlement.

On completion of this work the party then returned to a point on our located Muskoka Road Line at about five miles north of the Bridge Site on the north branch of the Muskoka River and commenced the survey of an exploration line passing westerly between Lakes Muskoka and Rosseau to near the Indian Village now Port Carling, and crossing the Indian River thence westerly and southerly north of Lake Muskoka to a crossing on the Moon River, a branch of the Muskosh below the site of now Bala Village and eventually reaching the Georgian Bay at the mouth of the Muskosh River where the sawmill was situated.

We found the country for upwards of twenty miles northward of the Georgian Bay very rocky and swampy and totally unfit for settlement and, therefore, the mouth of the Muskosh was abandoned as a shipping port for the Muskoka District.

Our next scene of operations was to commence an Exploration Line at Parry Sound, and to carry this out Mr. Dennis instructed the party to disband and we hired a sail-boat at the Muskosh mills and sailed across the Georgian Bay to Penetanguishene— a lovely moonlight night and pleasant sail of about twenty miles. The men were discharged and the surveying staff returned to Toronto via stage to Barrie and thence by rail to Toronto.

A new party was organized by Mr. Dennis about the 1st of November, 1860, for the survey of an Exploration Line from Parry Sound extending fifty miles eastward to the Bobcaygeon Road Survey Line. The staff selected for this survey were J. L. Oliver, H. J. Cambie,[67] Milner Hart and V. B. Wadsworth. We proceeded as usual by rail and stage to Penetanguishene and found our men, who had been hired by Alfred

[67]Henry J. Cambie (1836–1928) was born in Ireland, came to Canada as a young man, and qualified as a land surveyor July 8, 1861. He had a long and colourful career as a surveyor both in eastern and western Canada. He was employed on railway surveys in the west, and was in charge of the construction of the railway through the Fraser Canyon.

Thompson,[68] ready to accompany us. They were picked men and experts in all kinds of bush life. Mr. Dennis did not accompany us on this survey.

There were no steamers in those days so we hired a sailing bateau, large enough to carry our whole party, provisions, etc. and started off on our fifty-mile lake trip, making Moose Point the first night and there camped. The next evening we reached Parry Sound, passing by the inner channel, and found the place consisted of three houses and a sawmill and a few people there. The sawmill was closed down for the season. The mill and whole establishment was owned by the Gibsons[69] of Willowdale, York Township, one of whom was the father of the late Peter Gibson, a well-known Provincial Land Surveyor.

We settled on the starting point of this Exploration Line on the east side of the Parry Sound Bay and by Christmas Day had completed some thirty miles of survey. The whole party then returned to Parry Sound for a fresh supply of provisions and to obtain our snowshoes as the snow was getting quite deep, and the men made toboggans to help in the transportation of our supplies for the remainder of the survey. This line when completed passed at about what is now the village of Scotia Junction on the Canadian National Railway, and we reached the Surveyed Line of the Bobcaygeon Road in due course.

The country passed through was well suited for settlement, rocky in parts but well timbered. There were not many lakes and as the consequence of this report the Government decided to adopt Parry Sound Harbour as the lake port on the Georgian Bay for an outlet for the settlers in that district, and the Government decided then to extend the road from the Muskoka Road near Bracebridge to Parry Sound passing northward from Lakes Rosseau and Joseph. After completing in February this fifty miles of Exploration Line, the party returned to Parry Sound and then started on the ice of Georgian Bay for Penetanguishene.

Although the cold and exposure experienced was intense, with no heating of tents by sheet-iron stoves as is customary now, all kept well and the party reached Penetanguishene in perfect health after their arduous journey. The staff then proceeded by stage and rail to Toronto and the men were discharged at Penetanguishene.

Immediately on arriving at Toronto I was called upon by Mr. Dennis

[68]Alfred A. Thompson (d. 1885) and his brother Henry Horace Thompson (b. 1826) were early settlers at Penetanguishene. They established the Thompson store and carried on a fur-trading business. A. A. Thompson was appointed a justice of the peace, April 3, 1857. He was father of Alfred B. Thompson who was later member of the Ontario legislature for Centre Simcoe. H. H. Thompson disposed of his interest in the store in 1876 and opened a private bank.

[69]David Gibson (1804–1864) was born in Scotland and became a surveyor and engineer before coming to Canada and qualifying as a land surveyor in Upper Canada, December 27, 1825. He took part in the Rebellion of 1837 and fled to the United States, but returned to Canada in 1848. He became Inspector of Crown Lands Agencies and Superintendent of Colonization Roads in 1853 and held the position until his death. He was the father of James Alexander Gibson and Peter Silas Gibson who were also surveyors. His home was at Willowdale.

to assist in surveying into farm lots the northern part of Rama Township, which fronts on Lake Couchiching and the east branch of the Severn River. The men were hired at Penetanguishene, and the staff consisted of J. S. Dennis, J. J. Francis,[70] Edward Webb, V. B. Wadsworth and John McLennan. This survey was completed in April, 1861.

In July, 1861, Mr. Dennis organized a survey party to carry on surveys of the colonization roads in the Muskoka and Parry Sound Districts and accordingly the survey party, the staff consisting of J. S. Dennis, Arthur Bristow,[71] William Oliver and V. B. Wadsworth, met at Gravenhurst— the axe-men and packers having been hired in Penetanguishene— and proceeded thence by canoe and sail boat (the first sail boat on those lakes brought from Kingston, Ontario) to the head of Lake Rosseau, now known as Rosseau Village, passing through the Indian Village now Port Carling and thence to the head of Lake Rosseau where a store camp was established on the site where Pratt's Hotel was afterwards located and we cleared about an acre of land there. We then proceeded to survey an Exploration Line westward to Parry Sound passing north of Lake Rosseau and Lake Joseph. The length of this line was about 25 miles. We reached Parry Sound in due course, much to the delight of the few people who lived there, as the construction of the road would enable them to get out to civilization in winter by land instead of travelling on the ice of the Georgian Bay to Penetanguishene.

We passed through a rough rocky country on this line and came to many lakes, which we crossed on rafts. The timber was principally pine, hemlock and hardwood in places of good quality.

Returning on our surveyed line to our store camp at the north end of Lake Rosseau, we commenced from that point the survey of an Exploration Line which would intersect our Muskoka Road line herebefore run north of Muskoka Falls, now Bracebridge, being at the point where we ran the line to the Indian Gardens. On this line we discovered Three Mile Lake and several other lakes and passed through a rough country. The surveyor in charge was Arthur Bristow for a short time, and thereafter Frederick Baldwin, Provincial Land Surveyor, took charge of the Party.

After completing this surveyed line we proceeded to the Muskoka Falls, now Bracebridge, and obtained provisions there. We found the bridge (now in the centre of Bracebridge) across the River partly constructed and three families settled there and the Muskoka Road constructed four or five miles. That was in December, 1861.

[70]John James Francis (1834–1916) was appointed land surveyor on October 16, 1861. In 1862 he surveyed Harburn Township, and later subdivided much of the land around Sarnia.
[71]Arthur Bristow (1827–1892) had been a civil engineer in England before he came to Canada and studied under J. S. Dennis. He qualified as a land surveyor on April 28, 1851, and carried on surveys in several parts of Canada including work for the Intercolonial Railway. In 1879 he entered the Surveys Branch of the Department of the Interior.

We then proceeded to survey a line from the Muskoka Road Line east at a point where Huntsville is now situated on Vernon River out to the Bobcaygeon Surveyed Line and north of Mary, Fairy and Peninsula Lakes.

On completing this work we returned to the Skeleton Lake region and started a survey line from the Parry Sound Road Line to connect with the Surveyed Muskoka Road Line at Vernon River, now Huntsville. This was in January 1862. Before completing this connecting survey line, Mr. Dennis appeared one morning in January 1862, at our camp near Skeleton Lake with two Penetanguishene packmen and informed Mr. Baldwin that the surveys in the Muskoka District by our party would be abandoned for the present as he was then surveying ten townships for the Canadian Land and Emigration Company in the Minden-Haliburton District and our party was to survey into farm lots the Township of Guilford. This was situated east of the Bobcaygeon Road and fronted on the Peterson Road and about twenty miles distant from Minden Post Office. We accordingly packed up and broke camp and passed over Three Mile Lake and down Lake Rosseau on the ice through the Indian Village on through Muskoka Lake to the site of Bracebridge and thence to the Falls on the south branch of Muskoka River and thence by the Peterson Road to Guilford Township, having travelled on foot about 80 miles to reach our destination.

The Peterson Road for most of the distance was cut out but not travelled by teams excepting by timber teams in the winter and there were not more than a dozen settlers on our whole route of travel.

We spent the rest of the winter and until July in surveying the Township of Guilford. Then the party disbanded and returned to Toronto and the men to Penetanguishene.

I was then engaged in other surveys for a time and having served my term of apprenticeship, I passed my final examination and became a licensed Surveyor in April, 1864.

In November, 1864, I was instructed by Mr. Dennis to survey the Rosseau and Nipissing Road Line commencing at Cameron's Bay at the north end of Lake Rosseau and terminating at the mouth of South River on Lake Nipissing. I proceeded to Penetanguishene and hired the necessary axe-men, cook and packers for this survey and crossing in canoes over the Georgian Bay, we proceeded up the Muskosh River to Lake Muskoka and joined Mr. Dennis and staff at South Bay. The staff associated with Mr. Dennis were V. B. Wadsworth, O.L.S., in charge of survey, Milner Hart, O.L.S., Archibald McNabb, O.L.S., and Charles Mackenzie, explorer, and twelve men. We proceeded up Lakes Muskoka and Rosseau to Cameron's Bay and there built a store camp and commenced the work. We reached the crossing of the Magnetawan River on Christmas Day and then returned to our store camp for supplies for the next link in our survey from the Magnetawan River to South Bay, Lake Nipissing, a distance of about thirty-five miles. The men were engaged in packing in supplies for this remaining survey and the balance of the party located the roadway to the Magnetawan River where Magnetawan Village is now situated.

Thereafter the line was carried through to South Bay, Lake Nipissing, and we completed same and returned to the store camp on Lake Rosseau where our canoes were located, after walking back on our surveyed Line about eighty miles, and then proceeded down Lakes Rosseau and Muskoka to where Bala Village is now situated, and thence down the Muskosh River to the Georgian Bay and thence across the Bay to Penetanguishene where the men were discharged and the rest of the party returned to Toronto via stage to Barrie and the railway to Toronto. . . .

E. THE COLONIZATION ROADS

The Government and the Roads

E 1 "ROADS IN THE EASTERN AND MIDDLE SECTIONS OF UPPER CANADA, TO BE OPENED BY THE COLONIZATION GRANTS,"[1] 1854 [*Canada, Legislative Assembly*, Journals, *1854, app. MM*]

That portion of Upper Canada referred to in the Resolutions[2] of the Legislative Assembly of the 8th November 1852, lying between the Ottawa river and the Georgian Bay on Lake Huron, and extending from the counties fronting on Lake Ontario to Lake Nipissing and the French River, comprising an area of about eleven and a half million of acres or eighteen thousand square miles, presents an almost unbroken field for Colonization. . . .

After a careful examination of the reports, plans and field books of all the surveys and explorations made in these sections of the Ottawa and Huron country, the following works were projected with a view to opening it up for Colonization.

1st. A road from Pembroke up the Southerly bank of the Ottawa, to the mouth of the River Mattawan 98 miles, and from thence along the river Mattawan to Lake Nipissing, 40 miles, and to be subsequently extended along the French River to Lake Huron.

. . .

The road along the river Mattawan forms part of an important communication between the Ottawa and Lake Huron, which when completed, will not only develope the agricultural resources of the country, but enable the lumberers on the upper waters of the Ottawa to procure their supplies from the west at nearly the Montreal prices.

2nd. A road from the present head of steamboat navigation on the Ottawa, at Farrell's point, in the township of Horton, to the mouth of the River Maganatavan or of the French River, or to such other point in the Georgian Bay, as affords a good harbour, adopting the road line drawn by P.L.S. Robert Bell, from Farrell's point 220 miles to the Great Opeongo Lake on the head waters of a branch of the Madawaska

---

[1]This information was supplied by the Bureau of Agriculture in "Return to an Address of the Legislative Assembly to His Excellency the Governor General, dated 25th September, 1854, praying that His Excellency will be pleased to cause to be laid before this House a Statement in detail of the objects to which the sum of £60,000, (or any part thereof,) appropriated in the Session of 1852–53, for opening up the Waste Lands of the Province, has been applied."
[2]See D 8.

river. The length of Mr. Bell's line is 100 miles, and from the Opeongo Lake to the Georgian Bay about 120 miles. This road opens up the interior of the Ottawa and Huron country, benefitting equally the farmer and the lumberer. Mr. Bell's line crosses the red pine section where it presents most fertile land; he has selected the location with much care and judgment.

. . .

For the further development of the Ottawa and Huron territory, I would respectfully recommend . . . to open up the southern part of the hardwood section, by the construction of a road from Mr. Bell's Ottawa and Opeongo road line to the best harbour at the southern extremity of the Georgian Bay, leaving the Opeongo road a few miles westerly of Clear Lake, crossing the Madawaska about two miles above the mouth of York river, joining to Mr. Bell's Muskoka road line about two miles farther, following it to the High Falls on the Muskoka River, and continuing westerly to the southern extremity of the Georgian Bay at the best site for a harbour. The length of this road would be about 150 miles.

6th. A road from Bobcaygean, in the township of Verulam, northward as far as the 6th concession of Somerville, to open up the vacant Crown Lands in that locality. The length of this road will be about 10½ miles.

Provincial Land surveyor John Reid has recently been tracing the line for this road and opening it for winter travel, as far as the southern boundary of Somerville. . . .

Bureau of Agriculture
30th September, 1854.

E 2   FREE GRANTS ON COLONIZATION ROADS
[*Buchanan*,[3] Canada 1863, for the Information of Immigrants, *pp. 10–1*]

. . . Government has opened several great lines of road on which free grants of one hundred acres are given to actual settlers. . . .

The roads in Upper Canada are:—

1st. The Ottawa and Opeongo Road, which runs east and west, and will connect the Ottawa with Lake Huron; Resident Agent, T. P. French, Clontarf. Route, by Grand Trunk Railway and Ottawa River, or railway to Ottawa City, thence by stage and steamer to Farrell's Landing.

. . .

[3]Alexander Carlisle Buchanan (1808–1868) was appointed immigration agent at Quebec in 1838. He was noted for his kindliness and efficiency in dealing with immigrants.

5th. The Burleigh Road, running through the Townships of Burleigh and Anstruther; Resident Agent, Joseph Graham,[4] Peterborough. Route, by Grand Trunk Railway to Cobourg and Peterborough.

6th. The Bobcaygeon Road, running from Bobcaygeon, between the Counties of Peterborough and Victoria, north, and intended to be continued to Lake Nipissing. Resident Agents: for southerly portion, R. Hughes,[5] Bobcaygeon; for northerly portion, G. G. Boswell,[6] Minden. Route, by Grand Trunk Railway to Cobourg and Peterborough, and thence by steamer to Bobcaygeon.

7th. The Victoria Road, running north through the County of Victoria to the Peterson Road, Resident Agent, G. M. Roche,[7] Lindsay. Route, by Grand Trunk Railway to Port Hope and Lindsay.

8th. The Muskoka Road, running from Lake Couchiching to the Grand Falls of Muskoka; Resident Agent, R. J. Oliver,[8] Orillia. Route, by Northern Railway from Toronto to Barrie, thence by steamer to Orillia.

By means of these roads access is obtained to Townships recently surveyed by Government and now open for settlement. They are chiefly of excellent quality, and well adapted, in respect of soil and climate, to all the purposes of husbandry. . . .

E 3   J. W. BRIDGLAND TO JOSEPH GRAHAM
[*P.A.O., Colonization Roads Papers, Letter Book 2, pp. 83–4*]

Toronto, 12 June 1865.

I have yours of the 7th. and proceed immediately to answer the questions contained in the latter part of your letter.

The *Strike* you speak of should have been the immediate occasion for you to have discharged every man who subscribed to it and this would have enabled you to have engaged those to whom you were not

[4]Joseph Graham was appointed Crown Land Agent for the Burleigh Road on May 31, 1861, and for part of Victoria and Peterborough and the Bobcaygeon Road on March 31, 1865.

[5]Richard Hughes was appointed Crown Land Agent for part of Victoria and Peterborough and for the settlement on the Bobcaygeon Road, November 25, 1858 (F 9).

[6]George G. Boswell was appointed Crown Land Agent for the northern part of the Bobcaygeon Road on December 4, 1861, at $4 per day. He died in or before September, 1865.

[7]George M. Roche was appointed Crown Land Agent for part of the County of Victoria, October 22, 1858 (F 9). He was brother of the surveyor John K. Roche.

[8]Richard Jose Oliver, Orillia, was appointed Crown Land Agent for the Muskoka Road in the summer of 1859 (F 13). At the beginning of October he met the settlers at Severn Bridge and issued the first location tickets.

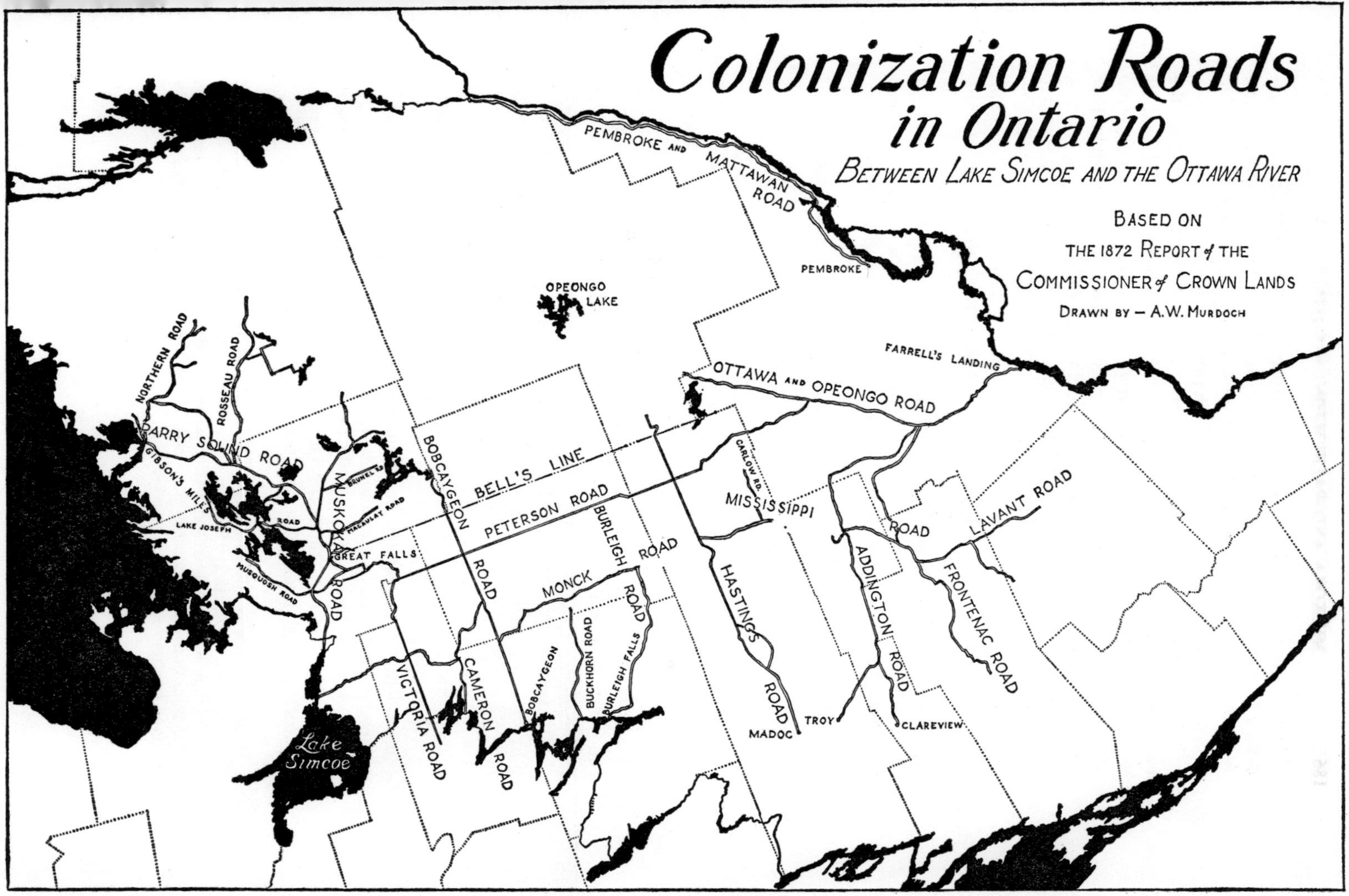
Colonization Roads
in Ontario
Between Lake Simcoe and the Ottawa River
Based on
The 1872 Report of the
Commissioner of Crown Lands
Drawn by – A.W. Murdoch
Pembroke and Mattawan Road
Pembroke
Opeongo Lake
Farrell's Landing
Ottawa and Opeongo Road
Northern Road
Rosseau Road
Parry Sound Road
Gibson's Mills
Lake Joseph
Road
Brunel Rd.
Macaulay Road
Muskoka Road
Great Falls
Musquosh Road
Bobcaygeon Road
Bell's Line
Peterson Road
Burleigh Road
Monck Road
Carlow Rd.
Mississippi Road
Lavant Road
Frontenac Road
Addington Road
Hastings Road
Madoc
Troy
Clareview
Victoria Road
Cameron Road
Bobcaygeon
Buckhorn Road
Burleigh Falls
Lake Simcoe

FIGURE 8

able to give employ. I am a little surprised that you should have submitted to parley a moment with men engaged under such circumstances. We cannot submit an instant that those who are hired under charitable considerations should dictate to us the terms of contract.

This circumstance proves one of two things to me; either that the men are not worthy of pity or that they have not been truthful in their assertion about their destitution. *I will not sanction a farthing of increase in wages* what if they do pay 12/6 per week for board, on various other roads they are doing the same, and their wages will then be as good as the laboring classes receive any where else. However to cut the matter short there is just one simple method of action— *discharge the dissatisfied*— dont keep grumblers on the work they'll infect the good. Act firm and prompt in this matter or your men will get the mastery over you.

About "Right of Way" Communicate formally with the *Councils* of the localities and say, if you prepare the way *free* for us we will make the changes. Let this be a finality and if *negatived* keep to the old line.

E 4   ANDREW RUSSELL TO JOHN CARROLL,[9] PETERBOROUGH
[*P.A.O., Colonization Roads Papers, Copy Book 1865–8, p. 118*]

Ottawa, 7th May, 1866

In reply to your letter of the 4 May last with reference to the rate of wages allowed for foremen of gangs on the Burleigh road I have to call your attention to the regular rate named in the rules viz $1 $\frac{25}{100}$ per diem.

On special application by the overseer of works and certificates from him that the individual in whose behalf the request is made for an increase of the rate is more than ordinarily qualified for the duty and in every respect worthy of a higher remuneration as compared with others, the regular rate may be increased to 1 $\frac{50}{100}$ but no more.

With regard to a knowledge of road making it is presumed and expected that the Overseer in charge is competent to the duty; to devise, lay out and practically direct all the operations of the service.

The duty of foreman is simply to receive his instructions and carry them out in detail to watch the laborers and the course and progress of the work as explained in Section No. 9 in the printed Rules.

[9]John Carroll was appointed Crown Land Agent for the Burleigh Road, October 27, 1863, and on April 2, 1867, he was made overseer of the work to be done on the Burleigh Road that season. After a lengthy dispute with the Crown Lands Department concerning construction costs on the road he was dismissed from both positions on June 15, 1868.

E 5   ANDREW RUSSELL TO R. J. OLIVER, ORILLIA
[*P.A.O., Colonization Roads Papers, Copy Book 1865–8, pp. 169–70*]

Department of Crown Lands
Ottawa 18th June 1866.

In reply to your letter of the 22nd. ult. in which you state that the men to be employed by you in repairing the Peterson road will be able to board themselves, I have to inform you that you are in no case to depart from the Rules established by this Department. The laborers are to be boarded in *one* place and not at their respective homes.

The Department in the interest of the road works has invariably refused compliance with applications to permit such a course as you describe.

There are two substantial reasons for this.

1st. The men to work simultaneously and equally must have the advantage of the same local proximity to the works.

2nd. No other course than that adopted by the Department it is considered will so well provide uniformly, sufficient and substantial food for the laborers What ever arrangement therefore you make as to who shall contract for boarding the men employed, the above principles must be carried out.

E 6   BRIDGLAND TO ALEXANDER CAMPBELL
[*P.A.O., Colonization Roads Papers, Reports, 1862–8, pp. 283–5*]

Ottawa, 16th. Novem. 1866.

There is a subject, connected with Colonization Roads which I have been desirous for some time past to bring under your notice.
It is briefly thus;
I have found in all my road examinations in the new districts that fully two thirds of the benefit to be derived from our Road improvements is enjoyed by that Class of operators styled lumberers.

In scarcely a single instance has any new road we have made had time to settle into a compact state before it has been ploughed into the deepest ruts and mudholes by the heavy provision loads of lumbermen, so that the roads have not only been mainly used by them, but most unfairly made to suffer in their tenderest condition.

To supply a single shanty gang during one season it would require at least 100 heavy loads of provisions and furnishings &c.

Often the stores of four or five shanties pass up the same road; so that it can easily be understood that the whole market produce of all the settlers on one of these roads would very little exceed (and in some instances it would fall below) the amount required to supply the united gangs of the adjacent lumberers.

The deduction from these facts is plain and incontrovertible that while we build our roads ostensibly for settlers lumberers are the parties who are really benefitted by them.

While these persons therefore, through the Hon. Mr Skead[10] and others, call urgently for consideration with regard to their favourite lines it must be remembered that, of the advantages to be derived from the road improvements already effected, they have ever taken the lion's share.

My object in laying this matter before you is one of simple justice to the poor settlers and of reason with reference to the Government.

If, as every one will admit, good roads are of the most essential importance to the commerce of lumberers, so much so that from their available existence their expenses of transport are materially diminished and their profits as a consequence augmented why should not some portion of the fees paid into the revenue by them be made to contribute to the support of the Colonization roads.

It goes to the public in our annual reports that the profits from our Woods and Forests are enormously large while the settlement of our new lands is a losing investment, and that not the least item in the profit & loss account is the expenditure for Colonization roads, while equitably in my opinion two thirds of that amount should be deducted from the Forest revenue and also from the expenditure connected with "New Settlements."

The whole Timber revenue is given in the Crown Lands Report for the year ending June 1865 as $306,483.

If an addition of 5 % were added to the fees now collected and then 10 % of the whole fund appropriated for the benefit of all the leading roads through the respective Counties in proportion to the collections, with the understanding that that amount in addition to what the Legislature should see fit to grant; should be actually expended on such roads, then I think the wants and claims of both lumberer and settler would be more equitably adjusted, but so long as the case stands as it is at present the following difficulties will exist

1. The poor settlers are charged with the cost of a large expenditure from which they derive but a very small benefit in comparison with that class who realize the advantage without sharing in the charges.

2. These roads cannot be maintained without almost the same yearly outlay in as much as the lumber traffic, in a country so difficult to make roads as the Ottawa & Huron Territory, destroys in one season the improvements of that which preceded it.

[10]James Skead (1817–1884), timber merchant and manufacturer, was a member of the Legislative Council from 1862 to 1867, and was appointed to the Senate in 1867.

E 7   LIST OF COLONIZATION ROADS, COMPILED BY THE COMMISSIONER
OF CROWN LANDS, STEPHEN RICHARDS[11] DECEMBER 30, 1867
[*P.A.O., Colonization Roads Papers, Reports, 1862–8, p. 345*]

Name of road	Date of survey	Work began	Length of line in Miles	Miles con-structed	Expenditure to Dec. 31, [ms blurred, probably 1866]
1 Addington	1854	1855	56	56	53,743
2 Bobcaygeon	1858–9	1856	28	65	49,363
3 Burleigh	1860	1862	56	34	19,771
4 Buckhorn	1863	1865	34	8	7,707
5 Cameron	No survey	1861	15	15	3,699
6 Flinton	do	1861	15½	15½	7,992
7 Frontenac	1858	1861	65	46	27,984
8 Hastings	1851	1855	100	70	58,274
9 Lavant	1858	1860	17	17	6,820
10 Mississippi	1857	1859	75	43	36,948
11 Monck	1864–5	1866	100	8	9,567
12 Muskoka	1856	1861	50	44	27,220
13 Northern (Great)	1857–8	1859	138	70	79,008
14 Opeongo	1850	1861	100	78	45,246
15 Parry Sound	1863	1863	45	45	18,249
16 Pembroke & Mattn.	1853	1854	100	40	24,553
17 Peterson	No survey	1858	114	114	39,640
18 Renfrew & Addin.	do	1859	22½	22½	9,260
19 Victoria	in part 1862	1861	39	40	19,745
20 Northern from P. S.	1865	1867	150	10	4,750
					$549,539

Major Roads of Muskoka and Haliburton

THE MUSKOKA ROAD

E 8   JOSEPH CAUCHON, INSTRUCTIONS TO CHARLES UNWIN[12]
[*Ontario, Department of Lands and Forests, Instructions
to Land Surveyors, Book 6, no. 84*]

Instructions to Provincial Land Surveyor Charles Unwin to survey a
line for a road from the foot of Steamboat navigation on Lake Simcoe

[11]Stephen Richards (1820–1894), lawyer and politician, represented Niagara in
the Legislative Assembly of Ontario from 1867 to 1875. He was Commissioner of
Crown Lands and Provincial Secretary in the Sandfield Macdonald administration.
[12]Charles Unwin (1829-1918) came to Canada from England in 1843. He qualified as a surveyor, April 12, 1852, and did much government work in the next few
years. For a time he was in partnership with Vernon B. Wadsworth. He served for
thirty-two years as an assessor for the city of Toronto and from 1905 to 1910 as
the city surveyor. Unwin's reports on the surveys to the east and west of Lake
Couchiching done under instructions in E 8 and E 9, are found in the Colonization
Roads Papers.

to Provincial Land Surveyor Robert Bell's road line from the Ottawa to the Great Falls on the Muskoka River.

In obedience to an Order-in-Council dated the 15th day of September 1856 authorizing the above-mentioned survey, I have to direct you to proceed to the performance thereof, in conformity with the accompanying general instructions, without unnecessary delay, and you are not to engage in any private surveys or other business until you have completed and transmitted your returns of survey.

Tracings from Provincial Land Surveyors William Hawkins[13] and J. W. Bridgland's[14] plans of their explorations in the above mentioned section of Country are enclosed herewith for your information. . . .

Toronto, 11th. October 1856.

E 9   CAUCHON, FURTHER INSTRUCTIONS TO UNWIN
[Ontario, Department of Lands and Forests, Instructions to Land Surveyors, Book 5, p. 295]

C.L.D. Toronto 17th April 1857.

With reference to your Survey of a road line from Lake Simcoe to the High Falls on the Muskako at the termination of P.L.S. Bell's road line, I have to instruct you to make an exploration on the westerly side of Lake Couchiching with a view to ascertaining which side of the Lake presents the most favorable location for the road, both as regards the fitness of the land for cultivation and its suitableness for road making.

The termini of your exploration are the village of Orillia and the High Falls on the Muskako.

E 10   DAVID GIBSON, "REPORT ON THE PRESENT STATE OF THE ROADS MADE FROM THE COLONIZATION AND IMPROVEMENT FUNDS"
[Canada, Bureau of Agriculture, Report, 1857]

Willowdale, 23rd March, 1858.

Muskoka Road.
It is intended to construct this road from the termination of the navigation at Washago Mills, on the extreme north of Lake Couchiching to the Great Falls of Muskoka, where it meets Bell's Line. Two trial lines for this road were run by Provincial Land Surveyor Unwin; one from Orillia, and the other from Atherly; both terminating at said Falls. But as on both of these there seemed to be many obstacles to overcome, involving expensive outlay, I was directed to make an examination of

[13]The survey directed by Lieutenant John Carthew in 1835.
[14]Probably a reference to the survey of 1852 (D 9).

the country, and endeavor to find a less costly line. I accordingly made a survey of the country, on a course about North 13° East from Washago Mills, till I intersected the Easterly or Atherly line, run by Mr. Unwin. This point of intersection is about nine miles distant from Washago Mills; and over that extent, though there are a good many granite ridges, I think the country is adapted for settlement. By deviating slightly from the course where it is crossed by these ridges, a good line of road is obtained till within about half a mile of the Atherly line. From this point, I mean to prosecute my survey to the Falls when the season admits of this being done.

Meantime, as instructed, I have given out contracts for constructing a bridge over the Severn River, and for making a part of the road from it northwards. The portion of the country lying between the Severn and Washago Mills, belongs to the proprietor of these, who is to establish a right of way from them to the bridge, between which points there is now a winter road. When established, this portion of the road will be given out on contract.

By selecting the termination of the lake navigation at Washago Mills, where a wharf is about to be erected, for the commencement of the line of road to Muskoka Falls; instead of beginning at either Orillia or Atherly, a saving of about twelve miles of road is effected.

. . .

At the date of my last report, the prices exacted for works on roads and bridges were very high. Since then, a great change has supervened. Provisions and labor have both fallen, and, in the new settlements, particularly, the scarcity of money disposes the settlers to take work in a much more reasonable manner than for some years past. From these causes, I have lately been enabled to let out contracts at upwards of 30 per cent less than I could twelve months ago. For the same money, therefore, I am now accomplishing about one-third more work, and it is thus obviously a very favorable time to let out such works as are to be proceeded with.

E 11   ANDREW RUSSELL, INSTRUCTIONS TO CHARLES RANKIN[15]
        [*Toronto Public Library, Charles Rankin Papers*]

Crown Lands Department
Toronto 18th Novr. 1858.

I have to instruct you to survey the Severn & Muskoka Road and to lay out free grant lots of one hundred acres each on both sides thereof.

You will commence your survey at the Bridge constructed across the

[15]Charles Rankin (1797–1886) became a land surveyor December 27, 1820. He lived for many years at Owen Sound and carried on extensive surveys of roads and townships.

R. Severn, as represented at the point A on the accompanying projected plan. You will then lay off lots of twenty chains in perpendicular width by 50 chains in depth, containing 100 acres each and plant posts and mark bearing trees along the road at the limits or front of each lot, and allow one chain for a road between every fifth and sixth lot, until you intersect the south Boundary of the township of Muskoka. You will then continue to lay off the lots in the township of Muskoka to the point B in the 4th Concession removing the lot posts on your former survey as far as altered by the present.

You will continue to make a traverse from B. to the Great Falls on the River Muskoka, so as to define the position of the road through the township of Muskoka. You will survey each of the side roads lines only as are marked red in the accompanying projected plan & conform as far as the nature of your survey will permit to the accompanying General Instructions and you will act with the Strictest economy in the performance of this Service.

E 12   RANKIN TO ANDREW RUSSELL
[*Toronto Public Library, Charles Rankin Papers*]

Owen's Sound Feby 19th. 1859

I had contemplated proposing to you that we should defer the little work to be done at Muskoka until the snow should be off, in the spring— upon the consideration of the possibly better chance then than now, in some places, of getting the posts well planted— but having recently met a son of your agent, Mr Gibson, and been told by him that there are already several settlers on the road, north of Severn, it occurs to me that you will desire the work to be done at once,— in such case I beg leave— referring to the 11th clause of your printed general Instructions— to request that you will sanction my sending out my partner — Mr Spry[16]— who as you are aware, is now an authorized surveyor, to do this work—

Am myself at this moment engaged in getting ready the Returns of survey of the little village plot, and am withal at present suffering inconveniences from an attack of influenza.

E 13   RANKIN TO THE COMMISSIONER OF CROWN LANDS,
P. M. VANKOUGHNET
[*Ontario, Department of Lands and Forests, Field Notes, no. 2229*]

Owen Sound May 24th. 1859

In forwarding to you herewith the returns of the Survey & posting the Severn & Muskoka roads, as ordered by you on the 18th Novr. last,

[16]William Spry (1831–1906) qualified as a land surveyor on July 19, 1858. He made his home at Owen Sound, and was active in surveying and railway construction.

there is but little, calling for remarks beyond what is given in the field notes.—

The line of road itself having been previously surveyed by Mr. Gibson, his report[17] probably has already conveyed to you a description of the features & character of the country bordering it— and moreover the depth of snow on the ground at the time of this survey, altho. not retarding the main object for which it was ordered— viz the posting into lots, was in the way of making observations on the character of the surface, except in the particular places where posts were planted in.

The best tracts, or those freeest from rock at the surface appear to be between lots Nos 16 & 23,[18] and again in Muskoka township from No 5 to No 10[19]—

I forward a list of the squatters— either resident or who had made more or less improvement, at the time of the survey— the particulars however may before this time in some cases have materially altered.

E 14   J. W. Bridgland, "Report on the Inspection of Surveys and Examination of Colonization Roads in Canada West," 1861 [*P.A.O., Colonization Roads Papers, unbound*]

The Muskoka Road

This road lies to the Northward of Lake Simcoe and from its peculiarly advantageous position for access, is rapidly filling up. It forms likewise an agreeable and ready mode of ingress to that part of the Peterson road lying Westward of the Bobcaygeon Road opening up for settlement in connection with the above first named road the newly surveyed township of Draper, Macauley, Ryde, and Oakley.

The Northern Rail Road — Steamboat on Lake Simcoe, and ferry daily from Orillia, conducts to the foot of Lake Couchiching where the road commences. The first two miles traverse Orillia Island. This is a generally level, stony bed tolerably passable in the dry season. At the end of this distance the Severn River is crossed by a Wooden bridge, supported by log crib piers and three sets of King posts— The Piers are weak and ill founded— the King posts and brace beams too ponderous for the foundation— the result is shown in the swerved and sunken condition of the Bridge. The Abuttments are likewise very poor— The approaches are not carried out far enough to admit of an easy ascent so that in its present condition a short abrupt hill with a mud hole at its base has to be overcome from each side in order to ascend the bridge— The road from the Severn bridge for about two miles or more is in a wretched state— Bad mud holes, bad roots, and bad stones abound— indeed nothing but positive ingenuity, or invention,— offspring of necessity, avails a traveller to conquer certain impediments of the above

[17]See E 10.
[18]Lots 16 to 23 of Morrison Township are north of the Kahshe River.
[19]Lots 5 to 10 of Muskoka Township are in the Gravenhurst area.

nature. The bad state of this part of the road is accounted for, from the fact that at the commencement of snow fall last Winter the sub contractor had not finished this part of the road; The contractor waited his convenience for beginning again in the Spring, but up to the time of my visiting (14th June last) nothing had been done and the road remained in the same wretched and unfinished condition

Occasionally from the end of this defective part there are rough portions but the greater part of the remainder of the road to the Falls is in a very tolerable condition. There are some very long crossways very well made of good Pine, Cedar and Hemlock logs— No covering or Chinking however relieves their naked deformity— Somewhere on the fourth mile South of the Falls occurs a series of broken stone ridges of no great magnitude. The last two or three miles ere reaching the Muskoka River, are exceedingly level and good— Quite a settlement is being made in the vicinity of the Great Falls[20] and in the adjoining lands in Draper. Two or three very respectable emigrants passed in during my short visit here. A very good plain and substantial bridge is thrown across the Chasm of the Falls. Immovable natural abuttments of solid granite render the structure perfectly secure; and from it a very picturesque view of the River and Falls is had.

The Peterson Road commences at this point, diverging first through the township of Draper; The contractor is now engaged forming this part of the road—

The settlements and improvements on the Muskoka line of road are certainly all that can be expected, within the short space of two years. Of course the clearances are all small, consisting of from two or three, to ten and twelve acres each. Free grant settlers, it may be reasonably supposed are not rife in pecuniary means, hence time and laborious patience must supply the lack of money for at least a few years. It was on this road line that the Mamoth prize turnip was raised last year weighing 35½ lbs.

Department of Crown Lands
Quebec 22nd. August 1861

E 15   BRIDGLAND, "GENERAL REPORT ON COLONIZATION ROADS
IN CANADA WEST"
[*P.A.O., Colonization Roads Papers, Reports, 1862–8, pp. 87–8; also printed in Canada, Department of Crown Lands, Report, 1863*]

Quebec December 1863.

Muskoka Road

Runs from the foot of Lake Couchiching northward through Morrison, Muskoka, Draper, Macaulay and Stephenson.

[20]South or Muskoka Falls.

This road is completed to the vicinity of Fairy and Vernon lakes,[21] and passes through much good and fast improving country;— indeed the land, all the way from the Falls, (24 miles beyond which the road is made) is of the best quality to be found in this latitude. At about the ninth mile the Parry Sound road branches off from this road in a north-westerly direction, passing between Skeleton and Rosseau Lakes, and leading to a large section of tolerably good land for settlement in that direction. Hence it will be seen that the Muskoka road is, for 30 miles of its length, not only the highway to the Section of country for the opening up of which it was directly undertaken, but also to that lying to the North-west, which is subsequently to be reached by the Parry Sound road, which branches off from it, at the above recited distance.

At a distance of about twelve miles on this road it approaches within 40 chains of a bay of Muskoka Lake, whence in the summer season convenient access by boating can be had to the country lying to the westward of Lake Joseph, and also (though by a somewhat circuitous route) the South and north falls of the Muskoka river.

The great public utility of this road, and its special claim to support, in the interest of general settlement, induces me to recommend sincerely a small grant to improve it, as far as the Town plot, laid out at and north of the South Falls. There are here about twenty miles of road which a judicious expenditure of the above amount, would render very passable country road. A road that never was tolerably good, and of which it cannot be said, it has relapsed from a creditable condition to its present almost impassible one by the neglect of good keeping, certainly has a claim to consideration that does not belong to others under opposite circumstances.

E 16   PETITION[22] FOR EXTENSION OF THE MUSKOKA ROAD
        [University of Toronto, Muskoka Papers]

Township of Chaffey.
Huntsville,
May 4th 1871.

At a public meeting of the settlers, held this day, it was resolved that a petition be drafted, praying the Government to extend the Muskoka road north, through the township, towards the Maganetewan river, with a bridge across the East River.

. . .

PETITION

We, the undersigned settlers in the township of Chaffey, beg to state that we settled on the Crown lands in this township under the impression

[21]The road did not actually reach the river between Vernon and Fairy lakes (the site of Huntsville) until 1870.

[22]A clipping from an unidentified paper, signed "George Hunt" (University of Toronto, Muskoka Papers).

that the Muskoka road would be pushed through without delay. We have endured very great hardships during the past winter for want of a road, having had to carry in our provisions for miles through the bush, through some three to four feet of snow. Many of us were unable to do this during the whole of the winter, the expense having been too much for our means. We have been informed that it is not the intention of the Government to carry the road further north, this year, than the bridge at Huntsville, Lot 14, 1st Con. We beg to state, that unless a road is made as far as and a bridge thrown across the East river, most of the settlers north of the river will have to throw up our lands and beg our way out of the country completely ruined.

We request, Honorable Sir, that our isolated position may be taken into consideration, and that a sufficient amount may be granted to carry the road through the centre of the township, as above: And, as in duty bound your petitioners will ever pray, &c., &c.

E 17   LETTER FROM "CHAFFEY" ON THE MUSKOKA ROAD
[*Toronto,* Daily Globe, *May 23, 1871*]

I saw a letter published in your paper the other day, stating "That the Muskoka district is a fine country for farming." So it is; it could not be better adapted for dairy farming and grazing. But how sadly will all these advantages be counterbalanced if the Government still persists in keeping us back another year, by not granting money to continue the Muskoka road through the centre of the townships that are taken up, and so drive out of the country settlers that have done a little work on their farms, who are now leaving the district on account of the expense and difficulty they are put to in getting in provisions, &c., for their families, by not having a road through the township.

We were promised a road last year, but I suppose that was like some of the promises that are made to immigrants to induce them to take up land, but are postponed to an indefinite period.

I am informed on good authority that at the present time there are two hundred immigrants now in Muskoka looking for land, and that from ten to twenty intended settlers are leaving the district every day, because we have no road; and I think if the Government were aware of this, they would take active measures at once. And should they put the road through there would not be an acre of ground not taken up in Chaffey or the surrounding townships that is worth having.

In conclusion, I can only say that I should advise immigrants not to come into Muskoka until the road is made or ordered to be made.

One of the sufferers,
CHAFFEY

May 16, 1871.

E 18   A Traveller on the Muskoka Road, 1871
[[*Mrs. King*[23]], Letters from Muskoka by an Emigrant Lady, *pp. 24–9*]

. . . We landed at Washage, and after standing for more than an hour
on the quay, took the stage-wagon for Gravenhurst, the vehicle being so
crowded that even the personal baggage most essential to our comfort
had to be left behind. Oh! the horrors of that journey! The road was
most dreadful— our first acquaintance with "corduroy" roads. The forest
gradually closed in upon us, on fire on both sides, burnt trees crashing
down in all directions, here and there one right across the road, which
had to be dragged out of the way before we could go on. Your brother
with his arm around me the whole way (I clinging to the collar of his
coat), could hardly keep me steady as we bumped over every obstacle.
In the worst places I was glad to shut my eyes that I might not see the
danger. Your poor sister had to cling convulsively to the rope which
secured the passengers' baggage (ours was left behind and we did not
see it for weeks) to avoid being thrown out, and for long afterwards we
both suffered from the bruises we received and the strain upon our limbs.
At last, long after dark, we arrived at Gravenhurst, where we were
obliged to sleep, as the steamer to Bracebridge could not start before
morning on account of the fog. The steamboat had no accommodation
for sleeping, but we had a good supper on board, and a gentlemanly
Englishman, a passenger by the stage and well acquainted with Muskoka,
took us to a small hotel to sleep. The next morning we went to Bracebridge. . . .

The drive from Bracebridge to Utterson, the nearest post-town to our
settlement and distant from it six miles, was a long and fatiguing stretch
of fifteen miles, but unmarked by any incident of consequence. The
forest fires were burning fiercely, and our driver told us that a week
before the road had been impassable. At times when the trees were
burning at each side of the narrow road we felt a hot stifling air as we
passed rapidly along. It was a gloomy afternoon, with fitful gusts of
wind portending a change of weather, and we were almost smothered in
clouds of Muskoka dust, much resembling pounded bricks. When we got
to Utterson we were obliged to remain for two hours to rest the poor
horses, as no fresh ones were to be got. . . .

[23]Mrs. Harriet Barbara King, an English settler who had lived for some time
in France, emigrated with some of her family to Muskoka in 1871 to join her son
Charles Gerrard King who had already settled on lot 18, concession 12 of Stephenson Township, near Utterson. Mrs. King settled on lot 20 of the same concession
and remained until 1875 when she left the "Bush" in despair. A book which relates
her experiences, *Letters from Muskoka by an Emigrant Lady*, was published anony-
mously in 1878.

THE PARRY SOUND ROAD

E 19   ANDREW RUSSELL TO JAMES A. GIBSON,[24] WILLOWDALE
[*P.A.O., Colonization Roads Papers, Letter Book 1, pp. 35–7*]

Instructions to locate Parry Sound Road

18 Dec '62

I have to instruct you to proceed with all possible dispatch to locate a road leading from a certain point (hereinafter more particularly defined) in the Muskoka Free Grant road line, & to extend thence in a general northwesterly direction to Parry Sound. P.L.S. Dennis has already made an exploration of the country through which this line of road is intended to pass, & has delineated on his plan of the said exploration a proposed road route, which (except in two or three instances) conforms generally very closely with his base line of exploration. A copy of the said exploration plan is herewith transmitted to you, which will be your chief guide in making a more detailed examination for the permanent location of the road. While you are expected of course not to confine yourself to the line delineated as the proposed route, saving over that portion already actually located by the above named Surveyor, viz: the most southerly six miles of the route adjoining the Muskoka road, you will at the same time pay a first and most particular attention to such delineation & if your judgement coincides with the recommendation alluded to, you will adopt P.L.S. Dennis's suggestion without further exploration. If, however, any observation you may have it in your power to make suggest an improvt., you are to consider no time wasted in testing such suggestions to a proof & carrying them out into practical detail. Your point of commencet. for examination & location of this road will be that where Mr Dennis diverges from the old Home & Simcoe district line in marking out that portion which he has located, shown upon his plans as being about the centre of the 9th. Con of Macaulay, & at the same point where the Muskoka road line & the same surveyor's exploration to the mouth of the Muskoka river diverge from the said old district line, but if any decided improvement from personal observation is suggested to you in the connection of this road with the Muskoka at its commencet. you are at liberty to make the alteration. From this point, therefore, you will proceed & define the road in general conformity with the accompanying plans & projections as far as the mills at Parry Sound, erected at the mouth of the Seguin river by David Gibson Esq. . . . .

---

[24]James Alexander Gibson (1831–1908) was a son of the surveyor David Gibson of Willowdale. He received his commission as surveyor April 7, 1855, but shortly after his father's death in 1864 retired from survey work and purchased a book store.

E 20   J. W. Bridgland, "Report on Upper Canada
Colonization Roads"
*[P.A.O., Colonization Roads Papers, Reports, 1862–8, pp. 244–5; also
printed in Canada, Department of Crown Lands, Report for the Half
Year Ending 31st December 1865]*

PARRY SOUND ROAD.

A great amount of work has been accomplished upon this new road
this season (1865), although, owing to divers causes, all that was contemplated in the spring has not been effected.

Mr. W. Beatty,[25] of Thorold, C.W. (who had entered into a contract
with the Commissioner of Crown Lands, to construct this road from
Parry Sound south-eastward as far as the 20th mile on Gibson's line,
a distance of 23 miles), has succeeded in completing 13 miles of the
same.

He has further chopped, logged and crosswayed seven miles more,
or nearly to the limit of his contract as above described.

For fourteen miles further, the line has been underbrushed. Some
crossway has also been made on this part, so that a winter sledge can
now be driven from Parry Sound through the whole length of the road,
43 miles, and the mails are now actually sent through once a week.

Besides the above road works Mr. Beatty has built a bridge over the
Seguin River, at the Sound, for the purpose of connecting the settlements on the north side of the river with the road in question, and also
to render the steamboat landing, located on that side of the river, accessible to the settlers on the south.

The returns of this work are not yet transmitted, consequently I can
not give the cost thereof.

In addition to the improvements effected by Mr. Beatty, six miles on
the south-east end of the road have been completed under R. J. Oliver,
Esq., C.L.A. These six miles were partly made in 1863–4, under Jas.
Cooper who failed in his contract and abandoned the work.

The amount paid for works this season, under charge of Mr.
  Beatty, is $11182 90
The amount paid for works this season, under charge of Mr.
  Oliver 2484 30
Paid balance due in 1864 .... 469 70

  Total expenditure in 1865 .... 14136 90

Ottawa, Feby. 27, 1866

[25]William Beatty was born in Ireland in 1835. He graduated from Victoria
College, Cobourg, in 1860 and later obtained an M.A. and an LL.B. He was a
partner in J. & W. Beatty & Co. (see H 2). A strong temperance advocate, and an

E 21   William Beatty to the Commissioner of Crown Lands,
Alexander Campbell
[*P.A.O., Colonization Roads Papers, Section 5, Reports, 1864–66,
pp. 107–8*]

Ottawa Jany 31st. 1867

I beg leave herewith to submit a report of the work done by me on
the Parry Sound Road during the past season

The contract which I had to complete the unfinished portion of the
road for the gross sum of $8500, I have by working late in the season
been able to complete with the exception of a small portion which I
shall hereafter mention so that there is now a good waggon road over
the entire distance from Parry Sound to the Muskoka Road

I found it impracticable to construct a road over a considerable portion of the surveyed line in consequence of the roughness of the Country

The principle deviation is from the 12th to the 22nd. mile where I
was obliged to leave the surveyed line altogether— This deviation has
lengthened the road 1 mile and 24 chains. At this point the road passes
near Lake Rosseau and goes through the newly surveyed Village of
Rosseau. The entire length of the Parry Sound Road is now constructed
from the bridge over the Seguin to the Muskoka Road is 45 miles and
70 chains

The work done by me under contract is as follows viz: 17½ miles
chopped logged crosswayed 22¾ miles graded and finished 5¼ miles
stumped and levelled. The portion which now remains unfinished is the
5¼ miles just referred to and which is situated between Rosseau Village
and a point 1⅞ mile east of Rosseau River This portion is however passable for waggons and will be finished as soon as the snow leaves in the
spring

In addition to the work done under contract I have by the direction
of the superintendent of Col Roads done some further work on that
portion of the road constructed in 1865 by day labour and also built
two single trussbridges the one over Rosseau River and the other over
Skeleton River

A pay list for the day labour in repairs of 10 miles of old works has
been duly forwarded to the Department

The two bridges above mentioned are substantially built and consist
of two piers each with hewed stringers and King posts and sawed planks
on the stringers The dimensions are as follows

Skeleton Bridge— 2 piers 12X16 feet 15 ft high— span 32 feet
length of stringers 44 feet   length of bridge 90 ft including crossway at
each end

---

important figure in the development of Parry Sound where he was known as
"Governor Beatty," he opened a large store there which is still in business. He was
for some years a member of the Legislative Assembly.

Rosseau Bridge— 2 piers 12X15 ft 10 ft high— length of span 43 ft with stringers 53 ft long—entire length of bridge 198 feet including crossway

The greater part of the country through which the road passes is fit for settlement and since the opening of the road nearly every available lot on it has been taken up and settled upon

THE BOBCAYGEON ROAD

E 22   W. S. CONGER[26] TO P. M. VANKOUGHNET, MINISTER OF AGRICULTURE
[*P.A.O., Colonization Roads Papers, Section 1, Box 10, Correspondence no. 83*]

Peterboro 19th Augt *1856*

I have just this moment since rd a letter from Mr. David Gibson in which he informs me that he has instructions to open a road along the eastern boundary of Somerville.

When I left Toronto it was understood that Mr Gibson should in the course of two or three weeks come down to my county, and with me visit the different sections of country proposed to be opened and improved,— in order that by personal observation, and a consultation with me the best route might be selected, and the most economical means of construction adopted.

After remaining at home for nearly six weeks daily expecting Mr Gibson, I receive a letter saying that he had instructions from the Crown Lands department, and had advertysed for Tenders to open a Road on the eastern boundary of Somerville—

Now it does appear to me that I have some reason to complain of the treatment I have recd.— I do not suppose that any member of the Govt. intended anything wrong,— but the effect upon me is nevertheless the same.—

In the first place what is doing *now* should have been done a *month* since,— 2 ly, a Road starting from the rear of Harvey, might as well for any practical good it could be to us here,— start at Bells Line,— for the reason that— 8 miles of road must be made through a wilderness from Bobcaygeon to rear of Harvey in order to reach your Road— And again if you intend this Road to become a leading road to the interior,— it must leave the boundary line between the Townships at the *rear* of Harvey and bear easterly so as to cross what is called the "Granite Ridge" at right angles, and at the narrowest point—

I need only say that I have spent some time & money in examining the country in rear of this county— and may therefore be supposed to know as much about it,— as parties who never saw it—

[26]Wilson Seymour Conger was Sheriff for the County of Peterborough and was elected member of the Legislature for Peterborough in 1854.

What I desire is to have the money properly laid out— In 1852 I obtained a grant of £600 for the same road, which was through the interference of Langton[27] entirely thrown away— and I do not intend that this shall occur again while I am in Parliament if I can by any means prevent it—

This Road to do any good must commence at Bobcaygeon— thence north between the Townships of Verulam & Harvey— to the rear of Harvey,— thence in a North Easterly direction through the country we desire to open— by this Route I believe we shall not only secure a good line of road but shall pass directly through the best portion of country.

E 23   CONGER TO VANKOUGHNET
[*P.A.O., Colonization Roads Papers, Section 1, Box 10, Correspondence no. 94*]

Peterboro 16th. Sept 1856

Mr Gibson and myself have made a personal inspection of a portion of the proposed Road, from Bobcaygeon northward, between the Counties of Peterboro & Victoria, and that gentleman agrees with me that it is very important this road should *commence* at Bobcaygeon,— The road opened by Mr Bird[28] being useless as a portion of the great road to the interior. He has therefore received tenders for this portion of the road also, and you will be kind enough to obtain an order in Council authorizing him to open it.— I would wish this road to be called "The Bobcaygeon Road."

It is also necessary in order to promote the settlement of Burleigh and east side of Harvey, to open up a few miles of road from "Buckhorn" Bridge, to the centre of Burleigh, as shown upon the accompanying Diagram.— This Road can hereafter be extended north through a favourable part of the Country, and if afterwards found advisable, extended to Bells Line.— The length of this road from Buckhorn, to its present proposed terminus in Burleigh will not exceed 13 miles, and to make this a good winter road, (which is all that is necessary at present) would not cost more than about £600— This road should be called "The Buckhorn Road"[29]

The Diagram sent herewith not only shows the direction of both these roads,— but it also shows the vacant lots along the line of each which I have marked by cutting them up in 100 acre parcels.— I would sug-

[27]John Langton (1808–1894) was born in England, came to Canada in 1833, and settled near Peterborough. From 1851 to 1855 he represented Peterborough in the Legislative Assembly. He was appointed Auditor General of public accounts in 1855, and was Auditor General for the Dominion from Confederation to 1878.

[28]Robert Bird, a road builder, was a member of a pioneer family of the Township of Sidney.

[29]The Buckhorn Road was surveyed in 1863 and subsequently built from Hall's Bridge or Buckhorn, north through the townships of Harvey and Cavendish to the Monck Road in Glamorgan.

gest that these vacant Lots be given to the actual settlers on same terms as the unsurveyed portions.—

I would also strongly recommend the Govt. to stop the sale of all Lands in these Counties to other than actual settlers.— Speculators are ruining the Country by picking up all the valuable Lands and Selling them at ruinous prices.

E 24   MICHAEL DEANE'S "REPORT OF THE SURVEY OF THE
BOBCAYGEON ROAD FROM SOMERVILLE TO BELL'S ROAD"
[*Ontario, Department of Lands and Forests, Field Notes, no. 2210*]

Lindsay 7th Sept. 1858

In obedience to instructions[30] dated the 22nd March 1858, to survey the frontages on the Bobcaygeon Road from Somerville to Bell's line, I beg leave to report that I entered on that duty on the 26th April on which day, and the two following, I hired men, procured supplies, brought my boats from Bobcaygeon and got them repaired— On the 29th of April I started with my party from Lindsay and arrived at my destination on the Bobcaygeon Road on the 1st of May— I beg leave to refer you to my Diary and field-notes for the details of my proceedings from the 1st of May to the 21st July when I completed the survey— on the 22nd July I started for home and arrived in Lindsay on the 23rd and discharged my party.

Having in a former report[31] described the lands on the Bobcaygeon Road, I consider it unnecessary now to enter into details, further than to state that the land generally is well adapted for agricultural purposes and is filling in rapidly with a good class of settlers.

The Road is now open for wheel travel about one mile north of the Burnt River, and its continuation to Bell's line is a matter of the greatest importance in the settlement of the back country— and while urging the importance and necessity of making the Road I am of opinion that the free grant system has but very little effect in the colonization of the country— Access is all that is needed and the sales of the frontage lots would create a fund almost sufficient to open the road.

E 25   ANDREW RUSSELL TO CROSBIE BRADY[32]
[*Ontario, Department of Lands and Forests, Instructions to
Land Surveyors, Book 5, pp. 424-5*]

Crown Lands Department
Quebec 22nd September 1859

Owing to the death of the late Mr J.K. Roche[33] P.L.S. who was employed by this department to survey and explore a line of road from

[30]Instructions to Land Surveyors, Book 5, p. 346.   [31]See D 11.
[32]Crosbie Brady qualified as a land surveyor on July 11, 1856.
[33]John Knatchbul Roche (1817–1859) came to Canada from England as a

Bell's Line in continuation of the Bobcaygeon Road, I have to instruct you to proceed to Lindsay and procure any memorandums, Field notes & documents relating to the said survey which may be in possession of his Brother George M. Roche Esqr C.L. agent;

You will then, with the least possible delay, proceed up the Bobcaygeon Road and complete the Survey from where Mr Roche left off, to Lake Nipissing.

You will make no change in the party, and when you arrive at the field of operations you will report without delay the progress and extent of Mr Roche's survey and the state of the party as you found them, also what supply of provisions, stores &c has been laid in for the survey.

The advance of $400.00 which was made to you on the 12th instant on account of the survey of the township of Hindon, you will apply,— instead, as an advance on account of the present Survey.

A copy of the Instructions issued to Mr Roche is herewith enclosed and by which you will be governed in carrying out the survey.

With reference to the Accounts for the Survey you will on taking charge of the party ascertain the quantity of provisions on hand, and their cost, and debit yourself with that amount, & commence your pay list of the party from the day you arrive at the camp. Mr Roche's Executor will make up an account of the survey including the Surveyor's pay till the day of his death— and that of the men until the day you join them also the payments made by Mr Roche for transport

E 26   BRADY, "FINAL REPORT ON THE BOBCAYGEON NIPISSING ROAD SURVEY"
[Ontario, Department of Lands and Forests, Field Notes, no. 2209]

Lindsay
1st. September 1860

I have the honor to inform you that the Survey of that portion of the Bobcageon & Nipissing Road Line with which I was intrusted was completed on the 23d of June last— and now beg to submit for your approval a final report thereon together with the necessary plan, field notes &c.—

On receipt of your instructions, 26th. Sept. /59, I hastened to Lindsay for the purpose of informing myself as to the position of the late Mr Roche's party & found that Mr Bell, his chief assistant, would probably continue the Exploring line until his then small stock of provisions was exhausted— when he would, of course, return to the settlements.—

I then proceeded to forward Northward with all possible dispatch, the supplies requisite for our winter's campaign— & on the 26th. Oct.

young man and qualified as a land surveyor on December 1, 1841. He drowned crossing Balsam Lake in a canoe, September 13, 1859. Instructions had been issued to Roche "to survey a line for a road in continuation of the Bobcaygeon Road from Bell's Line to Lake Nipissing," May 19, 1859 (Instructions to Land Surveyors, Book 5, pp. 400-2).

met Mr Bell returning with his party.— He had carried the Exploring
line to the 45th. mile.—

We were then occupied in transporting provisions to that point—
until the 6th. of Jany. when the survey was resumed.—

On my return from Lake Nipissing, Feby. 10th., whither I had gone
to procure some necessaries from the H.B.Company, I found one of my
party, David Roche, very ill & two others also suffering from a disorder
which, on their arrival at at [sic] Lindsay, was pronounced by medical
men a description of scurvy.—

I immediately dispatched them, attended by 5 men, towards Gull
River— Poor Roche died on the journey— thus being the second of his
family who had lost their lives in this survey.—

With the remainder of the party consisting of Mr Bell, my brother &
3 axemen, I finished the exploring line & road line, from the 45th. mile,
to Lake Nipissing which was reached on the 30th. of March.—

I then returned to survey the southern part of the road line completing it on the 16th. of June & discharging the party at Lindsay, on the
23d of the same month.

Our progress was of course materially retarded by the reduction of
our force already mentioned & reference to the diary will show that the
weather throughout was most unfavorable.—

The country traversed is generally timbered with hardwood, very
hilly to the 19th. mile— There is however, some excellent land to the
westward of the line & along the southern shore of the Lake of Bays.—

From the 19th. to the 37th. mile a generally good tract is found which
I have been informed extends & improves to the source and along the
banks of the Nahmanitigong[34] River.—

From 37 to 52 it again becomes hilly but good locations frequently
occur.—

Then to Lake Nipissing, the country is more level & some good tracts
for settlement were observed.—

On the whole, I think that, as the road is pushed Northward, there
is reason to anticipate a successful colonization in its neighborhood.—

Mr Murray's geological description of the banks of the Muskoka &
Magenatawan rivers will apply to the whole of this section— the rock
exposed being invariably gneiss.—

The road line, where it deviates from the straight course, presents, in
many places, unsightly bends, but with a due regard for economy, no
improvement in this respect could be made. . . .

E 27   J. W. BRIDGLAND, "REPORT OF INSPECTION OF SURVEYS AND
    EXAMINATION OF COLONIZATION ROADS IN CANADA WEST," 1861
        [P.A.O., Colonization Roads Papers, unbound]

Bobcaygeon Road

. . . The Bobcaygeon as far as the Burnt river eighteen miles from

[34]South River.

the Village is on the whole a pretty passable road. More labour appears to have been spent on the road bed than upon the former described roads. It is well cut out and being tolerably level and pretty free from bad swamps presents a more than ordinary civilized appearance. From Burnt river the character of the road changes very suddenly being neither so well made nor located on as favourable a site as the first described section, and after passing the first four miles, we travel over about six miles intensely rough and stony— one mile or two before reaching Gull River the road becomes rather better in surface— From Gull River for a distance of two miles the road is a pretty fair one; then succeeds another change, gradually, for the worse. One of the long log crossways here has floated out of position with the Spring flood and is at present in an impassable condition. The road hence becomes more hilly, and grows gradually worse in its finish until we arrive at the junction or Peterson Road forty two miles from Bobcaygeon Village— The last two or three miles have never been finished at all— It is a thoroughly bad road in this part, it being just possible to thread through the logs, brushwood, mud holes and rocks— I walked out three miles further on this line — where a sub-contractor is at work extending the road. I found also another gang commencing operations on the Peterson road here under the order of another sub-contractor.

On the whole this road (the Bobcaygeon) is a more passable one than the Hastings— the improvements are more general and considerable— the general character of the land of a better description and somewhat less stony.

The land around Burnt River[35] for some two miles is very sandy; the improvements however look healthy and advancing; and according to the statements of resident settlers the produce of the soil is extraordinary, viz: from three to four hundred bushels of Potatoes, six hundred bushels of turnips and thirty bushels of wheat per acre. Both Spring and Fall wheat are raised. A very good Saw-Mill has been erected on Burnt River, fifty by thirty feet, and an addition upon the South end of twenty four feet is being arranged and furnished with a run of Mill Stones bolts and necessary gearing for a gristing Mill. This is on lot 1 in the 13 Concession of Somerville— There is likewise about twenty-five acres cleared. A good barn and stabling, Tavern, Shop and Post Office. Mr. Joseph Hunter is the owner of this improvement. On the North side of the River also there is a further improvement, of clearance, two or three houses, Tavern, Store, Stables &c

Burnt River is here spanned by a wooden bridge standing firm at the present time. Queen posts and straining beams support the roadway, There are Log end abuttments and two intermediate piers awkwardly placed with their cutwaters sidelong to the current. The land surrounding Gull River is of similar character to that on Burnt River. This is a

[35]In the neighbourhood of Kinmount which is situated where the Bobcaygeon Road crosses the Burnt River.

deep stream about six rods wide crossed by a framed bridge supported by piers and King posts. Piers weak, with bad foundations. The Southerly one has dropped on one side, throwing the bridge very much out of position— if not soon relieved it must come down with the weight of the superstructure— About forty or fifty acres of clearance are here made— the crops look promising— I visited the mill site about one and a half miles up the river— It is a splendid water power with from 20 to 30 feet fall, offering great natural advantages to render it available. Further up the road about one and a half miles, there is a very good saw mill in operation, And about three miles distant from Hunters Mill on Burnt River on the same stream another Mill is in active progress of erection.

On the whole I judge this to be a very thriving road, and considered in connection with the large extent of promsing Country surrounding it, (just surveyed, and now in process of survey) must speedily become a very public one. . . .

Quebec, 22nd August 1861.

E 28   J. S. DENNIS'S REPORT TO WILLIAM MACDOUGALL (MCDOUGALL),[36] COMMISSIONER OF CROWN LANDS, ON RESURVEY OF FREE GRANTS ON BOBCAYGEON ROAD
[Ontario, Department of Lands and Forests, Field Notes, no. 2212]

I have the honour to report to you the completion of the service on the Bobcaygeon Road instructions[37] for which I received dated the 31st of July last—

This service involved the laying out of a range of free Grants on each side of the said Road in the Townships of Ridout Franklin Sherbourne and McClintock and the Survey and readjustment of the Fronts of the Free Grants upon the Road South of Bells line down to the North Boundary of Somerville. . . .

It is as a general thing a Hardwood country but hilly and Stony— in some places taking the latter character to a degree which will seriously interfere with its prospects of settlement. At the same time I think the greater part of the Lands will be taken up—

The Country abounds in Lakes as may be seen by the Maps some of which are of considerable extent— particularly those connected with the Trading Lake in the Township of Ridout.

[36]William McDougall (1822–1905) had a long political career. He was elected to the Legislative Assembly in 1858. From 1862 to 1864 he was Commissioner of Crown Lands, from 1867 to 1869 Minister of Public Works for Canada. In 1869 he was appointed Lieutenant Governor of Rupert's Land and the North West Territories but was turned back at Pembina by the Red River insurrection. He resigned the appointment and later returned to political life in the Ontario and Dominion governments.
[37]Instructions to Land Surveyors, Book 5, p. 510.

Should this part of the Country become entitled to importance as a settlement the locality around Trading Lake will no doubt be a favourite one from the beauty of the scenery and the better quality of the Land in the Neighbourhood.

Should it be still the Policy of the Government to reserve plots for Town or village Purposes— I would suggest a reservation with that view at Cedar Narrows[38] Lot 30— each side of the Road in Ridout and Sherbourne— and on both the North and South sides of the River.

Toronto July 15th 1862

E 29   WALTER BEATTY[39] TO THE COMMISSIONER OF CROWN LANDS, ALEXANDER CAMPBELL
[P.A.O., Crown Lands Papers, shelf 15, no. 9]

Delta November 11th. 1864

In accordance with your instructions dated August 27th 1864 requiring me to furnish your Department with an estimate in detail of the Amount required to put the Bobcaygeon Colonization road into reasonable condition for travel— I herewith transmit such estimate.

The amount required between Bobcaygeon Village and Muskoka river is $15784 $^{81}/_{100}$.

I am of opinion that the road would be very much improved in some places by making deviations from the present track and have made my estimates accordingly. I wrote your department about six weeks ago for instructions about making such deviations but have not yet received an answer.

One of the most important changes I have recommended in the road is that around Scotts Hill, South of Gull river. Said hill is of Granite rock and one hundred and nineteen feet in height— may be avoided altogether on the route described in Estimate thereby saving a Considerable Sum of money and at the same time opening up the best portions of the Minden Town plot (see Plan of Minden in your office) enough of which would sell in the Course of One Year to pay the expense of building new road which would otherwise remain unsold for many years.

With respect to the expediency of the work I am fully satisfied that bad roads have done more to retard settlement in this part of the country than bad lands, in proof, I may state that every 100 pounds which passes over the road from Bobcaygeon to Gull river a distance of twenty eight miles costs from one dollar to one dollar and a quarter, for freight.

---

[38]Now Dorset.
[39]Walter Beatty (1836–1911) passed his examinations as a land surveyor July 19, 1858. He subdivided Stisted, Chaffey, and other townships of Ontario, and was one of the pioneers in surveying the public lands of western Canada. He made his home at Delta, Ontario.

I do not think it would be expedient to do anything on the road between Trading Lake and Muskoka river. I found no one living north of Cedar Narrows (Trading Lake) There are two shanties and a small clearing at Muskoka river. South of Trading lake there is a good deal of good land which would no doubt settle if the road were good.

That portion of the road between Cedar Narrows (Trading lake) and Muskoka has been carried over a number of hills which should be avoided if such a thing be possible for it is not possible to make a good road over them. My estimate for this portion is what is absolutely necessary to make the road passable [,] good it cannot be made without involving a thorough exploration of the lands adjoining. This I did not consider my instructions would warrant me in taking the time necessary.

THE BURLEIGH ROAD

E 30   J. W. Fitzgerald, Report of Survey of the Burleigh Road [*Ontario, Department of Lands and Forests, Field Notes, no. 2215*]

Peterboro September 9th. 1861

In obedience to your instructions[40] dated August 9th. 1860 to explore for and locate a line of road from the vicinity of Burleigh Rapids to the Peterson Line. I have the honor to inform you that I have completed the survey of said road and furnish herewith the plan &c of same.

Having made all preliminary arrangements I started with my party, supplies &c from Peterboro on the 13th. Sept. 1860 and on the 14th. arrived at Burleigh Rapids. . . .

. . .

. . . I ran . . . to the boundary line between the townships of Monmouth & Cardiff which I struck about 4 miles north of the north boundary of Anstruther, having passed through a country very similar to that already described in Chandos. This boundary between Monmouth and Cardiff I followed for a short distance until it became so very rough & broken that I found it quite impracticable to continue it any further. I then made a deviation to the west and after proceeding a short distance crossed the South East branch of the Burnt River at this place about 40 feet wide— and connecting two pretty Lakes, seperated by a very beautiful level tract of land, which, ascending a short distance west of the road affords a commanding view of the above Lakes and the surrounding country— from this to the Peterson Road the whole country is well

[40]These instructions covered only from Burleigh Rapids to the rear of the Township of Burleigh and were supplemented by instructions of December 24, 1860, to continue to the Peterson line (Instructions to Land Surveyors, Book 5, pp. 477 and 485).

adapted for settlement being principally composed of undulating hard-wood land interspersed with small swamps—Cedar & Spruce— and some fine Beaver Meadows capable of affording the early settler an abundant supply of hay, the soil is a sandy loam having in some places where I have tried been as deep as 4 feet. A small Lake west of the 46 mile post is the first and farthest South of the waters flowing into the Ottawa, all the others I met with north of this flow into that River. These Lakes I have no doubt abound in fish tho' unfortunately for myself & party we had not been able to take advantage of so great a luxury from our extreme anxiety to work out from the flies.

The Peterson Road where I struck it (about 1 mile west of Buck Lake) appeared to me to be well cleared out the full width and the grad-ing executed in a very creditable manner.

The geological features of the section of the country traversed by the Burleigh Road differ little if any from those which pervade almost the entire central part of the Ottawa and Huron district, the formation being gneiss or granite and with very little change in the proportions of the ingredients which compose it, namely Felspar, quartz & mica.

Having now reviewed the entire country from Burleigh Rapids to the Peterson Road along the route of the Burleigh Road, and representing as nearly as possible its true nature, I have no hesitation in saying that it is capable of becoming in the course of a few years one of the most pros-perous of any of the new Colonization Roads being now opened up for settlement in Canada, and will yield to the industrious husbandman a profitable return for his labor for beside possessing the great advantage of passing through an uncommonly fine country I have taken great pains and trouble to select the best possible route that could be found between its two extremities and tho' I admit having occupied some extra time for this object, I have the satisfaction of knowing that it ought to reduce the expense of the construction by a very considerable percentage.

Trusting that this brief Report with the accompanying plan &c will deserve the approval of the Department.

E 31   J. W. BRIDGLAND, "GENERAL REPORT ON COLONIZATION
ROADS IN CANADA WEST," 1863
[*P.A.O., Colonization Roads Papers, Reports, 1862–8, pp. 83–4, 107*]

Department of Crown Lands
Quebec December 1863

Burleigh Road

Runs from Burleigh rapids through Burleigh, Anstruther, Chandos, Cardiff, Monmouth and Dudley to Peterson road.

About twenty-three miles of this road have been made by contract. Twenty more are now under contract to William Lackey of Mount Forest for the gross sum of $4,952.50. $9,000 are appropriated towards its extension $1,500 was appropriated for the settlement of last contract by O.C. of the 24th of October, 1862; so that after completing the present contract there will remain, of the last appropriation, a balance of $2547.50.

The completion of this contract will carry improvements on the Burleigh road as far as the 43 mile. There will then remain about 13 miles of unfinished line to reach the Peterson road. It is highly desirable that this remaining portion of the road should be made. About eight miles of the distance will pass through the Township of Dudley, one of the Canada L & E. Company's Townships, and four through the upper part of our Township of Monmouth. . . .

Supplementary Memorandum

. . . On the subject of the Burleigh road, I have suggested its continuation Northward to unite with the Peterson, but the formation of the Monck road will also render this unnecessary, and as the present contract on the Burleigh will carry it to or a little beyond the location of the Monck road, I beg to withdraw the suggestion of the Report as the existing appropriation is sufficient for the latter view. . . . Feby 10/64

E 32   ANDREW RUSSELL TO R. W. ERRIT (ERRETT),[41] PETERBOROUGH
[*P.A.O., Colonization Roads Papers, Letter Book 1, pp. 237–8*]

Quebec 8th. Aug. 1864

Mr. Wm. Gibson, under the instructions of this Department has reported in detail the damages done by the late fire upon the Burleigh road. He particularizes the same as follows,

North of Burleigh Bridge—

on	1st.	mile	5	rods	crossway	floated
"	7th.	"	14.85	"	"	Burnt
"	9th.	"	3.50	"	"	"
"	10th.	"	.25	"	"	"
"	11th.	"	8.85	"	"	"
"	15th.	"	4.33	"	"	"
"	23rd.	"	32.00	"	"	"

Total 68.75 rods

Bridges burnt

on	11th	mile	1—	66	feet long,	50	feet span
"	do	"	1—	59	do	35	do
"	15	"	1—	44	do	25	do

[41]Richard William Errett (b. 1827) moved to Peterborough in 1861 and obtained a government contract for building the Burleigh Road. In 1872 he was appointed clerk of the Division Court.

With reference to the original cost of the above works Mr. Gibson further reports the same to have been as follows,

For Crossway	68.78 rods		$105.10
Large Bridge on	11th mile		320.76
Small one on do		} together	
Do on	15th "		
			60.58
	Total original cost		$486.44

As you report it of material consequence especially for your own convenience and interest that these bridges be built immediately, you are hereby authorized, if you think fit, to proceed without delay, and reconstruct the impaired crossway, at the price which was paid for it under the first contract.

The Bridges will be planned and reported to the Department forthwith, after the original style and pattern, and these, when prepared and accepted, you can also undertake at the original rates, if you desire.

E 33   BRIDGLAND'S REPORT ON THE BURLEIGH ROAD, 1866
[*P.A.O., Colonization Roads Papers, Reports, 1862–8, pp. 293–4*]

The Burleigh Colonization Road suffers from irregular, tortuous and injudicious location, especially in its first distance.

There appears to have been no clearly conceived purpose, as to where its general direction should lie or tend.

Hence for the first six miles it passes through a section of country the most desolate and incorrigible to be conceived of. A region denuded of timber, destitute of soil, and broken into ravines and ridges composed of inconvertible granite, where the superficial labors of one year disappear from the next, through the actions of the floods and freshets of one spring tide. On the upper end of this road, through the townships of Chandos and Cardiff the land is of very tolerable average, and a respectable and healthy settlement is progressing.

If ingress could only be obtained into the settlement by a more rational route than at present made use of— say by the east side of Otanabee river, and across the Stony Lake Narrows so as to join the sharp elbow formed by this road on the 8th. lot in the 6th Concession of Burleigh— there would then be some hope of constructing a thoroughfare into the better settlement upon the road which could be made to stand without an expensive yearly improvement.

The operations upon this road have extended from the 24th mile post on the road to a distance of 11 miles from this point.

Over three miles of this distance an entirely new road has been made, and the remaining portion of eight miles has been carefully repaired.

Several bad hills have been avoided and a good many difficult places judiciously repaired.

Expenditure for the season $3858 ^{42}/100.

THE PETERSON ROAD

E 34   ROBERT BELL TO A. J. RUSSELL[42]
[P.A.O., Colonization Roads Papers, Section 1, Box 10, Correspondence, no. 144]

Ottawa 8 June 1857

I have this morning received yours of the 6th Inst and in reply to your question respecting the country between the Ottawa river and Lake Huron explored by me in 1847 and 1848, beg to say that the fullest information that I can afford on the subject is given in my report made in 1848— Since that time however I have ascertained that the country lying south of my explorations, especially that in the vicinity of York river is of much better quality than the country I examined, the surface of these tracts being less uneven and the portions of good land more extensive. I can see no difficulties in the way of settlement on a large scale if the line of road laid out by me and that surveyed by Mr. Elmore[43] were made passable, on the contrary I would regard it as being a favorable opening for settlement were these roads made

E 35   A. J. RUSSELL TO WILLIAM HUTTON,[44] SECRETARY OF THE BUREAU OF AGRICULTURE
[P.A.O., Colonization Roads Papers, Section 1, Box 10, Correspondence, no. 181]

Crown Timber Office
Ottawa 3d. Dec. 1857

I have received a letter from Mr. Bird respecting the line of road for which he has been exploring from the bridge site on the Madawaska to the Hastings Road where it intersects Mr Bells Muskoka Road line. He mentions that a line from the bridge site to a point on the Hastings Road about seven *miles* south of Mr Bells line had been recommended by Mr

[42]Alexander Jamieson Russell (1807–1887) was a surveyor and engineer, employed on the construction of the Rideau Canal and in building roads and bridges in Lower Canada. In June, 1846, he was appointed Crown Timber Agent.

[43]Publius Virgilius Elmore (1798–1857) was appointed surveyor June 2, 1821, and did many surveys of township boundaries. In 1847 he ran an exploration line in the rear of Victoria, and in 1857 surveyed a tier of lots on both sides of the Hastings Road.

[44]William Hutton (d. 1861) was Secretary of the Bureau of Agriculture from 1853 to 1861.

Peterson[45] the surveyor engaged in subdividing the township and petitioned for by a number of the settlers on the Hastings Road, but that the proposed line was considered objectionable by the Bureau as deviating too far from Bells line to be consistent with the continuation of it westward hereafter

In a former communication I mentioned that Mr Bell was of opinion that this part of his road line could be changed with advantage as there is much bad and rough ground on it from the crossing of the River Madawaska to the distance of three miles westward of Bark Lake where the good land on his line commences. At the time he traced his road line he believed that there was better ground to the southward but his instructions did not admit of his carrying the line there which in this part of it would have been desirable. Indeed the selection by Mr. Papineau then Commissioner of Crown Lands of a general site for the line knowing that it would in this part encounter two such serious engineering obstacles as Bark Lake and Lake Kiminiskeck to the east of it was unfortunate, requiring a great and very objectionable detour to avoid the still greater difficulty of ferrying over them

I enclose a copy of a letter to me from Mr. Bell in which he still more decidedly expresses his opinion that a better site for this part of the line could be found to the southward The accompanying trace will shew that even were it necessary to adopt the line proposed by Mr Peterson and Mr Bird (marked B.B.B.—) as far as the Hastings Road and thence to slope north-westward to Mr. Bells line it would be no departure from the general direction of the line with the view of carrying it westward— nor would the distance be in the slightest degree increased.— while it is not improbable that as exploration advances a site even better than Mr Bells Muskoka line may be found by continuing on this parallel of six miles south of it for the greater part of the way to the River Muskoka

There is another consideration also worthy of being noticed. This road from the Hastings Road to the Opeongo Road will form not only a useful thoroughfare from the settlements on the Ottawa to those behind Belleville and on the Lake shore generally besides giving access for the settlers on the Hastings Road to the markets on the Ottawa. As such it would be thirteen miles shorter by the proposed line B.B.B. than by going north to Bells line and then descending again to the Bridge sites by the present crooked line by Bark Lake and Kiminiskeck.—

I have gone so much into particulars in order that Mr. VanKoughnet may have all the information and considerations before him if he has not yet decided on the subject and if the contractor be not too far advanced to admit of the proposed route or something like it being adopted. I think from the nature of Mr Birds contract with Mr Neilson it would be immaterial to the contractor which line was taken

[45]Joseph S. Peterson qualified as a land surveyor on June 8, 1842. He made numerous surveys in the Kingston, Belleville, and Trenton areas, and later went to the United States.

E 36   ROBERT BIRD TO HUTTON
[*P.A.O., Colonization Roads Papers, Section 1, Box 10,
Correspondence, no. 183*]

Belleville December the 12 1857

Yours of the 9 inst. is before me and I beg to state that the decision
you have come to in regard to the Bell line road is just what that section
of Country requires, I am perfectly satisfied that the present Ministry
and particularly the Agriculture departments object is to adopt the best
plan for the settlement of the Country and in changing the line South at
the Hastings road will be a great advantage to the Settlement of that
Country and as Mr Russel says will not, in the event of proceeding with
the road west ward deviate much from a direct line I have delayed the
Commencement by Mr Nealson except in getting provisions back as far
as York Branch untill I get word from Mr Russell and I must say I am
much pleased that you have fell in with his views on the subject Mr
Nealson is not at home and I cannot see him for about two weeks as I
have to start back on Monday next for the purpose of giving his foreman
directions on the new line however I hereby garrintee that I will get a
letter from him to Mr Gibson that the change or any deviation we make
from the Bells line mentioned in his contract will not efect his contract in
any way except in the length of the road which is not particularized in
the contract and I think the South rout is not as long as the Bell line rout.
I will take care of the small map and will send it to you in about two
weeks

E 37   ROAD PROGRESS, MADAWASKA RIVER TO MUSKOKA ROAD
[*Canada, Bureau of Agriculture, Report, 1857*]

Bell's Line.

The portion of this line of road lying between the River Madawaska
and the production of the Hastings Road was contracted for in November last and is now in progress. The road is to be carried westward to a
point near Lake Muskoka, called the great falls, where it will meet the
Muskoka road running from the termination of the navigation on Lake
Couchiching at Washago Mills.

E 38   DAVID GIBSON'S REPORT ON THE PETERSON ROAD,[46] 1859
[*Canada, Bureau of Agriculture and Statistics, Report, 1859, p. 26*]

At the date of last Report this road had been made from the Madawaska River to the south-west angles of the Township of Wicklow, where
it intersects the Hastings Road,— a distance of nearly 21 miles. It has

[46]The *Report* of the Bureau of Agriculture and Statistics for 1858 stated that
the Peterson line of road had been adopted in place of Bell's line.

since been completed from the Hastings Road to the north-west angle of the Township of Herschell, a distance of over 10 miles,— making in all about 31 miles of a finished and good road.

The portion connecting with the Muskoka Road leaves that road about one-quarter of a mile South of the great Falls of Muskoka, on the District line, and runs south-easterly to the line between Lots 5 and 6 of the Township of Draper; thence southerly along that line to the line between Concession 5 and 6, and thence along the last mentioned line till near the East boundary of that Township, where a deviation has to be made round the North side of a small lake. This line was explored last Autumn. It passes through a tract of good land, and a contract for the road was entered into in November last. It is expected that it will be completed this season.

E 39   WILLIAM MORRISON'S[47] REPORT ON THE PETERSON ROAD, 1863
[Canada, Department of Crown Lands, Report, 1863]

This road was finished at the date of last report, with the exception of certain hills in the township of Oakley over which it is carried. These have now been all improved by excavation and embankment— the grades formed admitting of an ordinary wagon conveying 15 cwt. over them.

The whole road is thus completed between the Muskoka road and the Madawaska river, where it is connected with the Opeongo junction road, (now generally considered part of the Peterson road). Its entire length between these points is 101¼ miles, and its total cost was $ 35,589.97, gving an average mileage of $ 352.49, inclusive of bridges and super-intendence.

On the portion of the road passing between the townships of Guilford, Harburn and Bruton, on the north, and Dysart, Dudley and Harcourt, on the south, the underbrush has sprung up and is rapidly increasing. This and the strong growth of timothy grass, which covers that portion of the road in summer, render it difficult to be travelled. A small amount — probably $5 per mile — would now clear out the obstructions, and make the road free for traffic. As this portion runs through the lands of the Canada Land Emigration Company, it may be proper, if it be liable to maintain the road, that it be requested to clear out the underbrush before it acquire more strength and present greater impediments to the traffic.

E 40   J. W. BRIDGLAND TO THE COMMISSIONER OF CROWN LANDS, ALEXANDER CAMPBELL
[P.A.O., Colonization Roads Papers, Reports, 1862–8, pp. 201–2]

Quebec 28th. February, 1865

. . . I think it my duty also to draw your attention to the Peterson Road which from the important position it occupies in some of its sec-

47William Morrison was Superintendent of Colonization Roads.

tions relative to settlement merits, I consider that some action should be taken for its improvement. This road is more than 100 miles in length from the Great Muskoka Falls to the Opeongo Road.

The average cost has been about $338 per mile.

This amount, for the making of a road through a granite country, generally rough and difficult even if economically applied, every person practically acquainted with the business of Wild woods road making, will at once see is very insufficient; and when it is further considered that the expenditure has been made under extremely deficient checks and supervision of the work there can be no doubt I think on the mind of any one that the Peterson road in its character must be a very inferior affair. Having travelled very considerable portions of this road immediately after the same were pronounced completed and received off the contractors hands, I can certify [?] to you of the very inferior character of this road in the parts thus referred to. Besides this very soon after, that part of the road lying to the West of the Hastings road was completed a fire destroyed in a great many places the high crosswaying rendering the road at once impassable, So that I doubt whether the road has really ever been travelled by waggons throughout its whole length at all, and hence as a grand communication between the Ottawa and Lake Huron has never been a realization. . . .

E 41   ANDREW RUSSELL TO J. A. SNOW[48]
[*P.A.O., Colonization Roads Papers, Letter Book 2, p. 226*]

Ottawa, 27th June 1866.

R. J. Oliver, Esq., overseer of repairs now in progress on the Peterson road has been instructed to open a short branch road[49] from the angle of the said road in Draper, where the direction in the present travelled line leading to the Muskoka Falls leaves that line between the 5th. and 6th. concession of Draper and surveys at right angles, to the Northwestward to intersect the Muskoka road.

The position of the projected line is shown on a small sketch transmitted this day to Mr. Oliver. At any time when you can conveniently and safely leave the Monck road for a season to supervise Mr Oliver's work as directed in Departmental letters of the 16th inst., you will assist him in exploring the route through, and in locating the road line upon, the most favourable site.

[48]John Allan Snow (1824–1888) became a surveyor in 1847. He was employed by the government in the construction of colonization roads such as the Hastings and the Monck. In 1867 he was sent to build a road from Lake of the Woods to the Red River Settlement, which proved so unpopular that it contributed to the outbreak of the Rebellion.
[49]This branch road provided a more direct route to the Muskoka Road.

THE MONCK ROAD

E 42   BRIDGLAND, "GENERAL REPORT ON COLONIZATION ROADS IN
CANADA WEST, AND SUGGESTIONS FOR APPROPRIATIONS TO
PROLONG OR REPAIR THE SAME"
[*P.A.O., Colonization Roads Papers, Reports, 1862–8, pp. 81 and 107*]

Department of Crown Lands
Quebec December 1863.

. . . The Mississippi Road[50] is thence, viz. from its intersection with
the Hastings, projected westward to the bridge over the East branch of
the Severn River, as forming a grand middle road between the Peterson
Road and the navigable waters of Sturgeon, Buckhorn, Salmon, and
Stony Lakes, passing thro. Faraday, Cardiff, Monmouth, Glamorgan,
Snowdon, Lutterworth, Digby, Dalton, and Rama, and when completed
will form a nearly direct road line of communication between the Ottawa
and Lake Simcoe. The full completion of this road, however, cannot be
accomplished in one year. But its creation is, in my opinion, so desirable
and even necessary to forward the settlement of this vast tract of yet
comparatively unsettled country, that I strongly recommend its progress
not to be lost sight of, and in pursuance of this object, that a sum of not
less than $10,000 be appropriated to be expended the ensuing summer
upon it— on carrying it on from the Addington to the Hastings
Road. . . .

Supplementary Memorandum
A more matured consideration of the advantages and effects produc-
ible by the formation of the Monck Road,[51] also certain other additional
and highly necessary improvements which had escaped my observation
now leads me to append this supplement. On the subject of the Cameron
road[52] I have suggested in the Report that no further extension thereof
seemed desirable, but as the Monck road will probably pass within 4
miles of the Cameron I now think it judicious to recommend that the
latter be prolonged Northward to effect a junction and that $1200 be
appropriated for that purpose. . . . Feby 10/64

    [50]The Mississippi Road was to run from the Mississippi River in the Township
of North Sherbrooke to the Hastings Road.
    [51]In the interval between the report, December, 1863, and the "Supplementary
Memorandum," February 10, 1864, the name Monck appears to have been given
to the road.
    [52]The Cameron Road ran north from the river which connects Balsam and
Cameron lakes, along the east side of Balsam, crossed the Gull River at Coboconk
and continued a few miles north.

E 43   BRIDGLAND TO THE COMMISSIONER OF CROWN LANDS,
ALEXANDER CAMPBELL
[*P.A.O., Colonization Roads Papers, Reports, 1862–8, p. 143*]

D.C.L.   Quebec July 28 /64

. . . The Mississippi road line I consider a very important avenue of communication to the unsettled lands of the Crown, especially under the present aspect of the times, with Ottawa, as the seat of Government, the natural and easy connection of that city with the great St. Lawrence, and its' short and eligible communication with Perth and the commencement of the Mississippi road.

It will, no doubt, under such circumstances, become *a great*, if not *the* channel for the tide of emigration which will flow to the available new lands of Canada.

E 44   A(NDREW) R(USSELL) TO THOMAS WEATHERALD[53]
[*P.A.O., Colonization Roads Papers, Letter Book 1, pp. 276-7*]

Quebec, 4th. Oct. 1864.

I have to instruct you to complete the Survey of the Monck road line, viz: that part of the same lying between the Western terminus of the Mississippi road at its Junction with the Hastings, and the intersection of the above Monck road with the Bobcaygeon as surveyed by Provl. Land Surveyor Gibson,[54] all of which you will find delineated on the accompanying map of the Huron and Ottawa Territory.

For this purpose you will proceed either by the Hastings road to the terminus of the Mississippi road first indicated, or by the Bobcaygeon to the East end of Mr Gibson's line. Your preference of either route will of course depend upon its superiority for facility and economy in the transport of your provisions and luggage required upon the survey. . . .

E 45   WEATHERALD TO THE COMMISSIONER OF CROWN LANDS,
ALEXANDER CAMPBELL
[*P.A.O., Crown Lands Papers, Shelf 15, no. 16*]

Goderich Feby 6th. 1865.

In compliance with your letter of the 17th. January last I have made a Plan of that portion[55] of the Monck Road Surveyed lately by me. You

[53]Thomas Weatherald (1834–1917) qualified as a land surveyor January 12, 1856. He carried on many surveys, and for some time was in partnership with T. N. Molesworth.

[54]On September 24, 1864, Peter Gibson received $735.33 for the survey from Lake Couchiching to the Bobcaygeon Road (Colonization Roads Papers, Letter Book 1, p. 268).

[55]Easterly from the Bobcaygeon Road, 10¼ miles.

will observe that the route chosen is very crooked, caused by the excessively rough and hilley country through which it runs, from the commencement of my work to its termini I did not see 1000 acres of good ploughable farming land— We crossed several patches of hard wood, but the surface even there was invariably stoney, what soil did exist was composed of a fine red sand, in many places along the rout of road the Granite Rock is nearly bare, in others the surface is sprinkled with loose pieces of the same description of rock weighing from 100 to 1000 lbs each— High precipitous ridges of granite are very numerous through this Township their prevailing direction being North Westerly and South Easterly— averaging a height of about 80 feet; In my survey I noted the configuration of the Country only on my straight exploration line and "Road Proper" I deemed it unnecessary to loose time in making measurements to show the Topography of the Country to any distance North or South of the location of road, and merely walked up & down the side roads formerly run in the Township Survey choosing the best location for my road within the prescribed distance North and South of my straight exploration line— You will see on my Plan when I observed considerable Magnetic local attraction twice close to swamps and once on a side hill— the attraction at the latter place being very great (20° East of North) I obtained a specimen of the rock which I send you herewith— The ridge from which it is obtained is about 100 feet high and slopes away to the Westward at about one perpendicular to two base— this ridge runs along the southerly side of Bow Lake (as shown on Plan) I did not observe any other description of rock but granite throughout the whole route—

The swamps Tamerac and Cedar have generally a depth of three or four feet of black muck with rock beneath— they afford when crossed by the road line a sufficient quantity of good timber for all crossway purposes—

I have endeavoured to locate the road so that the grades will be the easiest possible through such a country, always bearing in mind the necessity of keeping as close as practicable to the straight line between the termini of the Monck Road, avoiding rock cuttings altogether (or very nearly so) The steepest natural grades do not exceed I think one perpendicular to ten base— and these in most cases can easily be made from 1 in 12 to 1 in 15 by cutting through loose stone and sand— In the accompanying Estimate of cost construction I have included any cuttings necessary in the price fixed to grubbing & ditching

There are only two unimportant Bridges on this portion of road the remarks I have made on the Plan & in the Estimate will be sufficient for them— the commonest bridge construction is all that they require

I look upon the Country traversed by my survey as almost unfit for settlement on account of its exceeding hilley and poorness of soil, even when soil does exist it is so stoney that it cannot be ploughed— I deem it best adapted (after being cleared) to raise sheep, and for grasing purposes—

There is considerable good Pine both red and white but the lumber men are fast thinning it out.

I have had no use for the blank agreement for "Right of Way" furnished me by the Department not having seen any settlers or clearings along the whole rout— with the exception of a small deserted clearing on the Bobcaygeon road at the commencement of my survey— I therefore return them—

Annexed to this please find my Estimate showing the cost of construction in conformity with specifications furnished me

E 46   ROBERT GILMOUR[56] TO THE COMMISSIONER OF CROWN LANDS,
ALEXANDER CAMPBELL
[P.A.O., Crown Lands Papers, Shelf 15, no. 16]

Paisley 22nd. January 1866

I have the honor to report that in accordance with your instructions dated the nineteenth June 1865, I have surveyed and located the line of the Monck Road— from the point where it was relinquished by Provincial Land Surveyor Wetherald to the Western terminus of the Mississippi Road and have succeeded in obtaining the best line the nature of the Country would admit of, and this without encountering any heavy hill cuttings (with one exception) or extensive swamps. A great deal of pains was taken in ascertaining the best site and for this purpose a very careful examination of the whole country through which the road runs was made.

. . .

The total length of road surveyed by me from its beginning in Snowdon to the Hastings Road is three thousand two hundred and thirty chains and ten links: from the Hastings Road to the old track of road above referred to sixty five chains and thirty one links all of which will have to be chopped and graded, in addition to the special works required and shewn on the plan, and twenty one chains and seventy two links from the latter place to the Mississippi Road. . . .

If I might be permitted I would recommend that the portion of the Monck Road lying between the Hastings Road and the Burnt River be first constructed as the bulk of the good land along the line of the Monck Road lies in between these two points; besides, this portion will be the cheapest to build. . . .

[56]Robert Gilmour (1833–1903) became a land surveyor April 11, 1856. He surveyed the Monck Road in 1865 and carried on extensive work in northern Ontario.

E 47   J. W. Bridgland to Alexander Campbell
[P.A.O., Colonization Roads Papers, Reports, 1862–8, p. 243]

Monck Road.

The operations upon this road line, during the season of 1865 have consisted of:—

1st. The completion of the survey and location of the line from the easterly boundry of the Township of Snowdon to the Hastings Road.

2nd.— An exploration at the westerly end of that part of the line surveyed by Provincial Land Surveyor Gibson, the object being to discover, if possible a more favorable terminus and avoid a good deal of flooded land passed over in the first location requiring expensive high crossway.

The first duty was performed by R. Gilmour, Esq. whose survey has been completed. The whole distance of located road is about 40½ miles.

The second work was done by Jno. A. Snow, Esq. whose exploration was successful in obtaining an excellent improvement in the above terminus.

Amount paid R. Gilmour on account of survey in 1865	$1400.00
Amount for Mr. Snow's exploration	121.88
Paid balance due P. Gibson for survey in 1864	266.33
	$1788.21

. . .

Ottawa, Feby. 27, 1866

E 48   Bridgland to Alexander Campbell
[P.A.O., Colonization Roads Papers, Reports, 1862–8, pp. 274–6]

Ottawa, 9th. July, 1866

Under the present somewhat war like aspect[57] of our Country, I beg again to revive the consideration of constructing the Colonization Road line called the Monck Road the works upon which are already commenced at the western terminus) as a Military Highway.

The line will extend from Ottawa to the water of Lake Simcoe.

An air line distance between the above points will be about 175 miles, but as a great portion of the country through which the road must necessarily pass, is exceedingly broken, the circuity of the route will much increase the length thereof.

[57]The Fenian Raids on the Canadian border in the spring and summer of that year.

Adopting the Monck road line as at present located, and the Mississippi as now travelled as a continuation of the road towards Ottawa and afterwards the public lines as now opened and travelled leading through Playfair's Corners, Lanark, Carelton [sic] place & Bell's Corners to Ottawa the total distance will be about 231 miles

Thus

    Monck road   = 90 miles
    Mississippi   = 71 ..
    Thence to Ottawa = 70 ..

         Total   231 miles

This distance, however, may be considerably shortened by the necessary corrections and improvements to be made beyond those contemplated simply for colonization purposes, the additional outlay for which will be warranted upon the consideration of the great public benefit to be confered in a Military point of view. . . .

The great advantage of a thorough internal communication road from the navigable waters of Lake Huron to those of the Ottawa by which Military stores & troops may be transported and deposited can hardly be overestimated, indeed it seems to have become in the present threatening emergency an indispensible necessity.

You will observe also that this Grand Trunk line will be tapped by all the various Colonization roads leading from the frontier, many of which have been so far improved within the past 4 years as to render them available with very little further improvement for Military service and communication with the line in question, so that should transport on the St. Lawrence at any time at some particular point be impeded the Monck line can thro' means of any of these be reached and the necessary transit go on thro' it to any point east or west which it is required to reach.

There will also be no difficulty in selecting eligible points along the line for block houses and arsenal depots, at convenient distances of 30 or 40 miles intervals; where an abundant supply of water can be had, and even in some cases where an internal water route can be made available for a great distance towards the frontier, as by Gull and Burnt river and Balsam Sturgeon Pidgeon Stony Buckhorn & Salmon trout Lakes and other connecting rivers and lakes. With the additional expenditure of between 3 & 400 dollars per mile on the amount which is now found necessary to complete our ordinary Colonization roads— this amount to be expended in widening the grade diminishing curves and angles and increasing the strength and capacity of bridges and culverts,— the Monck road can in my opinion be made very satisfactorily to serve the important purpose now before you for consideration.

E 49   J. A. SNOW'S REPORT ON THE MONCK ROAD
[P.A.O., Colonization Roads Papers, Minute Book, 1864, pp. 99–101]

Hull Novr 6th. 1866

On the twenty third of May last, I had the honor to receive my appointment to the oversight of the Monck colonization Road, with instructions to commence operations as soon as practicable.

Accordingly on the first of June I advertised for tenders to supply the men, that should be employed, with board and lodging, and repaired myself to Orillia, to receive them.

On account of the extremely high price of provisions, I only received two tenders for this service, and both at the same rate, Three dollars per week, of seven days, Having consulted with the superintendent of roads, who was in Orillia at the time, the contract was given to J. P. Cockburn,[58] Esq. Merchant of that place, and signed on the ninth of the month.

Mr. Cockburn was very slow in organizing his camp, and it was not till the Eighteenth of June, that the work in the field was fairly commenced. Since that period, it has been pushed forward with all the men that could be obtained at the wages allowed by the Department

During the months of June, July, and August, men were remarkably scarce, owing to the low rate of wages, and the fact that the wealthy farmers, in the neighbourhood, were paying one dollar per day, and board to the same class, that on the works only received fifty seven cents, with board only on the days they worked. Beside this, nearly all the hands had small farms in the adjacent townships, and would only come here, on condition of being allowed to attend to them, when absolutely necessary, In consequence of this, the attendance of the men was irregular.

After the first of September, men came on in greater numbers, and remained steadily up to the close of the work, on the fourth of November, as will be seen by the Pay lists.

The Work on this road, was begun where the line between the 12th. and 13th. concession of the township of Mara meets the road leading from the village of Atherly to the Indian Village of Rama, and near the boundary between Lots 28 and 29 . . . The entire length of road worked over is about Eight and a quarter miles About one quarter in the Eighth mile is unfinished

At the time when the work on this road commenced, and up to a late period in the season, it was expected by the Superintendent that this road would be built upon a broader, and more substantial basis, than the ordinary Colonization Roads, that in case of necessity, it might be useful for military purposes, and the works were commenced, and so

[58]John P. Cockburn, brother of A. P. Cockburn, was proprietor of the "Montreal Store" at Orillia, and later postmaster at Gravenhurst for about thirty-seven years.

far conducted with a view to meet the probable requirements, The line has been grubbed, to the width of 22 feet, and the graded road-way, made 18 feet with crosslays and bridges 16 feet wide, The drains have been made continuous on each side, with discharge drains, and culverts in each hollow. . . .

Before closing this Report, I beg leave to suggest that some changes be made, in the manner of boarding and lodging the men, employed on the works. The present system, does not work well, as the contractor has no interest in the work, other than to make all the money he can, and to effect his object, in nine cases out of ten, Indeavouring to force the men, to use provisions, more or less damaged. This has been particularly apparent this season, no doubt partly arising from the high price of sound pork and beef, the articles on account of which, the principal complaints have been made. It would certainly be more conducive to the advancement of the work, and the comfort of the men, if the overseer had the charge of providing both food and shelter, at the same time being confined within certain limits in regard to maximum cost, which should be varied to suit the fluctuations of the market.

E 50   State of the Monck Road
[*Orillia,* Times, *April 8, 1875*]

This important thoroughfare is in a most deplorable state at present, bridges are out of repair and one has already been almost entirely swept away. The settlers along the road through the townships of Mara, Rama, Dalston [*sic*] and Carden are about to present a Petition (which is now in circulation) to Government, representing the impracticable state of it in those townships, particularly during the Autumn and Spring seasons. It must be remembered that this Road was opened up by the Government some years ago for the purpose of, like other Colonization Roads, promoting the settlement of the Crown Domain, and since then the settlers have been obliged to keep it in repair which they have only been partially able to accomplish owing to the small number of those resident along the road. The Government have afforded some slight assistance but the money expended has almost been thrown away. We are reliably informed, however, that the energetic member for North Ontario, Mr. Thos. Paxton,[59] M.P.P., has managed to obtain a small grant from Government to aid in improving it, and that he expects to get more. One fact, however, is certain, that this important outlet to a large section of valuable land should not be neglected. The farmers as far if not beyond Mr. R. Young's[60] hotel make this their market town, and the merchants and business men of this place are largely interested in retaining their trade. . . .

[59]Thomas Paxton was a sawmill owner, and member of the provincial legislature for the riding of North Ontario.
[60]Young's settlement was about eleven miles east of Lake Couchiching.

F. THE BEGINNINGS OF AGRICULTURAL SETTLEMENT

Proposed Land Companies in the 1830's

F 1   ROBERT SHIRREFF[1] TO VISCOUNT HOWICK[2]
[P.R.O., C.O. 42, v. 412; also printed in P.A.C.,
Report, 1900, pp. 49–51]

London 29th. Septr. 1832

When I had last the honor of an interview with Mr Hay I mentioned that I was very desirous of submitting to His Majestys Government a plan for opening a direct communication between Montreal and Lake Huron by way of the Ottawa, and for settling the neighbouring country and I now beg leave to lay before your Lordship a few observations on the subject.

An undertaking of this kind was first suggested in a pamphlet[3] published in London by my brother in 1824, and both he and my Father have since been at great pains to ascertain the nature of the country with a view to the objects already mentioned. A description of a part of it which the former explored for that purpose at a very considerable expense, and which was previously a blank in the maps, accompanies this.

In countries which have been long occupied, the object for increased facilities to communication is generally to accommodate bodies of population already formed, tho' even in that view, an increased activity of intercourse is always reckoned on in calculating the cost. In more recently settled countries, the object of such facilities is often to encourage, and in some measure to guide the progress of settlement. . . .

. . . Should we unfortunately however, be involved in hostilities with our powerful rival, this short and safe cut to Lake Huron, together with a militia and population of English feelings in that part of Canada, would add greatly to our resources; whereas without them, a reference to the maps will at once show that the enemy, by the settlement of his Michigan and North Western Territories, will have turned our flank. . . .

The co-operation necessary on the part of Government and the Legislature, would be the giving at a valuation, and on certain conditions, to a Company either already, or to be formed, an extent of land and a charter that would enable them to combine both the settling effectually that part of the country, with the completing the navigation of the

[1]Robert, son of Charles Shirreff of Fitzroy Harbour.
[2]Sir Henry George Grey, Viscount Howick and afterwards third Earl Grey (1802–94), was undersecretary for War and the Colonies, 1830 to 1833.
[3]This pamphlet has not been identified.

Ottawa as far up, if necessary as Matawowen Bay, and the connecting that river by canals or railroads with the navigable waters between it and Lake Huron, so as to carry forward the line of communication to the latter.

If the writer may venture to hope that his views on this subject accord with those of His Majesty's Government, there are one or two points which he would respectfully state, as appearing to him very important.

The first of these is the delaying, for a short time, to make any grants or sales of land in the Midland District of Upper Canada north of the River Madawaska, in the Newcastle District north of the 45th. degree of latitude, and in the Home District north of the same degree and nearer to the Muskoka river and lake than 3 miles. The late season of the year will prevent this being inconvenient, whereas partial settlements north of the above limits might very much embarass the arrangements with a Company and their subsequent operations.

In the next place that in consideration of the risk and expense of opening this line of communication, an Association willing to undertake it should have the preference in choosing conditionally a tract of land between the Ottawa and Lake Huron, north of the boundary above specified. The extensive space unfit for cultivation immediately in the rear of the present surveyed Townships in the Midland and Newcastle Districts, and the obstructions which the falls and rapids of the Ottawa cause to settlements beyond that space, make it essential to the opening up of the country to the South of Lake Nipissing, that the command of the most desirable part of the land there and the removal of these obstructions should go hand in hand. . . .

F 2   "PROJECTORS OF AN OTTAWA COMPANY" TO
E. G. STANLEY,[4] AUTUMN, 1833
[*P.A.C., Q 219, pt. 2, pp. 300–3*]

To Rt. Hon. Edward G. Stanley, M. P. His Majesty's Principal Secty. of State for the Colonial Dept.

We beg leave on behalf of ourselves, and other gentlemen, connected with the trade of London to make the following representations to His Majesty's Government

Impressed with the expediency of enlarging the inducements to Emigration generally and looking to the numerous class of persons, whom the expiration of the East India Company's charter will immediately throw out of employment, as well as a similar change about to take place in our West India Colonies, it appears to us that Canada affords

[4]Edward George Geoffrey Smith Stanley, later fourteenth Earl of Derby (1799–1869), was Secretary of State for War and the Colonies, 1833–4.

the best Resource for parties who may thus be deprived of their present means of support, and for employing their labour and capital in future.

With this object before us, we have been induced to direct our attention to the settlement of the country on the higher part of the Ottawa, and from the advantages which it would possess, both in a commercial and military point of view, we feel ourselves justified, in soliciting for such an undertaking the favorable consideration of His Majestys Government.

The idea is, to form a Company to carry this desirable object into effect, which by assisting industrious Settlers with small loans, might convert that part of Canada from its present uninhabited and unproductive state, into fertile and populous settlements, and must necessarily lead by the formation of roads, and improvement in the navigation of rivers, to a direct communication between the Ottawa and Lake Huron.

The proposed Settlements would not in any way interfere with the Canada, or North American Land Companies, the operations of the former being confined to the South Western Extremity of Upper Canada and those of the latter, to the Eastern Townships of Lower Canada. In fact the additional influx of capital, and population consequent on the formation of a third Company would enhance the Value of the land belonging to the others.

As it regards the Canadian Lumber trade, the removal of obstructions in rivers and the cultivation of the lands in a part of the Country where the Pine Forests are so extensive would considerably lessen the cost of procuring the timber.

We moreover respectfully suggest that any extensive operations in the proposed line of settlement, must greatly facilitate if not ultimately accomplish the grand object of a direct communication between the Ottawa and Lake Huron, opening a Channel for an extensive Commerce, between Montreal, and the Shores of Lakes Huron, Michigan and Superior. From the information we have obtained of the Country between the former, and the Ottawa to effect this as well as to render that part of Canada accessible to Settlers, a large Capital would be required, which alone can be obtained by the intervention of a Company. This consideration we trust will induce Government to favor the Establishment of an Association for the purpose of carrying into effect a work of such national importance.

For the purpose above stated, a grant would be required in that part of Upper Canada, situated on the Ottawa, Lake Nipissing and the Eastern shore of Lake Huron, and in order to ensure to the Company an equitable remuneration, for any part of their capital which might be expended, either in removing those natural impediments which at present render many parts of the Ottawa unnavigable, or in opening the communication between that river and Lake Huron, it would be necessary to include a strip of Land along the Lower Canada shore. This would be the more expedient as it would prevent the expense and delay which might be occasioned by persons possessing themselves of Land, in the line of the proposed improvements.

F 3   R. W. HAY TO SIR JOSIAH COGHILL[5]
[*P.A.C., Q 219, pt. 2, pp. 257–9*]

Downing Street
11th. November 1833

I am directed by Mr. Secretary Stanley to acknowledge the receipt of your Letter of the 31st. ultimo, and to express to you his regret that the former communication to which it alludes, had accidentally remained unanswered.

I am now to acquaint you that Mr. Stanley has taken into his consideration the plans of the proposed Association, and that the proceedings which they contemplate for the Encouragement of Emigration, appear to him very much to correspond with what is actually done by the Government.— The enclosed notice put forth last year, will shew you that agents for the reception and gratuitous assistance of Emigrants are placed at the principal Ports of disembarkation in the Colonies of North America.— An Agent has also been appointed at Liverpool, and it is possible that officers of the same description may be stationed at the other Ports in the United Kingdom, where there shall appear an exigence for their Services.— Under these circumstances it seems probable that the chief object of the projected association would be sufficiently secured by cooperating with the Government in imparting the necessary information in this Country to persons contemplating Emigration, and by directing them to the Government Agents at home and in the Colonies.

With respect to the disposition of the Gentlemen who propose the formation of the Society to purchase Land — Mr Stanley desires me to acquaint you, that no Land could be sold except for a fixed price, of which the period of payment should also be fixed, and not contingent upon the number of persons whom the Society might be able to settle upon the Allotment.— The extent of the purchase which it is proposed to effect, appears disproportioned to the means which the Association expect to raise, since, in the least favourably situated Districts, Land could not be sold in any of the Colonies, to which Emigrants resort, at a lower price than from three to five Shillings per Acre.— if, however, the Gentlemen who recommend the incorporation of this Society wish to treat for Land to a less extent, Mr. Stanley will be very willing to consider any specific offer which they may make. Subject to the indispensable conditions above described.

[5]Sir Josiah Coghill Coghill, third Bart. (1773–1850).

F 4   THE EARL OF FITZWILLIAM[6] AND OTHERS TO T. SPRING-RICE[7]
[*P.A.C., Q 219, pt. 2, pp. 293–6*]

London 24th. June, 1834.

Two applications being already before His Majesty's Government on the subject of colonizing Lands on the Ottawa, one addressed to the Right Honorable Lord Howick on the 29th. of September 1832 by Mr. Robert Shirreff, and the other to Mr. Secretary Stanley in the Autumn of last year, signed by Mr. Ravenshaw, Mr. Solly and Mr. Douglas on behalf of themselves and others connected with the trade of London; and likewise a representation by Mr. Hamilton, on behalf of the North American Colonization Association of Ireland,[8] dated the 29th. of November 1833;

We now, jointly, beg leave to bring the subject again under the notice of the Colonial department, and to request your early and favorable consideration of it, so as to enable the United Company, proposed to be formed, to take prompt measures properly to prepare in Upper Canada for the reception of Labourers from the United Kingdom, and, in particular from Ireland.

The tract of country which we have in view to colonize with the sanction of His Majesty's Government, is that which lies between the River Ottawa and Lake Huron, to the South of Lake Nipissing, and in the rear of the present Settlements in the Newcastle and Midland districts, but separated from them by an extensive and barren space.— The precise boundaries are more particularly pointed out in the paper[9] and map [10] which accompany this. Although the above tract appears to be extensive, yet it is ascertained that a great proportion of it is land, unfit for cultivation, and much of the surface, water.

We likewise respectfully submit, that as the plan of Emigration which we have in view is an extensive one, embracing the population of Ireland and Scotland, as well as England, a proportionably large tract of land in Canada will be necessary to carry the proposed objects into effect.—

We shall again merely allude to the advantages likely to arise from

[6]Charles William Wentworth Fitzwilliam, third Earl of Fitzwilliam (1786–1857), was a member of the House of Commons from 1807 until his elevation to the peerage in 1833. He was an advocate of parliamentary reform and the repeal of the Corn Laws.

[7]Thomas Spring-Rice, later Baron Monteagle of Brandon in Kerry (1790–1866), was Secretary of State for War and the Colonies for a few months in 1834.

[8]The North American Colonial Association of Ireland was formed as the result of a meeting called July 21, 1833, to consider emigration. The President was the Earl of Fitzwilliam, and the association was closely related to the English company called the North American Colonial Association, of which Sir Josiah Coghill Coghill was chairman for a time.

[9]See F 5.

[10]See map by Maria Knowles, Plate III.

the above mentioned part of Canada being occupied by a body of Settlers closely connected with the Mother-Country, and attached to its institutions; and likewise to the tendency which these Settlements must have, to establish a direct communication between Montreal and Lake Huron, by the way of the Ottawa; and to increase, not only the internal trade of the Canadas, but likewise their commercial intercourse with those flourishing parts of the United States, the Michigan and North Western Territories.—

Should Government be pleased favorably to entertain this proposal, the projected Company is intended to embrace the Irish Association already alluded to, the whole to be conducted under the control of a Board of Directors in London, consisting of a Governor, Deputy Governor and ten Directors, with Branch Committees in Ireland and Scotland. The London Board to consist of English, Irish and Scotch Gentlemen.— The Committees in Scotland and Ireland to be formed of Gentlemen of those countries respectively.

It is intended to invite Sir Josiah C. Coghill, Bart., George A. Hamilton, Thomas Popham Luscombe, Robert Rowe, and Thomas Wilson, Esquires, as a temporary committee for Ireland to assist in carrying into effect the objects of this application. . . .

F 5   TRACT OF LAND PROPOSED TO BE COLONIZED, JUNE 24, 1834[11]
[*P.A.C., Q 219, pt. 2, pp. 297–9*]

The Tract of Land proposed to be colonized, in connection with the improvement of the Navigation of the Ottawa River, may be traced on the accompanying map[12] as follows.

First, the ungranted Land in the Island formed by the Canadian Mississippi, near Fitzroy Harbour,[13] being about 1500 acres; here immediate steps would be taken to form a Town as a depôt and resting place for the Settlers, and, where by the establishment of regular markets the new comers would be supplied by the old colonists with their produce.

Second, The ungranted Lands in the Township of Horton (excepting the Crown and Clergy Reserves):— thence from the North West corner of the said Township, then by its north line extended to the depth of a Township; then by a line touching the said extended line at a right angle and terminating where it shall touch the River Bonnechere or Norway Lake Then along the middle of the River Bonnechere or Norway Lake, to the head of said Lake, and from thence to Lake Ronde, and along the middle of it to its head;— from thence to the South-west end of Lake Pittoiwais; from thence to the head waters of the Muskoka, near Cranberry Marsh; thence down the middle of the

[11]Dated from covering letter F 4.
[12]See Plate III.
[13]Fitzroy Harbour was the home of the Shirreff family.

Muskoka water to Lake Huron:— From the mouth of the Muskoka along the shore of Lake Huron to the head of a deep bay or sound about twelve miles West of the French River, being part of what is called Collins's Sound.— From the head of the above Bay or Sound to the North West point of Lake Nipissing; then along the north shore of said Lake to its North-East point: then from said point by a line drawn so as to touch the North End of the largest Turtle Lake; and extended 'till it touch the Ottawa, above Mattawowen Bay.

In Lower Canada, the boundary would be as follows: . . .

The Space thus described is coloured *Pink* in the map.

F 6   NORTH AMERICAN COLONIAL ASSOCIATION TO EARL OF
ABERDEEN,[14] MARCH 2, 1835[15]
[*P.A.C., Q 224, pt. 2, pp. 479–90*]

To the Right Honorable the Earl of Aberdeen His Majestys Secretary of State for the Colonies. &c &c &c

The memorial of the undersigned, The President, Vice President, Governor, Deputy Governor, and Directors of the North American Colonial Association. Respectfully Sheweth.—

That your memorialists have witnessed for a Series of years the deplorable State of this Country, and the destitution and misery of thousands of its inhabitants, who have been thereby driven to the daily commission of crime, and become the ready instruments in the promotion of disturbance and disaffection.

That your memorialists have reason to believe that much of this wretched condition of the people of Ireland may be attributed to the state of population which far exceeds the present means and opportunity of employment in this Country, and therefore that relief will be most readily and most effectually given by a well regulated and extensive system of Emigration.

That these sentiments having met with the hearty concurrence of many of the most influential and intelligent persons of this Country, the North American Colonial Association has been formed, with a view to encourage and facilitate Emigration, and also to improve the System on which it has hitherto been conducted.

That at this moment there are many thousands of poor in Ireland, who feeling that they have no opportunity at home of employing their Industry which is their only capital, have the wish without the power to emigrate, that there are others who anxious to better their condition, are enabled barely to raise as much money as will provide them with a passage to America. That of these latter a great proportion sail in vessels so ill found and ill provided, that they either perish at sea, or arrive

[14]George Hamilton Gordon, fourth Earl of Aberdeen (1784–1860), was Secretary of State for War and the Colonies from December, 1834 to April, 1835.
[15]The memorial is undated but the covering letter is March 2, 1835.

in a foreign land the victims of disease, and with few exceptions, those who reach the ports of America, are reduced to wretchedness and despair, from a want of the means to employ or the information to direct their energies. . . .

That your memorialists further state, that the Association was brought under the notice of Lord Stanley, when he was at the Head of the Colonial Department, and his Lordship approving of its plans and objects, consented to make a grant on fair terms of a tract of not less than 500.000 Acres of land, for the operation of the then proposed Capital of £200.000— That in consequence of His Lordships Resignation of that office, a deputation proceeded from Dublin to London, last May, in order to enter into treaty with Mr. Spring Rice, his successor in office, when it was then suggested to the Noblemen and gentlemen interested in the Success of the Association, that a mixed Settlement of English, Irish and Scotch, would be more beneficial to the Empire and the Colony than one exclusively Irish.

That in consequence of this Suggestion, an application was made to the then Secretary of State for the Colonies, on the part of this association together with several highly influential English and Scotch Capitalists, who expressed themselves favorable to the formation of an Imperial Association; and a proposal under date of the 24th June last, was drawn up by the London gentlemen, Signed by the Noblemen and gentlemen named in the margin, and submitted to Mr. Secretary Spring Rice proposing to purchase a tract of unappropriated Forest Land, lying between the River Ottawa and Lake Huron in Upper Canada, and to which proposal memorialists respectfully beg leave to refer your Lordship.

That the District in question has been selected as a proper Site for the proposed new Settlement, for many reasons of which the following may be mentioned; It is at present wholly unappropriated. It is situated at a considerable distance from the Territories of the Canada Company and of the American Land Company, and cannot therefore interfere with their prosperity. It borders upon the Ottawa one of the largest Rivers in that Continent, and the most capable of the greatest improvement in its navigation, which being extended through Lake Nipissing, and along the French River to Lake Huron, would afford the greatest facilities for commercial intercourse to the Inhabitants of that portion of Canada. . . .

Your memorialists beg leave to submit to your Lordship, and His Majestys government: that in order to effect these great objects a fair return for Capital is a legitimate expectation, and without being able to hold out such an inducement subscribers for the necessary Capital could not be had, and consequently the primary objects of your memorialists vizt. that of releiving the country from the effects of a superabundant unemployed population would fail. . . .

. . . Memorialists beg also to intimate their hopes, that His Majestys Government will be pleased to grant a charter to incorporate the Association so soon as the usual portion of the Capital necessary for the undertaking shall be Subscribed, and an instalment of ten per cent paid to the trustees, and likewise, that His Majestys Government will give its support to a Bill to limit the liability of individual Shareholders, to the amount of capital for which each may subscribe, and will afford generally toward this Association the same facilities and accommodations which have been so largely conceded to the American Land Companies already established.— It is extremely gratifying to memoralists to be enabled to acquaint your Lordship and His Majestys Government that intense anxiety prevails amongst the population where branch societies have been formed to avail themselves of the advantages and facilities promised to be given to Emigrants by your memorialists, it is therefore of the first consequence, that memorialists and the Directors of local Branches, should be enabled to give effect to the expectations which have been thus raised of speedy and certain relief. . . .

Fitzwilliam President

Vice Presidents H. Winston Barron, F. Ponsonby, Rob. Chaloner, H. Bruen, John Rowe, Robt. Hughes.

Directors—Josiah Coghill Coghill, Govr, Rich H. Wall W. W. Fitzwm Hume, Dep Govr. E. Hayes, Walter Berwick, D. Henchy

[Names added in margin:] The Earl of Fitzwilliam, Earl of Gosford, Viscount Clifden, Lord Bishop of Derry, Sir Robt. Ferguson, Major Genl. Sir R. Dundas, Alderman Copeland, Colonel Percival, Colonel Verner, Mr. Barron, Mr. Ravenshaw, Mr. Edgar, Mr. Gordon Duff, Mr. Chas. Douglas, Mr. Hawthorne, Mr. McGarry, Mr. Reid, Mr. Chaloner, Mr. White, Mr. Sheriffe, Mr. Henry Hobhouse.

F 7   FINAL REPLY OF LORD ABERDEEN TO J. G. RAVENSHAW
[*P.A.C., Q 224, pt. 3, p. 746*]

Downing Street
April 1835.

I am directed by the Earl of Aberdeen to acknowledge the receipt of your letter of the 8 Instant on the Subject of the proposed Land Company on the Ottawa, and urging upon his Lordship's notice the inconveniences which may result from any delay in coming to a favourable decision upon this question. In answer I am to observe that you have entirely mistaken Lord Aberdeen's meaning in supposing that his Lordship looked upon the establishment of the proposed Company as a measure which was only deferred until some future period. On the contrary it was the intention of my letter of the 2d. Instant to convey to you the conviction to which his Lordship had been led by a consideration of the documents connected with the Subject, that it is not expedient to establish any new Land Company whatever in Canada.

The Opening of Muskoka and Haliburton

F 8   "AN ACT TO AMEND THE LAW FOR THE SALE AND THE
SETTLEMENT OF THE PUBLIC LANDS"[16]
[*Canada*, Statutes, *1852–3, 16 Vic., c. 159*]

(*Assented to 14th June, 1853.*)

Whereas it is expedient to amend the Law concerning the Sale and Settlement of the Public Lands: Be it therefore enacted by the Queen's Most Excellent Majesty, by and with the advice and consent of the Legislative Council and of the Legislative Assembly of the Province of Canada . . .

. . .

II. Except as hereinafter provided, no free grant of Public Land shall be made to any person whomsoever.

. . .

IV. The Governor in Council may from time to time fix the price per acre of the Public Lands, and the terms of settlement and payment.

. . .

IX. Notwithstanding any thing in this Act contained, it shall and may be lawful for the Governor of this Province, with the advice of the Executive Council, to appropriate as free grants any Public Lands in this Province to actual settlers, upon or in the vicinity of any Public Roads in any new settlements, which shall or may be opened through the Lands of the Crown, under such regulations respecting such settlements as shall from time to time be made and declared by the Governor of this Province in Council: Provided always, that no free grant shall exceed one hundred acres.

. . .

F 9   APPOINTMENTS OF CROWN LAND AGENTS
[*P.A.C., State Book T, pp. 115–16*]

10th September 1858.

On a Report from the Hon. the Commissioner of Crown Lands, dated 25th August 1858, recommending that Mr. Richard Hughes, who has been employed by the Bureau of Agriculture in making the Bobcaygeon Road (to be opened for free grants by Order in Council of the 4th. of May 1857) be appointed Agent for the settlement of the said line of Road, and also Agent for the sale and settlement of the lands in the

[16]This is the act under which sales of Crown lands, and free grants on public roads, were made in Muskoka and Haliburton before 1868.

adjoining Townships, vizt.:—Somerville, Galway, Snowdon, Lutterworth, Mindon, Anson, Stanhope and Hindon, partly in the County of Peterboro', and partly in that of Victoria.

And further, that Mr. G.M. Roche, of Lindsay, be appointed agent for the sale of public lands for the remainder of the County of Victoria, in the place of Mr. Walter Crawford who is at present Agent for the United Counties of Peterboro' and Victoria, but whose great age and place of residence render it extremely inconvenient for intending Settlers in Victoria to do business with him.

The Committee advise that the appointment of Mr. Richard Hughes and Mr. G.M. Roche as recommended by the Commissioner of Crown Lands be approved.

F 10   DRAPER AND MACAULAY OPENED FOR SALE
[*Toronto*, Canada Gazette, *July 23, 1859*]

Crown Lands Department,
Toronto, 15th July, 1859.

Notice is hereby given that the Lands in the Townships of Draper and Macaulay, in the County of Victoria, U.C., will be open for sale on and after the SEVENTEENTH of NEXT MONTH.

For lists of the lots and conditions of sale, apply to G.M. Roche, Esquire, Crown Land Agent, at Lindsay, in the Township of Ops.

Andrew Russell,
Assistant Commissioner.

F 11   MUSKOKA TOWNSHIP OPENED FOR SALE
[*Toronto*, Canada Gazette, *July 23, 1859*]

Crown Lands Department,
Toronto, 22nd July, 1859.

Notice is hereby given, that the lands in the Township of Muskoka, in the County of Simcoe, U.C., will be open for sale on and after the TWENTY-FOURTH of NEXT MONTH.

For lists of the lots and conditions of sale, apply to John Alexander, Esquire, Crown Land Agent, at Barrie.

Andrew Russell,
Assistant Commissioner.

F 12   TOWNSHIP OF MINDEN OPENED FOR SALE
[*Toronto*, Canada Gazette, *July 30, 1859*]

Crown Lands Department,
Toronto, 29th July, 1859.

Notice is hereby given that the lands in the Township of Minden, in the County of Peterborough, U.C., will be open for Sale, on and after the TWENTY-FOURTH of NEXT MONTH.

For lists of the lots, and conditions of sale, apply to Richard Hughes, Esquire, Crown Land Agent, at Bobcaygeon, in the township of Verulam.

Andrew Russell,
Assistant Commissioner.

F 13   APPOINTMENT OF R. J. OLIVER, AGENT FOR SETTLEMENT OF THE SEVERN AND MUSKOKA ROAD
[*Toronto*, Canada Gazette, *August 20, 1859*]

Crown Lands Department,
Toronto, 19th August, 1859.

Notice is hereby given that His Excellency the Governor General[17] has been pleased to appoint Richard Jose Oliver, Esquire, (to reside for the present at Orillia) Agent for the settlement of the Severn and Muskoka Road, upon which grants, limited to one hundred acres, will be made, subject to actual settlement.

F 14   SIMCOE COUNTY MEMORIAL ON LAND SALES
[*Simcoe County, Municipal Council,* Proceedings, *June, 1865, pp. 67–8*]

To His Excellency the Governor General, &c.,
The Memorial of the Municipal Council of the Corporation of the County of Simcoe, in Council assembled,
RESPECTFULLY SHEWETH,
   That your Memorialists consider that the manner in which the farming lands in this Province have, and are being disposed of by the Crown has been injurious to the best interests, and materially retards the progress and settlement of the country.
   They feel satisfied that the giving of free grants of land, with proper conditions as to actual settlement, is the true policy by which the government of a new country should be guided in the disposal of its lands, inasmuch as rapid settlement tends more than anything else to increase the wealth and material prosperity of the community, and by increasing the numbers of contributors to the public exchequer more than makes up, in a pecuniary point of view, for the increased direct outlay which would in such a case have to be made in connection with the Crown Lands Department. Your Memorialists, while regretting the great injury which they believe to have accrued to the province from the policy pursued in respect to this important matter in times past, consider that even now some advantage might be gained by adopting the system, which they would beg respectfully to recommend to your Excellency's

[17]Sir Edmund Walker Head, Baronet (1805–1868), Governor General of Canada, 1854 to 1861.

best consideration. They would, therefore, suggest that all Crown Lands in Upper Canada which are yet at the disposal of the Crown, and of the ordinary description suitable for farming purposes, and not above the actual value $4 per acre, shall in the future, be offered for sale at a nominal price, sufficient to cover the expenses of survey, to the same description of purchasers, but accompanied by the most stringent regulations as to actual settlement; and further that all lands not occupied, or held by actual settlers, the purchase money of which is in arrears to the Crown, shall be declared forfeited so soon as the same can be legally done, and at once offered for settlement as an encouragement to immigration; and to obtain for settlement a large quantity of the wild lands of the province now held by speculators to the great injury of the agricultural interests of the country.

Your Memorialists would further suggest for the consideration of your Excellency in Council the advisability of relieving settlers in backward townships, such as Morrison and Muskoka, and others recently opened for settlement, in this part of the province, with scant means of making money, and living a long distance from market, from the payment of arrears on their lands where certain improvements have been or shall be made thereon within a specified time, as your Memorialists have reason to believe that such settlers are greatly in need of encouragement and assistance, and are prevented from exerting themselves in making improvements to the extent that they otherwise might do, by the consciousness of having a claim hanging over them with its accumulating interest that they see no prospect of being able to pay.

Your Memorialists feel satisfied that the adoption of the suggestions which they have taken the liberty to make, would tend to the advantage of this province, and meet with the general approbation of all classes, and humbly trust that they may receive the early and best consideration of your Excellency in Council.

And your Memorialists as in duty bound will ever pray.

F 15   "AN ACT TO SECURE FREE GRANTS AND HOMESTEADS TO
       ACTUAL SETTLERS ON THE PUBLIC LANDS"
       [*Ontario*, Statutes, *1867–8, 31 Vic., c. 8*]

(*Assented to 28th February, 1868.*)

Her Majesty, by and with the advice and consent of the Legislative Assembly of the Province of Ontario, enacts as follows:—

1. This Act shall be called and known as "The Free Grants and Homestead Act of 1868," and may be so cited or designated in all Acts or proceedings whatsoever.

. . .

4. The Lieutenant-Governor in Council may appropriate any Public Lands considered suitable for settlement and cultivation, and not being Mineral Lands or Pine Timber Lands, as Free Grants to actual Settlers, under such regulations as shall from time to time be made by Order in Council, not inconsistent with the provisions of this Act.

5. Such grants or appropriations shall be confined to lands surveyed or hereafter to be surveyed, situate within the tract or territory composed of the Districts of Algoma and Nipissing, and of the lands lying between the Ottawa River and the Georgian Bay, to the west of a line drawn from a point opposite the south-east angle of the Township of Palmerston north-westerly along the western boundaries of the Townships of North Sherbrooke, Lavant, Blithfield, Admaston, Bromley, Stafford and Pembroke to the Ottawa River, and to the north of the rear or northerly boundaries of the Townships of Oso, Olden, Kennebec, Kaladar, Elzevir, Madoc, Marmora, Belmont, Dummer, Smith, Ennismore, Somerville, Laxton, Carden, Rama, and of the River Severn.

. . .

7. No person shall be located for any land under this Act or said regulations unless such person shall be of the age of eighteen years or upwards, nor shall any person be so located for any greater quantity than one hundred acres.[18]

. . .

9. No patent shall issue for any land located under this Act or under said regulations until the expiration of five years from the date of such location, nor unless nor until the Locatee or those claiming under him or her or some of them shall have performed the following settlement duties, that is to say: shall have cleared and have under cultivation at least fifteen acres of the said land, whereof at least two acres shall be cleared and cultivated annually during the five years next after the date of the location, to be computed from such date, and have built a house thereon fit for habitation at least sixteen feet by twenty feet, and shall have actually and continuously resided upon and cultivated the said land for the term of five years next succeeding the date of such location, and from thence up to the issue of the Patent, except that the Locatee shall be allowed one month from the date of the location to enter upon and occupy the land, and that absence from the said land for in all not more than six months during any one year (to be computed from the date of the location) shall not be held to be a cessation of such residence, provided such land be cultivated as aforesaid.

[18]This was amended to two hundred acres by "An Act to Amend 'The Free Grants and Homestead Act of 1868'," 32 Vic., c. 20, 1868–9. An extra allowance of land was also given on request to compensate for rocky areas.

On failure, in performance of the settlement duties aforesaid, the location shall be forfeited, and all right of the Locatee, or of any one claiming under him or her, in the land, shall cease.

10. All Pine trees growing or being upon any land so located, and all gold, silver, copper, lead, iron, or other mines or minerals, shall be considered as reserved from said location, and shall be the property of Her Majesty, except that the Locatee or those claiming under him or her, may cut and use such trees as may be necessary for the purpose of building, fencing, and fuel, on the land so located, and may also cut and dispose of all trees required to be removed, in actually clearing said land for cultivation, but no pine trees (except for the necessary building, fencing, and fuel as aforesaid,) shall be cut beyond the limit of such actual clearing before the issuing of the Patent, and all pine trees so cut and disposed of (except for the necessary building, fencing, and fuel as aforesaid,) shall be subject to the payment of the same dues, as are at the time payable by the holders of licenses to cut timber or saw logs. All trees remaining on the land at the time the Patent issues, shall pass to the Patentee.

. . .

F 16   "NOTICE[19] TO IMMIGRANTS & SETTLERS"
[P.A.O., Immigration Papers, Miscellaneous]

Department of Crown Lands,
Toronto, 18th April, 1868.

Notice is hereby given, that the Lands in the Townships of Humphrey, Cardwell, Watt, Stephenson, Brunel, Macaulay, McLean, Muskoka, and Draper, in the Territorial District of Muskoka, and in the Townships of McDougall and Foley, in Parry Sound, (Georgian Bay), are open for location under "The Free Grants and Homestead Act of 1868."

Applications for locations in the Townships of McDougall, Foley, Humphrey, and Cardwell, are to be made to John D. Beatty,[20] Esq Crown Land Agent, at the Village of Parry Sound; and for locations in the Townships of Watt, Stephenson, Brunel, Macaulay, McLean, Muskoka and Draper, applications are to be made to C. W. Lount[21] Esq. Crown Lands Agent at Bracebridge, in the Township of Macaulay.

[19]This is a government notice inserted in newspapers. Text is from an unidentified newspaper (P.A.O., Immigration Papers).
[20]John D. Beatty resigned his position as Crown Land Agent on August 17, 1875, and was replaced by Thomas McMurray.
[21]Charles W. Lount (d. 1890) was the son of George Lount, a land surveyor at Orillia. He lived at Bracebridge and held a number of offices including that of Crown Land Agent, Registrar, and Stipendiary Magistrate.

Locatees, in addition to obtaining the Free Grant of 100 acres, will be allowed to purchase an additional 100 acres, at 50 cents an acre, cash, subject to the same reservations and conditions, and the performance of the same settlement duties as are provided in respect of free grant locations by the 9th and 10th sections of the Free Grant Act, except that actual residence and building on the land purchased will not be required.

For further information respecting the conditions on which the lands will be granted apply to the above named Crown Lands Agents, or to the Department at Toronto.

S. Richards,
Commissioner of Crown Land.

Note.— The Route to Parry Sound is by the Northern Railway to Collingwood, and thence by steamer, once a week to the Sound; and to Bracebridge by the Northern Railway to Barrie or Bell Ewart, thence by steamer on Lake Simcoe (daily) to Washago, on the river Severn, and by stage thence to Gravenhurst, on Lake Muskoka, and by steamer on the lake and river to Bracebridge.

Department of Crown Lands,
Toronto, 10th June, 1868.

Notice is hereby given, that part of the Lands in the Townships of Cardiff, Chandos, Monmouth and Anstruther, in the County of Peterborough, are open for location under the provisions of the Free Grants and Homestead Act of 1868.

Applications for locations are to be made to Wheeler Armstrong,[22] Esq. Crown Lands Agent in the Township of Cardiff.

Locatees, in addition to obtaining the Free Grant of 100 acres will be allowed to purchase an additional 100 acres at 50 cents an acre, cash, subject to the same reservations and conditions, and the performance of the same settlement duties as are provided in respect of free grant locations by the 9th and 10th sections of the Free Grants Act except that actual residence and building on the land purchased will not be required.

For further information respecting the conditions on which the lands will be granted apply to the above named Crown Lands Agent, or to the Department at Toronto.

S. Richards
Commissioner of Crown Lands.

September, 1869.

[22]Wheeler Armstrong of the Township of Cardiff was appointed agent for location of free grants and sale of public land in Cardiff, Monmouth, Chandos, Anstruther, and Burleigh, 1868.

F 17   Monck Township, Petition[23] that Arrears on
Lands be Cancelled
[*P.A.O., Ontario Sessional Papers, Petitions, 1870–1, no. 11*]

To the Honourable The Legislative Assembly of Ontario in Parliament
Assembled
The petition of the Municipal Council of the Township of Monck in
Council assembled as well as of the undersigned inhabitants
Respectfully Sheweth

1st. That the hardy pioneers who first entered into the woods of the
said Township with axes on their shoulders to carve out a home
for themselves had to contend with the greatest hardships, many
even depriving themselves of the necessaries of life in order that
they might pay an instalment upon their land in order to secure
the same thus crippling the already too limited means of all, considering the hardships they had to contend with, viz want of roads,
loss of crops and other casualties which are incident to a new
settlement in the backwoods, whereas those who are now locating
under the Free Grant Act not only reap all the advantages attend-
ant upon the progress of the settlement but also get their land free,
Therefore it would simply be a matter of Justice to cancel all
arrearages upon the lands in the District of Muskoka, and issue
patents for the same upon the due performance of the settlement
duties,

2nd. That as our neighbouring Government is still holding out great
inducements to emigrants, it is highly important that similar inducements should be given to those loyal and patriotic subjects
who have borne the burden and heat of the day and who would
endure the same difficulties twice over, sooner than seek shelter in
a foreign land where politicks and oath of naturalization are dia-
metrically opposite to that of our beloved country,

3rd. That the original settlers in this District are not able to pay up the
aforementioned arrearages without serious injury to themselves and
families thereby retarding the advancement of the settlement,

4th. That the District is considerably broken by ridges of rock rendering the concession and side lines in many places impassable therefore it is of great importance that right of road should be reserved
through all lots for which the patents are not yet issued in order
that the several municipal councils may obtain deviations from the
original lines wherever it is found necessary, without having to pay
for them as they are now compelled to do,

Your petitioners therefore pray
That your Honourable assembly will take the matter into your earnest

[23]Presented to the Legislative Assembly by A. P. Cockburn, December 9, 1870.
Similar petitions were presented by other townships on the subject, and a memo-
rial was addressed to the Lieutenant Governor in Council by the Simcoe County
Council (Simcoe County, Municipal Council, *Proceedings*, June, 1870, pp. 20–1).

consideration and cancel all arrearages in this District of Muskoka issuing patents for all lands upon which the settlement duties have been duly performed and lastly reserving right of way through all lands affected by this petition in the same manner as through Free Grant Lands, and your petitioners as in duty bound will ever pray

The Settlement of Muskoka

F 18   THE MUSKOKA ROAD OPENED FOR SETTLEMENT
[*Canada, Department of Crown Lands*, Report, *1859, pp. 18, 74–75*]

. . . The Muskoka road leading from Lake Simcoe to the High Falls on the river Muskoka was open for settlement during the past year, and in the month of August last Mr. Jose Oliver was appointed resident agent. He has reported 54 locations. Most of the locatees have taken possession of their lots, and have built shanties and made small clearings. The lands on this road are not generally of so good a quality as on the other Colonization Roads, but they are easily accessible by the Northern Railway[24] and steamer on Lake Simcoe, and the road itself was undertaken, and has been completed, as a most important means of communication,— leading as it does from the head of the navigable waters of Lake Simcoe into the interior of the country, and meeting the great leading road now nearly completed,[25] which connects the river Ottawa at Farrell's Point with the Georgian Bay. . . .

Crown Lands Department   P.M. Vankoughnet
Quebec, February 28, 1860.   Commissioner

Appendix 28
R.J. OLIVER'S REPORT ON THE MUSKOKA ROAD.

A great number of lots are registered for by parties from a distance, who could not bring on their families this Winter, but have promised to do so in the Spring. These are a better class of settlers whom I have favored as an alternative. In most cases I have got them to commence chopping.

Several of those about to settle will also purchase Crown Lands in the rear, and have chosen their front lots with that object in view. Some of them have desired me to get Crown Lands secured for them, preparatory to their purchasing them in the Spring.

The settlers already in are a mixture of Irish, English and Scotch, with three Germans; and upon the whole are intelligent and apparently industrious— the Symington family[26] especially. Steps are being taken

24To Bell Ewart.
25This is an exaggeration. See *supra*, lxviii.
26Early settlers in Morrison Township.

to secure a post delivery[27] once a week. On my journey up the Road last week, this was universally called for, and I have promised to see to it. A subscription has also been entered into for building a school-house and a house for Public worship, which will be accomplished in the Spring.

The "rock" prejudices are giving way, and the settlers generally are satisfied that their homes will ultimately become profitable to them, looking to the probability of the road being extended into the better land Northeast of them, and thereby creating a large tract of agricultural and milling country.

F 19   R. J. OLIVER, REPORT ON FREE GRANTS ON THE SEVERN AND MUSKOKA ROAD
[*Canada, Bureau of Agriculture and Statistics,* Report, *1860*]

Orillia, Jan. 10th, 1861.

I have the honor to submit the subjoined statement as marking the progress on the free grants on the *Severn and Muskoka Road,* to the 31st *December,* 1860.

The shortness of the time since its settlement, and the necessarily brief Report of last year, (the road then only being a few months opened up) makes this the *first* regular Report of Progress; and although the data are still comparatively meagre, yet they afford tangible evidence of the development and incipient growth of a country that, a little over two years since, could boast of neither habitation nor name.

GENERAL PROGRESS[28]

Number of lots located	48
Number of actual settlers	41
Total population	190
Houses built	15
Shanties built	37
Stables and outhouses	15

Houses built in 1860	12
Shanties	12
Stables, &c.	10
Number of acres cleared	170
Number of acres cropped	87

NATIONALITY

English	9
Irish	14
Scotch	11
German	4
Canadian	3

[27]In his report for 1861 Oliver said: "There are in operation now two offices, one at the Severn and the other at the Great Falls of Muskoka."

[28]These figures cover free grant lands only.

AVERAGE YIELD OF CROPS.

Crop	Acres	Bushels to acre	Total bushels	Price	$	¢
Wheat,	25 acres,	25 bushels to acre,	525 bushels at	90c	$ 472	50
Oats,	7 ”	30 ” ”	210 ”	30	63	00
Peas,	¼ ”		10 ”	50	5	00
Barley,	¾ ”		35 ”	70	24	50
Potatoes,	30 ”	200 ” ”	6000 ”	30	1800	00
Corn,	4 ”	25 ” ”	100 ”	40	40	00
Turnips,	20 ”	170 ” ”	3400 ”	20	680	00
Maple sugar, 750 lbs.				10	75	00
Molasses, 59 gallons				75	43	05
Garden produce					199	00
Shingles, 50,000				125	62	50
					3464	55

GENERAL STOCK.

Horned cattle	33
Horses	7
Pigs	15
Poultry	153

The crops of wheat and oats given above is a maximum average, but the smallness of the returns will not of course admit of an elaborate deduction.

The yield of the free grants do not alone convey a full estimate of what has been done on the Severn and Muskoka Road, for it must be borne in mind that considerable accession to the settlement has been made since harvest, and whose industry therefore will not be apparent until the close of the present season. The Pioneers, however, have done much to render their position comfortable in many ways that cannot be reduced to figures.

One drawback has, this year, been partly remedied in the improvement of the road from the village of Orillia to the Severn Bridge, though much more requires to be done to make it a convenient highway for the extensive transit growing out of the settlement. The township council of Orillia, appreciating the importance of the trade of the settlement, last year appropriated a small sum for repairing the road, but its condition is such, teams not being able to pass over it in spring and fall— that several years must expire before the road can be made a good one if dependent on the small amounts at the disposal of the Council. The settlement suffers in consequence, whereas $200 or $300, added to the grants of the Council, would make the road at once an available one. If there is a public fund from which the money could be granted, its investment in this case would be a great and an immediate gain to the settlement.

In the season of navigation the necessity for the road is not so much felt, as Lake Couchiching affords easy access to within 2 miles of the bridge; but the transit has to be made in small boats, and a melancholy casualty last summer, resulting in the drowning of four of the settlers, has created a feeling of aversion among many to travelling by water, and hence confine themselves to the road.

The improvements made on the Severn and Muskoka Road this year, have done much to induce settlers and others to explore the back country; and on the new road, now nearly completed, through the township of Draper— (which is intended to connect with the Bobcaygeon Road)— and also on the newly surveyed road northward, on each of which large districts of excellent land are found, so that already, when scarcely more than surveyed, applications are made daily for free grants — (which it is presumed will be made)— and for crown lands in Draper and Macaulay, which however, are not within my present jurisdiction. Over fifty lots have been asked for, and so anxious are they to secure them, that several persons have squatted down this winter in order to make sure of them. From personal observation, corroborated by those of others, I will venture to affirm, that in no district in Canada are the same advantages to be obtained as here— when good land, the moderate price set on it, water and market privileges, and other considerations are taken into account.

At the commencement of the Road, Severn Bridge, Morrison Township, is the nucleus of a thriving village. A well kept tavern, two stores, a weekly post, a school house in building adjacently— (which is intended also for a place of worship, services being now occasionally performed by a minister from Orillia)— together with a number of families settled on the crown lands in the rear, among which are some mechanics following their respective avocations,— are indications warranting the assertion I have made.

I would suggest to your consideration the reservation of a village Plot[29] near the Great Falls of Muskoka, either on the East or West side of the River. There are many natural advantages that must ensure its becoming a centre of business as the diverging roads get settled— together with the superiority of land around in each direction, and its proximity to Muskoka Lake. The vast amount of water power can be easily applied to all practical purposes. Here, too, Peterson's Line, which intersects the other Colonial Roads, will be connected by the Draper Road, and by a further extension, an outlet to Lake Huron will be formed from the Muskoka Road— thus creating a great centre of travel at the Falls. So thoroughly convinced is every one who visits this beautiful and picturesque locality of its becoming a place of business, that many respectable and enterprising men are determined to settle there when the roads are fully opened— well knowing that the Muskoka Road, from its close connection with Lakes Huron and Simcoe, and the Northern Railroad to Toronto, must ultimately be the outlet of an extensive population.

The health of the settlement has been unexceptionable— no sickness

---

[29]A village plot was laid out here by W. H. Deane and known as South Falls or Muskokaville, and later as Muskoka Falls. It was soon surpassed, however, by Bracebridge which was about three miles away.

of any kind and perfectly free from malarious influences. The settlers are in general happy and contented, feeling satisfied that the efforts they put forth here will yield them a return as ample as are the expectations they have formed.

The settlement enjoys advantages not often met with in new districts. Orillia village, an excellent market, and within a day's travel from Toronto, is only 14 miles distant, and in summer can be reached by 2 miles land travel. Fish and game are abundant. Lumber for building can be obtained, within 2 miles, for about $4 50 per 1000 feet. A mill is now ready for work 2½ miles on the road from the Bridge, and another mill is erecting on the same stream near Sparrow Lake, to which a run of stones for gristing will be added. The latter is on the Crown Lands, in Morrison, where about fifty lots have been squatted on, waiting for the land to be brought into the market. These settlers have built good houses on most of their lots, and appear generally in the possession of means. They cropped the past season about 63 acres, yielding fine samples of grain and roots. About 40 head of cattle are owned by them, and they are steadily receiving accessions to their members.

I might mention here that on the free grants samples of spring wheat were grown equal to any in the County of Simcoe. The potatoes also were superb— large and dry, and the yield equal to any I have ever seen. I have a white turnip in my possession, grown on lot No. 9 East Morrison, that weighs 32½ lbs— the largest, I believe, ever grown in Canada.

In conclusion, I would beg to draw your attention to the advantages to be derived by establishing a Crown Land Agency in connection with the free grants, in this place, immediately connected with the Muskoka Road, embracing, at present, the townships of Morrison, Muskoka, Draper and Macaulay. Seekers for land on the road very naturally suppose that all particulars can be learned at this Agency; and frequently when registering for a free lot, desire also to purchase Crown Lands in the rear. In the case of the two former, I have to refer them to Barrie; and the two latter, to Lindsay. For three quarters of the year Orillia is alone the natural— because accessible— point of ingress and egress for the settlement, as at present; and will become still more important when the Roads connecting with the Severn and Muskoka Road are completed, affording, as it does, the only direct route to the central City of Upper Canada, Toronto. Lindsay, at no time of the year, can be conveniently reached by the settlers, or intending settlers, in Draper and Macaulay, there being no direct or convenient road thereto; thus entailing upon them more trouble and expense than they will readily encounter; whereas Orillia is at all times easily reached, and, only at such a distance from the remotest part of the Road as can be travelled over in one day. Another reason, that with much force might be adduced, is the fact, that the Crown Lands in these townships have a condition attached to them different from other Crown Lands— that of *absolute settlement,* and hence require such a jurisdiction as is now exercised over free grants to ensure its enforcement.

This matter is capable of much enlargement, but I simply desire to draw your attention to it, in obedience to demands made upon me, knowing it will receive that consideration it deserves.

The Postage account of the Agency from August, 1859, to 31st December, 1860, is $16 90.

F 20   OLIVER, REPORT ON THE MUSKOKA ROAD, 1862
[*Canada, Department of Crown Lands,* Report, *1862*]

CROWN LANDS AGENCY
ORILLIA, December 31st 1862.

I have the honor to submit a report of the general improvements on the Muskoka Road, up to 31st December 1862.

FREE GRANTS.

Number of lots located	99
Actual settlers	76
Total population	287
Houses	39
Shanties	49
Barns and outhouses	49
Lumber mill	1
Acres cleared	275
Acres chopped	165
Houses built in 1862	5
Barns, &c	31

NATIONALITY.

Irish	116
English	73
Scotch	65
Canadians	19
French	5
Germans	8
American	1
	287
Increase during the year	38

LIVE STOCK.

Horses	8
Cattle	36
Cows	25
Pigs	57
	126
Increase during the year	43
Emigrants (English) during year	12

PRODUCE OF 1862.

Wheat,	61	Acres,	915	Bushels,	at	$ 0.70	$ 603.90
Barley	4	"	60	"	at	0.70	42.00
Oats	33¾	"	665	"	at	0.40	266.00
Corn	1	"	20	"	at	0.50	10.00
Buckwheat	2½	"	50	"	at	0.50	25.00
Peas	10	"	150	"	at	0.45	67.50
Potatoes	46¾	"	9350	"	at	0.30	2805.00
Turnips	47	"	5640	"	at	0.20	1128.00
Hay			7¼	Tons	at	15.00	108.75
Shingles			88	m.	at	1.50	132.00
Sawn Lumber			130	m.	at	7.00	910.00
Maple Sugar			950	lbs.	at	0.10	90.00
Molasses			75	Gal.	at	0.75	56.25
Garden produce							275.00
Furs							75.00
							$ 6594.40
Increase in 1862							1694.17

The above covers only 10 miles of Free Grant Road, no addition of Free Grants having been made during the past year. Several miles of the extended roads, which will undoubtedly be Free Grants, are already occupied, and considerable improvements made, but they are accounted for in the general progress of the settlement, and not embraced in the above return.

Hitherto the settlers on this road have hired out the greater part of their time, and, as a consequence, their improvements have been neglected; but a marked change has recently taken place, every settler being now busily engaged on his own lot, pushing forward the required duties.

CROWN LANDS.

The four townships under my charge, viz.: Morrison, Muskoka, Draper and Macaulay, were placed in my hands in October 1861. Since then 16,000 acres have been sold.

NATIONALITY

Irish	220	Houses	83
English	146	Shanties	120
Scotch	145	Barns, &c	84
Canadian	126	Lumber mills	2
German	80	Acres cleared	350
French	20	Acres chopped	333
American	6		
	743		

EMIGRANTS DURING 1862.

English	41	German	13
Irish	12	Scotch	5

YEAR'S RETURNS.

Wheat	3675	Bushels	at	$	0 70	$	2422.50
Oats	810	”	at		0 40		336.00
Barley	400	”	at		0 80		320.00
Potatoes	13250	”	at		0 30		3975.00
Turnips	15175	”	at		0 20		3035.00
Corn	20	”	at		0 50		10.00
Peas	2272	”	at		0 45		129.00
Hay	20	Tons	at		15 00		300.00
Maple Sugar	2000	lbs.	at		0 10		200.00
Molasses	100	Gals.	at		0 75		75.00
Shingles	100	m.	at		1 50		150.00
Sawn Lumber	300	m.	at		7 00		2100.00
Garden Produce							200.00
Furs							150.00
							13402.50

SUMMARY.

	Population	Houses	Shanties	Barns,&c.	Live Stock	Lots occupied	Years returns
Morrison	290	46	46	58	212	75	$10401.20
Muskoka	56	8	5	6	8	17	610.50
Draper	159	19	20	16	47	65	1358.80
Macaulay*	220	10	50	6	30	57	1032.00
Free Grants	287	39	36	49	126	69	6594.40
Total	1012	122	157	135	423	283	19996.90
Years increase	342	44	42	75	93	116	7846.17

*This embraces Macaulay and the unsurveyed neighborhood.

The past season was very unfavorable for grain crops, a drought having set in early in the spring and continued until the grain was in the ear. This reduces the yield in cereals very materially; but in most instances where the grain was sown early, a good yield was obtained. The root crops were abundant, one settler on a free grant lot having raised 1000 bushels of potatoes of excellent sample. Turnips of from 20 to 25 lbs. each were frequently met with.

In a new settlement, however, it is not fair to expect more than a moderate average of crops, for late tillage is so general, that the best of land cannot be depended on. New settlers are anxious to obtain some crops, and they hasten to do their best, but it would be wiser to save the seed than to sow it late, on half prepared land.

The general progress of the settlement is very gratifying. A distinctive feature is the character of the buildings, so many good houses are to be seen. The Taverns in particular are commodious, and the accommodation excellent.

Three Post Offices, Schools, Lumber Mills, a Grist Mill in building, Stores, & c., are among the prominent improvements. Religious services, by resident and other ministers, are regularly held. Water power has been much sought after, and preparations are being made for the erection of other mills. The North Falls[30] of Muskoka is destined to become a village. A new Tavern, Store, Lumber Mill and other buildings are now in the course of erection, and water power leased for a foundry, grist mill, and other machinery.

During the year, Peterson's Road, through Draper, has been finished, thus opening up a continuous and good road from Muskoka Road on the West, to the Opeongo Road on the east; nearly every lot on this road through Draper is occupied. Several miles have also been added to the Muskoka Road through Macaulay and Stephenson; and six miles of the Parry's Sound Road has been contracted for. This line passes through an unsurveyed tract, but is already thickly squatted on, as is also the road through Macaulay and Peterson. The land in these districts is good, the timber being of the best description of hardwood.

The Muskoka Settlement offers to settlers advantages not usually met with in new districts. Although considerable belts of rock intersect the country, yet good farming lands abound, especially on the upper Roads. Extensive Lakes and rivers, offering beautiful sites for residences; Fish, and the ordinary varieties of game, are plentiful. Other townships of good land will soon be added.

With a view to the development of the Great North West, a branch of this road is to be pushed on to Parry's Sound, and from thence to Sault Ste. Marie and the Manitoulin Islands, thus forming a direct communication from the Ottawa valley to the upper shores of Lake Huron. This is an important desideratum in connection with the Muskoka Road, and the rapid influx of intelligent settlers, some of them with considerable means, is an evidence of the value set upon it. Taking the number of squatters in conjunction with those who have purchased lands during the past year and few instances can be found of so rapid a growth of population, in new districts.

Facilities for travel have been increased during the year. A steamboat has been put on the Muskoka route, running daily during the season of navigation; thus enabling parties to reach the settlement from Toronto in *eight* hours. Teams meet the boat to convey goods and passengers to all parts of the settlement.

To the Immigrant, this settlement will offer advantages in the extension of Free Grants. It is to be hoped the Government will provide liberally for the reception of the Emigrant, as an important means of settling wild lands. The chief Agent of the Emigration Office has displayed much energy and thought upon this point; yet undoubtedly more will be done. Most of the Emigrants, with families, leave their homes with a view to farming, and they will not be content with a few acres of land, nor will they like to become for years the servants of others. If in possession of 100 acres they feel that a right beginning has been made, and are more ready and willing to bear the difficulties or hard-

[30]Bracebridge.

ships of forming a new home for themselves. A spirit of independence is at once engendered, calling into exercise their best energies. To secure this to them, requires some sacrifice in the bestowal of land; and no doubt the desire to found a home for the Emigrant now so fully expressed by the Heads of Departments, will ultimate in a scheme yet more attractive and more practicable. The race now existing between the United States and ourselves for securing the tide of Emigration demands our most serious attention, and upon the liberal character of our policy will our success depend, it is not enough to entice people to our shores; care must be taken that discouraging accounts shall not be sent home to those of their friends who intend to follow.

Ere I close my Report I would again refer to the necessity existing in this increasing population for magisterial control. The township of Morrison will soon be an organized township, and many minor offences might be disposed of on the spot, if commissions of the Peace were granted.

F 21   J. W. BRIDGLAND TO THE COMMISSIONER OF CROWN LANDS,
ALEXANDER CAMPBELL
[P.A.O., Colonization Roads Papers, Reports, 1862–8, pp. 143–4]

D.C.L. Quebec July 28 /64

. . . The Muskoka road I next visited; I was also accompanied by Mr. Oliver, the agent, and gentleman appointed to oversee the contemplated repairs to be made. Every thing was done in this instance, as in those already enumerated, to ensure a prompt and proper performance of the designed improvements.

Mr. Oliver commenced his active preparations immediately.

I am happy to be able to state that in so short a space of time as that intervening between my visit[31] to this road in Oct. last and the present, notable evidences of increasing improvement in this interesting section of country present themselves— Expanding clearings, comfortable buildings, clacking mills and accomodative ferries are among the proofs of thrift and prosperity. Many very respectable persons and men of capital and business intelligence have located themselves in the Muskoka country and that noble and picturesque stream but eleven years ago (when I first explored its dark waters) the resort only of the Indian hunter and his victims, is now the boundary of many a prosperous white man's home and the fashionable summer resort of yachting and fishing parties.

At the town plot recently surveyed preparations have been made for the erection of a good hotel. Two decent houses of accommodation already exist— one at the South— the other at the North falls.

[31]The report of this visit is found in Colonization Roads Papers and is printed in the *Report* of the Commissioner of Crown Lands for 1863.

F 22   FORMATION OF A SETTLERS ASSOCIATION[32]
[*Orillia,* Orillia Expositor, *November 1, 1867*]

. . . A.P. Cockburn,[33] Esq., M.P.P. addressed the meeting at some length on the subject of forming a Settlers Association,— the object of which would be to give reliable and useful information to intending settlers. He stated that very often people had come in here with exaggerated ideas of the country and had left in consequence of the disappointments they had met with. He thought the organization of such a Society or Association would be of great value to parties intending to settle, as they would be in possession of the true facts of the case, and know what to bring in, the best routes to travel, where to find good land, &c. The subject was one that had long occupied his attention and he believed that every settler in the north was equally impressed with the importance of having a society of the kind organized to afford information that could be relied on to persons who were totally ignorant of the facilities for settlement of this section of Canada.

The following gentlemen were then named as a committee with power to add to their number for the purpose of drafting a constitution and adopting a motto and emblem for the association, viz: Messrs. A.P. Cockburn and Joseph Piercy, Muskoka; Moses Davis, and J.H. Jackson, Morrison; Walter Sharpe,[34] Draper; D. Hogoboam,[35] Stephenson; George Milne, Humphrey; J.B. Browning,[36] Monck; Matthias Moore,[37] Macaulay; H.J. McDonald, Bracebridge; Richard Lance, Watt.

In pursuance of the formation of the above committee and the and

---

[32]At a meeting of the Settlers Association on April 2, 1868, papers were read on various aspects of Muskoka. These formed the basis for a publication, *Muskoka District Settler's Guide,* which was at least partially reprinted in the *Orillia Expositor,* July 31, 1868.

[33]Alexander Peter Cockburn (1837–1905) was one of the most active promoters of the Muskoka district. As a young man he was in business with his father in Victoria County, and served as postmaster at Kirkfield and as reeve of Eldon (I 12). In 1865 he made a tour of Muskoka and became interested in its development. He placed the first steamers on the Muskoka Lakes, and was active in the retail and lumbering businesses. From 1867 to 1872 he represented North Victoria in the Ontario legislature, and from 1872 to 1882 Muskoka, and from 1882 to 1887 North Ontario in the Canadian House of Commons. In politics he was a Liberal. He wrote a number of immigration pamphlets and in 1905 published *The Political Annals of Canada.*

[34]Walter Sharpe was a farmer at Muskoka Falls and a member of the Council for Draper, Macaulay, Stephenson, and Ryde.

[35]David Hogaboam (with variant spellings) was a merchant and lumberman and served as first reeve of Stephenson Township.

[36]"The Brownings, of an old family from Newcastle (Eng.) especially J. B., were a highly cultivated family and thoroughly posted in modern literature" (Hamilton, *Muskoka Sketch,* p. 18). J. B. Browning, who lived in Bracebridge, advertised as "attorney, solicitor in chancery, conveyancer, notary public, &c."

[37]Matthias Moore was a member of the Council for Draper, Macaulay, Stephenson, and Ryde.

the [sic] adoption of Mr Cockburns suggestion a meeting is to take place at the Victoria Hotel, Bracebridge, at 1 o'clock p.m. on Thursday, 7th Nov., for the adoption of the constitution, the appointment of officers, and general dispatch of business.

F 23   SALE[38] OF STOCK AND IMPLEMENTS ON MUSKOKA FARM
[Orillia, Northern Light, *February 4, 1870]*

IMPORTANT SALE OF FARMING STOCK, MACHINERY, IMPLEMENTS, &c IN MUSKOKA

The undersigned being about to relinquish Farming, is desirous of disposing of the following

FARMING IMPLEMENTS STOCK &c

Three Milch Cows,
Two three year old Heifers, (first calf this Spring.)
Two two year old do,
One Heifer Calf,
A well bred Bull Calf, (Durham & Devon.)
20 Breeding Ewes and Lambs,
15 Lambs, (Ewe and Wether.)
2 Well Bred Rams,
A yoke of Steers rising three years,
2 Breeding Sows,
A thorough bred Berkshire and Suffok Boar,
A superior Threshing machine,
An eight horse power for Threshing machine,
Drum and Band for increasing speed,
An improved Sawing Machine for stovewood, by Noxon of Ingersoll,
A large Chaffcutter for horse or hand power, by Whitlaw of Paris,
A powerful screw Stumping machine, by Masey[39] Newcastle,
An improved Turnip Cutting machine,
A Fanning mill,
A strong tilt Cart for Oxen,
A strong Waggon nearly new,
Two Ox Sleighs,
A well finished Sleigh on bobs complete with box,
A strong Sleigh with steel runners,
A set of Double Harness,
A set of single do

[38]A sale of the stock and equipment of the farm offered for sale in F 24.

[39]A misspelled reference to the farm implements factory at Newcastle which was run by Hart Almerrin Massey, later president of the Massey Manufacturing Company.

About 30 Bushels Spring Wheat, 1st prize at Agricultural Show,
&c., &c., &c.

The above can be inspected and further particulars on application to

A.J. Alport,[40]
"Maple Grove."
Muskoka

F 24   MUSKOKA FARM FOR SALE
[*Orillia*, Northern Light, *May 27, 1870*]

MUSKOKA DISTRICT
VALUABLE
FREEHOLD PROPERTY
For Sale

A Farm containing 657 acres of which 100 are well cleared and substantially fenced. (A portion under crop with fall wheat, Oats and potatoes.)

Upon the premises are a good substantial Dwelling House with comfortable and extensive family accommodations.

A good garden, well furnished with fruit trees and vegetables.

Good barns, stables and other out-buildings (new) well adapted for farm and Stock purposes.

The above property is delightfully situated on the Muskoka Lake and River, in the Township of Muskoka, with a water frontage of about five miles, and within its boundaries there is a small lake, of nearly 100 acres, which offers great attraction to parties fond of fishing and shooting.

The steamer in connection with the route for Toronto passes daily, calling at the wharf on the premises when required.

Title indisputable, the owner being patentee of the Crown.

Full particulars can be learned on by [*sic*] application to the undersigned

A.J. ALPORT, Proprietor,
Alport;
FRANK EVANS,
Orillia;
or   J.A. DONALDSON,
Emigration Office, Toronto.

[40]A. J. Alport and his family came from New Zealand to take a free grant in the Muskoka district about 1862. As well as developing one of the best farms in Muskoka, A. J. Alport was a justice of the peace and took an active part in community affairs. In 1872 he was given a testimonial dinner by his fellow citizens (Orillia, *Northern Light*, April 17, 1872). His farm was later the property of E. G. Muntz.

F 25   THOMAS MCMURRAY[41] TO ARCHIBALD MCKELLAR,[42]
COMMISSIONER OF AGRICULTURE
[*Ontario, Department of Agriculture and Public Works,*
Annual Report on Immigration, *1872, pp. 29–30*]

Bracebridge, 7th November, 1872.

I have the honour to submit the following report for the season of 1872.

From various causes the flow of immigration has not been so great as was anticipated. However, it is generally conceded that most of those who have arrived are well adapted for the settlement.

I find that 382 immigrants have found their way to Muskoka during the season. Besides this, a large number have settled in the Parry Sound district.

As to their nationality, about three-fourths are English, the remainder being Irish, Scotch, German, and others.

It is encouraging to know that many of those who have been bene-fited by emigration are sending home money, to bring out their friends and relatives, so that next year we may look for a much greater influx.

Another noticeable feature in connection with the operations of this season is the fact that many from the United States have been attracted hither, and their universal testimony is, that all things considered, they can get on better here than on the other side.

. . .

During the season a number of gentlemen interested in emigration have visited the district with a view of obtaining correct information concerning the Free Grant Lands. Mr. O.W. Gjerdrum,[43] of Norway,

[41]Thomas McMurray (b. 1831) was born in Paisley, Scotland. After some ad-ventures at sea and in America he settled in Belfast, Ireland, where he was con-nected with the Irish Temperance League. In 1861 he emigrated to Canada, started the *Northern Advocate* at Parry Sound in 1869, and in 1870 moved it to Brace-bridge. There he opened a general store and real estate business, built a large home, and served as reeve of Draper, Macaulay, Stephenson, and Ryde. About 1874 he had serious financial difficulties and returned to Parry Sound where he began the *North Star*, and served as land agent for Parry Sound. He was one of the most active promoters of Muskoka and published *The Free Grant Lands of Canada* (Bracebridge, 1871). His early life is given in his *Temperance Lectures, with Autobiography* (Toronto, 1873).

[42]Archibald McKellar (1816–1894) represented Kent in the Legislative Assem-bly of the Province of Canada from 1857 to 1867 and in the Legislative Assembly of Ontario from 1867 to 1875. From 1871 to 1875 he was Commissioner of Public Works, Minister of Agriculture, and Provincial Secretary.

[43]O. W. Gjerdrum gave his impression of the Free Grant district in a letter to Archibald McKellar (Ontario, Department of Agriculture, *Annual Report on Im-migration*, 1872, pp. 38-9).

and Mr. Alexander Somerville,[44] "The Whistler at the Plough," were here in April. The latter gentleman has since written several letters giving an interesting account of his trip, which have been widely circulated throughout Great Britain and Ireland.

The Ontario Press Association[45] made their annual trip to the beautiful lakes of Muskoka in July, the members of which expressed themselves delighted with the evidences of prosperity which they witnessed, a full account of which appeared through the press.

The Rev. Mr. Stobo,[46] from Scotland, made a visit in August, exploring beyond the Maganetawan River.

The Rev. Horrocks Cocks,[47] from London, who spent some time in the district a year ago, made a second visit in October last, and conferred with those emigrants who had been assisted by the League with which he is identified.

It is gratifying to add that the crops throughout the entire districts of Muskoka and Parry Sound have been much in excess of former years. Labour is also plentiful at good wages, and general contentment reigns.

The erection of emigrant sheds has been agitated for some time, and I consider it important that such should be provided. Most of those who arrive have large families with only limited means; for such to stop at hotels is simply to use up what is absolutely required to enable them to go upon their land; hence, if sheds were built at suitable points, and the same furnished with cooking stores [sic], the families of land seekers might remain at such places at a trifling cost, until the heads thereof selected their lots, put up their log shanties, and made the necessary preparations to enable them to commence operations upon their own land, which could not fail to prove a great boon to many.

Muskoka's Critics and Defenders

F 26   McMURRAY TO THE EDITOR OF THE *Montreal Daily Witness*
(1869?)
[*Ontario, Department of Agriculture and Public Works,* Emigration to Canada; the Province of Ontario, *pp. 32–3*]

Mr. Editor,— My attention has been called to a paragraph which appeared in the Montreal *Witness* some time ago, headed "Cruelty of sending newly arrived Immigrants to worthless Free Grant Lands,"

[44]Alexander Somerville (1811–1885), a Scottish writer, came to Canada in 1858. He did journalistic work and was for a time editor of the *Canadian Illustrated News*. Among his best known works were *The Autobiography of a Working Man*, and *The Whistler at the Plough*.

[45]Error for the Canadian Press Association. See J 10.

[46]Edward John Stobo (1838–1918), clergyman and author, was ordained a minister of the Baptist Church in Scotland and came to Canada in 1872. He occupied a number of charges in Ontario and Quebec.

[47]The Reverend Horrocks Cocks of Kensington, England, Secretary of the National Emigration League.

where you have copied from the Sarnia *Observer*, an account given of a visit to Muskoka by a Mr. Simpson, where he describes the great poverty of an old couple from Paisley, Scotland. Now, as such statements are calculated to make false impressions, I beg leave to state a few facts in reference to that much admired and sometimes despised district.

I was the first settler in the township of Draper, having gone there on my arrival in Canada in May, 1861. Ever since that time, I have been closely watching the growth of this section, and my opportunities exceed those of a transient visitor; and for the benefit of your numerous readers, I beg to state that when I settled in Draper, there was not a soul living in, nor a tree cut in the following townships, viz: Draper, Macaulay, Stephenson, Oakley, McLean, Brunell, Monk, Watt, Humphries, Spence, &c.

Our nearest Post Office was the Severn Bridge, 21 miles distant, our nearest village and grist mill, Orillia, 35 miles off, and we had only one neighbour within ten miles of us; while now we have advanced so far as to have three grist mills, one oatmeal mill, and five saw mills. We have also four prosperous little villages, eleven post-offices with a daily mail from Toronto. There are clearances stretching for miles, with good barns and comfortable houses, and thousands of settlers.

Several churches and meeting houses have been built, and five ministers live in the neighbourhood, and work with a zeal worthy of their noble calling. We have day schools and Sabbath schools, and are well supplied with the means of Grace.

I admit there are some few cases of poverty here, but such is the exception not the rule. I know of no place in Ontario, considering the population, where there is less pauperism than in Muskoka, excepting Bridgewater and Garden Island; and the reason why there is not a single case of poverty in the above mentioned places is, in my opinion, because the proprietors, the Hon. Billa Flint[48] and D.D. Calvin,[49] Esq., M.P.P., have prohibited liquor from being sold there.

The settlers of Muskoka, for the most part, are a highly intelligent and very industrious class of settlers; and it is strange that some visitors can only record a solitary case of suffering, and omit to relate that hundreds are comfortable and contented, happy and prosperous.

In the *New Dominion Monthly* for March 1868, there is an account of "A Trip to Muskoka Lake," by the Rev. John Todd,[50] D.D. of Pittsfield, Mass., where he gives an account of a poor German family at Sparrow Lake, who were in great want. Now, there are few places, either

[48]Billa Flint (1805–1894), merchant at Belleville, member of the Legislative Assembly and later of the Legislative Council, and, after Confederation, of the Senate.

[49]Delano Dexter Calvin (1798–1884) was reeve of Garden Island for many years, four times warden of Frontenac County, and was elected member for Frontenac in the Ontario legislature in 1868, 1872, and 1877.

[50]John Todd (1800–1873) was a widely known Congregational clergyman and author.

in town or country, free from cases of extreme destitution, and it is not my present intention to inquire into the causes of such poverty, but I consider it unfair to write an account of a visit to a place, and then only to give the dark side. We have rich as well [as] poor; we have the noble as well as the mean; those enjoying all the comforts of life, as well as a few who are not so highly favoured.

. . .

. . . While I would not hold out an inducement for all newly arrived immigrants to come to Muskoka, yet I believe that if the right class will only come, they will do well. Here each actual settler of 18 years of age and upwards will get 100 acres of land as a free grant from the Government; and if they have a little means, and are industrious, they will soon have comfortable homes and become independent. We have three Paisley men in our township, all doing well; one of them owns 828 acres of excellent land.

The great mistake that some immigrants make is this: They settle down upon inferior lots on the road, and expend their means there in preference to going back a mile or two into the bush, where they might have good soil that would sustain their families. There is an abundance of good land in the Muskoka district; only let the settler make a wise selection. It is worthy of notice that the population of the district has doubled itself during the past year.

The Government has kindly given a grant of $35,000 towards improving the navigation in this section, so that in spring, Locks will be built connecting Lake Rosseau with Lake Muskoka, so that the beautiful little steamer "Wenonah" (i.e. first born) may be enabled to ply between the village of Gravenhurst on Lake Muskoka, and the village of Rosseau on Lake Rosseau, thereby precipitating the communication into the interior of this rapidly improving district.

A railway is about to be constructed between Washago and Gravenhurst, called the "Simcoe and Muskoka Railroad," thereby giving us direct railroad and water communication between Toronto and Bracebridge, the future county seat. For the information of intending immigrants, I might state that in winter the route is by Northern R.R. from Toronto to Barrie, thence to Bracebridge by mail stage, which goes daily on the arrival of the morning train.

Mr. Charles W. Lount, the Crown Land Agent, resides at Bracebridge.

F 27   "FARMING IN MUSKOKA"[51]
[Toronto, Mail, July 20, 1872]

The general character of the country traversed by your correspondent may be given in very few words. It is bold, picturesque, diversified with

[51]The second instalment of an article "Annual Excursion of the Canadian Press Association."

hill and dale, well-watered, almost devoid of swamp, and contains from 70 to 75 per cent. of good farm land, with from 25 to 30 per cent. of protuberant and often rampant-looking rock. The soil is, for the most part, an excellent loam, with patches here and there, of sand or of clay. The rock is seldom bare of vegetation; but is, for the most part, thinly wooded with trees that have sprung from seeds deposited in crevices and fissures, and by a slow dogged growth, have become of considerable size. In too many instances the settlers have made the mistake of clearing off the timber from the rocks, perhaps because being somewhat thin and sparse, it was easy to get at and dispose of it. The result has been that the soil being no longer held by the fibrous roots of the trees, is readily washed away by the rains, so that the rocky protuberances look and really are more marked and bare than ever. . . .

From a careful and impartial survey of the country, I do not hesitate to pronounce its agricultural capabilities, rich and varied. The crops of all kinds are looking remarkably well, quite as well as in any other part of this Province which I have had the opportunity of visiting the present season. Oats, peas, barley, spring-wheat, potatoes and all the grasses, all testify to the excellence of both soil and climate. Muskoka seems to be especially fitted for grazing, dairying and stock-farming. Finer timothy and clover cannot be found anywhere than I have seen growing during the past few days. Timothy, especially, makes a most luxuriant growth. Your correspondent measured stalks five feet and even more in height, and heads full nine inches in length. The woods everywhere display a rank and luxuriant vegetation, and the cattle roaming through them look sleek, fat and thriving. . . .

It is to be borne in mind that in all the free grants made by Government no account is taken of rock in measurement. When a settler locates 100 or 200 acres, he has only to furnish testimony proving that five, ten, twenty, thirty or more acres of his plot consist of rock, to have an equal quantity of good land given him in lieu of it. His farm is thereby enlarged in area by so much rock as he has upon it. . . .

F 28   Mrs. King's Observations on Muskoka[52]
[[*Mrs. King*], Letters from Muskoka by an Emigrant Lady, *pp. 133–7*]

I begin this letter with a few observations in support of my oft-repeated assertion that poor ladies and gentlemen form the worst, or at least the most unsuccessful, class for emigration to Canada. I must give you a slight sketch of the class of settlers we have here, and of the conditions they must fulfil before they can hope to be in easy circumstances, much less in affluent ones. Of course I am speaking of settlers from the "old country," and not of Canadians born who sometimes find their way from the front to try their fortunes in the backwoods. The settlers in this neighbourhood, for a circuit of about eight miles, are all of the lower

[52]Purports to have been written in 1872.

classes; weavers from Scotland, agricultural labourers from England, artisans and mechanics from all parts. Whatever small sum of money a family of this class can collect with a view to emigration, very little of it is spent in coming over. They are invariably steerage passengers, and on landing at Quebec are forwarded, free of all expense, and well provided for on the road, by the Emigration Society, to the part where they intend settling. Say that they come to the free-grant lands of Muskoka. The intending settler goes before the commissioner of crown-lands, and (if a single man) takes up a lot of a hundred acres; if married and with children, he can claim another lot as "head of a family." He finds the conditions of his tenure specified on the paper he signs, and sees that it will be five years before he can have his patent, and then only if he has cleared fifteen acres, and has likewise built thereon a log-house of certain dimensions. He pays some one a dollar to point out his lot, and to take him over it, and then selecting the best site, and with what assistance he can get from his neighbours, he clears a small patch of ground and builds a shanty. In the meantime, if he have a wife and family they are lodged and boarded for a very small sum at some near neighbour's. When he and his family have taken possession, he underbrushes and chops as much as he possibly can before the winter sets in; but on the first approach of the cold weather he starts for the lumber-shanties, and engages himself to work there, receiving from twenty to twenty-five dollars a month and his food. Should he be of any particular trade he goes to some large town, and is tolerably sure of employment.

It is certainly a very hard and anxious life for the wife and children, left to shift for themselves throughout the long dreary winter, too often on a very slender provision of flour and potatoes and little else.

When spring at last comes, the steady hard-working settler returns with quite a little sum of money wherewith to commence his own farming operations. . . .

Now it is obvious that ladies and gentlemen have not, and cannot have these advantages. The ladies of a family cannot be left unprotected during the long winter, and indeed are, for the most part, physically incapable of chopping fire-wood, drawing water, and doing other hard outdoor work . . .

F 29   JOSEPH DALE'S[53] WARNING TO ENGLISH IMMIGRANTS
[*Dale,* Canadian Land Grants in 1874]

Having recently returned from Northern Canada where I remained some little time in what is at present the "Free Grant District of the Province of Ontario," it occurred to me that the few following pages might be of some assistance to those who are about to take such an important step as to emigrate. I would beg the reader to understand that

[53]Joseph Dale's pamphlet is perhaps the most critical of all the material written about Muskoka. The preface is dated "London, June, 1875."

my observations are not addressed to those who are about to make the settled districts of Canada their future home, but to that class of men with families and a little capital who go out with the intention of making a home in the bush, and who, fully prepared to undergo many hardships and severe toil, leave the old country in the hope that their efforts and the expenditure of their hard earnings will give them such a reward as they might reasonably expect, and which settlers years ago have worked for, and realised.

. . .

The nearer we approach to Severn Bridge the more the impression comes upon us that we are entering upon a new and stony country, but when arrived there, we get a first view of the sort of land which emigrants from the "old country" are invited to settle on and cultivate. Hence we take the mail carts to a place called Gravenhurst, through a most dismal, rocky, and wild country. About three or four years ago a great bush fire passed over, and completely revealed its barren nature. No doubt this (some say fortunate) fire has done much to produce an unfavourable impression as to the desirability of a settlement in Muskoka, but on the other hand it unmistakeably shows the traveller what sort of country he is passing through, and is likely to meet with for many miles. On all sides are great masses of granite, containing veins of plutonic origin on which it is a wonder how anything, even a birch tree, can grow; here and there are to be seen a few poverty-stricken shanties and attempts at settlements, most of them deserted, the unfortunate settler having been compelled to leave such an ill-favoured, unremunerative spot, and seek to retrieve his lost time and labour, in the "front"— i.e., the settled country. The country speaks for itself, where although there is daily communication with Toronto all along this road, yet these semi-clearings remain deserted. Some time ago a number of hardy Norwegians were induced to settle in this barren region, and even they, used as they were to a rugged country, were obliged to abandon their clearings and return home ruined men. We now, however, reach Gravenhurst, a very languishing village which but for the summer tourists, would probably soon have to put the shutters up. Gravenhurst is on the borders of Lake Muskoka, which, like most of the lakes in this district, is very pretty and rocky. The water is of that dark brown colour peculiar to lakes in a rocky region. Here the traveller embarks on the steamboat, which, in about two or three hours, will take him up the Muskoka River to Bracebridge. On either side of the river and lake are clearings, but as usual most of them display the rocky nature of the soil, and some of them are nothing but patches of rock. The settlers here have however one advantage, and that is, a water communication with Bracebridge, and from thence with the "front" to one which is available both in summer and winter.

At Bracebridge we reach the falls of the Muskoka River, and navigation is at an end. Beyond that, communication with the front practically ceases.

The traveller is now in the highlands of Canada and in its most recent village. Bracebridge is about thirty miles from Severn Bridge, the terminus of the Northern Railway of Canada; fifteen miles of this distance, as the reader will notice, is traversed by two or three small mail carts and the rest by steamboat. From want of communication by rail with Severn Bridge, Bracebridge, although about three years old, is not a flourishing village, the two or three small hotels in the place being the only houses doing any good business. The hotels naturally pay, because of the number of visitors from the "front" to the "sporting regions of Muskoka", as the railway guide calls them.

. . .

. . . Starting from Bracebridge the emigrant will soon find himself on the Colonization or Government road which ends at a place called Baysville. The road for some distance out of Bracebridge is fairly kept, and an enthusiastic emigrant will not mind a few steep hills at starting. Soon however he will begin to pass allotments which have been merely "slashed", others slightly cleared and with tenantless log huts upon them. Some have capital beaver-meadows attached to them, and being so near the high road and not far from Bracebridge, the emigrant will naturally wonder how it is that better progress has not been made upon these allotments, when he has done his day's weary tramp in search of his intended allotment many miles off. I shall, therefore, explain here why this anomaly exists. Directly a Free Grant District is opened up, and before it becomes generally known in England, a rush of Canadians from the "front" takes place, and those allotments nearest to a town, and through which a road at Government expense is likely to come, or which possess the advantage of a beaver-meadow, are at once taken up. The information says, "The settlement duties are to have fifteen acres on each grant of 100 acres cleared and under crop, of which the last[54] two acres are to be cleared and cultivated annually for five years, to build a habitable house, at least 16 X 20 ft. in size, *and to reside* on the land, at least, six months in each year."

In reality, however, the people who take up these allotments are, in many cases, Canadians carrying on business in the settled districts, who lead thereon persons whom they call "agents." This practice is a most pernicious one, and tends greatly to retard the settlement of a new country. These agents are mostly men of a low class, without a farthing of capital, and who have neither interest in the land, nor care for the duties of settlement. All they have to do is to perform just so much of those duties as the Homestead Act compels them to do to secure the complete grant of the lands on which they are placed by their employers.

[54]Misprint: "the last" should read "at least."

The result of this is, that these ambitionless agents clear as little of the land as possible, neglect the roads which pass through the lands they live on, and during the summer, when harvest work is to be had, desert them. The employers, in the meanwhile, wait till emigrants with families and a little money from the old country, obliged thus to pass by these sham allotments, have pushed further on, and by their toil and expenditure so improved the roads and the country as to enhance the value of the lands on which the agents are located. The agent's employer then hopes to sell. Thus, whilst this agency farce goes on, the *bonâ fide* settler from England has been made a tool of, and is laughed at by his uncongenial neighbour. All that is left for the emigrant is the rejected lots . . .

. . . The emigrant, at last arrived on his allotment, and having never perhaps as yet used a backwoods-man's axe, will find it necessary to employ one or two axemen— Canadians, who have been used to this sort of thing all their lives. In fact, they will be on the look-out for a job at his expense, and will discuss his coming with keen and anxious faces. An emigrant from the old country, a little advanced in life, seldom or never learns to swing an axe, and without the assistance of these axemen, would make such slow progress as still further to diminish his ability to tide his family and cattle over the next year. The axemen, then, are hired, and of course, have to be fed during this engagement; and rare appetites they have. What with the money paid for their services, and the cost of their board (enhanced by bringing it over such a road as before described), the emigrant will soon find them a considerable item of expense. Having cut so many acres of land, the next thing will be to wait till the snow melts, and then begin to "log", or get the fallen timber together for burning. But what is the emigrant to do without cattle for this purpose? And how is he to keep any cattle, horse, mule, or other animal, to do the necessary hauling of timber? It is with great difficulty and expense that he can get sufficient food over such roads for himself, to say nothing of cattle, &c. Even if he purchased cattle at £25 a yoke, how is he to get them through such a swampy country without breaking their legs, or getting them mired? So few and far are the spots where sufficient grass can be obtained, and so quickly is anything like fodder snapped up in such a country, that the whole of the emigrant's time with the labour of his cattle would be consumed in getting sufficient fodder. To log by hand is impossible, besides being too slow for any practical purpose, and so the land remains encumbered. Those spots, which by desperate labour have been cleared by hand, reveal to the emigrant nothing but rock, rock, rock, covered here and there with a thin stratum of vegetable mould, without any secondary strata whatever. Then again, these ridges and little hills of rock cause corresponding depressions, and an infinity of swamps, both large and small. How are these swamps ever to be drained without great expense? for portions of rock must be blasted through to make anything like a systematic drainage for them. I have known instances where so great is the quantity of rock that the ground has had to be made; and a mound of earth has been sought for, and looked upon as a treasure. These painful facts are not perceptible to an emigrant when viewing the land covered with underbrush and forest; but when it is a little cleared, and burned by logging there is no doubt about it. We will now suppose the summer to be coming on, the winter stock of provisions running short, and the emigrant in want of fresh meat, pork or other necessaries, a supply of which the sleighing in the winter enabled him to procure. What is to be done to obtain a supply, over such a road, without beasts of burthen? He must perforce start on a weary journey to Bracebridge, and carry back over this toilsome road almost every little article he may want, besides a weight of provisions only fit for a beast of burden, and this has to be done in almost tropical weather. There is nothing the settlers dread more than this "backing" of provisions; and well they may. One whole day is wasted in going and another day in coming back. Two precious days are thus gone, and the expense of staying at Bracebridge incurred. . . .

. . .

As the food supply is one of the most important items to the emigrant, it would be as well that he should understand that although the bush may abound with deer and other game, yet that the hunting for it as a matter of food is a most precarious thing, when even experienced trappers find a great difficulty in getting sufficient to live on; how much greater, then, must be the difficulty of an emigrant? To hunt in the bush as a matter of necessity requires the cunning of an Indian and a life as nomadic. Any settler who attempts such a thing must neglect everything else. Nothing but an organised hunt by a number of settlers and dogs will accomplish anything worth the trouble, and such an organisation is seldom or never made. The emigrant must not look, therefore to the bush for a supply of animal food.

Our emigrant having been settled down on his land for eight or twelve months, will now, perhaps, begin to reflect upon his position, which, I venture to say, is a most painful one.

Where now is gone that little capital which he has so industriously saved and got together in England? Wasted upon a worthless block of rock. He has found out at a ruinous cost that the accounts given in books on settlement in the bush in Canada, which were written some years ago, and spoke in glowing terms of settlements rapidly rising around the industrious settlers, and of lands which by labour and self-denial have developed into an inheritance, do not apply to the Free Grant District of 1874.

. . .

No doubt I shall be contradicted in the accounts I have just given of the Free Grant District of Ontario, in 1874, and subjected to attacks by those who hold lands there, and employ agents. As, however, I speak from personal observation, and from facts which have come direct to me from those who have suffered, and whose veracity I have no reason to impeach, I shall be quite prepared to meet them.

. . .

The Settlement of Haliburton

F 30   EXCERPT FROM J. W. FITZGERALD'S "SURVEY OF
TOWNSHIP BOUNDARIES"
[*Ontario, Department of Lands and Forests, Field Notes, no. 1904*]

St. Mary's June 1st. 1858

. . . I left Fenelon Falls about 1 P.M. on the above day[55] (having procured an additional supply of flour at Lindsay) with my party of twelve men, about 29 cwt. stores beside camps, baggage, &c.— I arrived at the survey on the 15th having crossed eleven portages, the longest of which is about two miles. The following three days were occupied in arranging supplies &c from this to the 22nd. the day on which I commenced the survey the time was occupied in preparing axes, adjusting instruments taking observations &c—

Before referring more directly to the actual survey I would beg to make a few observations on the improvements which I have noticed on the route and on the general features of that section of the Country, with those around Cameron's and Balsam Lakes I presume you are already conversant. I will therefore pass on to the River[56] flowing from Mud Turtle into the latter, upon it a good saw mill is in operation capable of turning out five thousand feet of lumber daily. There are over twenty families about this place. The line which divides the crystaline limestone from the granite or gneiss formations passes through Mud Turtle Lake in a direction a little north of west. The limestone outcrops on the east shore in stratified horizontal layers forming a vertical cliff from five to twenty five feet high. There are several squatters on the west shore of this Lake on the unsurveyed lands[57] north of Bexley one of them a Frenchman by the name Couternance has made a clearing of 30 acres and has erected a good house, barn &c— this poor man died on my return from the survey having left a wife and young family— A saw mill is being constructed on the river between this lake & Moore's lake it is expected to be shortly in operation. There are several valuable mill sites on this River, the land along its west shore as well as that along Moore's Lake is all nearly occupied by squatters, not fewer than ten shanties were erected from September till my return in March. The land about the shores of Gull lake although very rough is being fast taken up by squatters, there is a large tract of good land a short distance to the east of this

[55]October 6, 1857.   [56]Gull River.   [57]Now Laxton Township.

Lake. The whole west front and part of the East of Gull River from the head of this Lake to the long portage probably five miles is either occupied by actual squatters or claimed by persons not yet on the land, the soil is a rich sandy loam— the river is over 60 feet wide in the narrowest part and with the exception of two short gentle rapids in between 6 and 10 feet deep. There is one squatter near this portage who has erected a very comfortable shanty and cleared several acres during the past Fall he rendered much assistance to myself and party. There is another squatter[58] north of this in the township of Stanhope, on a peninsula between Big & Little Bushkonk Lakes, he has lived there six years and has about 10 acres well cleared. . . .

F 31   RICHARD HUGHES TO THE COMMISSIONER OF CROWN LANDS,
P. M. VANKOUGHNET
[P.A.O., Crown Lands Papers, R. Hughes volume]

Crown Land Agency—
Bobcaygeon March 12th 1859

I beg to enclose my returns for the month of February 1859 the amount received is very small and I find that a great majority of the settlers are very poor, in fact if the work does not go on during the summer on the road I think some will have to leave— I trust that the Government will adopt some measure for the relief of poor settlers in these new settlements as many of them have spent all in getting here

It would be a great pity that so large a quantity of land as is now cleared and capable of giving an abundant crop without any fear of vermin destroying it should remain untilled for want of seed to put in it.

If seed were provided for such as cannot get it themselves, it would give a great impetus to the settlement and save many from *want* . . .

F 32   HUGHES, REPORT ON THE BOBCAYGEON ROAD, 1859
[Canada, Department of Crown Lands, Report, 1859, pp. 73–4]

BOBCAYGEON ROAD, Dec. 31, 1859.

Herewith I have the honor to submit statements of the number of settlers on the Free Grants on the Bobcaygeon Road to the 31st December, 1859; shewing the number of lots located, number of actual settlers, number of persons in each family, acres under crop, acres cleared, houses, barns and stables built— viz.:

Number of lots located	195
” actual settlers	168
Total number of persons in families	697
Houses built	126
Barns and stables	32

[58]Mr. Hunter. See I 34.

ACTUAL SETTLERS

English	31
Irish	96
Scotch	14
Canadians	22
Swedes	3
Germans	2
	168

Number of acres cleared		776		
" " acres under crop		371		

As follows —

90 acres wheat, 1620 bushels	@	$ 1 00		$1620
138 " potatoes, 20700 bushels	@	50		10350
87 " Turnips, 15400 do	@	20		3080
25 " Corn, 500 do	@	1 00	p.100	500
150 tons Beaver Meadow Hay	@	8 00		1200
8000 lbs Maple Sugar	@	10		800
400 gals. Molasses	@	60		240
50,000 feet Lumber sawn	@	6 00		300
10,000 shingles	@	1 50		150
10 tons Timothy Hay	@	20 00		200
200 Deer	@	3 50		700
Furs				1500
6 brls. Potash	@	25 00		150
Total				$20,790

The balance of the 371 acres under crop were planted with vegetables which, although of great value to settlers, may not be worthy of being included in a report.

The quantity of crop raised on the lands sold in the Townships opened up by the Bobcaygeon Road will, for this year, be somewhat inferior to that on the Free Grants, but I feel sanguine that next year they will be larger, as you will see by the following memorandum of sales in Galway, Sommerville and Minden, which latter Township was opened for sale on the 1st September last, and at the same time it will be taken into consideration that Somerville was nearly all sold before this agency was established, and that Galway has not been half surveyed.

Lands sold in Galway in 1859	2700	acres
" " in Sommerville	7000	"
" " in Minden in 4 months	4200	"
Total	13900	

Besides these sales many arrearages have been paid on lands in Sommerville in consequence of the increased value caused by the opening of the Bobcaygeon Road, and I have no doubt that when the lands in the lately surveyed Townships of Snowdon, Lutterworth and Anson are placed in the market, as also the Townships of Stanhope and the balance of Galway, now under survey, the sales will be more than double what they are now, this will be proved by the fact that more than 100 persons have offered payment already, and many of them wish to pay in full for lots in these Townships, which could not be accepted, as the lands have not yet been placed in market, and so determined are these persons to secure the lots, that most of them have moved out and are in actual possession and working on the lands.

Twenty-five families are settled on and near the boundary line between Stanhope and Minden, where, and to the Eastward, land of excellent quality is reported by those who have gone so far.

I would respectfully recommend that a road be located as soon as possible, running Eastward and Westward from the Bobcaygeon Road, commencing at the boundary between Minden and Stanhope, and to run to the Hastings Road, to Mr. Peterson's line, and Westward to the Muskoka Road, and that the lots on this road be Free Grants.

I would also suggest the propriety of surveying Lot. No. 3 Free Grant, in Minden, reserved, and laying it off into a village flat. I have had several applications from mechanics and traders for lots, they stating that if allowed to purchase a village lot each, they would move out at once.

One person[59] has squatted already, and has built a store, and is now doing a good business. I have every reason to believe that a town would spring up rapidly if it was opened for sale.

A saw-mill has been erected at Kinmount during the last six months, and is found of great benefit to the settlers, as it saves 18 miles of carriage for lumber.

Mills are very much wanted at Gull River and in the townships adjacent, and parties are prepared as soon as the privileges are ready for sale to erect mills at once to meet the demand.

We have to thank the Hon. the Postmaster General for opening three Post Offices during the year, viz.: one at Silver Lake, in Galway, nine miles, one at Kinmount in Sommerville, eighteen miles, and the other at Gull River,[60] in Minden, thirty miles from Bobcaygeon; these have been of great benefit to the settlers. . . .

F 33   HUGHES, REPORT ON THE BOBCAYGEON ROAD, 1861
[*Canada, Bureau of Agriculture and Statistics,* Report, *1861*]

Crown Lands Agency
Bobcaygeon, 31st December, 1861.

In accordance with directions from the Department of Crown Lands, I beg to submit my annual report of the progress made by the settlers on the Bobcaygeon Road . . .

Three post offices have been established up to the 31st December, at Galway, Kinmount, and Minden respectively. I understand that, in reply to a petition by the inhabitants, it is the intention of the Honorable Post

59Probably Thomas Young who opened the first store at Minden. See I 29.
60The name was later changed to Minden.

Master General, during the winter, to extend the postal facilities as far as Stanhope, and to give the settlers two mails per week.

Houses of entertainment can be found at distances along the road of from four to six miles, and are ten in number. The number of stores has been increased on the road during the past year and now amounts to six. Settlers can generally obtain all the necessaries of life at either of them.

Three Saw Mills on the road have been completed, one at Kinmount, one at North Britain, and the third at Minden, on a Branch of the Gull River. Two Blacksmith's shops have been put in operation during the past year. Mr J.H. Cummings has also erected a building large enough to put in a planing machine, shingle mill, turning lathe, and one or two run of mill stones, all of which he intends to complete during the next year, under the same roof with his saw mill now nearly completed.

Only one Grist Mill has been completed, north of Bobcaygeon as yet, viz: at Kinmount, by John Hunter, Esq., and the quantity of grain for grinding is steadily increasing. Two other grist mills will be finished, according to conditions, during the ensuing summer.

Of School-houses four have been built, and four school sections have been established. Three of the schools have been in successful operation during the year, and have been well attended. The other school house is just completed, and it is the intention of the inhabitants that the school shall be opened after the new year. . . .

I should have said that the school houses on the road are open to all denominations, and that services are held at several places nearly every Sunday. Ministers of the various denominations pay frequent visits to the back country, and hold services in the different localities. A minister of the Church of Scotland, and another of the Methodist persuasion, live on the road, and hold regular services.

F 34   HUGHES, REPORT ON THE BOBCAYGEON ROAD, 1862
[*Canada, Department of Crown Lands, Report, 1862, app. 31*]

FREE GRANT AGENCY.
Bobcaygeon, January 1st 1863.

. . . One or two school sections have been established on the Road during the year 1862, and the old ones are becoming more efficient.

Several missionary stations have been established by the different denominations, and services take place at each of the different villages along the road, every sabbath.

Lime has been burned at Gull River, of the best quality from chrystalized limestone, found in the immediate neighborhood.

Brick clay exists in large quantities on the road at Gull River, and it is the intention of persons who have purchased farms and moved out for the purpose of making brick, to commence in the Spring. All the bricks made use of there at present, being carried at least 50 miles over a rough road.

As to the lands sold to actual settlers since the establishment of this Agency in January 1859, I beg to say that about a thousand lots have been sold, containing over ninety thousand acres, and that when the final payments are made on these lands, the whole expenses of the construction of the Bobcaygeon Road, now completed to the North branch of the South Muskoka, a distance of seventy miles North of Bobcaygeon, and the cost of the survey of most of the townships now opened up on each side of the road, will have been paid and a new country opened up, which has hitherto been altogether misunderstood.

Three saw mills are now in course of erection in the townships of Stanhope and Minden, and a saw mill and grist mill have been completed on Gull River, in the immediate neighborhood of the town plot of Minden, by Amos Moore, and a saw mill is now in successful operation on the Burnt River in the third concession of the township of Snowdon, by H.W. Casey; and these with other mills before erected are causing a steady increase in the settlement of the surrounding townships.

Lumbering operations are now being carried on extensively in the neighborhood, and the great traffic over the road has had the effect of cutting it up in some places, so as to make it difficult for heavily loaded teams to travel a reasonable distance each day. I would respectfully suggest that a small sum be appropriated to make slight alterations where required, and to repair the road where statute labor is insufficient.

During the year 1862 two contracts have been completed on this road, one between the Peterson Line and Bell's Line and the other North of Bell's Line, the latter about twenty miles in extent; two bridges have been built, one at Cedar Narrows and the other on the North branch of the South Muskoka River.

F 35   GEORGE G. BOSWELL, "REPORT OF THE AGENT FOR THE
        NORTHERLY PART OF THE BOBCAYGEON ROAD"
      [*Canada, Department of Crown Lands, Report, 1863, app. 27*]

Minden, January 16th, 1864.

I have the honor to transmit a statement of the settlers and produce on the northern section of the Bobcaygeon Road, for the year 1863.[61]

In consequence of the great distance north, and the short time the settlers have been located, my present Report is rather limited.

The parties located seem content and happy in their new homes; nevertheless, there has been but little improvement in the place during the year. The principal cause is the bad state of the road north of Bell's line, which, although taken out of the contractor's hands, has not yet been finished.

The settlement at and near the Narrows of the Lake of Bays is in a

[61]Boswell's first report, to January 1, 1863, is printed in Guillet, *The Valley of the Trent*, pp. 82-3.

thriving condition, there being very good land along the road as well as a large tract in rear of the Free Grants.

Number of lots located	54
Number of lots settled on, or having small clearings in readiness for moving into this winter	39
Total population	130
Number of acres cleared	144

NATIONALITY

English, heads of families	17
Irish	20
Scotch	14
Canadian	14
Total	54

TOTAL QUANTITY OF PRODUCE AND VALUE

Wheat	530	bushels	@	$1 00	$530 00
Oats	1265	"	@	0 45	569 25
Indian Corn	100	"	@	0 75	75 00
Potatoes	3110	"	@	0 25	777 50
Turnips	6290	"	@	0 12½	786 25
Timothy Hay	29	tons	@	11 00	319 00
Beaver "	54	"	@	7 00	378 00
Furs					780 00
Maple Syrup	1160	lbs	@	0 08	92 80
					$4307 80

STOCK

Cattle	48
Horses	3
Pigs	12
	63

The Canadian Land and Emigration Company

F 36   "Regulations[62] for the Sale and Management of the Public Lands, Approved by His Excellency the Governor General in Council"
[*Toronto,* Canada Gazette, *January 15, 1859*]

1. That the lands in townships which have already been delineated or shall hereafter be delineated on Survey by the exterior lines only, may be offered for sale *en bloc* on the following terms, viz:

2. That the price shall be one half dollar per acre, payable at the time of sale.

3. That the purchaser shall cause the lands to be surveyed at his own expense into lots comprising either one hundred or two hundred acres of land in each lot; and on the north shore of Lake Huron into quarter

[62]These are the regulations under which the Canadian Land and Emigration Company began its negotiations for the purchase of land.

sections of 160 acres in each, except in spots where the configuration of the Township may render such exact quantities impracticable, and then as near to those allotments as possible.

4. That such survey shall be made by a duly licensed Provincial Land Surveyor approved of by the Commissioner of Crown Lands, and acting under his instructions, who shall make his return with Field Notes, &c., &c., in the usual method observed by Surveyors, to be also approved by the Department.

5. That one third of the quantity of land in the township shall be settled upon within two years from the time of sale; one-third more settled upon within the following five years, that is seven years from the time of sale; and the residue within the further period of three years, *i.e.* ten years from the date of sale, the settlement required being that there shall be at least one *bona fide* settler in authorized occupation for every two hundred acres of land; all land not so settled at the expiration of ten years from the time of sale to become forfeited and revert to the Crown absolutely, except such portions thereof as shall be found unfit for settlement, or such portions as are of very inferior quality and by reason thereof have remained unoccupied, in respect to which the Governor in Council may, upon application, dispense with the forfeiture and cause the same to be conveyed to the original purchaser or his assignee.

6. A Contract of sale to be made with the purchaser from the Crown, subject to the foregoing and following conditions; but Patents for the land to issue only to the occupants of the lots purchased deriving claim under the vendee of the Crown, or to the assignees claiming under such purchasers and occupants who shall have complied with the conditions of settlement hereinafter mentioned, upon a certificate or other evidence that they have paid such vendee or his assignee or complied with the contract with him, for or in regard to such particular lot; and upon evidence that the party applying, or some one under whom he claims, has been a resident upon the said lot for at least two years continuously, and that upon the same (not exceeding two hundred acres) at least ten acres for each one hundred acres have been cleared and rendered fit for cultivation and crop, and have been actually under crop, and that a habitable house in dimensions at least sixteen by twenty feet is erected thereon, and upon payment of the sum of four dollars as Patent Fees to cover expenses, &c. The nature and description of proof above referred to to be settled and prescribed by the Commissioner of Crown Lands.

7. All lands which shall, under the foregoing conditions revert to the Crown, shall be exposed to sale at Public Auction at such times and places and on such upset price as the Commissioner of Crown Lands shall fix.

. . .

Crown Lands Department,   P.M. Vankoughnet,
Toronto, 13th January, 1859.   Commissioner.

F 37   JOHN BEVERLEY ROBINSON[63] TO THE COMMISSIONER OF
CROWN LANDS, P. M. VANKOUGHNET
[*Ontario, Provincial Secretary,* Return to an Address of the
Legislative Assembly (Sessional Papers, *1868–9, no. 34*)]

Toronto, January 27th, 1859.

Having seen the advertisement issued from your Department, for the
sale of Crown Lands *en bloc* I have to inform you that, for some months
past, I have been in communication with parties in England, asking me
on what terms blocks of land could be purchased, the quality of the land,
&c. Their object is to send out persons to settle the land at once. As
these seem to be the description of purchasers that the Department in
their prospectus invite, I desire to know if I can obtain a map shewing the
situation and character of the soil, and also, as the purchasers are in
England, whether you would give me the refusal on behalf of my cor-
respondents of certain townships for 4 months, from 1st February next.
This would give them time to decide after the inspection of the maps, &c.

F 38   VANKOUGHNET TO J. B. ROBINSON
[*Ontario, Department of Lands and Forests, Instructions to Land Surveyors, Canadian Land and Emigration Company, p. 6; also printed
in Ontario,* Sessional Papers, *1868–9, no. 34*]

Department of Crown Lands
Quebec 26th. April 1860

In accordance with my letter to you of yesterday's date, I now forward
to you the names of the ten Townships that the Canada Agency Association may dispose of for the Government.

They are Dysart, Dudley, Harcourt, Guilford, Harburn, Bruton, Havelock, Eyre, Clyde, and Longford.

As the object of the Government is the speedy settlement of the
Country I must limit the time to the Association to sell these Townships
to the 1st November next.

In placing these Townships with the Company for sale, I reserve to
myself the right to withdraw any one or more of them for sale to any
other person who shall contact me for the purchase, before the Company
shall have effected a sale.

[63]John Beverley Robinson (1821–1896) was the second son of Sir John Beverley
Robinson. He was called to the Bar in 1844, was mayor of Toronto in 1857, and
was elected to the Legislative Assembly as one of the members for Toronto in
1858. From 1880 to 1887 he was Lieutenant Governor of Ontario. Robinson's
connection with the Canada Agency Association and with the newly formed Canadian Land and Emigration Company was broken off in the summer of 1861 after
a disagreement concerning his charges for legal fees.

F 39   VANKOUGHNET TO J. B. ROBINSON
[Ontario, Department of Lands and Forests, Instructions to Land Surveyors, Canadian Land and Emigration Company, p. 1; also printed in Ontario, Sessional Papers, 1868–9, no. 34]

Department of Crown Lands,
Quebec, 26th. February 1861.

In accordance with the request made by you, as Agent for the purchasers of certain townships referred to in our previous correspondence, I consent that Mr. B. W. Gossage,[64] Provincial Land Surveyor, shall act for the Dept. and the purchasers in the surveys to be made of these townships lying between the Bobcaygeon and Hastings Road. Mr. Gossage will be paid by the Government for the surveys of the outlines of the townships— The Company must remunerate Mr. Gossage for the survey and subdivision of each township into separate lots according to instructions from this Department— A duplicate of the plan and report thereof must be furnished to, and approved by, the Department.

Upon the approval of Mr. Gossage's report, the quantity of land to be paid for by the purchasers will then be ascertained.

You must understand that I cannot give longer delay than the time I have already named.

F 40   "MEMORANDUM OF ASSOCIATION OF THE CANADIAN LAND AND EMIGRATION COMPANY LIMITED"
[P.A.C., Canadian Land and Emigration Company, microfilm from Board of Trade 31]

1st. The Name of the Company is "The Canadian Land and Emigration Company Limited."
2nd. The Registered Office of the Company is to be established in England.
3rd. The Objects for which the Company is established are

The purchase holding alienation sale lease and disposal of lands or property of any kind in the Province of Canada — the survey improvement clearance and cultivation of the lands belonging to or under the control of the Company— the promotion and encouragement of Settlement thereon by the loan of money to Settlers and others and the establishment of Schools and the erection of places of Worship— the opening making improving and maintaining of roads railways and other communications and the subscription to any Railway Undertaking with a view to

---

[64]Brookes Wright Gossage (1832–1899) came to Canada from England in 1853 and qualified as a land surveyor April 11, 1857. For a time he was in partnership with Colonel J. S. Dennis and later with Vernon B. Wadsworth. He had a colourful personality and an unusually strong physique, and was a noted sportsman.

the Settlement cultivation and improvement of such lands— the promotion of Emigration into the said province from the United Kingdom of Great Britain and Ireland or elsewhere and generally the performance of such acts matters and things as are incidental or otherwise conducive to the attainment of the before mentioned objects or any of them and also such additional or extended objects as the Company may from time to time by special Resolution determine and resolve.

4th. The Liability of the Shareholders is Limited.

5th. The nominal Capital of the Company is Two hundred and fifty thousand pounds divided into Fifty thousand Shares of Five pounds each.

. . .

Dated the Eleventh day of April 1861

F 41   B. W. GOSSAGE TO VANKOUGHNET

[Ontario, Department of Lands and Forests, Instructions to Land Surveyors, Canadian Land and Emigration Company, pp. 10–1]

Camp Drag Lake
June 29th. 1861.

Agreeable to the Instructions which I received from the Chairman of the Canada Land & Emigration Company in England, a copy of which I had the honor of enclosing to you. I beg to state that I have examined four of the townships which— according to your letter of the 22nd. of May you considered were those purchased by that Company, the township of "Dysart" being one of the ten named I would respectfully request to be furnished with Instructions for the subdivision of that township as the first one the Company would desire to offer for sale.

I believe Instructions have already been issued to Mr. Rykert[65] P.L.S. and that the Department were under the impression that the survey was commenced which is not the case

There are three squatters who have commenced to make small improvements in this Township on Lake Kashagawigimog two of which have taken in their families.

I would be obliged by being furnished by the Department with a list of those Townships from which a selection can be made should it be found desirable to exchange one or two of those already named, as mentioned in your letter already referred to

I would desire in the interest of the Company that as little delay as possible should take place, in my being furnished with the Instructions and also the list of the townships, in which case I hope to be able in about five weeks from this date to report fully to the Department of my

[65]George Zacharias Rykert (1829–1869) qualified as a land surveyor on April 12, 1852. In 1861 he surveyed the Township of Dysart.

exploratory survey and to name the ten I shall recommend the Company to choose, as those to embrace their purchase.

F 42   GOSSAGE TO ANDREW RUSSELL, ASSISTANT COMMISSIONER OF CROWN LANDS
[Ontario, Department of Lands and Forests, Instructions to Land Surveyors, Canadian Land and Emigration Company, p. 28]

The Junction Bobcaygeon Road
February 12th. 1862

I have the honor to request that a further advance of Four thousand dollars on account of the survey of the Canada Land and Emigration Companys' Lands should be made to enable me to meet the heavy current expenses and to get into the neighbourhood of the townships my supplies for the summer while the sleighing is good. I find that a great saving in transport would thus be effected.

I trust that the Department will feel satisfied that the work is sufficiently advanced to entitle me to that sum

I may be allowed to state for your information that monthly advances have to be made to the families of most of the men in my employ, which when all told count between Sixty and seventy men.

I would desire that the cheque should be sent to Toronto, as it is my intention to go there about the 20th of this month to make my purchases

F 43   E. M. MILES[66] TO F. T. ROCHE[67]
[Ontario, Provincial Secretary, Return to an Address of the Legislative Assembly (Sessional Papers, 1868–9, no. 34)]

Toronto, February 5th, 1864.

With reference to the classification of the lands in your townships, according to their qualities, I beg to certify that the schedule herewith marked A, contains a correct statement of five of these townships, and the result of actual and personal inspection of each lot.

I further certify that my standard, or basis for such classification, is as follows:—

First-class lands contain 84 per cent. of land fit for cultivation.
Second   ,,   ,,   68   ,,   ,,   ,,
Third   ,,   ,,   34   ,,   ,,   ,,
Fourth   ,,   unfit for settlement, but contain merchantable timber.
Fifth   ,,   unfit for settlement.

[66]Edward Madan Miles (1835–1868) passed his examinations as land surveyor on July 13, 1857. He was appointed a surveyor to the Canadian Land and Emigration Company and laid out the town site of Haliburton.

[67]Frederic T. Roche of Toronto was appointed agent for the Canadian Land and Emigration Company in December, 1861.

I also certify that the schedule hereto annexed, marked B, contains a true statement of Mr. Gossage's classification, as drawn up by me from the returns and maps performed by him, and now in your possession.

Name of Township	1st Class Lands	2nd Class Lands	3rd Class Lands, rocky and broken	4th Class marketable Timber unfit for settlement	5th Class unfit for settlement
	Acres	Acres	Acres	Acres	Acres
Dysart	3949	11710	11714	1270	10233
Dudley	1452	22040	13307		1166
Harcourt	4042	19849	6178		2600
Harburn	150	12154	20646	800	4200
Guilford	2901	15652	18616	859	2400
Total	12494	81405	70461	2909	20599

A

Toronto, February 5th, 1864.

Edwd. M. Miles,
P.L.S.

Name of Township	1st Class Lands	2nd Class Lands	3rd Class Lands, rocky and broken	4th Class marketable Timber unfit for settlement	5th Class unfit for settlement
	Acres	Acres	Acres	Acres	Acres
Dysart	19038	15963		881	2994
Dudley	3992	17317	12884	969	2803
Harcourt	3716	13724	10617	1334	3278
Harburn	20096	10298	5154		2402
Guilford	8866	14864	12887	2360	617
Total of five Townships	55708	72166	41542	5544	12094
Bruton	15229	10905	9162	3740	828
Havelock	2176	19079	19032	996	936
Eyre	23691	14918	676	1236	7765
Clyde	16951	16143	11370		2385
Longford	5621	8977	17015	6272	988
Total of ten Townships	119356	142188	98797	17788	24696

B

Certified correct copy from Mr. Gossage's Returns.

Edwd. M. Miles,
P.L.S.

F 44   MEMORANDUM BY A(NDREW) R(USSELL)
[Ontario, Department of Lands and Forests, Instructions to Land Surveyors, Canadian Land and Emigration Company, p. 102; also printed in Ontario, Sessional Papers, 1868–9, no. 34]

Department of Crown Lands
Quebec 10th. November 1864.

The area of the ten townships sold to the Canadian Land and Emigration Company Limited is 403,125 acres from which deducting for swamps as per Agreement 41,000 acres — 362,125 remain to be paid for at 50 cents an acre, amounting to $181,062$\frac{50}{}$
The area subject to settlement duties is 261,544 acres. One ninth of which 29,060 $\frac{4}{9}$ acres are to be settled within three years from the 1st. of January next; four ninths,= 116,241 $\frac{7}{9}$ acres within ten years from do. and four ninths, = 116,241 $\frac{7}{9}$ acres within fifteen years from do.

29,060 $\frac{4}{9}$ — $\frac{1}{9}$ th.   3 years
116,241 $\frac{7}{9}$ — $\frac{4}{9}$ths. 10 ..
116,241 $\frac{7}{9}$ — $\frac{4}{9}$ths. 15 ..

One tenth of the purchase money is to be expended by the Company on Roads—

The purchase money is	$181,062$\frac{50}{}$
The amount to be expended	$ 18,106$\frac{25}{}$

F 45   ANNUAL GENERAL MEETING OF THE COMPANY, LONDON, 1865
[Toronto, Globe, March 20, 1865]

At the annual general meeting, held on the 1st instant, in London, the following report was received and adopted:—
The following information extracted from the despatches of Mr. Blomfield[68] and Mr. Stewart,[69] will show the progress that has been made in the settlement of the townships and the satisfactory position which the Company has assumed in the Province.

[68]Charles James Blomfield (b. 1831) was the son of the Right Honourable and Reverend C. J. Blomfield, Lord Bishop of London. He came to Canada in 1857 and in 1860 entered the office of Crooks, Kingsmill, and Cattanach. He was made secretary to the local board of directors of the Canadian Land and Emigration Company, and in 1868 became manager. He lived at Haliburton for many years, and in 1885 moved to Lakefield where he went into business. In 1906 he went to British Columbia where he died a few years later.
[69]Charles Russell Stewart (1826–1905), after some experience in journalism in England, came to Canada as agent for the Canadian Land and Emigration Company in 1862. He built the first home on Head Lake, prepared for the arrival of the settlers, and helped them establish schools and churches. He left the service of the Company in 1866 and became agent for Mossom Boyd. In 1872 he established the *Bobcaygeon Independent*. He was a brother of the H. C. Stewart mentioned in F 53.

	Acres
Farm lots	3,732
Town plot of Haliburton, 12 lots	6
	3,738
In the Township of Guilford	60
	3,798

About 1,000 acres may be added to this for applications under consideration. The above statement does not include any of those lots on which retaining fees have only been paid, many of which will be taken up.

The receipts on account of land transactions for the same period were	1,348.37
Allowed on account of work on roads, &c, being in effect cash	325.86
	1,674.23

Mr. Stewart in a letter addressed to the directors on the 19th February last, says: "The settlers who have recently come in are of the very best description, Canadians chiefly, accustomed to the woods, and in every instance men of respectability and means. I may say that we have been signally fortunate in securing settlers of respectability, for the character of the first settlers in a new country stamps it for ever after either with a good or a bad reputation. The means that have latterly been adopted by building a church, bringing in a surgeon, establishing schools, &c, secures to the settlement the most desirable class of settlers, and independently of all moral considerations, will be found excellent pecuniary investments."

Mr. Blomfield states "that the progress made in the sale of land since 1st April last, when we had many serious drawbacks to contend with, to which it is unnecessary for me to more than allude, will I trust, under the circumstances, be considered very satisfactory as promising large sales at no far distant date. Many of our settlers who have recently taken up land are men of some means and education. The local improvements in the last few months have been very considerable, and the advantages to settlers much more substantial than heretofore. The settlers are contented and hopeful, and the settlement generally may be considered in a very flourishing condition. The name of the Company wherever it is known now stands well from Quebec to Haliburton."

The following are Mr. Stewart's remarks as to future progress:—
"Of the future of the Company I can speak most hopefully. There is an excellent prospect of a substantial success. The majority of the new settlers take leases of their land at a rental of $10.50 per 100 acres. This

at once secures a 7 per cent interest on an upset price of $1.50. Estimating the cost to the Company at 75 cents, this gives 14 per cent. interest on the original purchase money, and the lots when sold will realise a profit of 100 per cent. Higher prices than these will in time be obtained but it would be most injudicious to raise the price at present. I can finally only repeat my former observations, that I believe the Company is in a fair way to substantial success. The opening of the Lindsay and Peterborough roads will remove the greatest difficulty in the way of settlement; and as the great advantages offered by the Company become known, and the really excellent quality of their lands become recognized, the influx of settlers will be rapidly augmented, and the prosperity both of the settlement and the Company be secured."

Mr. Blomfield reports that "The proposed establishment of a Norwegian, or, more properly speaking, a Scandinavian settlement, which had the approval of the directors in England, is being now put in a practical form, in accordance with the views expressed in their despatches on the subject. We hope soon to introduce a Norwegian clergyman, thoroughly reliable and of good business habits, to settle in one of our townships, who will act as a medium of communication between his countrymen and the English settlers, and in remunerating him for his services it is anticipated that we shall obtain some assistance from Government. We cannot at first expect to induce among the Norwegians, Swedes, or Danes, many men of means to settle in our township, but such will soon follow on hearing of the success of their countrymen, and the nucleus once formed, the growth of the settlement may be considered as secure. . . . From the nature of the operations of the Company, the shareholders cannot, of course, expect any immediate return for the capital invested, but notwithstanding some loss of time and money in the commencement, there is every prospect of a dividend being declared in a shorter time than in the case of the Canada Company, who were considered to have purchased some of the best land in the country on peculiarly favourable terms. In addition to these favourable reports, the directors are glad to state that indications of minerals of commercial value have been traced in the Company's lands, and it is hoped that further research will prove this a source of considerable profit to the Company. It is intended to pay interest for the year 1864 at the rate of 3 per cent on the paid-up capital, in the same manner as was done last year. On the establishment of the Company, it was anticipated that calls to the amount of £2 10s. per share would be very shortly required, and it was so stated in the prospectus. From the delay in the settlement with the Government only £2 per share has yet been called up. The directors therefore, propose an immediate call of 10s per share, and in order to complete the amount required for the settlement with Government, this will be followed, at not less than three months' interval, by another call of 10s, making in all £3 paid up per share. . . .

At the meeting of the above company, the report, which had been previously issued to the shareholders, was taken as read.

In the absence of Mr. Haliburton,[70] who arrived during the meeting, Mr. Montgomerie[71] was elected to the chair and moved the adoption of the report, which he was glad to say was the most satisfactory that had hitherto been issued to the shareholders, ...

F 46   MEMORANDUM[72] FROM THE COMPANY TO THE COMMISSIONER
OF CROWN LANDS, ALEXANDER CAMPBELL, MAY, 1867
[*Ontario, Provincial Secretary*, Return to an Address of the Legislative
Assembly (Sessional Papers, *1868–9, no. 34*)]

The Canadian Land and Emigration Co., (Limited,)
No. 84 Gresham House, Old Broad Street, E.C., London.

Whereas by an agreement entered into the 9th of August, 1864, between the Honorable the Commissioner of Crown Lands and Messrs. F.H. Heward,[73] C.J. Campbell,[74] and Adam Crooks,[75] acting for and on behalf of the Directors of the Canadian Land and Emigration Company, (Limited,) it was agreed that on payment of the balance of the purchase money in respect of 362,125 acres of good land, composed within the townships of Longford, Dysart, Dudley, Harcourt, Bruton, Harburn, Guilford, Clyde, Havelock, and Eyre, a patent from the Crown should be issued to the said Company, granting them in fee simple the townships referred to.

Upon survey of the lands so purchased, 261,544 acres were deemed fit for settlement and liable to the conditions set forth in the said agreement of August, 1864 ...

Several causes have occurred to delay the sale or leasing of the land so acquired by the Company. Among which may be mentioned the war in the United States, commencing shortly after the negotiations for the purchase of the land were completed, and which altogether turned aside the tide of Emigration upon which the Company had calculated for the settlement of their land.

[70]Thomas Chandler Haliburton (1796–1865), author of *The Clockmaker* and other humorous and historical works, was born in Windsor, Nova Scotia. In 1841 he was appointed to the Supreme Court Bench, and in 1856 left Canada to live in England. He was Chairman of the Canadian Land and Emigration Company and his name was given first to the village and later to the County of Haliburton.

[71]Hugh Edmonstone Montgomerie of Gracechurch Street, London, a merchant.

[72]Covering letter from the Toronto office of the Company is dated May 22, 1867.

[73]Francis H. Heward, Toronto, Manager of the Royal Insurance Company.

[74]Charles J. Campbell, Manager of the Commercial Bank, Toronto.

[75]Adam Crooks (1827–1885), solicitor for the Canadian Land and Emigration Company, was called to the Bar in 1852. He was elected to the Legislative Assembly of Ontario in 1871 and in turn held the offices of Attorney General, Provincial Treasurer, and Minister of Education.

This abnormal condition of affairs had scarcely ceased when it was followed by the Fenian invasion, producing in the minds of the German people (whom the company were then seeking as emigrants, through the medium of an agent specially employed for that purpose,) a strong feeling of distrust and a disinclination to select Canada as their future home, added to this the subsequent war in Germany rendered the outlay incurred by the Company in sending their agent altogether useless. These difficulties of immigration, which were also seriously felt in Great Britain, were further increased by an outbreak of cholera on board the vessels taking out emigrants.

The Company have used every effort to make known the advantages of settlement in Canada by advertising in that Province, in the United States, in the German and Norwegian papers, and in England, and also by the distribution of pamphlets in those countries. Having also by the expenditure of more than $10,000 in the opening of roads, by advances for the building of Saw and Grist Mills, and for the establishment of steam communication in the townships, and by every other means at their command, exhibited a *bona fide* intention faithfully to carry out their engagements and to fulfil the conditions of the bond, the Directors believe they have a fair claim for consideration and that the Government will be pleased to extend the date[76] from which the time for fulfilment of settlement duties should reckon, from the 1st January, 1865, as specified in the agreement to 1st January, 1868.

The Company beg it to be understood that their exertions will be in no way slackened by such a concession but that they will still continue, by the low price at which they offer their lands, and the other inducements they hold out, to urge on settlement so far as to fulfil at as early a date as possible the conditions stated in the agreement. . . .

F 47   THE COMPANY'S PETITION FOR RELIEF
[*Ontario, Provincial Secretary*, Return to an Address of the Legislative Assembly (Sessional Papers, *1868–9, no. 34*)]

To His Excellency the Honorable W.P. Howland,[77] Lieutenant Governor of the Province of Ontario, in Executive Council.

The humble petition of the Canadian Land and Emigration Co., (Limited,)

RESPECTFULLY SHEWETH AS FOLLOWS:

That your petitioners are incorporated under the Imperial Joint Stock Company's Act, and the shareholders of the said Company are principally resident in Great Britain.

[76]The Department of Crown Lands agreed to this extension (Andrew Russell to C. J. Blomfield, May 27, 1867, *Sessional Papers*, 1868–9, no. 34).

[77]William Pearce Howland (1811–1907) was Lieutenant Governor of Ontario, 1868 to 1873. In 1879 he was created a K.C.M.G.

That in the year one thousand eight hundred and sixty one, they laid out a capital of forty thousand and seventy-seven pounds, seven shillings and eight-pence, sterling, in the purchase of ten townships, containing four hundred and fifty thousand acres of land, in the Province of Ontario, and since that date they have expended the further sum of eighteen thousand and fifty-four pounds, fifteen shillings and two-pence, sterling in expenses connected with the management of the Company's affairs, surveys and preparation of the land for settlement and furthering emigration, and that while Canada has been benefited by so large an expenditure, various causes beyond the control of the Company have so much and so injuriously affected the settlement of the Company's land, notwithstanding the favorable terms and low price at which it has been offered for sale, that your petitioners have as yet been unable to obtain but a small return of the capital invested.

That their efforts to obtain settlers will be still further impeded now that the Government has offered to the public free grants large tracts of land in the immediate vicinity of the lands of the Company, and that had such been the announced intention of the Government at the time of the negotiation for the purchase of the townships now held by the Company, it is obvious that the purchase would either have been declined or such terms only would have been acceded to as, in the face of such competition, would have given them a rational prospect of fulfilling the settlement duties required.

Your petitioners therefore humbly pray that, under the circumstances, either that your petitioners may be placed in the same position as the free settlers by the restitution of the capital paid by them to the Government, or that they may be relieved of the performance of settlement duties.

And your petitioners, as in duty bound, will ever pray, &c.

Sealed with the Company's seal in the Province of Ontario, and signed by its attorney this twenty-second day of August, A.D., 1868.

F.H. Heward, [Seal]
C.J. Campbell.
Attorneys and Trustees.

Witness, Chas. Jas. Blomfield, Secretary.

F 48 "THE CANADIAN LAND AND IMMIGRATION COMPANY," 1869
[*Ontario, Department of Agriculture and Public Works, Emigration to Canada, the Province of Ontario, pp. 29–30*]

This is the youngest of our land companies, having bought so recently as 1861 the ten townships of Dysart, Dudley, Harcourt, Guilford, Harburn, Bruton, Havelock, Eyre, and Clyde (in Peterboro' Co.), and Longford (in Victoria Co.) These Townships— all in one block— were unsurveyed, and after a survey, which cost the Company $31,810, it appeared that they covered 403,125 acres, from which, after deducting

41,000 acres for the area covered by swamps, &c., there remained 362,125 acres, to be paid for at the rate of 50 cents per acre. The amount paid by the Company to Government was $195,043. The ordinary settlement duties upon these lands are to be performed within 18 years from January, 1865, and ten per cent of the purchase money is to be refunded to the Company for the construction of leading lines of road, subject to Government inspection. Besides these expenses, the Company has paid nearly $10,000 more for additional surveying, road-making, &c., besides considerable sums in preparation of their estate for settlement, the furtherance of emigration, &c. In all, besides payments to Government, over $100,000 have been expended to date.

Some 25 miles of new road have been constructed, and 25 miles of the old Government Peterson road have been brushed out and repaired. The Company has shared the expense of many of these improvements, with municipalities interested. In conjunction with a lumber firm of the district, the Company is now energetically extending other roads into the forest, and damming the principal lake, so as to keep the water up to high water mark, and allow a steamer, which it subsidizes, to run the whole summer through. The Company's officers are now engaged in promoting a plan for a wooden railway to run into the property, to facilitate lumbering and settlement.

The village of Haliburton, beautifully situated on Lake Kushog, is rapidly increasing, several stores have been established, and there is a saw and grist mill on the spot. The company pays half the stipends of a resident clergyman, and has given free grants of lands for churches and schools.

An arrangement has just been made whereby a portion of the valuable pine timber on the property will be gradually taken off by a firm who have undertaken to find work in the shanties, during the winter, for all willing and industrious hands. By this means a ready market for years to come is secured to the farmer at the highest prices, and the settlers will have the opportunity of earning good wages for themselves and their teams throughout the winter.

The settlement in Harcourt has hitherto not made rapid progress owing to the want of communication with the front; but now that there is every prospect of an immediate extension of the Burleigh road, the land being reported to be the best on the company's territory, they are about to erect a grist mill, which, with the saw mill already there, will form the nuclus of a prosperous village. To improve the means of communication 3000 acres are now offered as free grants along the Peterson road, and for these early application should be made, as a like opportunity will not easily be obtained. The price at which the Company now sells is:— In Dysart, $1.50, and in other townships $1.00 per acre, cash; or $2.00 in Dysart, and $1.25 in other townships, in five annual instalments, with interest at five per cent. Or the Company will rent for 17 years, for 15 cents per acre in Dysart, and ten cents in other townships, and the right of pre-emption at the end of the term, at $2.00 and $1.35 respectively. Half acre lots in the village of Haliburton are for sale at $20 each. Settlement duties have to be pre-paid on farm lots and town property. The sales have chiefly been made to Canadians, but the Company has just perfected arrangements for an active emigrant agency in England.

The return of produce in Dysart, made by the Company in the spring of 1868 is as follows:— Spring Wheat, 1,336 bushels; Fall Wheat, 425 bushels; Oats, 1,201 bushels; Potatoes, 5,430 bushels; Turnips, 5,380 bushels; Barley, 212 bushels; Hay, 111 tons; Pork, 6,830 lbs.

The office of the Canadian Land and Emigration Company is at Peterborough.

F 49   FIFTEENTH ANNUAL MEETING OF SHAREHOLDERS
[*Toronto*, Canadian Monetary Times, *March 23, 1869*]

The fifteenth[78] annual meeting of the shareholders of this company was held at the London Tavern, London, on the 3rd inst.

The Chairman, in moving the adoption of the report referred to the reconstruction of the Board, and the completion of such arrangements as would have the effect of giving more harmony to their deliberations. The directors, as you are aware, have shelved for some time the question of remuneration except such as should be voted to them at the annual meeting of the company. Now with regard to Canada. The Toronto board ceased to exist on the last day of last year, at the general wish of by far the greater part of the shareholders, and we believe that the time has come when its services are no longer required. We are at a great distance from the scene of the operations of the company, and it is important that we should have a gentleman there as manager in whom we could place thorough reliance, but upon whom there should be a check. Mr. Blomfield has been appointed— a man in whom, from all accounts, and from our experience of him for three years, we can place an implicit confidence; and we are agreed that within certainly defined limits he should have the fullest liberty to act for us to the best of his ability. Up to this time he was hampered by the Toronto board, to whom he acted as secretary, on the one hand, and on the other by fear of mis-representations sent home. . . .

The Rev. Mr. Tucker . . . thought it would be of advantage to the company to give away to *bona fide* settlers certain portions of land, say 100 acres, for they had now to compete with Government, who gave away gifts of land to the extent of 100 acres to any one who proved themselves to be a *bona fide* settler. And unless they did so, how could they expect men to take land from them? He would counsel the board

[78]By the Memorandum of Association of 1861, two General Meetings were held each year, and by the revised articles of 1870 only one General Meeting was held. The numbering of the reports varied accordingly.

to take the question into consideration, and to try it at least for two or three years. He wished to say nothing more, only to reserve to himself the right of proposing a director at the proper time.

Mr. Montgomerie (director) said— With regard to free grants of land by the Government, the company had made a remonstrance with them, not to ask them to give this up, but to say that it was scarcely fair to the company, considering the terms on which they had taken their lands. The Government recognized the justness of the complaint, and expressed themselves ready to discuss the questions with the company. But it was already a fact that we had given several free grants of land upon the roads through their lands where it was necessary to keep them open for traffic. The land was given upon the condition that the settlers kept the roads free from underbrush. So that there was considerable difference between their free lands and those of the Government; for by the means of their free lands they kept open the roads upon their estates, which the Government did not undertake to do. And so great was this benefit, that all persons who had any money to buy land preferred to buy the land of the company rather than take the free lands of the Government. With regard to forfeitures, he thought that the directors could scarcely be blamed for pressing upon these persons to pay; they had abstained from doing so as long as they could with justice to the other shareholders. . . .

. . .

A shareholder asked if the directors had any fresh news from Canada.

The Chairman— Yes, we have sold more acres of land than ever before, and in leasing we have done a great deal. We have leased 1,800 acres during the past year, while during the whole previous course of the company the leasings amount to only 7,500 acres, which I consider a very encouraging return. They are at ten cents per annum. . . .

F 50 EIGHTEENTH REPORT OF THE COMPANY
[*Canadian Land and Emigration Company Papers. Copies in possession of H. Cummings, Ottawa*]

18th Report— Annual General Meeting— 27th April 1871 held at the London Tavern

In presenting their Eighteenth Report to the Shareholders of the Canadian Land and Emigration Company, the Directors have to state, that the payment to the Shareholders recommended at the last Annual Meeting of 2s.6d. per share, amounting to £2,444.7s.6d., has been carried out.

They are happy again to be able to report favourably on the condition and prospects of the Company.

The proceedings taken in accordance with a resolution passed at the last Annual Meeting with regard to the Articles of Association, together with the recommendations of the Committee appointed for the purpose, have been already laid before the Shareholders. The new Articles of Association which were approved and confirmed at Extraordinary General Meetings held on the 12th and 29th of July last, will, it is anticipated, provide for the more efficient and successful working of the Company.

The Board announce with great satisfaction that, as will be seen from the Balance-sheet, all arrears of calls have now been paid up. Besides this, the former holders of 860 shares which had been forfeited for nonpayment of calls have, since the last Annual Meeting, made application to the Board for permission to resume possession of the shares in question, and the Board have, in exercise of their powers, arranged for their doing so, on payment of all arrears.

Lumbering operations have been carried on with great vigour during the past season in the Company's townships, and the high prices obtained by this means for all the produce raised in the district will give, it is hoped, a sensible stimulus to the settlement of the land.

Mr. Boyd's[79] operations have been carried on during the past season with great activity, and his payments alone to the Company, during the coming year, are estimated at $14,000. He has a large farm in Havelock, of which the following account is given by Mr. C.R. Stewart his agent there:

"Your farm in Havelock is now in good working condition. Nearly seventy acres will be under cultivation, and the whole of the buildings are in a thoroughly efficient state. The land cleared proves to be of excellent quality, and the farm is one of the best in the back country. Strangers who have visited it have been both surprised and encouraged by the fine crops raised there last year, and have spread such good reports of the district that we may reasonably expect a fine settlement will be established in the neighbourhood."

A provisional arrangement was entered into with Mr. R. Strickland[80] (who visited in England in August last) on terms similar to those of the agreement with Mr. Boyd, in virtue of which he has continued the Burleigh Road to the south boundary of Harcourt, thus giving a new and more advantageous access to the townships. This road will be continued this summer to Kenneway village.

[79]Mossom Boyd (1815–1883) was born in India, came to Canada in 1834, and settled in Bobcaygeon. For a time he was associated with John Langton in the lumber business, then operated his own company. Until the 1870's he was active in the square timber trade with Great Britain but after that period exported mainly sawn lumber to the United States. He bought mills at Bobcaygeon and carried on an extensive lumbering business in the Haliburton area.

[80]Probably Roland C. Strickland of the R. and G. Strickland lumbering company which had large mills at Lakefield.

Mr. Strickland has taken out timber to the amount of $1,500 from Harcourt, and an arrangement has been made, on favourable terms, with Messrs. Bronson and Weston,[81] superseding their hitherto uncertain and unsatisfactory relations to the Company.

The expenses incurred during the past year in road-making have been heavy, but it is the opinion of the Board that settlement can be best encouraged in this way: the greater portion of the cost will, however, be repaid out of the 10 per cent. reserve in the hands of the Government.

The purchase of the mills at Haliburton, recommended in the last report, has been carried out and improvements made in the machinery, which will prove to be of great benefit to the surrounding district. A good stock of sawn and seasoned lumber is now on hand, and the building trade is expected to be very brisk this year in Haliburton. Directions have now been sent to the Manager to seek for an eligible tenant at a rent sufficient to give an adequate return upon our outlay.

The Manager's return to 31 December last, shows the land sold or leased during the past year to be 4,883 acres, making a total of 16,560 acres sold and leased, of which 2,226 acres are cleared. . . .

The free grants of Government lands in the immediate vicinity continue to operate disadvantageously to the rapid settlement of our territory. The effect will not ultimately be adverse, and the intention of the Government to give assistance to railroads seems to hold out a real prospect of our obtaining that much-desired access to our lands. The Board are anxious that the Shareholders should contemplate the possibility of their being called upon, at no distant date, to decide whether they will make some present sacrifice to ensure these advantages.

On the broad contemplation of the results of last year's work, the Board consider the financial position of the Company such as to warrant their taking action under the 7th clause of Section V of the Articles of Association, and they therefore give notice of their intention to make a return of 2s.6d. per share in reduction of the Capital of the Company; leaving the amount paid up in each share £3.7s.6d. This step, they have no doubt, will meet with the approbation of the shareholders.

In accordance with the Articles of Association, Mr. Charles Gurney retires from the Board at this meeting, but, being eligible, offers himself for re-election. . . .

In pursuance of the powers contained in clause 8 of Section XIII of the Articles of Association, the Auditors have, with the approbation of the Directors, appointed as local Auditor in Canada, Mr. John Carnegie,

---

[81]Bronson and Weston were successors to Harris and Bronson, lumbermen in the Ottawa Valley. When the Canadian Land and Emigration Company bought the ten townships, part of the land was under timber licence to Harris and Bronson. According to an agreement, Harris and Bronson were to pay timber dues to the Company on these lands on the same terms on which they would have paid the government.

representative of the County of Peterborough, in the Provincial Parliament of Ontario, and the Canadian accounts, as audited by him, are embodied in the Balance-sheet certified to by the London Auditors, and herewith submitted.

By order
J.W. Collins
Secretary.

F 51   Twenty-third Report of the Company
[*Canadian Land and Emigration Company Papers. Copies in possession of H. Cummings, Ottawa*]

23rd Report of the Directors— Annual General Meeting— April 28, 1876 held at the London Tavern

In submitting their Twenty-third Report to the Shareholders of the Canadian Land and Emigration Company, the Directors have to announce that the return of Capital to the Shareholders of 6d. per share recommended at the last Annual General Meeting, amounting to £510.12s.6d. has been carried out. This further sum reduces the paid-up Capital to three pounds per share.

Your Board have to express their sincere regret that the substantial improvement which they were led to look for in the affairs of the Company has not been realized, but that, on the contrary, the serious stagnation which continues to depress the timber trade has diminished the receipts from timber sales during the past year by no less a sum than £1,898. The utmost endeavours of the Board have been used to stimulate activity on the part of the lumbermen, but these declare their inability to clear off stocks now on hand and bring fresh lumber to market except at ruinous loss. . . .

This state of things also acts injuriously in other respects upon our townships where the settlers, owing to the reduced establishments of the lumbermen, are deprived of the market to which they have been accustomed to look for the disposal of their produce. Under these circumstances the land sales have realized only £771, being £98 less than last year.

The attention of the shareholders must be called to the fact that the annual instalments received on account of the Township of Longford, and which have formed the chief item in our land sales of late years, will now cease the final payment having been made in 1875. It may be hoped that the nearer approach of railway communication will effect an improvement.

The negotiations for the purchase of your property by the Victoria Railway company have not been renewed during the past year. That Company has, however, just obtained a grant from the Dominion Government of $33,000 out of the Railway appropriation for the purpose of its extension to Kinmount, a distance of about 20 miles from Haliburton, to which place it will afford the readiest means of access. The latest reports received from the Manager give an almost positive assurance that the rails will be laid for traffic to Kinmount in the course of the ensuing summer.

It, therefore, now becomes the duty of your Board to consider on what terms it may be possible to procure an extension to Haliburton. We may fairly ask that we should not by reason of our proprietory being English, be exposed to any exceptional disadvantages in comparison with favours granted to other districts, and that the amount of money spent by us in the townships, and the benefit of our expenditure on roads, mills &c from which we have had so little return, should be set to our credit. The remarks of the Provincial Secretary, Mr. Wood, as to this may be noted: he said, "That when the Victoria Road reached Kinmount it would be entitled to receive aid as a colonization road, provided the English Land Company granted a reasonable bonus. The road would pass some thirty miles through the Company's lands, would add several hundred thousand dollars to the value of these lands, and it was but fair to demand from them that reasonable aid."

Contemporaneously with the great falling off in the receipts the Board regret to say that, from circumstances over which they had no control, the taxation of their property has largely increased, having risen from £735 in 1874 to £1,017 in 1875. Of this nearly £100 is raised on the County Assessment for railway purposes, and we are now taxed for the northern townships, not hitherto included in the assessment.

In view of such adverse circumstances in the past and the uncertainties of the year on which we are now entering, your Directors regret that they do not feel justified in recommending any return being made to the Shareholders on the present occasion, while the affairs of the Company are in a state of transition.

Your Board have lost no opportunity of urging upon their officers in Canada the necessity of the closest economy in the conduct of the Company's affairs. They are glad to be able to report that the general expenditure, not including taxation in Canada, notwithstanding the increase in the Manager's salary, the claim for which it was impossible for them reasonably to resist has been reduced from £1,144 to £1,022. The utmost endeavours of your Board will be used to effect still further reductions under this head.

In accordance with the Articles of Association, Mr. H. E. Montgomerie retires from the Board by rotation, but being eligible offers himself for re-election.

The Auditors, Messrs Fry and Lovelock, also offer themselves for re-election.

By Order
J.W. Collins
Secretary

F 52   A. PARSONAGE[82] TO CHARLES PARSONAGE
[P.A.C., Parsonage Papers]

Dysart November 19, 1865

. . . we have had a terrable time of it out here in the Bush many times on the borders of starvation leaving out the immence amount of Labour required to make a farm in what might be called the Wilderness but such appears to be the general fate of first Settlers who come out without capital for all the money we could muster in the world when we landed in Quebec was two shillings and ten pence with a journey of six hundred miles before us but Providence protects the Shorn Lamb— there are no Workhouses out here and very few Goals and with all its drawbacks it is still a large and beautiful Country. We are now in the midst of our Indian Summer which began about a week since, it will sometimes last three days and sometimes three weeks after which the snow begins to fall and the ground is covered for about five months until the [MS torn] of May when it quickly disappears and in a week the trees are out in full leaf— I am happy to say we are in a much better position than we where this time last year when we could scarcely get Potatoes to eat we have about 9 acres chopped two thirds of which we have had under crop— it has been a splendid harvest— we have been diggin Potatoes since the 10 of July and we have now 200 Bushels with 300 Bushels of Turnips 50 Bushels of Indian Corn a nice stack of Wheat the produce of [MS torn] Acres a good patch of Oats with a fine lot of vegetables allowed to be the best Collection in the whole Township including Cabbages Carrots Beets onions cucumbers mellons squashes Pumpkins Tomatoes and several other kinds and you may perhaps think I am [MS torn] but we have now in the House a squash that would fill the bottom of a small Donkey cart I can assure you it takes a strong man to raise it off the ground we have Cucumbers a yard in length and our 300 Bushels of Turnips was the produce of two ounces of seed and no more, many of them will quite fill an ordinary pail— the Township appears to be filling up fast most of what are called the best Lots are taken, we have a resident Clergyman living on the next Lot to ours Little Fred and Marian go there to School almost every day, Everet has been out camping in the Woods with one of the Trappers who resides in the next Townships we where glad to send him for the sake of his meals but after staying a fortnight he came home with the carcuse of a Beaver on his back not fancying the howling of the wild animals round the Camp during the night— he is growing a fine Lad

[82]A. Parsonage and his wife Annie with their youngest children came from England and settled in Dysart Township on Lake Kashagawigamog on "the old Indian Portage which means *Road* leading the nearest way from the Kahshagawigamog Lake, the Indian name for long and crooked, to the Burnt River" (Guillet, *The Valley of the Trent*, p. 81). The letter quoted was written by Mr. Parsonage to his son Charles who apparently remained in England.

but of course still very young nothing can exceed the joyeous merriment of the children out here their spirits seem almost uncontrolable not one single sigh of regret at parting from their native Land— I believe it is a great measure owing to the pureness of the atmosphere we have not had a half dozen foggy days since we have been out here. I am strongly recomended to start in my own line of Business as I am the only Butcher in the whole district and being one of the first comers of course known to every one I have no doubt there would be a good demand for meat if they only knew where to go to get it as when any of the Settlers have had meat to sell it as all been bespoke before hand it takes very little to start a Butcher in this Country the meat being less than half the price it is in England . . .

F 53   C. L. MacDermott,[83] an English Settler in Haliburton in 1868
[MacDermott, Facts for Emigrants]

It was on the 16th of May, in this year, 1868, that I sailed from London for New York, on my way to Canada. I had long been desirous of emigrating to Canada— an opportunity of a favourable character presented itself— I accepted the chance, and am at this moment writing at my new home in the depths of the wilderness. Many of my friends had begged that I would send them accurate and full information of the country, of the voyage, of the expenses, of the journey, of the prices of commodities, of the rate of wages, and so forth. I promised I would do so, and am now performing my promise.

. . .

. . . A delightful trip of about three hours, through lakes where the scenery is of the most charming character, took me to Bobcaygeon, a little village that stands at the commencement of the Government Road of that name, and upon the short river that connects Pigeon Lake with Sturgeon Lake. Bobcaygeon owes much of its prosperity to the energy of Mr. Boyd, an English gentleman who settled here when the forest was yet untouched, and who now carries on a very large business in sawed timber. He has powerful saw mills, and his operations extend a distance of fifty miles into the as yet only partially settled country to the north. He annually exports some millions of feet of pine boards to the States. I should here note that the fare from Chemony Lake to Bobcaygeon is two shillings sterling.

At Bobcaygeon, Simpson's Hotel is an excellent house to stop at, and Mr. Simpson is always ready to give information and assistance to those who are going to the "Back Country."

[83]Charles Landy MacDermott (b. 1852?) was born in London, England, of Irish parents. As a boy he came to Haliburton where he had friends, then returned to England and published *Facts for Emigrants*.

A stage from Bobcaygeon runs three times a week to Minden, a village thirty miles on the Bobcaygeon road; Tuesdays, Wednesdays,[84] and Saturdays up the road, and the alternate days down to Bobcaygeon; Fare 1 dol. 50 cents or 6s. sterling.

At Minden there are three hotels, and on my arrival I stayed at Buck's Hotel, a house that I can speak of in the best terms.

From Minden a waggon took me and my luggage and some fellow travellers to the port of Lake Kashagawigamog, a distance of three miles and a half, and here a small steamer was in waiting and conveyed me to my destination at Haliburton, a distance of about fourteen miles.

I have been particular in giving distances and expenses, in the hope that it may serve as a guide to future emigrants travelling in this direction; and I may say that from the moment I landed at Port Hope, I had no difficulty whatever in making my way to Haliburton. Mr. H. C. Stewart of 41, Great Percy Street, Pentonville, had supplied me so fully with information as to the line of road, that I travelled it as easily as though it were a once a week journey. Indeed if at any moment a difficulty arose, I had only to mention his name, or that of his brother Mr. C.R.Stewart of Haliburton, and I at once found myself in possession of an unfailing passport.

. . .

WAGES.

It is not easy to give a clear idea of the scale of wages in this Back Country. It is so involved with the subject of board and lodging that the old countryman cannot at once comprehend its nature. The wages of a carpenter,— a good workman,— who understands the nature of this country well, may be taken at 1 dol. per day and his board and lodging. The usual charge for board and lodging is 2 dol. 50 cents per week. In Haliburton there is a very nice little hotel, supplied abundantly with venison and salmon through the skill of the proprietor, Mr. Holland, and I believe that the usual charge for a week's board and lodging is from 2 dols. 50 cents to 3 dols. per week. The wages of a man hired to work on a farm, a man who can chop and is thoroughly familiar with the axe and all the work of clearing new land, may be taken at from 12 dols. to 15 dols. per month and his board and lodging. It must not, however, be supposed that an emigrant fresh from the old country will obtain these wages. If a raw hand can earn enough to pay for his board and lodging he should consider he is doing well. In fact the emigrant when he first arrives is not of much use to anyone. He can't chop,— he can't drive oxen,— he can't cradle,— he can't split rails,— and it is very few who can even hill potatoes or Indian corn. Since I arrived here a very industrious Englishman,— a hard working man,— came out and at once took a job,— chopping a piece of new land. He worked honestly at his job from sunrise to sunset, and in twelve days had scarcely finished half an

[84]Probably a misprint for "Thursday."

acre. The market price of chopping an acre of ordinary land is seven dols. and it takes an average axeman six days. There are men who say they can chop an acre in less, but I think seven days might be taken as an average. It will take at least two months for even a quick and apt old countryman to learn to swing an axe, and it will be a year before he makes a good axeman. The wages of girls are high, and they are in great request. A girl will obtain from four dols. to six dols. per month.

PRICE OF LAND.

Haliburton is the centre of the operations of the Canadian Land Company,[85] who own nearly half a million of acres in this district. In the Company's townships the land is selling from one dol. per acre to one dol. and fifty cents according to terms and locality. The townships immediately adjoining the Company's block are either totally unoccupied, or are otherwise only partially settled. In many of these townships the Government system of Free Grants is adopted, and an emigrant can choose his lot, take possession of it, cultivate it, and after five years' residence has the title deeds handed over to him. It is a serious question with the emigrant whether he should take a Free Grant, or purchase of the Canadian Land Company. The quality of the land may be assumed to be about equal; for a man who takes time can pick an excellent lot in either case. If the emigrant has sufficient funds, it is in my opinion better for him to purchase from the Company, who it must be observed, give either five or ten years to pay the money. The emigrant who purchases from the Company has at once the advantage of living on a good road,— he is near to saw mills and grist mills,— he is enabled to procure his supplies without difficulty, and to sell his produce, when he has any to spare. Moreover, he is close to schools, where his children are taught free of expense, and the local taxation is chiefly borne by the Company. Lastly, but most important, he is among well-to-do people, and when he runs out of funds, he can hire out to some of his neighbours and earn money to keep him until his farm begins to be productive. The man who takes a Free Grant must, if he chooses a good lot, be in the heart of the woods,— he is isolated from other settlements,— he has no road, no market, no school, no agricultural society, no post office, no mill, no church, He is living among settlers as poor as himself, and he cannot consequently hire out for wages, and whatever is done has to be done solely by the settlers themselves, without any extra assistance. Settling on a Free Grant in the townships just opened by the Government, means several years exceedingly heavy labour and much privation and hardship. These are not to be avoided by settling on the Company's lands, but they are greatly reduced, and the life of the woods is altogether made much more endurable. Still, the question is a serious one for the emigrant and must

[85]The Canadian Land and Emigration Company.

be determined according to the nature of his means. For my own part I prefer paying the one hundred dollars for the one hundred acres and sharing in the advantages offered by the Company.

NATURE OF THE COUNTRY AND QUALITY OF THE SOIL.—

The first impression that an emigrant forms of the back country is not favourable. He has been accustomed to the pastures and beautifully tilled corn fields of England, and when he sees the clearing of a settler,— the blackened stumps, the scattered logs, the rough and ugly faces,— he is disposed to take an unfavourable view of the whole affair. The land, too, is seldom level, and the surface is frequently encumbered with stones. Stone, indeed, is the great drawback of the whole of Canada, and especially of those districts that are yet unsettled. In looking for land in this neighbourhood, the only point to consider is whether it is free from stone— for the soil itself is universally good. The soil is high and loamy and sometimes sandy, but the subsoil is almost invariably a compact clay. Its fertility is abundantly manifested in the fine crops of wheat, Indian corn, oats, barley, peas, potatoes, and clover that are raised. A very moderate amount of skill and care will keep it in good heart; and the safest way, indeed, the only paying system is to take one or two crops off new land, and then seed it down with grass seeds for hay and pasture. In five years from the time of chopping, it can be readily ploughed, most of the stumps coming out with the plough. It is heavily timbered with hard wood, such as beech, and maple, and birch,— and there is sufficient cedar for fences. The whole country is thickly studded with lakes, and their effect is sensibly to ameliorate the climate. The winter is of the same length as on the shores of Ontario; the snow is seldom deep enough for good sledging before the middle of December, and it is off the ground by the first week in April. The lakes are closed for navigation about the middle of November. The Bobcaygeon road passes through a very bad country. It is the point of junction between the limestone formation and the granite. As soon as I passed the village of Minden, I noticed the difference at once, and we came into a country where it is evident agriculture can be carried on successfully.

COST OF CLEARING LAND.

It may be taken that the price of clearing land is 16 dols. per acre. This clears and fences the land and leaves it in fit condition for crops. A raw hand ought to clear the first winter at least five acres, and some men have cleared as much as ten. A practised axeman would chop ten or twelve acres during the winter, without working very hard.

AVERAGE CROPS.

Potatoes, two hundred bushels per acre.
Spring wheat, sixteen bushels per acre.

Fall wheat, twenty-four bushels per acre.

Oats, thirty bushels per acre.

Hay, (timothy) from a ton to a ton and-a-half per acre.

BEST TIME TO ARRIVE HERE

Emigrants should arrive here in July. They have then leisure to look for land, to build a shanty, to underbrush a piece of land, and to meet the winter fully prepared. It is not desirable to come earlier, as it is best to come here after the fly time is over. The flies are in full power from the last week in May, until the second week in July. The woods are then almost unbearable to a new comer; black flies and mosquitoes making life in the woods a misery. This annoyance becomes less every year. In the old settlements black flies are unknown, and mosquitoes scarce; but in the woods they are very numerous and fierce in their attacks.

EXPENSE OF SETTLING.

The Government papers say that a settler in going into the woods should have £40 of capital. The government is right, though many a man carves out an independence who carries nothing to the woods but his axe. It is clear that for twelve months a new settler must live on his own resources, for he cannot raise any crops in less time than that; and the first year he seldom does more than raise enough potatoes and flour to supply him, until his second crop comes to hand. In this settlement a man has a better chance than elsewhere for the Company have works in progress that employs much labour, and he can get a job of work at almost any period of the year. An instance is before me at this minute, of two young men aged seventeen and twenty-two, who came to Canada five years ago. They hired out for the first year, and saved a little money. They then bought two-hundred acres near Haliburton, and now they have forty acres under crop,— have live stock worth 250[86] dols., and will sell this season probably 200 bushels of wheat and other produce in proportion. They are now building a substantial farm house, and last year put up a large barn 80 feet long. Any man who is prepared to work hard can become independent here, and have a good farm, the necessaries of life in abundance, and some of the luxuries. Schooling is free, the schools in this settlement being maintained by a local taxation of which the bulk is borne by the Land Company. I find that though there is no political feeling of any kind, there is a perpetual skirmish going on about local affairs throughout each settlement I have passed through. Each settlement is divided into two or three parties, and the contentions between them are none the less acrimonious from the causes being paltry and small. Religious contentions take the lead, and the various sects manifest a most vigorous dislike to each other, in fact this is one of the disturbing influences of all new settlements. Municipal

---

[86]The printing of these figures is not clear.

affairs also give rise to numerous local squabbles of the most petty and contemptible character. But however violent may be these animosities, it is pleasing to find that if a man is in a difficulty, if his work gets a head of him, or he is in need of help, then his neighbours come to his aid; a "bee" is called, and one and all join to lend him a hand.

. . . I shall be happy to give any other information that my friends may apply for; and those who contemplate emigrating to this particular section of Canada, I strongly recommend to apply to Mr. H. C. Stewart, of 41 Great Percy Street, who is intimately acquainted with Canadian affairs, and who is now engaged in establishing a cooperative system of farming in Canada, with a view to the more speedy and practical settlement of the wild lands. One such farm is now in course of formation near Haliburton, and several settlers have arrived from the old country, all of whom speak in the most favourable manner of the project. As a conclusion to these somewhat disjointed memorandums, I append a copy of Mr. Stewart's prospectus of the Haliburton Co-operative Farm.

The Haliburton Co-operative Farm is situated in the County of Peterborough, in the Canadian Province of Ontario. It is on the shore of Lake Kashagawigamog, (now known as Lake Kushog) and within half a mile of the rising village of Haliburton. Haliburton has been formed about four years, and possesses Saw and Grist Mills, and the Shops that usually mark the commencement of a village in the Backwoods.

Each person employed on the Farm will be provided with a separate Cottage furnished with provisions and necessaries at cost prices, receive fair weekly wages for his work, and for the work of those members of his family whose industry is available,— and will be entitled to an equitable share of the yearly profits of the Farm proportionate to the wages he has received.

The following are among the advantages offered to the emigrant. He has at once a destination to proceed to on landing in Canada, and is thereby saved loss of time, expense, anxiety, and uncertainty;— and on arriving at the Farm he is ensured fair wages and constant employment for himself and family,— a comfortable home,— cheap provisions,— Schooling at the lowest cost,— and association with persons having similar objects, and of congenial habits.

Should the emigrant wish, after a time, to purchase land, and commence farming on his own account, the Managers of the Farm will assist him in making his purchase; and should he desire to remain in co-operation with the Farm they will locate him on lands immediately adjoining the property.

Further particulars and references may be obtained of
Mr. H. C. Stewart,
41, Great Percy street, Islington, London, England; or,
Mr. C. R. Stewart,
Post Office, Haliburton, Township, Dysart, County Peterborough, Canada West.

G. LUMBER, FUR, AND GOLD

Lumbering in Muskoka

G 1 T. G. ANDERSON TO S. P. JARVIS
[P.A.C., Indian Affairs, R.G. 10, v. 124, no. 18]

Coldwater 1st. December 1837

In compliance with your letter of the 24th. Novr.ult., I enclose a copy and an Extract from letter directing me to put the Indians in possession of the Severn Saw Mill[1] and the rest of the property at Coldwater and the Narrows and, it must be in consequence of that Surrender that John Aisence finds himself authorised to sell the Severn Saw Mills.—

This Mill was built by a Contractor named Lewis, I think in 1830, and for which he was paid £430 or upwards— It has been unemployed for Several years, and consequently much impaired, It was to save it from going to ruin that, in my "Official communication of the 23d Nov. 36" I recommended that Saw Mill being let to a Gentleman at the Narrows who had applied for it.

The Mill is Situate on the first Fall after entering the River; a few hundred Yards from the lake and to which larger Boats can go— It is, I understand, built on a Crown Lot—. Not having seen the Land, beyond the vicinity of the Mill I am not prepared to describe its quality — but immediately about the Mill there is very little Soil, and as far as I have seen is principally Granite Rock.

The Mill in its present State would probably sell for, betwixt £50 and £100.

I have been told lately, that Mr. A. Borland & Mr. Andrew Mitchell have offered John Aisence £75.— for it.—

G 2 W. M. DAWSON[2] TO ALEXANDER WILLIAM POWELL[3]
[P.A.O., Crown Lands Papers, Woods and Forests, Letter Book, 1852–6, p. 131]

C. L. D. 20th: June 1855.

I have the honor to inform you that His Excellency the Governor General has been pleased to appoint you Crown Timber Agent for the "Huron & Superior Territory."

[1]This mill at the mouth of the Severn River was mentioned by Baddeley in 1835 (B 27).

[2]William McDonell Dawson (1822–1890) Crown Land Agent at Ottawa and member of the Legislative Assembly for Trois-Rivières, 1858 to 1861.

[3]On August 10, 1863, the Governor in Council dispensed with the services of A. W. Powell and united the territories formerly under his charge with the Ontario agency under the superintendence of J. F. Way (Crown Lands Papers, Woods and Forests Letter Book, 1861-3, pp. 377-8).

Your Agency so far as it comes in contact with other organized Agencies will be bounded by the river Severn & Lake Simcoe to the mouth of Talbot River, thence by the North westerly boundaries of the Townships of Thorah, Eldon & Bexley and the height of land between the tributaries of the Severn and Trent and thence by the height of Land between the rivers falling into Lakes Huron & Superior, and those falling into the Ottawa.

Your salary has been fixed at £250 (Two hundred & fifty pounds) per annum.

You will require to open an Office and reside at such point as may be determined most convenient for persons having to transact business with you, and best calculated to enable you to exercise a general supervision over the territory; but on this head further communication will be made to you after you have been enabled from personal inspection to report on the present circumstances and prospects of your Agency to which it is desirable that you should repair at as early a date as possible in order to secure the duties on any Timber that may have been cut there during the past season.

You will require to visit the Crown Land Agent, Alexr: Mc:Nabb Esqr at Saugeen who has heretofore managed the affairs of the Territory, and obtain from him all such records and documents as appertain thereto, with such other information as he can supply. Such further instructions as may be necessary will be forwarded to you, and in the meantime you will be pleased to inform the Department of your movements and where you may be addressed.

G 3   TIMBER LICENCES IN MUSKOKA, 1856, SELECTED FROM "RETURN OF LICENSES GRANTED AND DUTIES ACCRUED IN THE SEVERAL TERRITORIES"
[*Canada, Legislative Assembly,* Journals, *1857, app. 25*]

LICENSES GRANTED

Names	Date	No.	Area in square miles	Amount of ground rent			Localities
				£	s.	d.	
Huron and Superior Territory A.W. Powell, Agent	1856						
Quetton St. George	Jan. 2	38	50	6	5	0	River Severn.
George Caswell & al	Feb. 13	51	25	3	2	6	River Severn.
do	do	52	25	3	2	6	do
Jos. Smith	23	53	40	5	0	0	do Muskoka.
do	do	54	20	2	10	0	do
do	do	55	40	5	0	0	do
do	do	56	20	2	10	0	do
Geo. Caswell & al.	Mar. 1	75	8	1	0	0	Islands in Severn River.

Names	Date	No.	Area in square miles	Amount of ground rent			Localities
				£	s.	d.	
Wm. M. Gibson	Apr. 4	76	50	12	10	0	Seguin River.
Jas. A. Gibson	do	77	50	12	10	0	do
Gzwoski⁴ & al.	23	78	25	3	2	6	Moon River.
do	do	79	25	3	2	6	do
do	May 19	7	25	3	2	6	Moon River.
do	do	8	25	3	2	6	do
Andrew Heron	Oct. 6	31	50	6	5	0	Severn River.
W.M. Gibson et al	Nov. 1	45	50	6	5	0	Seguin River.
Savigny & Co. & al	Dec. 24	47	50	6	5	0	Muskoka do
do	do	48	50	6	5	0	do
do	do	49	50	6	5	0	do
do	do	50	50	6	5	0	do
W.O. Hamilton	Dec. 24	56	15	1	17	6	Muskoka River.
do	do	57	15	1	17	6	do
do	do	58	30	3	15	0	Black River.
do	do	59	15	1	17	6	do
G. Caswell and F. Clemow	do		25	3	2	6	River Severn.
N. Caswell and F. Clemow	do		25	3	2	6	do
W. Moberly	do		50	6	5	0	do
W. Moberly	do		50	6	5	0	River Severn.
G. Caswell and Clemow	do		25	3	2	6	River Severn.
do	do		25	3	2	6	do
Joseph Smith	do		40	5	0	0	Muskoka River.
do	do		20	2	10	0	do
do	do		40	5	0	0	do
do	do		20	2	10	0	do
Geo. Caswell and Frs. Clemow	do		8	1	0	0	River Severn

G 4 L. V. Sicotte,⁵ Report on Muskoka River Sawmills
[*P.A.O., Crown Lands Papers, Woods and Forests, Report Book 1, pp. 300–1*]

Crown Land Department
Woods & Forests Branch
Toronto 5th. March 1858.

Report.

On application of Charles Kelly, Esquire, of Hamilton, to obtain a lease of 200 acres of land, in two separate blocks situate on the Muskoka River on which he has built a Saw Mill⁶ and other buildings, also a wharf.

⁴Misprint for Gzowski.

⁵Louis Victor Sicotte (1812–1889) was Commissioner of Crown Lands from 1857 to 1858, and Commissioner of Public Works from August to December, 1858.

⁶The mills were built in the interval between Alexander Murray's trip up the river in the spring of 1853 and the writing of his report February 1, 1854 (D 10).

The two blocks of land applied for, are shewn on the accompanying plan which is drawn on a scale of 20 chains to an inch. Block A. is to cover the Saw Mill built on an Island in the River, at the first fall, as seen on the plan, also the buildings and improvements on the main land, within the area indicated.

Block B. is to cover a wharf at the mouth of the said River, also the buildings and improvements on the main land within the second area indicated.

The Commissioner of Crown Land has the honor to recommend that a lease for the term of seven years, of the Block above described, forming a total area of two hundred acres, be granted to the applicant, subject to the conditions, restrictions and rent recommended in the report of this Department of the 2nd July 1856, on the general question of the disposal of mill sites in the unsurveyed lands of that section of the Province.

G 5   ANDREW RUSSELL TO A. W. POWELL, WINDSOR
[*P.A.O., Crown Lands Papers, Woods and Forests, Letter Book 2, p. 326*]

C.L.D. W. & F. Toronto, 2nd. Augst., '59

In connection with the Departmental Circular of the 16th June last and your answer of the 30th. of the same month, I have the honor to inform you that the Commissioner is of opinion that it is better to postpone the proposed sale of Timber Berths in the Huron & Superior Territory, until next year. The surveys now being proceeded with, and the new Road lines now being explored will lead to the Territory being better known, and the state of the Lumber market will, it is almost certain, be improved.

G 6   TIMBER LICENCES IN MUSKOKA, 1860 TO 1867, SELECTED FROM "STATEMENT OF TIMBER LICENSES GRANTED IN THE HURON AND SUPERIOR TERRITORY"[7]
[*Ontario, Legislative Assembly, Sessional Papers, 1868–9, no. 6, pp. 188–209*]

According to William Gibbard in 1860, "These mills were built in the first place by W. B. Hamilton, of Penetanguishene, — were sold to Kelly and others — were worked in 1859 by Mr. Tyson, of Collingwood; they are now idle." The mills were built above the first fall, and the lumber was taken over the portage by team or rafted down, and sent mainly to Chicago, but some to Owen Sound and Collingwood (Department of Crown Lands, *Report*, 1860, app. 29).

[7]This statement was supplied as part of "Return to an Address voted to His Excellency the Lieutenant Governor, praying for a Return shewing the number of licenses granted since 1860, to cut timber in the wild lands of this Province."

Date of issue of license	No. of license	Area in square miles	Amount of ground rent paid	Amount of bonus paid	To whom granted	Locality
1860						
[Oct.] 30	7	50	25 00		Andrew Heron and Alex. R. Christie	River Severn[8]
[Nov.] 30	37	5	8 00		J. Tyson & Co.	River Muskoka
do	38	5	8 00		do	do
Nov. 30	39	5	8 00		J. Tyson & Co.	River Muskoka
do	40	5	8 00		do	do
do	41	5	8 00		do	do
do	42	5	8 00		do	do
do	43	20	10 00		do	Black River
do	44	10	5 00		do	do
do	45	15	7 50		do	do
Dec. 1	46	8	4 00		W.F. Powell	Islands on River Severn
do	47	50	25 00		do	River Severn
do	48	50	25 00		do	do
Dec. 1	49	8	8 00		W.F. Powell	Severn Islands
do	50	50	25 00		do	River Severn
1861						
[Oct.] 4,	12	13½	6 75	84 00	John McGregor	Muskoka
do	13	12	6 17	84 00	do	Morrison
do	14	21½	10 75	88 00	Cook & Bros.	Ryde, No. 1
do	15	18½	9 25	75 00	do	do No. 2
do	26	12	6 00	65 00	John McGregor	Draper, No. 1
do	27	19	9 50	90 00	G. Cook and J. Cameron	do No. 2
do	28	19¾	9 84	85 00	John McGregor	do No. 3
do	29	15⅓	7 67	82 00	Cook & Bros.	do No. 4
do	30	20	10 00	108 00	McAulay & Platt	Macaulay, No. 1
do	31	20	10 00	112 00	M.E. Tobin	do No. 2
do	32	25	12 50	104 00	G. Cook and J. Cameron	do No. 3
1862						
Jan. 14	42	25	12 50		G. McMicken	Ryde and Dalton
do	43	25	12 50		do	Rama and Morrison
Feb. 5	44	50	25 00		A. Heron and A. R. Christie	River Severn
[Nov.] 26	8	50	25 00		Peter Christie	River Severn
[Dec. 5]	28	21½	21 50		[Cook & Bros.]	Ryde, No. 1
do	29	18½	18 50		do	do No. 2
do	30	25	25 00		G. McMicken	Ryde and Dalton
do	31	25	25 00		do	Rama and Morrison
do	32	19	19 00		G. Cook and J. Cameron	Draper, No. 2
do	33	15	15 34		Cook & Bros.	do No. 1
do	34	25	25 00		G. Cook and J. Cameron	Macaulay, No. 3

[8]A full description of the limits for this and some of the other licences may be found in the original list.

Date of issue of license	No. of license	Area in square miles	Amount of ground rent paid	Amount of bonus paid	To whom granted	Locality
1863						
Sep. 25	8	50	25 00		Peter Christie	River Severn
[Nov. 4]	19	25	50 00		G. McMicken	Rama and Morrison
do	20	5⅓	30 68		Cook & Brothers	Draper No. 4
do	25	21½	43 00		do	Ryde, No. 1
do	26	18½	37 00		do	do No. 2
do	27	25	50 00		G. McMicken	Ryde and Dalton
1864						
[Sept.] 25	3	50	25 00		Peter Christie	River Severn and Georgian Bay
[Dec. 5]	30	25	12 50		G. McMicken	Rama and Morrison
do	31	21½	10 75		do	Ryde, No. 1
do	32	18½	9 25		do	do No. 2
do	35	25	12 00		do	Ryde and Dalton
do	38	15⅓	7 67		[Cook & Brothers]	Draper, No. 4
do	61	6	4 00		Peter Christie	River Severn— Blocks and Islands A and B
1865						
[Oct. 3]	9	50	25 00		Peter Christie	River Severn
do	10	6	4 00		do	Blocks and Islands A and B
[Nov. 21]	42	21½	21 50		[Cook & Bros.]	Ryde, No. 1
do	43	18½	18 50		do	do No. 2
do	44	15⅓	15 34		do	Draper, No. 4
do	45	25	25 00		G. McMicken	Rama and Morrison
do	46	25	25 00		do	Ryde and Dalton
1866						
July 17	9	50	50 00		A.R. Christie	River Severn
do	10	8	8 00		do	Blocks and Islands A and B
[Aug. 8]	17	15⅓	30 68		Cook & Brothers	Draper, No. 4
do	18	18½	37 00		do	Ryde, No. 2
do	19	21½	43 00		do	do No. 1
do	21	25	12 50		G. McMicken	Rama and Morrison
do	22	25	12 50		do	Ryde and Dalton
[Oct. 4]	27	18	9 00	1890 00	H.W. Sage & Co.	Oakley, No. 1
do	28	19½	9 75	1825 00	do	do No. 2
Oct. 4	29	14¼	7 50	1278 00	H.W. Sage & Co.	Oakley, No. 3
do	30	13¾	7 00	1278 00	do	do No. 4
do	35	29½	15 00	1770 00	John Cook	Monck
1867						
[April 20]	12	50	25 00	57 00	J. & W. Beatty & Co.	Moon River
do 24	13	2	12 00		W.F. Powell	Islands on Severn River
do	14	50	75 00		do	River Severn
do	15	50	75 00		do	do
do	16	8	12 00		do	Severn Islands
[June] 25	8	50	25 00		A.R. Christie	River Severn and Georgian Bay
do	9	6	4 00		do	Blocks and Islands A and B, River Severn

G 7   M. C. CAMERON,[9] REPORT ON TIMBER, SEPTEMBER 26, 1871
[*P.A.O., Crown Lands Papers, Woods and Forests, Report Book 1,
pp. 556–7*]

The Commissioner of Crown Lands has the honor to report the following in connection with timber on unlicensed lands in Townships open for sale and location under the "Free Grants and Homestead Act of 1868", in the Districts of Muskoka and Parry Sound—

The following Townships, not under Timber license, have been placed under the operations of the said Act viz:— Muskoka, Draper, Watt, Stephenson, Hagerman, Ferguson, McKellar, Christie, Humphrey, Cardwell, Macaulay, Brunel, McLean, Stisted and Chaffey and large numbers of sales and locations have been made to Settlers in each of the Townships in question.

Considerable quantities of timber and Saw logs have been taken during the past two years from located lands, some of which were cut by Locatees in actually clearing their land for cultivation and crop and disposed of under authority of the 11 Section of the Act referred to, the greater quantity however was upon examination found to have been cut in trespass and was treated accordingly.

During the past summer fires have been raging in some of the Townships, and large quantities of timber is believed to have been so injured that it will be quite worthless unless cut during the coming winter.

In consideration of the many applications that have been made for the right to cut. The large demand for timber. The great difficulty in preserving the timber in a country being rapidly settled from destruction by fire: and the great benefit it would bestow upon the Free Grant Settlers in providing occupation in the lumbering shanties during the winter months. The Commissioner recommends that he be authorised to have lists prepared of all lands remaining unsold and unlocated on the 1st proximo, and to offer the same for sale as Timber limits, in berths not to exceed 20 sq. miles in area on such a day and place and at such upset price as he may deem advisable. . . .

G 8   LUMBERING OPERATIONS IN 1871
[*McMurray*, The Free Grant Lands of Canada, *p. 67*]

Few can estimate the extensive importance of the lumbering operations carried on in these parts. Here we have at work five of the largest and wealthiest lumbering firms on the *American Continent*— Messrs. Dodge & Co.,[10] Messrs. Clarke, White & Co., Messrs. Hotchkiss, Hugh-

[9]Matthew Crooks Cameron (1822–1887) became Provincial Secretary for Ontario in 1867 and was Commissioner of Crown Lands for some months in 1871. He was later appointed a judge, and created a Knight Bachelor in 1886.

[10]Dodge and Company carried on extensive operations in both the United States and Canada. The head of the company, Anson G. P. Dodge of New York, was

son & Co., Messrs. Cook Brothers,[11] and the Bell Ewart Company. The first-named concern employs 800 men, and the others in like proportion. Who, then, can estimate the benefits derived by the united operations of those gigantic establishments? Another source of wealth to the settlers is the income derived from the sale of their saw-logs. Those who have obtained their patents realize the *entire proceeds* of their logs, and thus they are enabled to make greater improvements; hence the wonderful rapidity of the growth and development of Muskoka.

G 9   "RESOURCES AND GROWTH OF MUSKOKA"
[*Orillia,* Northern Light, *November 10, 1871*]

Rod and Rifle
In Camp on Muskoka Lake,
Canada, October 7, 1871.

Muskoka, with a population approximating 10,000 persons; is yet all a wilderness. . . . Its almost exhaustless growths of pine are contributing wealth to our country, and afford a tempting field to American enterprise and capital. The great lumbering firm of Dodge & Co., of New York, employ more than 1000 choppers here, and will put into American and Canadian marts more than 80 million feet of pine lumber the present year. Messrs. Silliman and Beecher, of Albany, are also getting out lumber at the rate of 25 or 30 million ft. per annum, preparing to extend operations largely in the future, while numerous other firms from different portions of the United States are here engaged in extensive lumbering enterprises. So that while Muskoka presents to the traveller only the rude appearance of the newest type of pioneer civilization, in its log cabins, clearings that abound with charred pine stumps, and are yet resonant with the sound of the woodsmans' ax and odorous with the smoke of burning timber, there is still an evidence of energetic, vigorous enterprises among its increasing population that is decidedly American, and potent also in subduing its forests, and promoting its opulence and thrift.

. . .

also president of the Georgian Bay Lumber Company and vice president of the Toronto, Simcoe and Muskoka Junction Railway. Dodge and Company became involved in serious financial difficulties in the depression of 1873 in the United States.

[11]Several of the Cook family were lumbermen. The best known in Muskoka was Herman Henry Cook (b. 1837), member of the Dominion Parliament for North Simcoe, 1872 to 1878, member of the Ontario legislature 1879 to 1882, and member of the Dominion Parliament from 1882 to 1891. During 1871-2 he built a sawmill at Midland with a capacity of 20,000,000 feet of lumber per season.

G 10 "Timber Berths in the Muskoka and Parry Sound Free Grant Districts, Sold or Offered for Sale at Public Auction 23rd November, 1871"[12]
[*Ontario, Legislative Assembly,* Sessional Papers, *1871–2, no. 47, pp. 9–10*]

Township.	No. of Berths.	Name of Purchaser.	Area in Square Miles.	Bonus Per Mile. $ c.	Amount of Bonus. $ c.	Amount of Ground Rent.	Total.
Muskoka	1	Cook Brothers	18	220 00	3960 00	36 00	3996 00
Watt	1	do.	10	165 00	1650 00	20 00	1670 00
	2	do.	11	165 00	1815 00	22 00	1837 00
Cardwell	1	(Withdrawn from sale.)	16			32 00	
	2	(do.)	13			26 00	
	3	Cook Brothers	19	175 00	3325 00	38 00	3363 00
	4	James Metcalf	10	225 00	2250 00	20 00	2270 00
	5	Cook Brothers	10	200 00	2000 00	20 00	2020 00
Humphrey	1	do.	11	465 00	5115 00	22 00	5137 00
	2	do.	12	375 00	4500 00	24 00	4524 00
	3	do.	9	210 00	1890 00	18 00	1908 00
Christie	1	do.	17	210 00	3570 00	34 00	3604 00
	2	do.	18	135 00	2430 00	36 00	2466 00
	3	McArthur Brothers	15	265 00	3975 00	30 00	4005 00
	4	do.	14	360 00	5040 00	28 00	5068 00
McKellar	1	Cook Brothers	14	330 00	4620 00	28 00	4648 00
	2	do.	19	315 00	5985 00	38 00	6023 00
	3	H.B. Rathburn & Son	16	250 00	4000 00	32 00	4032 00
Hagerman	1	do.	18	175 00	3150 00	36 00	3186 00
	2	A.G.P. Dodge	19	130 00	2470 00	38 00	2508 00
	3	D. Switzer & Son	16	115 00	1840 00	32 00	1872 00
	4	A.G.P. Dodge	15	110 00	1650 00	30 00	1680 00
Fergusson	1	H.B. Rathburn & Son	13	140 00	1820 00	26 00	1846 00
	2	A.G.P. Dodge	9	140 00	1260 00	18 00	1278 00
	3	do.	12	300 00	3600 00	24 00	3624 00
	4	do	12	215 00	2580 00	24 00	2604 00
Stisted	1	William Doran	14	100 00	1400 00	28 00	1428 00
	2	(Withdrawn from sale.)	18			36 00	00
	3	do.	15			30 00	00
Stephenson	1	A.G.P. Dodge	13	180 00	2340 00	26 00	2366 00
Macaulay	1	do	7	111 00	777 00	14 00	791 00
Draper	1	do	7	260 00	1820 00	14 00	1834 00

[12]This list was supplied as "Return called for by Resolution of the Legislative Assembly 14th February, 1872, of Timber Berths in the Muskoka and Parry Sound Free Grant Districts, sold or offered for sale at public auction 23rd November, 1871, with names of purchasers, amount of Bonuses received on each Berth, &c., &c."

Township.	No. of Berths.	Name of Purchaser	Area in Square Miles.	Bonus Per Mile. $ c.	Amount of Bonus. $ c.	Amount of Ground Rent.	Total.
McLean	1	do.	14	225 00	3150 00	28 00	3178 00
	2	Cook Brothers	12	300 00	3600 00	24 00	3624 00
	3	do.	12	300 00	3600 00	24 00	3624 00
Brunel	1	do.	16	275 00	4400 00	32 00	4432 00
	2	do.	17	350 00	5950 00	34 00	5984 00
Chaffey	1	do.	10	350 00	3500 00	20 00	3520 00
	2	James Metcalf	12	500 00	6000 00	24 00	6024 00
	3	Cook Brothers	16	415 00	6640 00	32 00	6672 00
			549		117672 00	1098 00	118646 00
		Deduct Berths Withdrawn	62			124 00	
		Total realized	487		117672 00	974 00	118646 00

G 11   REVENUE FROM TIMBER, 1863–71
[Ontario, Legislative Assembly, Sessional Papers, 1873, no. 75]

A Return of the amount realized from Timber Dues, Sales of Timber Limits, and Licenses, and all other charges or revenue arising from Timber and Lumber in the Muskoka, Parry Sound, and Algoma Districts respectively, collected and carried to the Revenue Account of the Province (Canada and Ontario), from 1st January, 1863 to 31st December, 1871, and designating the amounts collected from the several Townships therein respectively; called for by the Honourable the Legislative Assembly of Ontario by resolution, dated 2nd February, 1872.

MUSKOKA DISTRICT.

TOWNSHIP, &C	AMOUNT	TOWNSHIP, &C	AMOUNT
Ryde	$1,054 88	Watt	$4,090 20
Morrison	3,449 94	Stephenson	3,283 62
Muskoka	18,174 99	Brunel	10,416 00
Draper	4,735 93	Humphrey	11,569 00
Oakley	35,677 31	Cardwell	5,383 00
McLean	10,426 00	Muskoka River	10,714 00
Macaulay	1,155 50		
Monk	4,308 95		$124,439 32

PARRY SOUND DISTRICT

TOWNSHIP, &c	AMOUNT
Chaffey	$16,216 00
Stisted	1,428 00

. . .

Moon River	879 50

. . .

G 12   ROBERT DOLLAR[13] IN MUSKOKA, 1872
[Dollar, Memoirs, 3rd ed., pp. 13–14]

Up to 1872, I had succeeded in saving some money, and had been persistently working on my education, having taken a good many books of standard authors to the camps and read them during the long winter, so that isolation from the world was a benefit in that way.

At that time I left the Ottawa River and went to a new country, the Muskoka district, north of Toronto, where in partnership with Mr. Johnson, we bought timber on land owned by farmers and started lumbering for our own account, making our headquarters at Bracebridge, Ontario. It was a new country just opened by the Government, and there was a good opportunity. Business was booming at this time and we did not sell our logs, expecting to get a higher price when we would deliver them at the market the following summer; but at that time along came Black Friday in New York, which paralyzed business throughout not only the United States but Canada as well. When we came to sell our logs we found we had made a loss of what little money we had put in as well as about $5000.00 more. . . .

In order to pay up the debts, my partner and myself had to go to work on wages. We divided up the indebtedness, each agreeing to pay half. For my part, it took three years' hard work to get even with the world again.

I had previously been in the employ of H.H. Cook. At this time he tried to get me to go into partnership with him, but I absolutely refused until I had paid up all my debts. I then started with him. He furnished the money and I the brains and hard work. Having the experience of previous years I was extremely cautious and careful, and made a success of the new venture from the start.

. . . In 1876 I had started eight camps in Muskoka district, and besides these I started a camp to get out saw logs on one of the islands of Georgian Bay . . .

G 13   T. B. PARDEE,[14] COMMISSIONER OF CROWN LANDS,
MEMORANDUM ON IMPROVEMENTS FOR MUSKOSH RIVER
[P.A.O., Crown Lands Papers, Woods and Forests, Report Book 1, pp. 643–5]

Memorandum

On application of Messrs. Cook Bros. of Toronto dated 15th. ulto. addressed to the Hon. the Attorney General, that a sum of money may

---

[13]Robert Dollar (1844–1932) was born in Scotland, came to Canada with his father in 1858, and soon began work in the lumber mills and shanties in the Ottawa district. In 1872 he went to Muskoka, married, and made his home in Bracebridge for seven years, while he carried on a lumber business. He then transferred his business to the United States, and some years later organized the Dollar Steamship Line to the Orient.

[14]Timothy Blair Pardee (1830–1889) was Provincial Secretary from 1872 until his appointment in 1873 as Commissioner of Crown Lands.

be expended in facilitating the descent of timber and saw logs down the Muskosh River from Lake Muskoka to Georgian Bay, or failing an appropriation from the revenue for that purpose, that the government would favour an act of the Legislature authorizing the applicants to improve the river and levy tolls on timber &c passing such improvements to recoup them for outlay.

The Commissioner of Crown Lands begs to report that for years past complaints have been made verbally to his Department by parties holding licenses and getting out logs and timber on the Muskoka and Muskosh rivers (the latter being a continuation of the former) that large quantities of timber and logs have annually been destroyed in passing over chutes (falls) and rapids on these streams, which destruction it is alleged might have been averted by a comparatively small expenditure in building slides.

The Commissioner would also call attention to the fact that recently the Department of Public Works of this Province has built slides and dams (and acquired such works previously built by private individuals) for the purpose of facilitating the descent of timber on the Gull River, Burnt River, and at Fenelon Falls, and established a pro rata charge on all timber &c passing over the works with a view to the repayment of principal and cost of repairs and superintendence.

The Commissioner cannot approve of the proposition of the applicants that they should be authorized by Legislative enactment to build such works as they might consider necessary on the rivers mentioned, and be empowered to levy tolls in connection therewith, as he considers that it would be more satisfactory to all concerned that such works if to be built should be erected as public works and be under the control and superintendence of that Department—

The Commissioner recommends the application of Messrs. Cook Bros. to the consideration of the Government

Toronto November 1874.

G 14   PETITION[15] FOR REDUCTION OF TIMBER DUES, 1876
[*Ontario, Legislative Assembly,* Sessional Papers, *1877, no. 47*]

PETITION OF LICENSE-HOLDERS
FOR REDUCTION OF RATE OF DUES ON PINE TIMBER
ON CERTAIN LANDS
IN MUSKOKA AND PARRY SOUND DISTRICTS; AND REPORT[16]
OF COMMISSIONER OF CROWN LANDS THEREON.

To the Honourable T.B. Pardee,
    Commissioner of Crown Lands for the Province of Ontario.
    The Memorial of the undersigned Mill-owners and Manufacturers of the Districts of Muskoka and Parry Sound

[15]The petition is not dated, but the Commissioner's report on the petition is October 18, 1876.
[16]The Commissioner's report, after considering the points in the petition one by

Humbly Sheweth:—

That your Memorialists are placed at a great disadvantage by an inconsistent and excessive rate of duty chargeable on timber and saw logs cut in the aforesaid Districts, being double the rate charged in other sections of the Province; which your Memorialists consider manifestly unjust to them and injurious to the Province, both as to present revenue, and the future value of our timbered lands, for the following reasons, which we most respectfully submit:—

1. Consequent upon the opening up of the Townships of Draper, Muskoka, Macaulay, McLean, Brunel, Chaffey, Stephenson, Stisted, Cardwell, Watt, Humphrey, Christie, McKellar, Ferguson, and Hagerman, for settlement under the Free Grants and Homestead Act, it was considered advisable by the Government to offer for sale by Public Auction as timber limits, the unlocated lands in the townships in question, at the Department in Toronto, on the 23rd day of November, 1871. This sale realized a cash bonus of $118,646, being an average of $241.62 per square mile, or 37¾ cts. per acre for every acre of land, rock, and swamp contained in the entire area sold. This sale was made, and the bonus realized under a special rate of timber dues, fixed at $25 per M cubic feet, on square timber, and $1.50 per M feet, board measure on saw logs. Owing to the inflated state of the timber market at the time of the sale, and as we believe the impression that it must so continue for a sufficient time to enable the purchasers to remove the timber, which they were required to do, under the terms of the Free Grants Act, within five years from the date of location of each lot, your Memorialists and others were induced to bid, and pay the large bonuses heretofore named.

. . .

4. The sale in question having been made so late in 1871, little or no work was done upon the said lands during the winter of 1871–72, and the severe depression which commenced in the fall of 1872, and has continued to increase in severity until the present time, has prevented any large quantity of timber being cut upon the said lands, a large portion of which have subsequently been located by Free Grant settlers; and the time for removing the timber is so short, that in any case your Memorialists will be forced to relinquish from 40 to 50 per cent of the lands purchased before it would be possible for them, even under a favourable market, to cut and remove the timber from the said lands. This loss of territory will about double the cost of that remaining.

5. Freights on sawn lumber from Ottawa to New York or Albany, are, on an average, $3 per M. feet less than from the Georgian Bay, and the cost of taking square timber to Quebec is still more largely in favour of the Ottawa producer.

---

one, concluded, "The Commissioner, therefore, respectfully recommends that the prayer of the Petitioners be granted, subject to ratification by the Legislative Assembly at its next meeting."

6. The present rate of timber dues on the lands in question is prohibitory. No timber can now be cut thereon at a profit, and even should the market revive, the choice lumber only could be taken, which may be placed at 25 per cent. of the entire quantity of 311,680,000 feet, which the entire area of 487 square miles in question is estimated to contain, . . .

. . .

8. The timber in the territory in question is known to be inferior, both in quality and quantity to that on the Ottawa, where no bonus was paid, where large expenditure in improving the streams has been made, where the tenure is more secure, the freights cheaper, and the dues exacted are only one-half of those charged your Memorialists.

9. The sale in question has defeated its object; no timber of consequence has been taken out under it; no such dues have been paid; no timber can be taken out, or such dues paid, without involving the ruin of those engaged in the trade.

10. In consequence of this prohibitory tariff, the lumber interests of the districts are languishing. The settlers are suffering for want of employment, and the fires are annually destroying this most valuable of Canadian products, in greater ratio than could be done by the lumberman's axe, thus causing a direct waste and loss to the Government, to the settlers of the districts, and to your Memorialists.

. . .

By giving this matter your immediate and favourable consideration, you will, we are convinced, confer a great boon on the country, and much relieve your humble Memorialists.

G. McLean,
And eighteen others.

Lumbering in Haliburton

G 15   APPOINTMENT OF JOSEPH FRASER WAY[17] AS CROWN TIMBER AGENT
[*Quebec,* Canada Gazette, *May 13, 1854, p. 843*]

CROWN LANDS DEPARTMENT
Quebec, 12th May, 1854.

HIS EXCELLENCY THE ADMINISTRATOR OF THE GOVERNMENT has been pleased to appoint Jos. Fraser Way, Esquire, of Belleville, to be Crown Timber Agent for the Territory lying between the westerly boundary of the County of Grenville and Toronto, extending back to the Agency of A.J. Russell, Esquire, of Bytown, at the height of land between the Tributaries of the St. Lawrence and the Ottawa.

[17]A. N. Morin, Commissioner, notified Way of the appointment on May 6, 1854, and stated the salary as £300 per annum (Crown Lands Papers, Woods and Forests Letter Book, 1852-6, pp. 91-2).

G 16 Timber Licences in Haliburton, 1860 to 1863, Selected from "Statement of Licenses Granted... in the Ontario Territory"[18]

[*Ontario, Legislative Assembly,* Sessional Papers, *1868–9, no. 6*]

Date	No.	Area	Ground Rent	Bonus	To whom granted	Locality
1860						
[Oct.] 2	20	11 23-32	6 00	320 00	Thos. Short	Lutterworth.
do 30	33	11 23-32	6 00	370 00	Gillies & McLaren	Lutterworth.
Dec. 4	61	9⅜	5 00	310 00	Curry & McAulay	Lutterworth.
do	62	2 13-16	4 00	98 40	Walter Gouin	do
do	71	9⅜	5 00	540 00	R.H. Scott	Lutterworth.
do 31	106	11⅞	6 00	311 60	Walter Gowin	Anson.
1861						
[July 16]	29	9⅜	5 00		[Geo. Kempt]	Lutterworth.
do 31	31	2 13-16	4 00		Walter Gouin	Lutterworth.
do	32	11⅞	6 00		do	Anson.
[Oct. 1]	67	11 23-32	6 00		Thos. Short	Lutterworth.
do [31]	71	7 1-32	4 00	100 00	Platt & Bissonette	Minden.
do	74	13 9-32	6 00	175 00	W. McDougall & Co.	Stanhope.
do	75	21¼	11 00	115 00	do	do
do	77	8⅛	4 00	85 00	do	Lutterworth.
[Nov. 2]	79	11 23-32	6 00	105 00	[Thos. Buck]	Anson.
	132	9 27-64	12 00		M. Boyd	Snowden.
Dec. 7	133	9 17-32	5 00		Gillies & McLaren	Lutterworth.
	135	6 3-32	4 00		R.H. Scott	Lutterworth.
1862						
April 30	149	3½	4 00	200 00	McAulay & McBean	Minden.
do	150	8 7-16	6 00	95 00	do	do
do	151	13 19-32	7 50	75 00	do	do
do	152	7 1-32	5 00	100 00	do	Stanhope.
[June 2]	45	9¼	10 00		M. Boyd	Snowdon.
do	53	8⅝	4 50		Gillies & McLaren	Lutterworth.
do	54	5⅝	4 00		R.H. Scott	do
July 1	74	11¾	13 00		W. McDougall & Co.	Stanhope.
do	75	20⅞	21 00		do	do
do	77	8	8 00		do	Lutterworth.
[Sept. 27]	85	2¾	8 00 ⎱		J.F. Flindall	Lutterworth.
do	Fine		8 00 ⎰			
do	86	11¾	6 00 ⎱		do	Anson.
do	Fine		6 00 ⎰			
do	89	11¾	12 00 ⎱		[Thos. Buck]	Anson.
do	Fine		12 00 ⎰			
[Nov. 5]	106	9⅜	5 00		[Geo. Kempt]	Lutterworth.
do	108	10¾	5 50 ⎱		Thos. Short	Lutterworth.
do	Fine		5 50 ⎰			
do 29	113	4⅛	8 00		Platt & Bissonette	Minden.
1863						
[March 10]	160	9¾	5 00	115 00	Boyd & Cumming	Snowdon.
do	161	11¼	6 00	400 00	M. Boyd	do
do	162	15⅛	8 00	445 00	S.H. Hanker	do

[18]Information supplied by Joseph F. Way, January 20, 1868, in "Return to an Address voted to His Excellency the Lieutenant Governor, praying for a Return shewing the number of licenses granted since 1860, to cut timber in the wild lands of this Province."

Date	No.	Area	Ground Rent	Bonus	To whom granted	Locality
[March 24]	166	8½	9 00		[Samuel Dickson]	Snowdon.
do	167	18¼	19 00		do	Stanhope.
do	168	7¼	8 00		do	Anson.
do	169	12½	13 00		do	do
do	170	11¾	12 00		do	do
April 30	173	6¾	8 00		A. Dennistoun	Lutterworth.
[June 1]	32	9¾	5 00		Boyd & Cumming	Snowdon.
July 3	65	9¼	5 00		M. Boyd	Snowdon.
do	66	11½	6 00		do	do
do	67	15⅝	16 00		S.H. Hanker	do
do 10	70	2¾	16 00		J.F. Flendall	Lutterworth.
do 13	71	11¾	12 00		do	Anson.
do [15]	73	9⅜	5 00		[Geo. Kempt]	Lutterworth.
do	75	10¾	11 00		do	Lutterworth.
do 18	77	11¾	6 00		Wm. McDougall & Co	Stanhope.
do	78	20⅝	10 50		do	do
do	80	8	4 00		do	Lutterworth.
[Sept. 9]	115	8½	18 00		[S. Dickson]	Snowdon.
do	116	18¼	38 00		do	Stanhope.
do	117	7¼	16 00		do	Anson.
do	118	12½	26 00		do	do
do	119	11¾	24 00		do	do
[Sept. 22]	126	5⅝	8 00		[W. A. Scott]	Lutterworth.
do	127	8¾	9 00		Gillies & McLaren	do
[Oct. 16]	135	19¼	10 00		Platt & Bissonette	Minden.
do [30]	147	21	10 50	810 00	J.R. Rodgers	Monmouth, No. 2.
do	148	24	12 00	605 00	do	Glamorgan, No. 3.
do	149	6⅜	16 00		J.F. Dennistoun	Lutterworth.
[Dec. 31]	169	18	9 00	450 00	R.C. Smith	Monmouth, No. 4.
do	170	18	9 00	425 00	J.C. Hughson	do No. 3.
do	171	16	8 00	533 60	M. Boyd	Glamorgan, No. 2.
do	172	20	10 00	667 00	do	Monmouth, No. 1.
do	173	36	18 00	625 00	S. Baker	Cardiff, No. 1.
do	174	21	10 50	1000 00	do	do No. 2.
do	175	15	7 50	450 00	do	do No. 3.
do	176	13	6 50	433 55	do	do No. 4.
do	178	20	10 00	500 00	W.A. Scott	Glamorgan, No. 1.
do	179	17	8 50	805 00	do	do No. 4.

G 17 Way to the Commissioner of Crown Lands, P. M. Vankoughnet

[*P.A.O., Crown Lands Papers, Belleville Letter Book, 1860–4, p. 68*]

C. T. O. Belleville 28th. Feby 1861

In compliance with your letter of the 5th Nov last with reference to the dispute which took place between Mr James Devlin and John McArthurs men relative to timber cut in trespass by them in the Township of Anson I have the honor to inform you that I proceeded to the Township of

Anson to make the seizure agreable to instructions but found the snow too deep to inspect the lots and make the seizure upon enquiring into McArthurs complaint I was informed by disinterested parties that neither Mr Devlin nor McArthur were present when the dispute took place between their men it seems both had purchased standing timber from Squatters on the lots in dispute and the lots were so mixed up that it was difficult to cut the Timber without interfering with each other and as is usually the case the men disputed about Timber which neither had a right to cut, without Mr Devlin or McArthur knowing anything about it untill it was over.

G 18   Way to the Commissioner of Crown Lands,
WILLIAM McDOUGALL
[*P.A.O., Crown Lands Papers, Belleville Letter Book, 1860–4, p. 336*]

C T. O Belleville 16 April 1863

I have the honor to inform you that on my tour of inspection last winter I found that many parties were cutting timber on lots not patented without authority of License I of course warned them against so doing as far as they came under my observation In many instances they told me that the parties from whom they purchased the timber said that they had deeds for their land and I am satisfied that there are many settlers who think that they have a right to sell the timber on their lands notwithstanding the trouble we have taken to notify them to the contrary there are cases where parties should be severely dealt with when they knowingly and willfully try to evade the law in such cases it would be well to make examples of such parties the past year has been a very trying one in this part of the Country. I know many people who have been considered in good circumstances are without bread seed or food for the cattle, it is hard to say what must be the lot of many of the poor before another harvest such was the failure of crop that Farmers have been compelled to sell cattle as low as $4 to keep them from starvation and have been compelled to sell timber and everything that they could to furnish bread for their families If the Depart. would defer carrying out the law rigorously for the present year and allow the people to have the benefit of timber (even cut in trespass when it does not interfere with private rights) at a low rate of dues, you would confer a great boon on the country

G 19   ANDREW RUSSELL TO WAY, BELLEVILLE
[*P.A.O., Crown Lands Papers, Woods and Forests, Letter Book,
1861–3, pp. 373–4*]

D. C. L. Quebec 10th August 1863

From a Departmental Notice inserted in the Canada Gazette of the 25th ultimo you will have seen that a sale of Timber Berths in your Territory is to be at your Office on the 5th of October next, and 60 slips of the Notice of sale were mailed to your address on the 30th ultimo for distribution. The Berths to be offered are those in the Townships of Glamorgan Monmouth and Cardiff

The vacant space in the Township of Faraday lying within your Territory will also be offered at an approximate area provided that the boundary between the Ottawa and Ontario Territories, as shewn by A. J. Russell Esquire, on Mr Dennis's plan of the Huron & Ottawa Territory (of which you have a copy in your office) is ascertained to be sufficiently correct to enable such estimate to be made. This will be ascertained in a few days. . . .

The Township of Glamorgan has been open for sale since the 4th of March last, but as yet no sales have been returned to this Department by the Agent Mr Hughes. You will please ascertain from him previous to the sale of Berths, what lots may have been sold. If there are any vacant lots in other Townships which you think ought to be offered at the sale you can offer them ascertaining however that they are really unsold.

G 20   WAY TO COMMISSIONER OF CROWN LANDS,
WILLIAM MCDOUGALL
[*P.A.O., Crown Lands Papers, Belleville Letter Book, 1860–4, p. 380*]

C T O Belleville 15 Sept 1863

In reply to your letter of the 11 Instant concerning letter from M Boyd Esqr and J.W. Dunsford Esqr M P P. relative to improvements made by Mossom Boyd Esqr on Burnt River[19] I have the honor to state that I have been informed that M Boyd removed the collection of flood wood that had been accumulating for many years in or near the mouth of Burnt river. I have frequently heard Lumbermen estimate the cost of the removal of flood wood from the mouth of the river at four thousand dollars.

I am not aware of what amount of money M Boyd expended in clearing out that stream but there is one thing certain that all the men who Lumbered on the Stream received or will receive an equal benefit with M Boyd in proportion to the amount of Lumber that they have already got or may get on the Stream

In many instances lumbermen expend a large amount of money to make roads for their Limits available, when they are the only parties benefited, having the exclusive right to the Limits on the stream. In the present case all the lumber on the Burnt River must pass this accumulation of flood wood, which could not be done without its removal. . . .

[19]A large proportion of the timber from Haliburton went down the Burnt River to the Trent system.

G 21   WAY TO THE COMMISSIONER OF CROWN LANDS,
STEPHEN RICHARDS

[*P.A.O., Crown Lands Papers, Belleville Letter Book, 1865–9, pp. 483–6*]

C. T. O. Belleville 26 Nov 1867

In compliance with a promise made to you, a few days ago at Toronto, I have the honor to define as near as possible the relative positions occupied by the Settlers and the Lumbermen in the Lumber districts of the Ontario Territory.

In the first place the Lumbermen hold Licenses which cover nearly all the vacant Public Lands lying to the North of the old Settlements in the Ontario agency, which they obtained either by application or purchase, in either case they have invested large sums of money in the shape of Ground Rents or Bonus to secure them. In addition to the Ground Rents and Bonus they have also invested a large amount of money in the opening of Roads and the improvement of Streams, necessary to make their limits available, Taking it all together the Lumbermen have a large investment in the Lumber districts— an amount of capital that neither the Lumbermen nor the people of this country can well afford to have sacrificed; It seems to be the popular opinion that these limits, held by Lumbermen, are a great monopoly— that they retard settlement, and place a large amount of Public property in the hands of a few individuals. I cannot view the affair in the same light. Any privileges the Lumbermen possess have been amply paid for, and have been open to the public and abundantly advertised so as to be brought within the reach of every one. It is currently reported that there is a great antagonism existing between the Lumbermen and Settlers. From my own Knowledge of the operation of Lumbermen and the operations of Settlers in the Lumber district, I know the Lumbermen have been a prey to the Settlers. The Regulations have all been on the side of the Settler. The new Townships have been advertised as open for Sale for Timber limits for which Lumbermen have paid heavy bonuses, and immediately after such sales the same Townships have been opened for Settlement under Regulations, which allow the Settler to purchase any lot (covered by the Lumbermens License) which he may choose to select, even the best Timbered lot in the limits, and entirely unsuitable for settlement by complying with the following conditions viz. To enter upon the lot within one month after the purchase, to build a house 18 x 24 feet and clear five acres, then the settler would be entitled to a settlers License and the benefit of all the Timber on the lot notwithstanding the Timber had been previously sold to the Licentiate or Lumberman and paid for at a high rate, which is certainly monstrous injustice to the Lumberman. As the present Regulations hold out encouragements to the settler to select the best timbered lots in a Lumberman's limits, to profit by the Timber and not by the Land. In many cases, as high as $2 per tree bonus in addition to the Tariff dues has been paid to the Settler, on lots purchased out of Lumbermens limits, which Timber would have had no value as there was no way open by which to bring it to market until the Licentiate improved the stream upon which it was situated. And even after all the expenditure of the Licentiate, the settler would not sell the Timber to him, as he could not afford to pay as much for it as the other Lumbermen who had neither paid any bonus, nor expended anything in the improvement of Streams to bring this Timber to market. While such is the fact that the settler has every guarantee— everything to protect him if he carries out the stipulations of purchase, on the other hand the Lumbermen have little or no security for their investments, and yet Public opinion is treating the settler as a greatly abused man, and the Lumberman as a highly privileged one. While the Lumberman does not get that protection which he deserves, the settler is allowed to recover a large amount of revenue, which justly belongs to the Government. Take for instance a lot of 200 acres, estimating at Timber at 223 trees of 80 feet average, the Tariff dues under a settlers License would pay for the lot, and leave the settler $446. bonus, or in that proportion, it might be very much more or it might be less. There would not be so much objection to that policy, if the settler selected lots suitable for settlement, and did not deprive the Licentiate of the value of the Timber that justly belonged to him, as the Timber had no market value when sold to the Lumbermen, until he improved the stream to enable him to bring the Timber out.

Under a judicious policy there could be no antagonism between the Lumberman and Settler; They would be a mutual benefit to each other, and if proper restrictions were placed on the Settler, he would necessarily be compelled to select such lands as would be suitable for agricultural purpose (if any such are to be found) and leave the timbered lands, which are seldom suitable, in the new Townships, to the operations of Lumbermen.

One of the best evidence of the unsuitableness of the land for settlement is that about three fourths of the lots, which were taken up at first, on some of the Colonization Roads, have been abandoned; the cutting of Timber having passed by them, and gone further into the interior, they have been obliged to abandon their old homes and follow up the trade, to enable them to live: this is another evidence of the Lumberman benefitting the settler. The settler well knows if he has any produce to sell he can get a larger price for it from the Lumberman, than in the best Markets on the frontier.

While the Government has done a great deal in the way of building Colonization Roads, to facilitate Settlement, the Lumbermen have done a great deal more. The only difficulty between the two classes is that the settler is allowed to buy the Lumberman's land and become a Lumberman instead of a Farmer, I think the only judicious and fair way to settle this dispute between them, would be to open up the Public Lands for settlement, and not allow the settler the benefit of the Timber beyond what he requires for the improvement of the farm or what he cuts in the process of clearing, until he has continuously occupied for five years, and made all the necessary improvements. Such a course would confine Settlers to such lots as are suitable for settlement, under such restrictions, at the expiration of five years, the settler would have the benefit of all the Timber which the lot contained at the time of purchase.

For the encouragement of settlement the Government might exercise as much forbearance with regard to payments as deemed expedient.

I do believe I have given, in this report a fair exposition of the relations which exist between the Lumbermen and the settlers: my conclusions are based upon twenty years experience with the Lumbermen and Settlers.

G 22   WAY TO JOHN RODGERS,[20] PETERBOROUGH
[*P.A.O., Crown Lands Papers, Belleville Letter Book 4, p. 169*]

C. T. O. Belleville 29th Apl 1870

I have the honor to enclose herewith, schedules of lots liable to crown dues in the following Townships Viz Verulam, Harvey, Somerville, Galway, Snowdon, Minden, Stanhope, Lutterworth, Anson, and Sherborne. I have not had time to make out schedules of lots covered by lumberers' licenses. You will please proceed on Monday next to Bobcaygeon and see Mr. Crown Lands Agent Graham who has a list of all lots so covered in the above named Townships. Mr Graham and yourself will come to an understanding as to what townships you will inspect. After you have made a thorough examination of each lot Trespassed upon you will report on the situation of the same as follows. Give the Township Concession and lot. The name of the party in occupation of the same, a description of the buildings, the number of acres cleared on each lot, and the number and description of the timber, logs or whatever may have been cut on the lot: also give the number of days employed. You will keep expenditure as reasonable as the efficiency of the service will warrant. You will not examine any lots covered by Lumberer's licenses unless you receive special instructions so to do, but if you know or learn of any thing wrong in reference to their returns or of their cutting timber you will be pleased to inform me of the Circumstances and I will order a special examination to be made. As the season is getting so far advanced you will please be as expeditious as possible to enable me to grant clearances or permits to the lumbermen when called for. The season has been so unfavorable that it would have been impossible to have made satisfactory inspections earlier. You will therefore do the best you can to make your inspection efficient.

[20]John Rodgers of Peterborough was a forest ranger for J. F. Way.

G 23   C. J. BLOMFIELD TO MOSSOM BOYD
[*P.A.C., Boyd Papers, v. 148*]

The Canadian Land & Emigration Company.
Peterborough, Ont., July 20th. 1870.

Mr Niven[21] writes that Mr Barnhart[22] informs him that you propose getting out from Havelock next season if possible about 50,000 logs that you intend to have 5 shanties on Keneses & Redstone Lakes & a clerk in each shanty who shall among other things measure & mark all the logs cut in that shanty—

I shall be glad to know if these are your arrangements— It appears to me that it will be to our mutual advantage to have these logs measured in the woods— They need not then be detained a day by us for measurement in the water in our Townships, & I should object to measurement lower down— It would be also satisfactory to both of us that our measurements should agree at the time so that no dispute would arise on the question. I shall be glad therefore to learn from you that in the event of my sending in to Havelock Mr West or other competent measurer you will instruct your clerks to give him every facility for measuring & also if possible to arrange to measure with him & to agree returns from time to time— Please also let me know whether you intend to take out any Squared Timber from Havelock.

I had proposed to make an arrangement, probably with Mr. West, as I mentioned to you to measure all your Timber & logs in the woods but your operations are likely to be too extensive to allow Mr. West to perform the duty to the satisfaction of the Company & the advantage of himself.

Mr. Niven thinks that your Guilford logs & timber can be measured in the water in Grass Lake without detaining them, as they will be held back by you until joined by Havelock drive. If so we can each send a man to measure & agree measurement on the spot—

He also writes that "The Dysart & Dudley timber & logs can be measured in the spring before passing over the Haliburton slide & there need be no delay because the measurement can be proceeded with just as fast as the timber and logs can be got down the creek or as fast as it can be put through the slide"—

If this can be done it will be satisfactory but it appears to me that it would be a difficult matter with a large quantity of timber & logs or a heavy freshet. However raising the dam at Haliburton & erection of Dam at Mud

[21]Alexander Niven (1836–1911) qualified as a surveyor, July 8, 1859. He was employed by the Canadian Land and Emigration Company first as a surveyor and in 1868 as resident agent, and took an active part in the development of Haliburton. He left the service of the Company in 1879.

[22]Norman Barnhart, bush superintendent for Mossom Boyd, has become almost a legendary figure among lumbermen. He was a man of great physical strength and determination (Thompson, *Up to Date, or the Life of a Lumberman*, pp. 30-1).

Lake may make a difference & I suppose Niven is well informed in this matter—

It is of importance I think that we should arrange a plan for measurement & I shall be glad to hear from you at an early date on the above points.

G 24   CHARLES R. STEWART TO BOYD
[*P.A.C., Boyd Papers, v. 148*]

May 27, 1872

In accordance with your wishes I have made enquiries with regard to the logs in your Harburn and Havelock limits, and have given the subject careful attention.

The information I have gathered with reference to the Harburn limit is full and sufficient, but as regards Havelock the information is scarcely complete. I have, however, ascertained that your Harburn limit is the best of the two.

In the two seasons operations in Harburn you have taken out somewhere about the equivalent of 30,000 logs, and there are now 50,000 standard logs remaining in the township of a quality similar to those already taken out. The quantity of inferior logs may be ascertained with a certain degree of accuracy by comparison. It is a fair estimate that the limit would yield proportionately two inferior trees for every good one. There would, therefor, be 160,000 inferior logs in the township, assuming the yield of first class logs to be 80,000

The above estimate of the quantity of first-class logs yet uncut is founded on the reports of your several foremen, of your chief superintendent, and of your forest ranger. This estimate when compared with the quantities obtained from these portions of your limits where the cut of first-class logs have been completed shows a larger yield than has yet been obtained. Thus in your Guilford limit of four concessions you obtained about 14,000 logs. This gives 3,500 to a concession or 45,500 to a township, but Harburn is better timbered than the Guilford limit, and that limit has not been cut very close. I think you may calculate with safety that 50,000 first-class logs can be obtained in Harburn and also 160,000 coarse logs, making a total for the township of 240,000 logs. This estimate (in proportion) largely exceeds the number taken out of Guilford by Messrs Campbell, but still I think the estimate is reliable.

The question of what is to be done with this large number of inferior logs is one of great importance both to you and the Company, and as you have nearly exhausted the first-class cut of logs in the south-west quarter of the township it is necessary to come to an early conclusion.

It is of course desirable to both parties that you should purchase these logs, and several arrangements suggest themselves. In the first place you could buy them at a reduced price per log. Another plan would be to buy for a lump sum all the timber left on a limit after you have taken off the first-class timber, or, again, the company might cut the logs, hand them over to you to manufacture, and the profits, if any, be divided by agreement. But each of these plans would be attended with many difficulties, and each would place the Company in so disadvantageous a position with regard to yourself, that it would be injudicious even to propose them to the Board. The best and safest plan would be for you to buy the whole of the timber in the township for a fixed sum, and this sum can be ascertained with fairness & precision.

The value of the 50,000 first-class logs you can fix with some accuracy. By the price of lumber last year you had to pay the Company altogether somewhere about 37c. per log. You would probably be safe in giving 35c. per log— or $17,500. The inferior logs, would, I should think, pay you at 10c. per log, or $16,000 for the whole quantity. Together this would amount to $33,500. You would therefore, I think, be justified in giving $30,000 for the whole of the timber, as it now stands, in Harburn, and taking into consideration the risk of fire, the chance of miscalculation of quantity, and various contingencies, that sum is the largest amount you could safely offer. This amount of $30,000 added to that already accruing to the Company, would realise about one dollar per acre on the whole township.

G 25   BLOMFIELD TO BOYD
[*P.A.C., Boyd Papers, v. 148*]

The Canadian Land & Emigration Company
Peterborough Ont. Sept 5th. 1873

Mr. Niven who was here the other day informed me that the return of your logs got from our Townships in season 1872–3, given him by your foreman was 18642 pieces which he thinks would average 16 inc; this would give 8841 standards which tallies pretty well with the estimate Mr. Niven gave me a little time ago but which I fancied could hardly be accurate the amount being so very small & short of Company's expectations.

Taking 10 per cent off pro tem there would be, say, 8000 standards which at 30¢ give $2400.

I shall feel obliged if you will send me a cheque for this amount on account as I am short of funds.

The Squared Timber will I presume be shipped over the Port Perry & Whitby R.R. and you will send me Certificate of Agent shewing measurements as hitherto.

Mr. Niven mentioned your desire to cut up all your own logs before commencing on ours which you take about beginning of next year. I told him to let you know that I had no objection to this.

G 26   BLOMFIELD TO BOYD
[P.A.C., Boyd Papers, v. 148]

The Canadian Land & Emigration Company
Peterborough, Ont.
Sepr. 30th. 1873.

As directed by the Board I hereby give you formal notice that you are
required to continue to cut and deliver logs under terms of Agreement
of 30th Sepr. 1869 until the expiration of the full term of ten years from
that date— v—cl.6. of Agreemt.

The term of the Agreement so far as regards price have been, in
accordance with tenor of letter from Sir John Kennaway[23] to you & as
notified you by Telegram on Saty. last, altered for this seasons operations only to 30c per standard, without share in price of lumber, on
your getting out sufficient to yield the Company a revenue of $6,000—
Provided that what is short this season be made up in future seasons.

You will observe by reference to Agreement that 40,000 Standard
logs are required to be got out each season.

Referring to your letter of 28 Sep Mr Niven & I were discussing the
subject of improving the road N. of Haliburton when I was last there.
The Council have certainly been extremely remiss in the matter & I
intended to speak myself to the Reeve but I had not an opportunity of
seeing him. I understand that the repairs were to be undertaken at once
& Mr Niven was to attend to this— I telegraphed him yesterday afternoon & will write to the Reeve tomorrow— our regular mail day —
unless I get satisfactory reply before.

G 27   GEORGE S. THOMPSON'S[24] REMINISCENCES OF LUMBERING
IN HALIBURTON IN THE 1870's
[Thompson, Up to Date, or the Life of a Lumberman, pp. 20–3, 26–7]

. . . I engaged with Norman Barnhart, bush superintendent for
Mossom Boyd, the lumber king of the Trent River, to go up to one of
the shanties in the capacity of shanty clerk. My wages were to be, I
think, twenty dollars a month, board, lodging and tobacco free. The
shanty I was assigned to was located in the township of Harburn, fifteen
miles north of Haliburton. Mr. Boyd had acquired the right to cut and
remove the pine timber from the English Land Company,[25] and the
season I went up was about the first cutting done in that township. My

---

[23]Sir John Kennaway, second Bart. (1797–1873), was High Sheriff of Devon-
shire and one of the directors of the Canadian Land and Emigration Company.
[24]George S. Thompson, lumberman from the 1870's to the 1890's. The story of
his adventurous life, probably somewhat fictional, is given in his autobiography,
Up to Date, or the Life of a Lumberman.
[25]The Canadian Land and Emigration Company.

shanty had a crew of about fifty men; the foreman and the majority of the crew were French Canadians; the crew were civil, obliging and a hard-working lot. They treated me very kindly, and I soon got to be a great favorite with them, and soon I was right at home in the bush. My duties consisted in keeping the men's time, and charging up to the men such articles as they required, and looking after the supplies, plant, &c., received, consumed, or sent away from my shanty. I also had to keep strict account of the number of pieces timber and sawlogs made and hauled to the stream each day. Our crew that winter made both square timber and sawlogs. The two gangs of timber makers— five men in each gang, went through the bush ahead of the sawlog makers, and selected and cut down the trees suitable for square timber. A timber gang would make about six pieces of timber per day, on an average, equal to about 400 cubic feet. A gang of sawlog cutters in those days consisted of five men— three to chop the trees down and cut and top the tree square with their axes when felled, and the other two men to saw the tree into lengths required for sawlogs, usually in 12 to 16 feet sections. Five logs to the tree was a good average, to get from the trees, and 75 logs was a good average day's work for the gang of five men to cut. In those days nothing less than 14 inch diameter at top end would pass for a sawlog, and it had to be straight and sound at that. Three knots or more in a log made a cull of it; even butt logs with a hollow or the least bit of shake had to be cut of [sic] and left in the woods to rot. It is needless to say that such a system caused a great waste of wood, for the extent of territory a crew would run over in one season was enormous— only about one third of the standing trees would make such a class of logs, and therefore the balance were left untouched, probably to be soon afterwards burnt, for the chips left by the timber makers, and tops of the trees that had been felled, along with brush heaps piled up in making places for railways or skidways and roads which were opened in order to have the timber and logs hauled to the stream, tell [sic] the bush full of inflammable material. The least spark of fire the next summer set the bush in a blaze. In this way millions of dollars worth of pine and other wood have been destroyed. . . .

I have already stated how twenty out of our crew of fifty men were employed; about fifteen more are kept cutting trails or roads, so that the horses and oxen could get to the timber and logs and haul them to the stream or railways. The sawlogs if any distance from the stream would in most cases have to be piled up on skidways or rollways, . . . so that no time would be lost when the sleighing came in collecting a load and hauling to the stream. The square timber had to be collected together in much the same way. The balance of our crew were teamsters and loaders, with the exception of the cook and his helper, or "devil," as he is usually called. The size of our shanty was about forty feet square. The walls were made of large pine logs, notched and dovetailed together, and were six logs high. On top of the walls from end to end were two

enormous stringers or beams to hold up the roof which was also made
of pine logs formed of halves of trees hollowed out, called scoops, and
the greatest expense in building a shanty is making the scoops or roof.
The walls of the shanty and the roof were stuffed with moss on the
inside, and the walls on the outside plastered with mud. A large opening, about eight feet square, was left in the centre of the roof and a
wooden tapered chimney, about six feet high, built up to carry off the
smoke from the fire place or camboose, which was built of sand and
stone in the centre of the shanty. The opening in the roof, or the
chimney, let in lots of daylight, so no windows were required, and at
night the huge fire supplied all the light necessary. Sometimes a floor of
logs was put in, but just as often none. One door, about five feet square,
and the shanty was ready for the bunks or sleeping berths of the men,
which was built of poles around one side and end. The other side and
end was occupied by the foreman, clerk and cook, and there was an
unwritten law which strictly prohibited any of the crew occupying or
taking up the foreman's side of the shanty. A stable built in the same
rough way to hold about ten pairs of horses, and a small storehouse
and granary completed the set of buildings. The cost of the lot would be
about three hundred dollars, for the crew would often put them up and
have them completed in the space of three days. . . . The cookery outfit
of a camboose shanty, in the early days, consisted of half a dozen bake
kettles for baking bread, and one for baking beans in ashes, which is
done by covering the kettles with hot ashes. . . . In addition to the half
dozen kettles there are two large pots and a tea boiler; that, with a
butcher knife and a fork, completes the cooking utensils. . . .

    . . . Very little timber is made or logs cut after Xmas, the snow
usually being too deep for the men to do such work to advantage.
Anyhow the hauling of the timber and logs, generally takes up all the
time of the foreman and the crew until about the middle of the month
of March; then preparations have to be made for the drives— for the
streams clear themselves of ice mostly in the month of April, and then
the real hard work of the raftsmen or river driver commences, for the
timber and logs must be got down the same stream by the spring
freshets, or if the flood of water is allowed to run off and get ahead of
the drive then the timber and logs will have to remain in the stream
until the next spring. That is what lumbermen call "sticking" or "hanging up" a drive, and it is a great loss to the owner as well as being
thought a disgrace to the foreman and crew who worked on it, and a
foreman who sticks more than one drive soon loses his reputation and
gets reduced to the ranks. . . . The objective point for the square timber
is Quebec, and the sawlogs on the Ottawa river to the owner's sawmill at
Ottawa and other points on that river. Sawlogs on the Trent go to
Fenelon Falls, Bobcaygeon, Peterborough and Trenton; on the Georgian
Bay, they mostly go to Waubaushene, Midland, Little Current and many
are sawn up at the mills at the mouth of Spanish, French, and other

rivers tributary to the Georgian Bay. Since the Americans have came over to Canada enormous numbers of sawlogs are towed across Lake Huron to Bay City and other points in Michigan. . . .

Those among our crew who were engaged for the run, when our shanty broke up that spring were sent to the depot or headquarter shanty, where they could be best employed until navigation opened. The depot shanty, is where all the provisions and all the supplies are forwarded to from the nearest railroad point, and from there are distributed as required to the other shanties on the limit. It is where the bush superintendent, chief clerk, bush rangers and log scalers make their head quarters, and where all men leaving are settled with and paid off. The books and accounts of the whole operation are kept there, and the clerks in the working shanties make a weekly return to the chief clerk of all work done in their shanties— the company's or concern's head office is probably hundreds of miles distant from the depot shanty, and as some of the big lumber concerns have as many as two thousand men in the bush, scattered perhaps over hundreds of miles of territory, the only feasible way is to have a bush superintendent for about every five hundred men, and a travelling agent to overlook the whole outfit. The operations must necessarily be scattered along the banks of several streams, as the smaller tributaries to the main rivers would not be able to carry out the enormous output of timber and sawlogs in one season that some of the large operators take out. . . . Large clearings are usually made in order to pasture the horses and cattle during the summer season. Villages and even towns often sprung up around these lumber depots.

Fur Trapping and Trading

G 28   "JEAN BAPTISTE SYLVESTRE'S NARRATIVE"
[*Osborne*, "The Migration of Voyageurs from Drummond Island to Penetanguishene in 1828," *Ontario Historical Society*, Papers and Records, *v. 3, 1901, pp. 142–3*]

I was born at Mackinaw on All-Saints' day in 1813, the second year of the American War. My father's name was Jean Baptiste Sylvestre, who went up with the North-West Company, became a soldier in the British army and fought at Mackinaw. He received his discharge, moved to Drummond Island with the troops, and started business as a fur trader. . . . My father came to Newmarket with his furs. He met tribes of Indians in the west clothed in deer and rabbit skins, and who had no axes, knives or iron instruments. He traded among the Muskoka lakes and at Sylvestre's Lake in Parry Sound. He took me with him on one trip. We got short of provisions, and he sent two Indians out for more. They got drunk and did not return. Father was obliged to eat moss[26]

[26]Probably *tripe de roche, Umbilicaria Dillenii*, an edible lichen.

from the rocks and kill our little dog to save our lives. At last we reached the Narrows, near Orillia, where Francis Gaudaur,[27] a half-breed lived. . . . My father traded with Gordon,[28] who lived at Penetanguishene Bay long before the troops moved from Drummond Island. . . .

G 29   FUR SALE AT PENETANGUISHENE, 1865
[*Toronto*, Globe, *June 12, 1865*]

Large Sale of Furs— Mr. Thompson's sale of furs at Penetanguishene took place last week, when the lot was sold at fourteen thousand nine hundred and fifty-nine dollars. The furs are sold by private contract, and this year competition ran so close that we believe in two estimates amounting to nearly fifteen thousand dollars, only thirty dollars difference was found between two of the tenders.— *Barrie advance.*

G 30   HUDSON'S BAY COMPANY AGENT
[*Orillia*, Orillia Expositor, *May 3, 1867*]

THOMAS GOFFATT,[29]
LINEN AND WOOLEN DRAPER, HOSIER, GLOVER,
HABERDASHER
AND LACEMAN,
GENERAL MEN'S MERCER
and Fashionable
Millinery Establishment.
Also, Agent for the Hon. Hudson's Bay Company.
The Highest Price paid in cash for all kinds of Raw Furs
Peter Street, Orillia.

G 31   TRAPPING IN HALIBURTON IN THE 1870's
[*Thompson*, Up to Date, or the Life of a Lumberman, *p. 18*]

In those days there were numbers of hunters and trappers in the Haliburton district, and they brought in great quantity of furs— beaver,

[27]Francis Gaudaur's name was also spelled Goodor, Gaudor, etc. Gerald Alley said of him, "I have a fine young man with me, he is part French but very active & was with the Indians last winter when I brought them out to Yonge St. his name is Francis Goodor— His Mother is full squaw daughter of Chief Big Shilling— his father is French." (Alley to S. P. Jarvis, November 30, 1838, P.A.C., R.G. 10, v. 124).

[28]George Gordon became an apprentice clerk of the North West Company in 1807. Ten years later he began trading for himself at Fort William and later at Drummond Island. In 1825 he moved to Penetanguishene and was already established there when in 1828 other traders migrated there from Drummond Island which had been declared to be in American territory.

[29]Thomas Goffatt (b. 1844), merchant, was an agent for the Hudson's Bay Company in Orillia from about 1862 to 1877, and made expeditions into the north to purchase furs. He is said to have had an outpost on Bigwin Island in the Lake of

otter, bear, wolf, martin, mink and muskrat being the principal furs. Occasionally a silver fox would be caught; the country also abounded in such game as moose and red deer, the latter being plentiful. I have often counted twenty deer playing on the ice, and so tame would they become towards spring that they would actually come into the yards around the lumber shanties to eat the hay that was thrown out of the stables, and after I went to work in the lumber woods and got to be superintendent I always had quite a number of pets around my shanties. Those early days a trapper would often realize five hundred dollars for his pack of furs. Haliburton had two great sale days— the 24th of May and the 5th of November— in each year. On these days the hunters and trappers would come to the village for hundreds of miles around to meet the fur buyers who came from New York, Boston, Toronto, Quebec, Peterborough and other cities and towns. Most of the trappers in the Haliburton district were white men, though quite a number were Indians.

G 32   A TRAPPER'S LIFE
[Watson,[30] The Sportsman's Paradise, pp. 57–9]

We found Dr. Pokorney[31] well versed in deer-hunting, and at the same time intelligent and companionable. His son, a lad of sixteen, brave and hardy, frequently amused me by the narration of his exploits in the Canadian forests at mid-winter, while engaged as a companion to an old beaver-trapper. His story, although not entirely new, was indeed very interesting. The boy said, "It was in the latter part of the month of January that I started in company with old Ben, to go back into the bush about seventy-five miles in order to trap beaver. The weather was very cold and the snow was nearly three feet deep, and we were compelled to use snow-shoes. The hardest part of our work consisted in carrying in our provisions, traps, and other things required in trapping. When we started from this lake I carried a pack which weighed about fifty pounds. The first day out we travelled about ten miles, halted for the night and cleared the snow from a space large enough for the fire and our bed. The required amount of wood and the balsam boughs were gathered, the fire built and the bed arranged, after which we prepared and ate our supper, and then wrapped ourselves in a woollen blanket, with which each was provided, and lay down for sleep." I inquired of the lad, "Were you able to sleep?" thinking the cold would probably act as a potent barrier in this instance. The reply came promptly from the hardy lad, "Oh yes! I slept very well, for Uncle Ben

Bays, which may have been the origin of the persistent tradition that the Hudson's Bay Company had a trading post on that island. After his retirement from the Company he became postmaster at Orillia.

[30]Beriah André Watson (1836–1892), a physician, was born at Lake George, New York, and died in Jersey City, New Jersey. The quotation is taken from an account of a hunting trip in the Lake of Bays district about 1878.

[31]According to the author, Dr. Pokorney was a well-educated Polish settler in the Lake of Bays area.

kept up a good fire all night." He then added, "The next morning, after breakfast, we again shouldered our packs and pushed forward about six miles into the forest, when we marked the spot and buried our luggage." In answer to my inquiry he informed me that they buried their packs, consisting of provisions and traps, to keep other trappers, who might chance to pass that way, from appropriating these articles to their own use, which might otherwise happen. The hiding having been completed, the old trapper and his assistant retraced their steps to the log cabin from which they had originally started on their journey to the woods. Here they remained only until the following morning, when they again started with other packs. This severe work of packing lasted more than two weeks, when they reached the locality that had been selected for trapping beaver. . . . They were in the woods nearly three months, without the protection of even a canoe, tent, or any other shelter, during that portion of the time in which they were engaged in transporting their provisions and traps to the new field of labor. Having reached their destination they then erected huts, which they occupied as long as they remained.

Rumours of Gold and Other Minerals

G 33   MICHAEL DEANE TO JOSEPH CAUCHON, COMMISSIONER OF CROWN LANDS
[Ontario, Department of Lands and Forests, Field Notes, no. 1926]

. . . There is a very current tradition existing among the Indians formerly resident on Balsam Lake that there is a very valuable mine of lead and silver in the vicinity of Miner's bay in Gull Lake, and so late as the beginning of the present century, numerous and valuable specimens were easily obtained by the fur traders; the secret was only known by the Chief and his immediate successor, but, owing to the unconquerable steadfastness of the Indians, and their well known aversion to reveal to white men the locality of mines, the place has remained undiscovered. The currency of this tradition as well as mineral indications in the rocks on the margin of Gull Lake induced some parties in 1850 to make mineral explorations, they blasted great quantities of granite rock but no traces of lead or silver were discovered, however, a specimen sent to England from their "diggings" and tested in the laboratory of an eminent chemical manufacturing firm in NewCastle, was pronounced to be a very pure specimen of "Iron Pyrites," the best that had come under their observation. . . .
Lindsay 8th Feby. 1856

G 34   MINERALS IN MUSKOKA
[Orillia, Orillia Expositor, May 17, 1867]

We are now in a position to speak positively as to the result of the specimens of minerals of various kinds, which Mr. J.P. Cockburn has

had tested during his recent visit to Montreal, in the office of Sir
William Logan.[32] The Officials showed Mr. Cockburn all the attention
possible, examined the specimens, and pronounced one to be rich in
copper, which would yield fully thirty per cent. Another to contain the
finest iron, now much sought after in the manufacture of a superior kind
of steel. The specimens of gold and silver were also considered excellent. We may soon expect to hear of a mining company being formed to
take advantage of the recent discoveries in the Muskoka territory.

G 35   GOLD AT SPARROW LAKE
[Orillia, Orillia Expositor, *September 20, 1867]*

We are informed from reliable authority that gold has undoubtedly
been discovered at the mine of Messrs. Hatch, Blain & Skinner, at
Sparrow Lake. We understand that specimens have been tested and
pronounced to be so rich, both in quality and quantity, that the fortunate possessors anticipate that their mine will yield at least $500
worth of gold per day. The Company expects to have a crushing mill in
operation shortly, when we will be able to give fuller particulars.

Specimens from the above mine can be seen at this office.

G 36   "GOLD AT SKELETON LAKE"
[Orillia, Orillia Expositor, *October 25, 1867]*

We are informed that Mr. J.A. Pickering has commenced operations
in the vicinity of the above lake. He states that he has found better
indications of gold bearing quartz in that locality than he had at the
Golden Carey Mines, California, where he has had four year's experience as a practical miner. Mr. Pickering is at present employed by a
New York firm (with which he was also connected while in California)
to prospect in the unsurveyed tract north of Skeleton Lake, and is quite
sanguine as to the results. It appears, however, that the expense of
sinking shafts in that region is very great on account of the extreme
hardness of the rock so that considerable capital will be required to
successfully prosecute the business of mining; nevertheless, a few are
engaged in the work, amongst whom are Messrs. Skinner & Blair and
Dr. Dellenbaugh.[33] When the crushing mills are put in operation the
wealth how [sic] in the rocks will be poured out and will assist to
stimulate all other industrial enterprises in the northern country.

[32]Sir William Edmond Logan (1798–1875) was appointed director of the Canadian Geological Survey when it was organized in 1843 and continued in that position until 1870.

[33]This may have been Dr. F. Dellenbaugh whose advertisement appeared in the
Orillia Expositor, May 22, 1868, "Dr. F. Dellenbaugh, German Physician of Buffalo, N.Y., Will be at Fraser's Hotel, BARRIE, on Tuesday the 2nd of June, 1868,
where he can be consulted on all forms of Lingering Diseases. CONSULTATION
FREE."

H. TRANSPORTATION

Stages

H 1   BAILEY'S STAGE, ORILLIA TO BRACEBRIDGE
[*Orillia*, Orillia Expositor, *November 29, 1867*]

BRACEBRIDGE
AND ORILLIA

Bailey's Line of Stages
Will leave the "Victoria Hotel," Bracebridge, daily, at 8 a.m. for Orillia.
Returning will leave the "Royal Hotel," Orillia, daily at 8 a.m. for
Bracebridge, stopping at Washago, Gravenhurst and Muskoka Falls,
and connecting with the stage for Parry Sound. Charges Moderate.

A. BAILEY.
Proprietor.

Bracebridge, Dec. 1st, 1867.

H 2   BEATTY'S[1] STAGE, PARRY SOUND TO BRACEBRIDGE
[*Parry Sound*, Northern Advocate, *December 14, 1869*]

ROYAL MAIL.
Parry Sound
to
Bracebridge,
AND VICE VERSA

THE Subscribers have much pleasure informing the inhabitants of Parry
Sound and Muskoka Districts, that on and after
December 2nd, 1869,
they will put on a Line of
MAIL STAGES
TO RUN BETWEEN
PARRY SOUND
AND
BRACEBRIDGE
Single Fare, $2.00.
The stage will
LEAVE Parry Sound
AT SIX O'CLOCK, A.M.
Monday and Thursday
MORNINGS

[1]J. & W. Beatty & Co. of Thorold bought a sawmill and timber limits at the
mouth of the Seguin River, now Parry Sound, in 1863. They operated boats on
Georgian Bay and Lake Huron as well as the stage service to Bracebridge.

Returning will
LEAVE Bracebridge
on
Tuesdays and Fridays
AT NOON
J. & W. BEATTY, & CO.
Proprietors.

Parry Sound, Nov. 22, 1869.

H 3   Harvie's[2] Stage, Washago to Gravenhurst
[*Parry Sound*, Northern Advocate, *December 14, 1869*]

HARVIE'S LINE OF
ROYAL MAIL
STAGES

The Subscriber begs leave to inform Tourists, and those in search of land in the Free Grant District of Muskoka, that he keeps a line of
STAGES RUNNING DAILY
BETWEEN
Washago & Gravenhurst.
Connecting with the steamers on Lake Couchiching, and the *Wenonah*, on Lake Muskoka.

John Harvie,
Proprietor

H 4   Gunigle's[3] Stage, Bobcaygeon to Minden
[*Lindsay*, Lindsay Expositor, *October 21, 1869*]

Royal Mail Stage
BETWEEN
MINDEN AND BOBCAYGEON

The above stage leaves Minden every Monday, Wednesday and Friday morning, at six o'clock, and arrives at Bobcaygeon at 12 o'clock, noon.

Returning, leaves Bobcaygeon every Tuesday, Thursday and Saturday, at 12 o'clock, noon, and arrives at Minden at 6 o'clock p.m.

[2]John Harvie (or Harvey), stage coach owner, was the eldest of seven sons of John Harvie who came from Scotland to south Orillia Township in 1832. At least two of his brothers, Andrew and Charles, transported freight, especially from Orillia to Toronto, before the days of the railway. John Harvie ran a stage coach from Barrie to Orillia, and later he and James Millard ran a stage to Gravenhurst, starting from Washago in summer and Orillia in winter. He was assisted for a time by his son J. T. Harvie (1847–1923?). As new settlers came to Muskoka Harvie extended his service further to the north and employed an increasing number of teams hauling passengers and freight.

[3]Bryan Gunigle (or Gunigal) was born in Ireland in 1838 and settled in Victoria County in 1856. He was the proprietor of livery stables at Lindsay and owned land in Ops Township.

Fares reasonable. Parcels at the owners' risk unless booked and paid for

Bryan Gunigle,
Proprietor.

H 5   Thomson's[4] Stage, Minden to Haliburton
[*Lindsay,* Lindsay Expositor, *December 23, 1869*]

Thomson's stages
Leave Haliburton for Minden every Tuesday, Thursday and Saturday, at 6.30 a.m., returning the same day.
Comfortable conveyances and fares moderate.

Boats

H 6   Vernon B. Wadsworth's Reminiscences of the First
Boat on the Muskoka Lakes, 1861
[*Ms in possession of W. R. Wadsworth, Q.C., Toronto*]

In 1860 J. S. Dennis, Provincial Land Surveyor, was instructed . . . to proceed to the unsurveyed and unsettled region North of the Severn River and Sparrow Lake and the Georgian Bay and locate Colonization Road lines, commencing from the Falls of South Muskoka River on to the North Falls, where the Town of Bracebridge is situate, and thence onward to Lake Nipissing and westward to Parry Sound . . .

Mr. Dennis carried on the surveys in the District during the year 1861— and it became apparent a boat was absolutely necessary to carry on the work and freight supplies of food for the survey-party. Mr. Dennis purchased a good substantial sailing boat from the O'Gormans who were boat builders in the City of Kingston— The boat was about 20 ft. in length with iron centre board well equipped with mainsail and foresail and suitable for the purpose. Harvey a freighter of Orillia delivered the boat on the shore of South Bay, Muskoka. There was of course no wharf there at that time.

The boat was sailed up the waters of Lake Muskoka and on to Lake Rosseau (moved across the portage at "Indian Gardens" now Port Carling, on rollers), and used that summer on Lake Rosseau for transport-work and was usually moored at the mouth of Shadow River, where we had a store-camp, and the road line was being surveyed to Parry Sound. . . .

---

[4]"Steve" Thomson (or Thompson) ran a stage from Haliburton to Minden in the winter, and in the summer a freight boat and a mail skiff from Haliburton to the foot of Lake Kashagawigamog and a stage from the landing, three and a half miles, to Minden. An account of the service, probably somewhat coloured by the author's personality is given in G. S. Thompson's *Up to Date, or the Life of a Lumberman*, pp. 11–18.

As winter approached the housing of the boat became a question, as there was no dock on Lake Rosseau or suitable building at that time— so at the first snowfall I was instructed to take the boat on shore at some safe and convenient point near the head of Lake Rosseau; so with one man and an Indian camped there on a site opposite the present Monteith Inn site. We proceeded along the East shore to what is now called Lawson's Bay and found a suitable place at the end of the Bay at the mouth of a small creek there situate— We hauled the boat out, covered it with balsam brush and placed the sails and equipment on a platform of trees there situate.

Our surveying operations were transferred in 1862 to the Haliburton District; and, although I returned in 1864 to the head of Lake Rosseau to survey the Nipissing Road Line, I never heard of the boat again— but she was the first wooden boat of any description to navigate the Muskoka Lakes (excepting, of course, birch bark canoes).

H 7   THE *Wenonah*,[5] FIRST STEAMER ON LAKE MUSKOKA, 1866
[*Toronto*, Globe, *July 7, 1866*]

Cockburn's Royal Mail Line.
(Established June 1866.)
The only expeditious and reliable route between
Washago, head of Lake Simcoe,
and
LAKE ROSSEAU.

Comfortable stages connect (daily) at Washago, (head of Lake Simcoe navigation) running to Gravenhurst, (foot of Muskoka navigation) overland (route 14 miles) and on Muskoka Lake (also upon the Indian and Muskoka Rivers), the fine new side wheel steamer
"WENONAH,"
33 HORSE-POWER,
Makes regular trips, calling at Alport, Bracebridge, Indian Village, and intermediate places.

This steamer was built during the last winter, and is comfortably fitted up for passenger traffic and excursions. Dimensions, length, 87 feet and breadth, 26½ feet; average speed 10 miles per hour. The Wenonah also connects, at the Indian Village, on Mondays, Wednesdays and Fridays, with an open boat which plies upon Lake Rosseau.

The new region now attracting the attention of business men and farmers, and for pleasure-seekers, tourists and sportsmen, it is quite unsurpassed in Upper Canada, the trout fishing is this season (as usual) most excellent.

Charges very moderate

[5]The *Wenonah* was a side-wheeler, listed at 62 tons. Before the lock was opened at Port Carling, the *Wenonah* usually ran on Lake Muskoka, but in 1871 it was warped over the portage during high water in the spring to Lake Rosseau.

For further particulars apply to

N. Milloy,
Toronto

A. P. Cockburn,
Orillia, July 7.

H 8   RATES ON THE *Wenonah*
[*Orillia*, Orillia Expositor, *May 22, 1868*]

District of Muskoka
1868   Steamer   1868

"Wenonah"

Will commence her regular daily trips on Monday, 1st June, and should sufficient encouragement and support warrant it, will ply during the season of navigation for the conveyance of Freight and Passengers

PASSAGE

Gravenhurst to	Alport	$0 50
	Bracebridge	0 50
	Tonden Island	0 50
	Baisong Rapid[6] (In. village)	0 60
	Little Currant[7] (Muskos)	0 60
Bracebridge to	Alport	0 15
	Gravenhurst	0 50
	Tonden Island	0 40
	Little Current (Muskos)	0 60
	Little Current	0 60
	Baisong Rapids (I. village)	0 00 [*sic*]

EXCURSIONS.

For the Day– not to interfere with regular trips. $30.

FREIGHT—FIRST CLASS.

Dry Goods, Glass and Earthenware, Leather and Implements, 15c per 100 lbs. Household Furniture double rates.

SECOND CLASS.

Groceries, Shelf Hardware, 12½c per 100 lbs.

THIRD CLASS.

Provisions, Heavy Castings, Nails, Bar Iron, &c., 10c. per 100 lbs.

LIVE STOCK.

Horses (aged)	80c each
Oxen "	75c "
Cows "	70c "
Hogs "	35c "
Sheep "	12½c "

Young stock in proportion to above.

---

[6]Baisong Rapids (now Port Carling) was better known as Indian Village or Obajawanung, with variant spellings. The name Baisong was taken from the Indian name for the river.

[7]The name Little Current was used for a short time for a settlement in the southwestern part of Lake Muskoka.

MISCELLANEOUS.

Wheat, corn, peas, rye, potatoes,	5c per bushel
Oats, Barley	4c ”
Hay pressed in bales	$2 per ton
” loose	$3 ”
Sawn lumber	$1 per m. ft.
Shingles	20c per m.
Lime (carefully packed in boxes or barrels)	5 per bushel.
Brick	$2 50 per m.
Two Oared Skiffs	37½c each
Sail Boats, from	50c. each
Bark Canoes	25c. each
Storage and Wharfage at Gravenhurst free	

Agent at Orillia— M. Burton.
    ”   Washago— H. Whitney.
    ”   Gravenhurst— Cockburn & Son.
    ”   Bracebridge— Alex. Bailey.
    ”   Baisong Rapids— M. Bailey.[8]

H 9   STEAMER ON SEVERN RIVER, 1875
[*Orillia,* Times, *April 8, 1875*]

Mr. Thomas Stanton, the well-known engineer, is placing a neat little steamer[9] on the Severn waters. She is intended to ply between the Severn Bridge and Sparrow Lake, and no doubt will prove a boon to the settlers around Sparrow Lake, who at present labor under great inconveniences and numerous disadvantages in consequence of the almost impracticable state of the roads through that portion of Morrison and North Orillia. In fact we understand there is nothing but winter roads about the Severn River and Sparrow Lake.

H 10   "HISTORY OF MUSKOKA NAVIGATION" TO 1878
[*Kirkwood and Murphy,* The Undeveloped Lands in Northern & Western Ontario, *pp. 72–3*]

Since the bulk of the traffic, whether immigrant or commercial, of Muskoka and of those portions of Parry Sound, which are tributary to Rousseau and Bracebridge, is carried over the lakes Muskoka, Rousseau, and St. Joseph, and also the Muskoka river, a history of the progress of navigation will form no slight index of the growth of the district.

It is needless to inform the reader that the first craft utilized for the navigation of these waters was the bark canoe of the red man, and it is probable that the same class of craft was employed by John Beal, the first settler, in reaching the Township of Macaulay in 1861. He is said

---

[8]Michael Bailey was one of the first white settlers at Port Carling. His land was at the north end of the present settlement.

[9]On April 15 the *Times* reported that the steamer was launched "last week."

to have spent five days in discovering the mouth of the river in order to reach the North Falls (now the flourishing village of Bracebridge), Mr. James Cooper[10] introduced the first wood-boat in 1862, to be followed by McCabe's sail-boat in 1863, and Mr. James Sharpe's[11] in 1864. All three boats were employed in the business of carrying passengers and freight to various points on the lakes. The rates then charged were 75cts. per cwt., between Washago (the head of Lake Simcoe route) and Gravenhurst, by land and water transportation, or $1 per cwt., all land carriage. Mr. Holditch,[12] about this time constructed a large flat boat to be propelled by horse-power. The boat was built at the North Falls (Bracebridge) and made a trip to McCabe's Bay (Gravenhurst), but never returned again, the craft, or rather its propelling arrangements, being a failure. The boat occupied upwards of twelve hours in going on her trip. About the same time, the Bradley Bros. built an expensive sloop for the trade, but it, like the horse-boat was a failure.

In September, 1865, Mr. A.P. Cockburn (now representing Muskoka and Parry Sound in the Dominion Parliament, but) then merchant and Reeve of the Township of Eldon, County of Victoria, made an examination of the Muskoka region, including the Lake of Bays, Peninsula, Fairy, Vernon Lakes, and the Maganetewan river, returning by way of Lake Muskoka, and he was much impressed with the beauty and importance of these lakes. He returned shortly afterwards, and in company with Mr. James Cooper, sailed over Lake Muskoka to examine the reputed natural obstructions to navigation at the Indian village, now Port Carling. Mr. Cockburn then forwarded a paper on the back country to Hon. T.D. McGee,[13] the then Commissioner of Agriculture, with a report of his observations, and some practical suggestions of a policy of road and other improvements, which, if the Government would promise to make, he (Mr. C.) would undertake to place a steamer on the lakes to facilitate settlement. Mr. McGee and the Government felt highly pleased and interested in Mr. Cockburn's representations . . . The result of these negotiations was, that the keel of the *Wenonah* was immediately laid, and this steamer opened up steam navigation trade by making her first trip in 1866, arriving at North Falls (Bracebridge) when there were not twenty people in the place to greet her arrival. The rate of freight from Washago to North Falls was reduced at once from 75c.–$1 per cwt.,

[10]James Cooper, father of Joseph Cooper, was a squatter on land now in Bracebridge, on both sides of the falls. Alexander Bailey later bought out his claim. Cooper built a tavern in Bracebridge about 1865.

[11]James Sharpe (b. 1820) came to Canada from Scotland and went to Muskoka about 1861. He served as shipping agent for the Muskoka Navigation Company for twelve years, emigration agent for a number of years, and inspector of weights and measures.

[12]Probably William Holditch, one of the first persons to own land in Bracebridge.

[13]Thomas D'Arcy McGee (1825–1868) was Minister of Agriculture from 1864 to 1867.

down to 40c. per cwt., and freight was always brought through punctually from McCabe's Bay (Gravenhurst). The *Wenonah* continued to ply alone, and generally at a loss to her owner, until in 1869, the *Wabamik* was brought up to assist in the despatch of the growing traffic. In 1871, the fine low-pressure steamer *Nipissing*[14] was added, and in the spring of 1876, the powerful steam-tug *Simcoe* formed another auxiliary to the Muskoka fleet. . . .

June 18, 1877, was a fresh steamboat epoch, the paddlewheel steamer *Northern,* having been launched on that day at Port Sydney. Her owners and builders, Messrs. Denton and Smiley, had a very successful season which closed early in December. The *Northern* is a paddle wheel steamer designed to carry 400 passengers, 80 feet X 24 beam, tonnage, 60; cost, $7,000. She runs 25 miles from Port Sydney to the head of Lake Vernon, and returning goes to Huntsville and Fairy Lake, making a distance of 56 miles for the entire route. She traverses Mary, Fairy and Vernon lakes, and has seven ports of call. . . .

A vista of future extensions of Muskoka navigation opens before us, when the Lake of Bays, the Maganetawan River, and Lake Nipissing shall have been provided with steamers. Even now the timbers and knees have been ordered and partly got out, for a steamer on the Lake of Bays, where there would be at least thirty miles of navigation, without counting the return journey. . . .

Canals and Locks

H 11   J. W. BRIDGLAND TO THE COMMISSIONER OF CROWN LANDS,
ALEXANDER CAMPBELL
[*P.A.O., Colonization Roads Papers,* Reports, *1862–8, p. 199*]

Quebec 28th. February 1865

. . . I beg also here to mention, that, I think it desirable, I should receive your sanction to visit the Rosseau Lake Narrows, while in that region during my anticipated visit to the roads next Summer for the purpose of ascertaining whether some moderate improvement of the same (in connection with the important navigable access to the two roads above described) at a cost commensurate with the advantage to be gained thereby, can be made.

In high water navigation, no peculiar difficulty, I believe, is experienced in passing through these straits; but in time of drouth some shallows and rapids will necessarily much impede the passage. A small amount might therefore be profitably expended in improving the Channel

[In margin] very well A.C.

[14]The *Nipissing* was a side-wheeler of 52 tons, and carried both freight and passengers. It is often called the "first" Nipissing to distinguish it from a later steamer on the Muskoka Lakes of the same name.

H 12   BRIDGLAND TO ALEXANDER CAMPBELL
[*P.A.O., Colonization Roads Papers, Reports, 1862–8, pp. 322–5*]

Toronto, 24 June /67

I have the honor to report that in obedience to your instructions I have made a cursory examination of the site and surroundings of the proposed Obigewanah Canal— to connect and render uninterrupted the navigation of Lakes Rousseau and Muskoka.

I found the shortest distance between the small landing Bay on the Rosseau side and the River on the opposite and Southern side, immediately below the rapids to be 110 feet and the difference of level, at the present time, to be but one foot seven and 1/3 inches.

There is a pretty strong current in the river at the point which continues for some 10 or 12 rods further, although not sufficient to prevent the passage of row boats to the terminus alluded to or the steamer which now lands freight and passengers close by.

I found the bench marks and section and outline stakes of the recent survey by Mr Baillargé.[15]

After considering well the extent of the traffic now existing and the augmentation of the same which may probably ensue in the future for many years, my opinion is that the expenditure of so large a sum as that estimated by Mr Baillargé for the projected canal would not be waranted.

I do not think it necessary to enter at all elaborately into the discussion of this question but shall merely place one or two facts before you, from the consideration of which I am confident you will arrive at a similar conclusion.

1st. The country above this point is at present sparsely populated and is intersected with good roads (The Muskoka and Parry Sound)

2nd. The Collingwood and Parry Sound route, will, as a line of ingress, in spite of any such improvement (were it made) draw off the major portions of the settlement tending Eastward

3rd. The amount Estimated for the Canal must be largely supplimented by a further allowance for a Lock-house and a yearly stipend for a Lock-master, while the whole duty he would perform would be to admit and pass through the lock one boat 3 times a week.

4th. And mainly because a comparatively inexpensive improvement could be made to supply all the wants of the country with more general satisfaction in my opinion than the Canal in question.

The simplest improvement would be a tram road across the narrow neck of land with a wharf & water break pier on the South side and a simple wharf on the North Bay.

A freight house or shed for general convenience could also be built and a block tackle and crane for the purpose of hoisting goods upon the track.

15G. F. Baillairgé (also spelled Baillargé), of the Public Works Department, also prepared a report on the Trent waterway.

A small boat such as that which now plies upon Lake Couchiching called the "Dean of Montreal" valued at about $1500 could be placed on the upper Lakes and complete the connection.

This latter improvement would, I doubt not, be the result of private enterprise as a respectable and well to do settler on Lake Rosseau has, I am credibly informed expressed his readiness to enter into such an investment.

All the improvements I have above suggested in place of the Canal Lock, including the boat alluded to, might be constructed for $4000 and upon the whole would, in my opinion, as I have before suggested, give more general satisfaction than the Lock.

In my review of the subject I cannot but think that however much my judgement may err as to the ultimate future advantage of the Lock, the present condition of things in the locality and vicinity, would render the immediate construction of it premature and extravagant.

I examined also the various points on the Rousseau river below the Lock site where shallows occur. There are some three or four places where, at low water, the channel is contracted and shoal. A little dredging would correct all of these obstructions, save one perhaps where a rocky bottom is found.

This upon examination, may also be found to be capable of being deepened, but I had neither the means nor the time at my disposal to make such an examination. It can be readily done in the future.

As however the present level of the water (which is quite sufficient for the Steamer Wenonah now plying upon Lake Muskoka) does not injuriously effect [sic] any land occupied or improvements by the settlers, a dam I think might be made at Muskoka Falls to kepe the water at nearly its present level and by one such improvement overcome all the obstructions alluded to.

[Note at end] I concur in Mr Bridglands reasoning against the Canal project and in favour of a tram road with freight shed and hoisting tackle — but probably the last two items may be left to private enterprise— whoever worked the tram road would probably build the shed and provide the crane & tackle A.C. [Alexander Campbell] C.C.L. 28th June '67

H 13   PETITION[16] FOR IMPROVEMENT OF NAVIGATION BETWEEN
LAKES MUSKOKA AND ROSSEAU
[P.A.O., Ontario Sessional Papers, Petitions, 1868–9, no. 895]

Unto the Honourable Legislative Assembly of the Province of Ontario
The petition of the undersigned inhabitants of the Townships of Muskoka, Macaulay & Monck
Humbly Sheweth
That your petitioners are (most respectfully) desirouse of impressing

[16]Presented to the Legislative Assembly by A. P. Cockburn, December 17, 1868.

upon your Honourable body the importance of our Inland navigation which is so constituted by nature and with a little government aid will supply a high way for 7 months of the year, for the Transportation of freight and passengers, through the very heart of the district, at a very moderate cost compared with land conveyance, the distance being shorter by water, and journeys by steamer can be accomplished, between Gravenhurst Bracebridge & Rosseau, with greater expedition and ease and at less than half the cost now incurred by land travel which can scarcely be undertaken at all except in sleighing

That your petitioners wish to explain that the removal of certain obstructions in the River between Lakes Muskoka & Rosseau are necessary before the benefit of the above system of navigation can be made properly available.

That your petitioners would call the attention of your honourable House, that there are vast tracts of land, surrounding this chain of Lakes, still unsettled, but once the navigation is extended, the country will be developed in a short period of time, hoping that you will at once undertake this much needed work,

Your petitioners as in duty bound will ever pray,

H 14   REPORT OF T. N. MOLESWORTH,[17] ASSISTANT ENGINEER ON
PUBLIC WORKS, DECEMBER 30, 1870
[Ontario, Department of Agriculture and Public Works,
Annual Report on Public Works, 1870, p. 17]

LOCK AND WORKS ON ROSSEAU RIVER,[18] MUSKOKA.

This work was commenced in July, 1870, and from difficulties in connection with the blasting of the rock, high water, and other causes, has progressed very slowly, but I have reason to hope it will be ready for the navigation of Lake Rosseau early next season; the excavations of the rock are far advanced; the material is all on hand and ready for the platforms, mitre sills, side walls, gates and other details; and preparations are now in hand for laying down the upper mitre sill and platform, and for building the walls of the upper recesses and wings. The sides of the chamber of this lock will be formed of the natural rock, which will have longitudinal and upright timbers, bolted on to protect vessels in passing from striking any roughness or projections of the rock. The walls forming the quoin piers, recess walls, and wings will be built of timber crib-work, filled with concrete, stone and puddle; they were to have been built of rubble masonry, of the stone coming out of the chamber, but this has been found unsuitable to dress for the purpose, and no other stone is to

---

[17]Thomas Nepean Molesworth (1824–1879) was born in Ireland, came to Canada in 1848, and qualified as a land surveyor April 25, 1851. In 1868 he was appointed Assistant Engineer on Public Works.
[18]The Indian River, not the present Rosseau River.

be obtained around the lake, and therefore this part of the work has been changed.

The entire expenditure on this work, is as follows:

Payments to contractors on materials and work	$12,750 00
Cost of surveys, superintendence, and sundries	3,450 90
Total	$16,200 90

Dredging and the removal of rocks in the river approaching the lock, and in the Muskoka river leading up to Bracebridge, form parts of the details included in the appropriation for these works, and the following amounts have been expended thereon:

Dredging on Muskoka and Rosseau Rivers	$2,046 50
Blasting and removing stones and rocks	523 20
Total	$2,569 70

The unexpended balance of the appropriation will be sufficient to complete the unfinished portions of these works.

CHANNEL BETWEEN LAKES JOSEPH AND ROSSEAU.

This work is designed to connect the navigable waters of Lakes Joseph and Rosseau, and is being excavated through a sandy neck of land between the two lakes. The work was let to Mr. George Blain, on the 5th of February, 1870, for the sum of $7,865, for the excavation of the channel, dredging at both entrances, and crib-work piers at each end; and $1,500 for retaining walls of crib-work throughout on each side, to meet the piers at each entrance. The whole crib-work rests on a stratum of hard clay, which gives an excellent foundation.

The crib-work along the entire north side of the channel is built up above water surface, and has a length of 350 feet.

The crib-work along the south side is laid for a length of about 200 feet to above the surface of the water, and requires about 150 feet to complete its length, and on both sides the walls require finishing up to their permanent level.

The excavation of the channel connecting the lakes, between the crib-work is nearly finished, and the waters are connected; but the dredging, especially in Lake Joseph, requires to be done, and this, as well as the crib-work, will be finished early in the summer of 1871.

The expenditure on this work is as follows:

Payments to contractor on works	$6,630 00
Do on surveys and superintendence	164 30
Total	6,794 30

The whole will be finished within the estimated cost.

H 15   THE CUT BETWEEN LAKES ROSSEAU AND JOSEPH
NAMED PORT SANDFIELD, SEPTEMBER, 1870
[*Marshall,*[19] The Canadian Dominion, *pp. 58–60*]

I had the honour of suggesting a name for a spot that may possibly attain to importance. At a certain point the waters of St. Joseph approach within about two hundred yards of Lake Rousseau; a strip of sand, easy to work, forming the division. Some thirty men were at work cutting this through, and embanking the channel solidly with stone. We encamped here one night on a wooded knoll overlooking the two lakes. I took a lesson in wood-chopping, and felled, but with many a wasted stroke, two trees. It was a pleasant experience to stand back, just after the last blow, and see the tottering tree sweep down from among its fellows with a thundering crash. It was more difficult to stand on the trunk afterwards and cut it into logs by strokes directed between the outstretched feet.

Before our canvas tents blazed a magnificent fire of pine logs. Here we broiled our fish and pork and cooked our tea. A recent settler prayed our acceptance of the first potatoes grown on Lake Joseph; they turned out from our pot white, flaky balls of unequalled deliciousness. Another settler brought out from his pocket a specimen ear of Indian corn about a foot long, and excellently ripened.

We ate suppers hearty enough to have given us all nightmare in any spot less free and wild than this. Then members of Government sang patriotic songs, and some backwoodsmen, and the men on the works close by, attracted to our camp, sang songs, sentimental and comic. The stars were long out when we crawled into our tents, rolled ourselves in blankets, and fell asleep.

. . .

In the morning a great plank was procured. In open block letters I inscribed on it the name newly decided on for the place. The plank was nailed up to a pine before the assembled party. In the name of Her Majesty Queen Victoria and of the Dominion of Canada, the Reverend Mr. Herring[20] christened the place Port Sandfield. We added our acclamations.

[19]Charles Marshall, who came from England for a tour of the United States and Canada, was invited by the Premier of Ontario to join the members of the government in a visit to Muskoka in September, 1870 (J 8).

[20]The Reverend Armine Styleman Herring, B.A., was incumbent of St. Paul's, Clerkenwell, London. He was active in promoting emigration especially to the Free Grant lands, and made a visit to Muskoka in 1870. He was chairman of the Clerkenwell and Central London Emigration Club and issued leaflets giving advice on emigration and settlement.

H 16   "LOCK BETWEEN MARY'S AND FAIRY LAKES"
[*Ontario, Department of Agriculture and Public Works,*
Annual Report on Public Works, *1873, p. 20*]

Department of Public Works, Ontario
Toronto, 22nd January, 1874.

. . . An appropriation of $20,000 was granted for this service in 1873, and surveys were made from which plans were prepared for a wooden lock similar in construction to that at Balsam river, but somewhat smaller in the area of the chamber.

. . .

The contract was let in June to Mr. John Carroll for the sum of $16,900, and although very little was done during the summer, except clearing off the ground, he is now getting out all the timber required for the construction of the works.

The completion of the lock will open a navigation through Mary's Lake, 13 miles from Bracebridge, up the north branch of the Muskoka river into Fairy, Vernon and Peninsula lakes, around all of which there are now promising settlements, with a considerable per-centage of good land interspersed amongst the high rocky hills. The Village of Huntsville is prettily located on the margin of one of these lakes, and will, therefore, be accessible by this navigation.

The expenditure on this work in 1873 has been as follows:—

Payments on account of the contract $425 00
Cost of survey, laying out works and printing 594 31

Total .... $1,019 31[21]

The balance of the appropriation will be required for revote for the completion of these works.

Railways for Muskoka

H 17   T. C. KEEFER'S[22] EVIDENCE ON THE OTTAWA-HURON TRACT
[*Canada, Legislative Assembly, Committee on Ottawa and Georgian Bay Territory, Report, June 15, 1864 (Legislative Assembly,* Journals, *1864, app. 8)*]

. . . The peculiarity of the Ottawa and Huron tract as a wilderness one, is, that unlike the valley of the St. Maurice, and the Saguenay, it is

[21]In his *Report* for 1877 the Commissioner gave the total expenditure to December 31, 1877, as $29,209.74.

[22]Thomas Coltrin Keefer (1821–1915) was a surveyor and an outstanding hydraulic engineer. He worked on the Erie and Welland canals and on the Ottawa and St. Lawrence River.

not necessarily a *cul-de-sac,* but if opened through, would form one of the shortest routes between the most important points east and west. In the face of other attractions it is hopeless, for the present, to expect that emigration and settlement can be attracted to this district by existing means of communication. If inveigled there, no valuable element of population will long remain cut off from communication with the railway world, in a country where this state of things is the exception rather than the rule.

A railway from the city of Ottawa, to the port of the Georgian Bay on Lake Huron, would nourish existing settlements and give birth to new ones within 30 miles on either side, wherein there was a suitable tract of land. It would drop the better qualities of sawn lumber from interior mills into the Hudson River boats at Ottawa, and the commoner kinds into Chicago schooners on Lake Huron. It would reduce the cost of supplies to the lumberman, increasing his profit and to that extent compensate for its interference with his monopoly. It would find a market for the valuable fish known to exist in the inland lakes and the still more valuable minerals more than suspected to be on their borders. Nor would it be confined to a local traffic. It would form part of the shortest possible route between Montreal and Lake Huron, and for the grain traffic between Chicago, Milwaukie and Montreal . . .

H 18　Petition[23] for Railway from Toronto to Lake Nipissing
　　[*P.A.O., Ontario Sessional Papers, Petitions, 1867–8, no. 501*]

To the Honorable the Legislative Assembly of the Province of Ontario, in Parliament assembled.

THE PETITION OF THE UNDERSIGNED RATEPAYERS OF THE COUNTIES OF YORK AND ONTARIO,
HUMBLY SHEWETH:

That the large tract of Country lying between the City of Toronto and Lake Nipissing is without any means of Communication or of Transport, except such as is afforded by the common roads of the country.

That in the judgment of your Petitioners, the construction of a Railroad through that section of country, would materially aid its settlement, and the development of its resources.

Wherefore, your Petitioners humbly pray your Honorable Body, that a charter may be granted for a Railway from Toronto to Lake Nipissing, traversing the Counties of York, Ontario, and Victoria; and that said charter contain a clause binding the said railway to carry cordwood, or any wood for fuel, at a rate of not to exceed two-and-a-half cents per

[23]Presented to the Legislative Assembly by A. P. Cockburn, February 10, 1868. On verso: "Petition of certain inhabitants of the Counties of York and Ontario praying for a charter for the Toronto and Nipissing Railway."

mile per cord, for all stations exceeding fifty miles, and at a rate not exceeding three cents per cord per mile, for all stations under fifty miles.

And your Petitioners, as in duty bound, will ever pray.

Toronto, this [blank] of [blank], 1867.

H 19   RATEPAYERS' INVITATION TO OFFICERS OF NORTHERN RAILWAY TO VISIT MUSKOKA
[*Orillia*, Orillia Expositor, *August 20, 1869*]

A meeting of the ratepayers of the District of Muskoka was held at Gravenhurst, on Wednesday, the 18th inst., for the purpose of extending an invitation to the Northern Railway officials. The meeting was a very influential one, though not numerously attended, owing to this being the busy season, and also to the fact of Mr. McMurray's large sale taking place on the same day. Besides the ratepayers of Muskoka township present, we observed several gentlemen from the townships of Morrison, Monck and Medora. A.J. Alport, Esq., Reeve of Muskoka, was, on motion, called to the chair, and J.T. Kirkpatrick[24] appointed secretary.

The Chairman explained at some length the object of the meeting, and in a most happy and encouraging strain, adverted to their past and present circumstances, and to the future prospects of the District, convincing all present that he is a genuine railroad man. Before resuming his seat, he called upon A.P. Cockburn, Esq., M.P.P., to address the meeting.

Mr. Cockburn showed that it was not possible for them to become a very prosperous people without a railway. He read an extract from a letter received from Mr. Cumberland,[25] which elicited applause. Mr. Cockburn concluded by moving the following resolution, which was seconded by J. Scott,[26] Esq., J.P.,

"That this meeting fully recognises and appreciates the urgency and importance of securing easier, quicker, and cheaper means of transportation, with a view to the more rapid development of the vast tracts of agricultural, mineral and pine timbered lands contained in and to the north of the District of Muskoka." — Carried unanimously.

The Chairman next called upon Joseph Piercy, who made a neat and pointed speech, and concluded by moving the following resolution, which Mr. E. Hewett[27] seconded:

"That whereas the District of Muskoka contains nearly intact a large lumbering field, conveniently intersected by lakes and rivers, tributary to the very considerable lakes of Muskoka, Rosseau, and Joseph, as well as a large traffic necessarily incidental to a thriving settlement, it is

[24]Probably James Kirkpatrick, a merchant at Gravenhurst.

[25]Frederic William Cumberland (1821–1881), engineer and architect, was managing director of the Northern Railway from 1860 until his death.

[26]John Scott of Severn Bridge.

[27]Edward Hewitt of Gravenhurst.

the opinion of this meeting that the Muskoka District offers no mean inducements to an enterprising Railway Company, for the construction of a line through this part of the country."— Carried.

The Chairman called upon Mr. D. Wright,[28] who expressed himself as being ready to assist to the utmost of his power to obtain the desired boon, and moved the following resolution,—

"That this meeting fully appreciates the substantial aid rendered by the Northern Railway of Canada during the past eight years, in the settlement of the Muskoka region, and hereby proffer said company the preference of our patronage and pecuniary aid, providing that a satisfactory understanding can be arranged with the said company."— Carried.

Mr. James Sharpe in seconding the resolution, spoke strongly in favour of it.

Paul Dane, Esq., of Monck, was requested by the chairman to address the meeting, which he did in a humorous and pithy speech. Mr. Dane moved the last resolution, which was seconded by Mr. Livingstone, who also supported it in a few appropriate remarks.

"That this meeting deem it highly expedient, in the interest and prosperity of this large District, that a cordial invitation be extended to the President, Managing Director, and others immediately connected with the Northern Railway Co., to visit our principal Lakes, Rivers, and Colonization roads, and that Messrs. Alport, Davis, Browning, Piercy, Fuller, Wright, Sharpe, Kirkpatrick and Cockburn, be appointed a Committee to confer with Mr. Cumberland, and to carry out the objects of this resolution."— Carried unanimously. . . .

H 20 MUSKOKA AND THE RAILWAY COMPANIES
[*Toronto*, Weekly Globe, *September 17, 1869*]

. . . There are three companies each of whom might lay claim to the Muskoka district being legitimately within the sphere of their operations. These are the Northern Railway, the Lindsay and Port Hope, and the Toronto and Nipissing lines, and to each of these, different sections of the community have been looking for aid in the matter. By far the greater number, however, are in favour of an extension of the Northern Railway, and a few days ago the Reeves of the various townships invited the Directors of that road to take a tour through the district, examine into its resources and capabilities, and so prepare themselves for any advances that might be made to them by the people of the territory. The Directors at once accepted the invitation, and last Monday morning, along with a considerable number of gentlemen from Toronto, they set out on their exploratory excursion. . . .

[28]Probably David Wright of Gravenhurst.

H 21   "An Act to Incorporate the Toronto, Simcoe and
       Muskoka Junction Railway Company"
       [*Ontario*, Statutes, *1869, 33 Vic., c. 30*]

(*Assented to 24th December, 1869.*)

Whereas A.J. Alport,[29] W.D. Ardagh, Noah Barnhart, G.L. Beard-more, A.H. Browning, Hugh M. Clarke, Henry Creswick, A.P. Cock-burn, Dalrymple Crawford, Fred. Cumberland, M. Davis, Wm. G. Deacon, N. Dickey, A.P. Dodge, Wm. Elliot, R.J. Griffith, Wm. Hamilton, Robert Hay, C. Harvie, Alex. Henderson, W.H. Howland, Robert Leadlay, Wm. Lount, David Morrow, Thos. McConkey, J.D. Merrick, A.R. McMaster, Donald McKay, Hon. J. McMurrich, Angus Morrison, F.H. Medcalf, G. Perceval Ridout, R.J. Reekie, D.L. Sanson, Robert Simpson, Jno. Steele, Frank Smith, Thos. Smith, Robert Spratt, S.B. Harman, J. Teviotdale, D. Thurston, Jno. Turner, John Wallis, Robert Walker, Robert Wilkes, and Jno. World, have petitioned the Legislature for an Act of Incorporation to construct a railway from some point on the Northern Railway of Canada, within the County of Simcoe, to unite the waters of Lake Simcoe with those of Lakes Muskoka and Rousseau, through and within the Counties of Simcoe, Ontario, and Victoria, with branches and extensions to the Georgian Bay, and it is expedient to grant the prayer of the said petition; Therefore Her Majesty, by and with the advice and consent of the Legislative Assembly of the Province of Ontario, enacts as follows:—

. . .

3. The said Company shall have full power and authority to lay out construct and complete a double or single iron railway from some point on the Northern Railway of Canada, within the County of Simcoe, connecting the waters of Lake Simcoe with those of Lakes Muskoka and Rousseau, through and within the Counties of Simcoe, Ontario and Victoria, or any of them, with branches and extensions to the Georgian Bay, and with full authority to pass over any of the country between the points aforesaid, and to carry the said Railway through the Crown lands lying between the points aforesaid.

. . .

32. The said Railway shall be commenced within one year, and completed from the point of junction with the Northern Railway of Canada to or near the village of Orillia within two years after the passing of this

[29]The names of the petitioners include Muskoka, Simcoe County, and Toronto names. Among the best known from Muskoka and Simcoe are A. J. Alport, W. D. Ardagh, warden of Simcoe County, A. H. Browning, A. P. Cockburn, and J. Teviotdale. Among the Toronto names are G. L. Beardmore, Fred. Cumberland, and W. H. Howland.

Act, or else all rights and privileges conferred upon the said Company
by this Act shall be forfeited, and the said Railway shall be completed
within six years.

. . .

H 22   Thomas McMurray, "Toronto, Simcoe, and
Muskoka Junction Railway"
[*Bracebridge*, Northern Advocate, *January 27, 1871*]

Nothing affords us greater pleasure than the *fact*, that already operations have been commenced for building the T.S. & M.J. Railway from
Barrie to Washago, when this is built it will be a great advantage to the
settlers, as then we will be (taking Bracebridge as a centre), only 25
miles from railroad communication; whereas, at the present we are
removed not less than 65 miles from such facilities *via* Barrie, because
we have Railroad and water communication all the way from Toronto in
summer, excepting 14 miles between washago and Gravenhurst does
not do away with the great necessity which exists for direct railway
communication between this and Toronto; true the want is more keenly
felt in winter; but still, over and above our water facilities, railroad
communication is indispensible to the growth and development of this
rising country.

The settlers here are alive to the importance of this matter, and are
willing to the utmost of their ability to assist the undertaking; but is it
[*sic*] too much to expect them to build the road, hence a petition has
been prepared, and numerously signed by the settlers, praying that
Government aid be granted to assist in building the road from Washago
to Bracebridge, the centre of the Free Grant district. To this petition
nearly one thousand settlers have affixed their names, and the hope is
fondly cherished that the Government will not turn a deaf ear to their
prayer.

The great advantage of railroads is now so fully established, that a
very few can be found who will stand in the way of obtaining that which
is so essential to our advanced civilization; and if ever there was an
enterprise which justified Government aid it is the extension of the T.S.
& M.J. Railway through the heart of the Free Grant District.

The crowning Policy of the present administration, has been the
settlement of our wild lands, and the way to insure a speedy settlement
of the same, is to build a railroad; if this were accomplished, thousands
would flock hither, and in a short time the country would be settled by
a loyal and industrious people. We have no hesitation in giving it as our
opinion that if the T.S. & M.J.R. was extended to Bracebridge, we
would have twenty settlers for one; the fact is, the country from Washago
towards Gravenhurst is so uninviting that multitudes have been so discouraged that they have turned right round and left in disgust. The land

now is well settled for several miles beyond this, and if emigrants could be hurried right through here by rail, it would hasten up the settlement of the district very much. . . .

> H 23   FRANK SMITH[30] AND WILLIAM F. MUNRO TO THE
>   PROVINCIAL SECRETARY, M. C. CAMERON
>   [P.A.O., Shanly Papers]

Toronto June 14th 1871

By authority of the Directors of the Toronto Simcoe and Muskoka Railway Company I have the honor to submit the following statement of its affairs for the purpose of obtaining aid towards the construction of the line under the terms of the Act 34 Vic: Cap 2— The Company was incorporated by Act 33 Vic: Cap 30 which received the Royal Assent on the 24th. December 1869— The Line starts from a Junction with the Northern Railway of Canada at Barrie, thence via Orillia, Washago and Gravenhurst to Bracebridge in the District of Muskoka, having a total mileage of 60 miles or thereabouts—

The Surveys of Location have been made to Washago and those of Exploration to Bracebridge. The Works between Barrie and Washago are now under Contract, tenders for which were received and accepted on December 10th. 1870.

The length and estimated cost of the Line are as follows, observing that for convenience and safety in finance and construction, the work is being dealt with in two Divisions, the first Division extending from Barrie to the West end of the Muskoka Colonization Road at Washago and the second having its Terminus at Bracebridge the County Town of the District of Muskoka—

Estimate of Cost

			$
1st. Division	Barrie to Washago	34 miles	565,224
2nd. ”	Washago to Bracebridge	26 ”	412,800
	Total cost of 60 miles		978,024
	Average mileage cost of $16,300		

. . .

We present these figures because we feel that the cost of this Railway in regard to Government aid under 34 Vic Cap 2 is entirely exceptional and without a parallel in the position of any other Railway, inasmuch

[30]Frank Smith (1822–1901) was a well-known Canadian capitalist. He was president not only of the Toronto, Simcoe and Muskoka Railway Company, but also of other companies such as the Dominion Bank, the Niagara Navigation Company, and the Toronto Street Railway Company. In 1894 he was created a Knight Bachelor.

as that its location for the most part is through an entirely unsettled Territory and that its Terminus being in the heart of the Free Grant District the Traffic of its Northern or 2nd. Division must be self created and that the public value of the Line is peculiar and palpable as being a Colonization Line which precedes rather than follows settlement and traffic—

In view of all the circumstances we respectfully submit that the maximum subsidy of $4000 per mile ought to be made applicable to the whole length (60 miles) of this Railway, in which event we could at once proceed with the construction of the 2nd Division, the contracts for which might at once be let— Any less subsidy upon any portion of our Railway will necessitate the postponement of the Second Division until such time as the Estimated deficit be provided, a postponement our Directors would deeply regret, but which would be unavoidable in view of the very light character of the Traffic which that portion of the line would yield until Settlers and Capital shall have lifted it up into Commercial value— It would, we humbly suggest, be more profitable to the Public and the Country to expedite the development of this Free Grant District by adopting the most liberal standard of subsidy authorized by the Act than by the adoption of a lower grant in aid to postpone indefinitely that portion of the Road which will chiefly promote the settlement of the District— The highest standard $4000 per mile/ permitted by the Act is less than 25 per cent of the actual cost of the works whilst it is indisputable that the Line is of far greater value as a Public than as a Commercial work.

As the construction of the 1st Division of the Line is proceeding with great rapidity we beg that we may receive an early intimation of the intention of the Government in regard to this application.

Wm F Munro Secretary   Frank Smith, President

H 24   ANNUAL REPORT OF THE NORTHERN EXTENSION RAILWAY
        [*Toronto*, Monetary Times, *March 21, 1873, pp. 821–2*]

. . . Although the contract has been let for the line between Washago and Gravenhurst, the Directors are not in a position to push the work with the vigour which it deserves. No steps have yet been taken by the district of Muskoka for the granting of the bonuses promised; indeed, there is a hesitation on the part of the local authorities which would seem to indicate a desire to avoid any burthen in aid of the work. Again, the serious advance which has taken place in the cost of every element of railway construction has reduced the value of the Government subsidy to a proportion of the cost of the line far below that which the Legislature intended to grant. That subsidy amounts, over a considerable portion of the railways, to $2,000 per mile, and over that part of them in actually unsettled territory does not exceed $4,000 per mile; and yet it is a fact that since these subsidies were determined upon as sufficient public aid to induce railway construction the rise in the price of the materials of the track alone (rails, &c.,) represents within a fraction of $2,000 per mile. Under these disadvantages, seeing that the municipal aid lingers, and that the parliamentary subsidy is wholly inadequate (especially in view of the nature of the territory) to the objects it was intended to promote and hasten, the Directors are of opinion that the works within the Muskoka District should be prosecuted with great caution, and distributed over such period of time as may ensure financial safety. They submit this recommendation with sincere regret, because the completion of the line to Lake Muskoka would greatly contribute to the traffic of the whole undertaking by opening out a wide field for lumbering and agricultural operation, now only awaiting railway service; and their regret is all the stronger because the postponement of railway service for two or three years will be a serious injury to the district, and a bar to industries and developments of great importance to the Province at large. . . .

H 25   GRAVENHURST'S CELEBRATION OF THE OPENING OF THE RAILWAY
[*Orillia*, Times, *November 18, 1875*]

The largest concourse of people ever seen in Gravenhurst assembled there on Saturday to celebrate the opening of the Northern Railway to the waters of the lakes of Muskoka. A special train brought the President and Directors of the Northern Railway Company, the majority of the members of the Corporation of the city of Toronto, and the members of the Corporation of the county of Simcoe, etc., in all making a party of over 250. On the arrival of the train at the Company's dock, where the steamers were waiting their arrival, a regular steam greeting took place, by the locomotives and steamers whistling without cessation for about five minutes, the brass band on the Nipissing playing an appropriate air. The company left the train and went on board the various steamers, where the members of the corporation of Muskoka received the visitors on board the steamer Nipissing, and during the trip on the beautiful bay, presented an address to Wm. Thompson,[31] Esq., President of the Northern Railway Co., who made a suitable reply. The company then landed, and proceeded to the new town hall, and partook of a sumptuous luncheon, gotten up by Mr. Webb of Toronto, the Reeve of Muskoka presiding.

The company broke up at 5 o'clock, all well pleased with the day's proceedings, when the special train returned to Toronto. . . .

[31]William Thomson, Vice President of the Royal Canadian Bank, became President of the Northern Railway in 1874.

Railways for Haliburton

H 26   CANADIAN LAND AND EMIGRATION COMPANY'S PETITION
FOR A RAILWAY
[P.A.O., Ontario Sessional Papers, Petitions, 1867–8, no. 341]

To the Honorable the Legislative Assembly of the Province of Ontario in Parliament assembled.

The Petition of the Canadian Land and Emigration Company Limited of England,

Humbly Sheweth

That the attention of your Petitioners has been called to the intended formation of a Company proposing to lay down a Railway between Toronto and Lake Nipissing to be called the Toronto and Nipissing Railway, thereby to open up further communication with the settlements in the County of Peterborough in which county your Petitioners possess a considerable territory, bounded by the Bobcaygeon and Hasting Roads and upon which a large sum has been expended by your Petitioners for the purpose of inducing further settlement and thereby adding to the population therein, your Petitioners are therefore anxious to support any proposition which may tend to an increased immigration to that part of the Province, and they are led to believe that these advantages will be attained by the proposed Railway.

The present restricted means of communication with the Townships north of Lindsay and Peterborough have proved a considerable drawback to the settlement of the Townships belonging to your Petitioners, and which they are satisfied the carrying out of the proposed Railway will tend very materially to remove.

Wherefore your Petitioners humbly pray your honorable body to give a favorable consideration to the proposed undertaking

And your Petitioners as in duty bound will ever pray &c

H 27   "AN ACT TO INCORPORATE THE PETERBOROUGH AND
HALIBURTON RAILWAY COMPANY"
[Ontario, Statutes, 1868–9, 32 Vic., c. 61]

(Assented to 23rd January, 1869.)

Whereas the construction of a railway from the town of Peterborough, or from some point north of the town of Peterborough, on the Peterborough and Chemong Railway, or the Cobourg and Peterborough Railway, to the Town Plot of Haliburton, in the township of Dysart, or to some point beyond the Town Plot of Haliburton, in the county of Peterborough, would develop the present resources of the county of Peterborough, and open for settlement a large tract of country now unimproved and waste, and it is expedient to grant a charter for the construction of such railway: Therefore, Her Majesty, by and with the advice and consent of the Legislative Assembly of the Province of Ontario, enacts as follows:—

1. P.M. Grover, John Carnegie jr.,[32] George Read, William Adam Scott, Elias Burnham,[33] William Hepburne Scott, James Stephenson,[34] S.S. Peck,[35] Nesbit Kirchoffer, Francis Beamish, Arthur Trefusis Henenge Williams,[36] Alex. J. Cattanach, Charles James Blomfield, together with such persons and corporations as shall, in pursuance of this Act, become shareholders of the said company hereby incorporated, are hereby constituted and declared to be a body corporate and politic by the name of "The Peterborough and Haliburton Railway Company."

. . .

H 28   Petition[37] for Aid for Peterborough and Haliburton Railway
[*P.A.O., Ontario Sessional Papers, Petitions, 1869, no. 123*]

To His Excellency the Honourable W P Howland— C B, Lieutenant Governor of the *Province of Ontario in Executive Council—*

The Petition of the undersigned *Inhabitants* and *Ratepayers* of the Town of *Peterborough* in the County of *Peterborough*

Humbly Sheweth—

That your *Petitioners* being deeply impressed with the importance of securing the early settlement of the *Crown Domain* in this *Province*; and believing that the great desideratum required to accomplish such an object, is cheap and expeditious modes of ingress and regress, for the settler and the products of his labor,—have viewed with special favor

[32]John Carnegie, Jr. (b. 1837) was a member of the Douro Municipal Council from 1859 to 1866, and for three years reeve of the Township. In 1867 he was elected to the Ontario legislature for the West Riding of Peterborough.

[33]Probably Elias Burnham (b. 1811), barrister and member of the Municipal Council of Peterborough for many years.

[34]James Stevenson (b. 1827) was born in Ireland, and went to Peterborough in 1843, where he became a successful businessman and railway promoter. He was President of the Peterborough Gas Company and owned a large part of the stock. He took an active part in municipal affairs, served on the Municipal Council and on the School Board, and was a justice of the peace.

[35]Samuel Stanley Peck (1829–1901) and his brother, Francis Peck, moved to Snowdon Township in 1860. S. S. Peck took a prominent part in municipal affairs and promoted the formation of the County of Haliburton and the building of a railway. In 1874 he became the first county clerk and treasurer for Haliburton and in 1879 was elected to the Legislative Assembly of Ontario as member for Victoria.

[36]Arthur Trefusis Heneage Williams (1837–1885) represented East Durham in the Ontario legislature 1867 to 1875, and in the Canadian House of Commons from 1878 to 1885.

[37]Signed by W. H. Scott, mayor of Peterborough, and 255 others. Presented to the Legislative Assembly by John Carnegie, November 17, 1869.

the inauguration of a system of Wooden Railways[38] which in the opinion
of your Petitioners are well calculated to supply the great want of our
new settlements a want which never can be supplied by the *ordinary
colonization Roads*—

While however the cost of a *Wooden Railway,* is trifling as compared with that of an *Iron Road*, and while it is only fair that a reasonable share of the Cost of the construction of these *Roads* should be
bourne by the localities to be more immediately benefitted thereby, your
Petitioners fear that they will be found to be beyond the unaided means
of those localities requiring them—

Remembering also that the *Province* as a whole is deeply interested
in the settlement of these lands, and is annually receiving a large revenue
therefrom, and which would be sensibly increased by the construction
of these Roads—your *Petitioners* are of opinion that no more judicious
expenditure could be made of the surplus now so fortunately at the
disposal of this *Province*, than by assisting in the construction of Railways calculated to open up the *Province*—

Among the several *Railway* projects now on foot, your *Petitioners*
desire to bring under your special notice that of the *Peterborough and
Haliburton Railway* which if carried to a successful termination is destined to do signal service in opening up and settling the *County of Peterborough*, no unimportant part of the *Huron and Ottawa Territory*—
within its bounds in the newly surveyed Townships are comprised no
less than (1,265,000) *one million, two hundred and sixty five thousand
acres of Land*, a large portion of which is well adapted for *agricultural
purposes*, while the operation of the *Galway Mining Company* and
others have proved beyond doubt that it is rich in *minerals*, particularly
Lead, and valuable *Quarries*— Besides these sources of wealth the
whole county abounds in forests of valuable *Birch, Maple* &c &c which
with proper facilities for transport would afford employment to thousands, and prove a source of wealth to the hardy *Pioneer*— instead of
a source of expense as at present.

Your *Petitioners* having reason to believe that the local *Municipalities*,
and individuals more immediately interested, are prepared to give liberally to this undertaking—

Humbly Pray that you will be pleased to take the subject matter of this
Petition unto your favourable consideration, and grant such aid to the
Peterborough and Haliburton Railway Company as will ensure its early
construction—

And your Petitioners as in duty bound will *ever Pray* &c

[38]Wooden railways were those which used wood for rails. In 1869 a report on
these was made by a Select Committee of the Legislative Assembly of Ontario
"appointed to enquire into and report upon the usefulness, and cost of Wooden
Railways as a means of furthering the settlement of the country" (Ontario, Legislative Assembly, *Journals,* 1869, app. 1).

H 29   C. J. Blomfield to Mossom Boyd
[*P.A.C., Boyd Papers, v. 148*]

The Canadian Land & Emigration Company.
Peterborough, Ont., March 23d. 1870

. . . I shall be glad to know whether there is any prospect of our being able to get a Wooden Railway from Bobcaygeon to Kinmount. A proposition is now being discussed and is receiving a good deal of support— for an extension of the Toronto & Nipissing Railway to Fenelon Falls either via Lindsay or direct from nearest point on the Cobiconk line, say Woodville—& for a Wooden Railway from Fenelon Falls to Kinmount & on to Haliburton— All the Municipalities would I believe vote for this & the T & N people are already beginning to see that this is the true line by which to keep the backcountry. I believe myself that if properly worked up the project will receive the support of the T. & N. people. I have arrived at the conclusion that we should take our wares to the best market. There is an enterprise about the Toronto people that we shall never see in Peterboro, probably never in Lindsay— They believe in opening up back countries & creating a trade— The T & N. Ry has this as its main object & it is now a strong Company and the construction of this road to some point near Balsam Lake is no longer doubtful. Toronto interest can secure Government aid to a road of this kind.

The aid that we should obtain from various & at present opposing interests to such a road as we proposed from Bobcaygeon to Kinmount would after all be very small even if we should get what we named & the aid & support that we could get from Toronto alone would far outweigh it.

Toronto is our best market for everything but lumber & on the whole it will be far the best point for our Township in a settlement view as most of our settlers come from the old part of the country. As far as that goes however I do not think it matters much where our R. R. reaches the front so long as have a Railroad.

I believe however that if we all work together we can get a road in connection with the T & N & I believe we can book it before long. After a conversation I had with some of the T. & N. people in Toronto I believe the present plan is the most feasible that has yet been advocated— As you have so large an interest now in our Township I hope you will give it your support.

H 30   Peterborough to Haliburton Railway Proposed
[*Toronto,* Monetary Times, *September 23, 1870*]

PETERBORO' AND HALIBURTON RAILWAY.— A meeting of the provisional directors of this undertaking was recently held in Mr. C.J.

Blomfield's office, Peterboro'. The scheme is as follows:— It is proposed to build a wooden railway from Peterboro' northward by way of
Buckhorn to Haliburton. With a view of connecting the town directly
with Chemong Lake, it is proposed to put down an iron rail to the lake,
providing that the wooden rail will not be answerable for the expected
traffic from that point. The distance from Peterboro' to Haliburton by
this route will be about sixty miles; the estimated cost per mile, including rolling stock, is $5,000. In order to provide the means for its con-
struction, it is proposed to ask for municipal bonuses from the county
and municipalities north of Buckhorn, to the extent of $60,000, and
from the town of Peterboro', $25,000 with an additional sum of $15,000
in the event of the iron rail to Chemong Lake being required. Having
obtained these bonuses, it is proposed to ask the Provincial Legislature
for assistance towards the work, to the extent of paying interest on half
the cost of construction for twenty years, in the same manner as assistance has been given by the Quebec Government towards similar undertakings in that Province. It is then proposed to issue bonds for half the
amount of the cost of construction, and ask the Government to guarantee
that their annual payment will be applied to the payment of the interest
on these bonds. This having been accomplished, there would remain but
a balance of $65,000 to be subscribed in stock; which amount of stock
the provisional directors, from information received by them, are of
opinion that, should the preceding conditions be fulfilled, there will be
no serious difficulty in obtaining and securing the construction of the
road in a reasonable time. A Board was elected, consisting of the following gentlemen:— John Carnegie, Jr., M.P.P., President; Lieut.-Col.
Williams, M.P.P., Vice President; C.J. Blomfield, Secretary; Jas. Stevenson, Treasurer.

I. COMMUNITIES AND INSTITUTIONS

The Establishment of Local and District Government

I 1 "AN ACT TO MAKE CERTAIN ALTERATIONS IN THE
TERRITORIAL DIVISIONS OF UPPER CANADA"
[*Canada*, Provincial Statutes, *1851, 14–5 Vic., c. 5*]

(2d August, 1851.)

. . . The County of Simcoe shall consist of the Townships of Orillia, Matchedash, Tay, Medonte, Oro, Vespra, Flos, Tiny, Sunnidale, Nottawasaga, Gwillimbury West, Essa, Tecumseth, Adjala, Tossorontio, Mulmur, Mono and Innisfil, together with the tract of land bounded on the East by the line between the late Home and Newcastle Districts prolonged to French River, on the West by Lake Huron, on the North by French River, and on the South by the River Severn and the Township of Rama, and the Islands in Lakes Simcoe and Huron, lying wholly, or for the most part, opposite to the said County of Simcoe, or any part thereof and contiguous thereto. . . .

I 2 "AN ACT TO ANNEX CERTAIN NEW TOWNSHIPS IN THE
COUNTIES OF VICTORIA AND PETERBOROUGH AND THE
NORTH RIDING OF THE COUNTY OF HASTINGS"
[*Canada*, Statutes, *1858, 22 Vic., c. 14*]

(Assented to 30th June 1858.)

Whereas the rapid settlement of the new Townships of Carden, Dalton, Ryde, Draper, Macaulay, Digby, Longford, Oakley, Lutterworth, Anson, Hindon, Laxton, Snowdon, Minden, Stanhope, Glamorgan, Dysart, Guilford, Monmouth, Dudley, Harburn, Chandos, Cardiff, Harcourt, Bruton, McClure, Herschel, Faraday, Wollaston, Wicklow, Monteagle, Dunganan, Limerick, Bangor, Carlow, Mayo and Cashel, which have been recently surveyed, and which adjoin the present limits of the Counties of Victoria, Peterborough and the North Riding of the County of Hastings, renders it expedient that the said Townships should be annexed to the said Counties respectively, in the manner hereinafter mentioned: Therefore, Her Majesty, by and with the advice and consent of the Legislative Council and Assembly of Canada, enacts as follows:
1. From and after the passing of this Act the said Townships of Carden, Dalton, Ryde, Draper, Macaulay, Digby, Longford, Oakley, Lutterworth, Anson, Hindon and Laxton, shall be attached to and form part of the said County of Victoria for all purposes whatsoever.
2. From and after the passing of this Act the said Townships of Snow-

don, Minden, Stanhope, Guilford, Dysart, Glamorgan, Monmouth, Dudley, Harburn, Bruton, Harcourt, Cardiff and Chandos, shall be attached to and form part of the County of Peterborough for all purposes whatsoever; And the said Townships of McClure, Herschel, Faraday, Wollaston, Wicklow, Monteagle, Dunganan, Limerick, Bangor, Carlow, Mayo and Cashel, shall be attached to and form part of the North Riding of the County of Hastings for all purposes whatsoever.

I 3 "A By-Law to Provide for the Union and Organization of the Townships of Morrison and Muskoka in the County of Simcoe for Municipal Purposes"
[*Simcoe County, Revised By-Laws, 1864, no. 139*]

Whereas certain settlers of the unincorporated townships of Morrison and Muskoka, in the County of Simcoe, have, by their petition addressed to the Corporation of the County of Simcoe, in Council assembled, set forth their desire to be united and incorporated for municipal purposes. And whereas said townships contain over 150 Freeholders and Householders,

Be it therefore enacted by the Council of the Corporation of the County of Simcoe, in accordance with chapter 54 sections 30 and 33 of the Municipal Institutions' Act of Upper Canada, as follows:—

1. That from and after the passing of this By-Law the unincorporated townships of Morrison and Muskoka, in the County of Simcoe, shall be united and incorporated for municipal purposes.

2. That Morrison shall be the senior and Muskoka the junior township.

3. That the Municipality shall be known and described as the Municipal Corporation of the United Townships of Morrison and Muskoka.

4. That the first meeting for the election of councillors shall be held at the home of John Scott. Esq., in the township of Morrison, on Monday, the second day of January, 1865, commencing at the hour of ten o'clock in the forenoon.

5. That James H. Jackson, of the township of Morrison, shall be the returning officer for holding said election.

Passed June 30, 1864.

I 4 Formation of Township Municipalities
[*Poole, A Sketch of the Early Settlement and Subsequent Progress of the Town of Peterborough, pp. 206–7*]

The municipality first[1] formed, in the back country,— as we suppose it must still be called,— was composed of the townships of Galway, Snowden and Minden, in the County of Peterborough, and those of Anson and Lutterworth in the County of Victoria, for as yet the two

[1]The author is referring only to the area later included in Haliburton County.

counties had not been separated. The municipality as thus formed came into official existence on the first of January, 1860, and continued to comprise the same townships for two years. At the close of 1861, Anson and Lutterworth, being on the Victoria side of the boundary line, withdrew on the separation of that county from Peterborough, leaving the municipality formed as mentioned below. Other withdrawals have gradually been made as new townships became possessed of a sufficient number of ratepayers to entitle them to a separate municipal existence of their own; so that in 1867 we find five distinct municipal councils, with their officers and legal powers, where six years ago, little save a wild wilderness, but partially surveyed, existed. Such has been the growth and prosperity of these new townships!

TABULAR STATEMENT

Of Reeves, Clerks, and Municipalities, composed of the new
Townships, from January, 1860, to January, 1867

Year	Townships comprising Municipalities	Reeve	Township Clerk
1860	Galway, Snowden, Minden, Anson and Lutterworth	Charles Austin	Wm. Hartle
1861	The same	Thomas Probert	Wm. McKelvey
1862	Snowden, Minden and Stanhope	S. S. Peck	Wm. McKelvey
1862	Galway	Thomas Probert	Wm. Leeson
1863	Snowden	Robert Ritchie	Wm. McKelvey
1863	Minden and Stanhope	William Gainor	Wm. McKelvey
1863	Galway	Thomas Probert	Wm. Leeson
1864	Snowden	S.S. Peck	Benj. Rothwell
1864	Minden, Stanhope and Dysart	Wm. Gainor	Wm. McKelvey
1864	Galway	Thos. McGaughey	Wm. Leeson
1865	Snowden	S.S. Peck	Francis Peck
1865	Minden, Stanhope and Dysart	Charles Austin	Wm. McKelvey
1865	Galway	Thomas Probert	Wm. Leeson
1866	Snowden	S.S. Peck	Francis Peck
1866	Minden and Dysart	John Lucas	Wm. McKelvey
1866	Galway	Thomas Probert	Christopher Irwin
1866	Stanhope (1st year)	James Mellville	George J. Rowe
1867	Snowden		
1867	Minden		
1867	Galway		
1867	Stanhope		
1867	Dysart, &c. (1st year)		

I 5   PETITION[2] FOR A DIVISION COURT[3]
[P.A.O., Ontario Sessional Papers. Petitions, 1867–8, no. 163]

The petition of the undersigned residents in the Townships of Morrison

[2]Presented to the Legislative Assembly by A. P. Cockburn, January 14, 1868.
[3]Division Courts hear civil cases involving small debts and claims.

Muskoka Monck Watts [*sic*] Humphrey Stephenson Brunel Macaulay and Draper

Sheweth

1. That for some time past there has been a growing need for a Division Court in some convenient place for the Townships above mentioned
2. That the inhabitants of the above Townships are partly divided for Division Court purposes between the Division Courts of Orillia Lindsay and the Territorial District of Nippissing
3. That none of these places afford a convenient centre for the bulk of the inhabitants of said Townships
4. That the Village of Bracebridge is rapidly progressing and forms the natural centre of the said Townships and is besides the place of all others most easy of access from all quarters indicated
5th. That the said District comprehends a dozen Townships containing at present upwards of 500 resident landholders and of course a population large in proportion and increasing

Your petitioners therefore pray

That the Townships above mentioned and such others as may seem meet be formed into a Division Court District—

That Bracebridge be appointed the place of holding the Court therefor

That a visiting judge be appointed

And lastly that steps be taken to constitute the District for registration purposes

And your petitioners will ever pray &c.

I 6   NOTICE OF DIVISION COURTS
[*Orillia,* Orillia Expositor, *May 22, 1868*]

District of Muskoka.
DIVISION COURTS
For 1868.

The Division Courts for the District of Muskoka, for the year 1868, will be held at the

Village of Bracebridge,

in the Township of Macaulay, on the undermentioned days, and at the places herein set forth, viz.:

AT THE COURT ROOM, BRACEBRIDGE,

Tuesday, 16th June, at noon,
Wednesday, 12th August, at noon,
Monday, 12th October, at noon.
Saturday, 12th December, at noon.

Stipendiary Magistrate,
D. Muskoka.

Bracebridge, April 24, 1868.

I 7 "PETITION[4] OF A. H. BROWNING[5] AND OTHERS OF MUSKOKA
DISTRICT PRAYING FOR THE PASSING OF AN ACT TO ERECT
THE DISTRICT OF MUSKOKA INTO A JUNIOR COUNTY"
[P.A.O., Ontario Sessional Papers, Petitions, 1869, no. 226]

Unto the Legislative Assembly of the Province of Ontario
The Petition of the undersigned settlers of the District of Muskoka
Humbly Sheweth
That your petitioners are inconveniently circumstanced from the fact
that the Muskoka settlement lies partly within the two different Counties
of Simcoe and Victoria, while the interests of each Muskoka Township
are identical and inseperable from the other the representatives of the
people in the County Councils are of course necessarily divided by
being compelled to sit in different County Chambers thus resulting in a
division of common force and action. Your petitioners would also
respectfully to impress upon you the importance of having all the
Townships united, and that they be empowered to raise means for the
material improvement of the whole District
Therefore your petitioners request that an act may be passed for the
purpose of uniting the Townships of the Muskoka District into a Junior
County to be styled the County of Muskoka, said county to be temporarily annexed to the County of Simcoe for County purposes and the
act to go into operation on the 1st Jany 1870
And your petitioners as in duty bound will ever pray

I 8 MEETING AT BRACEBRIDGE ON REJECTION OF BILL TO ORGANIZE
MUSKOKA INTO A JUNIOR COUNTY
[Parry Sound, Northern Advocate, January 4, 1870]

At a meeting of the settlers and ratepayers of the District, held after
the nomination of Municipal officers in the "Dominion House," Bracebridge, on the 20th ult., John Teviotdale, Esq., Reeve elect of the United
Township of Draper, Macaulay, Stephenson, Ryde, and Oakley, was
called to the chair, and R. J. Bell was appointed secretary, when the
following resolutions were put to the meeting and carried unanimously.
Resolved— 1st. That the thanks of this meeting be tendered to A. P.
Cockburn, Esq. M.P.P., for his indefatigable labors in behalf of the
Muskoka District, and the energetic manner in which he has tried to get
us the Bill through the Legislature, seperating and organizing the Townships of our District and forming a junior County.
2nd. That this meeting do express its regret and indignation at the
steps taken in the Legislative Assembly of Ontario, to throw out the
Bill to organize this District of Muskoka into a junior County, and to
add certain Townships thereto, as we are all convinced such a step is

[4]Presented to the Legislative Assembly by A. P. Cockburn, November 23, 1869.
[5]A. H. Browning was reeve of Monck Township.

calculated to injure our common interests, and will throw back this District very considerably,— it may be for years.

3rd. That the fact of the Legislative Assembly having refused the boon prayed for by petitions signed numerously by the settlers of the District, through the influence and efforts of one member,[6] this assembly hails with great dissatisfaction the intermeddling of any one member from personal or family interests.

R. J. Bell
Secretary.

I 9 SIMCOE COUNTY MEMORIAL ON COST OF ADMINISRATION IN MUSKOKA
[*Simcoe County, Municipal Council,* Proceedings, *January 1874, p. 51*]

To His Honor the Lieutenant-Governor of Ontario in Council &c., &c.
The Memorial of the Warden and Council of the County of Simcoe,
HUMBLY SHEWETH:

That from and by reason of the Muskoka and Parry Sound Districts being attached to and forming part of this County for Judicial and Criminal purposes, the County of Simcoe proper has to pay, annually, large costs and charges in the administration of justice from the Districts above named, and your Memorialists believe that said costs and charges are of such a nature that they should be paid out of and borne by the Provincial Exchequer.

And, further, your Memorialists would respectfully represent to your Honor that, from the many trials and hardships the settlers in the Muskoka District have to contend with, and being for the most part composed of a population not able to make such public improvements by building bridges, &c., as are required in the District, and having on several occasions applied for and received grants from this County, your Memorialists feel that, while unwilling to refuse such assistance, nevertheless deem it a hardship that they as a County should be required to contribute to the erection of bridges and other improvements in that District.

Your Memorialists would therefore pray that your Honor may be advised to make such grants of money for the purposes of public improvement in the Muskoka District as to you may seem just and right.

And your Memorialists, as in duty bound, will ever pray, &c.

I 10 "AN ACT TO INCORPORATE THE MUNICIPALITY OF HALIBURTON, AND TO PROVIDE FOR ITS BECOMING A PROVISIONAL COUNTY"
[*Ontario,* Statutes, *1874, 37 Vic., c. 65*]

(Assented to 24th March, 1874.)
Her Majesty, by and with the advice and consent of the Legislative Assembly of the Province of Ontario, enacts as follows:—

[6]A reference to William Lount, member of the Ontario legislature for the North Riding of Simcoe, and brother of Charles Lount.

1. The Townships of Lutterworth, Anson and Hindon, in the County of Victoria, the Townships of Snowdon, Glamorgan, Monmouth, Cardiff, Minden, Dysart, Dudley, Harcourt, Stanhope, Guilford, Harburn and Bruton, in the County of Peterborough, and the Townships of Sherborne, Havelock, Eyre, Clyde, McClintock, Livingstone, Lawrence and Nightingale, in the temporary judicial District of Nipissing, are hereby erected into a municipality to be called "The Municipality of the District of Haliburton."

. . .

3. A vote[7] of the ratepayers of the several townships within the said municipality, shall be taken upon Wednesday the twenty-seventh day of May next, upon the question of the formation of a provisional county, and as to the county to which the municipality shall be united for judicial purposes; which vote shall be, as nearly as may be, taken at the same places and in the same manner as votes are taken for the election of councillors, and shall be recorded in books prepared for that purpose; each voter in favour of such formation voting "yea" and each voter against such formation voting "nay;" each voter whether voting yea or nay, shall also state whether he prefers a judicial union with Peterborough or with Victoria, or if he has no preference shall state the fact, and such statement shall be recorded in like manner, and in separate columns.

. . .

I 11   MINUTES OF THE FIRST MEETING OF MUNICIPAL COUNCIL OF
THE PROVISIONAL COUNTY OF HALIBURTON
[*Haliburton County, Municipal Council,* Minutes of the Proceedings and
By-laws, 1874, 1875, 1876 & 1877, *pp 5–6*]

Town Hall, Minden,
June 18th, 1874.

The Municipal Council of the Provisional County of Haliburton met this day.
The following Reeves were present:—
A. Niven, Esq., Reeve of the United Townships of Dysart, Dudley, Harcourt, Guilford, Harburn, and Bruton.
James Langton, Esq., Reeve of the Township of Minden.
William Hartle, Esq., Reeve of the United Townships of Lutterworth, Anson, and Hindon.

[7]On May 27 "396 voted for a new county to 4 against and a unanimous vote was given to be united to Victoria for judicial purposes" (Toronto, *Globe*, May 28, 1874).

Philip Harding,[8] Esq., Reeve of the United Townships of Glamorgan, Monmouth, and Cardiff.

John R. Calvert, Esq., Reeve of Snowdon.

Joseph Beatty, Esq., Reeve of Stanhope.

Moved by Mr. Harding, seconded by Mr. Calvert,— That A. Niven, Esq., be Warden for this year.— Carried.

The Warden elect took the necessary declaration of office, and after returning thanks to the Council for the honour conferred, and the confidence reposed in him, took his seat as Warden.

Moved by Mr. Hartle, seconded by Mr. Harding,— That S. S. Peck, Esq., be Clerk and Treasurer for this County.— Carried.

Moved by Mr. Hartle, seconded by Mr. Harding,—That a by-law for appointing a County Clerk and Treasurer be now read a first time.— Carried.

On motion of Mr. Hartle the Council went into Committee of the whole on the second reading of the said by-law, Mr. Hartle in the Chair. Council resumed, and Chairman reported by-law read in Committee of the whole without amendment.

Moved by Mr. Hartle, seconded by Mr. Beatty,— That the above By-law be now read a third time, passed, signed, and Sealed.— Carried.

On motion of Mr. Beatty, the Council adjourned until ten o'clock to-morrow.

S.S. Peck,   A. Niven,
    County Clerk   Warden.

Politics and Elections

I 12   A. P. COCKBURN TO GEORGE BROWN[9]
[P.A.C., George Brown Papers, M.G. 24, B 40, pp. 269–72]

Orillia 7th. March 1867

I had the honor and pleasure of an introduction to you last July in Ottawa by Mr M'Conkey[10] M.P. and also addressed a communication to you upon some public matters, and have now taken the liberty of addressing you upon the subject of the political change, and ensuing general elections (under the new order of things) and to make a long

---

[8]Philip Harding (b. 1819) was born in England, became a settler in Haliburton, and served as first reeve of Glamorgan. In 1875 he gave up farming and began mission work for the Church of England in northern Peterborough County. For a time he officiated at Apsley on the Burleigh Road.

[9]George Brown (1818–1880) leader of the Reform party and editor of the Globe newspaper.

[10]Thomas David McConkey (b. 1815), member of the legislature for the North Riding of Simcoe.

story short, will observe that there is a probability of my being a candidate for the representation of the North Riding of Victoria in the Local Parliament. I need not observe that I have always been a staunch reformer, and a warm admirer of yourself and the *"Globe"* newspaper, and might refer you to Mr. Ault[11] M.P. or Mr Mattice ex M.P. of Cornwall, although I am scarcely 30 years of age I helped to fight some of the reform battles 10 years ago, since that time I have been doing more or less business in the County of Victoria and in 1863 I built a business premises in Kirkfield of which place I was Post Master, and in 1864 I was elected Reeve of Eldon, in 1865 again re-elected for Reeve, and but for a little over confidence would have been warden of Victoria. I might have taken the wardens chair by going into litigation, but did not think it worth while, also in autumn of 1865 I made a tour of the north, (see printed description forwarded to you last year), and became very greatly interested in the prospects of the Muskoka region, *so much so,* that I induced my Father to join me in constructing a steamer, and a large Saw mill at the outlet, (*the capacity of the latter to be 75000 ft per diem*) I have also a general store here, I leased the Kirkfield (Eldon) premises to a Mr. Russell of Ottonabee township, so all my stake is in the North Riding of Victoria, now that the Muskoka settlement is added to Victoria for representation purposes You will observe that I am thoroughly acquainted in the Riding, of which I fancy I have a greater knowledge than any other well known man, and have every reason to believe that I have been universally popular, the greatest drawback will be that many large settlements in the Riding are still unorganized, and also a large number where the Townships are organised are assessed too low to give them votes, and one of my prime objects in troubling you with so lengthy a communication, is to make particular enquiries, whether there will be any chance of the people voting on this springs assessment, the assessor in Morrison & Muskoka is raising the assessment suficiently high this year to make about 200 votes here, (in Muskoka).

In conclusion I request your influence in my behalf, should I happen to be the candidate chosen by the liberals. I have resided in Orillia since Octr. last, and am a member of the Revd. Mr Grays[12] congregation.

Apologising for taking up so much of your valuable time, knowing that you are over burdened with similar letters. Canada is the place of my nativity, and my parents left Berwickshire when very young themselves.

P.S.
I intend visiting the city early in April, and will endeavour to have an interview with you should I stand for the Riding.

[11]Samuel Ault, member for Stormont.
[12]The Reverend John Gray, first resident minister of the Presbyterian Church, Orillia.

I 13   A. P. COCKBURN'S ELECTION ADDRESS
[*Orillia,* Orillia Expositor, *August 23, 1867*]

TO THE ELECTORS OF THE NORTH RIDING OF VICTORIA

Gentlemen,— In accordance with the terms of the Act of Union, it will be your duty, at the approaching General Election, to choose your representatives to the House of Commons of the Dominion of Canada and the Legislature of Ontario.

At the request of a large number of Electors of the Riding, I offer myself as a candidate for the Representation of this Constituency in the Legislative Assembly of the noble Province of Ontario.

I am personally known to many of you in every township composing the Riding, having resided among you for the past eight years, and few persons are more thoroughly acquainted with every part of North Victoria than myself, and I may also be supposed to be acquainted with the struggles of early bush life, having been born in a country place in Upper Canada.

I am opposed to the system adopted lately in the management of our Crown lands, believing that through the influence of speculators, grants to absentees and to corporations have been made, operating injuriously against the settlement of the country; and not unfrequently through gross mismanagement we have failed to secure our legitimate share of European emigration. There being a large tract of arable land within the Riding, the immediate settlement of which would materially benefit the County of Victoria, and the Province generally, my best attention will be given to any and every scheme having for its object the settlement by actual settlers of this tract, and to the opening up and improving of roads therein, as well as those leading thereto. I am strongly in favour of giving Free Grants of the Crown Lands in the new townships to bona fide settlers.

The development of the vast mineral resources of the country shall receive my earnest attention.

It is my belief that the progress and social happiness of the people would be greatly promoted by the passage of a well-considered Homestead Law, by which settlers may apply money honestly their own, to the purchase of a farm or house, and set it aside by public registration for the benefit of their families, without liability to the claims of future creditors.

I will give special attention to the improvement of navigation on the lakes and rivers north of Fenelon Falls, for the purpose of rendering good and easy transit for steam-vessels to the different points in the Northern settlements.

In politics I am independent, and if I have the honour to be elected, the interests of the public shall not, be made subservient to my own, as

I have no other desire than to serve you impartially and faithfully, with-out fear, favour or affection.

I consider Confederation is a great boon, particularly in the Local Legislature, as it gives to us the entire control of all local matters, and I shall exercise my utmost efforts in aiding the harmonious and econo-mical working of our new Constitution.

I shall make it my business at an early day to see as many of you in your respective neighbourhoods as I can before the election takes place, when I shall be happy to give any information in my power and my views on any questions submitted to me.

Bracebridge, Macaulay, Co. Victoria,
July 15, 1867

I 14   T. R. FERGUSON[13] TO SIR JOHN A. MACDONALD,[14] OTTAWA
[*P.A.O., Alexander Campbell Papers*]

Barrie June 20th. 1872

I have been here since Monday morning, attending Co Council busi-ness and may be detained another week, Today I had a conversation with one of the *Reeves* from *Muskoka* he attended the Grit Convention held in that section of the Country on last tuesday. *Mr. A. P. Cockburn* was chosen Standard bearer for the party. The Globe once designated him *Traitor*.— *Martyr*, he will soon be called *Saint*. And nothing will be left undone to secure his election. Some of those who ought to be our friends, it appears, have joined the enemy. And Mr. *William Beatty* of the Parry Sound District— *one of them*. He attended the meeting and announced himself one of them and with them, and will doubtless carry a good many of his friends and neighbours along with him. And as I heard from *his brother "that the Govt. had favoured their line of boats"* and had promised *a postal subsidy* I fancied you could do a good deal to alter *even fixed principles* and therefore intrude this hasty information upon your early consideration. And would suggest your inviting a *private* interview with the *Messrs Beatty* at the earliest possible moment other-wise I fear our friend *Boulton*[15] will have difficulties *in his way* far beyond what he anticipated.

[13]Thomas Roberts Ferguson (1818–1879) came to Canada from Ireland in 1842 and became a merchant at Cookstown. He served as reeve of Innisfil Township, warden of Simcoe County, and member of Parliament for South Simcoe from 1857 to 1873, first for the Province of Canada and later for Ontario, and also repre-sented Cardwell in the Canadian House of Commons.

[14]Sir John Alexander Macdonald (1815–1891), Prime Minister of Canada, 1867 to 1873, and 1878 to 1891.

[15]D'Arcy Boulton (1825–1875), Q.C., grandson of the Honourable D'Arcy Boulton, was a Conservative in politics and a prominent member of the Orange Order. He was unsuccessful candidate for Muskoka riding in the House of Com-mons in 1872, but was elected to the Ontario legislature for South Simcoe in a by-election in 1873 and again in 1875.

Hoping you still enjoy good health and that you will excuse the liberty I have taken

I 15 WILLIAM BEATTY TO ALEXANDER CAMPBELL
[*P.A.O., Alexander Campbell Papers*]

Parry Sound
July 6th 1872.

I have received your letter with reference to election matters in Muskoka. In reply I would say that there are now two candidates in the field Mr. Bolton of Toronto and Mr Cockburn who was formerly M.P.P. at Toronto and who was a supporter of the late Mr Sandfield Macdonald[16] I have understood that both candidates were friendly to your Govt.

The contest does not seem to me to be of a political character but rather a personal one as Mr Cockburn lays claim to be a local candidate with a personal interest in the County while Mr Bolton is by many considered to have no interest in this section but is thought to be a political adventurer. In agreeing to support Mr Cockburn I did so because I thought him a more deserving man than his opponent and also because I thought he would be friendly to your Government.

I should be sorry if I have been mistaken in this latter respect. You are quite right in believing that I am friendly to your Govt. personally and also that I approve of your general policy, and I shall have pleasure in showing my friendship during the coming contest in several counties where I have some influence—

Endorsed: Dear Campbell
 I am afraid Beatty playcd false to us in this matter

J A McD

I 16 SIR JOHN A. MACDONALD TO CAMPBELL
[*P.A.O., Alexander Campbell Papers*]

Toronto
July 12/72.

. . . Things are looking pretty well in the West. We had a great meeting at Peterboro', & we made the most of the working men's excitement here last night, all of which you will see duly chronicled in the Mail. It is quite clear that Beatty has sold us in Muskoka. Cockburn is the choice of the Reform Convention and has pledged himself to vote against us.—
 Verily he shall have his reward.

[16]John Sandfield Macdonald (1812–1872), Prime Minister of the Province of Canada from 1862 to 1864 and of Ontario from 1867 to 1871.

Principal Early Villages

I 17   SEVERN BRIDGE IN 1871
[*McMurray,* The Free Grant Lands of Canada, *p. 29*]

This part of Morrison was first settled about 1858. The first settlers were James H. Jackson, William Johnston, and John Young. It was then the farthest point north that was settled. The next season five or six families more came in among them, the Messrs. Symingtons and a few families of Prussians. The first store was owned by O'Brien & Co., of Orillia, in the house now occupied by Mr. Mackenzie as an hotel. The next store was kept by a Mr. Gray, and H. W. Dillon opened a tavern. There is a good plank road, splendid water privilege, a first class hotel, two excellent stores, one kept by Mr. Jackson, the other by Mr. Samuel R. Thomson, who has named that part of "Severn Bridge" Sandy Row, in honor of that loyal part of Belfast, Ireland; they are first class stores and reflect credit on the enterprising proprietors. There is also a Town hall, Orange hall, blacksmith's shop, and carpenter's, and woodturner's shop.

I 18   GRAVENHURST IN 1867
[*Orillia,* Orillia Expositor, *October 25, 1867*]

Gravenhurst is the nucleus of a very fine village at no distant day if one were to judge by the numerous and commodious buildings now built and in process of being erected. The first is an Episcopal church, nearly completed, and reflects great credit on the architect, John Scott, Esq. Almost directly opposite, in the "Freemason's Arms," our late townsman Mr. T.B. Horton is comfortably domiciled and admirably discharges the duties of "mine host." A few minutes' walk brings us to another new house which is nearly finished and intended as a private residence and store for A.P. Cockburn, Esq., M.P.P. Immediately opposite, on the intersection of the Muskoka road with the wharf road Mr. Dougald Brown has built a very fine and commodious Hotel,[17] which, when completed will be one of the largest buildings in the Northern Region of Country— the indefatigable Dougald with his proverbial politeness and readiness to oblige will no doubt make an accommodating landlord.

About a quarter of a mile West from this point is the Big Bay of Muskoka, where the Wenonah's wharf extends out into the lake nearly 400 feet. From thence the march of progress is onward still onward and northward.

[17]Dougald Brown's hotel was called the Steamboat and Stage House and had forty rooms.

I 19   "A Short Sketch of the Rise and Progress of the
Village of Gravenhurst," 1871
[*McMurray,* The Free Grant Lands of Canada, *pp. 28–9*]

Ten years ago, the present site of the village of Gravenhurst was a
wilderness of pines which flourished in all their primeval grandeur. But
as the resources and advantages of the country became gradually known
to the outside world, eager immigrants from the mother country and land
seekers from the older settlements came here; amongst those Messrs.
Jas. Sharp, senior; David Wright, Joseph Brock, Edward and James
Hewitt, and Jas. McCabe, the last-named party also being proprietor of
the "Free Masons Arms" Hotel. The progress of Gravenhurst and
vicinity was necessarily slow for a few years.

Messrs. P. Cockburn & Son, commencing lumbering operations in the
country during the winter of 1865–'66, gave an impetus to industry and
advancement previously unknown; they purchased logs from the settlers
and gave them employment during the winter months, soon convincing
the inhabitants that pine trees were useful for other purposes than being
burnt into ashes. Mr. A.P. Cockburn, M.P.P., contributed very materially about this time to the welfare and progress of the settlement by
placing a steamer on Muskoka Lake, built near Gravenhurst wharf, and
known as the "Wenonah;" he also opened a general store, distinguished
as the "Montreal Store,"[18]— since that the country has steadily progressed.

Gravenhurst is pleasantly situated on a gentle declivity between Muskoka Bay and Gull Lake; it is distant from Toronto, 106 miles; from
Orillia, 26 miles; from Severn Bridge, 12 miles; and from Bracebridge,
11 miles. It is connected with Lake Couchiching by a new plank and
gravel road constructed during the past summer. The principal buildings
are Brown's hotel, Mr. Cooper's new building, the Queen's hotel, the
stores of Messrs. Cockburn & Co. and George Clarke, the Episcopalian
Church. Messrs. Sibbald & Chamberland are building an extensive
shingle mill, and Messrs. Cockburn & Co. a steam saw mill; a planing
machine and sash and door factory are also to be run in connexion with
the saw-mill.

A.P. Cockburn, Esq., is constructing a fine new steamer on Muskoka
Bay, which he expects to launch in the month of April next. I might
mention that James Sharp, senior, is general agent for the different
steamers and the "Union Line" at Gravenhurst. The lumbering firm of
Hotchkiss, Hughson, & Co., have an office at this point. The only places
of worship at present are the English Church and schoolhouse. Two new
churches and a public hall are in contemplation. The medical profession
is represented by Dr. J. Adams, of Nova Scotia. Amongst the expectations are the Toronto, Simcoe and Muskoka Junction Railway, and a

[18]The Cockburn store at Orillia was also known as the Montreal store.

branch of the Montreal Telegraph Line. Being situated at the foot of navigation, Gravenhurst does a large and increasing trade. The steamer *Wenonah* calls at the wharf twice each day. The village is favored with a daily mail, with a through mail from Toronto during the season of navigation.

I 20   THE FIRST DOMINION DAY IN BRACEBRIDGE
[*Orillia,* Orillia Expositor, *July 12, 1867*]

We are informed that the natal day of our new Dominion was celebrated with becoming loyalty and eclat, by the inhabitants of Bracebridge, as well as the settlers in the neighbourhood. A. J. Alport, Esq., J.P., whose liberality is proverbial on all occasions of the kind, took a leading part in the amusements of the day.

The programme consisted of various games, etc., and prizes were award [*sic*] to the successful competitors.

Before concluding the proceedings, the large assembly, amongst which might be noticed a fair proportion of the "fair sex," adjourned to where a platform had been erected, when H.J. McDonald, Esq., was requested to take the chair. After the assembly had been called to order, the following gentlemen delivered patriotic addresses appropriate to the occasion:— Messrs. Archer, Alport, Gillman, Willson, Bailey and R. Stewart.

With three hearty cheers for the Queen and three more for the new Dominion, the amusements of the day were brought to a close, all having enjoyed themselves to the fullest extent.

I 21   MEETING CONCERNING A MEDICAL MAN FOR THE DISTRICT
[*Orillia,* Orillia Expositor, *June 18, 1869*]

MEETING AT BRACEBRIDGE.— A meeting of the ratepayers of Draper and Macaulay was held in the Orange Hall, on Friday, 4th inst., for the purpose of obtaining an expression of the public sentiment in reference to levying a tax on the municipality to present to a medical who will settle in the District, in order that he might not be totally dependent on his fees, at least during the first year of his residence there. T. McMurray, Esq., Reeve, occupied the chair, and Mr. John S. Scarlett was requested to act as secretary. The municipal councillors of Draper, Macaulay, &c., and A.H. Browning, Esq., Reeve of Monck, were present. The atendance was not large, owing to unfavourable weather. After a somewhat lengthy discussion, Mr. Bell moved, seconded by Mr. Gow,[19] That the municipality of Draper, Macaulay, &c., be requested to give a grant of one hundred dollars, and the townships of Monck and Muskoka

19This may have been George F. Gow, one of the first to hold land in Bracebridge, owner of the Dominion Hotel, and at one time reeve of Macaulay.

each a similar sum.— Carried unanimously. The usual vote of thanks to the chairman concluded the proceedings.

I 22   ESTABLISHMENT OF THE *Northern Advocate,*
SEPTEMBER 14, 1869
[*McMurray,* The Free Grant Lands of Canada, *p. 56*]

The first newspaper in the Settlement was published by the author, on the 14th day of September, 1869, bearing the title of the *"Northern Advocate."* It was first printed at Parry Sound, but from the fact that Bracebridge was more central it has been removed thither.[20] The object of the publisher was to give reliable information about the Free Grant Lands, and his labours have been very successful. The circulation is 1,000 copies weekly. A great many copies go to England, Ireland and Scotland for the information of intending emigrants, and through its advocacy many have been induced to settle in our midst.

It is somewhat singular, that when the writer first came to Muskoka, he had to row across Muskoka lake, and when the first issue of the Northern Advocate was published, it so happened that the steamer was under repairs, and he had to row 16 miles across the same water in order to deliver the first number.

I 23   BRACEBRIDGE AS SEEN BY CHARLES MARSHALL, SEPTEMBER, 1870
[*Marshall,* The Canadian Dominion, *pp. 55–6*]

. . . In the morning we could see that a most romantic spot had been chosen for the little town. The narrow but deep and very lively Muskoka river winds round the place, with a set of falls in full view, and another at a short distance. Of course, saw-mills were in busy operation. At a bend in the stream floated a quantity of saw-logs. The log huts, and wooden cottages, and frame houses two or three stories high, at different elevations on the hilly ground, with a great variety of outline, gave the most picturesque views. All around were clearings in the wood, and fields still choked with stumps. There were a number of stores, and all were bustling and prosperous. Anything conceivable, apparently, was to be obtained there, and, as I discovered, at but a trifling advance upon Toronto prices. The artisan here has a hundred acres in the bush. Free public schools are opened. Presbyterian, Methodist, and Episcopal churches are already formed. "The Northern Advocate" has a circulation of 1,100 a week. The hotels— Victoria, the Royal, and the Dominion (signs significant)— at present sleep their superabundant guests in rows upon the floors, while their accommodation is being increased. The emigration agent here has disposed of 60,000 acres of land within the past two months. . . .

[20]The *Northern Advocate* moved to Bracebridge in 1870.

I 24   HUNTSVILLE IN 1871
[*McMurray,* The Free Grant Lands of Canada, *pp. 34–6*]

Huntsville is situated on the Vernon River, near its mouth or confluence with the waters of Fairy Lake, in the Township of Chaffey. The
Huntsville post-office was opened January, 1870. Two stores are now
being built, with cheering prospects, on the part of the spirited proprietors, of doing a good business. The Muskoka Road has been extended to
this place a few months ago, and a very substantial bridge spans the
waters of the Vernon. Lakes Vernon, Fairy and Peninsula, are all beautiful sheets of water in this vicinity, abounding with a great variety of
fish . . . The extension of the Muskoka Road to form a junction with the
Bobcaygeon Road, on the east of Franklin, would be a great boon to
this section of country. To effect this, a petition, numerously signed, has
been forwarded to Parliament. The influx of settlers to the vicinity of
these Lakes during last summer has been very great, yet there is much
good land to be given away. Preparations are being made for the erection of churches and mills next summer.

I 25   HUNTSVILLE IN 1878
[*Kirkwood and Murphy,* The Undeveloped Lands in Northern &
Western Ontario, *p. 82*]

Huntsville, within the chain of steamboat communication connecting
Fairy Mary and Vernon Lakes, twenty-five miles from Bracebridge, and
accessible from it by tri-weekly stage in the winter, or by steamer
Northern, from Port Sydney, in the summer, contains over 200 inhabitants, and being the centre of a good farming country will no doubt
flourish. A few rods from the site of the present printing office of the
Huntsville Liberal,[21] Mr. Hunt[22] put up his bark-roofed shanty, north of
which to Lake Nipissing an unbroken forest existed, save where lakes,
streams, or beaver meadows admitted sunlight. This was only eight years
ago. His shanty was then the focus and receptacle for all meetings, secu-
lar and religious, now there are two good-sized hotels, carpenters', shoe-
makers', blacksmiths', cabinet-makers', apothecaries', tinsmith's, and
pump and waggon shops; also dressmaker, etc. The Huntsville people
are ambitious, and not deficient in self-appreciation. Daily stage to
Bracebridge, and tri-weekly mail.

[21]The *Huntville Liberal* was established in 1875. It was printed in Bracebridge,
but edited in Huntsville by that community's first doctor, Francis L. Howland. In
1878 it was succeeded by the *Forester,* under the management of F. W. Clear-
water.

[22]George Hunt (d. 1882), captain in the militia, went from Montreal with his
wife and family to the present site of Huntsville in 1869, and was the first to build
a permanent home in the area later surveyed as a town. The land he selected was
on the east side of the river, near the place chosen for the crossing of the Muskoka
Road. He was very active in promoting settlement, and is regarded as the founder
of Huntsville.

I 26   A POSTMASTER FOR MINDEN — M. SWEETNAM[23] TO
FRANCIS KENT,[24] BOBCAYGEON
[*P.A.O., Miscellaneous Mss.*]

Post Office Inspector's Office,
Kingston, February 1859.

I have to hand you a Letter of Notification of your appointment to the Postmastership of an Office about to be opened at Gull River in the Township of Minden. The New Post Office will be named "Minden".

Be so good as return the enclosed form to me after filling in the names of two responsible persons who will be surety for the faithful discharge of your duty as Postmaster.

I 27   MINDEN IN 1860
[Peterborough Review, *October 10, 1860, as quoted in Poole,* A Sketch of the Early Settlement and Subsequent Progress of the Town of Peterborough, *p. 200*]

Gull river or what to the traveller on the Bobcaygeon road is recognized as such, is a busy spot. It is the centre for the fine district surrounding it, and Mr. Daniel Buck,[25] who keeps a tavern there, has his hands full, usually, to entertain his guests. He is making preparations to erect a large frame building to be used as an hotel; and hopes to have it up this fall. The lot opposite his place, lot three in Minden, forming the corner, bounded on two sides by the Gull river and the Bobcaygeon road, has been reserved by the Government, and the settlement of the place is somewhat retarded in consequence of this. A petition is now in course of signature praying the Government to cause it to be surveyed as a town plot, and placed on sale with settlement conditions.

I 28   GEORGE HENRY KENNEY'S[26] REMINISCENCES OF MINDEN, 1860
[*United Church Archives, photographic copy*]

In one of my appointments, now the County town there was a tavern, kept in a shanty couvered with scoops— scoops are logs split and hol-

[23]Matthew Sweetnam (b. 1831) spent his life in the service of the post office. In 1859 he was Post Office Inspector of the Kingston Division and in 1889 became Chief Inspector for the Dominion.

[24]Apparently Francis Kent did not accept the position because Daniel Buck is listed as the first postmaster in 1860.

[25]Daniel Buck and his wife were proprietors of Minden's first hotel which was in Anson Township on the Victoria side of the Bobcaygeon Road.

[26]George Henry Kenney (1833–1912) was born in Upper Canada, received his theological training at the New York Conference Seminary, and in 1860 at a conference in Belleville was received on trial as a minister of the Methodist Church. He was sent to Gull River, now Minden, in the fall of that year, where he remained until 1861. In 1879 he was stationed at the village of Haliburton.

lowed out,— two logs were laid lengthwise of the building on the top of the walls and these scoops are laid with the hollow sides up and another course breaking the joints of the first course, with their hollow sides down. They laid two courses on with one end of the scoops resting on the outer wall of the building and the other on the long logs running lengthwise of the building near its centre. This shanty was built to accommodate the men while building the colonisation Road. There was a small store in a little log house, and an other in a board shanty roofed with boards. This place also served as a stopping place for such travellers as had not the hardihood to put up at the tavern, a house with plank walls and shingled roof had been put [up] by a shoe maker, there the people assembled for worship. This was the germ of the future county town. I made my home when in the vicinity at the little store in the board shanty, and much kindness did I experience at the hands of the Young's, my hosts.

I 29   MINDEN IN 1867
[*Poole*, A Sketch of the Early Settlement and Subsequent Progress of the Town of Peterborough, *pp. 199–201*]

The village of Minden has the distinction of being, in a sense, the pivot around which the more remote of the new townships may be said to revolve. It is there that clergymen of the different religious denominations reside, who, by their ministrations, supply the spiritual wants of all the adjacent townships. Thither the settlers from a large area around flock to mill, market, store, Post Office and Division Court. . . .

Mr. Daniel Buck, it will be seen, was the first hotel keeper in Minden. He was also the first Postmaster, and the office, first opened in 1860, having then only a weekly, is now supplied with a tri-weekly mail. Mr. Thomas Young[27] opened the first general store in Minden in 1860, which was followed by that of Messrs. George and H. Andrews in the fall of 1862. To these have since been added the stores of Messrs. Wm. Dumble, Andrew Bell, Francis Mason[28] and James Langton.

A saw mill, at a falls about a mile above the village, was built in 1861, and a frame grist mill at the same place followed in 1862. The first mill had one run of stones, was commenced and partially completed by Mr. J.W. Cummings, and then passed into the hands of Mr. Francis Moore. . . .

The first school house in Minden was erected at the village in 1860,

[27]Thomas Young who had come to Canada from England, lived in Cavan Township before moving to Minden in 1860. He acquired five lots in the town and one hundred acres in concession A in Minden Township.

[28]Francis Mason (b. 1842) as a young man served as a clerk in a store in Peterborough. He went to Rochester for a short time, then returned and opened a general store at Minden where he remained for nine years. In 1873 he established a business at Peterborough.

of which the trustees were Messrs. Daniel Buck, senior, William Beavis and T.L. Moore.

The hotel already mentioned is [sic] kept by Mr. Daniel Buck, senior, was on the Victoria side of the Bobcaygeon road, and has since passed into the hands of his son John, and more recently is kept by his younger son, Daniel Buck, junior. The first hotel, actually in Minden, was that opened by Mr. Benjamin Sawyers in 1863. A second at some distance from the village, is kept by Mr. William Gervais.

A Division Court was established at Minden in 1865, at which His Honor R.M. Boucher, Esq., Judge for the County, presides. S.S. Peck, Esq., is Clerk, and Mr. R.C. Garrett, Bailiff of the Court. . . .

I 30   ESTABLISHMENT OF THE MINDEN *News*
[*Orillia*, Times, *July 23, 1874*]

The new county, Haliburton, had not long to wait for a representative journal. We have received the first number of the *News* published at Minden by Messrs. Robertson & Walsh, proprietors of the Peterborough *Times*. It is very neatly got up, and promises to be conducted with more ability than distinguishes the average country newspaper. Mr. Barr, of the Lindsay *Post,* is said to contemplate the publication of another journal in the same place. The latter will be the exponent of sound liberal views; the *News* professes to be independent in politics.

I 31   VERNON B. WADSWORTH'S REMINISCENCES OF
HALIBURTON VILLAGE IN 1864
[*Wadsworth*, Incidents of the Surveys, *pp. 15–6, from original in possession of W. R. Wadsworth, Q.C., Toronto*]

During one summer (1864) I was employed by Edward Miles, Provincial Land Surveyor, Manager of the Canadian Land and Immigration Company, to examine lands in some of their ten townships in the Haliburton country and part of the time I kept their store and post office and stayed with James Holland, who afterwards kept a hotel in Haliburton Village. Others there I knew were the Austins, Sawyers, and Bucks, who were hunters and farmers. . . .

When I was employed by Edward Miles, Manager of the Canadian Land and Immigration Company, Haliburton Village was only a dense forest. Drag Creek, the outlet of Drag Lake, passed through it and it also fronted on a lake there situate. Now[29] it is a thriving village and the terminus of a branch of the Canadian National Railway.

[29]Written in 1926.

On Drag Lake Dave Sawyer,[30] trapper and hunter, usually resided and I have hunted deer with hounds and speared salmon trout by the light of a birch bark torch with him and his sons when passing through there.

In reaching this Haliburton District from Toronto we proceeded via the Northern Railway to Belle [sic] Ewart and took the steamer there for Beaverton on Lake Simcoe, and then walked or drove over the Portage Road twenty miles passing through Kirkfield and reached Macginnis' Point on Balsam Lake on the Trent River waters. We hired boats or canoes there and crossing the lake entered the stream called the Gull River and passed through the village of Coboconk (a part of which I afterwards surveyed when the railway reached there) and up the stream and widening lakes about forty miles to the village of Minden and the intersection of the Bobcaygeon Road.

Our main store camp for the surveys was about four miles above Minden on Mountain Lake, kept by a man by the name of Shove.

By portage of a couple of miles to the east of Minden we entered Koshog Lake which empties into the Burnt River waters, which river is a tributary of the Gull River. . . .

I 32   THE VILLAGE OF HALIBURTON IN 1867
[City of Toronto Directory for 1867–8, p. 438]

In the township of Dysart there is already a flourishing settlement. There is a good road from the Bobcaygeon road, two miles below Minden, through Dysart to the Peterson road, and other roads are made, or being rapidly opened up. The Company[31] have granted aid to secure the running of a small steamer on Lake Kahshagawigamog or Kushog, during the summer months. A portage road of about three miles connects Minden with the foot of the lake, and from this point the steamer and a large row-boat run twice a week to Haliburton at the head of the lake, a distance of 14 or 15 miles, and touch at the landing on the south side of the lake, to take up passengers. The town plot of Haliburton, situate in the centre of Dysart, is now being rapidly settled. The Company erected an excellent grist mill, and the lessees, Messrs. Lucas and Ritchey have a saw mill adjoining. There are also at Haliburton, a post office supplying a tri-weekly mail, stores and boarding houses, a smith's forge and other conveniences. Lots have been granted to the various religious denominations for the erection of places of worship, and two school sections have been formed. An Agricultural Society has also been properly organized.

[30]Dave Sawyer was established as a trapper on Drag Lake before the Canadian Land and Emigration Company opened the area for settlement. He later lived in Dudley and Harburn townships.
[31]The Canadian Land and Emigration Company.

I 33   TELEGRAPH LINE TO HALIBURTON
[*Toronto*, Mail, *September 19, 1872*]

HALIBURTON.

Telegraphic Communication with the Back Townships.
(Special Despatch from Our Own Correspondent)
Haliburton, Sept. 18.— Telegraphic communication with this village
was completed yesterday, when the new office of the Montreal Telegraph Company was opened for business.

The Churches

I 34   EXTRACTS FROM GEORGE HENRY KENNEY'S
REMINISCENCES, *circa* 1860
[*United Church Archives, photographic copy*]

At the meeting of the Missionary Committee a man was wanted to
open a new mission in the Gull River country, which was being opened
up for settlement in the northern part of the counties of Victoria and
Peterboro, and I being available was sent.

. . . Mr Dowler[32] and his colleague had gone into the country once in
six weeks and preached until the previous Conference, when Gull River
was set off for a new mission, since which the people had been without
the services of a missionary until this time — about the close of
November.

. . .

The appointments of the next sunday were at 10.30 A.M. at Scotts
on the south side of Coshogwigamog Lake, at Mr. Peck's on the Minden
road at 2.30 P.M., and at Gull River at 7.30 P.M. On saturday I
started out and took dinner at Hunter's at Burnt River, (Kinmount) and
arrived at Mr. Peck's about three in the afternoon. My morning appointment was about six miles in the rear of Mr. Peck's. There was no road
to get to it, a road had been cut through the underwood, but the logs
had not been cut out, there was rapid river to be crossed, and there was
no bridge and no bridges over bogs and swamps and these were not
frozen up, and the only guide as to the course to take was the tracks
of two men who had come through several days before and their tracks
were nearly obliterated by freshly fallen snow. Mr. Peck tried to dis-
suade from attempting to go through especially as the afternoon was so

[32]The Reverend John A. Dowler, Methodist clergyman, commenced his work in
1854. He was at Bobcaygeon from 1858 to 1860.

near gone, but stay with them. I was very anxious to get through especially as this was my first time. I thanked him, and said that if he would
keep my horse I would make the attempt, this he consented kindly to
do, and I immediately set out. It was very hard walking, the snow being
about a foot deep and some places there were several inches of mud
under the snow. . . .

The country being new there was little feed to be got for my horse
within the bounds of my mission, besides there was only one road, the
Bobcaygeon Colonizing Road, and that was only opened as far north
as the Junction of Peterson's line, running as near as possible the line
between the Counties of Victoria and Peterboro, and my mission extended into nine townships and only along trails in the woods, or along
rivers and over lakes, I thought it better to get pasture for my horse in
the country outside and travel on foot. I knew it would be a great undertaking, but I could see no other way, therefore I left my horse near
Oakville[33] and went to my mission.

During this year I preached three times each sunday except once in
four travelling by bark canoe along rivers and over lakes, footing it
through woods and swamps frequently without as much as a trail. If I
got lost, I would keep a lookout for a blaze on the trees and then follow
it till I came to a corner stake, observe its number then on to the next
when I could ascertain the course to take. I visited everybody in the
country finding a welcome everywhere and making myself at home
everywhere and so finding a lodging place wherever the night overtook
me.

A few settlers having gone up lakes that constitute the head waters
of Gull River, I went up a few times to visit and preach to them.

The first trip I made, I walked up to Peterson's line and turning
eastward I followed a foot path through the woods till I came [to] the
Bushcong narrows, between Big and Little Bushcong Lakes. It was a
pretty spot. Here Mr. Hunter, a hunter and trapper had cleared the
narrow strip of land between these Lakes, built a shanty and made his
residence. Soon after the close of the Rebellion of 1837 Mr. Hunter,
who was said to have had something to do with the Rebellion, when it
closed, he thought to hide himself by burying himself in the forest, so he
took his canoe, and wife and went up through Balsam Lake, then up
Burnt River till he found a place sufficiently remote from human habitation and made a home, and made a subsistence by hunting and fishing.
In course of time his wife died, and he took her corpse in his canoe out
to the settlements to give her a burial. In after years settlers came in and
commenced to open up the country and he again took his canoe and
passing up the Burnt River into Lake Coshogwigamog thence by Gull
River and the chain of lakes from whose waters the Gull River was fed,
to Bushcong. There he made his home . . .

[33]His home was at Oakville.

. . .

Three or four families had gone further up the waters into the township of Stanhope and I was anxious to visit them. In the morning Mr. Cameron offered to go with me in his bark canoe. We started and went round to Beech River, the outlet of Beech Lake. When we came to the river we found it would be difficult to get up to the portage by which we might avoid the rapids in the river on account of the rapidity of the water caused by the spring floods. . . . We drew the canoe out of the water, got it on our shoulders and carried it across the portage. We passed a place where a mill was being erected on this river. Coming to Beech Lake launched out and passed to the upper end of the lake entering Maple River. Here was another rapid and we found the same difficulty as before. . . . We landed, as before, below the portage again getting our canoe on our shoulders we procededed [sic] to cross the half mile portage. When about half way, it occurred to Mr. Cameron that the waters might be too rough to proceed and it might be wise to lay our canoe down and go forward and see the condition of things at Maple Lake, which we did. When we came to Maple Lake we realized our fears were well grounded, but found a Mr. Mason living there who kindly gave us our dinners. As the waters of the lake were dangerous, and there was only one family above this we concluded, that it would not be wise to attempt to proceed accordingly we turned our faces the other way. . . .

I 35   FREDERICK BURT[34] TO LORD BISHOP OF TORONTO,
JOHN STRACHAN[35]
[*P.A.O., Strachan Papers*]

Huntingdon, C. E.
13 May 1865.

I beg to forward the "Letters testimonial" from his Lordship[36] of Montreal and now seek a license from you, my Lord, to officiate in Minden and places adjacent. My residence will be at Haliburton, township of Dysart.

I am permitted by the Bishop of Montreal to cease my labours here on the last Sunday of May. I hope then to proceed immediately to the locality above named to serve under your Lordship, supposing that by

[34]The Reverend Frederick Burt remained in Dysart only part of a year then moved to Minden where he lived until 1877. He was the first Anglican clergyman in Minden and established St. Paul's Church. As well as acting as clergyman he had one hundred acres which had been granted to the church in Minden Township, which he was expected to farm. He was also the county superintendent of schools, and, after 1874, inspector of public schools.

[35]John Strachan (1778–1867), first Anglican Bishop of Toronto.

[36]The Reverend Francis Fulford (1803–1868).

that date I shall have received the necessary papers from you as my Diocesan.

Asking the favourable consideration of your Lordship.

I 36   EXTRACTS FROM "DIARY KEPT BY THE REV. JOHN WEBSTER"[37]
[*United Church Archives*]

[July 5, 1871] Left Bracebridge at 3 P.M. for Port Carling, road on horse back, took the new road, that was opened last fall, I was never through it only in winter, before. It was better than I expected to find it, I called at Mr William Donally's[38] 5 or 6 miles from the Muskoka and Parry Sound road, took Tea and fed my Horse. I had been invited last winter to take up an appointment there, but could not make it convenient. I had officiated at the funeral of his wife in the winter. After Tea I again started on my journey at 10 minutes to Seven, had to ride 9 miles, the worst of the road had to be passed; got to the river 10 minutes after 9, could not get my horse over, took her back to a private residence . . .

6th. . . . I then started on foot to make a journey of 10 miles going and returning. Saw some few by the way side, talked a little to them about both worlds, and then went to Mr May's,[39] his wife was from home, talked to him about our work, took dinner with him (he is a first rate cook). I then called on another family (a young couple), they had a few hands logging, had prayer, then took a by path through the woods, as rough as any I ever travelled, over great mountains of rock, then descending into, and crossing vallies, reached Mr. Blain's Shanties where he has a Government Contract, making a canall at Port Sandfield, to connect Lake Joseph with Lake Rosseau, made an arraingement to preach, returned to Port Carling and preached in the evening in the new Orange Hall, and had again to put up at Thomeses Hotell.

The following day I returned home, visited some families, and made some arrangements for preaching. (I performed all this suffering from haveing a fractured ribb, jarring hurt it considerably, but it is now better.)

. . .

Aug. 11. On Sunday last traveled 25 miles and preached 3 times, led two classes and renewed the Quarterly Tickets.[40] Monday returned home.

[37]John Webster (b. 1823), Methodist minister, was born in London Township, commenced work in 1846 at Gosfield, and went to Bracebridge about 1870. In 1879 he moved to Simcoe County and lived for some time at Hillsdale.

[38]Probably William Donally who settled on lot 19, concession 11, of Monck Township, not far from Leonard Lake.

[39]This may have been Thomas May who lived on lots 25 and 26, concession 3, of Medora Township, a little beyond Port Carling.

[40]Tickets which granted the right to attend the "love feasts."

Married four couples in 2 weeks, three paid well paying $5 each, the other was a hard man and mean and the fee was accordingly.

. . .

Morrison Aug 22. On Sunday last (the 20) I rode 5 miles, preached in Draper and administered the Sacrement, I then started to Morrison, and drove through a heavy rain (it rained about half the way). I was to have preached in Morrison at 4 P.M. but was late on account of the roughness of the causeways, and a strap of my harness broke. I preached in the new Church, held a love feast[41] and administered the Sacrement. It was the first Quarterly Meeting held as the Morrison Quarterly Meeting. I drove (when I reached my stopping place) altogether 30 miles, preached twice, held one lovefeast, and administered the Sacrement at both places where I preached—

. . .

Fary[42] Lake Oct. 28th. 1871.
On the Morning of the 18 inst. we had a little snow. This morning the ground was covered; had about an inch of snow. I slept at Mr. Hogaboam's, las night, rose this morning a little after 5 oclock, started about day light, road 8 miles, before breakfast, breakfasted at Charles Hogaboam's[43] then road to Huntsville, took dinner at Mr. Hunts, could not get a man to take me across the Lake (Fary Lake). Mr Hunt had cut his foot and could not accompany me, but he told me to take his canoe, I did so, and came down the river to Fary Lake, and across the Lake to Mr Peter Fetterley's. The people are very much scattered, and I took a walk to see a new saw mill, and the land around it &c. there is some excellent land here. . . .

I 37   THE ROMAN CATHOLIC CHURCH IN MUSKOKA TO 1878
[*Kirkwood and Murphy*, The Undeveloped Lands in Northern & Western Ontario, p. 76]

The Roman Catholic Church:— Jesuit missions were established in the Huron and Parry Sound district 200 years ago, and for over that period, Catholic missionaries have visited the Georgian Bay and the Severn River. Father Proulx[44] ascended, about 1840, the river Severn

41A meal taken together by members of the church as one of the rites of the Methodist Church at that time.
42Fairy Lake.
43Charles Hogaboam, son of David Hogaboam and brother of Daniel A. Hogaboam, had land at Madills settlement.
44Probably Abbé Jean Baptiste Proulx (1808–1881) who was ordained at Montreal, July 26, 1835, and served as a missionary at Penetanguishene from 1836 to 1837, and at Manitoulin from 1837 to 1846.

to Sparrow Lake. The Manitoulin mission was organised about the beginning of the present century, and included the east shore of the Georgian Bay, and of Lake Nipissing and French River. On the 25th January, 1874, the Bishopric of Sarepta was established, which included Parry Sound, Muskoka, and part of the Nipissing district as far as the height of land between the watersheds of the Ottawa and Lake Nipissing. The Presbytery at Bracebridge was built in 1876. There is 1½ acres, value $700. Total value of church property in Bracebridge, $4,000. The congregation consist of 15 families in the village, and 24 in the country. In round numbers, there are 200 Catholics in Bracebridge and vicinity, and 160 in Gravenhurst; 100 at Port Severn; 100 at the Musquosh; 250–300 in Parry Sound Village and a circle of 10 miles round; 200 in Byng Inlet; and a fair proportion in Perry, Armour, Machar, Bethune, Proudfoot, Gurd, Himsworth, Nipissing, and Pringle. The Roman Catholic church in Muskoka and Parry Sound has its head quarters at Bracebridge, and with far-seeing insight into the present and future importance of that village as a religious centre, the Bishop of Sarepta (Monsignor Jamot,[45] a native of France), who takes his title *in partibus infidelium,* has made Bracebridge, if not his permanent residence, at least his head quarters and his home, in so far as a missionary Bishop can be said to have any home. . . .

The Schools

I 38   SCHOOLS IN MACAULAY, RYDE, AND STEPHENSON
[*Ontario, Education Office,* Annual Report of the Normal, Model, Grammar and Common Schools, *1868, app. A, p. 19*]

The Reverend Walter Wright,[46] Macaulay, Ryde, and Stephenson.—
. . . We have only had four schools in operation out of the ten sections, and none of these had anything about them particularly calling for remark. In the case of non-attendants at any of these schools, I believe the cause of their absence would be found to be the indifference of the parents. In two of the schools in operation, viz., No. 3, Draper, and No. 1, Stephenson, there was diligent attention paid to religious instruction;

[45]Jean François Jamot (1828-1886) was sent to Canada from France in 1855. In 1874 he became Bishop of Sarepta and Vicar Apostolic of Northern Ontario. In 1882 he transferred to the diocese of Peterborough. Contemporary favourable comment on him appears in Hamilton, *Muskoka Sketch,* pp. 22–3.
[46]The Reverend Walter Wright was a Congregational minister and acted as a local superintendent of common schools. A letter to the *Northern Advocate* outlining his opinion of religion, morality, and education in Muskoka is found in McMurray, *The Free Grant Lands of Canada,* pp. 91-2.

but as to what the regulations are, on this matter, neither trustees nor teachers know, for they have no School Manuals, but one, in the settlement, I believe. The want of the School Act has proved a very serious drawback. The teachers examined by me (according to the appointment of the County Council) were examined faithfully, and to the best of my judgment, without reference to any given programme, as none such was supplied to me. There is no library connected with any of these schools, and no distribution of prizes. . . . In all of the sections, excepting No. 4, Stephenson, there appears to be some action in school matters. I may mention that in several of these, the erection of school-houses is contemplated. For No. 1, Draper, we have secured a grant from Government of two half acre village lots, for a school site, through my personal application to Mr. Richards. It is intended that a school-house shall be built on it during the coming summer. Also in No. 2, Draper, and No. 2, Stephenson, they intend to erect school-houses as soon as the work can be done.

I 39   REPORT ON SCHOOLS IN 1869
[*Ontario, Education Office*, Annual Report of the Normal, Model,
Grammar and Common Schools, 1869, *app. p. 70–1*]

The Reverend Frederick Burt, Anson, Minden and Lutterworth.— . . . I can report that our Boards of Trustees evince quite an amount of anxiety for the welfare of the schools of which they are the chosen guardians. Three new sections have opened for active work in the past year, and another opens in April. . . . In the Township of Dysart, settlers are on the increase, and thus the schools are largely attended, nearly equalling that part of Minden Village (where I reside), or that of Kinmount, the second largest, being a small village school on the Bobcaygeon Road. The rest of the schools are small, owing to the standstill state of the country. . . .

The Reverend Walter Wright, Draper, Macaulay, Ryde, and Stephenson.— . . . Increasing interest is manifested through the whole settlement in general education, and there is reason to hope that eight or nine schools will be in operation this year. No. 2, Macaulay, has erected a very neat frame school house. No. 3, Macaulay, is about to erect one also. Nos. 1 and 2, Draper, also propose to build. Permit me to say that it seems very desirable indeed if not indispensable, that the Legislative Grant for this year should be considerably increased, if at all practicable, for the great mass of the population of Muskoka have to contend with very great pecuniary difficulties, so much so, that I doubt very much whether there be an equal section of country in Canada, where there is so strong a desire for educational advantages with so little pecuniary ability to gratify this desire.

I 40   A. H. BROWNING TO EGERTON RYERSON[47]
[*P.A.O., Education Department Papers, Incoming General
Correspondence, 1872, no. 7071*]

Alport P.O.
Muskoka
20th. May 1872.

I have been requested by Mr. Coulson[48] of the township of Monck
to submit the following case to you— He is a resident in the township
of Monck school Sectn. No 2 but owing to the distance from the
school House viz 4½ miles by road he finds it to be an utter impossibility
to send his child to school.

Previous to the New school act coming into force it was usual in this
new country where the population is so scattered to allow children to
attend the school most convenient in some cases a special rate was
imposed upon the children so attending but the trustees of school Sectn.
No 2 of the township of Macaulay refuse to allow any such attendance
for the future as there is no provision to that effect in the "Act" and
thus denying a child any chance of any education in a Common School.
Coulson & others were in hopes that from all schools being now free
schools that children would be allowed to attend the school most convenient where the trustees were willing to receive them, and where it
was clearly impossible that the children could attend at their *own Sectnl
school*. I should not have troubled you with matter had it not been the
exceptional position in which ratepayers are placed in Muskoka owing
to the scattered population and but few of the roads fit for travel—
Would you be kind enough to let me know if there is any way to get over
the difficulty I may further add that Mr Coulson of course would continue to pay his school rate to the section in which he is a resident but
is perfectly willing to pay such extra charge as the trustees of the school
at which the child may attend may deem fair

[Draft of reply on attached wrapper:] The only remedy for the difficulty
to which you refer is the establishment of Township Boards or the alteration in the boundaries of the Section

I 41   HENRY REAZIN'S[49] REPORT ON SCHOOLS, 1874
[*Ontario, Education Office*, Annual Report of the Normal, Model,
High and Public Schools, *1874, app. p. 52*]

Muskoka.— With one exception the School Sections are all poor,
and without the liberal provision made by the Legislature in providing

[47]Adolphus Egerton Ryerson (1803–1882) was Chief Superintendent of Education for Upper Canada and later Ontario from 1844 to 1876.

[48]This may refer to John Coulson who lived on concession 6 of Monck, on
the lot adjacent to the border of Macaulay Township.

[49]Henry Reazin (1831–1902) settled in Victoria County in 1863, and was later
appointed an inspector of public schools for West Victoria.

a poor School Fund for their assistance, very many of them could not exist, and large numbers of the children of those industrious pioneers who are now enjoying a Public School education would be entirely deprived of that blessing.

Ryde has two Sections formed and one School in operation, viz., No. 6, union with Draper.

Oakley, has no School yet. The settlers have asked for one, but are in my opinion scarcely strong enough yet to support a School. Their settlement is likely soon to be increased.

Draper has six Schools, including the union with Ryde. The Sections are all poor and difficult of access.

Macaulay has six Schools in operation, one at Bracebridge with three departments. They are all very poor with the exception of No. 1, which includes the Village of Bracebridge.

McLean has one School Section— extremely difficult of access.

Stisted has two Sections formed, with one School in operation.

Brunel has three Sections formed, but no School yet in operation.

Chaffey has four Sections formed, with two Schools in operation. (Chaffey is thirteen Townships north of Lake Ontario.)

Ryerson, McMurrich, and *Perry,* still farther north, have asked for assistance. I hope to be able to reach them during the year 1875.

Owing to innumerable lakes, rocky hills, swamps, the absence of roads, large forests, &c. the Schools in the above Townships are very difficult of access.

J. THE FIRST TOURISTS

J 1   McCabe's Tavern[1] Opened at Gravenhurst, 1861
[*McMurray,* The Free Grant Lands of Canada, *p. 14*]

Prominent amongst the early settlers stand the names of Mr. and Mrs. McCabe; they opened a tavern at Gravenhurst in 1861, and many a worn-out traveller has been glad to see their unpretentious log cabin where they might rest their weary limbs and get some refreshment to sustain nature. Never shall the writer forget his first interview with "Mother McCabe." When he arrived there, he was hungry and footsore; but he met with an "Irish welcome," and a dinner was served up by "Mother McCabe" which would not have disgraced any Hotel north of Toronto. The old log shanty looked dull outside, but within all was cleanliness and order; her clean white curtains kept out the musquitoes in summer and cold in winter, while her feather beds afforded sweet rest to many a weary land-seeker. How welcome was the sight of the dim low light through the bush, to the weary traveller, can only be fully appreciated by the early pedestrians when no horses or vehicles were on the road; there were hundreds in the settlement who remember them, and some of them have cause to bless "Mother McCabe" for her generosity.

J 2   Thomas M. Robinson[2] to James Bain[3]
[*James Bain Papers, in possession of Professor James Watson Bain, Toronto*]

Muskoka Bay, June 24/ 62.

It is with great pleasure that I atempt to be of any servace to you on your proposed expedition and since I received your letter last Sunday have made all the enquiries I have been able to do, but your letter not having arrived as soon here as might have been expected I thought it

[1]McCabe's tavern was described in less favourable terms by James Bain and John Campbell (Mason, *Muskoka; The First Islanders*, pp. 5–6).

[2]Thomas M. Robinson, an English sailor, first went to Muskoka in 1860 in search of land. He returned to England, came back with his wife in the following year and settled on Muskoka Bay, near Gravenhurst, where he soon became known for his ability as a guide on the Muskoka Lakes. For many years he provided board and room for tourists in his home. He wrote the article on Gravenhurst in *The Canadian Album, Encyclopedic Canada* (Brantford, 1896), v. 5, pp. 350–3.

[3]James Bain (1842–1908) as a young man was employed in the firm of James Campbell and Son, publisher, and was a close friend of John Campbell, his companion on several trips to Muskoka. These two young men who spent a week's holiday in Muskoka in 1860 may have been the first "tourists" in the area. From 1872 to 1882 James Bain was in the publishing business in England. In 1882 he returned to Toronto and in 1883 became the first chief librarian of the Toronto Public Library. He was one of the founders of the Champlain Society.

better not to deffer writing until next weeks mail, but send you all the information I could obtain at present.

In the first place the rout to Nippissing by the river[4] seems rather a doubtful affair, some of the Indians think it practicable, others do not but say the way is by Georgian bay and the french river and it is very difficult to get anything deffinate out of them: in the next place the distance is something like 100 miles more or less it is impossible to say exactly and I think your time altogether to short for that purpose. Again you would scarcely be able to do it with less than 2 Indians in each canoe and to make a forced march of it to Nippissing and back would find more toil than pleasure. The regular hire of the Indians is one Dollar per day. At the same time I would be far from discouraging you from attempting an undertaking of the kind as there is great inducements to something of the kind for since you have been here there has been another lake[5] discovered that was not before known to white men and connected to Lakes Muskoka and Rosseau which as you know are both very extensive being each about 12 or 14 miles by 9 or 10 in bredth and it is said by the surveyors that discovered this new lake that it is quite as large as either of the others, and the three are all connected together merely a fall of 5 feet from the one and 2 feet from the other which is no serious impediment to the passing of a small or light boat. Now what I would propose is this, if you could get a small or light handy boat that would carry the party comfortably in Toronto and bring it with you the expence would be a trifle compared to the other such a boat you could get for hire I have no doubt or even to buy it I have no doubt you could sell it here as boats are in great demand here at this time that is if you did not pay too much for it, in that case you would want no one to help you but one person or an Indian if you thought it necessary and I am much mistaken if the scenery of these most beautiful of lakes would not amply repay you. For as you have no doubt been informed Muskoka lake contains not less than 300 islands nor do I doubt it; for I was at the northwest part or the part nearest to Lake Rosseau this spring and I can safely say it was prettiest lake scenery I have ever seen in fact it is quite a collection of Islands.

The further we advanced the prettyer the scenery became because every island we passed showing more beauties and opening up another prospect more enchanting than the last. In fact a fortnight might be passed there alone without any fear of wearyness and I have no doubt the Fishing is excellent besides you will on the lakes be more free from these pests of the woods the flies which altho they will not be so very bad at the time you refer to yet will be in suficient numbers to prove

[4]The reference is not clear but may refer to a route by the North Branch of the Muskoka River, Vernon Lake, and a series of lakes and portages to the South River (B 24).

[5]Lake Joseph, although mapped by David Thompson in 1837, remained practically unknown to white men until surveyed by J. S. Dennis in 1860. The reference here, and the name given in Robinson's letter of July 6, suggest that Wadsworth's account of the origin of the name (D 16) is correct.

anoying in river navigation, if this plan meets with your approbation and you think of bringing a boat with you I can meet you in Orillia if necessary if you stait the day or if you like the plan and do not think of or cannot get a boat to answer I might try to get one in Orillia for you but the other would be the most satisfactory way; or if you still think the original project the best way you can do in that case is to get Rama Indians as they are more in the habit of going on expeditions of that kind and are all able to speak English You will be best able to get them your self as you come as this summer I am at home on Muskoka Bay living but in either case I will be but too happy to go with you as at that time my most urgent work will be over and as for the terms we will not quarrel about that but I have no doubt you will be satisfied. I hope you will write in time for our next mail which leaves Orillia every Thursday morning at McCabes that evening.

Please address Muskoka Bay, Simcoe
P.S. If you bring your own boat don't forget to bring the sails with you as they may be of much use also a tent if possible

J 3   Robinson to Bain
[James Bain Papers, in possession of Professor James Watson Bain, Toronto]

Muskoka Bay July 6th 1862

I had the pleasure of receiving yours of the 1st yesterday, and I hasten to answer it. I was sorry to know that after I sent the letter to you the person to whom I entrusted it and two others had made a mistake and paid a letter I had not intended to pay and left yours unpaid. I am very glad that you approve of the sujestion I made, I think you may do very well without an Indian.

Now to your first inquiry with regard to the portage[6] from Sparrow Lake to Muskoka Bay I think it could not be conveniently made as there is one portage on that route three miles in length and as the water in the numerous creeks is getting low for the passage of a boat

2nd I could meet you at Orillia on the 21st if you wish, so as to get to the Severn early and I will do my best to have a waggon ready to take you straight to the bay that night.

3rd I will try to get a canoe before that time

4th I must remember now what I forgot before to tell you that I think you had better bring hard bread or what is generally used at sea coarse biscuit with you as being preferable to flour as there is so much

[6]In 1896 T. M. Robinson described the route from the Severn to Lake Muskoka as follows: "the canoe route by way of the Severn River, through Sparrow Lake, thence *via* Morrison Lake to Leg Lake, and to Muskoka Bay, where Gravenhurst now stands, by the long portage on the route of the present Leg Lake road; or, with loaded canoes, by the longer route but shorter portages, by way of Pine Lake and Bear Bay, across what is now the Whitehead farm" (*The Canadian Album, Encyclopedic Canada*, v. 5, p. 351).

wasted by bad cooking but the fine Biscuits or Crackers are too dry for general use, you will no doubt be able to get the coarser kind in Toronto and as to quantity I think 100 lbs. or thair abouts suficient and as to meat I think ham or other dry salt meat from 60 to 90 lbs; if you think this to much you may reduce it, but you must remember you will not bring your City apatite with you and as for Tea or Coffee and sugar or any thing in that way you may bring just as it pleases you. As for further information respecting the other Lakes both Rosseau and St. Joseph there is so little known of them as to make it almost imposible much of them [sic] as only one or two parties of white men have been on Lake Rosseau and only one party of Surveyors in St. Joseph. The only thing can be said positively is that the fishing is splendid That seems to be acknowledged on all hands.

Now if you change your time of coming to Orillia, or do not mind me coming there to meet you or do not want the team & waggon or make any change in the arrangment please write and let me know by the very first opertunity or if you do not I shall come at the time proposed and make the other arrangement.[7] I take the first opertunity of sending this to Orillia by a friend to give you time to answer by this week's mail.

J 4   EXCERPT FROM BAIN'S "JOURNAL[8] OF THE MUSKOKA
EXPEDITION," AUGUST, 1864
[James Bain Papers, in possession of Professor James Watson Bain, Toronto]

Dramatis Personae

Captain	Mr Fraser[9]— alias "The Star" ex Stewart &c &c
Chaplain & Naturlist	Mr Campbell[10] ex Curate
Stewart & Secretary	Mr Bain alias Finn
Armourer	Master Jos Campbell[11] alias "The boy"
Do Do No 2	Master Ewart[12]
Ducens	Mr Robinson

[7]Bain and his companions made the trip which Robinson proposed in 1862, and that and subsequent expeditions are summarized in Mason's *Muskoka; The First Islanders.* In 1863 several of the group returned and the account of that expedition is printed in some detail (Bracebridge, *Muskoka Herald,* August 3, 1950).

[8]This excerpt, with its terse, broken style, is typical of the journals kept by James Bain and his friends on their early expeditions to Muskoka. Misspelled words in the Journal were no doubt deliberate. The members of the expeditions appear under assumed names which vary somewhat from year to year.

[9]J. C. Fraser, a bookkeeper in a wholesale drygoods firm in Toronto.

[10]John Campbell (1840–1904) graduated with a brilliant record from the University of Toronto, became a Presbyterian clergyman and professor of church history and apologetics at the Presbyterian College, Montreal. He was a leading member of the so-called "Muskoka Club" and later he and other members of the club built their cottages on Yoho and nearby islands in Lake Joseph.

[11]Josia Campbell (d. 1870) was a younger brother of John Campbell.

[12]John Skirving Ewart (1849–1933) was called to the Bar in 1871 and made a Q.C. in 1884. He became an outstanding lawyer and was also known for his writings on legal subjects and on the political independence of Canada.

Saturday August 13th Up at usual hour— Boy 2 cook— bathe— pack and start again for the top of the lake, lose a hook— tremendous expression of the Captains face while steering — land on rocky point for lunch— strong expression of the crew against the cheese— huckle- berry bushes— nothing on them— start— heavy pull against the wind — head of the lake hurrah! signs of a river— make exploration— sucessful at last— Ducks— fired at by the boys and missed— no passage through the marsh at the mouth of the river— land— boy shoots at or rather at [sic] a bittern— getting late and lake rough, deserted clearing— difficulty in finding a camping ground— succeed— stunning spot— dinner— pull out to catch fish for Sunday— land boys at the marsh with guns— good fishing— boys shoot nothing— return — glorious moonlight night— decidedly the prettiest camping ground and finest night we have had yet— Concert— to bed—

Sunday August 14th late in rising— heavy mist— breakfast— Cap- tain cook— general period of religious literature by all hands— morning service conducted by the Chaplain at eleven— sermon from Dr Guthries — lunch— reading resumed— Joe goes out in the boat to get water and has trouble in getting back— dinner grand!— Robinson goes to visit his friend and finds no one at home— rest of party asleep— tea— sacred concert— quiet day—

Monday August 15th— up at six— Joe and Ewart out after ducks— no go— Breakfast— Robinson cook— start at seven to explore Mud River with all hands aboard— shoot at snipe, usual result— delightful? portage— Bittern starts up close at hand and shot at as usual when out of reach— the river— slow sluggish stream about 40 feet wide, water deep and black— splendid alluvial land and fine timber, on each side principally— maple, hard and soft, ash, balsam, oak and elm. More ducks coolly go on before not at all put out by the shots— Ducens denunciations against the rascally shopkeepers for selling shot that always dodges the ducks— snags thick and progress slow— Botanist sees something on the shore and lands— 3 new speciments— remains of Indian clearings— stopped by snags— magnificent crane— return— snags again— more ducks getting "saucy"— Ducens enthusiastic on the soil— portage again— back to camp— all right— Boys challenge the remainder of party to shot at mark— Joe beats by 4 points and wins Captain prize— bathe— dinner— Ducens and Steward start out on a voyage of exploration— sail down the lake to "sou' east" tremen- dous cliffs— splendid bay with fine sandy beach— wigwam hurrah— land— bass bark tent— no one near— track leading into the bush— blaze with road to Parry Sound Road, follow it up— hark! female voices heard— sylvan dames gathering flowers and bark. Ducens accost the youth who accompanies them— interesting conversation— we learn all the information we require about the head of the lake— females very retired and backward in speaking— they accompany us to the boat without showing themselves possesed of the faculty of speech—

we start for the opposite shore due west— long pull— very deep bays — enter one— Ducens lands to examine the land— reports stunning location— All the land round the head with few exceptions covered with fine Sugar maple, beech and white ash— long pull home— Joe has shot 2 snipe and red headed woodpecker— Captain and boys go across to the marsh to shoot ducks— Ewart nearly kills a duck— cant be found— Joe hits a bittern it takes to a tree— Joe follows it— fire up and brings down a porcupine— Bittern nowhere— Captain comes to the conclusion that witchcraft has something to do with it— back to camp—

J 5   "Up the Muskoka and Down the Trent"
[*Toronto,* Globe, *October 4, 1865*]

Every summer witnesses the making up of small parties of neighbours and friends in the various cities and towns of Canada for excursions to one point or another of the Province, to the sea-side, to some fashionable watering-place to Europe, or to the backwoods in the fall, for the purpose of fishing and hunting. Your correspondent recently formed one of a party of four, bent upon a few weeks of sight-seeing and recreation upon the beautiful inland lakes and rivers to the north-east of Toronto. After due deliberation it was decided to take a round trip, beginning with Lake Simcoe, and ending with Lake Scugog, going up the north branch of the Muskoka river, at least as far as Vernon Lake, and crossing by whatever route might be found most practicable, to the head waters of the Trent. The engagements of several who had contemplated taking part in the trip, compelling them to forego the pleasure, the party was finally made up of the Reeve of Oshawa, D.F. Burk,[13] Esq., Mr. S. Luke,[14] one of the proprietors of the Oshawa Vindicator, Mr. J.E. Farewell[15], LL.B., of the same town, and the writer. The party left Oshawa on the evening of Wednesday, the 23rd of August, for the Severn river, their two boats and luggage being drawn by team to Beaverton, on Lake Simcoe. This season of the year was chosen in preference to an earlier or later date, on account of its more equable temperature. Earlier, the heat would have been too great and the black flies intolerable, while a month later, though the fishing and hunting would have been vastly better, the nights would not have been so

[13]David Francis Burk, reeve of Oshawa, lived on a farm just east of Oshawa. His grandfather was John Burk, one of the first settlers in Darlington, and his father was D. F. Burk of Bowmanville. Reeve D. F. Burk had a son, Captain David Francis Burk, after whom Burk's Falls was named.

[14]Samuel Luke (1834–1918) was born in Cornwall, England, and was brought to Canada as an infant in 1834. He was associated for many years with John Larke in running the *Oshawa Vindicator.* From 1876–8 he owned the *Oshawa Reformer.*

[15]John Edwin Chandler Farewell (1840–1923) was a member of the law firm of Farewell and McGee in Oshawa. In 1872 he went to Whitby as Crown Attorney. He was an authority on local history, and author of *The County of Ontario* (Whitby, 1906).

pleasant, or the promise of fair weather so good. Provisions sufficient for two weeks, independently of what might be caught or killed on the way, were taken, consisting principally of some twenty-five loaves of well-baked bread, two pounds of tea, and ten to fifteen pounds each of crackers, meal, bacon, fresh butter, salt, and dried fruit. The cooking utensils consisted of two frying-pans and a tin pail, and the table furniture of a tin plate, tin cup, knife, fork, and spoon for each man. For sleeping arrangements, a piece of common factory cotton, five yards by three, was taken as a tent, to be put up in the form of a house roof, with the boat sails to close the rear, leaving the front open; while a buffalo robe, five quilts and blankets and sundry overcoats formed the bedding, to be supplemented underneath, when time and opportunity permitted, by a spring mattress composed of pine, balsam, or hemlock boughs.

We give a few jottings from the diary of the trip, such as may prove generally interesting, and particularly to persons desirous of knowing something of the conditions of the country to the rear of the fine agricultural counties of Ontario, Simcoe, Victoria, and Peterboro, as well as those who may be contemplating a hunting or fishing trip in Canadian woods and waters:—

Thursday, Aug. 24— After two or three hours' rest in camp near Sonya, proceeded at daylight towards Beaverton, fifty miles north of Oshawa. Through misinformation as to the steamer's movements, reached the wharf about ten minutes after the Emily May had left for Orillia, twenty miles distant down Lake Simcoe. The lake being too rough for small boats, it was decided to hire a conveyance to take the party at once up to Atherley, in Mara township, where we arrived at dark, through the kindness of Mr. Perkins of Beaverton. On the way bagged three partridges, which formed a good breakfast. At Atherley camped upon the shore of what is called "The Narrows," connecting Lakes Simcoe and Couchiching. Over the Narrows there is a swing bridge connecting Ontario with Simcoe county.

Friday, Aug. 25— Put our boats in the water for the first time and pulled down stream three miles to the Indian village in Rama, nearly opposite Orillia. Here a well known Indian guide name Charles Jacobs, a son of the Rev. Peter Jacobs, was engaged to accompany the party in a small canoe, taking his own tent and some of our baggage. At 3 p.m., the steamer Fairy[16] arrived from Orillia, taking us to the north end of Lake Couchiching, at the end of the Severn River. Near the wharf at the Indian village, on a gentle eminence, a beautiful quarry-stone church is being erected by the Wesleyan Methodist denomination, to which body most of the Indians in Rama belong. It is to cost $1,100. The entire Indian population of the village is about 260; though called a village, it contains neither store, tavern, nor post-office, but has a good

[16]The steamer *Fairy* was later remodelled and renamed the *Cariella*.

common school, and there is also a R.C. separate school, which a few of the children attend, two families belonging to that persuasion. Nearly every man owns a good farm, though some have their homes in the village and join canoe building, fishing, hunting, &c., with farming. Their Chief, is a portly, well-educated gentleman named Benson, whose counsels are accepted by all as nearly akin to law.

Saturday, 26th— After a well relished breakfast on bread and bass — fish, not ale— the company proceeded down the river, past the Muskoka bridge, and took dinner at the head of Sparrow Lake, chiefly upon a maskinonge caught on the way with a trolling line. In the afternoon crossed the lake which was pretty rough, to a small island of a couple of acres, in the north-west quarter, on which our tent was no sooner erected than a storm of rain began to come down. Unfortunately the "drink" came right through the cotton and bid fair to give everything a general soaking, until under the direction of Charley, the superabundant poles were pulled out and the frame work made to consist of nothing more cumbersome than two upright crotches and a ridge-pole. Thus simply constructed, it answered every purpose most admirably. The island gave evidence of having been frequently camped upon by fishing parties, Sparrow Lake being a popular resort for fishing.

Monday, 27th — Spent a few hours fishing at the third fall, which occurs a short distance below the lake, and ran down as far as the fourth, the most beautiful of all, and furnishing the largest fish, all bass, of two different varieties. Leaving the majestic Severn to tumble and sweep along its rock-bound course to the Georgian Bay, we returned half a mile to the mouth of a creek entering it from Bear Lake,[17] which lies about five miles to the north. In passing up the creek, two portages were made of a few rods each, around falls, under which our guide informed us there were plenty of bass and sun fish, but they were passed by with indifference, after the feast obtained from the Severn. Bear Lake is about two miles long and one mile wide. Passing through it we entered Leg Creek, coming down from Leg Lake.[18] This, like Bear Creek, is a narrow and crooked stream, composed of dark-coloured water. It is about two miles in length, and contains four short portages, two of them of the wading description. These differ from ordinary portages in that one of the company gets into the water and successively hauls the boats, with their loads unbroken up the rapids; while in ordinary portaging everything has to be taken out of the boats, and carried to smooth water, beyond the obstruction, and then the boats themselves taken from the water, shouldered, and conveyed in like manner. Stopped at the second portage for dinner, where one of the company had the misfortune to cut his left foot rather badly, rendering him of no further use in portaging, though capable of performing his part in the canoe as well

[17]Now Morrison Lake.
[18]Now Muldrew Lake.

as before. After dinner, passed through four or five miles of Leg Lake, catching four large bass on the way by trolling, and camped for the night upon the half-mile portage across its largest peninsula. Leg Lake is a strange-shaped body of water, reminding one of a section of a large river, containing about thirty miles coiled up by sharp curves into eight or ten. A portage of half a mile across a neck of land, saves the labour of rowing some seven or eight miles up the lake, in travelling towards the Muskoka.

Tuesday, 28th.— Got the boats over the half-mile portage before breakfast, so that on breaking camp all hands moved on. A pull of a mile across the northern leg of the lake brought us to the two-mile portage into Muskoka Bay. Passing the boats and luggage over this rough and swampy portage, occupied the greater part of the day. The Indians, our guide informed us, call it two miles, while the white people call it three. The whole party came to the unanimous conclusion that the white men were right, and that the Indian measurement must have been made on snow shoes, or in other light travelling trim. In the evening, crossed the Muskoka Bay, a distance of a mile and a half, to a point where the Muskoka Road touches it, and camped for the night. Here we found an unfinished horse boat,[19] built some years ago to run from this point to the falls above and below Muskoka Lake, before the road had been finished, but failed to work satisfactorily, and was therefore abandoned.

Wednesday, Sept. 29th.— Breakfasted early, and started up the bay. A favourable breeze springing up, one of the boats took to sails, while the other took it easy with the oars, and passing through the eastern portion of the lake, reached the first fall on the north branch of the Muskoka river, a distance of fifteen miles, before noon. At this point there is quite a village, called Brace Bridge, consisting of a saw-mill, a new flouring mill, with its machinery nearly ready to run, a post-office, three stores, two taverns, a blacksmith's shop, and a cabinet factory. The flouring and saw-mill is owned by Mr. Alex. Thompson of Penetanguishene, and will prove highly remunerative both to the proprietor and to the settlement. At one of the hotels we met with Mr. Oliver, the Government agent in charge of the Muskoka road, to whom we are indebted for considerable information respecting the settlement. Although the free grants had been suspended, through the expiration of the time for which they were originally offered, yet settlers are occasionally coming along and taking up fresh lands, paying 70 cents per acre for them, in cash, or $1 on time. An industrious settler came in, and applied for a second lot during our conversation. There are at present in the settlement eight post-offices, four lumber mills, two flouring mills, and some three thousand inhabitants. The crops this season, we were in-

[19]Probably the boat built by Holditch (H 10).

formed by various parties, are most magnificent, beating everything in the memory of the oldest inhabitant, and quite fortunately a very large area of wheat was sown this spring. Upwards of three hundred bushels of seed were put in the ground above Three Mile Lake alone. Mr. Oliver is pushing forward the repair of the Muskoka road, under orders from the Government, and has some fifty-eight men employed upon different sections of it. Most of them are now upon the northern portion, connecting with the Parry Sound road. While our party were enjoying dinner, a tame deer belonging to Mr. Alex Bailey, the postmaster, came toward our camp, bringing visions of venison, and only escaping a shot from one of our guns by its boldness in coming forward. Presently it joined in our repast, taking bread and salt from our hands, and enjoying our caresses. But for this incident, too, a tame gull which lit on the river within gunshot, would certainly have fared badly, and the conclusion was eventually arrived at, that it would not do to shoot at any living thing in that neighbourhood, lest it might be somebody's pet. The afternoon was spent in a walk down the road to the famous Muskoka Falls, on the south branch of the river, two miles distant by the road from Brace Bridge. At these falls there is also a post office and village. The south branch is noted for salmon and speckled trout fishing, its waters being of a much clearer complexion than those of the north branch. In the dark red waters of the latter, very few fish are found, and those of an inferior description of bass, sun-fish and chubb.

Thursday, Sept. 31.— Took an early start up the stream,[20] and breakfasted at the first portage, which passes around a stiff rapid, of seven feet fall. During the forenoon, passed two other falls by portage, one of them twelve, and the other thirty-seven feet in height, and dined on Mountain portage. Here there is a magnificent fall of 59 feet in three chutes, and the portage has to be literally climbed, step by step, up the solid rock, nearly a hundred feet. In the afternoon, had three or four shallow rapids to pass through, two of which had to be used as wading portages. Camped for the night at the fourth fall, within a short distance of Mary's lake.

Friday, Sept. 1.— Had some sport shooting at ducks, but could not get near enough any one of them to bring it down. About ten o'clock, the two boats having passed on a mile ahead of the guide and his canoe, we were alarmed by his shouting at the top of his voice after firing his gun. Pulling back to him in haste, we found him tugging a deer from the shore into his canoe. It was a fine buck of fifteen months old, which had wandered to the brink and been maimed by a charge of duck-shot from Charley's trusty shooting-iron, after which he was soon captured, stunned, stripped, and turned to account in the course of sundry hearty breakfasts, dinners and suppers, of which particulars need not be related.

[20]The North Branch of the Muskoka River.

Suffice it is to say, that Charley is an admirable cook, and the invigorating exercise of rowing and portaging up the Muskoka, is calculated to awaken an appetite for substantial food. Took dinner on the fine sandy beach of Mary's Lake, described in Alex. Murray's geological charts. Discovered a new outlet of the lake, not laid down in the chart, about the middle of the south shore, and regretted want of time to follow it, with a view of discovering whether it runs to the south branch or returns to the north branch below the first fall. The latter is the most probable conjecture. In the afternoon, passed on through the lake and up the river towards Fairy Lake. Both these lakes are about the same size and have the same general appearance. They are about five miles long by two miles wide, and have each some half dozen islands. The land upon their banks, and in fact all the way up the river from Brace Bridge is unfit for settlement, except in little spots of a few acres. It is either rocky or marshy, and covered with pine, balsam and hemlock trees of moderate size. At some distance back from the water, the arable land is more abundant, but the amount of rock interspersed with it must ever render it a rather poor farming country.

Saturday, Sept. 2nd.— Passed into Fairy Lake, distant from Brace Bridge about thirty miles nearly due north. It is situated in the township of Brunel, while Mary's Lake is in the adjoining township of Stephenson. It is truly named Fairy Lake, being a most beautiful sheet of water, and having the peculiarity of carrying any ordinary sound from one end to the other with marvellous distinctness. On entering it, the laughing cackle of a couple of loons was heard, and they were supposed to be around a point close at hand, but a little investigation revealed the fact that they were fully four miles distant. On seeing our little fleet, their notes grew louder, and we enjoyed a perfect concert of melody from their clarion throats during our stay. While steering for the northern shore, we met a man and his wife in a canoe, who had with them the only deer-hound in the neighbourhood, and whose services we were in quest of, but he was pre-engaged. We then turned to the westward up a large river which comes down from Vernon Lake. This is a round-shaped lake, with several large bays, lying within two miles of Fairy lake, and nearly north of it. Here we met with the first settlement after leaving Brace Bridge, there being about a dozen clearings and log houses or shanties along the southern and eastern shores. The best farm and buildings are owned by an Indian who has reared a large family upon his farm, and appears to be getting along finely. Most of the shanties are surrounded with clearings of but one or two acres planted in potatoes and corn for use in the Fall, while trapping or trading for furs, and their owners cannot therefore be called settlers. Took dinner at the Narrows upon an island, and in the afternoon rowed up to a large and high island in the centre of the lake, distant, as we supposed when starting, one mile, but being actually about four miles away. From this point the echo of any sound is most marvellous, and a whole hour was spent in its enjoyment. Our attention was first attracted to it by the firing of a gun in a distant bay, which had the resemblance of a regular musketry fight between two hostile forces. Singularly enough the echoes all came to us from the southern hills, and with wonderful distinctness and prolongation. Satiated with echoes never to be forgotten, we turned southward, ran back into and through Fairy Lake, and up a very narrow and crooked stream[21] which flows into the north-east end of it from Peninsula Lake. This stream is a mile long, but is passable only half of its length for boats, and the other half mile has to be portaged. It being after dark when we reached the portage, we were obliged to camp upon it, though low and damp.

Sunday, Sept. 3rd.— In danger of being drowned out of camp by threatened rain, we determined on reaching higher ground, which was only found three miles down the south shore of Peninsula Lake, on the north end of the two mile portage which leads into Trading Lake, or Lake of Bays. Here the day was spent in an appropriate manner.

Monday, Sept. 4.— Made the portage into the Lake of Bays, which lies immediately south of Peninsula Lake, and is 102 feet higher above sea level. The maps have the Lake of Bays laid down as running into Peninsula Lake and down the north branch of the Muskoka River, but this is a great mistake. There is not the slightest connection between the two lakes. The Lake of Bays is a portion of the south branch of the Muskoka, which runs from its southern extremity in a circuitous manner to the south-west, and joins with the north branch in one river about three miles above Muskoka Lake. A small stream comes into the eastern end of Peninsula Lake, but the main stream of the north branch comes in through Vernon into Fairy Lake, while the main stream of the south branch is that which flows into the Lake of Bays from the north-east by way of Ox-tongue Lake, up which Mr. Alexander Murray explored, by the direction of Sir W.E. Logan, in 1855. He calls this stream the Muskoka River, as if it was the source of both branches, but it is only the upper portion of the south branch. The Lake of Bays is well named, though usually called Trading Lake, owing to the amount of trading for furs carried on upon its islands and peninsulas. It consists only of some dozen large bays, there being almost no lake proper. After crossing the portage into its northernmost bay we ran down its whole length, some twelve miles, to the mouth of the south Muskoka, and down this two miles to the first falls. Reached our destination after sundown, and caught a good string of fish of half a dozen varieties, but no speckled trout as anticipated. Went to bed determined on catching trout for breakfast.

Tuesday, 5th.— Unfortunately it rained during the night, and not a

[21]A canal was cut here in 1886–8.

fish of any kind was fool enough to bite, though coaxed with all sorts of bait and any amount of patience and perseverance. With a splendid breeze we hoisted sail, at ten o'clock, for Cedar Narrows[22] at the terminus of one of the eastern bays of the Lake, distant twenty miles, reaching our destination at five in the evening, with very little labour at the oars. Here the Bobcaygeon road crosses the bay over a substantial bridge, at the north end of which a rustic description of a store is kept by a family named Coles.[23] Obtained a supply of maple sugar and tea, and passed on up to the portage, half a mile east of the bridge.

Wednesday, 6th.— Tried trout fishing again at a little falls, on a creek emptying into the bay from the east, but owing to another shower that morning, caught nothing. During the forenoon made the portage of half a mile southward into a creek running toward Raven Lake. Followed this half a mile to a beaver dam, when another half mile portage was made, and dinner partaken of on the north bank of Raven Lake. This is a lake of several large bays, through about six miles of which we passed in a southern direction to Raven Rock. This is a rock of peculiar formation, rising with a perpendicular face of 150 feet from the water, and sparsely covered, on its top, with trees. It derives its name from the circumstance that all the ravens in this portion of the country are bred upon its high battlements. It is regarded by the Indians with a peculiar awe; and our guide scarcely lifted his eyes from it while visible. Raven Lake takes its name from this rock, and though not so depicted upon any map, is said by Mr. Jacobs, our guide, whose authority cannot be questioned, he having passed through the whole length of the river with his canoe, to be the head of the Black River, which empties with the Severn River a mile below Lake Couchiching. He pointed us out the spot where the river leaves the lake, at its southwestern extremity, but our course lay southward and through a beaver pond coming in from Pine Lake, along the south side of Raven Rock. To reach the pond a portage of forty rods or so was necessary. Next a portage in a southwesterly direction of half a mile brought us, after dark, and after a good deal of beating about the bush from having lost our path, upon the shore of Pine Lake. Last season this section of the country was laid waste by fire; all the leafy mould being consumed down to the sand earth underneath, for many miles in extent, destroying, among other things, the portage roads.

Thursday, 7th.— Brought over the boats before breakfast, and afterward crossed Pine Lake, which is about a mile long by half a mile wide, its waters is supposed to run through Raven Lake into the Black River. A portage of three-quarters of a mile, nearly south-westward, brought us into St. Nora's Lake, whose waters run southward through Gull River to the Trent, and enter Lake Ontario at Belleville. The raindrops upon

22Cedar Narrows was later called Dorset.
23Probably Zachariah Cole.

this portage divide along the ridge, some running into Pine Lake, through the Black and Severn Rivers, Georgian Bay, Lakes Huron, St Clair and Erie, and tumbling over Niagara Falls into Lake Ontario; while others take the more direct route by the Trent— to the same common destination. From St. Nora's Lake we passed directly southward through a narrow gorge[24] of rock into Lake Kashgowigamog,[25] which, being interpreted, means Long and Narrow Lake. This lake is upon the county line between Victoria and Peterborough counties. It is one of the most singular of the many lakes visited. Its eastern shore is almost a straight line north and south of about eight miles, while the lake itself is at some places only a respectable river, and at others two miles wide, giving it the appearance of a chain of little lakes placed in position by a "straight edge" on the eastern side. At the south end a bay turns up half a mile to the north-east from which a stream runs due east into Big Bushkong Lake. It being after dark, camp was formed in a clearing— the first seen since leaving Lake Vernon, five days previously— on the west side of the bay.

Friday, 8th.— Rose early, owing to a storm of wind through the clearing having played havoc with our slumbers, and made three miles before breakfast. First crossed the bay, and made a short half mile portage over a good sled road, past a saw-mill owned by a Mr. Buck, an old resident of this neighbourhood. Took breakfast at the bridge upon the Peterson road, a branch of the Bobcaygeon running eastward to the Hastings road. The bridge crosses the narrows between Big Bushkong and Little Bushkong Lakes, forming the line between the townships of Stanhope on the north and Minden on the south, both in the county of Peterborough. Passing on southward through Little Bushkong, we enter Twelve Mile Lake by a narrow passage, and go over about four or five miles of its southern end, until a fall of ten or twelve feet is met with, around which there is a portage of five or six rods into Mountain Lake. This is a neat little round body of water, about three miles in extent, to the east of which lies Horse Shoe Lake, into which it empties, and runs thence, by a small creek, southward eventually forming Gull River. The head of this river not being navigable for canoes, owing to the trees obstructing the channel, the usual course is to make a portage of a mile and a half through the farm of Mr. Frederick Shove, and along the county line between Victoria and Peterborough, into Gull River, leaving Mountain Lake at its southern extremity. Mr. Shove kindly drew our boats and baggage over the portage on his sled. He was engaged in hauling in an excellent crop of millet, for fodder, and represents the crops of every kind as being most excellent in that neighbourhood. No such yield of grain and roots of all kinds was ever known since those new townships were first settled. Oats are said to be producing eighty

[24]Ox Narrows.
[25]Now Kushog Lake.

bushels to the acre. Left the portage at 3 p.m., and ran to a mile below Minden village, where we camped in a rain storm.

Saturday, 9th.— Wishing to reach home on Monday, pushed on all day despite occasional showers, passing through Gull, Moore, and Mud Turtle Lakes, and on down Gull River to a few miles below Coboconk village, in the township of Somerville. Halted for the night at an early hour, and built a large fire to dry out our clothing, preparatory to reaching Fenelon Falls in the morning, instead of travelling late in the rain to reach it on Saturday night.

J 6   PRATT's[26] TOURIST HOTEL
[Orillia, Northern Light, August 26, 1870]

. . . At the head of Lake Rosseau, to which a little fast-going steamer[27] takes us from Port Carling, lives an enterprising American gentleman, named Pratt, who is erecting an hotel on a scale which has not (or rather will not have, when completed,) its equal north of Toronto. Mr. P. has "calculated" the resources and promise of the neighbourhood; he has noticed the scenic advantages, the profusion of speckled and salmon trout, bass and maskinonge; the haunts of the deer which abound there are not unknown to him,— and, let the tourist or sportsman come along, he can "fix" them as far as in an hotel keeper of the first order lies, and by the fall of 1871 will have his premises ready for the accommodation of family parties. . . .

J 7   "THE ONTARIO GOVERNMENT VISIT MUSKOKA,"
SEPTEMBER 14, 1870
[McMurray, The Free Grant Lands of Canada, p. 82]

The members of the Ontario Government and other celebrities visited the Free Grant Districts. I have pleasure in inserting the following, copied from the Northern Advocate published at Bracebridge, Muskoka.

On the 14th Sept., 1870, Bracebridge was visited by the Hon. John S. Macdonald, Attorney-General; the Hon. S. Richards, Commissioner of Crown Lands; the Hon. John Carling,[28] Commissioner of Public Works; the Rev. A. S. Herring, B.A., Incumbent of Clerkenwell, London (England); Charles Marshall, Esq., London (England); Fred. Cumberland, Esq., M.P.P.; Wm. Lount, Esq., M.P.P.; A.P. Cockburn,

---

[26]Pratt's hotel, officially called the Rosseau House, was built by W. H. Pratt, an American, at the head of Lake Rosseau in 1870. It was the most elaborate hotel in the north and entertained many of Muskoka's most important visitors. In 1875 it was enlarged but was destroyed by fire on October 6, 1883.

[27]Probably the Waubamik, owned by A. P. Cockburn.

[28]John Carling (1828–1911) was Commissioner of Agriculture and Public Works in Ontario, 1867–71, and Postmaster General of Canada, 1882–5. He was made a K.C.M.G. in 1893. Port Carling was named in his honour.

Esq., M.P.P.; the Hon. Sidney Smith,[29] John A. Donaldson, Esq., and a number of distinguished persons.

On the day of their arrival, the villagers got a hint of their intended visit, and resolved to give them a reception. Immense bonfires were kindled on the banks of the river just as the steamer "Wenonah" approached the wharf, and the effect produced by those illuminations was grand beyond description. A large concourse of people assembled at the landing, and gave the company three of as hearty cheers as ever greeted the ear of mortal. The party were then conveyed to the "Dominion House," where a splendid entertainment was got up by Mr. Ross, the well known host.

J 8 CHARLES MARSHALL'S VISIT, SEPTEMBER 14, 1870
[*Marshall,* The Canadian Dominion, *pp. 49, 55*]

It was my pleasant fortune to be invited by the Premier of Ontario to join him, with several members of the Government, upon a tour of inspection through the Muskoka district, a wide region of romantic lakes, and streams, and woods in the northern part of the province of Ontario. The object of the Government was to see the condition of the roads and bridges lately constructed under their order, to observe the suitability of the country for immigration, and to make themselves acquainted with the condition and wishes of the settlers. For myself, I wished to see something more of back-woods life, and to know what kind of land was given away without payment to the settler.

. . .

. . . The shades of night were falling as we reached Bracebridge. The moon rose above the great pine trees, and made a wide pathway of silver across the dark waters. Near the landing-stage, a mass of blazing pine-logs revealed the black shadows of the surrounding woods, and flecked the waters below with red and gold.

The news of our visit had preceded our arrival. A group of thirty or forty big, rough men welcomed the Attorney-General with ringing cheers. A second bonfire lit up the village itself. In a short time a supper, with ales and wines, was prepared for fifty or sixty persons. The reeve presided, and speeches, patriotic, and humorous, and explanatory, and promissory, were made up to two o'clock in the morning. The people wanted roads, railways, and a separate township, and were willing to tax themselves to assist in getting what they wished. They spoke good sense, in good English, some with a Scotch accent, and showed some natural pride in recounting what they had done within the past four or five years, and a great confidence in the future prosperity of the district.

. . .

[29]Sidney Smith (b. 1823) practised law in Cobourg and took an active part in municipal affairs. In 1854 he was elected to the Legislative Assembly and in 1858 was made Postmaster General.

J 9   Tourist Attractions
[*Bracebridge,* Northern Advocate, *June 30, 1871*]

As the time for sight-seeing has now arrived, we desire to bring the claims of the Muskoka and Parry Sound districts before the public, being fully satisfied that they have only to become known in order to be appreciated.

Those who are fond of the romantic and the picturesque can find an endless variety, while the contrast is very striking to those who have been residing in crowded cities or on well cultivated farms.

Our great attraction in this section is the beautiful chain of lakes, which, when the lock at Port Carling is completed and the cut at Port Sandfield is finished, will enable steamers to pass without interruption from Lake Muskoka into Lake Rosseau and thence into Lake Joseph, thus furnishing one of the most delightful sails to be found upon the entire continent.

Muskoka and Parry Sound are also very conveniently situated; they can be reached from Toronto in one day and at a trifling cost. A through ticket may be obtained from Toronto to Bracebridge for $3.75, and parties leaving Toronto by the afternoon train on Friday will reach Parry Sound (by the steamer "Waubuno" *via* Collingwood) on Saturday afternoon. . . .

Mr. Dwight[30] and Mr. Townsend,[31] of the Montreal Telegraph Company, from Toronto, have just returned from the south branch of the Muskoka river, where they have for nine years[32] past made regular annual trips. Their success has been good, as they caught 230 speckled trout, (nearly all three pounders,) in a few days. If others were only aware of the beauties and merits of this country the number of visitors would proportionately increase. . . .

J 10   Canadian Press Association in Muskoka
[*Toronto,* Mail, *July 16, 1872*]

ANNUAL EXCURSION OF THE CANADIAN PRESS
ASSOCIATION (FROM OUR OWN CORRESPONDENT.)

The route chosen for this year's excursion of the Canadian Press Association, being northward from Toronto to the region of country now known as the Muskoka District, the party took passage in the cars

[30]Harvey Prentice Dwight (b. 1828) worked as an operator at the Montreal Telegraph Company. In 1850 he moved to Toronto and later became president of the Great Northern Telegraph Company and active in several other companies.
[31]Probably John T. Townsend. He and H. P. Dwight were later members of the Dwight-Wiman Club which held hunting and fishing excursions in the Lake of Bays area.
[32]If Dwight and Townsend were making trips into Muskoka in 1863 they were among the first tourists.

of the N.R.C. at seven o'clock on the morning of Tuesday, July 9th, at the City Hall Station, and after a pleasant run through a beautiful country, reached Bell Ewart, and embarked on board the *Emily May* for Orillia. It being the steamer's day for calling at Beaverton, the excursionists had a somewhat longer voyage, and a better opportunity of seeing the beauties of Lake Simcoe than they would have done if the direct course had been taken from Bell Ewart to Orillia. By the time the arrival was made at Orillia (about 2 p.m.) every one was ready to appreciate a good dinner. That despatched, the party at once embarked in the *Ida Burton* for Washago, at the head of pretty little Lake Couchiching, which adjoins Lake Simcoe, and stretches northward about 15 miles.

. . . Washago was reached about 5 p.m. At this point the Muskoka territory may be said to begin and here your correspondent will commence to describe the journey with a little more minuteness of detail, since its course from Washago lies through a comparatively unknown region. A line of "Royal Mail" stages runs from Washago to Gravenhurst, owned by Messrs. Harvey and Millard. A sufficient number of these, to accommodate the party, awaited the arrival of the *Ida Burton,* and the transfer from steamer to vehicle was quickly effected. The ride from Washago to Gravenhurst was over an excellent plank and stone road, and through as hard, rocky, and unpromising a country as can well be found any where. Boulders to right of you, boulders to left of you, with little patches of greenness between, and here and there a somewhat more extensive bit of land out of which some determined settler was resolutely trying to coax a few garden vegetables or a crop of grain. The general feeling engendered by this ride of fourteen miles was that if this were a sample of Muskoka it was indeed a dreary region, unfit to dwell in. We were assured, however, that the road lay over a kind of rocky backbone, and that on either side of it there were stretches of excellent land able to repay the husbandman's toil.

Gravenhurst, the southernmost point and port of Lake Muskoka, was reached about sun-down. Here the steamer *Nipissing,* owned by Mr. A.P. Cockburn, and generously placed at the service of the party for a couple of days, awaited us, with steam up, ready to start for Bracebridge, some fifteen miles distant. Everyone was astonished to find so beautiful and well-appointed a craft plying on these northern waters. Not only was steam up, but an excellent tea was ready, to which the excursionists did speedy and ample justice. The shades of evening having now fallen, but little could be seen of the surroundings during the run across the end of Lake Muskoka, some nine miles to the mouth of the Muskoka river. The dim outlines of land and water could be detected. The passage of six miles up the river was very enjoyable. We cautiously crept up through a constantly retreating host of shadows, now apparently being just upon the land, and now having a stretch of watery expanse before us. The wooded banks produced a very beautiful effect in contrast with the dark, still waters through which our staunch little steamer was threading her devious and careful way. Bracebridge was reached about ten p.m. The villagers in considerable numbers awaited us at the wharf, a band of music greeted us with lively airs, a bonfire blazed in the middle of the main street, and one building was brilliantly illuminated. This proved to be the Agricultural Hall, where, to our surprise, a bountiful supper had been prepared in anticipation of our coming, and although at that hour beds would have been most acceptable to the now weary excursionists, and some of the ladies were obliged to retire from the scene, too fatigued to participate in the coming festivities, a very pleasant time was had in discussing the good things that had been provided, and delivering and listening to a number of speeches in reply to toasts. . . .

All were soon again on board the *Nipissing* and the six miles of river sailing done in the dark on the previous evening, was now done by day light and in the sunshine. The Muskoka is a beautiful stream, deep, still, and winding. Here and there clearances were to be seen on its banks, but for the most part they were thickly wooded, with a mixture of deciduous and evergreen woods. From the river, our course lay nearly due north to Lake Rosseau, which is connected with Lake Muskoka by a short stream only a few rods in length, but having a descent of some eight feet, and called Indian River. Here a substantial lock has been built by Government. A small village has sprung up at the locks named Port Carling, in honour of the late Commissioner of Agriculture and Public Works. From this point we proceeded to the head of Lake Rosseau, where there are some hotels and a number of private houses. Here the party were entertained at the Rosseau House by the proprietor, Mr. W.H. Pratt, who had provided an excellent supper, and made arrangements for an out-door ball. The supper was universally appreciated, but the ball was participated in by but a small minority of the party. Rosseau is a striking point,— being lofty and commanding,— and looking as if intended by nature as the site of a fortress. It has already begun to be a place of resort by tourists, and needs only to be better known to be visited much more than it is at present.

All Thursday was spent in voyaging upon Lakes Rosseau, Joseph and Muskoka. Rosseau and Joseph are connected by a cut, at which is a breakwater or pier, and where considerable dredging has been done to obtain sufficient depth of water. The scenery upon all these lakes is very much of the same character, exceedingly beautiful but not greatly varied. They are more or less studded with islands, some of which are mere rocks rising like large bald-heads out of the water, and others being of considerable extent of area, and covered with "old piney woods," Lake Joseph is the most picturesque and beautiful of these inland waters, being a singularly, clear, silvery, pellucid lake, and having a sort of sheen upon it and its surroundings. A hotel has been commenced at its northern point, proposed to be named Port Cockburn, and this spot, when better improved and better known, will doubtless be a place of even greater resort than Rosseau. . . .

J 11   VISIT OF THE GOVERNOR GENERAL[33]
[*Orillia,* Times, *August 6, 1874*]

Gravenhurst, July 27, 1874.

The true and loyal subjects of Her Majesty Queen Victoria, living in and near this place, were to-day cheered by a sight of the representative of that Sovereign and great was the enthusiasm in consequence. Too much cannot be said in praise of the taste and energy with which the arrangements for the reception were carried out. The principal object of attraction was a large archway flanked by two smaller ones, and composed of pine boughs— fitting emblems of Muskoka.— The principal arch was surmounted by a crown, below which on the south side were the words "Welcome to Muskoka," and on the north side "God save the Queen," while from four flagstaffs streamed in the smart north wind different versions of the national flag; while the brilliant green foliage bristled with small editions of the Union Jack. A little further on a splendid banner stretched completely across the street leading towards the wharf, with "Welcome Lord and Lady Dufferin."

The day fortunately could not have been finer, as the rain of yesterday had cooled the air and laid the dust, and although the sun shone brightly yet the breeze so tempered the heat as to render the day all that could have been wished. After several false alarms the expected party was seen to be approaching, and was met by the Township Council, headed by the Reeve, who escorted Lord and Lady Dufferin to a platform fitted up for the occasion, where an address of welcome was read and replied to by His Excellency, after which they again entered the carriages and drove to the wharf, where the *Nipissing* gaily dressed in bunting soon after started for Bracebridge. . . .

[33]Frederick Temple Hamilton-Temple Blackwood, first Marquis of Dufferin and Ava (1826–1902), was Governor General from 1872 to 1878. He and Lady Dufferin made several long journeys through Canada which she described in *My Canadian Journal* (London, 1891).

BIBLIOGRAPHY
AND
INDEX

BIBLIOGRAPHY

MANUSCRIPTS

CANADA

Public Archives of Canada (P.A.C.)
Mossom Boyd Papers, M.G. 28.
George Brown Papers, M.G. 24, B 40.
C Series, British Military Papers, R.G. 8.
C.O. 42, M.G. 11, microfilm of originals in P.R.O.
Canadian Land and Emigration Company, microfilm from Board of
    Trade, 31.
Haldimand Papers, M.G. 21, transcribed from originals in British
    Museum.
Indian Affairs, R.G. 10.
Indian Treaties and Surrenders, R.G. 10.
Parsonage Papers, M.G. 24.
Q Series.
David Thompson Letters, M.G. 19, A 8, 3.
Upper Canada State Papers, R.G. 1, E 3.
Upper Canada Sundries, R.G. 5, A 1.
Report on Water Communications, R.G. 11.
Map Division.
Print Division.

ONTARIO

Department of Lands and Forests
Field Notes.
Instructions to Land Surveyors.
Surveyor General's Office, Letters Written.
Surveyors' Letters.

Department of Public Records and Archives (P.A.O.)
F. H. Baddeley Exploring Report.
Alexander Campbell Papers.
C.O. 42, microfilm of volumes relating to Ontario from originals
    in P.R.O.
Colonization Roads Papers.
Crown Lands Papers.
Education Department Papers.
Immigration Papers.

Instructions to Land Surveyors, microfilm copies of originals in
Department of Lands and Forests.
Macaulay Papers.
Miscellaneous Manuscripts.
Ontario Sessional Papers.
Ontario Sessional Papers, Petitions.
Charles Rankin Papers, photographic copies of originals in Toronto
Public Library.
Percy J. Robinson Papers.
J. B. Rousseau Papers.
Shanly Papers.
Simcoe Papers.
Strachan Papers.
Surveyors' Letters, microfilm from originals in Department of Lands
and Forests.
David Thompson Papers.
Upper Canada State Papers, microfilm copies of originals in P.A.C.
Map Division.
Picture Division.

Toronto Public Library
Charles Rankin Papers.
T. H. Ware Diary.
John Ross Robertson Picture Collection.

Archives of the United Church of Canada, Victoria University, Toronto
G. H. Kenney Reminiscences, photographic copy.
John Webster Diary.

University of Toronto Library
George Gordon Papers.
Muskoka Papers (Harry Linney Collection).

Private Ownership
Dr. James Watson Bain, Toronto
James Bain Papers.
Mr. Harley Cummings, Ottawa
Copies of Canadian Land and Emigration Company Papers.
Mr. William R. Wadsworth, Q.C., Toronto
Vernon B. Wadsworth Papers.

ENGLAND
Public Record Office (P.R.O.)
Admiralty 1.
C.O. 42.
W.O. 55.

NEWSPAPERS

Bracebridge and Parry Sound, *Northern Advocate.*
Lindsay, *Expositor.*
Orillia, *Expositor.*
────── *Northern Light.*
────── *Packet.*
────── *Times.*
Peterborough, *Examiner.*
Toronto, *Canadian Monetary Times.*
────── *Daily Globe.*
────── *Weekly Globe.*
────── *Leader.*
────── *Mail.*

Some of the above are available in scattered issues only. The Orillia
papers are on microfilm at P.A.O., through the kindness of the *Orillia
Packet and Times.* Clippings from Muskoka newspapers, collected by
Mr. Harry Linney are found in the Muskoka Papers at the University of
Toronto Library.

STATUTES AND OTHER SERIAL
GOVERNMENT PUBLICATIONS

Upper Canada, *Statutes,* 1792–1840.
────── House of Assembly, *Journal,* 1792–1840.
Canada (Province), *Statutes,* 1841–66.
────── Legislative Assembly, *Journals,* 1841–66.
────── Legislative Assembly, *Sessional Papers,* 1860–66.
────── Bureau of Agriculture, *Report,* 1854–65. Name of Bureau
varies.
────── Department of Crown Lands, *Report,* 1856–66.
────── Geological Survey, *Report of Progress,* 1843– .
Canada Gazette, 1841–67.
Ontario, *Statutes,* 1867– .
────── Legislative Assembly, *Journals,* 1867– .
────── Legislative Assembly, *Sessional Papers,* 1868/9– .
────── Department of Agriculture and Public Works, *Annual Report
on Immigration,* 1869– .
────── Department of Agriculture and Public Works, *Report on Public
Works,* 1868– . Title varies.
────── Education Office, *Annual Report of the Normal, Model,
Grammar, and Common Schools,* 1868– . Title varies.
Haliburton County, Municipal Council, *Minutes of the Proceedings and
By-laws, 1874– .*
Peterborough County, Municipal Council, *Proceedings,* 1850– . Title
varies. Includes By-laws.

Simcoe County, *Revised By-laws.*

—— Municipal Council, *Minutes*, 1843– . Title varies. Includes By-laws.

CONTEMPORARY WORKS, DESCRIPTIVE ACCOUNTS, TRAVELS, AND REMINISCENCES

ABORIGINES' PROTECTION SOCIETY, *Report on the Indians of Upper Canada* (London, 1839).

ADAM, G. M., *Muskoka Illustrated, with Descriptive Narrative of this Picturesque Region* (Toronto [1888]).

ADAMS, E. H., *Toronto and Adjacent Summer Resorts . . . Souvenir and Guide Book* (Toronto, 1894).

BELDEN, H., & Co., *Illustrated Atlas of the Dominion of Canada* (Toronto, 1881). Simcoe County edition.

—— *Illustrated Atlas of the Dominion of Canada* (Toronto, 1881). Victoria County edition.

BIGSBY, J. J., *The Shoe and Canoe; or Pictures of Travel in the Canadas* (2 vols., London, 1850).

BUCHANAN, A. C., *Canada 1863 for the Information of Immigrants, Published by Authority* (Quebec, 1863).

BUSKIN, GEORGE, *More than Forty Years in Gospel Harness; a Tale of Truth Designed to Profit the Readers Young and Old* (Berlin, Ont., 1898).

CANADA, COMMISSION APPOINTED TO INQUIRE INTO THE AFFAIRS OF THE INDIANS IN CANADA, "Report," Legislative Assembly, *Journals,* 1844–5, app. EEE, and 1847, app. T.

—— DEPARTMENT OF CROWN LANDS, *Remarks on Upper Canada Surveys, and Extracts from the Surveyors' Reports, Containing a Description of the Soil and Timber of the Townships in the Huron and Ottawa Territory . . . Appendix no. 26 to the Report of the Commissioner of Crown Lands for 1861* (Quebec, 1862). Another edition 1863.

—— LEGISLATIVE ASSEMBLY, COMMITTEE ON OTTAWA AND GEORGIAN BAY TERRITORY, "Report," Legislative Assembly, *Journals,* 1864, app. 8.

—— SPECIAL COMMISSION TO INVESTIGATE INDIAN AFFAIRS IN CANADA, *Report of the Special Commissioners Appointed on the 8th of September, 1856* (Toronto, 1858).

CANADA (Dominion), DEPARTMENT OF AGRICULTURE, *. . . Muskoka and Lake Nipissing Districts* (Ottawa, 1880).

—— DEPARTMENT OF INDIAN AFFAIRS, *Indian Treaties and Surrenders* (3 vols., Ottawa, 1905–12).

Canadian Parliamentary Guide, 1862– (Quebec, 1862–).

CARTHEW, JOHN, BADDELEY, F. H., and HAWKINS, WILLIAM, "Report," Upper Canada, House of Assembly, *Journal*, 1836–7, app. 37.

CHAMPLAIN, SAMUEL DE, *The Works*, edited by H. P. BIGGAR (6 vols. and maps, Toronto, 1922–36).

City of Toronto Directory for 1867–8 (Toronto, 1867).

CLERKENWELL AND CENTRAL LONDON EMIGRATION CLUB AND SOCIETY, *Emigration to the British Colonies* (London, 1873?). A pamphlet issued by the Reverend A. Styleman Herring, Chairman.

COPWAY, GEORGE, *The Life, Letters, and Speeches of Kah-ge-ga-gah-bowh, or G. Copway, Chief Ojibway Nation* (New York, 1850).

The County of Victoria Directory for 1869–70 (Toronto, 1869).

CUMBERLAND, F. B., ed., *The Northern Lakes of Canada; the Niagara River & Toronto, the Lakes of Muskoka, Lake Nipissing, Georgian Bay, Great Manitoulin Channel, Mackinac, Sault Ste. Marie, Lake Superior* (2nd ed., Toronto, 1886).

DALE, JOSEPH, *Canadian Land Grants in 1874* (London, 1875).

[DE LA FOSSE, F. M.], *English Bloods, by Roger Vardon* (Ottawa, 1930).

DICKSON, JAMES, *Camping in the Muskoka Region* (Toronto, 1886). Reprinted by the Ontario Department of Lands and Forests, 1960.

DOLLAR, ROBERT, *Memoirs* (3rd ed., San Francisco, 1927).

DU CREUX, FRANÇOIS, *The History of Canada or New France*, translated with an Introduction by PERCY J. ROBINSON, edited with Notes by JAMES B. CONACHER (2 vols., Toronto, 1951–2).

DUFFERIN AND AVA, HARIOT GEORGINA (HAMILTON) HAMILTON-TEMPLE-BLACKWOOD, MARCHIONESS OF, *My Canadian Journal, 1872–8; Extracts from my Letters Home, Written while Lord Dufferin was Governor-General* (London, 1891).

GALINÉE, RENÉ DE BRÉHANT DE, "Exploration of the Great Lakes, 1669–1670, by Dollier de Casson and De Bréhant de Galinée . . . Translator and Editor, James H. Coyne," Ontario Historical Society, *Papers and Records*, v. 4, 1903, pp. 78–89.

GRANT, G. M., *Picturesque Canada; the Country as it Was and Is* (2 vols., Toronto, 1882).

——— *Picturesque Spots of the North; Historical and Descriptive Sketches of the Scenery and Life in the Vicinity of Georgian Bay, the Muskoka Lakes, the Upper Lakes, in Central and Eastern Ontario, and in the Niagara District* (Chicago, 1899).

GREAT BRITAIN, COLONIAL OFFICE, *Aboriginal Tribes (North America, New South Wales, Van Diemen's Land, and British Guiana)* (London, 1834).

——— *Return to an Address of the Honourable the House of Commons, Dated 11 June 1839, for Copies or Extracts of Correspondence since 1st April 1835 between the Secretary of State for the Colonies and the Governors of the British North American Provinces Respecting the Indians in those Provinces* (London, 1839?).

Guide to Muskoka Lakes, Upper Maganetawan & Inside Channel of the Georgian Bay (Gravenhurst, 1888?).

GUILLET, E. C., ed., *The Valley of the Trent* (Toronto, 1957).

HAMILTON, J. C., *The Georgian Bay; an Account of its Position, Inhabitants, Mineral Interests, Fish, Timber, and Other Resources* (Toronto, 1893).

HAMILTON, W. E., *Guide Book & Atlas of Muskoka and Parry Sound Districts; Maps by Jno. Rogers, Sketches by S. Penson* (Toronto, 1879).

—— *Muskoka Sketch* (Dresden, 1884).

—— *Peeps at my Life* (2nd ed., Chatham, 1895).

HATHAWAY, ANN, *Muskoka Memories; Sketches from Real Life* (Toronto, 1904).

[HEDLEY, J. A.], *Notes of a Hunting Trip with the Dwight-Wiman Club in the Muskoka District, Canada, October, 1884* (Toronto, 1884).

INDIAN CHIEFS AND PRINCIPAL MEN, *Minutes of the General Council of Indian Chiefs and Principal Men Held at Orillia, Lake Simcoe Narrows, on Thursday the 30th, and Friday, the 31st July, 1846, on the Proposed Removal of the Smaller Gommunities [sic], and the Establishment of Manual Labour Schools* (Montreal, 1846).

JONES, PETER, *History of the Ojebway Indians, with Especial Reference to their Conversion to Christianity* (London, 1861).

[KING, MRS. H. B.], *Letters from Muskoka, by an Emigrant Lady* (London, 1878).

KINTON, A. F., *Just One Blue Bonnet; the Life Story of Ada Florence Kinton, Artist and Salvationist, Told Mostly by Herself with Pen and Pencil, ed. by her Sister, Sara A. Randleson* (Toronto, 1907).

KIRKWOOD, ALEXANDER, and MURPHY, J. J., *The Undeveloped Lands in Northern & Western Ontario . . . Collected and Compiled from Reports of Surveyors, Crown Land Agents, and Others, with the Sanction of the Honourable the Commissioner of Crown Lands* (Toronto, 1878).

LAHONTAN, LOUIS ARMAND DE LOM D' ARCE, BARON DE, *New Voyages to North America, Reprinted from the English Edition of 1703* (2 vols., Chicago, 1905).

LANGTON, JOHN, "On the Age of Timber Trees, and the Prospects of a Continuous Supply of Timber in Canada," Literary and Historical Society of Quebec, *Transactions*, ser. 1, v. 5, 1862, pp. 61–79.

McADAM, J. T., *The Muskoka Lakes and the Georgian Bay, by Capt. Mac* ([Toronto], 1884).

MacDERMOTT, C. L., *Facts for Emigrants* (London, 1868).

[McDONELL, ALEXANDER], "Diary of Gov. Simcoe's Journey from Humber Bay to Matchetache Bay, 1793," Canadian Institute, *Transactions*, v. 1, 1889–90, pp. 128–39.

McMURRAY, THOMAS, *The Free Grant Lands of Canada, from Practical Experience of Bush Farming in the Free Grant Districts of Muskoka and Parry Sound* (Bracebridge, 1871).

————— *Temperance Lectures, with Autobiography* (Toronto, 1873).

MARSHALL, CHARLES, *The Canadian Dominion* (London, 1871).

OLIPHANT, LAURENCE, *Minnesota and the Far West* (Edinburgh, 1855).

ONTARIO, DEPARTMENT OF AGRICULTURE AND PUBLIC WORKS, *Emigration to Canada; the Province of Ontario, its Soil, Climate, Resources, Institutions, Free Grant Lands, &c., &c., for the Information of Intending Emigrants* (Toronto, 1869).

————— PROVINCIAL SECRETARY, "Return to an Address of the Legislative Assembly, dated 24th November, 1868, to His Excellency the Lieutenant Governor, for Copies of the Agreements between "The Canada Land and Emigration Company" and the Government, Respecting the Purchase of Ten Townships of Crown Lands, and all Orders in Council and Correspondence Respecting said Agreements," *Sessional Papers*, 1868–9, no. 34.

ONTARIO AGRICULTURAL COMMISSION, *Report*, app. R1–R2, Muskoka and Parry Sound (Toronto, 1881).

Picturesque Canada! the Northern Lakes' Guide to Lakes Simcoe and Couchiching, the Lakes of Muskoka, and Lake Superior via the Northern Railway of Canada (Toronto, 1875). Later editions have variant titles; *see* CUMBERLAND, F. B.

PODMORE, PERCY ST. MICHAEL–, *A Sporting Paradise, with Stories of Adventure in America and the Backwoods of Muskoka* (London, 1904).

POOLE, T. W., *A Sketch of the Early Settlement and Subsequent Progress of the Town of Peterborough, and of Each Township in the County of Peterborough* (Peterborough, 1867). Reprinted in 1941.

ROPER, EDWARD, *Muskoka, the Picturesque Playground of Canada* (Toronto, 1883). Portfolio of drawings.

RUSSELL, PETER, *The Correspondence, with Allied Documents . . . ,* edited by E. A. CRUIKSHANK (3 vols., Toronto, 1932–6).

SAGARD, GABRIEL (called Théodat), *The Long Journey to the Country of the Hurons*, edited by G. M. WRONG, translated by H. H. LANGTON (Toronto, 1939).

SHIRREFF, ALEXANDER, "Topographical Notices of the Country Lying between the Mouth of the Rideau and Penetanguishine on Lake Huron, by Alexander Sherriff," Literary and Historical Society of Quebec, *Transactions*, ser. 1, v. 2, 1831, pp. 243–309, and map at end of vol.

SHIRREFF, CHARLES, *Thoughts on Emigration and on the Canadas as an Opening for It* (Quebec, 1831).

SIMCOE, J. G., *The Correspondence, with Allied Documents . . . ,* edited by E. A. CRUIKSHANK (5 vols., Toronto, 1923–31).

SMYTH, SIR J. C., 1st bart., *Copy of a Report to His Grace the Duke of Wellington, Master General of His Majesty's Ordnance &c. &c. &c., Relative to His Majesty's North American Provinces by a Commission of which M. General Sir James Carmichael Smyth was President* (n.p. 1825). Lithographed from manuscript.

THOMPSON, G. S., *Up to Date, or the Life of a Lumberman* (Peterborough, 1895).

THWAITES, REUBEN GOLD, ed., *The Jesuit Relations and Allied Documents; Travels and Explorations of the Jesuit Missionaries in New France, 1610–1791* (74 vols., Cleveland, 1896–1901).

TODD, JOHN, "A Trip to Muskoka Lake," *New Dominion Monthly*, v. 1, March, 1868, pp. 361–3.

WADSWORTH, V. B., "History of Exploratory Surveys Conducted by John Stoughton Dennis, Provincial Land Surveyor, in the Muskoka, Parry Sound, and Nipissing District, 1860–1865," Association of Ontario Land Surveyors, *Annual Report*, 1926, pp. 156–67.

WALKER, W. W., *By Northern Lakes; Reminiscences of Life in Ontario Mission Fields* (Toronto, 1896).

WATSON, B. A., *The Sportsman's Paradise; or the Lake Lands of Canada* (Philadelphia, 1888).

WHITE, THOMAS, JR., *An Exhibit of the Progress, Position, and Resources of the County of Peterboro', Canada West, Based upon the Census of 1861, together with a Statement of the Trade of the Town of Peterborough* (Peterborough, 1861?).

SELECTED SECONDARY WORKS

ADAMS, F. D., and BARLOW, A. E., *Geology of the Haliburton and Bancroft Areas, Province of Ontario* (Canada, Geological Survey, Memoir 6, 1910).

ASSOCIATION OF ONTARIO LAND SURVEYORS, *Annual Report* (Toronto, 1886–).

BAIN, J. W., "Early Explorations in the Muskoka and Haliburton Districts," typescript.

———— "Surveys of a Water Route between Lake Simcoe and the Ottawa River by the Royal Engineers, 1819–1827," *Ontario History*, v. 50, winter, 1958, pp. 15–28.

BAKER, R. H., *History of the Provisional County of Haliburton, Province of Ontario* (n.p., 1930?).

CALDER, GEORGE, "A Geographical Survey of the District of Parry Sound," B.A. thesis, Department of Geography, University of Toronto, 1949.

The Canadian Album, edited by J. CASTELL HOPKINS and WILLIAM COCHRANE (5 vols., Brantford, 1891–6).

COATSWORTH, E. S., "When Muskoka Defended Toronto," York Pioneer and Historical Society, *Annual Report*, 1954, pp. 18–19.

COPE, L. M., *A History of the Village of Port Carling* (Bracebridge, 1956).

CROSS, M. S., "The Lumber Community of Upper Canada, 1815–1867," *Ontario History*, v. 52, Dec., 1960, pp. 213–33.

DE LA FOSSE, F. M., "Early Days in Muskoka," Ontario Historical Society, *Papers and Records*, v. 34, 1942, pp. 104–10.

DORMAN, ROBERT, *A Statutory History of the Steam and Electric Railways of Canada, 1836–1937* (Ottawa, 1938, with appendix, 1953).

DRURY, E. C., *All for a Beaver Hat; a History of Early Simcoe County* (Toronto, 1959).

FRASER, L. R., *History of Muskoka* (Bracebridge [1946]).

———— "Municipal History of Monck Township," *Bracebridge Gazette*, Jan. 7–Feb. 4, 1943.

History of the County of Peterborough, Ontario, Containing a History of the County, History of Haliburton County, their Townships, Towns, Schools, Churches, etc. (Toronto, 1884).

HODGETTS, J. E., *Pioneer Public Service; an Administrative History of the United Canadas, 1841–1867* (Toronto, 1955).

HOWE, C. D., and WHITE, J. H., *Trent Watershed Survey, a Reconnaissance, with an Introductory Discussion by B. E. Fernow* (Toronto, 1913).

HUNT, G. T., *The Wars of the Iroquois; a Study in Intertribal Trade Relations* (Madison, Wis., 1940).

HUNTER, A. F., *A History of Simcoe County* (2 vols., Barrie, 1909).

Huntsville's Old Home Week, July 31st to August 6th, 1926 (Huntsville, 1926).

JARVIS, JULIA, *Three Centuries of Robinsons; the Story of a Family* (Toronto, 1953).

JENNESS, DIAMOND, *The Indians of Canada* (5th ed., Ottawa, 1960).

JONES, A. E., "*8endake Ehen*," *or Old Huronia* (Ontario, Bureau of Archives, Report, no. 5, 1908).

KIRKCONNELL, WATSON, *Victoria County Centennial History* (Lindsay, 1921).

LOWER, A. R. M., "The Assault on the Laurentian Barrier, 1850–1870," *Canadian Historical Review*, v. 10, Dec., 1929, pp. 294–307.

———— *The North American Assault on the Canadian Forest, a History of the Lumber Trade between Canada and the United States* (Toronto, 1938).

———— *Settlement and the Forest Frontier in Eastern Canada* (Toronto, 1936).

———— "The Trade in Square Timber," University of Toronto, *Studies, History and Economics, Contributions to Canadian Economics*, 1933, pp. 40–61.

MACKENZIE, N. H., "The Economic and Social Development of Muskoka, 1855–1888," M.A. thesis, University of Toronto, 1943.

MASON, D. H. C., *Muskoka; the First Islanders* (Bracebridge, 1957).

MINDEN, CENTENNIAL PLANNING BOARD, *Minden Centennial, 1859–1959* (Minden, 1959).

MORRIS, J. L., *Indians of Ontario* (Toronto, 1943).

MULDREW LAKES COTTAGERS' CLUB, *The History of Muldrew Lake, a Record of Bygone Days in and around the Lake* ([Toronto], 1953). Mimeographed.

ONTARIO, BUREAU OF FORESTRY, "A History of Crown Timber Regulations, from the Date of the French Occupation to the Present Time, Compiled with the Assistance of Mr. Aubrey White," Ontario, Bureau of Forestry, *Annual Report*, 1899, pp. 29–139.

ORILLIA PACKET AND TIMES, *A Peek behind the Scenes; Issued on the Occasion of the Sixteenth Annual Convention of the Canadian Weekly Newspapers' Association* (Orillia, 1935).

OSBORNE, A. C., "The Migration of *Voyageurs* from Drummond Island to Penetanguishene in 1828," Ontario Historical Society, *Papers and Records*, v. 3, 1901, pp. 123–49.

PARRY SOUND, *Old Home Week Celebrations, Parry Sound, Ontario, August 9th to 15th, 1959* (Parry Sound, 1959).

PAUDASH, ROBERT, "The Coming of the Mississagas, Prepared by J. Hampden Burnham," Ontario Historical Society, *Papers and Records*, v. 6, 1905, pp. 7–11.

PINART, L. A., *Recueil de cartes, plans, et vues relatifs aux Etats-Unis et au Canada, New-York, Boston, Montréal, Québec, Louisbourg, 1651–1731* (Paris, 1893). Portfolio of maps.

Pioneer Days in Muskoka; Port Sydney (n.p., 1927?).

REYNOLDS, NILA, "In Quest of Yesterday; a History of Haliburton," *Haliburton County Echo*, July 7, 1960–March 29, 1962.

RICHARDS, J. H., "Land Use and Settlement Patterns on the Fringe of the Shield in Southern Ontario," Ph.D. thesis, University of Toronto, 2 vols.

—— "Lands and Policies; Attitudes and Controls in the Alienation of Lands in Ontario during the First Century of Settlement," *Ontario History*, v. 50, autumn, 1958, pp. 193–209.

ROBINSON, P. J., "The Chevalier De Rocheblave and the Toronto Purchase," Royal Society of Canada, *Proceedings and Transactions*, ser. 3, v. 31, 1937, s. 2., pp. 131–52.

—— "Galinée's Map of the Great Lakes Region in 1670," *Canadian Historical Review*, v. 20, Sept., 1939, p. 293.

—— "On the Derivation of Certain Place-Names in the Georgian Bay," Royal Canadian Institute, *Transactions*, v. 10, 1914, pp. 127–9.

—— "The Toronto Carrying-place and the Toronto Purchase," *Ontario History*, v. 39, 1947, pp. 41–9.

—— *Toronto during the French Régime* (Toronto, 1933).

—— "Yonge Street and the North West Company," *Canadian Historical Review*, v. 24, Sept., 1943, pp. 253–65.

SATTERLY, JOHN, "Mineral Occurrences in the Haliburton Area," Ontario, Department of Mines, *Annual Report*, no. 52, pt. 2, 1943.

—— "Radioactive Mineral Occurrences in the Bancroft Area,"

Ontario, Department of Mines, *Annual Report*, no. 65, pt. 6, 1956.

SAUNDERS, AUDREY, *Algonquin Story* (Toronto, 1947).

SPRAGGE, G. W., "Colonization Roads in Canada West, 1850–1867," *Ontario History*, v. 49, winter, 1957, pp. 1–17.

STEVENS, G. R., *Canadian National Railways* (2 vols., Toronto, 1960–2).

THOMAS, G. H. O., "Bracebridge in 1884, Being Reminiscences which Appeared in the Gazette in 1934," *Bracebridge Gazette*, July 27–Aug. 24, 1944.

THOMAS, R. M. S., "The Beginning of Navigation and the Tourist Industry in Muskoka," *Ontario History*, v. 42, April, 1950, pp. 101–5.

WALKER, F. N., *Four Whistles to Wood-up; Stories of the Northern Railway of Canada* (Toronto, 1953).

WALLACE, W. S., "The Early History of Muskoka," *Queen's Quarterly*, v. 49, autumn, 1942, pp. 247–50.

WHITTON, CHARLOTTE, *A Hundred Years a' Fellin';—Some Passages from the Timber Saga of the Ottawa in the Century in which the Gillies have been Cutting in the Valley, 1842–1942* (Ottawa, 1943).

WOLFE, R. I., "The Summer Resorts of Ontario in the Nineteenth Century," *Ontario History*, v. 54, Sept., 1962, pp. 149–60.

WURTELE, D. J., "Mossom Boyd, Lumber King of the Trent Valley," *Ontario History*, v. 50, autumn, 1958, pp. 177–89.

INDEX

References in italic indicate biographical or brief identifying notes.

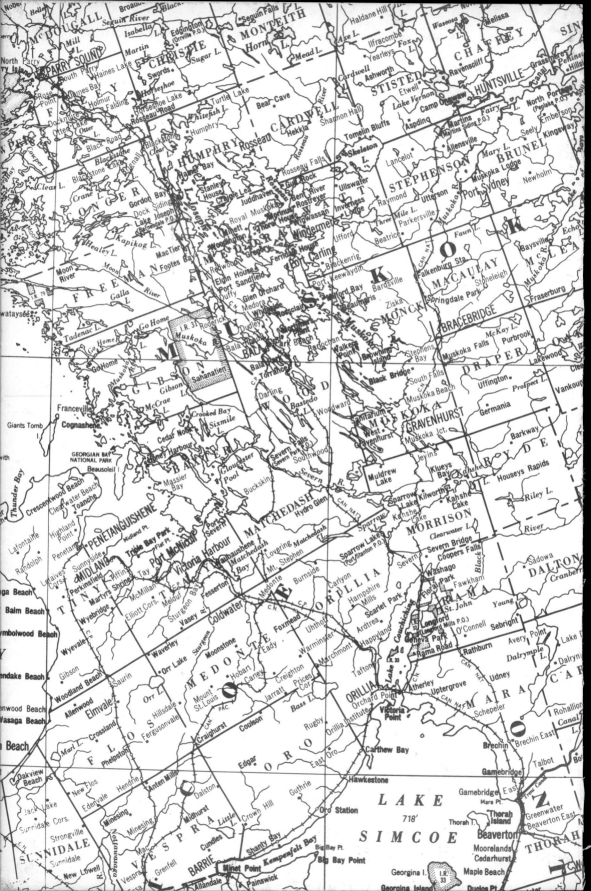